TRANSFORMING THE SCHOOL COUNSELING PROFESSION

Second Edition

BRADLEY T. ERFORD
Loyola College in Maryland

PEARSON

Merrill
Prentice Hall

Upper Saddle River, New Jersey
Columbus, Ohio

Library of Congress Cataloging-in-Publication Data

Erford, Bradley T.
    Transforming the school counseling profession / Bradley T. Erford.—2nd ed.
      p. cm.
    Includes bibliographical references and index.
    ISBN 0-13-170275-0
    1. Educational counseling—United States—Handbooks, manuals, etc.   I. Title.

LB1027.5.E67 2007
371.4—dc22   2005036193

Vice President and Executive Publisher: Jeffery W. Johnston
Publisher: Kevin M. Davis
Associate Editor: Meredith Sarver
Editorial Assistant: Sarah N. Kenoyer
Production Editor: Mary Harlan
Production Coordination: Thistle Hill Publishing Services, LLC
Design Coordinator: Diane C. Lorenzo
Cover Design: Thomas Borah
Cover Image: SuperStock
Production Manager: Laura Messerly
Director of Marketing: David Gesell
Marketing Manager: Autumn Purdy
Marketing Coordinator: Brian Mounts

This book was set in Garamond by Integra Software Services. It was printed and bound by Hamilton Printing Company. The cover was printed by Lehigh Press.

Pearson Education Ltd.
Pearson Education Singapore Pte. Ltd.
Pearson Education Canada, Ltd.
Pearson Education–Japan

Pearson Education Australia Pty. Limited
Pearson Education North Asia Ltd.
Pearson Educación de Mexico, S.A. de C.V.
Pearson Education Malaysia Pte. Ltd.

10 9 8 7 6 5 4 3 2
ISBN: 0-13-170275-0

This effort is dedicated to The One: the Giver of energy, passion, and understanding; who makes life worth living and endeavors worth pursuing and accomplishing; the Teacher of love and forgiveness.

PREFACE

Myriad societal changes have created significant academic, career, and personal–social developmental challenges for today's students. A short list of these challenges includes achieving high academic standards; suicide; substance abuse; technological changes recasting future labor-force needs; violence in schools, homes, and communities; and high-stakes testing. The prominence of these and many other challenges that confront the children and youth of today makes professional school counselors more essential than ever to the mission of schools.

In the past, many educators have viewed school counseling as an ancillary service. More recently, due to national school reform and accountability initiatives, school counselor leaders have encouraged professional school counselors in the field to dedicate their programs to the schools' mission objectives, which typically focus on academic performance, and the achievement of high academic standards by all students. Without question, school counseling programs with curricula emphasizing affective skills associated with academic performance help students become motivated to perform, "learn how to learn," and cope with the challenges of our diverse and changing world. Historically, professional school counselors have focused on career and personal–social needs as ends in themselves.

This new focus on academic performance in support of a school's educational mission is necessary to win the respect of school reform advocates and achievement-focused educators. Thus, professional school counselors must ensure that comprehensive developmental school counseling programs address career and personal–social issues with the end goal of removing barriers to, and improving, educational performance. To accomplish this goal, however, professional school counselors must develop programs offering a broad range of services aimed at the increasingly diverse needs of systems, educators, families, and students. *Transforming the School Counseling Profession*, Second Edition, was written to help accomplish this goal.

Designed as an introduction to the school counseling profession, this book may also serve as a school counseling program development resource. Its goal is to inform the reader about how the seemingly diverse roles of the professional school counselor fit together in a comprehensive manner. Some topics are treated more thoroughly than others. Whereas most school counselor educational programs offer entire courses on some of these topics, others are barely touched on before students encounter them in the field. This book will help professional school counselors in training to prepare for their entry into a career as a professional school counselor and help them avoid mistakes. Experienced professional school counselors and counselor supervisors interested in new ideas may also find the book stimulating in its offering of new perspectives and detailed descriptions aiding program development. At times both idealistic and futuristic, the authors attempt to be realistic and practical as well while pointing out more effective methods. Although our goal is primarily to educate the reader, we also seek to provoke discussion among professional school counselors, school counselors in training, school counselor educators and supervisors, and the broader educational community.

ORGANIZATION OF THE TEXT

Transforming the School Counseling Profession, Second Edition, begins with a glimpse of current barriers to effective implementation of a comprehensive developmental school counseling program and presents a vision for the 21st century. Dr. Reese House and Pat Martin, former directors of the DeWitt–Wallace Education Trust's School Counseling Initiative, present some interesting perspectives on how to remove barriers to academic performance.

In chapter 2, Dr. Edwin Herr of Penn State University and I provide a concise, yet comprehensive, synopsis of the history of the profession, and then highlight issues that will determine its future course. Chapter 2 concludes with an explanation of 10 roles emerging from the current school counseling literature that must be considered to effectively implement a comprehensive school counseling program.

Dr. Susan Whiston of Indiana University provides a concise summary of school counseling outcomes research in chapter 3, concluding that, although little research is available, existing research is generally supportive of school counseling services. In chapter 4, Dr. Lynn Linde of Loyola College in Maryland focuses on the importance of ethical, legal, and professional issues related to the practice of school counseling.

In chapter 5, Dr. Cheryl Holcomb-McCoy of the University of Maryland and Dr. Stuart Chen-Hayes of CUNY–Lehman bring their unique scholarly perspectives to bear on answering the question, "What does a multiculturally competent school counselor look like?" The vignettes and questionnaire provided are certain to provoke interesting classroom discussions!

In chapter 6, Dr. Deryl Bailey and Dr. Yvette Getch of the University of Georgia and Dr. Stuart Chen-Hayes of CUNY–Lehman provide practical, down-to-earth advice on how to advocate, and teach others to advocate, for academic success and social equity. This chapter focuses on the professional school counselor as academic and social advocate and is an exciting addition to school counseling literature and practice.

Beginning with chapter 7, the "how to" of a comprehensive data-driven school counseling program begins to take shape. Dr. Vivian Lee of the College Board and Dr. Gary Goodnough of Plymouth State University summarize the planning and implementation of a systemic data-driven

school counseling program. Dr. Gary Goodnough, Dr. Rachelle Pérusse, and I expand on the curriculum development and implementation processes in chapter 8 and extend into the classroom guidance component of a developmental program. Chapter 9, coauthored by Dr. Debbie Newsome and Dr. Sam Gladding, both of Wake Forest University, provides a basic introduction to the individual and group counseling components of a comprehensive program. In chapter 10, Dr. Spencer (Skip) Niles of Penn State University and Dr. Patrick Akos of UNC–Chapel Hill expand on the educational and career-planning component of a comprehensive program that, although historically focused on in high school, has received greater emphasis recently in K–8 curricula. Chapter 11 reviews the importance of consultation and collaboration, setting the stage for systemic collaboration and parent/community outreach. Chapter 12 explores the many facets of school counseling accountability, including needs assessment, program evaluation, service assessment, outcomes evaluation, and performance appraisal. School reform movements around the country have made accountability a critical element in all educational components, and professional school counselors are wise to become knowledgeable leaders in this area.

No discussion of school counseling would be complete without some attention to violence in the school and community and students who are at risk. Chapter 13 focuses on systemic solutions, as well as assessing and counseling youth who are at risk through just such systemic solutions. In chapter 14, Dr. Vivian Lee of the College Board and Amber Throckmorton, a Virginia professional school counselor, discuss developing conflict resolution and peer mediation programs in schools to combat violence and enhance interpersonal communication and problem solving. These programs currently enjoy great popularity at the high school level and are appearing at many elementary and middle schools. Innovative programs such as these are bringing down discipline referral rates across the country.

Dr. Elana Rock of Loyola College and Erin Leff, a lawyer who specializes in educational law, provide an exceptionally comprehensive look in chapter 15 at the professional school counselor's role in meeting the needs of students with disabilities, providing sufficient justification to protect the counselor from being overused in the special education process, while providing enough information to allow counselors to advocate for the needs of these students.

Finally, an excellent introduction to mental and emotional disorders is provided by Dr. Carol Kaffenberger and Dr. Linda Seligman, both of George Mason University, in chapter 16. Although professional school counselors may not diagnose these conditions in their workplace, knowledge of the medical model and characteristics of mental and emotional disorders will surely facilitate appropriate referrals, liaising with mental health practitioners, and integration of students with mental and emotional disorders into the school environment.

Transforming the School Counseling Profession seeks to be more than just an introductory text. Its purpose is to strike a chord with professional school counselors and school counselors in training all around the world and to lead the professional practice of school counseling in new and exciting directions that will benefit students, educators, parents, and the entire community. Professional school counselors can and must provide advocacy, leadership, and support in the school reform and accountability movements, helping to ensure that no student falls through the cracks.

SUPPLEMENTAL INSTRUCTIONAL FEATURES

Supplemental to this book are pedagogical tools helpful to school counselor educators choosing to use this book as a course textbook. The companion Instructor's Manual contains at least 30 multiple-choice questions, 20 essay questions, and 15 classroom or individual activities per chapter. In addition, a comprehensive Microsoft PowerPoint® presentation is available from the publisher for counselor educators to use or modify for classroom presentations. Case studies and vignettes included in the text can stimulate lively classroom discussions.

ACKNOWLEDGMENTS

This book is dedicated to the thousands of professional school counselors and school counselors in training who struggle daily to meet the seemingly ever-expanding needs of the students, families, educational colleagues, and communities they serve. This dedication extends to the thousands of counselor educators and supervisors who have devoted their lives to their profession, colleagues, and students. Thank you for making this a profession to be proud of! I especially want to thank the authors who contributed their perspectives and words of wisdom. They are all true experts in their specialty areas and are truly dedicated to the betterment of the profession. It is an honor to work closely with such an august group of scholars. As for myself, I owe much of my current thinking and perspective to the many conversations I have had with colleagues and graduate students. Kevin Davis and Sarah Kenoyer of Merrill/Prentice Hall deserve special mention for their stewardship during the editing of this book. Additional mention goes out to Mary Harlan, my production editor at Merrill/Prentice Hall, and Amanda Hosey Dugan, my project editor at Thistle Hill Publishing Services, for their outstanding service. I am also grateful to the reviewers, Jennifer R. Adams, University of Tennessee at Chattanooga University; Virginia B. Allen, Idaho State University; Douglas J. Mickelson, Mt. Mary College; Tarrell Portman, University of Iowa; and Tovah Sands, California State University, for their helpful and supportive comments. Finally, I am forever grateful to my family, whose tolerance for my periodic quest of solitude makes projects such as this possible.

DISCOVER THE COMPANION WEBSITE ACCOMPANYING THIS BOOK

THE PRENTICE HALL COMPANION WEBSITE: A VIRTUAL LEARNING ENVIRONMENT

Technology is a constantly growing and changing aspect of our field that is creating a need for content and resources. To address this emerging need, Prentice Hall has developed an online learning environment for students and professors alike—Companion Websites—to support our textbooks.

In creating a Companion Website, our goal is to build on and enhance what the textbook already offers. For this reason, the content for each user-friendly website is organized by chapter and provides the professor and student with a variety of meaningful resources.

Common Companion Website features for students include:

- **Chapter Objectives**—outline key concepts from the text.
- **Interactive Self-quizzes**—complete with hints and automatic grading provide immediate feedback for students. After students submit their answers for the interactive self-quizzes, the Companion Website **Results Reporter** computes a percentage grade, provides a graphic representation of how many questions were answered correctly and incorrectly, and gives a question-by-question analysis of the quiz. Students are given the option to send their quiz to up to four email addresses (professor, teaching assistant, study partner, etc.).
- **Essay Questions**—allow students to respond to themes and objectives of each chapter by applying what they have learned to real classroom situations.
- **Web Destinations**—link to www sites that relate to chapter content.

To take advantage of the many available resources, please visit the *Transforming the School Counseling Profession,* Second Edition, Companion Website at

www.prenhall.com/erford

ABOUT THE AUTHORS

EDITOR

Dr. Bradley T. Erford is professor of education and director of the school counseling program at Loyola College in Maryland. He is the recipient of the American Counseling Association (ACA) Professional Development Award, ACA Carl D. Perkins Government Relations Award, ACA Research Award, Association for Counselor Education and Supervision's (ACES) Robert O. Stripling Award for Excellence in Standards, Maryland Counselor of the Year, MACD Counselor Advocacy Award, MACD Professional Development Award, and MACD Counselor Visibility Award. He is also an ACA Fellow. He is the editor of five texts: *Transforming the School Counseling Profession* (2nd ed.; Merrill/Prentice Hall, 2007); *Professional School Counseling: A Handbook of Principles, Programs and Practices* (2004); *The Counselor's Guide to Clinical, Personality and Behavioral Assessment* (2006); *Assessment for Counselors* (2007); and *Research and Evaluation in Counseling* (2008). His research specialization falls primarily in development and technical analysis of psychoeducational tests and has resulted in the publication of numerous refereed journal articles, book chapters, and published tests. He is past president of the Association for Assessment in Counseling and Education (AACE), past chair of the American Counseling Association–Southern (US) Region; past chair of ACA's Task Force on High Stakes Testing; past chair of ACA's Interprofessional Committee; past chair of the American Counseling Association's (ACA) Public Awareness and Support Committee (cochair of the National Awards Subcommittee); past president of the Maryland Association for Counseling and Development (MACD); past president of Maryland Association for Counselor Education

and Supervision (MACES); and past president of the Maryland Association for Measurement and Evaluation (MAME). Dr. Erford is a Licensed Clinical Professional Counselor, Licensed Professional Counselor, Nationally Certified Counselor, Licensed Psychologist, and Licensed School Psychologist. Prior to arriving at Loyola, Dr. Erford was a school psychologist/counselor in the Chesterfield County (VA) Public Schools. He maintains a private practice specializing in assessment and treatment of children and adolescents. A graduate of the University of Virginia (Ph.D. in counselor education), Bucknell University (M.A. in school psychology), and Grove City College (B.S. in biology and psychology), he teaches courses in Testing and Measurement, Lifespan Development, School Counseling, Research and Evaluation in Counseling, and Stress Management.

CONTRIBUTING AUTHORS

Dr. Patrick Akos is an assistant professor of school counseling in the School of Education at the University of North Carolina at Chapel Hill. He is a former middle school counselor and was recognized as the American School Counselor Association's 2004 Counselor Educator of the Year. Dr. Akos's research focuses on school transitions, middle school counseling, and developmental advocacy. Currently, his research continues on how school personnel can promote successful transitions into and out of middle school (and the assorted configurations found in school districts) and how professional school counselors can intervene and advocate for optimal development of early adolescents.

Dr. Deryl F. Bailey is an assistant professor and program coordinator of the school counseling master's program at the University of Georgia. He earned a master's degree in guidance and counseling from Campbell University, in North Carolina, and Ed.S. and Ph.D. degrees in counselor education from the University of Virginia. His primary research areas are adolescent development, psychosocial development among adolescent African American males, school counseling, and issues related to multiculturalism and diversity. He is the developer of Empowered Youth Programs, an enrichment program that develops and nurtures academic and social excellence in children and adolescents with a special emphasis on African American males.

Dr. Stuart F. Chen-Hayes is associate professor of counselor education/school counseling at Lehman College of the City University of New York. Dr. Chen-Hayes has coordinated Lehman College's companion institution status with the Education Trust's National Center for Transforming School Counseling (NCTSC) Initiative since 1999. Dr. Chen-Hayes helped to write a $1.2 million Elementary and Secondary School Counseling Demonstration Act Grant for the New York City Department of Education to transform all elementary school counseling programs (with intensive staff development for all elementary school counselors, principals, and academic intervention team leaders in the ASCA *National Model* and the NCTSC principles) in New York City during the 2004–2007 school years, and he works as a lead trainer/consultant on the project with the Education Trust's NCTSC. Dr. Chen-Hayes has published many refereed journal articles and book chapters in school, family, and sexuality counseling. He is on the editorial boards of *Professional School Counseling* and *The Journal of LBGT Issues in Counseling* and has given more than 150 professional presentations and workshops in counselor education and advocacy related to transforming school counseling, family counseling, and sexuality counseling.

Dr. Yvette Q. Getch is an associate professor at the University of Georgia. She earned a B.S. in social work at the Florida State University, an M.Ed. in rehabilitation counseling from the University of Arkansas, and a Ph.D. in rehabilitation education and research from the University of Arkansas. Her primary areas of research include

advocacy skills training for students who have disabilities or chronic illnesses and accessible sexuality education materials for students who are deaf. Dr. Getch has developed self-advocacy training materials for students who are deaf and has coauthored training materials to assist school personnel helping young children cope with asthma and chronic illnesses in early education environments.

Dr. Samuel T. Gladding is a professor and chair of the Counseling Department at Wake Forest University, North Carolina. He is the past president of the American Counseling Association (ACA), Association for Specialists in Group Work (ASGW), the Association for Counselor Education and Supervision (ACES), and Chi Sigma Iota. He is the author of a number of professional texts on counseling, including books on group counseling, family counseling, the arts and counseling, and community and agency counseling.

Dr. Gary Goodnough coordinates the counselor education program at Plymouth State University, New Hampshire. He received a Ph.D. in counselor education from the University of Virginia in 1995 and is a national certified counselor and state-licensed clinical mental health counselor. A former high school director of guidance, Dr. Goodnough has authored several articles and book chapters and has made numerous regional and national professional presentations on school counseling.

Dr. Edwin L. Herr, NCC, NCCC, is distinguished professor emeritus of education (counselor education and counseling psychology) and associate dean emeritus, College of Education, Pennsylvania State University. Dr. Herr served as a school counselor, a local director of guidance, the first state director of guidance and testing and, subsequently, the first director of the Bureau of Pupil Personnel Services in the Pennsylvania Department of Education. From 1968 until 1992, Dr. Herr served as head of the Department of Counselor Education, Counseling Psychology, and Rehabilitation Services Education or other department iterations at the Pennsylvania State University. During this time, he also served as university director of Vocational Teacher Education and director of the Center for Professional Personnel Development in Vocational Education and as interim dean in

1972–1973 and 1998–1999. Dr. Herr received a B.S. in business education from Shippensburg State Teachers College in 1955 and an M.A. in psychological foundations, a Professional Diploma in coordination of guidance services, and an Ed.D. in counseling and student personnel administration from Teachers College, Columbia University, where he was an Alumni Fellow. Dr. Herr is past president of the American Association for Counseling and Development (now ACA), the National Vocational Guidance Association, the Association for Counselor Education and Supervision, and Chi Sigma Iota, the Counseling Academic and Professional Honor Society International. Dr. Herr was a member of the Executive Committee of the International Round Table for the Advancement of Counseling from 1976 to 1984, and of the Board of Directors of the International Association of Educational and Vocational Guidance from 1991 to 1999. He is the author or coauthor of over 300 articles and book chapters and 33 books and monographs, a former editor of the *Journal of Counseling and Supervision* (1993–1996) and *Counselor Education and Supervision* (1971–1974), and a member of several other editorial boards.

Dr. Cheryl Holcomb-McCoy received her Ph.D. in counseling and educational development from the University of North Carolina at Greensboro. She is an associate professor of Counselor Education in the Department of Counseling and Personnel Services at the University of Maryland at College Park. Her areas of research specialization include multicultural school counseling, school counselor multicultural self-efficacy, and urban school counselor preparation. She has written numerous book chapters and refereed articles on issues pertaining to diversity in counselor education. Dr. Holcomb-McCoy is a former national secretary of Chi Sigma Iota International (CSI) and was the recipient of the CSI Outstanding Research Award in 1998. She has served on the editorial boards of *Professional School Counseling, Journal of Counseling and Development,* and *Journal of Multicultural Counseling and Development.* She is currently serving as the American School Counselor Association's (ASCA) Diversity Professional Network Chairperson.

Dr. Reese M. House is a nationally recognized counselor educator. He is professor emeritus at Oregon State University, where he focused on preparing professional school counselors to be proactive change agents and advocates for social, economic, and political justice. He has experience working as a professional school counselor, community activist, and HIV/AIDS educator. Dr. House currently works at the Education Trust in Washington, DC, on the Transforming School Counseling Initiative.

Dr. Carol V. Kaffenberger is an assistant professor in the counseling and development program at George Mason University, Virginia. Dr. Kaffenberger teaches counselor preparation courses and supervises school counseling interns. She developed a school reintegration model for counselors serving students with chronic illnesses and provides training to practicing counselors. She has been a consultant for the NCTSC at the Education Trust and provides training for practicing school counselors locally and nationally in the use of data and the development of advocacy and leadership skills.

Dr. Vivian V. Lee is the Higher Education School Counselor Specialist at the National Office for School Counselor Advocacy of the College Board. Dr. Lee is a former teacher, secondary school counselor, director of school counseling, and counselor educator. She continues to teach school counseling courses as an adjunct at the University of Maryland at College Park. Her work includes research in the area of school counselor professional development, serving as a MetLife trainer with the Education Trust National Initiative for Transforming School Counseling, and has published articles and book chapters on developing school counseling programs, conflict resolution and violence, and group counseling. Dr. Lee worked in public education for 24 years before joining the College Board. She received her master's and doctoral degrees from the University of Virginia.

Erin H. Leff is an attorney, retired school psychologist, and mediator who has worked in special education for over 30 years. She earned an M.S. in Educational Psychology from the University of Wisconsin–Madison and a J.D. from Rutgers–Camden. Ms. Leff has worked as a school psychologist as well as a program administrator in multiple states. She has been a special education due process hearing officer, appeals officer, and mediator. Ms. Leff has provided training on various topics in special education and mediation. Currently, Ms. Leff is Deputy Special Master in the federal district court case regarding special education in the Baltimore City Public Schools.

Dr. Lynn Linde is an assistant professor of education and the Director of Clinical Programs in the school counseling program at Loyola College in Maryland. She received her Master's degree in school counseling and her doctorate in counseling from the George Washington University. She was previously the chief of the Student Services and Alternative Programs Branch at the Maryland State Department of Education, the state specialist for school counseling, a local school system counseling supervisor, a middle and high school counselor, and a special education teacher. She has made numerous presentations, particularly in the areas of ethics and legal issues for counselors and public policy and legislation, over the course of her career. Dr. Linde is the recipient of the ACA Carl Perkins Award, the ACES Program Supervisor Award, and the SACES Program Supervisor Award as well as numerous awards from the state association and from the state of Maryland for her work in student services and youth suicide prevention.

Patricia J. Martin is a nationally recognized leader in the reform of school counseling and efforts to design training opportunities to help practicing counselors become an integral part of the primary mission for schools. Pat holds a B.A. in mathematics and an M.A. in school counseling from Our Lady of the Lake College in San Antonio, Texas. Pat has more than 30 years of experience as a public school educator, having worked as a teacher, professional school counselor, district supervisor of counselors, high school principal, chief educational administrator, and assistant superintendent of schools in Prince George's County, Maryland. In her work as the senior program manager at the Education Trust, she provided the leadership and technical expertise that solidly launched the National Transforming School Counseling Initiative, which was underwritten by the DeWitt Wallace Foundation.

She is currently an assistant vice president at the College Board, leading the National Office for School Counselor Advocacy in Washington, DC. In this capacity, she continues working to establish a national presence in education reform for school counselors as they seek to advance the academic agenda for all students.

Dr. Debbie W. Newsome, LPC, NCC, is an assistant professor of counseling at Wake Forest University, North Carolina, where she teaches courses in career counseling, appraisal procedures, and statistics and supervises master's students in their field experiences. In addition to teaching and supervising, Dr. Newsome counsels children, adolescents, and families at a nonprofit mental health organization in Winston-Salem, North Carolina.

Dr. Spencer G. Niles is a professor of education and the head of the Department of Counselor Education, Counseling Psychology, and Rehabilitation Services at Penn State University. He served previously as professor and assistant dean in the Curry School of Education at the University of Virginia. He is a past editor of the *Career Development Quarterly* and serves on the editorial boards of other career-development journals. Niles has also served as president for the National Career Development Association. He received the David Brooks Distinguished Mentor Award and the Extended Research Award, both from ACA. He is also the author or coauthor of over 80 journal articles, book chapters, and books. Niles is a licensed psychologist and licensed professional counselor.

Dr. Rachelle Pérusse is an associate professor in Counseling Psychology within the Department of Educational Psychology at the University of Connecticut. Previous to this appointment, she was on the faculty at Plattsburgh State University since 1997 and was the school counseling coordinator in the Counselor Education Department. She received a Ph.D. in Counselor Education from Virginia Tech in 1997. Before becoming a school counselor educator, Dr. Pérusse worked with poor and minority youth as a high school counselor in a rural school district in Georgia. She is a national certified counselor and a national certified school counselor. Professionally, she has worked as a consultant with the

Education Trust and as a MetLife Fellow for the Transforming School Counseling Initiative, and is secretary for the Association of Counselor Education and Supervision (2005–2006). As a MetLife Fellow, she conducts consultations with school districts about the role of the school counselor and administration in relation to closing the achievement gap and advocating for poor and minority youth. Dr. Pérusse has several articles published about national trends in school counselor education and has coedited two books: *Critical Incidents in Group Counseling* and *Leadership, Advocacy, and Direct Service Strategies for Professional School Counselors.*

Dr. Elana Rock is an associate professor of special education at Loyola College in Maryland. Her responsibilities include teaching special education courses for the undergraduate education program and the graduate special education programs. Dr. Rock earned a B.A. from University of Pennsylvania, an M.A. in teaching children with emotional disturbance from New York University, and an Ed.D. in Special Education from Johns Hopkins University. Prior to earning her doctorate, Dr. Rock taught elementary and secondary students with learning disabilities and emotional/behavioral disorders. For the past 5 years, Dr. Rock has served as expert research consultant to the U.S. federal district court's Special Master overseeing special education service delivery in the Baltimore City Public Schools. Her research publications and presentations focus on children with concomitant high-prevalence disorders, evaluating service delivery in special education, and special education teacher education.

Dr. Linda Seligman is both an academic and a clinician. She is a faculty member at Walden University and also teaches at Johns Hopkins University. She is a professor emeritus at George Mason University in Fairfax, Virginia, where she was codirector of the doctoral program in education, coordinator of the Counseling and Development Program, and in charge of the Community Agency Counseling specialization. Dr. Seligman also is a licensed psychologist and licensed professional counselor with a private practice in Fairfax, Virginia. She has extensive experience in a variety of clinical settings, including psychiatric hospitals, college counseling centers, community mental health centers, substance abuse treatment programs, foster care, corrections, and private practice. Dr. Seligman received a Ph.D. in counseling psychology from Columbia University. Her research interests include diagnosis and treatment planning and the mind–body–spirit connection. She has written 11 books and over 75 professional articles and book chapters. In addition, she has lectured throughout the United States and Canada on diagnosis and treatment planning and is a nationally recognized expert on that subject. Dr. Seligman has been editor of *The Journal of Mental Health Counseling* and has served as president of the Virginia Association of Mental Health Counselors. She was selected as a distinguished professor by George Mason University and was chosen as Researcher of the Year by the American Mental Health Counselors Association.

Amber Throckmorton, NCC, is currently a professional school counselor with Newport News City Public Schools in Newport News, Virginia. She earned a B.S. in communications and an M.S.Ed. in school counseling from Old Dominion University. She has presented at regional, state, and national conferences and is a member of several professional organizations.

Susan C. Whiston, Ph.D., is a professor at Indiana University in the Department of Counseling and Educational Psychology. She has been teaching school counseling courses since 1986 and has published many articles concerning empirical support for school counseling. Prior to receiving her doctorate from the University of Wyoming, she worked in secondary schools as a counselor for low-income students.

BRIEF CONTENTS

CONTENTS

Note: Every effort has been made to provide accurate and current Internet information in this book. However, the Internet and information posted on it are constantly changing, so it is inevitable that some of the Internet addresses listed in this textbook will change.

TRANSFORMING THE SCHOOL COUNSELING PROFESSION

BRADLEY T. ERFORD, REESE M. HOUSE, AND PATRICIA J. MARTIN

Editor's Introduction: Welcome to an exciting career—and adventure. Transforming school counseling involves changing its substance and appearance. The changes encouraged in this book are not cosmetic but deep, meaningful changes that encourage professional school counselors to become agents of educational reform and social change. The effective professional school counselor seeks to remove barriers to educational, career, and personal–social development, whether for a single student or an entire society. Although usually pursuing a common purpose, each professional school counselor must understand and integrate the school's mission and goals, the needs of the school community, and his or her own strengths into a comprehensive developmental school counseling program. Such an approach adds uniqueness to each program while ensuring that needs are addressed in a comprehensive manner.

The 21st century brings a new age in the profession of school counseling, one in which traditional methods must be transformed to meet current and future challenges. Professional school counseling must evolve into a model that will both fit the needs of the students in this rapidly changing society and conform to the demands of school reform and accountability mandates. The changes suggested in this book are not cosmetic, but deep and meaningful changes that encourage professional school counselors to become agents of school reform and social change while working as leaders and advocates in schools to remove barriers to student success.

THE SCHOOL: THE PRIMARY WORKPLACE FOR SCHOOL COUNSELORS

The Context of Professional School Counseling

The word *school* in the title "professional school counselor" has incredible significance for what is expected of the professionals who hold this role in K–12 public schools today. School reform, based on the principle that the level of academic proficiency must be raised for all children, dictates that all professionals working in school settings must contribute to this bottom line or find themselves on the budget-cut list. And, the contributions that are valued in the "school setting" are those that have direct ties to increased student achievement. If this goal of raising achievement for all populations in the school settings does not occur, there are now sanctions for schools and school personnel who are unable to meet these demands. Never before in the history of public education has such congruency of purpose been the *rule du jour* for every professional working in schools. There are no exceptions for professional school counselors.

Inequities and Lack of Access Propel Changes in Schools

Educational equity in a democratic society requires that all children have equal access to quality education. However, data from states and local school districts show that students who are economically disadvantaged and students of color are systemically denied an education that will lead them to success in school and in the marketplace (Education Trust, 2005a). These data show a significant achievement gap between students from low-income and minority families and their more advantaged peers. Except for a few schools, students from low-income and minority families perform less well on all existing measures of academic proficiency. Thus, many of these children do not obtain the skills and knowledge necessary to participate successfully in the 21st-century economy. The achievement gap among students exists primarily because educators (a) expect less of children from low-income and minority families; (b) provide some students (usually White

and/or middle-class) with a rigorous, high-quality curriculum and others with a watered-down, weak curriculum; and (c) provide fewer material resources to students who have the greatest needs (Education Trust, 2005a).

The Continuing Call for School Reform

In the United States, two primary developments continue to fuel school reform efforts: the unrelenting call for accountability for educating all students to higher academic standards, and the economic demand for a more knowledgeable workforce equipped to work in an ever-expanding technological world. Concurrent with these demands, reform is driven by awareness that the student population is increasingly more diverse and now includes higher numbers of students from low-income and minority families living in urban and rural communities. Educational institutions have not served these populations well in the past and are faced with dire consequences if the job is not done better (Lee, 2005; Mohrman & Lawler, 1996).

Throughout the last 15 years, educators, policy makers, community groups, and business leaders have worked in venues as diverse as boardrooms, legislative arenas, school districts, universities, and even at kitchen tables across the nation to reform K–16 education (The National Center for Public Policy & Higher Education, 2000). Recently, these efforts received a very public boost when the National Governors Association (NGA) proclaimed high school reform in America as a highest priority and declared that students must graduate from high school ready for college, work, and citizenship (Gates, 2005).

The Standards and Accountability Movement

The Standards movement, adopted by most states and the Federal mandates outlined in the No Child Left Behind Act of 2001 (NCLB) legislation were instituted to address the inequities existing in schools. These mandates have redefined expectations for educational outcomes in schools. Standards for academic outcomes for all children define what all students should know and be able to do as the result of academic course content. Standards have made expected results for teaching and learning more transparent for all, including teachers, students, families, and the community at large.

The accountability provisions for NCLB require states to describe how they will close the achievement gap. All students, including those who are disadvantaged, must achieve academic proficiency. The Standards movement and NCLB have been prominent catalysts in propelling data-driven changes in the landscape of schools. In the past, the culture of schooling allowed acceptance of schoolwide student performance based on aggregate data, accepting the law of averages as opposed to attention to progress for all students.

Connecting School Counseling to School Reform

Today, professional school counselors must apply their skills and knowledge in a school setting that is under serious reform and scrutiny. School counselor educators and professional school counselors can neither minimize nor exclude this factor as a primary consideration in preparation programs or in practice. For professional school counselors to work effectively in schools, they must design data-driven school counseling programs that fit into the mission of today's schools of rigorous standards and accountability for all students.

Accountability for student achievement is everybody's business, but traditionally it has been seen as the turf of teachers, administrators, and central office personnel in charge of curriculum and instructional programs. In reality, accountability is the responsibility of everyone in the school setting, including professional school counselors as well as students, parents, and the community at large.

Until recently, professional school counselors have been left out of discussions regarding school reform, student achievement, and accountability. This omission is deleterious to the accomplishment of the goals for 21st-century K–12 school reform. School reform that constitutes systemic change for all students will not occur without the involvement of all the critical players.

Professional school counselors need to integrate themselves into school reform by collaborating with all school staff instead of

working as ancillary personnel removed from the instructional side of schools. In the ancillary model, professional school counselors focus on addressing individual issues and concerns, more often those that have to do with social and personal development. This role is most often seen as nonessential to teaching and learning. Indeed, it often is seen as an ineffective utilization of resources, as well as fiscal irresponsibility by policy makers, school boards, and school system leaders who are being held accountable for increasing student achievement.

A Call for Change in School Counselor Practice

As we move further into the 21st century, it is critical for professional school counselors to move beyond their current roles as "helper–responders" and become proactive leaders and advocates for the success of all students. To do this, professional school counselors must move out of the traditional mode of operation and begin collaborating with other school professionals to influence systemwide changes and become an integral part of their schools and school reform (Hayes, Dagley, & Horne, 1996; House & Hayes, 2002). This approach requires counselors to examine and question inequitable practices that do not serve the interests of all students.

To work as leaders and advocates to effect systems change, it is of paramount importance that the role of the professional school counselor undergo a transformative change (Capuzzi, 1998). To "transform" means to alter, to shift, or to change the way one works (Mezirow, 1994). For professional school counselors, it means moving away from a primary focus on mental health and individual changes to a focus on whole-school and systemic concerns that fit the schools' mission—academic achievement (see Table 1.1).

Through data-driven advocacy that purposefully highlights and focuses on marginalized populations, the scope of professional school counselor work will be expanded and transformed. The use of data allows professional school counselors to be accountable for their actions and to show they can make a difference in the academic success of all students. The results of these deliberate actions can be documented by "hard data" that move

TABLE 1.1
Transformation of the Role of Professional School Counselor

Present Focus	New Vision
Mental health issues	Academic and student achievement focus
Individual student concerns and issues	Whole school and system concerns and issues
Clinical model focused on student deficits	Academic focus, building on student strengths
Providing service, one-to-one and small groups	Leading, planning, and developing programs
Primary focus on personal/social	Focus on academic counseling, learning and achievement, supporting student success
Ancillary support personnel	Integral members of educational team
Loosely defined role and responsibility	Focusing on mission and role identification
Record keeping	Using data to effect change
Sorting, selecting course placement process	Advocating inclusion in rigorous preparation for all, especially students from low-income and minority families
Work in isolation or with other counselors	Teaming and collaboration with all educators in school in resolving issues involving the whole school and community
Guarding the status quo	Acting as change agent, especially for educational equity for all students
Involvement primarily with students	Involvement with students, parents, education professionals, community, and community agencies
Little or no accountability	Full accountability for student success, use of data, planning and preparation for access to wide range of postsecondary options
Dependence on use of system's resources for helping students and families	Brokering services for parents and students from community resources/agencies as well as school system's resources
Postsecondary planning with interested students	Creating pathways for all students to achieve high aspirations

school counseling from the periphery of school business to a position front and center in constructing and supporting student success.

Professional school counselors are ideally positioned in schools to serve as conductors and transmitters of information to promote school-wide success for all students. When professional school counselors aggressively support quality education for all students, they create a school climate where access and support for rigorous preparation is expected. In so doing, students who have not been served well in the past have a chance at acquiring the skills necessary to unconditionally participate in the 21st-century economy.

A CALL FOR CHANGE IN SCHOOL COUNSELOR PREPARATION PROGRAMS

For the role of professional school counselor to be one of leader and advocate working to make systemic change to benefit all students, professional school counselor preparation programs will need to change practices. Since the 1960s, most professional school counselors have been taught the three "Cs" as a way of defining their role in schools. The three Cs—counseling, consultation, and coordination—served the profession well over the years, but these roles are now too limiting and no longer provide enough breadth and depth of scope for professional school counselors to be effective. In addition, the older model does not provide a basis for serving all students. Instead of limiting professional school counselor training and practice to these roles, counselor educators and practitioners must broaden their roles to include leadership, advocacy, teaming and collaboration, counseling and coordination, and assessment and use of data (see Table 1.2).

Teaching professional school counselors these new approaches broadens the scope of the work so that it is systemically more inclusive and, thus, helpful to more students. The model allows competent professional school counselors to work as leaders and team members with parents and members of the educational community to create supportive pathways that allow all students to succeed. Examples of school counselor preparation programs preparing students in this transformed model can be found at the Education Trust Web site (www.edtrust.org) under the "Transforming School Counseling" tab.

THE ASCA NATIONAL MODEL: A FRAMEWORK FOR SCHOOL COUNSELING PROGRAMS

In 1997, the American School Counselor Association (ASCA) published the *National Standards for School Counseling Programs* (Campbell & Dahir, 1997) to provide a standardized basis for the creation of comprehensive, developmental guidance services. The nine standards, three each in the domains of academic, career, and personal/social development, were accompanied by suggested student competencies (i.e., knowledge and skills to be acquired) and led to the development of comprehensive developmental school counseling curricula by school systems around the country. The National Standards were a historical landmark that gave direction to a profession floundering for an identity and role in school reform.

Shortly after publication, leaders in the field realized that producing curricular standards and competencies was only the first step in transforming the school counseling profession.

A developmental curriculum is essential to educating students and provides the "what," but it falls short of the "how." At the same time, the Education Trust's Transforming School Counseling Initiative was gaining steam in school counselor education and public school venues. This initiative emphasized data-driven services and programs to address achievement disparities, particularly between racial or socioeconomic subpopulations, as well as more specific attention to issues of social advocacy and justice. To expand on and integrate the National Standards into a comprehensive framework that addressed the "how" of school counseling, ASCA (2003a) published the *ASCA National Model: A Framework for School Counseling Programs*. This model focused professional school counselors on a more comprehensive, systemic approach to four core elements or mechanisms for student success: program foundation, delivery, management, and accountability. As such, professional school counselors were encouraged to switch from the traditional focus on services for some needy students to program-centered services for every student in the school and, by extension, their families and community.

Program foundation, the "what" of a comprehensive school counseling program, makes clear "what every student will know and be able to do" (ASCA, 2003a, p. 22) and includes emphases on a school counseling program's beliefs and philosophies, mission, domains (i.e., academic, career, personal/social), standards, and competencies. These domains, standards, and competencies are amply described in *National Standards* (Campbell & Dahir, 1997) and included in appendix C of this book.

A delivery system discusses "how" professional school counselors should implement a comprehensive developmental program. It includes attention to the guidance curriculum (i.e., systematic developmental classroom guidance lessons), individual student planning (i.e., assistance in establishing personal goals and future plans), responsive services (i.e., individual or small group counseling, crisis counseling or consultation, peer mediation, referrals), and systems support (i.e., program maintenance

TABLE 1.2
New Vision for Professional School Counselors

Leadership	Advocacy	Teaming and Collaboration	Counseling and Coordination	Assessment and Use of Data
Promoting, planning, and implementing prevention programs, career and college activities, course selection and placement activities, social/personal management, and decision-making activities	Making available and using data to help the whole school look at student outcomes	Participating in or consulting with teams for problem solving; ensuring responsiveness to equity and cultural diversity issues as well as learning styles	Brief counseling of individual students, groups, and families	Assessing and interpreting student needs, and recognizing differences in culture, languages, values, and backgrounds
Providing data snapshots of student outcomes, showing implications and achievement gaps, and providing leadership for school to view through equity lens	Using data to effect change; calling on resources from school and community	Collaborating with other helping agents (peer helpers, teachers, principal, community agencies, business)	Coordinating resources, human and other, for students, families, and staff to improve student achievement (community, school, home)	Establishing and assessing measurable goals for student outcomes from counseling programs, activities, interventions, and experiences
Arrange one-to-one relationships for students with adults in school setting for additional support and assistance in reaching academic success	Advocating student experiences and exposures that will broaden students' career awareness and knowledge	Collaborating with school and community teams to focus on rewards, incentives, and supports for student achievement	Working as key liaison with students and school staff to set high aspirations for all students and develop plans and supports for achieving these aspirations	Assessing building barriers that impede learning, inclusion, and/or academic success for students
Playing a leadership role in defining and carrying out the guidance and counseling function	Advocating student placement and school support for rigorous preparation for all students	Collaborating with school staff members in developing staff training on team responses to students' academic, social, emotional, and developmental needs	Coordinating staff training initiatives that address student needs on a schoolwide basis	Interpreting student data for use in whole school planning for change

through professional development, consultation/collaboration, management functions).

The *management systems* element accounts for the "when," "why," and "on what authority" of a comprehensive school counseling program (ASCA, 2003a, p. 22) and is comprised of: management agreements (i.e., what accomplishments the professional school counselor is accountable for during the school year), advisory council, use of data (for student monitoring and closing of achievement/social disparities), action plans, distinctions between appropriate and inappropriate uses of time, and a school counseling program calendar.

Accountability answers the all-important question of "How are students different as a result of the program?" (ASCA, 2003a, p. 23). Accountability is provided by professional school counselors through results reports, performance standards, and performance audits. A *results report* is comprised of outcomes assessments that document changes in students and other stakeholders through systematic analysis of their performance within various program components. An example might be academic performance changes as a result of participation in a study-skills group. Monitoring changes in perceptions, process, and attitudes can also provide helpful evidence of professional school counselor effectiveness. *Performance standards* for professional school counselors include all local job and program expectations to help assess one's skill in implementing a comprehensive developmental school counseling program. *Program audits* are conducted to ensure that a school's comprehensive developmental program aligns with some set of standards, whether at the local or state level, or with the *ASCA National Model.* Such alignment is deemed critical in addressing the needs of all students. All of these accountability processes are aimed at program evaluation and continuous quality improvement.

The *National Model* (ASCA, 2003a) also encouraged professional school counselors to focus on local student needs and the local political context, and to use data to identify and meet these needs as well as to document program effectiveness (ASCA, 2003a). It also

emphasized four important themes: leadership, advocacy, collaboration and teaming, and systemic change. *Leadership* describes the activities of professional school counselors within the school and beyond to enact system-wide changes to facilitate student success. Professional school counselors work diligently to ensure that all students have access to rigorous academic programs and to close achievement gaps among student groups, particularly minorities and the materially poor. *Advocacy* involves the systematic identification of student needs and accompanying efforts to ensure that those needs are met. Professional school counselors help every student achieve academic success by setting high expectations and providing needed support and removing systemic barriers to success. *Collaboration and teaming* require that professional school counselors work with a wide array of stakeholders within the school, school system, and community. Collaborative efforts should focus on providing students access to rigorous academic programs, and other factors leading to academic success. Teaming with parents, educators, and community agencies to develop effective working relationships is critical to this goal. *Systemic change* encompasses schoolwide changes in expectations, instructional practices, support services, and philosophy with the goal of raising achievement levels for all students. A focus on data-driven programming allows professional school counselors to identify areas in need of improvement, leading to alterations in systemic policies and procedures that empower students and lead to higher performance and greater opportunities for postsecondary success.

The *ASCA National Model* (ASCA, 2003a) and its facets will be explored in greater depth in chapter 7 and applications of the model can be seen in every other chapter in this book. The *National Model* presents a cogent starting point for professional school counselors to implement effective comprehensive developmental programs that will benefit all schools.

The *National Model* also identifies appropriate responsibilities that professional school counselors should engage in and inappropriate activities that should be avoided (ASCA, 2003b, p. 168). For example:

1. Designing individual student academic programs . . . (NOT . . .) Registering and scheduling all new students.
2. Counseling students with excessive tardiness or absenteeism . . . (NOT . . .) Signing excuses for students who are tardy or absent.
3. Counseling students with disciplinary problems . . . (NOT . . .) Performing disciplinary actions.
4. Collaborating with teachers to present guidance curriculum lessons . . . (NOT . . .) Teaching classes when teachers are absent.
5. Interpreting student records . . . (NOT . . .) Maintaining student records.
6. Ensuring student records are maintained in accordance with state and federal regulations . . . (NOT . . .) Clerical record keeping.
7. Assisting the school principal with identifying and resolving student issues, needs and problems . . . (NOT . . .) Assisting with duties in the principal's office.

The *National Model* provides a solid framework on which responsive, proactive, comprehensive developmental school counseling programs can be built. These programs ensure that all students are exposed to rigorous academic curricula, treated equitably and with dignity, and held to high academic standards that enhance postsecondary career opportunities.

ACCOUNTABILITY: MAKING SCHOOL COUNSELING COUNT

School counseling programs that are accountable are built around specific strategies utilizing student data to create vision and targeted change. These strategies include clear indicators that the school counseling program is producing results. In this accountability model, professional school counselors are key to removing barriers to learning and achievement and promoting success for all students. Removal of these barriers is critical to the future success of students and their families. Holding low expectations and believing that students cannot achieve due to life circumstances causes irrevocable damage to their future life options. To act as agents of

school and community change, professional school counselors must:

1. Provide and articulate a well defined developmental counseling program with attention to equity, access, and support services.
2. Routinely use data to analyze and improve access to, and success in, rigorous academic courses for underrepresented students.
3. Actively monitor the progress of underrepresented students in rigorous courses and provide assistance or interventions when needed.
4. Actively target and enroll underrepresented students into rigorous courses.
5. Develop, coordinate, and initiate support systems designed to improve the learning success of students experiencing difficulty with rigorous academic programs.

New Vision Practice

Advocating for high achievement for all students by serving as a leader and team member (see Table 1.1) in schools becomes the key role for counselors in this new approach to school counseling. It places professional school counselors at the center of the mission of school and school reform. In addition to counseling skills, professional school counselors will need to:

- Expect all students to achieve at a high level
- Actively work to remove barriers to learning
- Teach students how to help themselves (e.g., organization, study skills, and test-taking skills)
- Teach students and their families how to successfully manage the bureaucracy of the school system (e.g., teach parents how to enroll their children in academic courses that will lead to college, make formal requests to school officials on various matters, and monitor the academic progress of their children)
- Teach students and their families how to access support systems that encourage academic success (e.g., inform students and parents about tutoring and academic enrichment opportunities, and teach students and parents how to find resources on preparation for standardized tests)

- Use local, regional, and national data on disparities in resources and academic achievement to promote system change
- Work collaboratively with all school personnel
- Offer staff development training for school personnel that promotes high expectations and high standards for all students
- Use data as a tool to challenge the deleterious effects of low-level and unchallenging courses
- Highlight accurate information that negates myths about who can and cannot achieve success in rigorous courses
- Organize community activities to promote supportive structures for high standards for all students (e.g., after-school tutoring programs at neighborhood religious centers)
- Help parents and the community organize efforts to work with schools to institute and support high standards for all children
- Work as resource brokers within the community to identify all available resources to help students succeed

What Prevents Professional School Counselors from Changing?

The call for change in the role of professional school counselor is not new. Although professional school counselors are identified in educational literature as being important to the success of students in schools (Hayes, Dagley, & Horne, 1996), it seems that the profession has changed very slowly until recently. The following obstacles, or barriers, to changing the way professional school counselors practice may help explain why.

- Homeostasis: There is sometimes an unwillingness to change, that results in maintaining the status quo.
- Administrative practices can dictate the role of professional school counselors, even if the dictated role is different from counselor training.
- Professional school counselors can be pliable, often accepting responsibilities that are not part of their counseling role and function (e.g., bus duty, cafeteria duty).
- Pressure from special-interest groups may dictate the role of professional school counselors.

- Many counselor educators have little or no ongoing involvement with K–12 institutions, including little or no follow-up with recent graduates.
- Special education mandates for assessment, documentation, and ongoing services take too much of the counselor's time.
- Large numbers of practicing professional school counselors are functioning as highly paid clerical staff and/or quasiadministrators.
- Professional school counselors sometimes function as inadequately trained therapeutic mental health providers with unmanageable client loads.
- The role of professional school counselors is frequently determined by others, rather than by the counselors' developing their own purposeful, comprehensive programs.
- Little or no professional development is provided for professional school counselors.
- Crisis management on a day-to-day basis usurps too much of the professional school counselor's time.
- Professional school counselors may choose not to be involved in school reform efforts in school buildings.
- Professional school counselors may not see academic achievement as their goal or mission.
- Professional school counselors generally work to change students, not the system in which the student functions. Thus, the student, not the system, is assumed to be the "problem."

Professional school counselors who continue to use these "excuses" to avoid change often serve as maintainers of the status quo, advocating for the school system rather than for students and marginalized groups. They become "sorters and selectors," perpetuating the accepted placements and systemic barriers that cause an inequitable distribution between achievers and nonachievers based on race and socioeconomic status (Hart & Jacobi, 1992).

A Sense of Urgency Is Propelling Change

The sense of urgency to help all students be successful in school is propelling professional school counselors to change. Indeed many professional school counselors are seizing the opportunity to be leaders in schools and work as advocates for students. The *ASCA National Model* (2003a) provided the structure to implement a comprehensive approach to program foundation, delivery, management, and accountability. The model provides the mechanism with which professional school counselors and school counseling teams design, coordinate, implement, manage, and evaluate their programs for students' success. It provides a framework for the program components; the professional school counselor's role in implementation; and the underlying philosophies of leadership, advocacy, teaming and collaboration, and systemic change.

In many states, professional school counselors are working as a part of school reform efforts to increase access and opportunity for students. Project 720 in Pennsylvania is a high school reform effort that identifies key components that schools must address to improve student achievement. School counseling and advocacy is one component under review, and professional school counselors are actively involved in the planning and implementation of this school reform effort. More information about this project can be found at the following Web site: www.pde.state.pa.us. This is one example where professional school counselors are at the table and integrating themselves into school reform by collaborating with all school staff. They are integrally involved in planning systemic changes in schools that have the goal of closing the achievement gap and increasing proficiency of all students.

LIVING THE TRANSFORMED ROLE

The question becomes not whether the role of the professional school counselor will continue its transformation, but what shape this transformation will involve. This book focuses on the importance of a comprehensive program and some possible specialty roles, each of which has a great deal to offer a school community. But for a professional school counselor alone in a school to adopt only one of these roles would likely result in an ineffective program, or at least one in which many needs will not be addressed. Likewise, professional school counselors who attempt to focus on all roles will likely become overwhelmed. No one can do it all. School counseling services involve a complex interplay of student and school community needs with counselor strengths. Balance is needed, and it is quite possible that a professional school counselor who is "unsuccessful" in one school venue can be very successful in another venue in need of his or her particular strengths and talents. Thus, the transformed role of the professional school counselor will be multifaceted but flexible and practical.

It is helpful to think of the transformed role in terms of the confluence of rivers. When two or more rivers join, the resulting flow is dependent on a complex interplay of factors, including the volume of water (e.g., school, societal, and individual needs) and topographical features (e.g., services and resources). If the water volume of various rivers is heavy and the topography flat and featureless, a messy flood occurs! However, if the topography allows for channeling and measures of control such as deep collecting pools that make for calm appearances, or even steep, narrow walls with a rock-strewn path that sometimes leads to an appearance of controlled turbulence, the situation can be managed. In many ways, a skilled, competent professional school counselor can make a huge difference in very important ways. Likewise, professional school counselors who partner with stakeholders to provide a pool of resources and services can often calm the flow or at least channel it in some positive directions. Either way, the needs of many students, parents, educators, and citizens will be addressed in a proactive manner.

Another helpful way of looking at this complex interplay is through the metaphor of nets of various sizes. A comprehensive developmental school counseling program with its focus on large-group guidance and prevention-based programs is the first and highest net attempting to catch students and keep them on track developmentally. But as fate would have it, some students' needs are more serious and not necessarily developmental in nature, thus requiring intervention services. The next level of netting attempting to catch students in need may be group counseling with students or consultation or collaboration with parents and teachers. While many students are put back on track through effective implementation of these services, some require additional interventions (nets) that are more individualized. Individual counseling, or referral to qualified mental health professionals when lack of time or skill requires it, serves as that next level of netting. However, even after individualized services, some students will still be present with unmet needs. These students are the ones who in the past have been described as "falling through the cracks" and require a more systemic service delivery approach. This is where school–community–agency partnering and social and academic advocacy come in. These systemic interventions (nets) are essential to ensure that the needs of all children in our society are addressed.

ON BECOMING A PROFESSIONAL SCHOOL COUNSELOR: YOUR DESTINY

Among the many important components of a school counseling program and roles of the professional school counselor, the professionals authoring the chapters of this book have advocated for the development of comprehensive developmental school counseling programs and establishment of school–community partnerships. We have underscored the importance of social advocacy to remove systemic barriers to student academic performance and social development. We have made clear that professional school counselors must attain and maintain a high degree of skill and competence in the various components of a comprehensive program to ensure that all students can succeed.

Transformations are visible at both surface and deeper levels. The lessons of this book will be wasted if readers simply make cosmetic changes to program and profession. The transformations advocated in this book cut to the core of our mission as educators and counselors,

indeed to the very essence of why we wanted to become professional school counselors.

Most professional school counselors get into the profession because they love to work with children or adolescents, want to make an important difference in students' daily lives, and believe in the power of education as an equalizing social force. Welcome to a profession in which you can do all that and more! But before you begin that journey, take a moment to visualize, in your mind's eye, what you see yourself doing as a professional school counselor.

Many professional school counselors in training picture themselves counseling a student in a one-on-one setting or, perhaps, a small group of students. While this is certainly part of what a professional school counselor does, it is but a single facet. The role of the professional school counselor in a comprehensive school counseling program is very broad and very deep—so broad and so deep that many counselor educators struggle to prepare professional school counselors who can "do it all." From a realistic perspective and as described earlier, this may not be possible for all counselors (or perhaps any). The job of the professional school counselor is complex and involves a complicated interplay of what the school community's needs are and the strengths and weaknesses of the individual counselor.

As you make your way through this book, try to picture yourself performing the described roles and implementing the suggested strategies. It is likely that your strengths and weaknesses as a counselor and learner, as well as your past life experiences, will make some roles feel natural while others may feel uncomfortable. This is the normal developmental process of becoming a professional school counselor.

Please do enjoy your wondrous journey in becoming a professional school counselor and transforming the school counseling profession— a journey on which hundreds of thousands have preceded you, but which will be as distinct and fulfilling a path as you choose to make it. Enjoy the struggles. Serve the students, their families, your colleagues, and the community. But most of all, always remember in your heart why you wanted to become a professional school counselor!

SUMMARY/CONCLUSION

The vision for professional school counselors presented in this book is cutting edge, compelling, and essential to maintaining the profession in the 21st century and beyond. This vision puts professional school counselors in the middle of school reform and gives them an opportunity to demonstrate that they do make a difference in the success of students. Professional school counselors will be valued when they demonstrate effectiveness in making systemic changes that allow all students access to rigorous programs and equity in academic success.

The importance of school reform is clear. Our global society is increasingly dependent on the development and better use of all of our human resources. As Elam stated in 1993, "high-level thinking, lifelong learning, and the capacity to make frequent career changes will be required in an increasingly competitive, high-tech, knowledge-driven, worldwide economy" (p. 276). His statement is even more true today. Not addressing the need for educational change and continuing to foster low expectations and inadequate academic preparation for low-income and minority students is paramount to benign neglect. Professional school counselors support this neglect when they intentionally or inadvertently become part of the system that relegates large numbers of students to limited career options and virtually closes the door on their futures.

As leaders and advocates, professional school counselors need to reexamine professional role patterns and think in a more systemic fashion. They must be willing to reach and influence people beyond their jurisdiction, have political skills to cope with conflicting requirements of multiple constituencies, and question the status quo. When working from this framework, professional school counselors will be active creators, definers, and participants in educational systems change, and not passive respondents or victims of environmental circumstance. This practice aligns professional school counselors with school reform, transforms the counselors' role, and places them in the middle of the changes needed to help all students achieve.

An appropriate mantra for professional school counselors might be: "Fix the system, not the student." This calls for substantial changes in both preparation and practice of professional school counselors. Professional school counselors, understanding the context or environment in which they work, clearly see the mandate to connect their work to the mission of the school, the building-level school improvement plan, and specific accountability measures to be effective and accountable for their work.

Now go to our Companion Website at www.prenhall.com/erford to assess your understanding of chapter content with "Multiple-Choice Questions," apply comprehension with "Essay Questions," and broaden your knowledge of the school counseling profession with related "Web Links."

ACTIVITIES

1. Research the schools in your local community. Find test scores, percentages of students who graduate, percentage of low-income students, and racial and ethnic breakdown. How would the specifics of the schools in your area affect your focus as a professional school counselor in one of those schools?

2. Brainstorm ways that a professional school counselor could conduct and transmit information to an entire school to promote success of all students. Design several activities or lessons a guidance department could implement to support student achievement for all.

3. Read the *ASCA National Model: A Framework for School Counseling Programs* (2003a). What appears to be some of the significant themes effecting change in the profession? How could you incorporate this model in a new program that you have been assigned to begin?

HISTORICAL ROOTS AND FUTURE ISSUES

EDWIN L. HERR AND BRADLEY T. ERFORD

Editor's Introduction: It has been said that to know who you are, you must understand where you came from. When attempting to discern the future, historical events provide intriguing perspectives. Likewise, when beginning a journey of professional transformation, it is essential to understand the profession's roots and key developmental events. In this chapter, Dr. Herr provides an exceptional synopsis of the historical roots of the school counseling profession and, from this perspective, offers a peek at some of the profession's likely future challenges.

THE RISE OF PROFESSIONAL SCHOOL COUNSELING IN THE UNITED STATES

It can be argued that school counseling is the earliest form of intentional or systematic counseling in the United States or, perhaps, in the world. It also can be argued that many of the philosophical ideas and process methods incorporated into what professional school counselors now do could be traced in a fragmented way into ancient history (Dumont & Carson, 1995; Miller, 1961; Murphy, 1955; Williamson, 1965) as elders, teachers, or mentors engaged in dialogues intended to provide guidance to young people. Throughout history, every society has found methods beyond the family by which to provide selected young people direction and support as they grappled with questions of who they might become and how to achieve such goals. In some instances, the persons who delivered such guidance were philosophers, physicians, priests or other clerics, medicine men or shamans, teachers, or masters to apprentices. But "guidance" or "counseling" of young persons was not equally available to all young people, nor was it planned and systematic.

Against such a context, it is fair to suggest that the pervasive, formal, and systematic provisions of guidance and counseling in schools is an American invention. Although notions that arose in European research laboratories about individual differences, assessment techniques, and psychological classifications and explanations for behavior were conceptually important in shaping some of the content and methods of school counseling, they were not the stimuli that caused school counseling to come into being.

Like other major social institutions, guidance and counseling in schools did not arise spontaneously, nor did it occur in a vacuum. Although there were visionaries, scholars, and early practitioners of guidance and counseling who were critical to the implementation of school counseling, the historical moment had to be right for the ingredients of change to take root and begin to flourish. In the last quarter of the 19th century in the United States, political and social conditions converged to prod the nation to educational reform and to sensitize it to emerging issues of human dignity and the exploitation of children in the workplace, to the dynamics of massive immigration, and to the demands for human resources by the burgeoning Industrial Revolution.

Various authors during the 20th century have identified the different conditions that gave rise to guidance and counseling in U.S. schools. Brewer (1942) contended that four of the most important conditions were the division of labor, the growth of technology, the extension of vocational education, and the spread of modern forms of democracy. Traxler and North (1966) contended that the guidance movement in schools could be traced to five divergent sources: "philanthropy or humanitarianism, religion, mental hygiene, social change, and the movement to know pupils as individuals" (p. 6).

Clearly, there were many background or contextual variables that influenced the rise of school counseling at the end of the 19th and the beginning of the 20th century. But there is general consensus that the beginnings of school counseling in this century were in vocational guidance. It also is clear that many of the concerns that gave rise to school counseling were focused on the quality and utility of existing educational processes. Embedded in both the emerging concepts of vocational guidance and of educational reform were issues of individual freedom of choice and dignity.

These three factors, interacted and intertwined as philosophies of school guidance and models of school guidance or counseling, were introduced by various pioneers in the field.

There are different persons who can be described as early visionaries or practitioners of school guidance and counseling. History has failed to record the names of many of them. But among those about whom we know, several persons have been worthy of special note: George Merrill, who in 1895 developed the first systematic vocational guidance program in San Francisco; Jesse B. Davis, who in 1898 began working as a counselor in Central High School in Detroit and in 1908 organized a program of vocational and moral guidance in the schools of Grand Rapids, Michigan; and Eli W. Weaver, principal of a high school in Brooklyn, who authored *Choosing a Career*. Although each made important contributions to the founding of vocational guidance, the person generally regarded as the primary architect of vocational guidance in the United States is Frank Parsons.

Parsons was a man with multiple interests and a social conscience. Trained as a civil engineer and as a lawyer, throughout much of his adult life Parsons was heavily involved in the activities of settlement houses in central Boston and in other cities along the eastern seaboard. It was there that he learned firsthand about the plight of immigrants and others trying to survive physically and find appropriate access to the rapidly growing occupational structure of the cities to which they had come. Such experiences fueled Parsons's concerns about the need to deal with what he viewed as the excesses of the free enterprise system and the management of industrial organizations that led, in his view, to the debasement of individual dignity.

As these experiences grew, he turned his attention to strengthening industrial education and creating the process of vocational guidance. His perception was that too many people, especially the immigrants from Europe, were not able to effectively use their abilities and to prosper economically and socially because of the haphazard way they found work and made the transition to the specialized world of the factory. In such a view, Parsons created not only a counseling approach, which will be described later, but also what to him was a moral and social imperative to value and facilitate the effective use of human resources. In this sense, Parsons's initiatives in vocational guidance were congruent with the growing emphases of the time on vocational guidance as the "conservation of human resources" (Spaulding, 1915), the effort to avoid the waste of human talent by identifying and maximizing its use.

After several years of experience in providing vocational guidance and counseling, Parsons founded the Vocations Bureau of Boston in 1908, serving as the director and vocational counselor. The setting was not a school, but rather the Civic Service House (Miller, 1961), with branch offices in the Young Men's Christian Association (YMCA), the Economic Club, and the Women's Educational and Industrial Union in Boston. Unfortunately, Parsons died only a few months after founding the Vocations Bureau in January 1908. His legacy to the field of vocational guidance was captured in his major work, *Choosing a Vocation,* which was published posthumously in 1909. This extraordinary book laid out the principles and methods of implementing vocational guidance, collecting and publishing occupational information, conducting a group study of occupations, carrying on individual counseling, and processing individual assessment. Perhaps Parsons's most famous contribution was what became known as a trait and factor approach: his articulation of the three broad factors or steps of the vocational guidance process. The approach called for the following:

> First, a clear understanding of yourself, aptitudes, abilities, interests, resources, limitations, and other qualities. Second, a knowledge of the requirements and conditions of success, advantages and disadvantages, compensation, opportunities and prospects in different lines of work. Third, true reasoning on the relations of these two groups of facts. (Parsons, 1909, p. 5)

Following Parsons's death, the work of the Vocations Bureau was extended to the Boston schools, and training of vocational counselors was undertaken. In 1917, the Vocations Bureau became part of the Division of Education at Harvard University. During the years following the publication of *Choosing a Vocation,* many leaders in American education began to recognize and adapt to the social significance of Parsons's paradigm of vocational guidance (Bloomfield, 1915). This process was compatible with the growing calls for educational reform in the nation's schools. Parsons himself, among many observers of the time, attacked the public schools for their specialization in book learning and advocated that "book work should be balanced with industrial education; and working children should spend part time in culture classes and industrial science" (Stephens, 1970, p. 39).

Such views targeted on the public schools, particularly in the cities, reflected both the rising issues of child labor—children aged 8, 10, or 12 working in coal mines and factories and not receiving the opportunity to go to school—and the dynamics of the industrial revolution that served as the backdrop for concerns about educational and social reform. In the late 1800s and early 1900s, the United States was in the midst of making the transition from a national economy that was, in general, agriculturally based to an economy that was increasingly based in manufacturing and industrial processes. As this transition ensued, urbanization and occupational diversity increased, as did national concerns about strengthening industrial education as a way to prepare young people to enter the growing opportunities in the workforce. To play out such goals effectively required information about how persons could identify and get access to emerging jobs. By the turn of the 20th century, particularly in urban areas, such information was so differentiated and comprehensive that families or local neighborhoods could no longer be the primary sources of occupational information or of the allocation of jobs; other, more formal mechanisms, including vocational guidance in the schools, became necessary.

The issues of vocational guidance in the schools and elsewhere in society became confounded by the changing demographics of the potential workforce. At the beginning of the 20th century, large numbers of immigrants from nations with poor economic opportunities were coming to the United States seeking new lives and options for themselves and for their children; so, too, people within the United States were migrating from rural to urban areas spurred by the concentration of large plants producing steel, furniture, automobiles, and other capital goods.

Such social and economic phenomena—industrialization, urbanization, and immigration—stimulated concerns about whether existing forms of education were appropriate in a rapidly growing industrial society, the need for less bookish and more focused industrial education, how to bridge the gap between schooling and the realities of the adult world, how to make the school-to-work transition, and how to accommodate the new educational theories being advanced (e.g., Progressive Education, the concepts of John Dewey, etc.) for use in the schools.

Stephens (1970), a historian, spoke about the relation between industrial or vocational education and vocational guidance:

> To many leaders of the vocational reform movement . . . it was apparent that vocational education was but the first part of a package of needed educational reforms. They argued that a school curriculum and educational goals that mirrored the occupational structure created merely a platform and impetus for launching youth into the world of work. What was clearly needed to consummate the launch were guidance mechanisms that would insure their safe and efficient arrival on the job. Without guidance experts it was argued, other efforts at reform would be aborted. . . . [T]he youth who had been carefully trained would also have to be carefully counseled into a suitable occupational niche. (p. xiv)

Thus, in this context, vocational education and vocational guidance were seen as a partnership. Certainly as one of the major roots of the professional school counselor's role, engaging in vocational guidance was seen as a significant emphasis.

Other forces were also at work shaping the role of the professional school counselor at the beginning of the 20th century. For example, Cremin (1964), also a historian, suggested that the clearest reminder in the schools of the impact of the Progressive Education movement, in the latter quarter of the 19th century and the first 50 years

of the 20th century, is the guidance counselor. He stated:

> [T]he craft of vocational guidance would serve not only the youngsters who sought counsel, but the cause of social reform as well. . . . [T]he effort to individualize education was at the heart of what came to be known as educational guidance. . . . Finally, the effort to develop a science of education, also at the heart of the progressive movement, was reflected in the spirited interest in tests and measurements that grew up in the United States shortly after the turn of the century. . . . [T]he idea developed of the guidance worker as a trained professional, wise in administering and interpreting scientific instruments for the prediction of vocational and educational success. (pp. 11–19)

THE ROLE OF THE PROFESSIONAL SCHOOL COUNSELOR IN THE 1920s, 1930s, AND 1940s

As the layers of expertise expected of the professional school counselor began to be defined in the 1880s and 1890s and in the first decades of the 1900s, debates about and approaches to the philosophy and the role of professional school counselors continued to occur in the 1920s, 1930s, and 1940s. These issues tended to be affected by other forces coming to prominence in schools and in educational philosophy at the same time. Some of these forces directly affected the extant perspectives about school counseling; others were more indirect. Hutson (1958) suggested that in addition to the importance of vocational guidance as a powerful force shaping the professional school counselor's role, there were five others: student personnel administration; psychologists, working as researchers and clinicians; personnel work in industry; social work; and mental health and psychiatry. Each deserves further comment.

Student Personnel Administration

This concept originated in higher education, where it essentially related to the identification of a specific official, often called the Dean of Students, whose responsibility was dealing with the personal and disciplinary problems of students. In time, this person would be expected to administer or provide leadership to all of the nonacademic services that facilitate the progress of the students through the institution. Included were such services as admissions, counseling, student orientation, financial aid, and placement. This concept was seen in the 1920s as having relevance to the secondary schools, and perhaps the elementary schools, as the functions of the professional school counselor took on an increasingly large array of responsibilities. Some high schools in the United States continued to use titles such as Dean of Students or Dean of Boys or Girls into the latter decades of the 20th century. Perhaps more important, this concept foreshadowed the creation of positions now commonly titled Director of Guidance Services or Director of Pupil Personnel Services or, in some larger school districts, Assistant Superintendent of Pupil Personnel Services.

Psychologists, Working as Researchers and Clinicians

The content and methodology of school counseling owes much to psychology as the major discipline providing insights into student development, cognition, behavior classification and analysis, and effective interventions. In his observations, Hutson (1958) referred to two particular contributions of psychologists. The first had to do with psychologists' research into the development of objective instruments for measuring human behavior (e.g., interest inventories, aptitude and achievement tests, diagnostic tests), without which many would see the role of professional school counselor as nothing more than "organized common sense." But the availability of these tools and their use gave professional school counselors areas of expertise and information that enriched their ability to engage in vocational guidance and increased their professional credibility.

The second contribution of psychologists in a clinical sense was to provide specialized services to specific groups of students experiencing particular learning or behavioral problems. To the degree that psychologists were available in school districts or child guidance clinics to deal with these students, professional school counselors could focus their energies on other segments of the student population.

Personnel Work in Industry

As personnel work in industry grew during the first 50 years of the 20th century, it provided job requirement specifications, motivation studies, and the tests for job application and vocational guidance purposes. Personnel work in industry also broadened the application of counseling to specific job-related problems such as meeting job requirements, getting along with fellow workers, and other factors that could interfere with a worker's job efficiency. Such information helped to broaden the content and processes of vocational guidance in schools.

Social Work

Starting with the visiting teacher movement that originated in 1906 and 1907 in settlement houses or civic associations and involved working with problem pupils and their parents, school social work was taking on its own identity in the 1930s and 1940s. School social workers represented an official liaison among the school, the home, and community social agencies. The introduction of social workers to school staffs replaced the former concepts of law and punishment of problem or delinquent children by truant officers, with such emphases as diagnosis, understanding, and adjustment. As school social workers became available to deal with specific problem children—those who were habitually truant and whose behavior was being monitored by legal or family services—the role of the school social worker also affected the role of the professional school counselor. Where social workers were available, professional school counselors tended to be less directly involved with home visits or with community social agencies. The social workers tended to be the community liaison; the professional school counselor was more school bound. In addition, as the school social worker and community agencies provided interventions for specific problem children, the professional school counselor could focus more fully on the children who needed primarily educational and vocational guidance.

Mental Health and Psychiatry

From the early decades of the 20th century, the National Association for Mental Hygiene, related organizations, and the rise of psychiatric attention to schools combined to disseminate the principles of mental health and information about various types of personality maladjustment, and advocated that the development of wholesome personalities "is the most important purpose of education" (Hutson, 1958, p. 13). In the 1920s and subsequent decades, psychiatry focused on combating juvenile delinquency and sought to establish "child guidance clinics" for the psychiatric study and treatment of problem children in the schools. While the direct impact of guidance clinics on problem children was small, the insights about maladaptive behavior and the principles of treatment subtly affected how professional school counselors were prepared, whom they referred to community agencies for treatment, and how they viewed the fostering of mental health as part of their role.

Each of these influences or forces shaped perspectives on why counselors were important in schools; how they needed to differ from, but be collaborators with, psychologists, social workers, and psychiatric specialists; and what functions they could serve in schools and with what groups of students. Such perspectives extended the analysis of the relationship of counselors to schools per se, to why schools should appoint counselors. Cowley (1937) reported three areas of emphasis that were evolving in the public schools: (a) guidance as the personalization of education, (b) guidance as the integration of education, and (c) guidance as the coordination of student personnel services. Like so many other issues and possibilities for action that occurred as guidance and counseling were taking root in the schools, these three areas continue to influence contemporary issues.

Guidance as the Personalization of Education

Cowley (1937) suggested that of most importance, "counselors have been appointed to counteract the deadening mechanical limitations of mass education" (p. 220). He decried the depersonalization of both higher and secondary education, the growing lack of close relationships between teachers and students, the lack of a personal touch in education, and the decreased concerns by administrators about student problems. All of these factors led Cowley to argue that

> No matter how expert personnel people may be as technically trained psychological testers or diagnosticians, the real test of a personnel program is the extent to which it makes the student feel that he individually is important— that he is not being educated in a social vacuum. . . . (1937, p. 221)

In more contemporary terms, guidance as personalization of education continues, with different language, to be embedded in statements about the professional school counselor's role as one in which the student is helped to achieve academic development (Campbell & Dahir, 1997).

Guidance as the Integration of Education

Cowley (1937) was particularly concerned with the explosion of knowledge and the rapid growth of curricular offerings: the movement away from a fixed curriculum, which all students took advantage of in elective courses, and toward the compartmentalization of knowledge and the specialization of instruction. Against such challenges, Cowley saw the professional school counselor as the person who would help students effectively sort through educational options and create for himself or herself a unified course of instruction; the person who would discover the student's talents and motivations and bring the resources of the institution to bear on developing these talents and motivations.

Guidance as the Coordination of Student Personnel Services

While Cowley saw educational counseling as the most important function that professional school counselors undertook, he felt it was necessary to coordinate the counseling function with the other functions professional school counselors engaged in, in relation to the role of other mental health workers (e.g., psychologists, social workers, and psychiatrists). He was concerned that a student could be "chopped up," seen as a person with a specific problem rather than as a whole person. Thus, Cowley argued that the professional school counselor should be responsible for coordinating all of the specialist services available to students, and for integrating those findings into a coordinated set of directions and support.

Arthur J. Jones provided additional perspectives on the needs of students and schools for counselors. In the two editions of his classic work, *Principles of Guidance*, Jones (1930, 1934) summarized both the need for providing guidance and the significance of the schools offering the guidance. He stated:

I.   Need for Guidance from the Standpoint of the Individual. The amazing and rapid increase in the complexity of industrial and economic life, the changes in the conditions of living, and the phenomenal development of educational facilities beyond the elementary school have greatly increased the dependence of the individual upon outside help, and this dependence is steadily becoming greater. The young person is now confronted with a bewildering complexity of choice, not only of occupations and of jobs within an occupation, but also of future schools and kinds of specialized training for life work. Intelligent choice can result only where the young person has adequate facts and experiences and receives careful counseling at all stages of his progress. These the school must provide. Delicate adjustments are necessary in the life of the youth of today that were not necessary half a century or more ago. The individual needs assistance as never before.

IV.   The Significance for the School. It is clear, then, that all the conditions of modern life point unmistakably to the increasing necessity for organized guidance, especially for our young people. This help may be given by all parts of the social order, the home, the church, the state, and the schools. Adequate guidance cannot be given unless all these agencies unite in a cooperative effort to give the assistance needed. But upon the public school must fall the major responsibility for initiating and carrying on the

work. It is the only agency that can provide such help in a form and to a degree that promises any adequate solution of the problem. Not only has it the children most of the time and at the most impressionable age, but its very organization makes possible expert assistance of a kind that home or church cannot provide. (Jones, 1934, pp. 30–31)

By the mid-1930s, when Jones (1934) was discussing the status of school guidance and counseling in the nation, the approach to school counseling often, but not always, followed a trait and factor, or directive, approach. Tests had increasingly become available, although the range of behavior they assessed was still limited primarily to "intelligence," aptitude, achievement, and interests. There were not yet any major theories of school counseling per se. Philosophies and principles of school counseling were being shaped by the Progressive Education movement, by psychiatry, and by other emerging theories. Indeed, Jones (1934) took pains in his book to explain why astrology, phrenology, physiognomy, and graphology were shortcut methods that scientific data did not support. He described these methods as "alluring" and widely used ways that "claim to list and classify types of individuals in such a way as to provide a quick and reliable method of discovering qualities of character and special aptitudes for certain occupations" (p. 205). Instead, he said that "every careful teacher and guidance worker should be on . . . guard against these methods" (p. 217). The preferred method, according to Jones, was the "long and tedious process of individual investigation" (p. 217), by which he meant case studies of students, the use of school records of attendance and grades, objective standardized instruments, and tryout and exploratory activities as methods of studying the individual. He also advocated the value of psychiatry, visiting teachers, and child guidance clinics as methods of achieving such goals. Jones also described "methods of guiding students," which in his view included counseling; homeroom guidance and group guidance; educational guidance with regard to choices of courses, schools, and colleges; "stay in school" campaigns; vocational guidance (beginning in the elementary school), including instruction, tryout, exploration, choice, placement, and follow-up relative to occupations; leadership guidance; and leisure-time guidance. Jones (1934) also explicitly stated that it is necessary to distinguish between counseling and the other activities that the counselor does.

> This distinction is not a trivial one. . . . Counselors are now so burdened with other work as to make it impossible to do counseling well. If we can focus the attention upon counseling as the center and core of the work, we shall do much to relieve the situation. (p. 273)

Focusing on the comprehensive and important work of Jones illustrates that many contemporary issues related to counseling versus guidance and the role of the professional school counselor have antecedents that have not yet been brought to closure. Support for and refinement of the techniques, the tools, and the philosophies of school counseling continued throughout the 1920s, 1930s, and 1940s. Space is not available here to analyze the continuing support for school counseling or the additional techniques made available to the professional school counselor through these three decades. Suffice it to say that during the 1920s, concerns about the dignity and rights of children flourished, as did concerns for greater emphasis on mental hygiene in the schools in which professional school counselors would be important players. In 1926, New York was the first state to require certification for guidance workers, and in 1929, New York State became the first to have full-time guidance personnel in the State Department of Education, providing leadership to school systems for the integration of professional school counselors in schools. Given the growing deterioration of the national economy, the need to certify and train people in school counseling was overshadowed by the need for the techniques and processes associated with vocational guidance counseling. One of these was the creation,

during the Great Depression of the 1930s, of a national occupational classification system that resulted in publication of the first edition of the *Dictionary of Occupational Titles* (U.S. Department of Labor, 1939) and, in 1940, establishment of the U.S. Bureau of Labor Statistics. In 1933, the Wagner-Peyser Act established the U.S. Employment Service. Several acts during the 1930s provided fiscal support for vocational guidance activities. In 1938, a Guidance and Personnel Branch was created in the Division of Vocational Education in the U.S. Office of Education. This unit continued until 1952 as the only federal office dealing with guidance in the schools, but restricting the federal emphasis to vocational guidance. The major issues of technological unemployment during the Depression tended to focus on vocational guidance as a placement activity, causing some debate about whether school counselors or vocational educators should undertake the vocational guidance activities funded by the federal government.

The 1940s were a period in which the expansion of testing grew dramatically in response to the need for worker classification by the armed forces as World War II ensued and, later, as veterans returned to society and were provided guidance services through schools, colleges, and community agencies. The *Occupational Outlook Handbook* was first published by the U.S. Bureau of Labor Statistics in 1948 (U.S. Department of Labor, 1949). During this period, federal support continued for vocational guidance and counseling in schools in support of vocational education.

In 1942, Carl Rogers published *Counseling and Psychotherapy,* which defined the counseling process as that concerned with other than traditional medical models, disease entities, and psychoanalytic approaches in which the counselor was a directive authority. Rogers's book heralded the beginning of client-centered counseling in which the counselor and client were seen as collaborators. Such perspectives were incorporated into the expansion of guidance techniques and increasing eclectic models of what school counseling might be.

SCHOOL COUNSELING COMES INTO ITS OWN: THE 1950S AND 1960S

In a sense, all of the important strides made in support of counseling and guidance in schools during the first 50 years of the 20th century were a prelude to the major events of the 1950s and 1960s. These were the watershed years of legislation and professional development that essentially defined the importance of school counseling for the remaining decades of the 20th century.

Until the 1950s, there were relatively few professional school counselors across the United States; the opportunities for the professional preparation of school counselors were relatively limited; the advocacy for professional school counselors by professional organizations was not systematic; and the legislative support for school counseling, other than for vocational guidance, was largely nonexistent. All of these conditions changed in the 1950s and 1960s.

Among the extraordinarily important indicators of support for school counseling in the 1950s was the founding of the ASCA in 1952 and its becoming, in 1953, a division of the American Personnel and Guidance Association (APGA), formed in 1951 from the merger of the National Vocational Guidance Association, the American College Personnel Association, the National Association of Guidance Supervisors and Counselor Trainers, and the Student Personnel Association for Teacher Education.

However, it is important to note that the perspective that the founding organizations brought to the creation of the APGA shaped for the ensuing several decades the language and the emphases within which professional school counselors were evolving. For example, the term *guidance*, not *counseling*, was the accepted term for all that counselors did (Sweeney, 2001)— school counselors were often called guidance counselors in the decades immediately before and after the founding of APGA. Frequently, what professional school counselors did was called personnel work. The term *guidance* was widely viewed as conveying the notion that the

professional school counselor was primarily involved in directive, advice giving to the students. Personnel work suggested that the professional school counselor was engaged primarily in administrative tasks related to maintaining student records about their schedules and progress. While these terms lost favor by the early 1980s, their residual effects were to distort the images by which professional school counselors were reviewed. Indeed, one could argue that many, if not most, of the members of the four founding organizations were themselves administrators, not counselors. For example, to this day, the American College Personnel Association is composed primarily of deans of students and related administrative personnel. The same was true of the Student Personnel Association for Teacher Education before it was renamed and significantly changed in purpose in 1974, when it became the Association for Humanistic Education and Development, and again in 1999, when it changed its name to the Counseling Association for Humanistic Education and Development (C-AHEAD).

Nevertheless, this federation of professional organizations speaking for counseling in K–12 schools, in institutions of higher education, and in workplaces gave credibility to and advocated for standards, ethical guidelines, and training of professional counselors working with various populations and in various settings. In 1953, the *School Counselor* was founded as the professional journal of the ASCA. Also in 1953, the Pupil Personnel Services Organization of the Division of State and Local School Systems was created in the U.S. Office of Education, a move that significantly broadened the view of school counseling as more than vocational guidance.

In 1957, APGA created the American Board for Professional Standards in Vocational Guidance; in 1959, the National Association of Guidance Supervisors and Counselor Trainers undertook a 5-year project designed to build a set of standards for education in the preparation of secondary school counselors.

In 1959, James B. Conant, the former president of Harvard, wrote *The American High School Today*, an influential analysis of the need for strengthened secondary school education. In the book, Conant argued for 1 full-time counselor (or guidance office) for every 250 to 300 pupils in each American high school, a criterion that has been used frequently, even though such a ratio of school counselors to students has rarely been met.

The National Defense Education Act, 1958–1968

By the 1930s, nearly every city of 50,000 or more inhabitants had some formal guidance work in the schools and professional school counselors employed to carry it out. Courses to train professional school counselors had been developed and were being offered in several universities (e.g., Harvard University, Teachers College, Columbia University; the University of Pennsylvania; Stanford University), and textbooks were being written to identify the techniques and assumptions on which such work could be undertaken (Jones, 1930). Guidance work in the schools continued to grow, and the number of professional school counselors multiplied through the 1940s and 1950s. But the major stimulus to the education and implementation of school counseling clearly was the National Defense Education Act (NDEA) of 1958 (Herr, 1979).

Although not often considered in this vein, the NDEA, like the legislation on vocational education and vocational guidance that preceded it, identified professional school counselors as sociopolitical instruments to achieve national goals. In the case of the NDEA, professional school counselors became indirect participants in the Cold War between the United States and the Soviet Union. To be more specific, in 1957, the Soviet Union launched *Sputnik*, the first human-made object to orbit the earth. As a result, although the United States was close to launching its own space vehicle, the Soviet launch precipitated a major national outpouring of news articles suggesting that the United States had lost the space race; that our science and engineering capabilities were inferior to the Russians'; and that once again, American schools had failed to produce students whose scientific

and mathematical skills were competitive with those of the Soviet Union. The NDEA was the result. Passed by the U.S. Congress in 1958, the NDEA required states to submit plans about how they would test secondary school students so that academically talented students could be identified and encouraged to study the "hard sciences" in high school and go on to higher education, emphasizing courses of study in the sciences, engineering, and mathematics. These legislative goals were not altruistic or concerned with the self-actualization of students. They were designed to increase the scientific capacity of the United States as it competed in the Cold War.

Central to the provisions of the NDEA were the training of large numbers of secondary professional school counselors and their placement in schools primarily to test students, to identify those capable of entering higher education in the sciences, and to encourage them to do so. These were basic elements of the secondary professional school counselors' role as seen by NDEA legislation, regardless of whether professional organizations viewed the role in the same manner. Title V-A of the NDEA, administered through state departments of education, allocated funds directly to schools that had submitted formal proposals to employ professional school counselors and to provide the resources (e.g., tests, occupational and educational materials, etc.) necessary to provide school guidance and counseling programs. Title V-B appropriated funds for the education of new secondary professional school counselors or for upgrading the qualifications of those who had been employed as secondary professional school counselors. To compete for Title V-B funds, universities needed to present proposals defining their programs to prepare professional school counselors in full-time, year-long guidance and counseling institutes, or offer more specialized programs (e.g., precollege guidance) in summer guidance and counseling institutes. The 1964 amendments to the NDEA emphasized guidance and counseling for all students, giving impetus to elementary professional school counseling and to counseling in technical institutes and other nonbaccalaureate postsecondary educational institutions.

It is not possible to discuss all of the effects of the NDEA, but there are several obvious results. With the full force of federal legislation behind the preparation and employment of secondary professional school counselors, the number of secondary professional school counselors and the high schools in which these counselors served exploded in number. So did the number of colleges and universities providing preparation programs. Literature on professional school counseling became more comprehensive, as did the state certification requirements for counselors. The programs were transformed from simply taking courses on a piecemeal basis until one had completed what was needed for certification, to more full-time, systematic, and integrated curricula, usually leading to a master's degree. Certainly, many more students in the United States were being served by professional school counselors in the 1960s and beyond than had ever been before; some state departments of education mandated that schools maintain specific counselor-to-student ratios to receive state funding. As the large amounts of federal support ended in the late 1960s, professional school counselors had become embedded in schools and were engaged in initiatives that went beyond the expectations of the NDEA. Even though the responsibility for funding school guidance and counseling programs shifted from the federal government to local school districts, by the end of the 1960s, professional school counselors were vital participants in achieving the multiple missions of schools (e.g., dropout prevention, academic scheduling, educational and career guidance, crisis intervention, etc.).

The Great Society Legislation of the 1960s

As the impact of the NDEA legislation unfolded during the late 1950s and throughout the 1960s, other major legislation was developed to address the Civil Rights movement, the beginnings of technological impact on the occupational structure, rising unemployment, poverty, and other social ills. In many of these legislative actions, education was viewed as the instrument to restructure society, and again, professional school counselors were supported. For example, the Elementary and Secondary Education Act (ESEA) of 1965 designated funds for guidance and counseling. The 1969 amendments to the ESEA combined funds from the NDEA's Title V-B with funds from the ESEA's Title III into one appropriation for guidance. The Vocational Education Act Amendments of 1968 advocated for career guidance programs; responses to people who were disadvantaged and people with disabilities; and the expansion of a broadened concept of guidance and counseling, including its extension into the elementary schools. These pieces of legislation stimulated a large number of national and state conferences on guidance and counseling and innovative projects in career guidance, counseling, and placement.

THE YEARS OF CONSOLIDATION AND REFINEMENT: THE 1970S AND BEYOND

The outpouring of federal legislation that specifically focused on guidance and counseling in the schools essentially reached its zenith in the 1960s. However, there were important legislative initiatives in the 1970s, 1980s, 1990s, and into the first decade of the third millennium. Much of the legislation in the 1970s focused on vocational education and career education. For example, career education was seen as a school reform initiative as it developed in the early 1970s, and as it was reflected in the Career Education Incentive Act of 1976. Career education indirectly institutionalized career guidance in schools and infused its concepts and experiences as part of the teaching and learning process. The educational amendments—the ESEA—of 1976 included major support for guidance and counseling in schools, a major emphasis on vocational guidance in schools, and the implementation of an administrative unit in the U.S. Office of Education. The purpose of this administrative unit was to coordinate legislative efforts in the Congress on behalf of guidance and counseling and to serve in a consultative capacity with the U.S. Commissioner of Education about the status and needs of guidance and counseling in the nation's schools.

During this period, a large amount of theory building took place, leading to the development of materials on decision making, career education, drug abuse prevention, and self-development, which became available for specialists in guidance and counseling. Fears of economic crisis and concerns about widespread unemployment among youth continued to spur development of career guidance initiatives. The impact of the Civil Rights and Women's Liberation movements, as well as legislation effectively mainstreaming all special education students, refocused the attention of professional school counselors to greater emphases on diversity in schools and the needs of special populations for guidance and counseling.

Multicultural Diversity

It is important to note that beginning in the 1960s, federal legislation and state and local educational initiatives began to incorporate responses to multicultural diversity in the schools. The Civil Rights legislation had essentially banned segregated schools and caused municipalities throughout much of the United States to embark on policies and tactics by which to integrate African American children into schools with White children. Such policies struck down notions of "separate but equal schools" and expected that children of all ethnic and racial backgrounds would be in the same classrooms and courses, athletic teams, musical groups, and social events. Children of different racial backgrounds, gender, or other special characteristics could no longer be the target of discrimination or segregation.

Schools and communities used many methods to integrate schools. Busing of children from one part of town to another or from one town to another to change the demographic mix of students in a particular school was a frequently used method. However, in many schools, professional school counselors were given responsibility to work with culturally diverse groups of students in classrooms, in group counseling, and in other settings to help these students to learn more about each other and to air their fears and concerns about integration, and to develop plans of action by which students could learn to respect each other and reduce conflict.

Part of the problem at the time was a lack of attention to issues of cultural diversity in counseling

theory and counseling practice. A major challenge to counseling processes in a culturally diverse world was that for most of its history in the United States, the assumptions and techniques of counseling ignored cultural differences or treated them as unimportant (Clark, 1987). Theories of counseling did not acknowledge the cultural distinctiveness of most people in the United States or the racial and ethnic traditions that shaped their behavior and affected their approaches to learning and decision making (Herr, 1999). Too often, students of cultural differences were treated as deficient, inferior, or abnormal rather than as distinct in their socialization. In response to such inappropriate behavior toward cultural differences, Vontress (1970), among others, talked about the issues involved when White counselors counseled African American students, how cultural differences affect the establishment of rapport between counselors and students, and that "sensitivity to issues of racial and ethnic diversity must be factored in as an important variable in counseling theory, practice, and research" (C. C. Lee, 2001b, p. 581).

During the ensuing 35 years, growing attention has been directed to embedding scholarship about ethnic and racial differences into counseling theory and practice. Such perspectives do not embrace deficit models; rather, they provide affirmations of the worldviews of different cultural groups and the implications of these for counseling process. Virtually all counselor education programs now have one or more courses, practicum experiences, or other methods by which to prepare professional school counselors to work effectively and sensitively in a culturally diverse world. Professional school counselor training now includes studies of how appraisal, ethics, interventions, and counseling competencies/standards are affected by cultural diversity (Sue, Arredondo, & McDavis, 1992). The refinement and application of these perspectives will be a constant presence in the training of professional school counselors throughout the 21st century.

The Latter Decades of the 20th Century

During the 1980s and into the 1990s, much of the legislative activity in the nation did not directly address school counseling; it focused on the need for professional school counselors to deal with issues such as child abuse, drug abuse prevention, and dropout prevention. Legislation supporting career guidance continued under new guises as well. Among the major legislation defining school guidance and counseling, with a primary emphasis on career guidance, was the Carl D. Perkins Vocational Education Act of 1984, the Carl D. Perkins Vocational and Applied Technology Act of 1990, and the subsequent amendments to these acts. These were the major federal sources of funding for guidance and counseling in the schools through the 1980s and early 1990s. In 1994, Congress passed the School to Work Opportunities Act, which reinforced the importance of career guidance and counseling as students contemplate their transition from school to employment. Throughout the 1980s and 1990s, the National Occupational Information Coordinating Committee (NOICC), created by congressional legislation as a joint effort of the U.S. Departments of Education, Defense, and Labor, provided career development and guidance program information and resources to elementary, middle, and secondary schools. Unfortunately, NOICC was disbanded in 2000.

However, in 2003, the National Career Development Guidelines Project was commissioned by the U.S. Department of Education's Office of Vocational and Adult Education. By 2005, the Guidelines Revision Project had reconceived the original NOICC Career Development Guidelines, aligned them with the goals of the NCLB legislation, and created a Web site by which information on the new guidelines; learning activities; and strategies for K–12 students, teachers, counselors, parents, and administrators and the business community could be delivered.

In 1995, the Elementary School Counseling Demonstration Act, which was expanded and reauthorized in 1999, represented the first major legislative departure for more than a decade from the emphasis on career guidance and related topics. This legislation, providing $20 million, assisted schools in providing greater access to counseling services and in creating a more positive ratio of professional school counselors to students. Given the reduction of direct support

for school counseling during the 1980s and 1990s at state and national levels, the current statistics indicate that rather than a ratio of 1 counselor to every 250 students, as recommended by the American Counseling Association (ACA), in 1999 the ratio across the United States averaged 561 students to 1 professional school counselor. The highest ratio was in California, where there is 1 professional school counselor per 1,171 students (ACA, 2000a). There were, however, some hopeful signs that more professional school counselors and innovative counseling programs were developing.

For example, by the beginning of the 21st century, the Elementary School Counseling Demonstration Act had been expanded to include secondary schools or and the word *Demonstration* was dropped. The Elementary and Secondary School Counseling Program is a discretionary program administered by the U.S. Department of Education to provide competitive grants to school districts that demonstrate the greatest need for new or additional counseling services or the greatest potential for replication or dissemination or that propose the most innovative program. For fiscal year 2004, some $33.8 million in federal funds were expended to meet the goals of the act. The more wide-ranging affirmation of the need for professional school counselors is embedded in the NCLB Act signed into law in January 2002. This comprehensive legislation requires the states to adopt a specific approach to testing and accountability intended to lead to higher achievement for all children, to take direct action to improve poorly performing schools, to raise the qualifications of teachers, and to make many other changes in schools to make them accountable for student achievement. The need for and support of school counseling is evident in many parts of the legislation relating to drop-out prevention, career counseling, drug and alcohol counseling, state and drug-free schools, facilitating the transition of students from correctional institutions back to community schools, identifying and serving gifted and talented students, and dealing with children who are neglected or delinquent or otherwise at risk of academic and social failure. These many legislative actions suggest the importance of counseling as a process that complements and is integral to the success of instructional methods and goals and, as such, allows, if not encourages, school districts to have professional school counselors engage in many complex roles.

FUTURE ISSUES FOR THE SCHOOL COUNSELING PROFESSION

Space limitations prohibit a comprehensive analysis of all of the trends cited in each of the decades discussed. For example, the use of computers in guidance and counseling began in the 1960s, with the first computer-assisted career guidance system becoming operational in 1965. In 1964, the Association for Counselor Education and Supervision published the *ACES Standards for Counselor Education in the Preparation of Secondary School Counselors,* the forerunner to standards developed by the Council for the Accreditation of Counseling and Related Educational Programs (CACREP). In the 1970s, pressure mounted for accountability in guidance and counseling. During the 1970s and 1980s, models were developed that envisioned school guidance and counseling as an integrated, planned, and systematic K–12 program rather than a loosely connected set of services (Gysbers & Henderson, 1994; Gysbers & Henderson, 2001; Herr, 2002; Lapan, 2001). Such efforts were designed, among other reasons, to clarify the expected results or outcomes of guidance and counseling programs in the schools. To that end, in 1997, ASCA published the *National Standards for School Counseling Programs* (Campbell & Dahir, 1997). These standards argued that school counseling programs should facilitate three broad areas of student development: academic development, career development, and personal–social development. Within these three areas are nine standards, each of which includes a list of student competencies or desired learning outcomes that define the specific types of knowledge, attitudes, and skills students should obtain as a result of effective school counseling programs. Among the other purposes of the *National Standards for School Counseling Programs* was a concern about clarifying appropriate and inappropriate counselor roles. The basic point was that the roles of school counselors need to be focused on addressing student needs, not performing noncounseling quasiadministrative tasks. Further, implementation of the *National Standards for School Counseling Programs* and, more specifically, the three broad areas of student development—academic, career, and personal–social development—requires counselor competencies that are important assets in student development and in achieving educational goals. These counselor competencies should not be ignored or misused if local programs are to be comprehensive, professional, and provided for all students (ASCA, 2003a).

In 2003, ASCA published the *National Model for School Counseling Programs* to help professional school counselors implement the National Standards and focus school counseling programs on four primary areas: foundation, management system, delivery system, and accountability.

In the quest for clarity, professionalism, and accountability of professional school counselors, in addition to the substantial program of content and delivery identified in the *National Standards* and *National Model,* the National Career Development Guidelines, briefly mentioned previously, provide another source of program content and delivery, particularly for the career development segment of the National Standards. The National Career Development Guidelines also address three broad areas of student development: personal–social development, educational achievement and lifelong learning, and career management. The three domains organize the content of the guidelines in 11 goals and in three learning stages: knowledge acquisition, application, and reflection (www.acrnetwork.org). These guideline domains, goals, indicators and learning stages can be the basis for a K–12 or K–Adult career development program, its delivery, and its evaluation.

Continuing Issues

In spite of the important contributions to the nation's schools and to its students made by professional school counselors, there continue to be basic issues that confront professional school counselors and school counseling programs. Some of these issues have been articulated by Paisley and Borders (1995), including the:

> lack of control school counselors have over their day-to-day work activities. . . . [S]chool counselors, for example, are [often] directly accountable to school principals and the school system's director of school counseling. . . . These two . . . supervisors may have very different agendas about the counselor's role in the school. . . . There is a second fundamental issue [for school guidance and counseling], the ongoing confusion and controversy about the appropriate focus for its practitioners. . . . [T]he first [issue] concerns their role in the delivery of a comprehensive developmental program [although] despite its centrality to the profession . . . such a program has rarely been implemented; and the second philosophical role question . . . is "What is counseling in the schools?" . . . The distinction between counseling and therapy is never clear, and it often seems to have little relevance. (pp. 151–152)

Herr (1998) has suggested that the future role of professional school counselors is based on several pivotal concerns. These concerns are presented in abridged form with added commentary as follows:

1. *The degree to which school counseling programs are systematically planned; tailored to the priorities, demographics, and characteristics of a particular school district or building; and clearly defined in terms of the results to be achieved rather than the services to be offered.*

ASCA and, indeed, other blue-ribbon panels and national organizations have increasingly advocated for planned programs of school counseling. Such planned programs are intended to clarify the expected outcomes of such programs and how these outcomes will be achieved; to maximize the efficient use of resources committed to school counseling; to prevent or modify student risk factors and promote social and educational competence; and to provide a structure by which to assess whether professional programs of school counseling are meeting the goals assigned to them.

2. *The degree to which school counseling programs begin in the elementary school or in the secondary school . . . [is] truly . . . longitudinal (K to 12) and systematically planned.*

For much of the latter part of the 20th century, as both secondary school counselors and, increasingly, elementary school counselors have been employed in schools, there has been support in professional literature for longitudinal programs of school counseling. Essentially, the advocates of such approaches have argued that students at every educational level have concerns, problems, and environmental circumstances that affect their behavior and productivity in school. While the issues and tasks that students experience vary developmentally from kindergarten through Grade 12, they are important at each developmental level and deserve the attention of professional school counselors and planned programs tailored to their needs.

3. *The degree to which school counseling programs are seen as responsible for the guidance of all students or for only some subpopulations of students, such as those at risk.*

A debate that has recurred throughout the history of professional school counseling has focused on whether all students should be served by school counseling programs or only selected groups of students (e.g., potential dropouts, those in crisis, those who are disruptive and act out). This issue has to do with how best to use the limited number of professional school counselors and to maximize their positive effects on students. The subquestions focus on whether all students need the attention and support of professional school counselors or whether subgroups of students who would benefit most from such services can be identified. Among the underlying assumptions are that many students can get along effectively without the help of professional school counselors; many students receive positive support and resources from their parents or other persons in their environment that replace the need for a professional school counselor; and a school should direct its resources to those students who cannot get adequate guidance outside of school or who are most in need of such support.

4. *The degree to which school counseling programs include teachers, other mental health specialists, community resources, parent volunteers, and families as part of the delivery system.*

Because the ratio of students to professional school counselors is so high (e.g., 1:500 or more) in many schools, it is necessary to broaden the network of persons who can augment the work of professional school counselors. Thus, in many schools, teachers, parents, and others are trained to perform specific functions (e.g., academic scheduling, coordinating a career resource center, helping students use educational and career resources, providing group guidance topics or workshops) that free professional school counselors to deal with student problems for which they are uniquely qualified. In such situations, professional school counselors coordinate, train, and support other persons who augment and extend the outreach of their functions.

5. *The degree to which school counseling programs are focused on precollege guidance and counseling; counseling in and for vocational education and the school-to-work transition; counseling for academic achievement; and counseling for students with special problems such as bereavement, substance abuse, antisocial behavior, eating disorders, and family difficulties (single parents, stepparents, blended family rivalries).*

The issue here is whether the school counseling program in a particular school offers a range of interventions that address the needs of all student subgroups or whether the program emphasis is on a restricted range of students (e.g., the college-bound, students in crisis).

6. *The degree to which professional school counselors should be generalists or specialists; members of teams or independent practitioners; and proactive or reactive with regard to the needs of students, teachers, parents, and administrators.*

This issue has to do with how professional school counselors should be educated and how they should function in a school. Should they be

trained to view children or adults in holistic terms and thus be prepared to deal with any type of problem they experience? Or should they be trained in a subspecialty (e.g., career, discipline, family, testing, substance abuse) and melded into a team of specialists who can combine to serve the needs of a particular individual? A further question is whether professional school counselors should be essentially passive and wait for students, parents, or teachers to come to them, or be assertive in marketing their program and providing services, workshops, and so forth in multiple and visible forms and potentially outside of counselors' offices.

7. *The degree to which professional school counselors employ psychoeducational models or guidance curricula as well as individual forms of intervention to achieve goals.*

As professional school counseling has evolved during the past 100 years, so has the range of techniques available for use. In addition, the knowledge bases that students need to acquire for purposes of self-understanding, educational and career planning, interpersonal effectiveness, conflict resolution, and decision making have expanded. The question is, given pressures for efficiency and accountability, can such knowledge, and the associated attitudes and skills, be best conveyed to students by individual counseling? Or are these types of knowledge best conveyed through group work or a guidance curriculum (e.g., workshops, units in classrooms) that is likely to disseminate this information more evenly to all students?

8. *The degree to which the roles of professional school counselors can be sharpened and expanded while not holding counselors responsible for so many expectations that their effectiveness is diminished and the outcomes they affect are vague.*

Clearly, the role of professional school counselors is complex and comprehensive. The range of concerns and problems that professional school counselors are expected to address continues to grow as the dynamics of the larger society affect the readiness and behavior of students in schools. Thus, the questions must be addressed: What can counselors do best? For what outcomes should they be held accountable? How should their workload be balanced and to what end? Which current duties should be eliminated and which emphasized? How can the responsibilities of professional school counselors be made explicit and achievable?

9. *The degree to which professional school counselors have a reasonable student load, 250 or less, so that they can know these students as individuals and provide them personal attention.*

If one of the important roles of professional school counselors is to help students personalize their education and make individual plans pertinent to their abilities, interests, and values, how is that best done when each professional school counselor is responsible for 400 to 1,000 students? Is the answer more group work; more use of technology; shifting selected functions of professional school counselors to other persons in the school or community, such as teachers, parents, mental health specialists; or limiting the responsibilities of professional school counselors to a specific and defined set of roles?

One possible response, now lost in the history of professional school counseling, is the Carnegie Foundation for the Advancement of Teaching's book, *High School: A Report on Secondary Education in America* (Boyer, 1983). This report was unequivocal in its support of guidance services and student counseling as critical needs in American high schools. According to the report's conclusions,

> The American high school must develop a more adequate system of student counseling. Specifically, we recommend that guidance services be significantly expanded; that no counselor should have a caseload of more than 100 students. Moreover, we recommend that school districts provide a referral service to community agencies for those students needing more frequent and sustained professional assistance. (Boyer, 1983, p. 306)

This very important, but long overlooked, recommendation has increased urgency in today's school environment fraught with pressures for

students and for those who teach and counsel them. It suggests that the needs of many students go beyond the capacity of the school to address and should be seen as a communitywide responsibility to coordinate and use all of the mental health resources available on behalf of the needs of its student population.

10. *The degree to which professional school counselors effectively communicate their goals and results to policy makers and the media both to clarify their contributions to the mission of the school and to enhance their visibility as effective, indeed vital, components of positive student development.*

This issue relates to how professional school counselors should use knowledge about what interventions work effectively, for which student problem, and under what conditions to help policy makers understand more fully their role. In this sense, professional school counselors must be statespersons for their field, able to interpret their goals, their skills, and the added value they represent to positive student development and to the mission of the school.

Many of the issues just discussed are reflected in 10 current and emerging roles, or specialty areas, that influence the practice of school counseling in various parts of the United States. They suggest that the transformed role of the professional school counselor is not singular but multifaceted and based on several "realizations" discussed in the beginning of the following section.

TRADITIONAL AND EMERGING ROLES AND PRACTICES

The transformed role of the professional school counselor is multifaceted and stems from several essential "realizations" that are listed in this section. Following the realizations are 10 current and emerging roles, or specialty areas, that influence the practice of school counseling in various parts of the country. It is essential to note that, depending on the school community's needs and the skills of the professional school counselor, some of these "roles" may predominate in a given school or even at certain times of the school year. However, necessary boundaries must be in place to ensure that no single role predominates. A comprehensive developmental school counseling program requires substantial attention to balance to meet the needs of *all* students.

Realizations Guiding the Transformation of the Professional School Counselor's Role

The first important realization is that, of all the educational professionals, professional school counselors receive the most extensive specialized training in consultation and collaboration and team and relationship building. It follows, therefore, that professional school counselors are among those most able and qualified to not only build collaborative relationships to fully implement a comprehensive developmental school counseling program, but also to move school reform work and task groups in positive directions leading to changes that will benefit all students.

Over the past several decades, many professional school counselors and counselor educators have come to realize that the job descriptions and role responsibilities, coupled with the work and caseload realities, are overwhelming for all but the superhuman. Add to this the challenge professional school counselors face in taking a leadership role in school reform, and experienced professionals would justifiably throw up their hands.

This leads to the second realization: Professional school counselors can't do it all! Societal problems are creating developmental and clinical problems for children and youth in record numbers, and most citizens and stakeholders are expecting school personnel to effectively address these issues. Children are developing serious psychological problems at younger ages and in greater numbers; teachers are leaving the field in droves, and fewer college students are choosing teaching as a professional career; professional school counselor caseloads and workloads are expanding; and governments and citizens demand improved test scores in high-stakes testing programs. In addition, school violence is increasing, technology is changing rapidly, and the challenges

stemming from an increasingly diverse student population are growing. How can one person, a professional school counselor, possibly do it all?

One person can't do it all—and shouldn't be expected to! For too long, the "lone ranger" attitude has pervaded the profession. In transforming the profession, counselors must look to resources beyond themselves: community agencies, local business partners, teachers, parents, grandparents, and, yes, even the students themselves, among many other possible partners. If school conflict and violence are increasing, professional school counselors can partner with students, teachers, and organizations to implement a teacher- or student-led developmental conflict resolution curriculum and peer mediation program while also tapping community organizations to provide workshops on personal safety. If substance abuse is a problem, professional counselors can partner with community mental health and substance abuse professionals, teachers, parents, and students to implement a substance abuse curriculum taught by teachers. Counselors can run groups with abusers and children of alcoholics (COAs) and harness the resources of local businesses and organizations such as the local Mothers Against Drunk Driving (MADD) chapter for a continuing program to help parents and their children cope with substance abuse. If children's reading scores are below expectations, professional counselors can partner with community organizations, grandparents, parents, and educators to hold book drives to procure books for use by preschoolers and school-aged children, organize community "read-ins" at local bookstores or the school or public library, facilitate coordination of a parent and grandparent volunteer reading program, and even ask older students to volunteer some time before or after school to listen to and help a younger child read.

The common denominator is that someone has to take the initiative to get things started, and the professional school counselor has the collaborative and human relationship skills to do it. Many traditional thinkers will reflexively demand that these are not the kinds of things that professional school counselors do, or should do. But think about it: Which of the partnering examples mentioned does not fit perfectly into the goals of a comprehensive developmental school counseling program? The key is that the examples describe different ways to achieve the goals, rather than having a professional school counselor counsel one child at a time or go into the classroom to teach one or several guidance lessons on these topics. While these traditional interventions are effective in their own way, the partnering plans use the gifts and talents of many other people who are more than willing to help, if invited to do so.

The third realization guiding the transformation of the professional school counselor's role is that well-organized and well-run comprehensive developmental school counseling programs are greatly needed in today's schools and work very well. Furthermore, if a professional school counselor fails to implement a comprehensive program in a school, no one else will. Establishing such a program must become the professional school counselor's top priority. Many schools lack a comprehensive program because of poorly trained and unmotivated counselors or counselors who believe their job is merely to put out fires, provide long-term individual therapy for a select group of students in need, or complete office work. When a counselor spends nearly all of his or her time providing one type of service, a comprehensive program does not exist. The exception is when a school has multiple professional school counselors engaging in specialties, but even in this case, professional school counselors expend a lot of effort integrating and coordinating their services in a comprehensive manner.

This leads to the fourth realization: All professional school counselors have strengths and weaknesses and, therefore, may provide varying-quality levels of service to varying populations. Thus, in many ways, specialization makes sense and is most efficient, but only if the remaining portions of a comprehensive developmental school counseling program are provided by other qualified individuals. It is here that the argument recycles to the discussion of partnering, including other professional school counselors, school personnel, or community resources. For professional school counselors, the key is to know what they are good

at and to specialize in those areas without upsetting the balance of the school counseling program. Counterbalancing is provided by counselor, school, and community collaboration.

The fifth and final realization is that many students are not getting what they need from our educational and mental health systems (Substance Abuse and Mental Health Services Administration [SAMHSA], 1998). Some professional school counselors view their role as something like "triage," which in medical terms means to sort, prioritize, or allocate the treatment of patients. Although this holds true in most instances, like it or not, as professional school counselors, they will encounter many students for whom they are the last and only hope. This is why counselor training is so broad and comprehensive and includes topics such as human and career development, counseling techniques and multicultural issues, appraisal, and special services. If counselors do not have the skills and knowledge to help those students, those students will likely not get help. This is also why professional school counselors need to become social advocates and members of their local, state, and national professional organizations. Oftentimes, working with an individual who has nowhere else to turn is like sticking a finger in the dike. A look to the left and right will often show other professionals using their fingers to plug a hole. By joining with other professional counselors in the same area, state, and nation and speaking with a united voice in advocating for the needs of students, they are seeking solutions not only for the students they are working to help, but for all students—those whom colleagues are seeking to serve and those who will seek help in the future. The counseling profession is based on the belief that all human beings have worth and dignity (ACA, 2005a). Professional school counselors seek to create solutions for students who are oppressed and marginalized so that their paths of development will also lead to successful life opportunities.

Although many of the services provided by professional school counselors are well known and accepted, others are gaining wider acceptance in various parts of the country and world. The purpose of this book is to explore not only what professional school counselors *do*, but also what *could be done*. There are a number of important roles and practices that appear to have value to the transformation of school counseling. These roles, practices, and initiatives will be reviewed briefly here and serve as a prelude to the chapters that follow.

The School Counselor as a Professional

By now, you have noticed the use of the term *professional school counselor*. This is the term preferred by the ASCA (ASCA, 1999a) and adopted by numerous counselor educators and professional school counselors around the world. It means something! Professional school counselors are first and foremost representatives of their profession. How one behaves, good or bad, reflects on all. School counseling literature is replete with articles emphasizing the importance of ethical, professional practice (e.g., Brott & Myers, 1999; Erk, 1999; Froeschle & Moyer, 2004; Guillot-Miller & Partin, 2003; Gysbers, Lapan, & Jones, 2000; Isaacs & Stone, 1999; L. S. Johnson, 2000; Mitchell & Rogers, 2003; Sealander, Schweibert, Oren, & Weeley, 1999).

Professional school counselors practice as professionals in three major ways, as addressed in this chapter and chapter 4. First, professional school counselors are aware of the history of guidance and counseling as well as the pressing issues guiding future transformations. When one is trying to know where one is going, it is generally helpful to know where one has been. Second, professional school counselors use effective techniques and practices implemented through legal, ethical, and professional means. Belonging to a profession requires one to adhere to the highest standards of that profession.

Third, professional school counselors maintain membership in professional organizations at the local, state, and national levels. At the national level, the ACA and the ASCA are the professional and political forces supporting the mission of professional school counselors. Each of these has branches or divisions in most states, and many local areas have affiliated chapters. All are ready to welcome professional school counselors into the profession, but it is the counselors' responsibility to join and support the efforts. It is

estimated that almost 90% of doctors belong to the American Medical Association (AMA) and 70% of licensed psychologists join the American Psychological Association (APA). Each organization has a powerful political and professional voice. ACA and ASCA estimate that less than 20% of counselors belong to either association! Until counselors develop an allegiance to the profession to a degree commensurate with that of psychologists and doctors, their political and professional voices will remain background noise. Being a professional school counselor means committing to the mission of the professional organizations. The money contributed annually to these organizations is small compared to the professional and political gains benefiting students and colleagues.

The Professional School Counselor as an Agent of Diversity and Multicultural Sensitivity

Referred to as the Fourth Wave, multicultural counseling and development is a strong influence on the counseling field today (e.g., Carter & El Hindi, 1999; Carter & Vuong, 1997; Constantine, 2001; Constantine & Yeh, 2001; Day-Vines, Patton, & Baytops, 2003; Durdoyle, 1998; Graham & Pulvino, 2000; Hijazi, Tatar, & Gati, 2004; Holcomb-McCoy, 2001, 2004; C. C. Lee, 2001b; Rayle & Myers, 2004; Reeder, Douzenis, & Bergin, 1997; Schwallie-Giddis, Anstrom, Sanchez, Sardi, & Granato, 2004; Williams & Butler, 2003; Yeh, 2001). With U.S. demographic projections estimating the trend toward a more diverse U.S. population will continue for decades, the demographics of teachers and professional school counselors, who are mainly White and female, will most likely also shift. Regardless, current professional school counselors must retool, and future professional school counselors must enter the field prepared to address the developmental and counseling needs of a diverse student population. Although professional school counselors are, by and large, ahead of other educational professional groups, the multicultural counseling movement is helping professional school counselors lead the way toward a more diverse, tolerant, and sensitive educational environment. Chapter 5 addresses this essential area of practice, and multicultural issues are infused throughout the other chapters of this book.

The Professional School Counselor as an Advocate for Academic and Social Justice

In some ways, this entire book is about preparing the professional school counselor as an advocate for social justice, but chapters 1, 5, and 6 specifically address the issue. Professional school counselors have an ethical responsibility to help students minimize or eliminate barriers to educational performance and career and personal–social development. Sometimes these barriers and inequities exist in federal and state laws, regulations, and funding mechanisms; sometimes in the policies and procedures of local school systems; and sometimes in the hearts and minds of students, their parents, the community, and, yes, even the teachers, administrators, and the professional school counselors themselves. Professional school counselors seek to address barriers and inequities, wherever they may exist, for the benefit of all. Fortunately, professional school counseling literature is beginning to give substantial attention to this emerging role (e.g., Baggerly & Borkowski, 2004; Bemak & Chung, 2004; Black & Underwood, 1998; Cali, 1997; Chung & Katayama, 1998; Cooley, 1998; Field & Baker, 2004; Fontaine, 1998; Lambie, 2005; Lee & Cramond, 1999; Marinoble, 1998; McCall-Perez, 2000; McFarland, 1998; McFarland & Oliver, 1999; Omizo, Omizo, & Okamoto, 1998; C. B. Stone, 2000; Trusty & Brown, 2005). If a single student is oppressed and treated unfairly, no one in that society can claim equity.

The Professional School Counselor as a Developmental Classroom Guidance Specialist

Professional school counselors are aware of recent national (ASCA, 2003; Campbell & Dahir, 1997), state, and local standards that guide implementation of a comprehensive developmental school counseling program. They have specialized expertise in planning and evaluating comprehensive programs (e.g., Brigman & Campbell, 2003;

Britzman, 2005; Dahir, 2001; Fitch & Marshall, 2004; Gysbers, 2004; Gysbers & Henderson, 2001; Gysbers, Lapan, & Blair, 1999; Herr, 2001; Lapan, Gysbers, & Petroski, 2003; Lenhardt & Young, 2001; Nicholson & Pearson, 2003; Paisley, 2001; Sink & MacDonald, 1998; Sink & Stroh, 2003; Sink & Yillik–Downer, 2001; Smith, Crutchfield, & Culbreth, 2001). Although many have not been teachers before entering the profession (Quarto, 1999), professional school counselors provide developmental educational and guidance instruction to classes and other large groups and prepare their lessons much as classroom teachers do. This means they write measurable objectives and plan interesting activities to meet the diverse learning needs of the students. Perhaps most important, professional school counselors must assess the effectiveness of their instruction and evaluate the outcomes of the comprehensive program (Lapan, 2001; Scruggs, Wasielewski, & Ash, 1999; Trevisan & Hubert, 2001). Chapters 7, 8, and 12 address these issues in detail.

The Professional School Counselor as a Provider of Individual and Group Counseling Services

While it may come as no shock to hear that the professional school counselor will continue to provide specialized group and individual counseling in the schools, the nature of the problems that usher students to counseling today differs from in years past. Today, students are much more likely to need assistance with special issues, exhibit clinical symptoms, or show resistance, all requiring a different approach. The professional literature for school counselors is addressing these changes (e.g., Abrams, Theberge, & Karan, 2005; Arman & McNair, 2000; Bardick et al., 2004; Carter & Mason, 1998; Cochran & Cochran, 1999; Cook & Kaffenberger, 2003; Erford, 1999; Fleming, 1999; Gabel & Kearney, 1998; Kahn, 1999; Kareck, 1998; Kizner & Kizner, 1999; Kress, Gibson, & Reynolds, 2004; Lambie, 2004; Lambie & Sias, 2005; Lockhart & Keys, 1998; McGlauflin, 1998; Mostert, Johnson, & Mostert, 1997; Post & Robinson, 1998; Ray, 2004; Stout & Frame, 2004; Webb & Myrick, 2003).

Chapter 9 briefly reviews the developmental facets so essential to a comprehensive approach to school counseling. Chapter 16 focuses on what professional school counselors need to know about clinical disorders and psychopathology to help ensure their students get appropriate help. Some view professional school counselors of the future as serving in a school-based clinical role; undoubtedly some professional school counselors are providing services to clinically diagnosed students already. Other school systems have hired licensed clinicians to provide counseling services (often receiving third-party reimbursement in the process), confining professional school counselors to those "noncounseling" functions of their role or, in a few instances, cutting school counseling positions altogether. While many professional school counselors, having received appropriate education, experience, and supervision, are licensed to provide clinical counseling services by state licensing boards, the practice of what some see as mental health counseling in the schools is likely to remain a professional issue receiving much attention and discussion.

The Professional School Counselor as a Career Development and Educational Planning Specialist

A number of states require that individual educational and career plans be developed for every high school student to serve as a guide for entering higher education or the workforce. School counseling claims career development as its roots and many secondary professional school counselors become specialists in career and lifestyle development. The trend is for elementary and secondary professional school counselors to provide more emphasis in this area as well. Chapter 10 provides an overview of the important developmental issues requiring attention. School reform and accountability movements in the United States demand that professional school counselors focus on academic performance and achievement. This is commensurate with the *National Standards for School Counseling Programs* (Campbell & Dahir, 1997) and the goals of a comprehensive developmental school counseling program (e.g., Bachay & Rigby, 1997; Barker & Satcher,

2000; Blackhurst, Auger, & Wahl, 2003; Bobo, Hildreth, & Durodoye, 1998; Carnevale & Desrochers, 2003; Dykeman et al., 2003; Feller, 2003; Granello & Sears, 1999; Gribbons & Shoffner, 2004; Jarvis & Keeley, 2003; Jones, Sheffield, & Joyner, 2000; Kraus & Hughey, 1999; Mau, Hitchcock, & Calvert, 1998; Mosconi & Emmett, 2003; Murrow-Taylor, 1999; Niles, Erford, Hunt, & Watts, 1997; O'Shea & Harrington, 2003; Peterson, Long, & Billups, 1999; Rosenbaum & Person, 2003; Sellers, Satcher, & Comas, 1999; Trusty & Niles, 2003; Wahl & Blackhurst, 2000).

The Professional School Counselor as a School and Community Agency Consultation/Collaboration Specialist

Chapter 11 addresses the basics of consultation/ collaborative models used with individuals and organizations, as well as how to engage parents in the educational process. Consultation has long been a part of the professional school counselor's role, but collaboration makes the professional school counselor a more active and vested participant in the problem-solving process, whether working with individuals or organizations (Keys, 2000a; Keys & Bemak, 1997). Collaboration has been receiving considerable attention recently in school counseling literature (e.g., Amatea, Daniel, Bringman, & Vandiver, 2004; Bemak, 2000; Brotherton & Clarke, 1997; Bryan, 2005; Bryan & Holcolm-McCoy, 2004; Carpenter, King-Sears, & Keys, 1998; Dimmitt, 2003; Fusick & Bordeau, 2004; Giles, 2005; Hayes, Paisley, Phelps, Pearson, & Salter, 1997; Kahn, 2000; Keys, 2000a; Keys & Lockhart, 1999; Luongo, 2000; Miano, Forrest, & Gumaer, 1997; Mullis & Otwell, 1998; Murphy, DeEsch, & Strein, 1998; Osborne & Collison, 1998; Ponec, Poggi, & Dickel, 1998; Porter, Epp, & Bryant, 2000; Shepherd-Tew & Creamer, 1998; Taylor & Adelman, 2000; Terry, 1999; Walsh, Howard, & Buckley, 1999).

In the future, working hand in hand with parents will become more important to all educational professionals because supportive parents are more likely to have successful students. For example, students who have at least one parent actively involved in their academic life are more likely to get high grades and less likely to get suspended. More than half of all Americans believe parents encounter circumstances when help is needed to raise their kids. Interestingly, the parents are not viewed as irresponsible, so much as overwhelmed at the time (U.S. Dept. of Education, 1998).

The Professional School Counselor as a School Reform and Accountability Expert

Another topic addressed throughout the book is the professional school counselor's role as an agent of school reform. School reform hinges on an understanding of what is and isn't working—a process called accountability. While chapter 12 introduces the topics of needs assessment and program evaluation, chapter 3 provides a whirlwind tour through counseling and guidance literature. Although one can take heart in knowing that there is validation for much of what professional school counselors do, what amazes many experienced counselors is the relative dearth of outcomes studies related to school counseling. For example, in comparison with other roles outlined in this book, outcome assessment has traditionally received the least attention, although recent attention has been given (e.g., Brown, Galassi, & Akos, 2004; Curcio, Mathai, & Roberts, 2003; Dahir & Stone, 2003; Ekstrom, Elmore, Schafer, Trotter, & Webster, 2004; Eschenauer & Chen-Hayes, 2005; Hughes & James, 2001; Isaacs, 2003; Johnson & Johnson, 2003; Myrick, 2003; Zinck & Littrell, 2000). This becomes another essential task for this generation of professional school counselors. Much more outcomes research and results evaluation of school counseling roles and activities are greatly needed to determine the effectiveness of what is currently done and lead the school counseling field in new directions.

The Professional School Counselor as a Safe Schools, Violence Prevention, At-Risk Specialist

Recent sensational news stories have created powerful "safe schools" and "at-risk" movements in the United States, and professional school counselors are positioned to play a pivotal role.

In an equivalent fashion, the professional interest in school counseling literature has kept pace with societal interest (e.g., Arman, 2000; Auger, Seymour, & Roberts, 2004; Beale & Scott, 2001; Brock, 1998; Brown & Parsons, 1998; Buckley, 2000; Canfield, Ballard, Osmon, & McCune, 2004; Carlson, 2003; Charkow, 1998; Cobia, Carney, & Waggoner, 1998; Cunningham & Singh Sandhu, 2000; Del Prete, 2000; Edmondson & White, 1998; Edwards & Mullis, 2003; Esters & Ledoux, 2001; Fryxell & Smit, 2000; Glasser, 2000a; Halverson, 1999; Hanish & Guerra, 2000; Hazler & Carney, 2000; Hernandez & Seem, 2004; Isely, Busse, & Isely, 1998; King, Price, Telljohann, & Wahl, 2000; King, Tribble, & Price, 1999; McFarland & Dupuis, 2001; Minden, Henry, Tolan, & Gorman-Smith, 2000; Pietrzak, Peterson, & Speaker, 1998; Popenhagen & Qualley, 1998; Rainey, Hensley, & Crutchfield, 1997; Riley & McDaniel, 2000; Schaefer-Schiumo & Ginsberg, 2003; Skovholt, Cognetta, Ye, & King, 1997; Theberge & Karan, 2004; Vera, Shin, Montgomery, Mildner, & Speight, 2004).

Chapter 13 addresses the professional school counselors' role in counseling students at risk, while chapter 14 covers important aspects of developmental conflict resolution curricula and peer mediation programs. It is hard to underestimate the importance of these components in the future of school counseling (Gerber & Terry-Day, 1999; Humphries, 1999; Scarborough, 1997; Tobias & Myrick, 1999). Conflict and violence are on the rise in schools and society, and the developmental and intervention components of a comprehensive school counseling program can address these problems on multiple levels.

The Professional School Counselor as an Advocate for Students with Special Needs

Over five million students aged 6 to 21 receive special education services in the public schools (Kupper, 1999; USDOE, 2005). The movement known as *inclusion* has resulted in numerous students with significant emotional and learning problems being returned to the regular educational classroom and being taught by regular teachers with little or no training to instruct children with special needs (Greer, Greer, &

Woody, 1995; Lockhart & Keys, 1998). Though the research has demonstrated neutral to positive outcomes for special education students, the impact on regular education students and teachers is largely unknown.

Professional school counselors are often the designated (and sometimes lone) advocates for children with special needs and their parents in an intricate and often intimidating educational bureaucracy. It follows that the more a professional school counselor knows about testing and special programs, including special education and Section 504, the more effective the advocacy will be. Increasing attention is being paid to this area in school counseling literature (e.g., Agnew, Nystul, & Conner, 1998; Bowen & Glenn, 1998; Durodoye, Combes, & Bryant, 2004; Erford, 1995, 1996a, 1996b, 1997, 1998; Erford, Peyrot, & Siska, 1998; Esters & Ittenbach, 1999; Garcia,

Krankowski, & Jones, 1998; Glen & Smith, 1998; Isaacs, Greene, & Valesky, 1998; Quigney & Studer, 1998; Reis & Colbert, 2004; Sabella, 1998; Scarborough & Deck, 1998; Schweibert, Sealander, & Bradshaw, 1998; Tarver-Behring, Spagna, & Sullivan, 1998; Thompson & Littrell, 1998).

It is essential that professional school counselors know all there is to know about school system standardized testing programs, the child study process, special education eligibility procedures and planning, Section 504 eligibility procedures and modifications, and group and individual assessment procedures and interpretation strategies. Professional school counselors who know the laws, ethics, policies, procedures, and loopholes serve as effective advocates for students, families, and schools. Chapter 15, which focuses on special education, serves as a primer on this subject.

SUMMARY/CONCLUSION

Professional school counseling in the United States rests on a rich heritage of ideas, techniques, and implementation approaches. The profession has evolved in response to institutional changes such as immigration; national defense, social, and school reform; economic circumstances such as poverty and programs for the economically disadvantaged; the integration of culturally diverse students who had been previously segregated in some parts of the nation; and growing knowledge about student development—changes that have shaped concepts of education and the role of school counseling.

The historical roots that have spawned the need for counselors in schools and the future issues that remain to be fully resolved at the beginning of the 21st century suggest that the role of the professional school counselor is not a rigid and static set of functions. Rather, it is in a constant state of transformation in response to the changing demands on American schools and the factors and influences that affect the growth and development of America's children and youth.

Across the 100 years or so that comprise the history of school counseling in the United States, the questions and issues have changed. However, there is no longer a question of whether professional school counseling will survive or whether it is relevant to the mission of the school. The questions today are how to make its contribution more explicit, how to distribute its effects more evenly across school and student groups, and how to deploy these precious professional resources in the most efficient and effective manner. These are the challenges that this generation of professional school counselors face.

Now go to our Companion Website at www.prenhall.com/erford to assess your understanding of chapter content with "Multiple-Choice Questions," apply comprehension with "Essay Questions," and broaden your knowledge of the school counseling profession with related "Web Links."

ACTIVITIES

1. Interview a school social worker, school psychologist, or a community-based mental health worker to find out what role his or her profession plays in student development.
2. Research a culture different from your own and brainstorm possible counseling issues someone from this culture may experience.
3. Talk to a professional school counselor or a school administrator to find out some of the noncounseling tasks counselors are often asked to perform in a school. Develop a plan of action to advocate for using counselor time for counseling and not for noncounseling-related tasks.

CHAPTER 3

OUTCOMES RESEARCH ON SCHOOL COUNSELING INTERVENTIONS AND PROGRAMS

SUSAN C. WHISTON

Editor's Introduction: The science of school counseling involves empirical study of the methods, techniques, and procedures used by professional school counselors in their day-to-day work. The transformation of the profession must be guided by knowledge and understanding of what works, rather than what or how much of something is done. Effective practices raise a profession to new heights, and it is with this focus that we explore what is known about the effectiveness of school counseling practices. As you will see, while some evidence exists regarding effective service provision, much more evidence is needed to document effectiveness and establish school counseling as an accountable profession. The transformed professional school counselor understands the vital nature of this mission and establishes collaborative partnerships to conduct field-based action research and outcomes evaluation to benefit students and the profession.

The remaining chapters of this book will discuss practices in the profession of school counseling with a focus on the evolving role of the professional school counselor. The services that professional school counselors provide are particularly important because of the diverse needs of children and adolescents. Epidemiological studies indicate that many children and adolescents suffer from some form of behavioral or emotional problems. For example, Costello et al. (1996) found that 20.3% of children ages 9 to 13 years meet the criteria for a mental disorder as defined by the *Diagnostic and Statistical Manual of Mental Disorders* (APA, 2000). This is consistent with Doll's (1996) findings that a typical school can expect to find between 18% and 22% of students with diagnosable psychiatric disorders, most frequently Anxiety Disorders, Conduct Disorder, Oppositional

Defiant Disorder, and Attention-Deficit Disorder. In secondary school populations, Doll found that depression and suicidal behaviors were also prevalent. The costs for addressing these issues can be substantial. Ringel and Sturm (2001) found the direct costs for the treatment of children with mental health problems (emotional and behavioral) who had insurance was approximately $11.75 billion in 1998. It may be argued that investing in school counselors may be a good investment as professional school counselors are often the ones who are on the "front line" in terms of addressing the needs of students who have difficulties and providing prevention programs.

Not only do professional school counselors have responsibilities for students with problems, but they also have a responsibility to assist all students in terms of their academic, personal–social, and career development. As we explore the professional practice of school counseling, it is important to examine whether the services professional school counselors provide are actually helpful to students. In this age of accountability in education, school boards, administrators, parents, and legislators want evidence that confirms the effectiveness of school counseling. Furthermore, many of these individuals want evidence not only that school counseling services are beneficial to students, but also that these services are cost effective.

In addition to providing accountability information on the effects of school counseling interventions and services, outcomes research can also provide pertinent clinical information to the professional school counselor. Counseling outcomes research can be a potentially useful source of this information because it is designed to identify which approaches and activities produce positive changes for students. Outcomes research can aid professional school counselors in selecting counseling interventions and guidance activities that have been shown to be effective. Some have argued that without empirical information, practitioners are making uninformed decisions. Lambert (1991) contended that without a thorough knowledge of the counseling outcomes research, a practitioner cannot ethically counsel. He argued that counselors are ethically bound to provide the best services to their clients, and without

thorough knowledge of the research, they will not know what has been shown to be the "best." Given the significant responsibilities that professional school counselors have, it is important they choose interventions that are effective.

However, it is not always easy to be a good consumer of outcomes research. Outcomes research is published in a wide variety of journals, and it is often difficult for counselors to keep abreast of relevant findings (Sexton, 1996). In addition, it is sometimes difficult to decipher results and identify valid and reliable findings that are pertinent to counseling practice. This chapter is designed to assist counselors by summarizing the outcomes research related to school counseling activities. Whiston (2002) argued that it is critical for professional school counselors to be informed about outcome research and know which activities are supported or not supported by research. The primary purpose of this chapter is to summarize the research in this area so that professional school counselors will have empirical knowledge when making decisions about what works best with which students.

The second purpose of this chapter is to provide information that can be communicated to other constituents. In these days of educational reform and accountability, school curriculums and activities are under close scrutiny. In some school districts, professional school counselor positions may be eliminated unless there is empirical support documenting the effectiveness of professional school counselor activities. This discussion of school counseling outcomes research is designed to address the following set of questions: Is professional school counseling effective? What students benefit from school counseling activities? What are the effective methods for delivering school counseling programs? Does a fully implemented school counseling program make a difference?

IS PROFESSIONAL SCHOOL COUNSELING EFFECTIVE?

The answer to the question of whether professional school counseling is effective cannot be determined with the results of just one study.

No single study can examine the multitude of duties performed by professional school counselors at all the different grade levels. Therefore, the answer to the question concerning the effectiveness of school counseling services resides in examining the accumulation of school counseling research. One valuable resource is research reviews on professional school counseling, and there are two types of research reviews. The first type is the more common qualitative reviews, where the reviewers examine the studies and summarize the findings and trends. The second type of review is based on meta-analytic techniques, where researchers seek to quantify the results by calculating an overall effect size (e.g., the mean of the control group subtracted from the mean of the experimental group divided by the standard deviation of the control group).

Results from qualitative reviews are generally supportive of the effectiveness of school counseling activities. Borders and Drury (1992) examined research studies and professional statements from counseling organizations published between 1960 and 1990. They concluded that school counseling interventions have a substantial impact on students' educational and personal development. Their review cited a number of studies that indicated students who received school counseling services showed improvements in terms of their academic performance, attitudes, and behaviors. In a systematic review of outcomes research in professional school counseling, Whiston and Sexton (1998) concluded that a broad range of activities professional school counselors perform result in positive changes in students. They found, however, that not all school counseling activities have been empirically investigated.

In addition to general reviews of school counseling research, a few qualitative reviews have focused on specific student populations. In a review of studies published on elementary counseling, Gerler (1985) concluded that school counseling programs can positively influence that affective, behavioral, and interpersonal domains of children's lives. At the middle school level, St. Claire (1989) found support for some programs and strategies utilized by professional middle

school counselors, such as a behavior management program, successful daily progress reports, and self-relaxation techniques. N. S. Wilson (1986) focused specifically on research related to the effects of counselor interventions with underachieving and low-achieving students. The results from this review indicated that many professional school counseling interventions have a positive influence on these students' grade-point averages.

Meta-analytic reviews, as stated earlier, provide a quantitative measure of the degree to which school counseling interventions and programs are effective. A recent meta-analysis conducted by Whiston, Eder, Rahardja, and Tai (2005) provided some quantitative evidence concerning the degree to which school counseling interventions are effective. These researchers examined the school counseling literature since 1980 and found 117 published and unpublished studies related to school counseling that contained sufficient data to calculate an effect size. An effect size is calculated by subtracting the mean of the control group from the mean of the treatment group and dividing by the pooled standard deviation, which results in a numerical index of whether the students receiving the school counseling intervention did better or worse on the outcome measure than the students who did not receive the intervention during the time of the study. In examining these 117 studies, Whiston et al. identified 153 school counseling interventions that involved 16,296 students. In terms of the effectiveness of all school counseling interventions, these researchers found an average unweighted effect size of .46; however, when weighting the effect size by the methods proposed by Hedges and Olkin (1985), they found a significant effect size of .29. An effect size of .29 is somewhat small, but it does indicate that students who received a school counseling intervention were almost a third of a standard deviation above those who did not receive the intervention. Whiston et al. also found that school counseling interventions were not homogeneous and there was variation among the interventions, which indicates that some interventions are more effective and others have much smaller effect sizes.

There also are four other meta-analytic reviews that have some relations to school counseling. Sprinthall (1981) found that primary prevention programs were effective; however, this meta-analysis included only six studies. A more comprehensive review of primary prevention strategies is that of Baker, Swisher, Nadenichek, and Popowicz (1984). The effect sizes varied, but a conservative estimate of effect size (ES) was .55, which would indicate that prevention activities are moderately effective. Two other meta-analyses have examined the effects of counseling or psychotherapy in school settings. In the first (H. T. Prout & DeMartino, 1986), researchers found a moderate effect size (ES = .58); whereas the second meta-analysis (S. M. Prout & Prout, 1998) found these types of interventions were very effective (ES = .97). It should be noted that these last two meta-analytic reviews (H. T. Prout & DeMartino, 1986; S. M. Prout & Prout, 1998) included interventions conducted by both professional school counselors and school psychologists.

If the results from these various meta-analytic reviews are coalesced, there appears to be support for the conclusion that school counseling interventions are moderately to highly effective. The qualitative reviews are also generally positive. As a caveat, however, these conclusions are based on a somewhat limited number of studies. Sexton, Whiston, Bleuer, and Walz (1997) found that significantly more is known about the effectiveness of individual and career counseling than is known about the outcomes of school counseling. Furthermore, Whiston et al. (2005) and Whiston and Sexton (1998) contended that many of the studies evaluating the effectiveness of school counseling have methodological limitations. Thus, conclusions about the outcomes of school counseling should be made cautiously.

WHICH STUDENTS BENEFIT FROM SCHOOL COUNSELING INTERVENTIONS?

Professional school counselors work with students at different grade levels, and there is some evidence that school counseling interventions may have a differential effect on students at different ages. Whiston et al. (2005) found that studies in the past 25 years have focused more predominantly on elementary school counseling; that is, 46% of the interventions researched were with elementary students, 21% with middle school or junior high students, and 28% with high school students. Whiston et al. found a weighted effect size of school counseling interventions with elementary students of .25, an effect size of .39 for middle and junior high students, and .34 for high school interventions. This study indicated that interventions are most effective with middle school students, which is not consistent with Nearpass's (1990) finding that interventions with upper-level high school students are most effective than interventions with younger high school students. H. T. Prout and DeMartino (1986) also concluded that older students seem to benefit more from school counseling interventions than younger students do; however, S. M. Prout and Prout's (1998) study found that interventions with elementary students produced the greatest gains. Additionally, Gerler (1985) found that elementary school counselors' interventions have a positive effect on elementary students. Hence, the findings regarding the effectiveness of school counseling at different levels is somewhat mixed and is probably related to differences in interventions at different levels. For example, although Whiston et al. found an overall effect size for elementary school counseling interventions of .25, they also found considerable differences among effect sizes depending on the type of interventions used with elementary students. This is often a problem when collapsing diverse interventions (e.g., individual counseling, group counseling, classroom guidance) across diverse domains (e.g., academic, career, personal–social) to arrive at general conclusions.

Concerning this area of research, a factor to consider is which students typically use school counseling services. A study by Lavoritano and Segal (1992) provided some insights regarding which students are typically referred by teachers for counseling. For example, they found that children from single-parent homes, students who had been retained, underachievers, students who had been suspended, and more males than females were referred for counseling. Mahoney and Merritt (1993) examined ethnic differences in the utilization of school counseling services. They found that a higher percentage of African American students than White students considered counselors to be important in helping them make their educational plans. Furthermore, African American students, particularly males, were more likely to seek school counseling services to overcome academic weaknesses than were White students. They also found this same trend concerning African American students' increased usage of counseling resources related to job and educational placement.

In terms of examining which students benefit from school counseling, a few studies have found that the effectiveness of an intervention will vary between males and females. Lapan, Gysbers, Hughey, and Arni (1993) found that a conjoint language arts and career guidance unit with high school students enhanced learning for girls, regardless of whether they were doing well in school. However, for boys, it only promoted learning for those already doing well in school. Another student characteristic that has been found to have an impact on counseling effectiveness is whether the students volunteered to participate or were required to participate. With low-achieving students, programs in which students volunteer to participate have been found to be more successful than programs where the students are forced to attend (N. S. Wilson, 1986).

There are other student characteristics that have not been found to be related to outcome. Student background characteristics or student academic variables did not predict middle school students' satisfaction with group counseling (Hagborg, 1993). Background characteristics that were not related to satisfaction were student's gender, age, grade level, socioeconomic status, parental marital status, and presence of an educational disability. A number of academic variables also were found to be unrelated to satisfaction with the group experience, including grades, attendance at school, and standardized achievement scores. These findings suggest that some of the stereotypes counselors may have

regarding who will view group counseling positively may not always be accurate.

In summary, the outcomes research in school counseling does not provide a clear indication about which students may benefit from school counseling activities. Increasingly, professional school counselors are required to serve *all* students in a school. Questions related to which students benefit from school counseling activities are probably not as important as questions related to how professional school counselors can deliver a school counseling program effectively to all students. The next section of this chapter examines the research related to the methods of delivering school counseling programs and the effectiveness of the different modalities.

WHAT ARE THE EFFECTIVE METHODS FOR DELIVERING SCHOOL COUNSELING PROGRAMS?

Increasingly, the field of school counseling is moving toward providing program-related services. Professional school counselors do not focus on helping select students find scholarships and helping other students who are experiencing a crisis. The role of professional school counselors is to implement a comprehensive program for all students that is a systematic component of the larger school's purpose and mission. For example, Sink and Stroh (2003) found that elementary students who attended schools with a comprehensive school counseling program for at least 5 years had slightly higher achievement scores than did students who attended schools with no systematic guidance program. In providing a school counseling program, counselors typically employ a variety of interventions and activities; hence, it is important to know which delivery methods result in the most positive benefits for students. As an example, professional school counselors may want to know if it is more effective to counsel using groups or whether students benefit more from individual counseling. ASCA (2003a) developed a national model, which suggested four components within the delivery system of a school counseling program (i.e., Guidance Curriculum, Individual Student Planning, Responsive Services, and System Support). In examining outcome research, these four areas of program delivery will be used to provide information on the effectiveness of these areas and examine particular types of activities that tend to be most effective.

Guidance Curriculum

Gysbers and Henderson (2000) suggested that professional school counselors incorporate guidance curriculum activities into their daily work with students. According to ASCA, guidance curriculum involves structured developmental lessons designed to assist students in achieving guidance competencies that are intended to provide all students with the knowledge and skills appropriate for their developmental level (ASCA, 2003a). In making decisions about guidance curriculum activities, professional school counselors need to consider whether students benefit from these activities and which guidance curriculum activities are the most beneficial.

Borders and Drury (1992) concluded that classroom guidance activities were effective; however, Whiston and Sexton (1998) did not find clear empirical support for classroom guidance activities. Whiston et al. (2005) identified 44 studies that evaluated guidance curriculum activities, which had an overall weighted effect size of .33. Hence, students who were in schools where guidance curriculum materials were implemented tended to score about a third of a standard deviation better than those students who did not receive these types of classroom and group activities. Of the guidance curriculum interventions evaluated, 40% were with elementary students, 26% with middle school students, 26% with high school students, and 7% with a mixture of students or with parents. Interestingly, although much of the research on guidance curriculum interventions is with elementary students, it seems like middle school or junior high students benefited the most (ES = .41) from guidance curriculum offerings. These researchers also found that high school students seemed to benefit with an average effect size of .39, while the

effect size for elementary students was somewhat smaller (ES = .29).

Related to guidance curriculum activities at the elementary level, Rowley, Stroh, and Sink (2005) found that elementary counselors were most likely to use guidance curriculum materials related to the personal/affective domain. Whiston and Sexton (1998) found that elementary classroom guidance activities that focused on improving self-esteem or self-concept had mixed results. This may be related to the difficulties associated with measuring self-esteem or self-concept. A study conducted by Omizo, Omizo, and D'Andrea (1992) described a guidance curriculum designed to promote wellness among elementary children, which positively affected self-esteem and knowledge of wellness. Hadley (1988) and R. S. Lee (1993) found that some guidance curriculum activities designed to increase self-esteem had a positive influence on academic achievement. It is important to note, however, that the findings related to the positive effects of classroom guidance activities on academic achievement are based on only two studies, which both had some methodological limitations. More recently, Brigman and Campbell (2003) and Campbell and Brigman (2005) evaluated a classroom guidance or small group curriculum with fifth and sixth graders called the Students Success Skills, which focused on improving academic, social, and self-management skills. Although the students who received the intervention had only slightly higher achievement test scores than those in the control group, the achievement scores for those students who participated in the Student Success Skills program increased substantially from before the program to after it. Concerning social skills training, Gerler (1985) concluded that interpersonal skills training was generally effective with elementary students. The efficacy of classroom-based social-competence programs is also supported in the work of Weissburg, Caplan, and Harwood (1991). They concluded that the short-term benefits of social skills training have been established for preschool, elementary, middle, and high school students.

At the middle and high school level, Whiston et al. 's (2005) findings support professional school counselors in providing guidance curriculum lessons. In a well-designed study, Schlossberg, Morris, and Lieberman (2001) found that counselor-led, developmental guidance units presented in ninth-grade classrooms have the potential to improve students' expresssed behavior and general school attitudes, while also addressing their developmental needs. A conjoint language arts and career guidance unit was positively evaluated both quantitatively (Lapan et al., 1993) and qualitatively (Hughey, Lapan, & Gysbers, 1993). Professional school counselors and English teachers worked cooperatively to develop a guidance unit that provided an opportunity for high school juniors to develop academic skills while exploring career issues.

The findings of Baker et al. (1984) are somewhat related to guidance curriculum activities, for they examined the effectiveness of prevention programs. These researchers determined that programs that emphasized career maturity enhancement, communication skills training, and deliberate psychological education tended to be effective. On the other hand, programs that emphasized cognitive coping skills training, moral education, substance abuse prevention, and blended values clarification with other strategies had smaller effects sizes.

Classroom guidance activities are a major emphasis of school counseling programs in some school districts; yet, the research in this area should be more extensive. Rowley et al. (2005) found that with a few exceptions (e.g., Missouri Comprehensive Guidance and Counseling Program), professional school counselors are predominantly using curricular materials that have not been well researched. They recommended the development and evaluation of guidance curriculum materials by grade level that meet the needs of students and correspond to national standards. This recommendation is of critical importance because developing empirically supported guidance curriculum material is a crucial step in transforming school counseling.

Individual Student Planning

Individual student planning involves professional school counselors coordinating ongoing systemic activities designed to assist students in individually determining personal goals and developing plans for their future (ASCA, 2003a). Whiston et al. (2005) found only 10 studies that addressed individual planning, and the majority of these were with high school students. The overall weighted effect size was statistically significant (ES = .27). Interestingly, these researchers found that for middle school or junior high school students, the effect size for individual planning activities was extraordinarily high (ES = 1.01), which means the students who received individual planning scored over a standard deviation above those who did not receive individual planning on the outcome measures. As a caveat, this effect size is based on only three studies, but it does indicate that individual planning activities might be particularly important for those in middle or junior high school.

According to Gysbers and Henderson (2000), professional school counselors often design individual planning around educational and career/vocational planning. In addition, one of the three areas in the *National Standards for School Counseling Programs* (Campbell & Dahir, 1997) is career development. It is important, therefore, to examine the research related to effective career guidance and counseling activities. Furthermore, there is evidence that both students and parents would like professional school counselors to put more emphasis on career guidance and development activities (Libsch & Freedman-Doan, 1995; Scruggs et al., 1999).

There is support for career counseling with clients at various developmental levels from both narrative reviews (Swanson, 1995; Whiston & Oliver, 2005) and meta-analyses (Oliver & Spokane, 1988; Whiston, Sexton, & Lasoff, 1998). The meta-analyses differ somewhat on the degree to which career interventions are effective. The first meta-analysis (Oliver & Spokane, 1998) indicated career interventions were highly effective, whereas the meta-analysis of more current research (Whiston et al., 1998) found career interventions to be moderately effective. These two meta-analyses were consistent in finding that individual career counseling or classes were the most effective methods of delivering career counseling services.

A recent study found that counselor-free interventions are not effective, and interventions that involve a counselor are significantly more efficacious (Whiston, Brecheisen, & Stephens, 2003). This finding is particularly important because many schools have purchased computerized career guidance programs or encourage students to use career resources on the Internet. Whiston et al.'s (2003) finding clearly indicated that students do not gain much when they use these resources alone; however, students do benefit from the use of computerized career guidance systems when they are integrated with other activities involving a counselor.

Concerning career interventions specifically in school settings, Baker and Taylor (1998) found that career education activities designed to assist students in the school-to-work transition also had a moderate effect size. Whiston and Sexton (1998) also supported the effectiveness of career interventions in a school setting. They determined that career counseling activities seemed to assist a wide range of students (e.g., students from minority families, students with learning disabilities, and students who are gifted). In addition, they cited two studies where adolescents' career development was positively affected by instructing parents on methods for assisting their children in the career area (Kush & Cochran, 1993; Palmer & Cochran, 1998).

In conclusion, professional school counselors can feel confident in reporting that career development activities are generally effective. Rowley et al. (2005) found that at the secondary level, professional school counselors are increasingly using guidance curriculum materials to address the career/vocational domain. This is a positive development because previous research had indicated this domain was often neglected in school counseling programs.

Responsive Services

Responsive services concern the role of the professional school counselor in assisting students with immediate issues that are usually affected by life events or situations in the students' lives (ASCA, 2003a). Gysbers and Henderson (2000) suggested this component of a school counseling program is consistent with systematic means for attending to students' topics or problems. Typical modalities employed in responsive services activities are individual counseling, group counseling, referral, consultation, and peer assistance programs.

In examining the school counseling research, Whiston et al. (2005) found 58 studies that examined 73 interventions, which were classified as being responsive services. Once again, the weighted overall effect size (ES = .35) indicated that those who received the responsive services scored a little more than a third of a standard deviation above those who did not receive the intervention. It should be noted that elementary children seemed to particularly benefit from these services, with an effect size of .40. Surprisingly, they found that only 10 interventions in the responsive services area were researched with middle school or junior high students, and these studies resulted in an effect size of .22. It is perplexing that so few findings have been conducted with this early adolescent population when these students are often experiencing physiological changes, social pressures, and behavioral problems. Whiston et al. (2005) found the evaluation of 20 responsive services interventions with high school students, and these studies produced an effect size of .34.

Individual and Group Counseling

Administrators, teachers, and parents sometimes question whether the time students spend in individual or group counseling is worth the time away from the classroom. The research findings are mixed on whether it is more effective for a professional school counselor to provide service primarily through group interventions or through individual counseling. S. M. Prout and Prout (1998) found that most research studies concerning counseling and psychotherapy in schools examined group approaches. Whiston et al. (2005) found group interventions were often evaluated and produced a weighted effect size of .36; whereas only three studies investigated individual counseling, and the average weighted effect size for these few studies was .06. N. S. Wilson (1986) found evidence that group counseling was more effective than individual counseling in increasing the academic performance of low- and underachieving students; whereas, Nearpass (1990) found that individual counseling is generally more effective than group counseling. Wiggins and Wiggins (1992) found that counselors who predominantly used individual counseling were more effective than those counselors who predominantly used classroom guidance activities. This finding, however, should be interpreted cautiously because of methodological problems with the study.

There are indications that individual counseling does not have to be lengthy to be effective. Littrell, Malia, and Vanderwood (1995) concluded that three approaches to brief individual counseling were effective with secondary students. There is also empirical support for using brief counseling approaches with students with learning disabilities (Thompson & Littrell, 1998). In a meta-analysis of the effects of school-based programs on aggressive behavior, Wilson, Lispey, and Derzon (2003) found that behavioral approaches and counseling showed the largest effects, and multimodal and peer mediation programs showed the smallest effects.

Borders and Drury (1992) pointed to a substantial number of studies that verified the positive effects of group counseling interventions. Whiston and Sexton (1998) also found this support for group counseling. They determined that there was substantial support for group approaches for social skills training, family adjustment issues, and discipline problems. In particular, there is sound research that indicates that groups designed to assist students whose parents have divorced have both short-term (Omizo & Omizo, 1988; Pedro-Carroll & Alpert-Gillis, 1997) and more long-term positive effects (Pedro-Carroll, Sutton, & Wyman, 1999). There is also support for relaxation groups and congnitive–behavioral approaches to group counseling with high school students (Bauer, Sapp, & Johnson, 2000; Kiselica, Baker, Thomas, & Reddy, 1994). In conclusion, the support for group counseling is primarily with younger students, and conclusions about the effectiveness of group approaches with high school students require further exploration.

Peer Mediation

In recent years, there has been an increased interest in peer mediation programs. Shepherd (1994) estimated that, in the early part of the 1990s, conflict resolution programs in the schools have increased by 40%. Some of the earlier reviews of research in this area indicated that there was empirical support for peer counseling and peer mediation programs at both the elementary and secondary levels (Borders & Drury, 1992; Whiston & Sexton, 1998). Whiston et al. (2005) found that peer mediation interventions were effective with a weighted effect size of .39; however, many of the outcome measures used involved assessing peer mediators' knowledge of the mediation porcess and did not involve measuring whether the peer mediation process had any effect on reducing conflict. Wilson et al. (2003) found that peer mediation programs had a small impact on aggressive behavior. M. W. Lewis and Lewis (1996) found that many of these peer helping programs were supervised by noncounseling professionals and questioned whether these individuals had the proper training to supervise the programs. This concern was legitimized when they also found that those schools with noncounselors supervising the peer helping programs had suicide rates higher than those of schools where a professional school counselor supervised the program. Gerber and Terry-Day (1999) argued there is not sufficient empirical inquiry to support the widespread use of peer mediation programs. M. W. Lewis and Lewis (1996) voiced this same concern in a detailed analysis of the research related to peer helping programs. Hence, professional school counselors should not assume there is conclusive empirical support for peer mediation programs; more research is certainly needed in this area.

Parent Education and Family Counseling

The benefits of parent training and family counseling are well established in the counseling and psychotherapy outcomes research (Kazdin, 1994; Weissburg et al., 1991). Furthermore, there is some evidence that with low- and underachieving students, the effectiveness of the counseling is significantly related to the amount of parental involvement in the counseling process (N. S. Wilson, 1986).

A growing movement across the country is to provide mental health, social services, and "wrap-around" services in school-based centers (Center for Mental Health in Schools, 1999; Melaville & Blank, 1998). These centers often involve providing health and mental health services to students and their families. Professional school counselors and professional organizations need to consider the role they are going to play in providing these services. In some communities, professional school counselors may be viewed as having primarily clerical responsibilities and will not be involved in the parent education and family counseling services provided through these centers. If professional school counselors ignore this trend of others providing mental health services in school settings, then in the future, professional school counselors may have little involvement with mental health issues and family counseling.

There is a significant body of evidence that indicates family counseling is one of the most effective methods for addressing issues related to juvenile violence and crime (Office of Juvenile Justice and Delinquency Prevention, 2000). In fact, the Centers for Disease Control has issued "blueprints" for addressing juvenile violence that are based on substantial empirical evidence. Two of these blueprints concern counseling services, and both of these involve family counseling approaches (e.g., multisystemic family therapy and functional family therapy). Functional family therapy has been found to be particularly effective in issues related to juvenile violence (Sexton & Alexander, 2002). Recent incidents of school violence have resulted in an increased interest in the professional school counselor's role in decreasing violence in the schools. Considering the empirical support for multisystemic and functional family therapy, professional school counselors should consider seeking training on these therapeutic approaches or at least establish a viable referral network with private family therapy practitioners. This may be an important time for professional school counselors to take an active role in responding to juvenile violence through the use of family therapy.

Consultation Activities

Consultation is typically considered an indirect method of providing psychologically oriented services. There is growing empirical support for the effectiveness of consulting as a means of remediating problems (J. J. Murphy, 1999; Zins, 1993). Professional school counselors are often involved in consultation activities with parents, teachers, and other educational professionals. Gerler (1985) concluded that consultation with teachers was an effective method of influencing elementary school children's behavior. Furthermore, Borders and Drury (1992) determined consultation activities to be effective at both the elementary and secondary levels. Professional school counselors often consult with teachers, and Otwell and Mullis (1997) found that a consultation workshop held with teachers resulted in more students being referred for counseling. Amatea et al. (2004) described a 3-year consultation project designed to promote strong working alliances among professional school counselors, teachers, and students' families. They developed family–school problem-solving meetings that focused on developing a plan to assist the student by involving parents in a nonblaming and respectful manner.

There are some indications that the verbal responses of professional school counselors conducting counseling and consultation sessions were very similar (Lin, Kelly, & Nelson, 1996). One of the few differences these researchers found is that professional school counselors provided more information and asked less open and closed questions in consulting, as compared to when they were counseling. In terms of skills that increase the effectiveness of consultation, Gresham and Kendell (1987) found problem identification to be the most important process variable. Zins (1993) found a direct approach to be most effective in enhancing consultees' problem-solving skills. He recommended that counselors directly train consultees in problem-solving, communications, and intervention techniques. He further recommended that counselors overtly model for their consultees the problem-solving process.

DOES A FULLY IMPLEMENTED SCHOOL COUNSELING PROGRAM MAKE A DIFFERENCE?

In the previous section of this chapter, the efficacy of components and activities of a school counseling program were reviewed. As the field moves toward comprehensive developmental school counseling programs, it is important to examine the research related to whether these programs make a difference. Lapan, Gysbers, and Sun (1997) compared schools with more fully implemented guidance programs to schools with a less programmatic approach. The students from schools with more fully implemented programs were more likely to report that (a) they had earned higher grades, (b) their education better prepared them for the future, (c) they had more career and college information available to them, and (d) their schools had a more positive environment. In another study (Gysbers et al., 1999), researchers found that school counseling programs that were more fully implemented rated themselves as having higher levels of engagement and more visibility in the community. In addition, although the results were somewhat mixed, those schools with more fully implemented guidance programs reported a reduction in the performance of nonguidance tasks such as clerical or student supervision duties. In a large study of schools in Utah, Nelson, Gardner, and Fox (1998) also found that students in highly implemented comprehensive guidance programs were more positive about their peers and felt their school had prepared them better for employment or further education than those students in schools designated as low in terms of implementing a guidance program. In addition, students in schools with highly implemented guidance programs tended to be more satisfied with the guidance they received as compared to those in schools with a low implementation rating.

There is also increasing evidence that comprehensive guidance programs have a positive influence on grades and academic achievement. These findings are particularly pertinent in the current educational environment, where there is an increasing focus on academic achievement scores. Lapan et al. (2003) conducted another

substantial study by surveying 22,601 seventh graders related to their feelings of safety and other educationally related outcomes. Once again, students from schools with more fully implemented school counseling programs reported better outcomes. Students attending middle shools with more fully implemented comprehensive programs reported (a) feeling safer in school, (b) having better relationships with their teachers, (c) thinking their education was more relevant and important to their future, (d) being more satisfied with the quality of education at their school, and (e) earning higher grades. Sink and Stroh (2003) found the academic achievement scores of elementary students who consistently attended schools with a comprehensive school counseling program were significantly higher than for students who were attending schools with no systemic guidance program. This positive finding regarding academic achievement is further substantiated by Sink and Stroh's study involving a large sample of 5,618 third and fourth graders.

Wiggins and Moody (1987) compared the counseling programs of schools that were evaluated by students and a team of evaluators as being highly effective, average, or below average. This study concluded that counselors in the highly effective programs spent more than 70% of their time in direct services (e.g., individual and group counseling activities) and very little time doing clerical activities. On the other hand, in school counseling programs that were rated as below average, the counselors spent between 24% and 43% of their time performing clerical tasks. Moreover, the researchers found that the professional school counselors who were spending their time disproportionately performing clerical activities were not always forced to do so by their administrators. Other research has shown that parents, students, and teachers felt that the least important activities for professional school counselors involved paperwork, clerical tasks, and coordinating testing programs (Schmidt, 1995). Furthermore, Wiggins and Moody found that professional school counselors in these below-average schools did not have organized school counseling programs, nor were the majority of these professional school counselors knowledgeable about implementing needs assessments and using such results for programmatic planning. The importance of a well-designed school counseling program was also found by Fitch and Marshall (2004). These researchers used achievement test scores to determine high-achieving and low-achieving schools and found that professional school counselors in high-achieving schools spent more time in program management and coordination. Furthermore, high-achieving schools were more likely to have implemented a school counseling program that aligned with national and state standards.

Overall, research studies suggested that professional school counselors should work toward developing and implementing a comprehensive school counseling program. A comprehensive school counseling program does not mean only

focusing on program administration, for the *ASCA National Model* recommends 80% of a school counselor's time be spent in direct services. In Utah, when there was a statewide focus on implementing comprehensive guidance programs in middle/junior high and high schools, the counselor–student ratio declined substantially from 1:500 in 1992 to 1:375 in 1999 (Utah State Office of Education, 2000). Furthermore, this concerted effort on implementing comprehensive programs in Utah also resulted in professional school counselors reporting they had more time to spend with students. This is encouraging as there is little empirical support for professional school counselors spending time doing clerical tasks. In conclusion, a multifaceted approach and comprehensively implemented school counseling program are not only desirable but are also supported empirically.

SUMMARY/CONCLUSION

Reviews of outcomes research in professional school counseling generally indicate that school counseling activities have a positive effect on students. The reviewers, however, vary somewhat on how substantial they believe the empirical support is. There is also meta-analytic support related to the effectiveness of school counseling interventions, with these studies indicating that school counseling activities are moderately to highly effective. The conclusion that many school counseling interventions are effective may be heartening to professional school counselors, but it may also be an important time to communicate these findings to principals, school board members, and legislators.

This review of the school counseling outcomes research indicates that many school activities have a positive effect, but not all activities produce beneficial results. Therefore, professional school counselors need to be cautious in selecting activities because not all interventions are supported by research. For example, at the elementary level, some guidance curriculum activities designed to increase self-esteem did not necessarily increase self-esteem. Moreover, many of the guidance curriculum activities at the elementary level had comparatively small positive effects.

On the other hand, a number of school counseling activities were supported by research. Research supports that more fully implemented comprehensive school counseling programs result in better outcomes than do nonsystematic approaches to school counseling activities. Studies suggest that within a comprehensive school counseling program, responsive services at the elementary level seem to be particularly effective, whereas guidance curriculum activities appear to be more effective at the middle school and high school levels. Middle school and junior high students seem to benefit greatly from individual planning activities. Furthermore, counselor involvement in career development activities is also supported, and schools should be discouraged from relying on counselor-free interventions (e.g., computer programs). Some approaches to group counseling are supported, such as groups designed to build social skills and assist children whose parents have separated or divorced. In addition, consultation activities have also been found to be an effective school counseling activity. Professional school counselors should consider communicating these positive results to others such as parents, teachers, and administrators. As an illustration, some principals may be more favorably inclined to allow group counseling for children whose parents have recently divorced if they know there is empirical support for these types of counseling activities.

In conclusion, this analysis of the outcomes research on professional school counseling indicates there is considerable need for more and better research in this area. If we are to examine the totality of counseling outcomes research, school counseling has the least amount of empirical evidence available to practitioners (Sexton, 1996). In reviewing all types of school-based mental health services, Hoagwood and Erwin (1997) identified only 16 studies that had methodological rigor. The field of school counseling may be at risk because there is no systematic and rigorous research that supports the effectiveness of school counseling programs. Education is frequently the focus of public interest, and currently there is close scrutiny of educational practices. The public is no longer interested in funding educational programs without substantial evidence that these programs contribute to increased student learning. This is a critical time for professional school counselors and researchers to join together and provide more compelling documentation concerning the positive effects that school counseling programs have on children and adolescents. There is also a particular need to examine the cost effectiveness of school counseling services. Without additional empirical support, some schools may eliminate professional school counseling programs.

Readers need to consider ways they can contribute to outcomes research on school counseling. Professional school counselors should encourage professional organizations to devote funds to research projects and welcome researchers into their schools. In addition, practicing professional school counselors can identify methods for evaluating themselves and their own programs and share these results with other professional school counselors. Students in the field of school counseling might consider taking additional research classes so they are prepared to contribute to the knowledge base and become involved in research projects related to school counseling during their graduate studies. The future of professional school counseling is at risk unless there is a shared commitment to conducting research that clearly documents how professional school counselors make a positive difference in students' lives.

Now go to our Companion Website at www.prenhall.com/erford to assess your understanding of chapter content with "Multiple-Choice Questions," apply comprehension with "Essay Questions," and broaden your knowledge of the school counseling profession with related "Web Links."

ACTIVITIES

1. Begin the basic process of a research project on a topic related to school counseling. What topic would you like to gather data and information about? Would you use a qualitative or quantitative study? What would you hope or expect to find?

2. Choose and attend a community program (e.g., Alcoholics Anonymous meeting, a speaker, community meeting, etc.). How do you feel about your participation? Were you interested in it since you had the choice of what to attend? How do you think you would have felt about the topic/information if you had been required to attend? How can this knowledge be applied to programs offered to students (those who are willing to attend compared to those who resist)?

3. Call a local school to find out if the counseling department offers peer mediation. Attend a peer mediation session and interview the professional school counselor in charge of the program. Has he or she noticed a difference in the student population since the program began? What are the main things the peer mediators are trained to do? Ask what studies are conducted or what documentation is collected to demonstrate program outcomes and effectiveness. How might this intervention be effectively implemented in all schools?

ETHICAL, LEGAL, AND PROFESSIONAL ISSUES IN SCHOOL COUNSELING

LYNN LINDE

Editor's Introduction: Before moving into the "how to" portion of this book, we must address some ethical, legal, and professional issues. Always remember that professional school counselors are first and foremost representatives of the school counseling profession. How you conduct yourself personally and professionally reflects on your colleagues. Knowledge and understanding of the issues reviewed in this chapter are but a starting point. Keep up to date with the laws, ethics, policies, and procedures that govern professional practice. The implementation of your professional responsibilities will require your undivided attention every day of your professional life.

One of the greatest challenges facing most professional school counselors daily is how to appropriately handle the many different ethical and legal situations they encounter. Due to the nature of school counseling, counselors must be prepared to help students who have a variety of problems. It is often difficult to know all that one needs to know. Fortunately, there are a number of resources and sources of information that can help guide counselors as they strive to assist students in an ethical and legal manner. The professional associations for counselors have created ethical standards for professional behavior and provide a wealth of current information, resources, and training. Federal and state governments continually enact laws and regulations that affect counselors, including the judicial branch in which courts hand down decisions that directly affect counselors' behavior. In addition, state boards of education and local school systems create policies, guidelines, and procedures that professional school counselors must follow. Each of these areas will be covered in detail in the sections that follow.

PROFESSIONAL ASSOCIATIONS AND CREDENTIALING ORGANIZATIONS

The ACA is the professional association for all types of counselors. The ACA's mission is to enhance the quality of life in society by promoting the development of professional counselors, advancing the counseling profession, and using the profession and practice of counseling to promote respect for human dignity and diversity. The ACA is a partnership of associations representing professional counselors who enhance human development. It comprises 18 divisions that represent specific work settings or interest areas within the field of counseling, 56 state or affiliate branches, and four regions, which represent major geographical areas. The ACA influences all aspects of professional counseling through its programs, committees, and functions. This includes credentialing of counselors and accreditation of counselor education programs, ethical standards, professional development, professional resources and services, and public policy and legislation.

The ACA has 15 standing committees that address much of the professional business of the association. One of those is the Ethics Committee, which is responsible for updating the ethical standards for the association and investigating ethical complaints. When joining the ACA, one must sign a statement agreeing to abide by the *Code of Ethics* (ACA, 2005a). This is covered in more detail in the next section. The other committees are Awards, Bylaws and Policies, Cyber-Technology, Financial Affairs, Human Rights, International, Interprofessional, Nominations and Elections, Professional Standards, Public Awareness and Support, Public Policy and Legislation, Publications, Research and Knowledge, and Strategic Planning. Each year, task forces are created to address time-limited concerns and business for the association; there are currently 10 task forces. Task forces last for 1 year unless it is determined that additional

time is needed, in which case they must be reappointed. The ACA and its affiliates offer many training and professional development opportunities through state, regional, and national conferences, workshops, and learning institutes. The journals published by the ACA and its divisions cover current research, professional practices, and other information valuable to the practicing counselor. Its monthly newsletter, *Counseling Today*, includes information about what is going on in the field as well as covering special topics and providing notes about members and a governmental relations update. The ACA also publishes books about counseling and current trends and topics in the field, some of which are used as textbooks in counseling courses. ACA staff are available for consultation on a variety of issues, represent ACA in Congress and before other organizations, and advocate for counselors and professional counseling. In summary, the ACA touches all counselors' lives, from the training they receive to the requirements they must achieve to be credentialed to the way in which they conduct themselves regardless of the type of counseling practiced to the professional development in which they engage.

The ASCA is a semiautonomous division of ACA and addresses school counseling issues. ASCA "supports school counselors' efforts to help students focus on academic, personal/social and career development so they achieve success in school and are prepared to lead fulfilling lives as responsible members of society" (ASCA, 2005a, p. 1). The ASCA targets its efforts toward professional development, publications and other resources, research, and advocacy specifically for professional school counselors.

The National Board for Certified Counselors (NBCC) began as a corporate partner of ACA and is now an autonomous organization. Headquartered in Greensboro, North Carolina, NBCC is the only national credentialing organization for professional counselors; all other licenses and certifications are granted through state and local entities. NBCC has established the National Certified Counselor (NCC) credential and several specialty area certifications. The National Counselor Exam (NCE) must be passed as part of the process for becoming nationally certified. The NCE is the exam frequently required by state counseling licensure boards for professional counselor licensure or certification.

CACREP is a corporate partner of ACA and is responsible for establishing state-of-the-art standards for counselor education programs. CACREP standards address program objectives and curricula, faculty and staff requirements, program evaluation, and other requirements for accreditation. Currently, more than 150 university school counseling training programs in the United States are CACREP accredited. Students who graduate from CACREP programs are usually in an advantageous position to be hired because their programs include 48 graduate credit hours and 700 hours of field placement.

ETHICAL STANDARDS AND LAWS

Counselors are sometimes confused by the difference between ethical standards and laws and what one should do when these appear to be in conflict with each other. It may be helpful to take a look at the origin of both. Ethical standards are usually developed by professional associations to guide the behavior of a specific group of professionals. According to Herlihy and Corey (1996), ethical standards serve three purposes: to educate members about sound ethical conduct, to provide a mechanism for accountability, and to serve as a means for improving professional practice. Ethical standards change and are updated periodically to ensure their relevance and appropriateness.

Ethical standards are based on generally accepted norms, beliefs, customs, and values (Fischer & Sorenson, 1997). The ACA's *Code of Ethics* (ACA, 2005a) is based on Kitchener's five moral principles of autonomy, justice, beneficence, nonmaleficence, and fidelity (Forester–Miller & Davis, 1996). Autonomy refers to the concept of independence and the ability to make one's own decisions. Counselors need to respect the right of clients to make their own decisions based on their personal values and beliefs and do not impose their values on clients. Justice

means treating each person fairly, but it does not mean treating each person the same way. Rather, counselors should treat clients according to client needs. Beneficence refers to doing good or what is in the best interests of the client. In counseling, it also incorporates the concept of removing conditions that might cause harm. Nonmaleficence means doing no harm to others. And fidelity involves the concepts of loyalty, faithfulness, and honoring commitments. This means that counselors must honor all obligations to the client.

Laws are also based on these same, generally accepted norms, beliefs, customs, and values. However, laws are more prescriptive, have been incorporated into code, and carry greater sanctions or penalties for failure to comply. Both laws and ethical standards exist to ensure appropriate behavior for professionals within a particular context to ensure that the best interests of the client are met. When the two appear to be in conflict with each other, the professional must attempt to resolve the conflict in a responsible manner (Cottone & Tarvydas, 2003). Counselors must make their clients aware of the conflict and their ethical standards. But, because there are greater penalties associated with laws, the counselor will often follow the legal course of action if there is no harm to the client. Many ethical standards recognize that other mandates must be followed and suggest that counselors work to change mandates that are not in the best interests of their clients.

Within the ACA, there are multiple codes of ethics. The ACA has its *Code of Ethics* (2005a), to which its members must adhere. Additionally, several divisions, including the ASCA, have their own codes of ethics; also the Association for Specialists in Group Work (ASGW) has developed guidelines for best practices in group work. These codes of ethics and guidelines parallel ACA's *Code of Ethics* but speak more directly to the specialty area. For example, the ASCA's *Code of Ethics* discusses what ethical behavior consists of in a school setting. Many counselors belong to multiple organizations, each of which has its own code of ethics. They may also hold credentials from organizations or state credentialing boards that have a code of ethics as well. It is often hard to know which code takes precedence. While each professional will have to make that determination individually, there are two general guidelines. First, what is the setting in which one is practicing, and is there a particular code that applies specifically to that setting? Second, in what capacity is the professional operating? Additionally, all the codes are similar, and all concern behaving in an appropriate professional manner; operating in the best interests of the client; and practicing within the scope of one's education, training, and experience. If a counselor is doing all of that, then the existence of multiple codes of ethics should not be a significant issue.

ACA Code of Ethics

The ACA revises its *Code of Ethics* minimally every 10 years. The sixth and most recent revision became effective August 2005. There are several significant changes from the 1995 *Code of Ethics and Standards of Practice*. The most obvious change is that the Standards of Practice section, which described in behavioral terms the aspirational ethics set forth in the code, has been incorporated into the body of the *Code of Ethics* and is no longer a separate section. Each section now begins with an introduction, which sets the tone for that section and is a beginning point for discussion (ACA, 2005a). Parts of the *Code of Ethics* have been updated to reflect current thinking and practice in the field, and several new issues have been added. Additionally, a glossary of terms has been added.

ACA states that the 2005 *Code of Ethics* serves five main purposes.

> The *Code* 1) enables the association to clarify to current and future members, and to those served by members, the nature of the ethical responsibilities held in common by its members; 2) The *Code* helps support the mission of the association; 3) The *Code* establishes the principles that define ethical behavior and best practices of association members; 4) The *Code* serves as an ethical guide designed to assist members in constructing a professional course of action that best serves those utilizing

counseling services and best promotes the values of the counseling profession; and 5) The *Code* serves as the basis for processing of ethical complaints and inquiries initiated against members of the association. (ACA, 2005, p. 3)

The 2005 ACA *Code of Ethics* (see appendix A) addresses the responsibilities of professional counselors toward their clients, colleagues, workplace, and themselves by delineating the ideal standards for conducting one's behavior. All members are required to abide by the *Code of Ethics*, and action will be taken against any member who fails to do so. In effect, as these are the standards of the profession, all professional counselors are held to the *Code of Ethics* by the mental health community, regardless of whether they are members of the association.

The *Code of Ethics* is divided into eight areas: The Counseling Relationship; Confidentiality, Privileged Communication and Privacy; Professional Responsibility; Relationships with Other Professionals; Evaluation, Assessment, and Interpretation; Supervision, Training, and Teaching; Research and Publication; and Resolving Ethical Issues. Each of these areas details the responsibilities and standards for that area. In general, the *Code of Ethics* discusses respecting one's client and the background each brings to the counseling setting; maintaining professional behavior with clients and other professionals; practicing with the best interests of the client in mind; and practicing within the limits of one's training, experience, and education. The last section provides direction for members resolving ethical dilemmas.

ASCA Ethical Standards for School Counselors

The ASCA (2004a) has developed a parallel set of ethical standards (see appendix B) that specifically addresses professional school counseling. The eight sections of the ASCA code are: Responsibilities to Students; Responsibilities to Parents; Responsibilities to Colleagues and Professional Associates; Responsibilities to the School and Community; Responsibilities to Self; Responsibilities to the Profession; Maintenance of Standards; and Resources. As in the ACA's standards, these standards discuss putting the counselee's best interests first, treating each student as an individual and with respect, involving parents as appropriate, maintaining one's expertise through ongoing professional development and learning, and behaving professionally and ethically.

Both the ACA and the ASCA have developed guides to ethical decision making that can be used when a counselor is concerned about a particular situation and needs to determine if an ethical dilemma exists. The ACA's model involves seven steps: (a) identify the problem, (b) apply the ACA *Code of Ethics*, (c) determine the nature and dimensions of the dilemma, (d) generate potential courses of action, (e) consider the potential consequences of all options; choose a course of action, (f) evaluate the selected course of action, and (g) implement the course of action (Forester-Miller & Davis, 1996).

C. B. Stone (2005) has taken the ACA model and applied it to the school setting. She named the nine-step model the STEPS Model for School Settings. The steps are:

1. Define the problem emotionally and intellectually;
2. Apply the ACA and ASCA ethical codes and the law;
3. Consider the students' chronological and developmental levels;
4. Consider the setting, parental rights, and minors' rights;
5. Apply the moral principles;
6. Determine your potential courses of action and the consequences;
7. Evaluate the selected action;
8. Consult; and
9. Implement the course of action. (pp. 17–19)

As Stone and others caution, counselors using either of these models or any other ethical decision-making model will not necessarily come to the same conclusion. There is seldom one correct way of handling any given situation, and each counselor brings different background, values, and belief systems to each dilemma. However, if one reflects on the moral principles and continues to practice with these in mind, it is likely that the dilemma can be resolved in the client's best interests.

Remley and Herlihy (2001) suggested four self-tests to consider once a decision has been made. First, in thinking about justice, would you treat others this same way if they were in a similar situation? Second, would you suggest to other counselors this same course of action? Third, would you be willing to have others know how you acted? And last, do you have any lingering feelings of doubt or uncertainty about what you did? If you cannot answer in the affirmative to the first three tests and in the negative to the fourth test, then perhaps the decision was not ethically sound. It is always appropriate and ethically sound to consult with a colleague when working through a dilemma to ensure that all aspects of the issue have been examined and that all possible problems have been discussed. Remley and Huey (2002) developed an Ethics Quiz for School Counselors that is one tool professional school counselors can use to test their knowledge of ethical codes and to reflect on their professional conduct.

SOURCES OF INFORMATION AND GUIDANCE

While the ethical standards provide an important foundation for guiding counselor behavior, there are a number of other sources of information with which counselors must become familiar if they are to maintain the highest standards of ethical and legal behavior. Each of these other sources is described below.

The Court System

Counselors are affected by three main types of laws: statutory law, which is created by legislatures; constitutional law, which results from court decisions concerning constitutional issues; and common law, which results from other court decisions. There are 51 U.S. court systems—the court systems for the 50 states and the federal system. Both state and federal courts can enact decisions affecting counselors, and both are usually composed of tiers. The structure of state courts varies but generally consists of trial courts that include courts of special jurisdiction, such as juvenile court or small-claims court, and courts of appeal. All states have a court that is the final authority to which cases may be appealed. The name of this court varies across states. In Maryland and New York, it is the court of appeals; in West Virginia, it is called the supreme court of appeals; in other states, it is called superior court. One must be careful in reading state court decisions to note which court rendered the decision as the names are not consistent across states. Cases from the highest court in each state may be appealed directly to the U.S. Supreme Court. Decisions from state courts are binding only on persons living within that state but may serve as precedent for a similar case in another state.

The federal court system is also a three-tiered system. The approximately 100 U.S. district courts form the basis of the federal system. These courts hear cases that involve federal law, disputes between citizens that involve over $75,000, and cases where the United States is a party (Fischer, Schimmel, & Kelly, 1999). There are 13 courts of appeals. Decisions from the circuit courts of appeals are binding only on those states within the court's jurisdiction (see Table 4.1). However, decisions from one court may influence the decision rendered by another court when the same issue arises. Cases from the circuit courts of appeals may be appealed to the U.S. Supreme Court, the highest court in the country.

Statutory Law

Statutory law is the body of mandates created through legislation passed by the U.S. Congress and state legislatures. Much of the structure of education and health and many of the policies that govern their implementation are found within these mandates. The federal government has authority to pass legislation related only to those powers specified in the Constitution, but a number of laws have been enacted that affect counselors who work both in schools and in other settings. The majority of legislation influencing schools and counselors is passed by state legislatures and concerns two types of legislation: creating state legislation to implement federal legislation, and enacting new, state-specific legislation. State laws may be more restrictive than federal legislation but may never be less restrictive.

State and Local Agencies

Most state departments of education have the ability to enact regulations that are binding on the school districts within the state. The state's board of education passes regulations that encompass areas not addressed through other state legislation or add detail to state legislation and may include implementation plans and more specific definitions. State agencies, including education, also develop policies, which are often detailed explanations of how to implement a specific law. Last, state agencies may also issue guidelines, which are actually suggestions about how to address a specific issue. Unlike regulations and policies, guidelines are not mandates and do not have to be followed. However, because they do represent the agency's current thinking regarding a particular issue, local policies generally do not deviate too far from them.

Although it is not a regulation, the state attorney general may issue an opinion or advice of counsel. This guidance is frequently in response to a new court case or law or on request of a state agency. The advice or opinion is the attorney general's legal interpretation of what that law or case means for the agency or agencies impacted and usually suggests what it needs to do to comply. The advice or ruling is often incorporated into policy or guidelines by the agency.

Local school systems and agencies may also develop their own policies, procedures, and guidelines. School systems, in particular, often take state regulations and policies and rewrite them to reflect their specific local situation; these are often then adopted by the local board of education. Local mental health departments or agencies may also further define state policies and procedures to reflect their jurisdiction-specific needs. Finally, individual schools or centers may have additional policies or guidelines in place for certain issues that further direct the manner in which a professional school counselor must act.

TABLE 4.1
Minors' Right to Consent to Health Care and to Make Other Important Decisions

State	Contraceptive Services	Prenatal Care	STD/HIV Services	Treatment for Alcohol and/or Drug Abuse	Outpatient Mental Health Services	Abortion Services	Drop out of School[1]
Alabama	NL	MC	MC[2,3,4]	MC	MC	PC	MD[6]
Alaska	MC	MC	MC	NL	NL	NL[8]	MD[6]
Arizona	MC	NL	MC	MC[2]	NL	NL[8]	MD[6]
Arkansas	MC	MC[10,11]	MC[4,11]	NL	NL	PN[13]	NA[14]
California	MC	MC[10]	MC[2,16,17]	MC[2,4]	MC[2,4]	NL[8]	NA[14]
Colorado	MC[7,18]	NL	MC[16]	MC	MC[4,19]	NL[8]	MD[6]
Connecticut	NL	NL	MC[16]	MC	MC	MC	PC
Delaware	MC[2,4]	MC[2,4,10,11]	MC[2,4,11,16]	MC[2]	NL	PN[20,21]	MD[6]
Dist. Columbia	MC	MC	MC	MC	MC	MC	NA[14]
Florida	MC[7,18]	MC[11]	MC[3]	MC	MC[23]	NL[8]	PC
Georgia	MC	MC[10]	MC[3,4,11]	MC[4]	NL	PN	MD[6]
Hawaii	MC[4,24,25]	MC[4,10,24,25]	MC[4,24,25]	MC[4]	NL	NL	MD[26]
Idaho	MC	NL	MC[3,24]	MC	NL	PN[13,29]	MD[6]
Ilinois	MC[7,18]	MC[11,18]	MC[2,3,4]	MC[2,4]	MC[2,4]	NL[8]	MD[30]
Indiana	NL	NL	MC	MC	NL	PC	PC
Iowa	NL	NL	MC[16,31]	MC	NL	PN[21]	MD[32]
Kansas	NL[12]	MC[11,33]	MC[4]	MC	NL	PN	MD[32]
Kentucky	MC[4]	MC[4,10]	MC[3,4]	MC[4]	MC[4,6]	PC	PN[6]
Louisiana	NL	NL	MC[4]	MC[4]	NL	PC	MD[34]
Maine	MC[7,18]	NL	MC[4]	MC[4]	NL	MC	MD[34]
Maryland	MC[4]	MC[4]	MC[4]	MC[4]	MC[4,6]	PN[21]	MD[6]
Massachusetts	NL[36]	MC[10]	MC	MC[2,37]	MC[6]	PC	MD[26]
Michigan	NL	MC[4]	MC[4,16]	MC[4]	MC[24]	PC	MD
Minnesota	MC[4]	MC[4]	MC[4]	MC[4]	NL	PN[13]	PC
Mississippi	MC[7,18]	MC[11]	MC[3]	MC[4,19]	NL	PC[13]	MD[34]
Missouri	NL	MC[4,10,11]	MC[4,11]	MC[4,11]	NL	PC	PN[26]
Montana	MC[4]	MC[4,11]	MC[4,11,16]	MC[4,11]	MC[6]	NL[8]	MD[39]
Nebraska	NL	NL	MC	MC	NL	PN	MD[26]
Nevada	NL	NL	MC[3]	MC	NL	NL[8]	MD[40]
New Hampshire	NL	NL	MC[24]	MC[2]	NL	NL	PC
New Jersey	NL	MC[4,11]	MC[4,11]	MC[4]	NL	NL[8]	MD[6]
New Mexico	MC	NL[42]	MC[16,17]	NL	MC	NL[8]	PC
New York	NL[36]	MC	MC[16]	MC[4]	MC[4]	NL	MD[6]
North Carolina	MC	MC[10]	MC[3]	MC	MC	PC[21]	MD[6]
North Dakota	NL	NL	MC[24,44]	MC[24]	NL	PC[13]	MD[6,26]

(*Continued*)

TABLE 4.1   Continued

State	Contraceptive Services	Prenatal Care	STD/HIV Services	Treatment for Alcohol and/or Drug Abuse	Outpatient Mental Health Services	Abortion Services	Drop out of School[1]
Ohio	NL	NL	MC[16,17]	MC	MC[24]	PN[21,29]	NA[14]
Oklahoma	MC[4,45]	MC[4,10]	MC[3,4]	MC[4]	NL	NL	PC
Oregon	MC[4]	NL	MC[3,11]	MC[4,24]	MC[4,24]	NL	MD[46]
Pennsylvania	NL	MC	MC[3]	MC[4]	NL	PC	MD[34]
Rhode Island	NL	NL	MC[16]	MC	NL	PC	MD[6]
South Carolina	MC[47]	NL[47]	MC[47]	NL[47]	NL[47]	PC[21,48]	MD[49]
South Dakota	NL	NL	MC	MC	NL	PN	MD[6]
Tennessee	MC	MC	MC[3]	MC[4]	MC[6]	PC	MD[34]
Texas	NL[50]	MC[4,10,11]	MC[3,4,11]	MC[4]	MC	PN	NA[14]
Utah	NL[50]	MC	MC	NL	NL	PN[52]	NA[14]
Vermont	NL	NL	MC[2,3]	MC[2]	NL	NL	MD[53]
Virginia	MC	MC	MC[3]	MC	MC	PN[21]	NA[14]
Washington	NL[54]	NL[54]	MC[3,11,24]	MC[23]	MC[23]	NL	MD[6]
West Virginia	NL	NL	MC	MC	NL	PN[21]	MD[30]
Wisconsin	NL	NL	MC	MC[2]	NL	PC[21]	NA[14]
Wyoming	MC	NL	MC[3]	NL	NL	PC	MD[55]
Total MC/MD	26	28	51	45	21	3	34
Total PC/PN	0	0	0	0	0	31	9
Total NL/NA	25	23	0	6	30	17	8

Notes. MC = Minor explicitly authorized to consent; PC = Parental consent explicitly required; MD = Minor allowed to decide; PN = Parental notice explicitly required; NL = No law or policy found; NA = Not applicable.

In all but four states, the age of majority is 18. In Al and NE, it is 19, and in PA and MS, it is 21; however, in MS 18 is the age of consent for health care.

[1]All states require minors to attend school until a certain age, beyond which the young person or, in a few states, the parents may decide whether the minor will stay in school.

[2]Minor must be at least 12.

[3]State officially classifies HIV/AIDS as an STD or infectious disease, for which minors may consent to testing and treatment.

[4]Doctor may notify parents.

[5]Minor must be a high school graduate, married, pregnant or a parent, or, in AL, at least 14.

[6]Minor must be at least 16.

[7]Minor may consent if a parent; also if married in DE, KY, ME, MD, MN, MS, MO, and NV; also if married or pregnant in CO, FL, IL, MA, MT, NJ, NY, and OK.

[8]Law has been blocked by court action.

[9]Law does not distinguish between minor and adult parents.

[10]Excludes abortion.

[11]Includes surgery.

[12]Any minor who is mature enough to understand the nature and consequences of the proposed medical or surgical treatment may consent.

[13]Involvement of both parents is required.

[14]Minor may not drop out.

[15]Minor parent must have a court-appointed guardian.

[16]Law explicitly authorizes minor to consent to HIV testing and/or treatment.

[17]Law does not apply to HIV treatment.

[18]Minor may consent if has a child or doctor believes minor would suffer "probable" health hazard if services not provided; in IL, also if minor is referred by doctor, clergyman, or Planned Parenthood clinic; in CO and MS, also if minor is referred by a doctor, clergyman, family planning clinic, school of higher education, or state agency.

[19]Minor must be at least 15.

[20]Applies to minors younger than age 16.

[21]Includes an alternative to parental involvement or judicial bypass. In MD, the law provides for a physician bypass but does not have a judicial bypass.

[22]A minor who is pregnant or, in DE, FL, GA, IN, MD, and OK, has a child may marry without parental consent; in FL, KY, and OK, the marriage must be authorized by a court; in IN and MD, a minor must be at least 15.

[23]Minor must be at least 13.

[24]Minor must be at least 14.

[25]Excludes surgery.

[26]Minor may drop out if employed and in MA, MO, and NE is 14, in HI is 15, in MA also if has completed the 6th grade; in NE also if has completed the 8th grade. Otherwise, a minor may drop out at 16 in these states.

[27]Minors need judicial authorization.

[28]The state's medical consent statutes allow "any person of ordinary intelligence and awareness" to consent to hospital, medical, surgical, or dental care. Although a later section authorizes parents to consent for a minor child, the attorney general's office "frequently" interprets the law as authorizing minors to consent. (R. Hardin, deputy attorney general, personal communication to P. Donovan, AGI, Oct. 22, 1990, reconfirmed to E. Nash, AGI, by R. Hardin, July 19, 2000.)

[29]A revised law that requires parental consent is currently not in effect; meanwhile, the parental notification requirements remain in effect.

[30]Minor may drop out of school before reaching age 16 if employed.

[31]Parent must be notified if HIV test is positive.

[32]A court may allow a minor to drop out.

[33]Minor may consent if parent is not "available" or in the case of general medical care "not immediately available."

[34]Minor must be at least 17.

[35]Court may waive parental consent if the minor is "sufficiently mature and well informed" or the adoption is in the child's best interest.

[36]The state funds a statewide program that gives minors access to confidential contraceptive care.

[37]Minor may consent if found drug-dependent by two doctors; bars consent to methadone maintenance therapy.

[38]Parents must be notified if either party is younger than age 21; however, female minors at least 15 and male minors at least 17 may marry without parental consent.

[39]Minor must be at least 16 or have completed 8th grade, whichever occurs later.

[40]After eighth grade, court determines whether the minor or the parents can make the decision.

[41]Court may require the consent of a minor parent's parent.

[42]Minor may consent to pregnancy testing and diagnosis.

[43]Law allows minors to consent when parent or guardian is not "immediately available."

[44]Parent must be shown the informed consent form for an HIV test before the minor signs it.

[45]Minor may consent if she has ever been pregnant.

[46]Minor must prove to the school board that the minor has acquired "equivalent knowledge" of the high school courses, or consent may be granted by the state school board for minors 16 and 17 who are employed.

[47]Any minor 16 and older may consent to any health service other than operations. Health services may be rendered to minors of any age without parental consent when the provider believes the services are necessary.

[48]Applies to minors younger than age 17.

[49]Minor who has completed 8th grade may seek court authorization to drop out to work.

[50]State funds may not be used to provide minors with confidential contraceptive services.

[51]Minors 14–18 may petition court for permission to marry.

[52]Law does not include a judicial bypass.

[53]Minor must be at least 16, have completed 10th grade, or be excused by the superintendent.

[54]Providers rely on *State v. Koome*, which held that minors have the same constitutional rights as adults, to provide confidential contraceptive services and prenatal care to minors.

[55]Minor must be at least 16 and have completed 10th greade.

Reproduced with the permission of the Guttmacher Report on Policy from: Boonstra, H., and Nash, E. Minors and the right to consent to health care. *The Guttmacher Report on Public Policy,* 2000, 3(4): 4–8. Table 1.

MAKING DECISIONS

Failure to understand the law, and by extension policies, procedures, and guidelines, is not an acceptable legal defense. It is incumbent on the professional school counselor to become familiar with all the various sources of information and guidance that are available to perform one's responsibilities in an ethical and legal manner. Fortunately, there are many ways of maintaining current information.

In most work settings, with the exception perhaps of private practice, counselors have a supervisor or other person in authority who can help them become familiar with the regulations, policies, and guidelines relevant to that setting. Most schools and many community agencies have administrative manuals that incorporate all these sources of information into continually updated binders. The ACA newsletter highlights issues and hot topics in counseling, as do other professional journals and newsletters. There are also a number of commercially available newsletters that cover recent court rulings and their impact in different work settings. The Internet has become an invaluable tool for current information and resources. Guillot-Miller and Partin (2003) identified over 40 sites that include information relevant to ethical and legal practices for counselors. The professional associations for counselors and other mental health professionals, institutions of higher education, state and federal government agencies, government-funded organizations, and professional and legal publishers all continuously update their Web sites and are good sources of current information.

There may be times when mandates appear to be in conflict with each other. In such cases, common sense should prevail. There may be a therapeutically logical reason to follow one particular mandate rather than another one. The counselors should follow the logical course of action and document what they did and why. For example, if a counselor is working with a suicidal student but believes that telling the parents will result in an abusive situation, the counselor should handle the situation as an abuse case and tell child protective services about the suicidal behavior. Additionally, if a

particular policy, guideline, or regulation is not in the best interest of the students in the counselor's work setting, as per the ethical standards, the counselor should work to change the mandate.

Two other issues are sometimes confusing for counselors. The first concerns the different ways in which counselors in different settings operate. Some mandates cover all counselors, particularly mandates that are the result of federal or state legislation or court cases. For example, child abuse and neglect laws apply to all counselors regardless of the setting in which they work. But the implementation of some mandates, particularly as they become policy and guidelines, may look very different in different settings. Schools have perhaps the greatest number of mandates under which staff must operate, yet professional school counselors seldom need permission to see students (Remley & Herlihy, 2001), particularly if there is an approved comprehensive developmental program. A mental health counselor, employed by an outside center or agency but working either in a school or in a school-based health center, needs signed, informed consent to see those same students. In some cases, local school systems have mandated an opt-in program, which is a program that requires signed, informed consent for students to participate in different aspects of the comprehensive guidance program. In such cases, professional school counselors working in nearby systems or even schools may operate very differently.

The second issue concerns counselors who hold multiple credentials. A counselor may work as a professional school counselor but hold state certification or licensure and work as a mental health counselor outside of school. The counselor may need permission to do something as a professional school counselor but not need permission as a mental health counselor or vice versa. Under which set of mandates should the counselor operate?

The answer to both of these questions is the same: Employees must follow the mandates that apply to their work setting. Counselors are required to operate under the mandates of the system that employs them or, in the case of volunteers, the mandates of the entity under whose auspices they are working. If a counselor is employed by a school system as a counselor, then he or she must follow the mandates of the local school system. Teachers who have degrees in counseling or another related mental health degree but who continue to be employed as teachers do not have the same protections as counselors because they are not employed in a mental health capacity. They need to check their system's policies carefully to see if they are covered by any protections such as confidentiality.

ADDITIONAL LEGAL CONSIDERATIONS

In developing an ethical stance, professional school counselors must take all of the aforementioned sources of information into account. However, there are several other influences that must be considered (Herlihy & Corey, 1996; Hopkins & Anderson, 1990; Stone, 2005). Each counselor brings to every counseling relationship the sum of experiences, education, and training. Each also brings to the setting that which makes one unique; that is, values, morals, and spiritual influences. Who a counselor is strongly influences the stance taken on issues. Professional school counselors must continually be aware of how their own beliefs and values impact the way they think about issues, the students and their needs, and the options that they perceive to be available. Counselors must also continually examine their behavior in light of cultural bias and multicultural understanding. When deciding on a course of action for a client, counselors always try to do what is in the best interests of the client.

Professional Competence

In addition to being knowledgeable about mandates, as was previously discussed, there are a number of further steps counselors should take to ensure ethical and legal behavior. Several of these are mentioned in the ethical standards, but it is important to reemphasize them. As reported in Hopkins and Anderson (1990) and Cottone and Tarvydas (2003), counselors should:

- Maintain professional growth through continuing education. While counselors must attend continuing education opportunities to renew national credentials, state credentials, or both, it is important to stay current with theories, trends, and information about clients and different populations.
- Maintain accurate knowledge and expertise in areas of responsibility. Information changes so quickly that counselors must ensure they are providing quality and effective services to their clients. One way of achieving this goal is through professional development, but counselors may also gain information through reading, consultation with colleagues, supervision, and other means.
- Accurately represent credentials. As stated in the ethical standards, counselors should claim only those credentials they have earned and only the highest degree in counseling or a closely related mental health field. Counselors who hold doctorates in non-mental health fields should not use the title "doctor" in their work as a counselor. This is a particular problem in school settings where counselors earn doctorates in administration and supervision, or related fields, but continue to work as counselors and use the title "doctor" in their job. Furthermore, counselors should not imply in any way that their credentials allow them to work in areas where they are not trained.
- Provide only those services for which qualified and trained. The easiest way for counselors to get into trouble professionally is to provide services for which they are not qualified, either by training or education. This is particularly true when using counseling techniques. Counselors should have training in using a particular technique before using it. Reading about a technique is not equivalent to implementing it under supervision. Professional school counselors should also not try to work with students whose problems go beyond their expertise. If professional school counselors are put in a situation where there are no other counselors to whom to refer the student, the counselor should consult with colleagues and ask for supervision to ensure the effectiveness of the counseling.

"Can I Be Sued?" and "What Is Malpractice?"

The answer to "Can I be sued?" is, of course, yes. Anyone can be sued for almost anything, particularly in our litigious society. But the more important question is, "Will I be found guilty?" The answer to this question is much more complex.

If professional school counselors fail to exercise "due care" in fulfilling their professional responsibilities, they can be found guilty of civil liablility; that is, the counselor committed a wrong against an individual. Negligence may be found if the wrong committed results in an injury or damages; in other words, if the duty owed to the client was breached in some way. In counseling, it is more common for counselors to be sued for malpractice. Malpractice is the area of tort law that concerns professional conduct. "Malpractice is professional misconduct or any unreasonable lack of skill in the performance of professional duties" (Lovett, as cited in Hopkins & Anderson, 1990, p. 48). Generally, for a counselor to be held liable in tort for malpractice, four conditions have to be met (C. B. Stone, 2005): A duty was owed to the plaintiff (client) by the defendant (counselor); the counselor breached the duty; there is a causal link between the breach and the client's injury; and the client suffered some damage or injury.

An example of negligence would be a counselor who failed to report an abuse case. The counselor had a duty to the client and failed to fulfill that duty. With malpractice, the client suffered due to lack of skill or appropriate behavior on the part of the counselor. An example of malpractice would be if a counselor treated a client with an eating disorder through hypnosis when the counselor was not trained to use the technique of hypnosis. The situation may be further complicated should this technique not be recognized as particularly effective for treating eating disorders.

The standard of practice will be used in any liability proceeding to determine if the counselor's performance was within accepted practice. The standard of practice question is, "In the performance of professional services, did the counselor provide the level of care and treatment that is consistent with the degree of learning, skill and ethics ordinarily possessed and expected by reputable counselors practicing under similar circumstances?" (ACA, 1997, p. 9).

The standard of practice will be established through the testimony of peers. These peers, who are called expert witnesses, are considered to be experts in the field under question. For professional school counselors, the expert witnesses will be other school counselors (C. B. Stone, 2005). The standard is an ever-evolving level of expectation and is influenced by two major factors: education and experience. The standard is not an absolute one, but a variable one. It will be much higher for a counselor who has practiced for a number of years and pursued advanced graduate training or professional development than it will be for a counselor in the first year of practice immediately following graduate school. The more training and experience a counselor possesses, the higher the standard to which the counselor will be held accountable. The assumption is that a counselor should know more each year he or she practices through experience and training and should therefore be held to a higher standard with each additional year. Using this standard of practice, a counselor will usually be found guilty of malpractice if one or more of the following situations occurs (Hopkins & Anderson, 1990):

- The practice was not within the realm of acceptable professional practice.
- The counselor was not trained in the technique used.
- The counselor failed to follow a procedure that would have been more helpful.
- The counselor failed to warn and/or protect others from a violent client.
- The counselor failed to obtain informed consent.
- The counselor failed to explain the possible consequences of treatment.

Several professional publications have reported that sexual misconduct is the primary reason that liability actions are initiated against counselors. School staff, counselors, and other mental health professionals have been accused of committing sexual abuse or misconduct. It may be that other problems, such as failure to use a more appropriate technique, are actually more common but that most clients lack the ability to recognize therapeutic problems and may just have a general sense that "it isn't working or helping" and choose to terminate.

While the number of professional school counselors who are sued is increasing, the number still remains very small. Parents are more likely to request their child not be included in certain guidance program activities or to complain to the principal or central administration about a program or behavior. In rare cases, parents may sue. The majority of cases against school counselors have been rejected by the courts (Fischer & Sorensen, 1997). In school settings, violating or failing to follow school system mandates will get a professional school counselor in trouble faster than almost any other behavior. Depending on the counselor's action, the system may choose to reprimand the professional school counselor. In extreme cases, the counselor's employment may be terminated. Professional school counselors must also be knowledgeable about their communities. They may have a legal right to implement certain programs or conduct certain activities, but if the community is not supportive of those activities, they are going to face opposition.

When a professional school counselor is faced with any legal action, the first thing the counselor should do is call a lawyer and then let the counselor supervisor, if there is one, know. Most agencies, clinics, practices, and schools are accustomed to dealing with such legal issues and may even have a procedure for what to do. Professional school counselors should never attempt to reason with the student or contact the student's lawyer without advice of counsel. It is important to not provide any information to, or discuss the case with, anyone except the counselor's lawyer or the person designated to help the counselor. Just as professional school counselors advise clients to get professional mental health help when they have personal problems, counselors must get legal help when they have legal problems.

Subpoenas

Many counselors will receive a subpoena at some point in their professional career. Probably the most common reason counselors, and particularly professional school counselors, receive subpoenas is in cases involving custody disputes, child abuse or neglect allegations, and special education disputes. In most cases, the client an attorney is representing believes that counselors may have some information that will be helpful to the case. Professional school counselors need to pay attention to subpoenas because they are legal documents. At the same time, consider whether the information being requested is confidential, because professional school counselors may be limited in what they can share. Under no circumstances should the counselor automatically comply with the subpoena without discussing it first with the client, the client's attorney, or both, or employing the agency's or school system's attorney. According to the ACA (1997), counselors should take the following steps when receiving a subpoena:

1. Contact the client or the client's attorney and ask for guidance. If you work for a school system, contact the school system's attorney to seek guidance.
2. If the above-mentioned parties advise you to comply with the subpoena, discuss the implications of releasing the requested information.
3. Obtain a signed informed-consent form to release the records. That form should specify all conditions of release: what, to whom, and so forth.
4. If the decision is made to not release the records, the attorney should file a motion to quash (or, in some areas, ask for a protective order). This will allow the counselor to not comply with the subpoena.
5. Maintain a record of everything the counselor and attorneys did; keep notes regarding all conversations and copies of any documents pertaining to the subpoena.

An attorney who wants information may ask a judge to issue a court order. A court order permits the release of confidential information but does not mandate its release. If both a subpoena and a court order are received, the counselor must release the information with or without the client's consent. Failure to do so may result in the counselor's being held in contempt of court.

The important things to remember about subpoenas are do not panic and do consult an attorney. Subpoenas are legal documents, but the counselor has enough time to consider the implications to the client of releasing the information and to seek legal advice.

CONFIDENTIALITY

For clients to feel free to share sometimes sensitive and personal information during a counseling session, they must feel that they can trust the counselor not to share what is disclosed during sessions with anyone else without their permission. This sense of trust and privacy, called confidentiality, is essential for counseling to be successful. Confidentiality is the cornerstone of counseling and is what separates the counseling relationship from other relationships where information is shared. Confidentiality belongs to the client, not to the counselor. The client always has the right to waive confidentiality or to allow information to be shared with a third party.

Counseling minors presents particular challenges to the issue of confidentiality. Every state sets the age of majority; for most states, it is 18 years of age. Most students are minors under the age of 18 who are therefore not legally able to make their own decisions. Thus, students have an ethical right to confidentiality, but the legal rights belong to their parents or guardian (Remley & Herlihy, 2001). Approximately twenty states protect professional school counselor–client confidentiality through statutes (Cottone & Tarvydas, 2003), but many include significant restrictions.

Professional school counselors often ask what to do if parents want to know what is discussed during counseling sessions with their children. Legally, parents, and only parents, have the right to know what is being discussed.

However, the child might not want the information shared with the parent. Section B.5.b, Responsibility to Parents and Legal Guardians, of the ACA *Code of Ethics* states that:

Counselors inform parents and legal guardians about the role of counselors and the confidential nature of the counseling relationship. Counselors are sensitive to the cultural diversity of families and respect the inherent rights and responsibilities of parents/gaurdians over the welfare of the children/charges according to law. Counselors work to establish, as appropriate, collaborative relationships with parents/guardians to best serve clients. (ACA, 2005a, p. 8)

This statement leaves counselors with a dilemma. To resolve this dilemma, Remley and Herlihy (2001) suggested that the counselor first discuss the issue with the child to determine if the client is willing to disclose the information to the parent. If the child will not disclose, then try to help the parent understand that the best interests of the child are not served by disclosure. If this does not work, then schedule a joint meeting with the parent and child to discuss the issue. If the parent still is not satisfied, then the counselor may have to disclose the information without the child's consent. Some counselors would suggest that this type of situation may be reflective of some deeper family issue. While the parent or guardian has a legal right to the information, there may be an underlying "family secret" that the parent does not want known and the counselor should be sensitive to any difficulties the child may be demonstrating. Or, this situation may be the result of cultural differences and the counselor needs to be more sensitive to the family's traditions and beliefs.

Many counselors suggest that at the beginning of the first session of each new counseling relationship, the professional school counselor should discuss confidentiality with the student, explain what it means, and point out the limits of confidentiality. Some counselors choose to hang a sign on the wall of their office that outlines this information as a reinforcement to what is discussed in the first session. While this issue appears to be simple on the surface, in reality it is a very complex issue that has generated a significant amount of research and professional discourse. As the use of technology increases in counseling settings, the discussions will continue and expand. There are significant challenges to keeping electronic information confidential.

Limits to Confidentiality

According to section B.1.a of the ACA *Code of Ethics* (2005a, p. 2), "Counselors respect client rights to privacy. . . . " Section B.1.c states, "Counselors do not share confidential information without client consent or without sound legal or ethical justification." Section B.1.d states, "At initiation and throughout the counseling process, counselors inform clients of the limitations of confidentiality and seek to identify foreseeable situations in which confidentiality must be breached." However, there are several instances in which counselors must break confidentiality. These are delineated within Section B.2.a. The most important of these is the "duty to warn." When a counselor becomes aware that a client is in danger of being harmed, such as in instances of abuse, or when the client is likely to harm someone else, the counselor may break confidentiality and tell an appropriate person.

The basis for the duty-to-warn standard began with the 1974 Tarasoff case in California. In this case, the client, a graduate student, told his psychologist about his intent to kill a girl (named Tarasoff) who had rejected his advances. The psychologist told the campus police and his supervisor but did not warn the intended victim or her family. The majority of the California Supreme Court ruled that the psychologist had a duty to warn a known, intended victim. This case established the legal duty to warn and protect an identifiable victim from a client's potential or intended violence and has formed the basis of many other court decisions across the country. In the ensuing 25 years, some cases have extended the duty-to-warn standard to include types of harm other than violence and foreseeable victims in addition to identifiable victims. The ACA's *Code of Ethics*, Section B.2.a, now reads, "The general requirement that counselors keep information confidential does not apply when disclosure is required to protect clients or identified others from serious and foreseeable harm. . . ." (p. 2)

Several other situations constrain the limits of confidentiality, as delineated in the ACA *Code of Ethics* (2005a):

- *Subordinates.* Confidentiality is not absolute when subordinates, including employees, supervisees, students, clerical assistants, and volunteers, handle records or confidential information. Every effort should be made to limit access to this information, and the assistants should be reminded of the confidential nature of the information they are handling.
- *Treatment teams.* The client should be informed of the treatment team and the information being shared.
- *Consultation.* The professional school counselor always has the right to consult with a colleague or supervisor on any case. In such instances, the counselor should provide enough information to obtain the needed assistance but should limit any information that might identify the client.
- *Group and families.* In group or family counseling settings, confidentiality is not guaranteed. The counselor may state that what goes on in the sessions is confidential, and the members may agree. However, because there is more than one client in the group, it is impossible to guarantee confidentiality.
- *Third-party payers.* Information will sometimes have to be sent to a mental health provider, insurance company, or other agency that has some legitimate need for the information. The counselor will disclose this information only with the client's permission.
- *Minors.* There are special considerations regarding confidentiality and minors that will be discussed in detail in the next section.
- *Contagious, life-threatening diseases.* Unlike the duty-to-warn standard, the ACA ethical standards state that the counselor is justified in disclosing information about a client to an identifiable third party if that party's relationship with the client is such that there is a

possibility of contracting the disease and the client does not plan on telling the third party. It should be noted that the word used is *justified*, not *should* or *must*. This wording leaves it up to the counselor to decide if the third party is at risk and must be warned.

- *Court-ordered disclosure.* Subpoenas were previously discussed. Even if ordered to reveal confidential information by a judge, counselors should limit what they reveal to only what is absolutely necessary.

In summary, confidentiality is a very complex issue but essential to the effectiveness of counseling. Clients have an ethical right to confidentiality, and counselors make every effort to ensure this right. However, there are specific cases where it is not only permissible but also essential to break confidentiality to protect the client, or others from the client.

Confidentiality and Privileged Communication

The term *confidentiality* is used in discussions about counseling, while the term *privileged communication* is the legal term to describe the privacy of the counselor–client communication. Privileged communication exists by statute and applies only to testifying in a court of law. The privilege belongs to the client, who always has the right to waive the privilege and allow the counselor to testify. Clients have an ethical right to confidentiality, and the ethical standards for the mental health professions detail the boundaries of confidentiality. Privileged communication is more limited; federal, state, and local mandates determine its parameters. Whether a client–counselor relationship is covered by privileged communication varies widely across jurisdictions. Even within a jurisdiction, a counselor in private practice may be covered by privileged communication, but the school counselors who work in that same jurisdiction may not be. It is essential that counselors become familiar with their local mandates and policies to determine the extent to which privileged communication applies to their situation.

MINOR CONSENT LAWS

All states have a minor consent law that allows certain minors to seek treatment for certain conditions, usually involving substance abuse, mental health, and some reproductive health areas. These laws are based on the federal regulation 42 USC §§290dd-3; 42 C. F. R. Part 2, which references the confidentiality of patient records for drug and alcohol abuse assessment, referral, diagnosis, and treatment. The law further prohibits the release of these records to anyone without the client's informed consent and includes clients under the age of 18 even if they are in school and living with parents or guardians.

Over the past 10 years, there has been a movement to increase the number of student assistance teams and student assistance programs (SAPs) in schools. These teams usually consist of an administrator, one or more student services professionals (e.g., professional school counselor, school social worker, pupil personnel worker, school psychologist, or school nurse), and teachers, and may include a substance abuse assessor from a local agency or similar professional. School staff refer students who are suspected of having a substance abuse problem to this team. The team is trained to deal with substance abuse issues and, if they believe the student has a substance abuse problem, have the student assessed and referred for appropriate assistance.

The controversy surrounding this program concerns the role of the parents or guardians in this process. Under the federal law, the student may go from referral through completion of treatment without the parents' or guardians' knowledge. Substance abuse professionals are divided regarding whether it is possible to successfully treat abusers without the family's involvement. Other professionals have concerns about the ability of young adolescents to seek treatment without any family knowledge or involvement.

As this federal law has been incorporated into state statute, states have taken different approaches to deciding to whom this law applies and for what. In general, the patient must be old enough to understand the problem, the treatment options available, and the possible consequences of each. Some states may have no age limits and maintain that a minor has the same capacity as an adult to consent to certain services. On the other hand, some states have decided on a specific age at which the minor may consent to mental health treatment, reproductive or substance abuse services, and treatment for sexually transmitted diseases (STDs) and AIDS/HIV. According to the Guttmacher Institute's *State Policies in Brief* reports (2000, 2005a, 2005b), 21 states and the District of Columbia allow all minors to consent to all contraceptive services, 25 states allow minors to consent to contraceptive services in one or more circumstances, and 5 states have no law for contraceptive services. Twenty-seven states allow minors to consent to prenatal treatment when pregnant, whereas 23 have no law. All 50 states allow minors to consent to treatment for STDs and HIV/AIDS; 44 states allow treatment for alcohol abuse, drug abuse, or both; 20 states allow outpatient mental health services, and 29 do not; 22 allow general medical care, and 29 do not; and 3 states allow abortion services, 30 require parental consent or notification, and 18 have no law. Where the numbers add up to 51, the law has provisions in that category that restrict some services but allow other services (see Table 4.1).

There is tremendous variation across the 50 states in what is permissible under the law. There is also some question as to the applicability of this law to school settings. The laws clearly cover medical personnel and certain conditions. A school nurse is covered, but a professional school counselor or school psychologist may not be covered. It is critical that counselors and other student services personnel become familiar with the minor consent law in the state in which they work to ensure compliance. Staff must also investigate local policies. A state law may allow a professional school counselor to address reproductive issues and substance abuse without parental consent or notification, but a local policy may prohibit such counseling. The laws cover minors seeking advice and/or treatment. If a minor

is not seeking help, then the law may not apply and the counselor would follow other policies or procedures in dealing with these issues.

The legal issues aside, this is the law that raises a tremendous number of ethical issues for counselors. There are a number of professionals who have difficulty with the ability of young adolescents, in particular, to access these services without the family's involvement. Should a counselor help a 13-year-old substance abuser seek treatment without the family's knowledge? How successful will the adolescent's recovery be? What about a 15-year-old who is abusing drugs and engaging in risky sexual behaviors? What is the counselor's ethical responsibility? The problem this law presents for many counselors is that it allows them to assist adolescent clients legally but may conflict with their personal beliefs. Some professionals believe that behaviors such as these can cause harm to oneself and therefore they have a duty to warn, which supersedes all other responsibilities. Other counselors work with the adolescent to help the adolescent involve the family, whereas others believe that telling the family will work against the adolescent's obtaining help.

Another issue is that many parents do not understand that their children can seek treatment in these areas without parental consent. Parents will be understandably angry and distrustful when they discover their child has an STD or is a substance abuser and the counselor knew and did not tell them about it. Counselors need to be prepared to deal with the aftermath of such discoveries. They need to think through their positions on these issues very carefully and be honest with clients about their beliefs. Counselors should not wait until they are faced with a situation to figure out where they stand on an issue.

RECORDS AND PERSONAL NOTES
Educational Records

Educational records are all the records of a student's achievement, attendance, behavior, testing and assessment, school activities, and other such information that the school collects and maintains. Schools frequently divide student records into cumulative records, health records, special education records, and confidential records, including psychological evaluations. In reality, this is done for the convenience of the school; all these records are considered to be part of the educational record. The only exceptions are personal notes, reports to Child Protective Services for abuse or neglect, and, in some states, reports from law enforcement agencies regarding students' arrests for reportable offenses.

The inspection, dissemination, and access to student educational records must be in accordance with the Family Educational Rights and Privacy Act (FERPA) of 1974 (20 U.S.C. 1232g). This law, which is often referred to as the Buckley Amendment, applies to all school districts, pre-K–12 schools, and postsecondary institutions that receive federal funding through the U.S. Department of Education. Nonpublic schools that do not accept federal funding are exempt from this law. FERPA has several provisions. The first provision requires that schools or systems annually send a notice to parents or guardians regarding their right to review their children's records and to file a complaint if they disagree with anything in the record. The system has 45 days in which to comply with the parents' request to review the records. There are penalties, including loss of federal funding, for any school or system that fails to comply. Second, the law limits who may access records and specifies what personally identifiable information can be disclosed without informed consent; that is, what constitutes directory information or pubic information. Under FERPA, only those persons "with a legitimate educational interest" can access a student's record. This includes the new school when a student transfers. The sending school may send the records without the parents' consent but should make every attempt to inform the parent that it has done so. The major exception to this relates to law enforcement; the school must comply with a judicial order or lawfully executed subpoena. The school must also make whatever information is needed available to the school's law-enforcement unit. In emergencies, information relevant to the emergency can be shared (see www.ed.gov/print/policy/gen/guid/

fpco/ferpa/index.html). All states and jurisdictions have incorporated FERPA into state statutes and local policies, with some degree of variance among such aspects as what constitutes directory information.

The rights of consent transfer to the student at age 18 or when the student attends a postsecondary institution. The law does not specifically limit the rights of parents of students over 18 who are still in secondary school. Noncustodial parents have the same rights as the custodial parent unless their rights have been terminated or limited by the courts. Stepparents and other family members who do not have custody of the child have no rights under FERPA unless the court has granted authority.

The Protection of Pupil Rights Amendment (PPRA) of 1978, often called the Hatch Amendment, gives parents additional rights. It established certain requirements when surveys are given to students in pre-K–12 schools; it does not apply to postsecondary schools as students can consent on their own. If the survey is funded with federal money, informed consent must be obtained for all participating students if students in elementary or secondary schools are required to take the survey and questions about certain personal areas are asked. It also requires informed parental consent before the student undergoes any psychological, psychiatric, or medical examination, testing, or treatment or any school program designed to affect the personal values or behavior of the student. The Hatch Amendment also gives parents the right to review instructional materials in experimental programs.

The NCLB act of 2001 included several changes to FERPA and PPRA and continued to increase parents' rights. The changes apply to surveys funded either in part or entirely by any program administered by the U.S. Department of Education (USDE). NCLB made minor changes to the seven existing categories concerning surveys and added an additional category. PPRA now requires that:

• Schools and contractors make instructional materials available for review by parents of participating students if those materials will be used in any USDE funded survey, analysis, or evaluation

- Schools and contractors obtain written, informed parental consent prior to students' participation in any USDE funded survey, analysis, or evaluation if information in any of the below listed areas would be revealed:

  - Political affiliations or beliefs of the parent or student
  - Mental and psychological problems of the family or student
  - Sex behavior or attitudes
  - Illegal, antisocial, self-incriminating, or demeaning behavior
  - Critical appraisals of other individuals with whom the student has close family relationships
  - Legally recognized privileged or analogous relationships such as those of lawyers, ministers, and physicians
  - Religious practices, affiliations, or beliefs of the student or student's parent (new)
  - Income other than such information as required to determine eligibility or participation in a program (20 U.S.C. 1232h)

The new provisions of PPRA also apply to surveys not funded through USDE programs. These provisions give parents the right to inspect, on request, any survey or instructional materials used as part of the curriculum if created by a third party and involves one or more of the eight aforementioned areas. Parents also have the right to inspect any instrument used to collect personal information that will be used in selling or marketing. Parents always have the right to not grant permission or to opt their child out of participating in any activity involving the eight previously delineated areas. PPRA does not apply to any survey that is administered as part of the Individuals with Disabilities Education Improvement Act (IDEIA).

As can be seen from the previous discussion, there are many constraints in schools to assessment, testing, and surveying students. As individual school systems or districts may have further defined this legislation, it is essential that professional school counselors become familiar with the requirements of the policies and procedures for their specific school system.

The word *parents* has been used in the preceding discussion about student records. The law does recognize the right of students over the age of 18 to access their own records and accords them the same rights as parents of students under the age of 18. However, the law does not specifically limit the right of parents whose children are over the age of 18 to also access their child's records, particularly in cases where the child is still living at home and is financially dependent on the parents. The law also gives noncustodial parents the same rights as custodial parents. Unless there is a court order in the child's file that limits or terminates the rights of one or both parents, both parents have the same access to the child's records. School personnel must also provide copies of records such as report cards to both parents if requested.

The word *parent* is used to reference the legal guardian of the child, who may not be the biological or adoptive parent of the child but some other legally recognized caregiver. Stepparents and other family members have no legal right to the student's records without court-appointed authority, such as adoption or guardianship. This is particularly problematic in situations where a relative provides kinship care; that is, the relative has physical custody 24 hours a day, 7 days a week, but no legal custody of the child. Legally this person has no educational decision-making rights for the child and cannot access that child's record or give consent. The crack epidemic and AIDS/HIV have created a situation where millions of children under 18 are involved in informal kinship care situations. Kinship care may be the best situation for children, but these situations present significant legal implications for schools.

Outside agencies may not access records of any student without the signed consent of the parent. Some states have worked out interagency agreements wherein a parent signs one form that designates what records may be shared with which agencies, making individual forms unnecessary. Local policies dictate whether signed informed consent is needed to share information at school team meetings such as SAP, IEP, or student services meetings, when the agency personnel are regular members of the team.

Personal Notes

Personal notes are those notes written by professional school counselors to serve as an extension of their memories; they are an impression of the client or session. These notes must remain "in the sole possession of the maker" and cannot be shared with anyone except "a substitute maker." A substitute maker is someone who takes over for the counselor in the counselor's position, in the same way a substitute teacher takes over for the regular teacher. A substitute maker is not the counselor who becomes responsible for the child the next year or in the next school.

The important point about personal notes is that such notes must remain separate from the educational record. Once any information in the personal notes is shared, it is no longer confidential. If professional school counselors keep their personal notes in their offices, they should keep them separate from all other records and secured, such as in a locked file cabinet. Some counselors go so far as to keep them in their car or house, but this is not necessary unless there are problems with security in their office. As technology becomes more common in counseling offices, professionals may prefer to keep their personal notes on the computer. That is not a good idea unless the counselor can absolutely guarantee that no one can access the program or break through firewalls. Even keeping the notes on disk is questionable. Stories of computer hackers breaking codes and paralyzing Web sites for hours are frequently reported in the news. It is preferable to keep notes separate and not tell anyone they exist, even if there is nothing of particular interest in them. The information is confidential, and the professional school counselor needs to ensure its security. Information from the notes would be shared only in those cases where there is a clear duty to warn or when a judge requires that confidentiality be broken and the information shared.

THE HEALTH INSURANCE PORTABILITY AND ACCOUNTABILITY ACT (HIPAA) OF 1996

The HIPAA of 1996 required that the U.S. Department of Health and Human Services (HHS) adopt national standards for the privacy of individually identifiable health information, outlined patients' rights, and established criteria for access to health records. The requirement that HHS also adopt national standards for electronic health-care transactions was also included in this law. The Privacy Rule was adopted in 2000 and became effective in 2001. The Privacy Rule set national standards for the privacy and security of protected health information. The rule specifically excludes any individually identifiable health information that is covered by FERPA. Thus, health records in schools that are under FERPA are specifically excluded from HIPAA. However, in reality, the situation is not quite that simple, particularly in the area of special education. Many schools receive mental, physical, and emotional health assessments of students that have been conducted by outside providers whose practices are covered by HIPAA regulations. In previous years, such assessments and reports automatically became part of the educational record. This may no longer be the case, particularly if the provider requests that the report not be redisclosed. As HIPAA continues to impact health information, school systems must develop policies and procedures to address any potential conflicts between FERPA and HIPAA. Professional school counselors must be aware of these issues and any school policies.

CHILD ABUSE

Another issue professional school counselors must deal with that has clear legal mandates is child abuse and neglect. Efforts to recognize and intervene in child abuse cases began in the late 1800s and were modeled on the prevention of cruelty to animals laws. In 1961, the "battered child syndrome" was legally recognized, and by 1968, all 50 states had laws requiring the reporting of child maltreatment. In 1974, the National Child Abuse Prevention and Treatment Act (P. L. 93–247) became a federal law. The act was later reauthorized with changes and renamed the Keeping Children and Families Safe Act of 2003. The law defined child abuse as physical or mental injury, sexual abuse or exploitation, negligent treatment, or maltreatment of a child under the age of 18 or the age specified by the child-protection law of the state in question, by a person who is responsible for the child's welfare, under circumstances that indicate that the child's health or welfare is harmed or threatened (42 USCS § 5101).

The law is very clear regarding who must report child abuse and neglect cases. Every health practitioner, educator, human services worker, and law enforcement officer must report suspected abuse or neglect, generally within 24 to 72 hours of first "having reason to suspect." It is incumbent on the person who first suspects the abuse or neglect to call Child Protective Services to report. The oral report must be followed up by a written report in most cases. Each state may have slightly different procedures for reporting; some states allow up to seven days for submission of the written report and identify different agencies to which the report must be made. What does not change is the legal mandate to report.

There is no liability for reporting child abuse, even if a subsequent investigation determines no evidence that abuse or neglect occurred, unless the report is made with malice. However, most states do have serious penalties for failure to report. These penalties may include loss of certification or license, disciplinary action, or termination of employment.

Parents or guardians have no rights to information during this process. The school or other entity making the report should not inform the parents that a report is being made. It is the responsibility of the department of social services and the law enforcement agency to contact the parent and conduct the investigation. It is critical that professional school counselors and other professionals understand the laws regarding child abuse and neglect cases and follow the procedures exactly. It should be emphasized that

the person submitting the report does not have to prove that abuse has occurred; it is enough to have reason to suspect.

Professional school counselors are sometimes put in an awkward position when they are not the first person to suspect abuse but the staff member who does is not willing to make the report and asks the counselor to do it. In such cases, if the staff member will not make the report, professional school counselors should do it but should apprise the administrator of the circumstances surrounding the report. Regardless of who submits the report, the student will need support and assistance throughout the process. Lambie (2005) suggested that "the counselor use sound and appropriate counseling skills" (p. 7) and assure the student of his or her concern.

SUICIDE

For many years, the standard that was used in the profession for dealing with potential suicide cases was Tarasoff, which was previously discussed. As a result of the Tarasoff, ruling, counselors had a duty to warn if there was a foreseeable victim. According to Remley and Herlihy (2001), subsequent court decisions interpreted the case differently; some judges ruled that the duty exists even when there is no foreseeable victim, if persons are unintentionally injured by the client, classes of persons of which the victim is a member, bystanders, and other individuals (pp. 97–98). In general, when dealing with a potentially suicidal client, the professional school counselor would conduct a lethality assessment, determine the seriousness of the threat, and then, based on the seriousness of the threat, decide whether the duty to warn was applicable. The Eisel case in Maryland changed the standard for many counselors. In that case, two middle school students became involved in Satanism and, as a result, became obsessed with death and self-destruction. Friends of Nicole Eisel went to their school counselor and told her that Nicole was thinking about killing herself. This counselor consulted with Nicole's school counselor. Both professional school counselors spoke with Nicole, who denied thinking about killing herself. Shortly thereafter, on a school holiday, Nicole's friend, who attended another school, shot Nicole and killed herself in the park behind the school. Mr. Eisel sued the school, the school system, and the professional school counselors. The circuit court dismissed the case. Mr. Eisel appealed to the court of appeals. Its decision of October 29, 1991, stated:

> Considering the growth of this tragic social problem in the light of the factors discussed above, we hold that school counselors have a duty to use reasonable means to attempt to prevent a suicide when they are on notice of a child or adolescent student's suicidal intent. (*Eisel v. Board of Education*, 1991)

On the facts of this case as developed to date, a trier of fact could conclude that the duty included warning Mr. Eisel of the danger. The case was remanded back to the circuit court to decide the issue of liability for both the school system and the professional school counselors. The case finally concluded 8 years after it began and found the school and professional school counselors had acted appropriately given the circumstances, their training, and the policies in place at the time.

However, the court's decision had a major impact on professional school counselors in the state of Maryland. This decision removed the counselor's ability to determine whether duty to warn is applicable. As a consequence, professional school counselors in Maryland must always tell the parent whenever there is any indication from a child or someone else that the child is thinking about suicide, regardless of the seriousness of the threat. Further, they must also inform the principal or the principal's designee. Many of Maryland's school systems now apply this procedure to all student services personnel employed by the school system.

While this case is legally binding only on professional school counselors in Maryland, it has become the standard by which subsequent cases have been decided. For example, a Florida court subsequently made a similar ruling in a similar case, and several other courts are following suit. Professional school counselors must be aware of the policies within their system. The courts clearly are ruling in favor of duty to warn, as opposed to counselor discretion.

SUMMARY/CONCLUSION

If one were to survey practicing counselors regarding the "hot issues" in counseling, the list would likely include eating disorders, HIV/AIDS, self-mutilation, autism and Asperger's syndrome, bullying, harassment, changing family structures, mobility, cultural diversity, sexual orientation, depression, loss and grief, students with special needs, emotional disturbance, gangs, and a host of other topics. So how does a counselor help the 13-year-old who believes he is gay? Or the 16-year-old who is starving herself to death? Or the incarcerated parent who wants the professional school counselor to read his letters to his children in school because the mother will not let him have any contact with his children?

Here are some final words of wisdom to help guide you as a professional school counselor.

- Always document in writing what you did and why you did it.
- If you did not follow a policy, document why you did not (e. g., not calling the parent in a suicide case because it was handled as an abuse case).
- Know federal, state, and local laws, regulations, policies, and guidelines.
- Consult with a colleague or supervisor when you have questions or doubts.
- Read and use resources.
- Consult with a lawyer when appropriate.

Professional school counselors must be prepared to deal with these issues and more every day of their professional lives. Many of these areas do not have clear laws, regulations, court cases, or policies to guide counselors toward legal and ethical behavior. Professional school counselors need to try to do what is in the best interest of their clients, and to help the clients see what that is. They must advocate for their students, because frequently the professional school counselor will be the only support that the student has. Professional school counselors must never stop believing and having faith that what they do makes a difference in the lives of children.

Now go to our Companion Website at www.prenhall.com/erford to assess your understanding of chapter content with "Multiple-Choice Questions," apply comprehension with "Essay Questions," and broaden your knowledge of the school counseling profession with related "Web Links."

CHAPTER 5

MULTICULTURALLY COMPETENT SCHOOL COUNSELORS

AFFIRMING DIVERSITY BY CHALLENGING OPPRESSION

CHERYL HOLCOMB-MCCOY AND STUART F. CHEN-HAYES

Editor's Introduction: The transformed professional school counselor is multiculturally competent, respectful of human diversity, and a school leader in ensuring that oppressive systemic barriers to academic, career, and personal–social development are removed. To achieve this goal, professional school counselors must explore and know their own culture and biases, then open themselves to, and seek to understand, the cultures of the diverse popularions they serve. This chapter includes a Professional School Counselor Multicultural Competence Checklist and several dilemmas and vignettes to help you on your journey to becoming multiculturally competent.

VIGNETTE 1

Janice is a middle-class, Jewish professional elementary school counselor in a wealthy suburban school district. In recent years, there has been a large influx of multilingual working-class Taiwanese students of indigenous ethnicity and Buddhist faith into her school. Because these students never self-refer for counseling and because she has never attended the local Buddhist temple or consulted with spiritual leaders of the local Taiwanese Buddhist community,

Janice erroneously assumes they have no school or family concerns.

VIGNETTE 2

John, a White middle-class professional urban high school counselor, is puzzled as to why there is an achievement gap at his school with Native American, African American, and Latino/a students, 90% of whom qualify for free and reduced lunch, who are overrepresented in special education classes, and who are accepted to college and universities at a significantly lower rate than White and Asian students are. He wonders what can be done to change the attainment gap that is evident because few of the school's poor and working-class Latino/a, African American, and Native American students who are accepted into college finish and graduate with diplomas.

VIGNETTE 3

Kay, a middle-class African American rural professional middle school counselor, feels uncomfortable providing developmental school counseling lessons to a class of recent Central American immigrant students of indigenous ethnic/racial identity, all of whom qualify for free and reduced lunch, who desire career and college development skills, and who want accurate information and educational/career/ college planning so that they have the opportunity to attend and graduate from college. Kay cannot speak Spanish, and the only Spanish-speaking staff member is a custodian.

VIGNETTE 4

Ricardo, an upper-class Latino urban professional middle school counselor, avoids academic, career/ college, and especially personal-social counseling with poor and working-class students of color; White students; and multiracial students whom he perceives as lesbian, bisexual, gay, or transgendered because he fears they will out him as a gay Latino.

The dilemmas faced by the professional school counselors in the above scenarios have become increasingly more commonplace. This is true because never before has American society been as multiethnic, multicultural, and multilingual as it is today (Marshall, 2002; Sue, 1991; Sue & Sue, 1990). Between 1980 and 1990, the White American population grew by only 6.01% while the African American and Hispanic populations grew by 13.8% and 53.02%, respectively (U.S. Bureau of Census, 1992; Wehrly, 1995). The current racial/ethnic

distribution among students in public schools in the United States is about 1.2% Native American, 4% Asian/Pacific Islander, 15.6% Latino/a, 17.2% African American, and 62.1% White/European (National Center for Education Statistics [NCES], 2001). These figures are expected to change due to increases in students of color enrolling in school each year, with the largest increases in student population among Latino/as and Asian/Pacific Islanders. Hodgkinson (1985) predicted that in the early 21st century, the non-White population will make up a majority of the U.S. workforce, and this is quickly becoming a reality.

Based on these rapidly changing demographics, the skills of affirming diversity and challenging oppression are key components of the professional school counselor's transformed role. In fact, multiculturalism as a key component of the school counseling profession is no longer viewed as desirable but mandatory. Professional school counselors, as is the case with other school professionals, are becoming more aware of the need to be knowledgeable about the manner in which culture and ethnicity affect the learning process, and more importantly, how students are differentially affected in their schools based on ethnicity, race, language, disability status, social class, and other cultural identities.

In many school districts, professional school counselors are preparing themselves for their diverse clientele by taking courses in foreign languages, enrolling in extensive multicultural counseling training, and consulting with ethnic minority community leaders. Professional school counselors are also beginning to play a major role in school reform initiatives and efforts to improve the academic achievement of ethnic minority students (e.g., Education Trust). At the same time, it is unclear whether professional school counselors are effective in their work with students from oppressed backgrounds. Some research has even suggested that professional school counselors maintain a status quo of educational outcomes for minority students (Fallon, 1997).

In response to the increasingly diverse caseloads of professional school counselors, the

American School Counselor Association (ASCA, 1999b) adopted the following position statement on multicultural counseling:

> *Cross/multicultural counseling:* the facilitation of human development through the understanding and appreciation of cultural diversities. ASCA recognizes cultural diversities as important factors deserving increased awareness and understanding on the part of all school personnel, especially the school counselor. Counselors may use a variety of strategies not only to increase the sensitivity of students and parents to culturally diverse persons and enhance the total school and community environment, but also to increase the awareness of culturally diverse populations.

In addition, in the 2004 revision of the Ethical Standards for School Counselors, multicultural, diversity, and antioppression competencies are addressed as follows in Section E.2, Diversity:

The professional school counselor:

a. Affirms the diversity of students, staff, and families.

b. Expands and develops awareness of his/her own attitudes and beliefs affecting cultural values and biases and strives to attain cultural competence.

c. Possesses knowledge and understanding about how oppression, racism, discrimination and stereotyping affects her/him personally and professionally.

d. Acquires educational, consultation, and training experiences to improve awareness, knowledge, skills, and effectiveness in working with diverse populations: ethnic/racial status, age, economic status, special needs, ESL or ELL, immigration status, sexual orientation, gender, gender identity/expression, family type, religious/spiritual identity and appearance. (ASCA, 2004a, p. 4)

Considering the ethical and professional obligation of professional school counselors to be culturally competent, this chapter's main objectives are to (a) clarify the language and terminology used when discussing multicultural competence, affirming diversity, and challenging oppression; (b) discuss the need for culturally competent professional school counselors;

(c) offer ways in which professional school counselors can integrate multiculturalism in their school counseling programs; (d) offer a checklist that can be used to assess professional school counselors' multicultural competence; (e) provide case studies of actual professional school counselors challenging multiple oppressions through closing achievement and opportunity gaps; and (f) offer vignettes that can be used to facilitate one's development of competence when working with students' multiple cultural identities and challenging oppression.

For clarification, the term *culturally diverse* is used throughout this chapter to denote distinctions in "the lived experiences and the related perceptions of and reactions to those experiences, that serve to differentiate collective populations from one another" (Marshall, 2002, p. 7). These distinctions are affected directly by the complex interactions of racial/ethnic classification, social status, historical and contemporary circumstances, and worldview. Racial/ethnic designations are used throughout the chapter when discussing cultural diversity and other factors such as social class, gender, religion, sexual orientation, language, disability, and immigration status have been incorporated into various discussions. Racial/ethnic and social class identities have been highlighted throughout the chapter because of their historical correlations with the achievement, opportunity, and attainment gaps that persist among cultural groups in U.S. schools (Education Trust, 2005b).

MULTICULTURAL AND ANTIOPPRESSION TERMINOLOGY

Much of the frustration in understanding multiculturalism and antioppression theory is due to misuse of and confusion about the terminology. S. D. Johnson (1990) suggested that more time be devoted to clarifying multicultural terminology in Counselor Education graduate programs. In his study of counselor trainees' ability to make distinctions between the concepts of "race" and "culture," he found that trainees offered definitions that were "badly confounded, containing vague and simplistic notions of culture and race" (p. 49). Culture, race, ethnicity, and various types of oppression are contrasted in this section.

The term *culture* has been defined in a variety of ways. Goodenough (1981) described culture as consisting of the follwing components: (a) the ways in which people perceive their experiences of the world so as to give it structure; (b) the beliefs by which people explain events; (c) a set of principles for dealing with people as well as for accomplishing particular ends; and (d) people's value systems for establishing purposes and for keeping themselves purposefully oriented. Drawing from a more traditional perspective, Wehrly (1995, p. 4) described culture as "a dynamic construct that includes the values, beliefs, and behaviors of a people who have lived together in a particular geographic area for at least three or four generations." Culture has also been described narrowly to include only an individual's ethnicity or nationality and from a more broad perspective, to include one's economic status, gender, religion, and other demographic variables. This lack of consensus in defining culture has created a debate as to how inclusive the construct of "multicultural counseling" should be (Pederson, 1988).

Similar to *culture, race* is a term that has been defined in various ways. For behavioral scientists, race has been used to denote genotypically homogeneous human groupings (Kluckhohn, 1985). However, according to Baba and Darga (1981), the practice of racial classification by biological characteristics is practically impossible. *Merriam-Webster's Collegiate Dictionary* (1993, p. 570) defines race (or racial group) as a "family, tribe, people, or nation of the same stock." Pederson (as cited in Ponterotto & Pederson, 1993) suggested that although the race construct has been discredited as a scientific and biological term, it remains an important political and psychological concept. In counseling and psychology, race has been used in three main ways: (a) differential sociopolitical and economic socialization, (b) biogenetic psychological characteristics inferred from the presence of observable "signs" commonly assumed to be racial, and (c) differential cultural (e.g., values,

beliefs, rituals) socialization (Helms, 1994). It is critical for professional school counselors to remember that race has been and continues to be used in schools to carry out such practices as segregation; stereotyping groups by students' academic achievement; tracking; selection of students for special education; and low teacher expectations for students of color, particularly students of color who are also poor, have disabilities, or are English language learners.

In contrast to race, *ethnicity* was defined by Schaefer (1990, p. 27) as "a group set apart from others because of its national origin or distinctive cultural patterns." It is within this ethnic identity that an individual is socialized to take on the group's values, beliefs, and behaviors. McGoldrick and Giordano (1996) referred to ethnicity as

> A common ancestry through which individuals have evolved shared values and customs. It is deeply tied to the family, through which it is transmitted. . . . The concept of a group's "peoplehood" is based on a combination of race, religion, and cultural history and is retained, whether or not members realize their commonalities with one another. The consciousness of ethnic identity varies greatly within groups and from one group to another. (pp. 1–2)

Oppression, in contrast to other terms in this chapter, can be defined in an equation: **Oppression = prejudice × power,** whereby prejudice is maintaining incorrect conscious or unconscious attitudes, feelings, and beliefs about members of a cultural group as inferior or that a group's cultural differences are unacceptable (Arnold, Chen–Hayes, & Lewis, 2002). Power is the ability to control access to resources, including control of, or over, the images of what is culturally appropriate. Power and power-over are maintained and used on individual, cultural, and systemic levels (Arnold et al., 2002; Hardiman & Jackson, 1997; Jackson, 1990). I. M. Young (1990) further expanded the definition of oppression by delineating five conditions of an oppressed group: exploitation, marginalization, powerlessness, cultural imperialism, and violence. *Exploitation* refers to the steady transfer of the results of the labor of one social group to the benefit of another. *Marginalization* refers to the process where individuals or groups of people are permanently confined to lives of social marginality because they are not attractive or perceived as "acceptable" to people in the dominant culture. Young emphasizes that marginalization is particularly harmful to people since it means being both expelled from participation in social life and being subjected to material deprivation. *Powerlessness* is defined as having to take orders without having the right to give them. *Cultural imperialism* refers to the dominance of one group's experiences and culture and its establishment as the norm. Young claimed that cultural imperialism occurs when the experiences and perspectives of oppressed groups seem "invisible" to the dominant group. Paradoxically, the oppressed group is stereotyped and marked out as the "other." Violence is a manifestation of oppression because of the social context, which makes violence possible and, in some cases, acceptable. Violence is systemic because it is often directed at members of oppressed groups simply because they are members of that group.

Other forms of oppression include individual, cultural, systemic, internalized, and externalized oppression. *Individual oppression* is behavior based on conscious or unconscious negative assumptions about people who are culturally or racially different. Examples are joke telling, staring at someone "different," and targeting a person for a crime solely because of his or her skin color. *Cultural oppression* is when the standards of appropriate actions, thought, and expression of a particular group are seen as negative (overtly or covertly). As a result, a member of the oppressed group must change her behavior to be accepted by the dominant group. An example of cultural oppression is when heterosexuality is the only sexual orientation mentioned or recognized in a school's curriculum. *Systemic/institutional oppression* includes unequal power relationships in institutions that result in inequitable distribution of resources. It can include inflexible policies and procedures unresponsive to cultural differences. Systemic oppression can involve the use of power to limit others based on their race, cultural background, or both. Examples include women and ethnic minorities being paid less for work comparable to that of White men (Arnold et al., 2002; Hardiman & Jackson, 1997; Jackson, 1990). Table 5.1 lists common forms of oppression.

Internalized oppression is characterized by an individual believing the stereotypes about one's group and then acting accordingly (Chen-Hayes, 2005). *Externalized oppression,* on the other hand, is when an individual targets members of nondominant groups for oppression, violence, coercion, and control based on a belief (conscious or not) that members of the nondominant group are inferior or otherwise deserving of control, coercion, or violence (Chen–Hayes, 2005).

Multicultural Counseling

As previously stated, it is the lack of clear definitions of terms that leads to the question, "What is multicultural counseling?" Locke (1990) referred to multicultural counseling as a counseling relationship in which the counselor and client differ as a result of socialization in unique cultural or racial or ethnic environments. However, C. E. Vontress (1988) noted, "[I]f the counselor and client perceive mutual cultural similarity, even though in reality they are culturally different, the interaction should not be labeled cross-cultural counseling" (p. 75). It has also been debated whether or not to narrowly define multicultural counseling as a relationship between two or more ethnically or racially diverse individuals. According to P. Arredondo and D'Andrea (1995), the definition of multicultural counseling provided by the Association for Multicultural Counseling and Development (AMCD) relates to "five major cultural groups in the United States and its territories: African/Black, Asian, Caucasian/European, Hispanic/Latino, and Native American or indigenous groups which have historically resided in the continental United States and its territories" (p. 28).

Other counseling professionals and professional organizations, including CACREP, view multicultural counseling from a universal perspective and include characteristics of not only race and ethnicity, but also gender, lifestyle, religion, sexual orientation, and so on (CACREP, 2001). CACREP's definition further emphasizes the implication of a pluralistic philosophy. The term *pluralistic* in the accreditation procedures manual and application is used to "describe a condition of society in which numerous distinct

TABLE 5.1
Forms of Oppression That Are Found Throughout Society, Including K–12 Schools

Ableism: Prejudice multiplied by power used by temporarily able-bodied persons against persons with disabilities (physical, developmental, or emotional) that limits their access to individual, cultural, and systemic resources.

Ageism: Prejudice multiplied by power used by persons age 18–49 against childern and youth and persons age 50+ that limits their access to individual, cultural, and systemic resources.

Beautyism: Prejudice multiplied by power used by persons with dominant standards of beauty against fat persons or persons with other nondominant appearances that limits their access to individual, cultural, and systemic resources.

Classism: Prejudice multiplied by power used by wealthy and upper middle-class persons against poor, working-class, or lower middle-class persons that limits their access to individual, cultural, and systemic resources.

Familyism: Prejudice multiplied by power used by persons of traditional family configurations against single persons, single parents, same-gender parents, same-gender couples, divorced persons, couples who live together, and adoptive/foster families, and limit their access to individual, cultural, and systemic resources.

Heterosexism and Transgenderism: Prejudice multiplied by power used by heterosexuals and traditionally gendered persons against lesbian, bisexual, gay, two-spirit, intersex, and transgendered persons that limits their access to individual, cultural, and systemic resources.

Linguicism: Prejudice multiplied by power used by dominant language speakers against nonspeakers or persons who speak with an accent that limits their access to individual, cultural, and systemic resources.

Racism: Prejudice multiplied by power used by Whites against people of color or multiracial people that limits their access to individual, cultural, and systemic resources.

Religionism: Prejudice multiplied by power used by members of a dominant cultural religious group (e.g., in the United States, Christians) against nondominant religious, spritual, or nonreligious persons and groups (Jews, Muslims, Hindus, Jains, Buddhists, Earth-Centered, Pagans, atheists, agnostics) that limits their access to individual, cultural, and systemic resources.

Sexism: Prejudice multiplied by power used by men or boys against women or girls that limits their access to individual, cultural, and systemic resources.

Source: "Multicultural Counseling Class Lecture," by S. F. Chen-Hayes, 2005, Bronx, New York: Lehman College of the City University of New York.

ethnic, racial, religious, and social groups coexist and cooperatively work toward interdependence needed for the enhancement of each group" (CACREP, 2001, p. 109). For the purposes of this chapter, the definition of multicultural counseling proposed by the AMCD will be used. This definition is central to the Multicultural Competencies proposed by AMCD as criteria for identifying multiculturally competent counselors.

Multicultural Competence

Perhaps one of the greatest challenges confronting the multicultural counseling movement is determining what constitutes multicultural counseling competence. When does one know he or she is multiculturally competent? According to Ponterotto and Casas (1987), multicultural competence is achieved when a counselor possesses the necessary skills to work effectively with clients from various cultural backgrounds. Hence, a counselor with high multicultural competence acknowledges client–counselor cultural differences and similarities as significant to the counseling process. On the other hand, a counselor with low multicultural competence provides counseling services with little or no regard for the counselor's or client's ethnicity or race.

Over the past 3 decades, the literature regarding multicultural counseling competence has focused on three main areas or dimensions: awareness, knowledge, and skills (C. G. Carney &

Kahn, 1984; D. W. Sue, Arredondo, & McDavis, 1992; D. W. Sue et al., 1982). The first area, *awareness*, stresses the understanding of personal worldviews and how counselors are the products of their own cultural conditioning. C. C. Lee (1991) further stressed that it is imperative for counselors, especially counselor trainees, to be aware of how their personal biases may or do interfere with counseling effectiveness. The goal of multicultural counseling training, therefore, is to "increase a counselor's intentionality through increasing the person's purposive control over the assumptions that guide his or her behavior, attitudes, and insights" (Pederson & Leafley, 1986, p. 138).

The second area, *knowledge*, reinforces the importance of understanding the worldviews of culturally different clients (D. W. Sue & Sue, 1990). D. W. Sue et al. (1992) pointed out that counselors must understand as well as respect their clients' worldviews. Traditionally, counseling, like disciplines, has accepted culturally different persons if they are willing to become acculturated and reject cultural distinctiveness (Midgette & Meggert, 1991). This "melting pot" philosophy creates negative consequences when counseling techniques designed for the dominant culture are used inappropriately with clients of ethnically dissimilar backgrounds. According to Midgette and Meggert, counselor education programs cannot continue to operate on an ethnocentric philosophy that is based on conforming clients to a homogeneous model of acceptable behavior.

Finally, the *skills* area deals with the process of actively developing and practicing appropriate intervention strategies needed for work with culturally different clients. According to D. W. Sue et al. (1992), studies have revealed that counseling effectiveness is improved when counselors use techniques and interventions that are consistent with the life experiences and cultural values of their clients.

In addition to D. W. Sue et al.'s (1982, 1992) three-dimensional framework of multicultural competence, other perspectives regarding multicultural competence have been offered. In another article, Holcomb–McCoy and Myers (1999) suggested that there could possibly be more than three dimensions to multicultural competence. They proposed that one must also have

knowledge of multicultural terminology and racial identity–development theories. Pope–Davis, Reynolds, Dings, and Ottavi (1994) suggested that multicultural competence in counseling is "an appreciation of and sensitivity to the history, current needs, strengths, and resources of communities and individuals who historically have been underserved and underrepresented by psychologists" (p. 466). Ridley, Mendoza, Kanitz, Angermeier, and Zenk (1994) proposed a conceptualized model of cultural sensitivity that is based on perceptual schema theory. Ridley and colleagues described cultural sensitivity as the ability of counselors to "acquire, develop, and actively use an accurate cultural perceptual schema in the course of multicultural counseling" (p. 130).

S. Sue (1998) offered a more scientific approach to cultural competence. He suggested that cultural competence consists of three characteristics: being scientifically minded, having skills in dynamic sizing, and being proficient with a particular cultural group. Being *scientifically minded* stresses the counselor's ability to form hypotheses rather than making premature conclusions about the status of culturally different clients. The second characteristic, having *skills* in *dynamic sizing*, reinforces the importance of the counselor's skills "to know when to generalize, when to individualize, and finally when to be exclusive" (p. 446). The counselor's ability to use dynamic sizing decreases his or her tendency to use stereotypes while still embracing the client's culture. In other words, the use of dynamic sizing is one's ability to appropriately categorize experiences and behaviors. Third, the characteristics of *being proficient with a particular cultural group* includes the counselor's expertise or knowledge of the cultural groups with which he or she works, sociopolitical influences, and specific skills needed to work with culturally different clients.

THE NEED FOR CULTURALLY COMPETENT SCHOOL COUNSELORS

As stated previously, professional school counselors are faced with the challenge of providing services that enhance the academic, career, and personal–social development of all students. One of major challenges, however, is the need to create developmental school counseling programs that help to close attainment, achievement, opportunity, and funding gaps among groups of students in K–12 schools. These gaps exist not only in terms of standardized test scores, but also in areas such as Advanced Placement (AP) course participation and test taking, high school graduation rates, college entrance and graduation rates, and earned income. For instance, scores on the 2003 version of the National Assessment of Educational Progress (NAEP; USDE, 2003b) test revealed the continued achievement gaps between African American and Latino/a students and their White peers. Scores on the reading portion of the test at the fourth-grade level showed that 75% of White students scored at the basic level or above, whereas only 44% of Latino/a students and only 40% of African American students did so.

The achievement, attainment, funding, and opportunity gaps are demonstrated in other ways as well. For instance, the Education Trust (2005b) reported that African American and Latino/a students were underrepresented on several different measures of academic and career/ college achievement. Students of color were underrepresented in AP test taking, compared to their percentage of the population (e.g., African Americans—17% of student population, 5% of AP calculus tests; Latinos—17% of student population, 8% of AP biology tests; Whites—60% of students, 72% of calculus tests, 67% of biology tests). High school graduation rates showed that about 72% of White students who began high school in 1997 graduated in 2001, whereas only 52% of Latino students and 51% of African American students graduated within 4 years. Finally, of those students who enrolled in college in the fall of 1998, 59% of White students graduated in 4 years; in contrast, only 36% of Latino students and only 40% African American students graduated in 4 years. Discussions regarding professional school counselors' role in addressing these inequities and disparities in student achievement and career/college access and achievement are relatively new in the school counseling literature. The Education Trust's

Transforming School Counseling Initiative (TSCI) sparked a dialogue among school counseling professionals regarding how professional school counselors can assist in closing the gaps between student groups (Education Trust, 2005b).

INTEGRATING MULTICULTURAL AND ANTIOPPRESSION TOPICS IN SCHOOL COUNSELING PROGRAMS

Professional school counselors can play a pivotal role in combating oppression and assisting culturally diverse students achieve success academically, in career and college attainment and in personal, social, and cultural skills. To begin, however, professional school counselors must recognize that traditional school counseling is embedded in White or European culture, and this limits its cross-cultural utility (Bolyard & Jensen–Scott, 1996). Professional school counselors typically lack specific training to address the problems and effects of oppression and multiple cultural identities because most counselor education programs do not offer consistent training (e. g., coursework, field experiences) that includes topics related to antioppression work and the cultural history and related awareness, knowledge, and skills needed to work effectively for multiple cultural groups and identities.

To effectively assist students of historically oppressed backgrounds, professional school counselors must engage in interventions that create social environments for students that support social justice. The concept of social justice is central to the practice of multicultural school counseling. Social justice refers to equity, equality, and fairness in the distribution of societal resources (Flynn, 1995). Social justice includes a focus on the structures and outcomes of social processes and how they contribute to equality. The professional school counselor's role is to develop practices that contribute to these aforementioned goals. For instance, professional school counselors might reach out to community members and organizations to develop school counseling services that are closely aligned with the community's goals for its students and families. More importantly, professional school counselors should be involved in community organizing that involves mobilizing people to combat common community problems and increasing community members' voices in schools. For example, a professional school counselor, as an advocate for improved housing for low-income parents in her school, might attend city council meetings with local community members and lobby for a new housing policy.

There is a limited amount of literature on strategies and interventions specifically designed for culturally diverse students. However, this section will include an overview of how multicultural topics, diversity topics, or both can be integrated into existing school counseling programs. To begin, empowerment-focused interventions will be described. Empowerment-focused interventions have been suggested in the literature as a means of promoting the well-being of culturally diverse persons. Next, discussions of how multicultural topics may be integrated into typical professional school counselor delivery modes and functions (e. g., individual counseling, group counseling, assessment, consultation, and data collection and sharing) will be offered.

Empowerment-Focused Interventions

Empowerment is a construct shared by many disciplines (e. g., community development, psychology, economics). How empowerment is understood or defined varies among these perspectives. Rappaport (1987) noted that it is easy to define empowerment by its absence but difficult to define in action as it takes on different forms in different people and contexts. As a general definition, empowerment can be defined as a process of increasing personal, interpersonal, or political power so that individuals, families, and communities can take action to improve their situations. It is a process that fosters power (i. e., the capacity to implement) in disenfranchised and powerless groups of people, for use in their own lives, their communities, and their society, by acting on issues that they define as important. Interestingly, the word *empowerment* can be disempowering, when it is understood to

mean the giving of power by the powerful to the powerless. Therefore, the appropriate role of the professional school counselor is to help students and parents build their own power base.

Empowerment is multidimensional, social, and a process. It is multidimensional in that it occurs within sociological, psychological, and economic dimensions. Empowerment also occurs at various levels, such as individual, group, and community. Empowerment, by definition, is a social process, as it occurs in relationship to others. Empowerment is a process that is similar to a path or journey, one that develops as we work through it. One important implication of this definition of empowerment is that the individual and community are fundamentally connected.

Although the literature on empowerment theory describes empowerment as a method that can incorporate multiple levels of intervention, most of the current work has focused on individual or interpersonal empowerment (Gutierrez, 1995; R. Parsons, 1991). The literature has discussed methods and strategies for moving individuals to a point where they feel a sense of personal power. One such strategy is the development of critical consciousness (Zimmerman, 2000). *Critical consciousness* has been described as involving three psychological processes: (a) *group identification*, which includes identifying areas of common experiences and concern with a particular group; (b) *group consciousness*, which involves understanding the differential status of power of groups in society; and (c) *self and collective efficacy*, which is described as perceiving one's self as a subject (rather than object) of social processes and as capable of working to change the social order. For individuals to understand that their problems stem from a lack of power, they must first comprehend their group's status in society as well as the overall structure of power in society. At the individual level, professional school counselors can help students feel empowered by facilitating discussions about one's group identification and helping them understand how their group membership has affected their life circumstances. Students can empower themselves by taking responsibility for their own learning, by increasing their understanding of the communities in which they live, and by understanding how they as individuals are affected by current and potential policies and structures. Equipped with this greater understanding and with new confidence in themselves, students can develop new behavior patterns and perspectives.

An empowerment approach to working with students requires that professional school counselors provide students with knowledge and skills to think critically about their problems and to develop strategies to act on and change problems (C. C. Lee, 2001a). Professional school counselors and students must work collaboratively to help students take charge of their lives. For instance, professional school counselors might help facilitate the problem solving and decision making of students by building on their strengths. Rather than focusing on counselor-assumed student problems, the focus should be on problems identified by the student. The problem-solving process can include problem identification selection of one problem, the choosing of a goal to solve or minimize the problem, the generation of activities to achieve the goals, and identification of available resources to assist in goal attainment (Gutierrez & Ortega, 1991).

Individual Counseling

Individual counseling is a mode of counseling that most professional school counselors are trained to implement in their graduate training programs. Individual counseling theories and techniques, however, tend to be based on traditional, Eurocentric theories that are often inappropriate for students of diverse cultural backgrounds. According to D'Andrea and Daniels (1995), one of the most serious problems in school counseling rests in the fact that "most counseling theories and interventions, which are commonly used in school settings, have not been tested among students from diverse student populations" (p. 143). Very few counseling approaches have been specifically designed and validated for use with specific cultural groups. For this reason, professional school counselors should seek and develop individual counseling strategies that are effective with culturally diverse students.

Professional school counselors should also be aware of the pervasive influence that culture has on the counseling process (Wehrly, 1995). In the school setting, counselors should be aware of the impact of culture on students' way of thinking, belief systems, definitions of self, decision making, verbal and nonverbal behavior, and time orientation. For instance, some non-Westernized cultures place more emphasis on "being" than on "doing." In the Native American and Asian cultures, self is not seen as a separate entity from the group or from nature. In addition, African Americans and other non-mainstream Western cultures see family as an extended unit that does not necessarily limit itself to "blood" relatives. These varied cultural beliefs and practices can be significant in the individual counseling process and have profound effects on the behavior of children and adolescents. Perusse and Goodnough (2004) contributed an edited text full of individual counseling suggestions from a transformative approach for professional school counselors across multiple domains (academic, career, and personal–social) and cultural groups.

Group Counseling

When implementing groups in schools, multiculturally competent school counselors must be able to facilitate the cultural development of group members. This can be done by understanding and acknowledging the reality that students are socialized within a society in which some groups have a history of suffering stereotypes, prejudice, oppression, and discrimination. When composing groups, professional school counselors should consider how students from differing cultural backgrounds are likely to relate to each other and to the group leader. Professional school counselors should be familiar with the literature on selecting and planning for culturally diverse groups (e.g., A. Brown & Mistry, 1994; Davis, Galinsky, & Schopler, 1995). For instance, when reviewing the strengths of same-sex and same-race groups, Brown and Mistry (1994) noted that these groups have advantages when the group task is associated with issues of personal identity, social oppression, and empowerment.

Professional school counselors who lead groups must remember that students bring diverse patterns of behavior, values, and language to groups. Students might bring experiences of oppression and particular feelings about themselves, their group identity, and the larger society to the group. When problems of dissatisfaction or conflict among group members occur, the professional school counselor should remember that the issues may be caused by cultural differences, not by an individual member's personal characteristics or flaws in the group process. Perusse and Goodnough's (2004) edited text on leadership and advocacy in school counseling contains multiple ideas for group counseling, including culturally competent small and large group outlines in academic, career, and personal–social development.

Consultation

Despite the attention focused on multicultural counseling, less emphasis has been placed on the significance of culture on the consultation process. Consulting is a significant responsibility for professional school counselors (Gerler, 1992; Kurpius & Fuqua, 1993). Given the vast amount of time professional school counselors spend consulting with parents, teachers, and administrators of diverse backgrounds, a discussion of multicultural competence of school-based consultants is warranted. Professional school counselors acting in the role of consultant should be sensitive to the cultural differences among the three parties in the consultation process: consultant, consultee, and client. Professional school counselors who consult with culturally different teachers and parents should ensure that the teacher or parent understands that his or her input is welcomed and in many cases is necessary for the success of the intervention. It is just as important, however, to consider the cultural differences of the client. Although the consultation process involves indirect contact with the client, the consultant should not forget that the client is the focus of the consultee's problem; therefore, the culture of the client will have an impact on the change process.

School-based consultants should also focus on conceptualizing the problem or concern of the consultee (e.g., parent, teacher) within a cultural context. Assessing the influence of culture on the consultee's and client's perception of the problem and interpersonal interactions is critical to the consultation process. For instance, a Taiwanese student who is overly concerned about involving her parents in her college choice should not be considered immature by a teacher because of his or her own cultural beliefs. Because the Taiwanese culture emphasizes parental respect, the consultant must ensure that the student is not penalized for behaving in a culturally appropriate manner.

School-based consultants should be able to identify and challenge a consultee's stereotypical beliefs and biases because, ultimately, these faulty perceptions can affect the consultation outcomes. Prejudicial attitudes within the consultation process may be manifested in outright rejection or the provision of inadequate interventions. Clearly, school-based consultants need to be vigilant about detecting and dealing with negative racial attitudes, negative cultural attitudes, or both (Rogers, 2000). By identifying the consultee's biased and prejudicial statements or assumptions, the school-based consultant is more apt to eliminate negative cultural attitudes that might possibly affect the consultee's or client's problem. Oftentimes, for example, teachers will consult with a professional school counselor but fail to recognize their own biased beliefs that are directly or indirectly creating a problem for a student.

Assessment

Given the prevalence of standardized achievement and aptitude tests in today's schools, it is imperative that professional school counselors understand the cultural appropriateness of assessment instruments used frequently in schools (Howell & Rueda, 1996). The assessment of students from diverse backgrounds is complex and needs to be performed with professional care and consideration. Professional school counselors should be able to evaluate instruments for cultural bias and identify other methods for assessing culturally diverse students. In addition, professional school counselors should be competent in relaying assessment results to culturally diverse students and parents. It is important to remember, however, that there is not one instrument that is totally unbiased. Therefore, professional school counselors should know that their judgments in assessing the cultural appropriateness of an instrument and providing unbiased interpretations are key in the process of culturally sensitive assessment. Biased interpretations, for instance, of a student's test results can lead to inappropriate decisions regarding a student's needs. Professional school counselors must always be cognizant of the presence of unjust assessment practices, which lead to tracking students of color and poor students in low-performing classes, excluding racially or culturally diverse students from gifted-and-talented programs, and disproportionately identifying students of color for special education services (Delpit, 1995).

And finally, professional school counselors should be aware of the testing options for English language learners. Generally the options for these students are to have a test translated, use interpreters, use tests that are norm-referenced in their first language, or use a bilingual test administrator (Figueroa, 1990). Professional school counselors must challenge linguicism (Chen–Hayes, Chen, & Athar, 2000) and ensure that bilingual students receive a fair and appropriate testing environment as well as an opportunity to receive a fair representation of their skills, abilities, and aptitudes.

School Counseling/Guidance Curriculum Lessons

Classroom school counseling curriculum lessons are used to relay information or to instruct a large group of students. These lessons, based on the *ASCA National Model* (2003a), are an effective way for professional school counselors to address cultural sensitivity and issues pertaining to race, gender, sexual orientation, disabilities, or any diversity-related issue (Bruce, Shade, & Cossairt, 1996). Perusse and Goodnough (2004) included multiple school counseling curriculum lessons on

culturally diverse topics by authors on academic, career, and personal–social development, looking at multiple oppressions, including ableism (Coker, 2004), racism (Bailey & Bradbury–Bailey, 2004), sexism (C. B. Stone, 2004), heterosexism (S. D. Smith & Chen–Hayes, 2004), and multiple oppressions, (M. Jackson & Grant, 2004) as they affect K–12 students. Adams, Bell, and Griffin (1997) published an entire text on how to focus on teaching multiple issues of oppressions in social justice skills training.

Professional school counselors can help students become more culturally sensitive by implementing classroom school counseling curriculum lessons focused on: affirming differences, accurate multicultural terminology, exploring one's biases, learning about ethnic/racial identity–development models, understanding diverse worldviews, and challenging the various oppressions. In addition to the above resources, sample classroom school counseling curriculum lessons might include the following activities related to multicultural issues:

1. Students are given case studies of students dealing with racism, classism, heterosexism, ableism, linguicism, sexism, multiple oppressions, and so forth. They are then asked to discuss the feelings of the students featured in the case studies and ways to solve problems dealing with oppressive behavior, particularly solutions for challenging systemic barriers that keep certain groups of students from achieving access and success.

2. Students are asked to define *stereotype* and then brainstorm stereotypes that students have or have heard about different groups of people. Discuss the dangers of stereotypes and where students can go to find accurate information about persons of diverse cultural identities.

3. Students are asked to interview a classmate or classmate's family members about their experiences with prejudice, power, and various forms of oppression. This activity is followed by a large group discussion of themes that have emerged and the similarities and differences with various oppressions.

4. Invite diverse persons from the community to discuss their personal ethnic/racial/

cultural histories. This activity can be done in a large auditorium with 60 to 65 students. Students should have prepared questions for the panelists about how they have dealt with prejudiced people, racism, and oppression.

5. Have students read excerpts from or the entire *A People's History of the United States* (Zinn, 2003), and ask them to do a family history on how their ancestors as well as current members have been subject to, or subjected others to, oppression based on ethnicity, race, gender, social class, language, immigration status, disability, and other identities.

School Counseling Program Coordination

Professional school counselors provide a variety of services directly and indirectly to students, parents, and teachers. At the same time, professional school counselors are responsible for coordinating school counseling program activities and services that involve individuals and programs outside the school. Professional school counselors' coordinating activities may range from coordinating a peer mediation program to coordinating family counseling services. Multicultural aspects of coordination include being sensitive to the diverse needs of those persons inside the school and in the community. Professional school counselors should coordinate schoolwide programs relevant to the needs of all students, particularly those from culturally diverse backgrounds. Schoolwide programs that promote skills to affirm all cultures and to handle conflict resolution promote respect for various worldviews.

Also, professional school counselors should take the time to meet and develop relationships with referral sources that are representative of their school's communities. Atkinson and Juntunen (1994) recommended that professional school counselors be familiar with services offered both in ethnic/racial communities and in the larger community. For instance, a professional school counselor in a community with a large percentage of Muslim students should contact and begin a working relationship with local mosques. Or, a professional school counselor seeing the numbers of out lesbian, bisexual, gay, and transgendered students should contact and assess the services provided by local agencies that specialize in working with gay and lesbian youth and their families, such as Parents and Friends of Lesbians and Gays (PFLAG; www.pflag.org) and the Gay, Lesbian, Straight Education Network (GLSEN; www.glsen.org).

Data Collection and Sharing

Collecting and analyzing meaningful data about the characteristics and academic performance of students, and about school organization and management, helps highly diverse schools "identify achievement gaps, address equity issues, determine the effectiveness of specific programs and courses of study, and target instructional improvement" (Lachat, 2002, p. 3). Data is collected, analyzed, and interpreted to make school counseling program improvements as well as total school improvements. The use of data to effect change within the school system is integral to ensuring that every student receives the benefits of the school counseling program. To create a data-driven school counseling program, professional school counselors must work with administrators, faculty, and advisory council members to analyze data to create a current picture of students and the school environment. This picture focuses discussion and planning around students' needs and the professional school counselor's role in addressing those needs. Professional school counselors should be proficient in the collection, analysis, and interpretation of student achievement and related data. Professional school counselors monitor student progress through three types of data: (a) student-achievement data, (b) achievement-related data, and (c) standards- and competency-related data.

Student-achievement data measure students' academic progress and include grade point averages, standardized test scores, academic standards-based test scores, SAT and ACT scores, graduation rates, and drop-out rates. Achievement-related data measure those fields the literature has shown to be correlated to academic achievement and include these data fields: course enrollment patterns; discipline referrals; suspension rates; alcohol, tobacco, and other drug violations; attendance rates; parent or guardian participation; homework completion rates; and participation in extracurricular activities. Standards- and competency-related data measure student mastery of the competencies delineated in the *ASCA National Model* (2003a) and can include: percentage of students with a 4-year plan on file, percentage of students who have participated in job shadowing, percentage of students who have set and attained academic goals, percentage of students who apply conflict-resolution skills.

Professional school counselors who strive to be culturally competent disaggregate data by variables to see if there are any groups of students who may not be doing as well as others. These data often shed light on issues of equity and focus the discussion on the needs of specific groups of students. Although there are many variables by which data may be separated, the common fields include gender, ethnicity/race, socioeconomic status, home language, disability, attendance, grade level, teacher(s). To determine whether specific programs are not working for certain students—underachieving students, students with excessive absenteeism, and dropouts—data can be disaggregated by courses taken or even by the teachers who taught them, to consider relevant school influences. The performance of students with similar personal characteristics can be disaggregated to determine which courses, instructional strategies, and so forth are most effective with them. Differences between student grades and scores on standardized tests can be reviewed to determine whether there are lags in course content or poor preparation for some types of tests (Lachat, 2002).

Finally, item analysis—the process of examining the group of students that missed a particular item on one test or similar items on several assessments—can determine what, if any, factors they have in common, such as the same teacher or limited opportunity to learn the material (Slowinski, 2002).

CASE STUDIES OF PROFESSIONAL SCHOOL COUNSELORS CHALLENGING OPPRESSIONS IN K–12 SCHOOLS

In this section, case studies of professional school counselors who have used the previously discussed strategies for becoming culturally competent will be highlighted.

Case Study 1

Having learned about the Education Trust's Transforming School Counseling Initiative and the importance of professional school counselors focusing on academic success for all students, James Martinez, a bilingual Puerto Rican professional middle school counselor, asked his assistant principal for data measuring the results of academic services for students who were failing three or more classes. James was overwhelmed with the response. The assistant principal not only gave him the data on students' failing grades, but wanted to give him more data on other issues. Based on the data, James developed a program to monitor the performance progress of students who were failing, and advocated for equitable academic services to support students' diverse learning needs. When the superintendent and the school board wished to know exactly what it was that professional school counselors do, he sent his newly created brochure on school counseling programs and services offered at Peekskill Middle School to the administrators along with handouts on transformative school counseling programs, as well as a summary data collection to challenge academic inequities.

Case Study 2

Winnie Lisojo, a Puerto Rican bilingual/bicultural professional school counselor was concerned about the academic success of the Puerto Rican and Dominican students at the school where she performed her internship and worked as a bilingual teacher. She realized that systemic linguicism was occurring. Winnie found that Puerto Rican students were often transferred into

English as a second language (ESL) classrooms simply because they possessed Latino/a surnames and without any screening of their language abilities. After months of advocating for a change in the policy of ESL inclusion, Winnie convinced the principal to place students on the basis of their language skills, not simply sorting them by surnames. Students, parents, administrators, and staff all benefited from her challenging linguicism.

Case Study 3

Theresa Wyre-Jackson, a Bronx high school counselor of Caribbean descent, realized that her school was focusing on "at-risk" students who were failing, as opposed to her preferred focus on "at-promise" students and building on their strengths and potential for academic, career, and college success. As she collected data on academic success at her school, she challenged her students and her teaching colleagues to strive for high expectations and high achievement. She created a series of workshops to directly challenge the internalized and externalized racism, classism, and heterosexism adversely affecting students and teachers. Through her school advocacy efforts, she created dissatisfaction with the status quo and instead created an environment in which *all* students learned to challenge oppressive myths.

Case Study 4

Inez Ramos, a professional school counselor at Health Opportunities High School in the Bronx, is Latina and bilingual and a strong student advocate. At a public meeting, she openly questioned the New York City Board of Education chancellor as to why he was not providing more financial and administrative support for the academic and emotional needs of K–12 students, particularly poor children of color. Her question was replayed on several New York City television stations and resulted in her being asked to discuss her concerns with the chancellor.

Case Study 5

Kimmerly Nieves, a middle-class professional middle school counselor of Puerto Rican descent in Westchester County, New York, works at Albert Leonard Middle School, a school with roughly 50% of its student body comprising poor African American and Latino/Chicano students and ethnic/racial identities and the other 50% made up of White and Jewish students of middle- and upper middle-class backgrounds. The staff was primarily White or Jewish. Kimmerly developed multicultural school counseling lessons and implemented them at her school. She found support from administrators, staff, and a diverse range of parents in her school. She found that many of the White teachers embraced her efforts to increase academic success for all students. Her unwavering work to include the concept that the cultural identities of all learners must be affirmed by all members of the school for greater academic success has modeled multicultural and antioppression competencies for the community. Her outreach to students and parents of color in particular was critical in demonstrating trust and credibility on the part of professional school counselors—and all educators—in ensuring academic success for all students.

INCREASING PROFESSIONAL SCHOOL COUNSELOR MULTICULTURAL COMPETENCE

As DeLucia–Waack, DiCarlo, Parker–Sloat, and Rice (1996) stated, "[M]ulticulturalism is best viewed as a process or a journey rather than a fixed end point" (p. 237). Because this is a process, it is important for counselors to have a variety of learning experiences that enhance multicultural competence. This section offers five ways in which professional school counselors can increase their level of multicultural competence: investigate one's own cultural or ethnic heritage; attend workshops, seminars, and conferences on multicultural and diversity issues; join organizations that are focused on multicultural issues; read literature written by ethnic minority authors or about ethnic cultures; and become familiar with multicultural education literature.

Investigate One's Own Cultural or Ethnic Heritage

Researchers and counselor educators have documented the importance of self-awareness as a requirement for working with others (G. Corey, Corey, & Callanan, 1998; Hulnick, 1977; Speight, Myers, Cox, & Highlen, 1991). Self-awareness is essential to becoming multiculturally competent. Speight et al. suggested that the acceptance of others' cultures and differences increase as one's self-knowledge increases. For this reason, many multicultural counseling courses and training seminars focus on increasing trainees' self-awareness.

Professional school counselors should explore their ethnic identity, racial identity, and other cultural identities. For many White counselors, this is a difficult process because they often don't see themselves as having an ethnicity or affiliation with a racial identity. However, almost everyone can trace his or her family history, values, and experiences, with the exception of some persons who have been adopted or have no access to family members. For some, this can mean exploring the values of their family of origin or examining written histories of their families' "roots." In addition to exploring one's family history, White counselors should spend time exploring the concept of White privilege and the issues that result from such privilege. For instance, White counselors should have an opportunity to explore what it means to be White, the benefits of White privilege, and the guilt associated with being a member of the dominant racial culture in terms of power and privilege in the United States.

Attend Workshops, Seminars, and Conferences on Multicultural and Diversity Issues

For many professional school counselors, one course in multicultural counseling is not the answer for their lack of multicultural competence.

In addition to the content learned in the course, most counselors need additional training when they are employed. Given the importance of multiculturalism in counseling, most counseling organizations have developed special workshops, weekend seminars, and annual conference presentations that cover issues related to multi-culturalism, various oppressions, and creative approaches for working with diverse clientele.

Join Counseling Organizations Focused on Cultural and Social Justice Equity Competency

It is important that professional school counselors not only attend workshops and seminars related to multiculturalism and diversity, but also join organizations that are focused primarily on increasing multicultural and social justice equity competencies. Such counseling organizations as AMCD, Counselors for Social Justice (CSJ), and the Association for Gay, Lesbian, Bisexual, and Transgendered Issues in Counseling (AGLBIC) are dedicated to combating oppression and increasing cultural senstivity in the counseling profession.

Read Literature Written by Culturally Diverse Authors

Literature can be a useful tool in learning about other cultures. Through reading about other cultures, the professional school counselor's worldview is broadened and she is introduced to the present and past realities of people of a certain cultural group. Cornett and Cornett (1980) indicated that the reading experience encourages readers to engage in critical thinking when they begin to realize how selectively some U.S. historical and sociopolitical events have been and still are reported. One of the authors uses Howard Zinn's (2003) *A People's History of the United States* to teach multicultural counseling because it uses a narrative format to illustrate the personal and systemic stories of how ethnic, racial, social class, and gender oppression have been intertwined for centuries in the United States and how members of oppressed groups and their allies have resisted and continue to resist oppression in the forms of racism, classism, and sexism in the United States and the rest of the Americas. It gives a powerful understanding to how affirming diversity is not enough; culturally competent professional school counselors must also be advocates for social justice and equity.

Become Familiar with Multicultural Education Literature

It is imperative that professional school counselors stay abreast of the literature and research pertaining to multicultural education. The teacher education profession has a long history of exploring teachers' lack of multicultural

competence and biased behavior in the classroom. For professional school counselors to play a pivotal role in changing some of the institutional barriers for ethnic minority students, they must be aware of the most current research related to multicutural pedagogy and curriculum.

PROFESSIONAL SCHOOL COUNSELOR MULTICULTURAL COMPETENCE CHECKLIST

Perhaps one of the first steps to becoming a multiculturally competent professional school counselor is determining areas of personal improvement needed. Figure 5.1 includes a

FIGURE 5.1
Professional School Counselor Multicultural Competence Checklist

Directions: Check whether you are competent (COMP) or not competent (NOT COMP) on each of the following items.

COMP   NOT COMP

Multicultural Counseling
1. I can recognize when my beliefs and values are interfering with providing the best services to my students.
2. I can identify the cultural bases of my communication style.
3. I can discuss how culture affects the help-seeking behaviors of students.
4. I know when a counseling approach is culturally appropriate for a specific student.
5. I know when a counseling approach is culturally inappropriate for a specific student.
6. I am able to identify culturally appropriate interventions and counseling approaches (e. g., indigenous practices) with students.
7. I can list barriers that prevent ethnic minority students from using counseling services.
8. I know when my helping style is inappropriate for a culturally different student.
9. I know when my helping style is appropriate for a culturally different student.
10. I can give examples of how stereotypical beliefs about culturally different persons impact the counseling relationship.
11. I know when my biases influence my services to students.
12. I know when specific cultural beliefs influence students' response to counseling.
13. I know when my helping style is inappropriate for a culturally different student.

COMP   NOT COMP

Multicultural Consultation

14. I know when my culture is influencing the process of consultation.
15. I know when the consultee's (e. g., parent, teacher) culture is influencing the process of consultation.
16. I know when the race and /or culture of a student is a problem for a teacher.
17. I can initiate discussions related to race/ethnicity/culture when consulting with teachers.
18. I can initiate discussions related to race/ethnicity/culture when consulting with parents.

Understanding Racism and Student Resistance

19. I can define and discuss White privilege.
20. I can discuss how I (if European/American/White) am privileged based on my race.
21. I can identify racist aspects of educational instructions.
22. I can define and discuss prejudice.
23. I can identify discrimination and discriminatory practices in schools.
24. I am able to challenge my colleagues when they discriminate against students.
25. I can define and discuss racism.
26. I can discuss the influence of racism on the counseling process.
27. I can discuss the influence of racism on the educational system in the U.S.
28. I can help students determine whether a problem stems from racism or biases in others.
29. I understand the relationship between student resistance and racism.
30. I am able to discuss the relationship between student resistance and racism.
31. I include topics related to race and racism in my classroom guidance units.
32. I am able to challenge others' racist beliefs and behaviors.
33. I am able to identify racist and unjust policies in schools.

Understanding Racial and/or Ethnic Identity Development

34. I am able to discuss at least two theories of racial and/or ethnic identity development.
35. I can use racial/ethnic identity development theories to understand my students' problems and concerns.
36. I can assess my own racial/ethnic identity development in order to enhance my counseling.
37. I can assist students exploring their own racial identity development.
38. I can develop activities that enhance students' racial and/or ethnic identity.
39. I am able to discuss how racial identity may affect the relationships between students and educators.

Multicultural Assessment

40. I can discuss the potential bias of two assessment instruments frequently used in the schools.
41. I can evaluate instruments that may be biased against certain groups of students.

(Continued)

FIGURE 5.1 (Continued)

                                                                        COMP   NOT COMP

42. I am able to use test information appropriately with culturally
    diverse parents.
43. I can advocate for fair testing and the appropriate use of testing of
    children from diverse backgrounds.
44. I can identity whether or not the assessment process is culturally
    sensitive.
45. I can discuss how the identification stage of the assessment process
    might be biased against minority populations.
46. I can use culturally appropriate instruments when I assess students.
47. I am able to discuss how assessment can lead to inequitable
    opportunities for students.

Multicultural Family Interventions
48. I can discuss family counseling from a cultural/ethnic perspective.
49. I can discuss at least two ethnic groups' traditional gender role
    expectations and rituals.
50. I anticipate when my helping style is inappropriate for a culturally
    different parent or guardian.
51. I can discuss culturally diverse methods of parenting
    and discipline.
52. I can discuss how class and economic level affect family functioning
    and development.
53. I can discuss how race and ethnicity influence family behavior.
54. I can identify when a school policy is biased against culturally
    diverse families.

Social Advocacy
55. I know of societal issues that affect the development of ethnic
    minority students.
56. When counseling, I am able to address societal issues that affect the
    development of ethnic minority students.
57. I can work with families and community members in order to
    reintegrate them into the school.
58. I can define "social change agent."
59. I am able to be a "social change agent".
60. I can discuss what it means to take an "activist counseling" approach.
61. I can intervene with students at the individual and systemic levels.
62. I can discuss how factors such as poverty and powerlessness
    have influenced the current conditions of at least two ethnic groups.
63. I am able to advocate for students who are being subjected to unfair practices.
64. I know how to use data as an advocacy tool.

Developing School–Family–Community Partnerships
65. I can discuss how school–family–community partnerships are
    linked to student achievement.
66. I am able to develop partnerships with families that are
    culturally different than me.
67. I am able to develop partnerships with agencies within
    my school's community.

COMP   NOT COMP

68. I can define a school–family–community partnership.
69. I am able to discuss more than three types of parent involvement.
70. I am able to encourage the participation of ethnic minority
    parents in school activities.
71. I am able to work with community leaders and other resources in the
    community to assist with student (and family) concers.

Understanding Cross-Cultural Interpersonal Interactions

72. I am able to discuss interaction patterns that might influence ethnic
    minority students' perception of inclusion in the school community.
73. I can solicit feedback from students regarding my interactions
    with them.
74. I can verbally communicate my acceptance of culturally
    different students.
75. I can nonverbally communicate my acceptance of culturally
    diverse students.
76. I am able to assess the manner in which I speak and the
    emotional tone of my interactions with culturally diverse students.
77. I am able to greet students and parents in a culturally
    acceptable manner.
78. I know of culturally insensitive topics or gestures.

Multicultural Career Assessment

79. I can develop and implement culturally sensitive career development
    activities where materials are representative of all groups in a wide
    range of careers.
80. I can arrange opportunities for students to have interactions with
    ethnic minority professionals.
81. I am able to assess the strengths of multiple aspects of students'
    self-concept.
82. I can discuss differences in the decision-making styles of students.
83. I integrate my knowledge of varying decision-making styles when implementing career counseling.
84. I can integrate family and religious issues in the career
    counseling process.
85. I can utilize career assessment instruments that are sensitive to
    cultural differences of students.
86. I can discuss how "work" and "career" are viewed similarly and
    differently across cultures.
87. I can discuss how many career assessment instruments are
    inappropriate for culturally diverse students.

Multicultural Sensitivity

88. I am able to develop a close, personal relationship with someone
    of another race.
89. I am able to live comfortably with culturally diverse people.
90. I am able to be comfortable with people who speak another language.
91. I can make friends with people from other ethnic groups.

checklist that can be used by professional school counselors to determine areas for additional multicultural counseling training and exploration. Based on the AMCD's *Multicultural Competencies and Explanatory Statements* (P. Arredondo et al., 1996) and multicultural education literature, the checklist encompasses those behaviors, knowledge, and awareness that have been noted as important for culturally competent work in school settings. The checklist can be completed by professional school counselors and counselors in training annually to monitor progress and needs for further exploration. In addition, professional school counselors in training benefit from case studies of actual professional school counselors creating culturally competent schools through challenging oppression and through the use of practice vignettes.

Practice Vignettes

Another step in the process of developing multicultural counseling competence is for professional school counselors to openly question their thoughts and behaviors when working with ethnic minority students: "What additional knowledge, awareness, or skills do I need to effectively work with this student?" "Am I effective when working with students of this particular ethnic background?" "How are my beliefs, values, and biases affecting the counseling process with this student?" These questions enable the professional school counselor to better understand his or her level of multicultural competence and need for further multicultural counseling training.

In addition to questioning one's thoughts and behaviors, professional school counselors can use case studies as a means to begin discussions with colleagues. Following are seven vignettes that describe cases involving a sensitive cultural issue in a school. The task of the reader is to think about how to work with the student(s), parents, and teachers involved and determine one's level of competence. These vignettes can be used for large- and small-group discussions with other counselors who are seeking to improve their multicultural competence.

VIGNETTE 1

You accept a position as a professional high school counselor in a predominately Latino/a and African American school. Your responsibilities include both academic and career counseling. Eduardo is a 16-year-old junior, a first-generation U.S. citizen who is bilingual. His parents fled to the United States from El Salvador many years ago. His parents have strongly encouraged him to earn high grades so that he will be able to be admitted to a prestigious college. Eduardo is uncertain about what he wants to do after high school, and admits that he has not really thought about a career for himself. He has stated that he resents the pressure put on him by his parents, and feels that they are trying to live out their dreams through him. Eduardo knows, however, that he needs to begin thinking about life after high school and is hopeful that you will be able to help him find some answers because he's not yet had any career or college counseling at the school.

VIGNETTE 2

You are a counselor in a rural school in Arizona. Parents of the Native American children in your school are upset when several of the bilingual Native American students are placed in a special education classroom designed for students with learning disabilities. Many of the parents complain that they received a condescending letter stating that their child was given a test and the results were very low, indicating severe learning disabilities. No White students, who speak only English and no native languages, have been placed in the special education classroom, and White students comprise 65% of the student population. Of the students, 100% are eligible for free and reduced lunch.

VIGNETTE 3

Brandon is a 15-year-old student at a high school in a predominately upper middle-class White suburb. Brandon has lived most of his life in this community but has recently begun hanging out in the African American section of the suburb and recently announced that he has converted to Islam from Christianity. Brandon is biracial; his mother is White and his father is African American. His parents are concerned about Brandon because he has become very angry at his parents' supposedly "White lifestyle" and has asked to live with his father's parents. His parents want you, the professional school counselor, to talk to Brandon about their concerns.

VIGNETTE 4

You are a professional school counselor at a diverse elementary school. The ethnic/racial composition of the student population is 41% White, 25% African American, 25% Asian, 5% Latino/a, 2% Native American, and 2% Jewish; 33% of the students are on free or reduced lunch; 29% of students are English language learners; and 22% of the students have one or more learning, physical, developmental, or emotional disabilities. The ethnic/racial makeup of the teaching staff is 95% White and 5% "other," and all are at least working class or middle class. There are no teachers who speak English as a second language and some teachers have physical and emotional disabilities. Since the student population has become increasingly diverse, you have become more cognizant of teachers making racist, classist, linguicistic, and ableist jokes and stereotypical comments about students of color, poor and working-class students, English language learners, and students with disabilities, in the teachers' lounge. You have become very uncomfortable with the comments.

VIGNETTE 5

You are a professional middle school counselor in a rural middle school composed of working-class and

middle-class families. It has come to your attention that the African American and multiracial students, particularly boys, are performing disproportionately lower than their White peers on achievement tests. Teachers have commented, "That's just the way it is." The principal has asked you to be a part of a task force to investigate the low performance of African American and multiracial students.

VIGNETTE 6

Maria is a bilingual Mexican 11th grader with severe asthma and obesity and is eligible for free and reduced lunch at the high school in which you are a professional school counselor. Maria has just received her SAT scores, which are very high (i.e., 1250). She has also received several letters from competitive colleges and universities. Nevertheless, Maria tells you that she doesn't want to go to college. Instead, she would like to find a job so that she can help her family financially.

VIGNETTE 7

Unhei, a bilingual seventh grader of Korean ethnicity and a working-class Christian family, comes to your office to discuss her class schedule for next semester. However, you can tell by her demeanor and nonverbal behavior that some other issue, not her class schedule, bothers her. You are aware that she has been hanging out with students who are in the school's Gay/Straight Alliance, but you are not sure if that is what she is concerned about. You decide to use a client-centered approach to get her to talk about her feelings. She abruptly leaves your office and never returns.

SUMMARY/CONCLUSION

With the increasingly diverse student population of today's schools, there is a critical need for professional school counselors who are able to provide effective school counseling programs that offer both culturally competent and antioppressive programs to all students to help close achievement, opportunity, and attainment gaps in K–12 schools. As professional school counselors work with larger numbers of students of color and students of other multiple cultural identities, they need to adjust their perceptions and school counseling programs to address students' diverse needs. This chapter has focused on several ways in which professional school counselors can integrate cultural competence; antioppression work; and multiple cultural identity awareness, knowledge, and skills into school counseling programs to increase student success and to demonstrate school counselor cultural competence. Although this chapter is an introduction, the goal for professional school counselors is to continue a journey of developing greater cultural competence. Engagement in the process of developing cultural competence and affirming diversity through challenging oppressions provides professional school counselors an unparalleled opportunity for personal and professional growth and demonstrable skills to better the lives of all students through data-driven school counseling programs.

This chapter began with an introduction to important multicultural and antioppression terminology because it is imperative that professional school counselors first know how to define and conceptualize cultural and oppressive incidents that occur in schools. In addition, a brief discussion of how cultural and antioppression practice might be integrated into components of developmental school counseling programs was provided. Considering that a major goal for professional school counselors is learning how to discuss oppression and cultural topics freely and openly in school settings, this chapter included case studies and vignettes to stimulate dialogue among counselors as to how they might react to or resolve issues related to oppressive school practices, students' cultural differences, or both. Continuous dialogue regarding issues of oppression in schools should be initiated by professional school counselors.

For professional school counselors who want to assess their multicultural competence, the Professional School Counselor Multicultural Competence Checklist is included at the end of this chapter. This checklist is unique in that it includes 11 dimensions of professional school counselor multicultural competence: multicultural counseling, multicultural consultation, understanding racism and student resistance, understanding racial and/or ethnic identity development, multicultural assessment, multicultural family interventions, social advocacy, developing school–family–community partnerships, understanding cross-cultural interpersonal interactions, multicultural career assessment, and multicultural senstivity.

Overall, this chapter has provided an introduction to the nature of multicultural counseling in schools and the ways in which oppressive beliefs and practices impact student success. It is important to note, however, that it is impossible to prepare in advance for all the different experiences one might encounter in schools. Instead, professional school counselors need to acquire the knowledge and skills that will allow them to critically assess and intelligently address the various challenges encountered by students and their families.

Now go to our Companion Website at www.prenhall.com/erford to assess your understanding of chapter content with "Multiple-Choice Questions," apply comprehension with "Essay Questions," and broaden your knowledge of the school counseling profession with related "Web Links."

ACTIVITIES

1. Collaborate in a small group on a developmental school counseling lesson plan outline and specific activities and content on awareness, knowledge, and skills needed by students and staff to combat at least two of the oppressions discussed in this chapter. Link this activity to the *ASCA National Model* or your state's school counseling model and specific state learning standards/outcomes for a specific grade and building level (e.g., 5th-grade elementary students, 8th-grade middle school students, 10th-grade high school students).

2. Discuss the multicultural demographics (ethnicity/race, gender, sexual orientation, disability status, social class, language status, religious/spiritual identity, and other

variables) as well as the multicultural competence level on the part of the teaching and school counseling staff of the K–12 schools that you attended. How will you be similar or different when you are working as a practicing professional school counselor?

3. Go to the Education Trust's Web site (www.edtrust.org) and find a piece of local or national data that most illustrates the racism and classism involved in a current achievement, opportunity, or attianment gap facing poor and working-class students or students of African American, Latino/a, or Native American ethnic/racial identity, including students who are English language learners, students with disabilities, or both. Once you have located the piece of data, what would you do as a culturally competent professional school counselor to challenge systemic barriers in a school that has those types of gaps?

CHAPTER 6

ACHIEVEMENT ADVOCACY FOR ALL STUDENTS THROUGH TRANSFORMATIVE SCHOOL COUNSELING PROGRAMS

DERYL F. BAILEY, YVETTE Q. GETCH, AND STUART F. CHEN-HAYES

> Editor's Introduction: Key to the transformation of the school counseling profession is the professional school counselor's advocacy for social justice and academic equity—also known as achievement advocacy—through transformative school counseling programs delivering measurable achievement competencies to all students via counseling, lesson plans, workshops, educational planning, and activities.

While some school professionals continue to refer to students "at risk," it is more empowering to think of all students as "at promise" (Swadener & Lubeck, 1995). This change in language provides a window for school counseling programs advocating to challenge the beliefs and views of some adults that not all students can achieve high levels of success in school. School counseling programs that use a strengths-based, "nondeficient" advocacy model are perceived as educational leaders in schools providing measurable equity, achievement results, and success for all students. In particular, students of color, poor and working-class students, students with disabilities, and English-language learners have traditionally not received equal access, opportunities, and resources for success from school counseling programs or from K–12 schools as a whole (ASCA, 2004a; Education Trust, 2005a; see also chapters 1 and 5).

Professional school counselors who develop and implement transformative school counseling programs based on the *ASCA National Model* (ASCA, 2003a) strive to empower and advocate for historically oppressed populations such as students oppressed because of membership in nondominant groups based on ethnicity, race, social class, language, disability, sexual orientation, gender, gender identity/expression, appearance, immigration status, family type, spirituality/religion, and so forth, as outlined in the *ASCA Code of Ethics* (2004a). Implementing a results-based transformative school counseling program such as the *ASCA National Model* is a form of systemic achievement advocacy that benefits all students. When professional school counselors develop and maintain a school counseling program based on advocacy with specific competencies and outcomes that demonstrate how professional school counselors assist students to succeed in academic, career/college, and personal–social achievement domains, they empower teachers, parents and guardians, and students to speak out and change unjust institutional and systemic practices perpetuated in a "one size fits all" school bureaucracy. In short, the transformed professional school counselor leads the way in removing barriers to student performance and overcoming social injustice through modeling and teaching social and academic advocacy strategies through implementing both a transformative school counseling program and a strong school counseling public awareness and support program. Creating public awareness and support for the school counseling program ensures that all stakeholders are clear on the transformative definition, roles, mission, vision, and specific outcomes for all students in grades K–12 (see chapters 1 and 5).

For over a decade, "All kids can learn!" has been the cheer heard around the United States in terms of school reform. It is the concept that schools need to focus on ensuring all students meet high standards and graduate from high school ready to pursue their dreams. Large groups of students of color, poor and working-class students, students with disabilities, and English-language learners are not achieving equitable results in schools when compared to their more privileged peers. Ongoing achievement, opportunity, attainment, and funding gaps continue in many K–12 public schools (Education Trust, 2005a).

Unfortunately, some gaps are maintained even under the guise of reform. Some school systems, hoping to encourage positive change, invite charismatic speakers whose goals are to motivate educators to make a difference in the lives of all children. Most often, this peaked motivation to serve all kids dissipates as quickly as it came. Shortly after the start of classes, educators can be found conducting business as usual and, at the end of the year, wondering why there continue to be so many students failing, suspended or expelled, dropping out, or just disappearing. A principal once explained this phenomenon in the following manner: "If you always do what you've always done, you'll always get what you've always gotten." While this statement may be flawed grammatically, it offers some valuable insight into why achievement gaps exist between various groups of students. Reports indicate that major achievement, opportunity, attainment, and funding gaps exist between students of color and White students as well as between students from low-income families (often students of color) and students from middle- and upper-income families (Brennan, 1999; College Board, 1999a, 1999b; Education Watch, 1998). Why are these achievement, opportunity, attainment, and funding gaps so wide between various groups of students if all students can learn?

Many school systems have taken bold steps to reform and as a result have demonstrated that students of color and students from low-income households can excel academically (Brennan, 1999). The Education Trust, for example, annually honors school districts and individual schools that have closed significant achievement and opportunity gaps throughout the United States (Education Trust, 2005b). Brennan reported that students from low-income families can match the achievement of affluent families "stride for stride" and that poor students from some school districts actually outperform students from affluent families. These findings were based on 1998 student achievement data from Kentucky and a national survey of high-poverty schools conducted by the Education Trust in conjunction with the Council of Chief State School Officers (CCSSO). According to another report released by the Education Trust (2005a), *Dispelling the Myth: High Poverty*

Schools Exceeding Expectations, successful high-poverty schools demonstrated the following characteristics:

1. Extensive use of state/local standards to design curriculum and instruction, assess student work, and evaluate teachers
2. Increased instruction time for reading and mathematics
3. Substantial investment in professional development for teachers focused on instructional practices to help students meet academic standards
4. Comprehensive systems to monitor individual student performance and to provide help to struggling students before they fall behind
5. Parental involvement in efforts to get students to meet standards
6. Accountability systems with real consequences for adults in the school

With these characteristics in mind, the advocacy, systemic change, leadership, and collaboration skills and services provided by professional school counselors via a transformative school counseling program based on the ASCA *National Model* (2003a) to ensure achievement advocacy for all students are critical. For example, school counseling programs should use state and local standards to design curriculum and instruction and assess student learning. School counseling programs can be major contributors by integrating student learning styles and other learning modalities and working directly with academic intervention teams and other educators collaboratively in school leadership teams to monitor student progress on a weekly basis and determine what needs to be done by all adults in schools to ensure equity and high standards are achieved by all students. In professional development, professional school counselors can collaboratively design and implement workshops for teachers, administrators, parents and guardians, and others to develop awareness of achievement, opportunity, attainment, and funding gaps and devise specific advocacy strategies, skills, and outcomes for systemic change.

Professional school counselors should play a pivotal role in monitoring student performance as well as providing assistance to students who struggle academically, in terms of career and college curriculum offerings and decision making or with personal and social concerns. Some professional school counselors resist and resent their involvement in student scheduling of classes. While professional school counselors should not be treated as high-paid clerks, it is imperative that professional school counselors be engaged in this task as consultants and advocates so that all students receive outstanding teaching and no students are marginalized or tracked with teachers who lack credentials or who do not believe all students can learn at high levels. What better way to monitor student performance and prevent students from being inappropriately placed in courses that are not challenging or that do not prepare them for future success (Baker, 2000)? Professional school counselors can also encourage parent and guardian involvement by ensuring parents and guardians are notified immediately when students begin to experience problems in school, and assisting the student and parent or guardian in working through these difficulties using a strengths-based advocacy perspective.

Bob Sexton, director of the Prichard Committee, a nonpartisan citizen advocacy group in Kentucky, believes that data from the Kentucky study proved "that there are ways to reach every child . . . [W]hy can't every school do the same?" (Brennan, 1999, p. 1). The gap in academic achievement, educational opportunities, college graduation rates, and equitable funding across public schools between the various groups of students continues and, in some instances, is increasing (College Board, 1999a, 1999b; Education Watch, 1998). This chapter focuses on professional school counselors as achievement advocates promoting systemic changes in schools and communities through transformative school counseling programs with measurable achievement results based on the ASCA *National Model* (2003a) and the work of the Education Trust's National Center for Transforming School Counseling (2005b). Professional school counselors as advocates assist in eliminating barriers that have traditionally impeded the growth and performance of all students, particularly students of color, poor and working-class students, English-language learners, and students with disabilities.

WHAT ARE ADVOCACY AND ACHIEVEMENT ADVOCACY?

Advocacy is the intentional effort to change existing or proposed policies, practices, and learning environments on behalf of all students and families (Ezell, 2001). Similarly, researchers (Kurpius & Rozecki, 1992) have defined advocacy as "a process for pleading the rights of others who for some reason are unable to help themselves" (p. 179). Advocacy has also been described as an act of promoting an idea, belief, or program that does not receive support from others (Glickman, Gordon, & Ross-Gordon, 1995). Osborne et al. (1998) presented a model of advocacy congruent with the aforementioned definitions. Their model encouraged counselors to take individual or collective actions on behalf of all students to promote justice and improve academic and environmental conditions.

For professional school counselors, achievement advocacy is defined as becoming a risk taker for all students, ensuring high levels of academic, career, college, and personal–social skills are delivered to all students as part of a school counseling program with specific results. The degree to which students struggle may change daily and depend on a number of variables. These variables include, but are not limited to, family and school environments, socioeconomic status, parental education levels, quality of teachers, access to educational and career opportunities and information, adult level of expectations for student performance, and, unfortunately, ethnicity and cultural backgrounds (Herr, 1989). Nonetheless, nearly all students will need a professional school counseling program to advocate on their behalf at some point during their school career. The question that remains is, are all professional school counselors ready, willing, and able to implement school counseling programs focused on achievement advocacy for all students? Are professional school counselors transforming the profession and changing the perception and roles of school counselors and school counseling programs to create positive achievement changes for all students? The latter question may sound extreme, but it is essential for counselors to speak out against policies or practices that have been a part of "business as usual" for the past decade or so in the form of achievement, opportunity, attainment, and funding gaps.

HISTORY OF ADVOCACY

Advocacy is by no means a new concept for counselors or counselor educators (C. Lee & Walz, 1998). In the early 1970s, Dworkin and Dworkin (1971) issued a call to action for counselors to become leaders in social change rather than sideline cheerleaders. Ironically, advocacy continues to be a concept that is far more likely to be talked about than to be widely adopted with practical application. Scholars have indicated that professional school counselors should take a more active role in advocating for all students. Professional schools counselors, in particular, should be expected to serve as advocates for all students and their families, with extra programmatic attention and interventions geared for students who demonstrate academic, career/college, and personal–social achievement concerns.

In the past, researchers and counselor educators have referred to advocacy with terms like *assertive change* and *assertive work* (Lofaro, 1982) and provided lists of characteristics for those wishing to adopt an assertive role (Kurpius & Rozecki, 1992). While this body of literature provides valuable information, these words often are not put into practice. Too often, professional school counselors become overwhelmed with administrative concerns (e.g., bus and hall duties, discipline, attendance, testing, lunch monitoring, running personal errands for the principal, relentless paperwork, schedule changes, constant crises), to the point of becoming entrenched in the system. As a result, professional school counselors who should be advocating for all students and encouraging changes in the system end up "gatekeepers of the status quo," supporting and maintaining an inequitable system that harms entire groups of students because professional school counselors cannot figure a way out from under the inappropriate roles and job responsibilities that take them away from counseling, delivering lesson plans, workshops, activities, and educational planning for all students (Hart & Jacobi, 1992).

R. M. House and Martin (1998) suggested that professional school counselors not support and maintain such ineffective systems, but instead become "catalysts and leaders focused on removing the institutional barriers that continue to result in an achievement gap between poor and minority youth and their more advantaged peers" (p. 284). R. M. House and Martin also encouraged professional school counselors to be "dream-makers" rather than "dream-breakers." Moreover, counselor education curriculums have often spoken of counselors as advocates of change, but do little in practical application and implementation for social change within the school community (Osborne et al., 1998). Academic achievement advocacy needs to be infused throughout the counselor education curriculum if new professional school counselors are to be properly prepared for their roles as educational change agents.

In addition to counselor education programs, professional organizations have traditionally been in an excellent position to provide valuable support for counselors as advocates, but even in this arena, words appear to have been more abundant than actual implementation. Initially, professional organizations such as the ACA and the Association for Counselor Education and Supervision (ACES) acted as "forces for change in that they include language that encourages individual members and organizational units to remove barriers to individual development" (Collison et al., as cited in C. Lee & Walz, 1998, p. 265).

In retrospect, these professional organizations appear to fall short of a directive statement that is a call to action for professional school counselors. ACA's mission statement and code of ethics speak of enhancing human development (ACA, 2005a) but do not include specific language to direct counselors to take on an advocacy role as part of their professional stance (Collison et al., as cited in C. Lee & Walz, 1998). In view of the fact that the professional school counselor's office is the most likely interface between student–teacher, student–administrator, teacher–parent/guardian, and school–community

interactions, it becomes the most logical place for academic, career/college, and personal–social achievement advocacy within the school community (R. M. House & Martin, 1998). To correct this history, both counselor education programs and professional organizations need to take a more proactive role in promoting particularly academic and career/college achievement advocacy as expected practice for professional school counselors. To this end, counselor education programs need to modify curriculum to make advocacy an integral part of the program, thus allowing students to learn how to advocate, practice advocacy, and, most important, observe faculty in advocacy roles (Osborne et al., 1998). As an indicator of important trends in this area, the *ASCA National Model* (2003a) proposed that advocacy serve as one of the cornerstones of effective school counseling programs. Thus, as the profession moves through the early part of the 21st century, advocacy services stand as a promising new direction for the profession.

The Importance of Advocacy: Challenging the Barriers

Over the past 4 decades, U.S. society has undergone a major facelift (C. C. Lee, 1997). The process began with the United States being recognized as a truly pluralistic nation. C. C. Lee suggested the turmoil of the Civil Rights movement of the 1950s and 1960s was the starting point. What was once a predominantly White society has become a multiethnic and multiracial society. Researchers (Herr, 1989; C. C. Lee, 1985) have been predicting this major shift in the population for some time now. On September 12, 2000, Bryant Gumble, host of CBS's *Early Show*, referred to America as a "melting pot." We now recognize the fact that people who came to America, either through migration or on slave ships, did not "melt" into one culture. Alternatively, it is perhaps a more appropriate metaphor to compare American society to a "tossed salad" (P. Arredondo & Locke, 1999), where every group maintains characteristics and customs that are unique to its culture. Just like with a tossed salad, no matter how much you mix things up, everyone retains his or her own cultural identity.

Similarly, student populations in many public schools across the nation have changed dramatically over the past 4 decades. The percentage of students of color has increased as well as those who speak English as a second or third language. Since 1972, there has been a 22% increase in the number of students identified as being a part of an ethnic or racial group of color. The number of school-age children who speak a language other than English at home has more than doubled since 1979, and many of these students are English-language learners lacking fluency (USDE, 2005). Additionally, the percentage of students identified as low-income or poor has also increased (Education Trust, 2004; Education Watch, 1998; C. C. Lee, 1985). By the year 2020, children of color will comprise more than 50% of public school students (Hodgkinson, 1995), and they already are the dominant group in most major urban areas, many older suburbs, and increasing numbers of rural areas in the United States.

Professional school counselors serve as advocates for all students and their families, especially those students for whom achievement, opportunity, attainment, and funding gaps continue to grow; namely, students who are African American, Latino/a, Native American, from low-income households, English-language learners, and students with disabilities (College Board, 1999a, 1999b; Education Watch, 1998; Herr, 1989; R. M. House & Martin, 1998). While high school graduation rates for Whites, African Americans, and Latinos have improved since 1971, and the gains (almost a seven percentage-point improvement) made by African American students have narrowed the gap between White and African American students, the gap between White and Latino/a students has remained virtually the same, and the gaps for Native American students are even larger when compared to White students (USDE, 2005). Specifically, out of every 100 White kindergartners, 94 graduate from high school. Out of every 100 African American kindergartners, 88 graduate with a high school diploma. Out of every 100 Latino/a kindergarteners, 62 earn a high school diploma, and the numbers are even lower for Native American kindergartners (USDE, 2005).

To be outstanding advocates for all students, professional school counselors and their colleagues must understand their own biases, recognize potential harm when dealing with culturally diverse students and parents, and be open to change in personal worldviews. When professional school counselors and other educators have developed multicultural competencies, they can understand the social and political forces operating around and within the school community. When professional school counselors and other educators recognize their own inappropriate and potentially harmful beliefs, attitudes, actions, and inactions, they can see how these work against their students and change their attitudes and behaviors to advocate for students and challenge inappropriate practices and barriers that disproportionately harm students of color, poor students, students with disabilities, and students who are English-language learners. If this recognition does not occur, professional school counselors may never be a proactive force for social change, equity, and achievement advocacy.

With these changes come new challenges for professional school counselors who believe that "all students can learn." Becoming sensitive to cross-cultural issues in school counseling is an important step for a professional school counselor who hopes to be an advocate for all students. Adapting this professional stance allows the professional school counselor to see his or her students within a more correct environmental context and to possibly redefine the direction of his or her action. Instead of a stereotypical view of the student that focuses on the student and the student's family as the source of his or her problems, a socially responsive professional school counselor recognizes external oppressive forces built into the social, economic, and political framework of the school and community as potential problem sources. The student's problem may be a response to various oppressions, poverty, or some other factor related to the inequities that exist in schools, communities, or society in general. This redirects the professional school counselor's response to one of empowering the student to discover ways to deal with the problem and formalize a plan for success within the system.

In addition, the professional school counselor needs to advocate for and encourage change within the school community so that all students feel safe and are served academically and socially and given full access to career and college development information and curricula throughout their K–12 experience. This approach, part of a transformative school counseling program, will help the professional school counselor move beyond treating problems or issues as single incidents and begin to recognize the commonalities of these issues among groups of students (ASCA, 2003a). Another challenge facing professional school counselors arises from the distance felt between the school and its community. Busing and large consolidated systems have contributed to this dilemma. Consequently, professional school counselors need to make a connection between the school and each community that feeds into it for smooth and successful transitions for all students.

WHO NEEDS AN ADVOCATE AND WHY?

Who doesn't need an advocate? At some point in every person's, organization's, or community's life, an advocate is needed to promote and facilitate positive action. Advocacy, as an approach, is based on the belief that action must be taken (either individually or collectively) to improve the conditions of a group or to alleviate injustices faced by individuals or groups (R. M. House & Martin, 1998). Thus, professional school counselors can take action either individually or collectively to facilitate positive change to benefit individuals or groups or to right injustices. The transformative school counseling program ensures that all groups of students are given access and high-level achievement skills with measurable results (ASCA, 2003a). Because professional school counselors interface with individuals and groups daily, it is essential that they recognize the different needs of both and how transformative school counseling programs can influence both in a positive way by advocating on their behalf.

Students Need Academic Achievement Advocates

All students need an advocate at some time in their academic life. It is sometimes easy to label particular groups of students as being "at risk" or "the ones" who need advocates, but that labeling also creates a stigma and a deficit approach. A strengths-based argument can be made that some individuals might need an advocate more often or for more reasons than others, but to really change our schools and communities, it is crucial for people to recognize that all students can learn and become active and valued citizens in our communities.

Transformed school counseling programs advocate for all students and focus on students being "at promise" (Swadener & Lubeck, 1995).

If all students are to succeed, transformative school counseling program advocates are needed to remove barriers and undo stereotypes. The students in most need are often those who are students of color in low-level classrooms and who come from low-income families (R. M. House & Martin, 1998). Specific groups of children are often labeled, neglected, and left unchallenged and forgotten in the lowest tracks in our schools (J. A. Lewis & Arnold, 1998). These groups overwhelmingly include children of color (specifically, African American, Latino/a, and Native American children), children from low-income families, English-language learners (J. A. Lewis & Arnold, 1998), and children with disabilities. Native American and African American children are more likely to be classified as having a disability than are their White, Asian, or Latino/a peers, and the numbers of children in poverty and English-language learners continue to increase (USDE, 2005). These children need advocates who will ensure that they are academically challenged in school and placed in classes that will prepare them for college entry. These children need educators who will monitor the progress of entire groups of students of similar backgrounds in the school system and challenge inequitable practices such as tracking and low expectations, which often combine to create inequitable results (Nieto, 1999, 2004).

Students in gifted and talented programs are also in need of advocates. These students often do not receive what they need, especially if they also have disabilities or are children of color (Ford, 1996). There are also children who do adequately in school but do not excel in any particular area and, unfortunately, often go unnoticed. There are students who are left out, teased, or ostracized by other students and teachers because of a pervasive culture of heterosexism, transgenderism, religionism, classism, sexism, beautyism, and other forms of oppression (see chapter 5). Some students come from homes where they are neglected, abused, or merely tolerated. There are students whose parents push them so hard and have set standards so high that the student may cave in under the pressure. There is no single description of a student in need of an advocate; rather, it can be said that all students need an advocate. However, certain groups of students may have particular issues that professional school counselors will need to recognize and provide interventions to address through transformative school counseling programs.

African American, Latino/a, Native American, and Low-Income Students Need Advocates

Why do achievement, opportunity, and attainment gaps exist? Simply put, society often provides less to those who need more (Education Watch, 1998). Children from poorer schools are 10% less likely to be enrolled in eighth-grade algebra (NAEP, as cited in Education Watch, 1998). When adults are asked why there is an education gap, the common response has been, "The children are poor . . . Their parents don't care . . . They come to school without an adequate breakfast" (Education Watch, 1998, p. 10). Many educators place the blame on the parents and children; however, when children are asked about the education gap, their responses differ from the adults'. Children respond that their teachers are not qualified, the curriculum is boring and unchallenging, and their educators and counselors do not believe they can achieve at high levels (Education Watch, 1998). It should be

noted that while some parents may not be overwhelmingly involved in their child's school experience, that does not necessarily mean they do not care. Some parents just do not know how to be involved (see chapter 11). For many parents, the school is not a welcoming environment. One need only visit the main office of some schools to experience the unwelcoming atmosphere that many parents experience. This is especially true for people of color, people with low incomes, and people with limited English proficiency.

According to Education Watch (1998) and the USDE (2005), the research data support the children's views. The data indicate that students from low-income families and secondary school students of color are more likely to receive instruction from teachers lacking a college major or minor in the content area they are teaching. Further analysis of data suggests that African American and Latino/a students are even less likely to be taught by fully qualified teachers. Recent research on teacher quality and student performance indicates that students with similar initial achievement levels had huge differences (30–50 percentile rank points) in academic outcomes based on the teachers to whom they were assigned. For example, eighth-grade students scored better in math when their teachers were math majors. Unfortunately, a disproportionate number of students from low-income families and students of color (particularly Latino/a and African American students) receive math instruction from teachers who do not have a college major or minor in mathematics. African American and Latino/a students are less likely to have algebra integrated into their eighth-grade curriculum than are White and Asian students. Even more striking is that those attending high-poverty schools are 14% less likely to have algebra integrated into their eighth-grade mathematics curriculum. In high-poverty schools, students may receive an A for work that they would receive only a C or D for in affluent schools. The bottom line is that educators often do not expect poor students to perform as well as affluent students and have lowered the standards for these students. However, evidence suggests that students from low-income families will meet high standards if they are provided adequate support and quality instruction and are expected to meet these high standards (Brennan, 1999; Education Watch, 1998).

Perhaps of greatest concern is that even when African American students attend school with White students, they receive an education that is not only different, but also inferior (Irvine, 1991). African American males are three times more likely to be labeled as having mental retardation and placed in special education classes. Conversely, they are underrepresented in classes for the gifted and talented (Carnegie Corporation of New York, 1984–1985; Ford, 1996). African American students are more likely to be in vocational or general tracks rather than college preparatory classes (Education Watch, 1998).

While educators recognize that students have different abilities and learning styles, the most disturbing fact about tracking is that African American students and students from low-income families are more likely to be placed in these lower ability tracks (Irvine, 1991). An argument can be made that a disproportionate number of students from low-income families, including large numbers of African American students, are placed in lower tracks based on social class and not academic potential. According to Irvine, "[T]he instruction is inferior and ineffective, and students suffer psychologically and emotionally" (p. 11). The overrepresentation of African American students and students from low-income families in these low-ability groups perpetuates stereotypes that African American students are intellectually inferior to White students. The myth that students of color are intellectually inferior may be taking a severe psychological toll on these students and appears to lead some students to perform below their capabilities even when they are challenged academically (College Board, 1999a). It is imperative that professional school counselors address these inequities within our school systems and communities.

African American students are more likely to be subjected to severe disciplinary practices that exclude them from classes and increase their feelings of maltreatment, isolation, and rejection (Irvine, 1991). These feelings may contribute to an increase in misbehavior. Carnegie study data (1984–1985) indicated that African American students were likely to be suspended at a younger age and were more likely to receive lengthier and repeated suspensions than their White peers were. Perhaps even more disturbing is that African American students are disproportionately suspended and expelled (Carnegie Corporation of New York, 1984–1985; M. C. Taylor & Foster, 1986). Unfortunately, many educators stereotype African American students and perceive these students, especially males, to be sources of classroom disruption. Teachers inappropriately perceive these students' antischool behaviors to stem from impoverished home environments (Irvine, 1991). Discriminatory disciplinary practices increase the likelihood that African American students, particularly males, will miss more school. If students perceive unequal treatment to be race related, they may become hostile, alienated, and aggressive, which may lead to failure in school.

Certainly, not all the news on educational attainment is negative. The NAEP results show that students at every grade level and across most racial groups have increased their scores steadily since 1990 (Education Watch, 1998; USDE, 2005). However, on closer observation of the data, a disturbing pattern emerges. Although virtually all groups are achieving higher scores, White students and Asian/Pacific Islander students continue to outperform African American, Latino/a, and Native American students in both mathematics and reading (USDE, 2005).

When examining achievement, opportunity, and attainment gaps, how culture is perceived in the school cannot be ignored. African American children and White children come from different ethnic and racial backgrounds. Specifically, Black cultures contain the following interrelated attributes: spirituality, harmony, movement, exuberance, affect, communalism, expressive individualism, oral tradition, and social time perspective (Boykin, 1986). Irvine (1991) cautioned that to be color blind (not acknowledge racial differences) denies the students' heritage, culture, and ethnicity and may contribute to misunderstandings, hostilities, and confrontations between teachers and African American students. Irvine also purported that there are three cultural characteristics that may be particularly problematic for African American children in public schools. These include style, use of Black English, and cognition. Style includes nonverbal communication such as "getting or giving skin," standing stances, and walking styles (Irvine, 1991). Style also includes dress and interpersonal communication. African American children's behavior may be more animated, confrontational, intense, and demonstrative (Hanna, as cited in Irvine, 1991; Kochman, 1981). Language is an important factor because teachers often judge students' abilities based on their use of language, and Black English is often considered to be inferior and an indicator that the child has poorer intellectual ability (Irvine, 1991). In the area of cognition, it has been posed that African American children may process information differently (Anderson, 1988; Hilliard, as cited in Hale-Benson, 1986; Pasteur & Toldson, 1982; Shade, 1982), and because of this, their academic achievement in school may be negatively impacted (Irvine, 1991). Latino/a, Native American, and some Asian students are also affected by systemic racism, linguicism, and mistaken cultural perceptions in schools.

Unless school systems and school counseling programs make drastic changes in how they educate and counsel students from these groups, the achievement, opportunity, and attainment gaps will widen. The academic outlook for these students will continue to be an uphill struggle plagued by significant barriers in their pursuit of academic excellence.

Empowering Students with Achievement Advocacy Skills

Professional school counselors and school counseling programs play an important role by advocating on behalf of all students and teaching students how to advocate for themselves and others. What kind of advocates do students need? Students need an advocate who will recognize when student needs are not being heard or met and when they are being squashed emotionally and intellectually by the very systemic policies and procedures designed to enhance their emotional, physical, and intellectual well-being. Perhaps there is no more effective way to do this that to model advocacy behaviors. Advocacy should not end with the students. Professional

school counselors should also advocate on behalf of all students, parents and guardians, teachers, and communities. In addition, these individuals need to be taught to advocate on their own behalf (i.e., become self-advocates).

To be an effective advocate, one needs to have the conviction, knowledge, and skills to advocate (Ezell, 2001). Perhaps most important, the entire community and its individual members (including professional school counselors) need to believe that all students can excel (Education Watch, 1998; R. M. House & Martin, 1998). Furthermore, professional school counselors must be able to convey this belief and expectation to all students. Counselors can convey their belief and students' ability to achieve by assisting students in recognizing inequities that exist and by taking action to change practices that are unfair or inequitable. For example, if a student is placed in a lower-level academic class but has the potential to succeed in a more advanced class, the professional school counselor can step in and advocate on the student's behalf or advocate alongside the student. More broadly, students can be empowered to challenge tracking practices all together and insist that all students receive high-level curriculum in all classes. Advocating with the student simply means that the professional school counselor helps point out the condition; ensures the student has the necessary information to express the discrepancy; helps the student meet with the necessary parties (parents, teachers, administrators); and provides support and direction to the student before, during, and after meetings.

Professional school counselors must recognize when it is necessary for them to take the lead in advocating on behalf of students, and when it is more beneficial to play a supportive role. There will undoubtedly be occasions when the professional school counselor will attempt to advocate on behalf of a student, and the student and even parents or guardians will fear the professional school counselor's help. Being an advocate for students does not mean doing what is easy, but what is right for that particular student and his or her educational goals. Too often in the case of students of color, low academic expectations dictate the decision made by professional school counselors, administrators, parents and guardians, and even the students themselves. Professional school counselors acting as advocates for students must explain the reason for their decision and then stand firm. The Personal Reflection discussing student fears of achievement advocacy is an example of such a scenario.

Professional school counselors can help students recognize external barriers that impact their well-being and academic achievement and then assist students in formulating plans to confront these barriers (Toporek, 1999). It may be necessary for counselors to accompany students when they initially approach the identified barriers and then gradually encourage students to take the lead in advocating for themselves. Remember, involving the student in the process gives the student ownership and empowers the student.

Professional school counselors must actively remove barriers to student learning (R. M. House & Martin, 1998). This includes identifying cultural attitudes, stereotypes, and misunderstandings that lead to students being placed in environments that are not conducive to learning and achieving at high levels. Examples include students being tracked in lower level classes, students who are taught by underqualified teachers, and groups of students who are placed disproportionately in special education. Overwhelmingly, this includes young men of African American, Latino, and Native American ethnic and racial identities. However, it is not enough for counselors to assist students and their parents in recognizing these inequities. Professional school counselors must take action to resolve the identified inequities. For too long, professional school counselors have reacted to individual situations (Paisley & Borders, 1995) and have not acted on larger, systemic problems (Keys, Bemak, & Lockhart, 1998). When advocating for removable barriers, professional school counselors need to work at the systemic, not just the individual level. By doing so, professional school counselors are simultaneously modeling social advocacy behaviors and conveying support to students and their parents and guardians.

PERSONAL REFLECTION: Student Fears of School Counselor Achievement Advocacy

As a professional school counselor, educational leader, and student advocate, I would at times advocate for students and find students fearful about my advocacy. On one occasion, an African American male student requested a schedule change that would have removed him from an honors-level class, placing him in an average-level class. After reviewing the student's academic records, speaking with teachers regarding his academic performance and potential, and reviewing the student's goal to attend college, I denied the student's request. I explained to the student that when I compared his previous academic performance to his present performance (lack of effort evidenced by missed assignments and poor attendance), it was evident that his poor performance was not because he could not do the work, but because he chose not to do the work.

The student and his parents were not happy with my decision and went to the principal to appeal my decision. I was immediately summoned to the principal's office. After explaining how and why I made the decision I did (sharing with him the information from teachers, student records, and the student's desire to attend college), the principal informed me, "As a counselor you are oftentimes the student's last hope. Therefore, you should be advocating for the student." I was stunned that the principal could not see that I was being an advocate for the student. I was very confident that the student could handle the work in the upper-level course, and this course would strengthen the student's chances of being admitted into college. It was for this reason that I did not honor the student's request. In the end, the principal honored the student's request.

Think: Based on your knowledge of school counseling and advocacy, how would you have handled this situation? How do the professional school counselor and the principal differ in how they perceive and use advocacy? What advocacy strategies could the school counseling program develop if this situation arises in the future?

Professional school counselors are also in a position to teach students how to advocate on their own behalf, as well as on behalf of peers. Professional school counselors can do this on a group level by teaching students how to use conflict resolution skills and peer mediation, and by assisting students with organizational skills, study skills, and test-taking skills (R. M. House & Martin, 1998). Students also need to learn how to advocate for career-development and college-development skills in elementary, middle, and high school to ensure they are well prepared for their future. Students need to learn self-advocacy skills for two important reasons. First, it is essential that students become more active in the decisions that affect their academic careers (Getch, 1996). Studies indicate that when decisions are made for students, motivation to cooperate with learning and preparation goals can decrease substantially (Van Reusen, Bos, Schumaker, & Deshler, 1994). Second, learning self-advocacy skills can be empowering for students and may increase student motivation to achieve goals (J. Miller, 1992). Professional school counselors must recognize that acquiring advocacy skills is a developmental task that takes time, effort, and practice (J. A. Kelly, 1982; Wilkinson & Canter, 1982). Students learn through experience to recognize what is happening, how to evaluate the situation, how to formulate potential solutions, how to evaluate possible alternatives, how to pick the best option, and then how to execute their choice (J. A. Kelly, 1982; C. M. Nelson, 1988; Wilkinson & Canter, 1982). Professional school counselors can teach students these skills and then provide opportunities for students to practice these skills in low-risk environments with supports in place before students move to riskier situations that provide fewer supports (V. A. Johnson, 1996). Professional school counselors are in a unique position to teach these skills and provide students with practice environments that are supportive and contain relatively few risks.

Counselors can also educate students and their parents and guardians to manage the bureaucracy of the school system (R. M. House & Martin, 1998). Far too often, students or parents and guardians do not possess these skills. Parents and guardians often approach schools and school personnel as the authority. When schools make decisions, parents and guardians many times assume the professionals making these decisions are acting in the best interest of the child. Professional school counselors can step in and point out the inequities or injustices that are present, and then assist students and their parents or guardians through the bureaucratic labyrinth to ensure students receive what they need to succeed.

Professional school counselors assist students and their families by informing them of resources in the school and community and how to access these resources (R. M. House & Martin, 1998). Connecting parents or guardians and children to these resources is vital. Although this can be done in a traditional group fashion, professional school counselors must recognize that some students and families may need systemic assistance in accessing resources. Professional school counseling programs need to take a leadership role in ensuring all materials in the school are provided in languages spoken by parents and guardians, and that parents, guardians, and students receive specific information on accessibility issues and accommodations that can be provided for various disabilities (e.g., learning, emotional, physical, developmental). Financial and transportation resources as well as child care during parent/guardian–teacher nights and meetings are also essential to advocate for and ensure students have family involvement in their schooling.

Last, students need to be empowered to become leaders for life in their elementary, middle, and high school communities. Professional school counselors develop leadership academies and peer tutoring and peer counseling programs and encourage and expect all students to participate in extracurricular activities such as student government, athletics, the arts, and academic-related subjects to increase their leadership skills, which, in turn, can provide students with a basis to learn advocacy skills. Students need to be encouraged to evaluate the success of the school and the school counseling program through anonymous surveys and needs assessments, and student representation on the school counseling program advisory committee should be ensured (ASCA, 2003a).

Empowering Parents and Guardians with Achievement Advocacy Skills

Parents and guardians often approach schools and school personnel as the "authority." When parents and guardians present issues and the school answers, parents and guardians often take that information as fact, or accept that this is "just the way it is." Parents and guardians often do not understand the political or bureaucratic nature of schools (R. M. House & Martin, 1998) and may not know what to ask, how to ask, whom to ask, or where to go to obtain the information needed to help their children succeed (Friesen & Huff, 1990). Professional school counselors inform parents and guardians about how the school operates. Although parents and guardians are often strong advocates for their children, collaboration between parents and guardians and professional school counselors increases the effectiveness of advocacy.

Educational professionals, particularly professional school counselors, help identify resources and discuss existing services with parents and guardians (Friesen & Huff, 1990). Professional school counselors assist parents and guardians to maneuver through unfamiliar territories to access services. Professional school counselors assist parents and guardians to understand and interpret information received from the school and to understand their rights as parents or guardians through Web sites, brochures on the school and the school counseling program, bulletin boards, letters, and handouts. Once parents and guardians have the information they need in an understandable form, they may need assistance in determining how and when to use the information.

Parents and guardians are often faced with many barriers, including lack of respite care or appropriate child care, repeated crises that place a strain on the family, isolation, lack of transportation, financial difficulties, work schedule conflicts, time constraints, guilt, and, sometimes, stigma related to disability issues (Friesen & Huff, 1990). These barriers make it difficult for parents and

guardians to become involved in support groups and advocacy activities. Professional school counselors assist parents and guardians in identifying resources to access the services they need, thereby reducing barriers to participation in the activities that are so important to their children.

Parents and guardians may need assistance learning how to effectively communicate their needs, desires, and concerns. Assistance may involve teaching parents and guardians the mechanics of communication, including compromise, persuasion, and negotiation (Cunconan-Lahr & Brotherson, 1996). Parents and guardians also may need assistance in identifying who to include in communication efforts and what needs to be communicated. Assisting parents and guardians, especially those from diverse cultural backgrounds, in recognizing the best or most appropriate time to address issues or take calculated risks is an important school counseling program objective.

Professional school counselors recognize when it is necessary to advocate on behalf of parents and guardians, because parents and guardians may be reluctant to disagree with professionals they perceive as having expertise or power (Friesen & Huff, 1990). In these cases, professional school counselors collaborate with parents and guardians and educational professionals to remove barriers to achievement. Professional school counselors often recognize when educators distort or lack sensitivity to parent and guardian concerns. Professional school counselors explain the content of written reports that are meant for parent and guardian review, such as standardized test score reports and career- and college-development information and applications, especially when written in convoluted professional jargon (Friesen & Huff, 1990). At these times, professional school counselors ensure that parent and guardian concerns are heard, and written reports accurately reflect the reality of complicated situations. Some parents and guardians may not possess the skills or resources to advocate on their own or their child's behalf. The professional school counselor as advocate is vital in these instances.

Oftentimes, families become more frustrated when they become more knowledgeable about their rights (Friesen & Huff, 1990). Parents and guardians may advocate on behalf of their child and run into a brick wall. When this occurs, professional school counselors may bear the brunt of parental and guardian frustrations. Professional school counselors should be candid with parents and guardians (Friesen & Huff, 1990) and share knowledge about the system, possible roadblocks, and possible delays or red tape that may be encountered. This action allows professional school counselors to maintain open communication with parents and guardians. Such precautions often reduce long-term parent and guardian frustration. Parents and guardians can also be valuable members of school leadership teams and school counseling program advisory councils (ASCA, 2003a). Last, many schools have moved to hire a parent/guardian coordinator. Professional school counselors can easily collaborate with this person to empower parents and guardians as achievement advocates for all students in schools.

Empowering Educators with Achievement Advocacy Skills

Professional school counselors assist teachers and other educators in recognizing inequities that exist in the school system and use data to correct them (ASCA, 2003a). These inequities include differential treatment of students from low- and middle- or high-income families, students of color and White students, students who are intellectually gifted and average, students with and without disabilities, and students who speak only English and students who are learning English and speak a different native language. Professional school counselors encourage and challenge teachers to examine their own biases and practices. Challenging teachers to do this has a risk, but it is imperative to do so if school counseling programs and schools in general are to change so that all students can achieve. In many ways, teachers are the school environment, and professional school counselors must encourage teachers to create an environment that supports all students, with data and evidence showing that all students learn at high levels in every classroom.

When professional school counselors witness stereotyping and self-fulfilling prophecies in action based on ignorance and misinformation about certain groups of students, it is their duty to challenge the misinformation as systematic advocates. What should professional school counselors do when overhearing teachers making defeatist statements like, "Kids from homes like that are doomed," "What do they expect us to do with 'those' children?" and "Why should I have to have a child with a disability in my class?" These statements clearly indicate biases, and these teachers do not believe that all students can learn and achieve. Professional school counselors can provide annual formal in-service training (Gysbers & Henderson, 1994) and frequent informal informational sessions or activities aimed at increasing teacher knowledge and effectiveness (Henderson & Gysbers, 1998). Informal activities might include sharing success stories, sharing empirical research, utilizing technology (e.g., Web pages, e-mail, etc.), discussing the professional school counselor's role, consulting with teachers (Ribak-Rosenthal, 1994), and using evidence-based practices collected by the Education Trust's National Center for Transforming School Counseling (2005b). Perhaps of greatest importance is that professional school counselors consistently model advocacy behaviors both systemically and individually. Not all teachers have the requisite skills to effectively work with students, parents and guardians, or administrators. Professional school counselors have training in communication, interpersonal relationships, problem solving, conflict resolution (M. Clark & Stone, 2000), collaboration, and team building that enables them to promote collaboration among school personnel, thereby promoting high achievement for all students. Teachers may look to the professional school counselor for assistance in solving classroom-management problems, problems with parents and guardians, specific learning issues with students, career and college development and counseling for students, and collegial support. Professional school counselors assist teachers in developing management, facilitation, and advocacy skills.

Professional school counselors provide in-service training on effective classroom-management skills and assist teachers in learning techniques to create a safe, equitable, and learner-friendly environment for all students. Professional school counselors also work with teachers to assist them in learning to more effectively communicate with parents and administrators. Training should include multicultural information so counselors can effectively communicate and collaborate with persons from various economic, linguistic, ethnic or racial, and other cultural backgrounds and with those with disabilities. Professional school counselors can assist teachers in advocating on behalf of students and parents and guardians by providing them with strategies and skills to facilitate the development and use of advocacy skills. Teachers who advocate genuinely care about students' needs, concerns, desires, and growth (Gatta, McCabe, & Edgar, 1997). Unfortunately, teachers are not typically taught advocacy skills, and some may not feel that advocacy is a teacher's responsibility. To be a true advocate, one must speak out about injustice and work to abolish barriers to students' success, well-being, and academic achievement.

Professional school counselors can encourage teachers to become leaders within the school and community. Strong leaders who believe in the potential of all students can change the school environment and influence others into making changes that facilitate the inclusion and achievement of all students. Professional school counselors can inform teachers of learning opportunities and should encourage teachers to become involved in the community.

It may be as simple as organizing a community service project for the year, whereby teachers participate in a project that facilitates interaction with people that they might not otherwise have an opportunity to meet. Professional school counselors can also encourage teachers to participate in school events and as extracurricular advisors for sporting events, club activities, recitals, art exhibitions, contests, and so forth. When teachers become actively involved in the school community and the larger community, they are more likely to recognize the needs, issues, and inequities that exist. Getting involved outside of regular academics provides teachers with an opportunity to network with others. In turn, students notice and appreciate teachers who take the time to attend events, and may internalize these efforts as evidence that teachers believe in them and support their efforts.

Most importantly, school counseling programs ensure that specific academic, career, college, and personal–social competencies are defined and delivered each year to all students. Working collaboratively with teachers as advocates to deliver developmental school counseling lessons in each of these areas is a key part of achievement advocacy. The ASCA *National Model* (2003a) delineates delivery of the school counseling curriculum as a shared task that is planned and systemic each year for each grade level. Successful school counseling programs have strong teacher input and collaboration and ensure that teachers are a vital

PERSONAL REFLECTION: Asthma Medication in a Secure Location

When my child was entering kindergarten, I met with the school principal to discuss his medical needs and to arrange for him to have his asthma medication with him at all times. When I asked about this, I was informed, "Medications must be in a secure location at all times . . . we keep them in the school office." I persisted and explained that my child needed his rescue inhaler with him at all times. I was then informed, "State policy requires that medication must be in a secure location." At that point in time, I said, "I'm aware of that, but if

necessary we can write a 504 plan to ensure he is able to keep his medication with him at all times." When I said that, the principal looked at me in a surprised manner (I could almost hear her thinking, "Oh no, informed parent here") and said, "Well, I'm sure we can work it out."

Think: How can a school counseling program help parents, guardians, and teachers understand the procedures for ensuring that children with special needs are well cared for in terms of individual and systemic advocacy policies and practices?

component of the school counseling program advisory committee (ASCA, 2003a).

Empowering School Systems for Achievement Advocacy

Professional school counselors work with students, parents, guardians, teachers, administrators, and all other school personnel. Working as a team is important; the most important task ensuring success of the school counseling program is for administrators to be "on board" and supportive of these efforts. Some principals may fail to support professional school counseling programs because of previous experiences with ineffective counselors (Keys, Bemak, Carpenter, & King–Sears, 1998). Educating principals and other administrative staff on the changing roles of professional school counselors and the key function of systemic advocacy for achievement is important. However, professional school counselors must keep in mind that principals are in charge of the schools (Henderson & Gysbers, 1998). Building effective relationships with principals and other administrators is essential if counselors are to take advocacy-related risks and become change agents within schools through school counseling programs. Several strategies that enhance relationships between counselors and administrators include maintaining a respectful demeanor, communicating effectively and often, and asking for overt signs of support for the school counseling program.

Professional school counselors can improve communication and be more effective in team building if they involve the principal and other administrators in school counseling activities. Professional school counselors may invite principals to attend education, career, or college information sessions; school counseling curriculum lesson planning sessions; conferences with parents and guardians; and other activities that do not breach confidentiality (Ribak–Rosenthal, 1994). Formal and informal meetings can also enhance communication among counselors and administrators because they provide an opportunity to not only share information, but also to build rapport. They also offer a mechanism whereby professional school counselors can bring forward ideas and

issues that impact students, teachers, and schools, ideally in school leadership team meetings where the professional school counselor is seen as an essential figure in advocating for academic achievement for all students.

Professional school counselors need to work collaboratively with all school personnel (R. M. House & Martin, 1998). To do this, counselors must utilize their skills in interpersonal communication, group process, human development, multiculturalism, assessment, leadership, advocacy, and counseling. Working collaboratively also means that all school personnel have an understanding of the role of the professional school counselor. Unfortunately, many administrators assign counselors inappropriate activities that are unrelated to counseling and are not cost effective (Hardesty & Dillard, 1994; Henderson & Gysbers, 1998; Hutchinson & Reagan, 1989). These activities may undermine the effectiveness of professional school counselors when they attempt to work with students, parents, guardians, teachers, and other school personnel (Henderson & Gysbers, 1998).

Professional school counselors provide staff development training and research data to promote system change (R. M. House & Martin, 1998). Staff development training should include emphasis on promoting high standards and expectations for all students. Counselors can share success stories of schools that have emphasized high achievement for all students, and case studies as telling examples of how important expectations are in achieving academic success. Counselors can also use these opportunities to "challenge the existence of low-level and unchallenging courses" (R. M. House & Martin, 1998, p. 289). As long as low-level courses exist, schools perpetuate old ideas that some students can achieve and others cannot. Many schools continue to disproportionately place students of color, students from low-income families, students with disabilities, and students who are English-language learners in these low-level courses. Thus, the students who need the most receive the least (Education Watch, 1998), and their academic, career, college, and personal–social opportunities are diminished by the actions, policies, and practices of educators and administrators.

Professional school counselors need to be visible in the school and the community in delivering the school counseling program. To do this, they must be out of their offices and in the classrooms, delivering school counseling curriculum lessons, as well as in public areas of the school on a daily basis (Cormany & Brantley, 1996). Professional school counselors need to be seen and involved. They should be proactive and implement outreach programs to inform students about educational, career, college, and social–emotional opportunities; motivate students to achieve at high levels; dispel myths that are harmful to students; and provide opportunities for students to develop their talents (Hart, & Jacobi, 1992). It is difficult to predict problems that may occur if the professional school counselor is not out and about in the school, communicating with students and school personnel. Visibility and accessibility are the keys, and administrators may be more apt to provide support when they view professional school counselors and school counseling programs as active, integral players in the achievement and success of students and schools.

Professional school counselors and school counseling programs assist administrators in creating student-, parent-, and guardian-friendly schools. These schools communicate that students, parents, and guardians are valued members of the community, and their input and presence are welcome. One of the most important values to convey is that all children and adolescents are expected to excel. Creating an environment that empowers students and parents and guardians enhances communication and collaboration among students, parents, guardians, and educators. When a safe, welcoming environment is established, it is more likely that parents, guardians, and students will communicate their concerns and needs to school personnel. This open communication creates an opportunity to recognize the needs and disparities that exist in schools and provides an avenue for productive, cooperative change.

Finally, administrators are welcomed as a key part of the school counseling programs' Advisory Committee (ASCA, 2003a) and assist in creating goals and objectives for the year for each grade level and the benchmarks that will be used to assess the results of the school counseling program in terms of student achievement each year.

Empowering Community Stakeholders with Achievement Advocacy Skills

Outside of the school environment, professional school counselors are presented with unique opportunities to work with the community as a whole. School counseling programs should have networks to connect parents, guardians, children,

---

PERSONAL REFLECTION: Individual Education Plan (IEP) Notice

One day, my partner called me at work in an absolute panic. He had opened our child's school folder and there was a letter requesting an IEP meeting. The letter stated that our child qualified for services and was signed by an SLP. There was no information explaining what the meeting was for (other than it was an IEP meeting) and a specific meeting time was set for us to check whether or not we would attend. My partner asked me, "What has our child done wrong now? Is there something going on that I don't know about? What in the world is an 'SLP'?" Fortunately, I am familiar with the terminology and reminded my partner that we had requested that our child's speech be evaluated earlier in the year, and that the letter indicates that he apparently qualifies for speech therapy. "SLP" is simply short for "Speech Language Pathologist." My partner's comment was, "Well, why didn't they tell us that in the letter?" The letter was a form letter; there was no information in the letter indicating that he had his speech evaluated and that the evaluation indicated a need for services. The letter merely stated that he qualified for services and requested our presence at an IEP meeting.

Think: How can a school counseling program ensure that institutional communications to parents and guardians build partnerships instead of raise defenses and concerns?

PERSONAL REFLECTION: But You Are Deaf

Exclusionary Practices Based on Disability

Todd and Bill had participated in a summer research project where they learned self-advocacy skills. More specifically, they learned how to be active participants in their IEP meetings. Both Todd and Bill were deaf and were getting ready to enter sixth grade. When Todd picked up his schedule, he realized he had been signed up for art as an elective. Todd went to his resource teacher and said, "I don't want art. I want music." The resource teacher said, "But you are deaf." Todd then said, "Do the other kids get to choose their elective?" The resource teacher said they did, and then Todd said, "Then my choice is music! I know that the other kids get to choose; then it is my right to choose." Todd's schedule was changed. When Todd met up with Bill, Bill was complaining that he had been assigned an art elective and he wanted music. Todd said, "Bill, remember the class this summer? You can choose music; it is your right!" Bill had his schedule changed too.

---

and adolescents with resources that will help all students succeed (R. M. House & Martin, 1998). Professional school counselors also can assist parents, guardians, and school personnel in organizing community efforts to assist schools in instituting a higher standard for all children and adolescents. To do this, professional school counselors must be involved in the community and be aware of available organizations and resources. Herr (as cited in Hart & Jacobi, 1992) suggested that professional school counselors should enlist the support of various community organizations, including civic organizations, places of worship, businesses, colleges, social service agencies, and individual volunteers. Unfortunately, important parties are often left out of the collaborative efforts of professional school counseling programs. These untapped resources include physicians, local mental health resources, politicians, lawyers, support groups, and other leaders in the community.

Connecting parents and guardians with organizations creates a network of support that can be used to change schools at a systems level. Professional school counselors encourage community involvement in education and facilitate activities that promote and provide support for students' academic achievement (Hart & Jacobi, 1992). Networking within the community facilitates the development of quality services and opportunities for students and encourages the development of a community culture that supports, values, and expects all students to succeed.

In doing so, the professional school counseling program can play an important role in integrating the community into the schools, thereby supporting and promoting system changes that will enhance the educational opportunities for all students. Community members also play a critical role as a part of the school counseling program's advisory council and are encouraged to take an active role in shaping the implementation and evaluation of the school counseling program each year (ASCA, 2003a).

PUBLICIZING THE PROFESSIONAL SCHOOL COUNSELING PROGRAM'S ROLE AS ACHIEVEMENT ADVOCATE FOR ALL STUDENTS

Both internal and external publics are important in the ongoing dialogue about the role and function of professional school counselors and school counseling programs. Internal publics include students, parents, guardians, educators, and other school system employees. The external public includes those outside of the school system who have a stake in student success, including politicians, businesses, agencies, and the general community. Part of the professional school counselor's essential role in schools is to ensure that school counseling programs are defined and affirmed as supporting the academic, career, college, emotional, personal, and social success of all learners in a school and use data to back up their results (ASCA, 2003a). If school counseling programs do not function in the role of achievement advocates for all students with demonstrable results, in an era of tight school budgets, professional school counselors are seen as expendable. The reality is that, most recently, the media have covered professional school counselors only during times of crisis, primarily during acts of violence occurring on school grounds. Rare is the news story that discusses the proactive role professional school counselors play daily in schools through comprehensive developmental school counseling programs. Professional school counselors need to create advisory councils that will assist in getting the word out inside and outside the school about the essential achievement advocacy function of school counseling programs.

Many superintendents, principals, teachers, and other related school personnel know little about what professional school counselors or school counseling programs do for student success. Therefore, professional school counselors and school counseling programs must undertake specific internal and external public relations strategies to spread the word about the professional school counseling program's role and mission in the school as academic success and achievement advocates for all students. The more aware all members of the school and community are regarding the professional school counselor's role and the role of the school counselor's role and the role of the school counseling program, the better the support from all stakeholders.

A strong internal and external public relations effort is essential to ensure that school counseling programs delivered by state-certified professional school counselors are seen by others as central to the school's mission of educating all students effectively. First, professional school counselors, school counseling programs, and their allies need to target external publics such as legislators, local politicians, community-based organization workers, clergy and members of places of worship, and workers in businesses and explain the specific benefits provided by professional school counselors through school counseling programs.

Second, internal publics such as students, teachers, administrators, parents and guardians, school social workers and psychologists, school counseling and teaching practicum and internship students, school secretaries, janitors, lunchroom personnel, and bus drivers must be informed of the professional school counselor's role and the school counseling program mission, services, activities, competencies, and achievement results (ASCA, 2003a) to ensure that professional school counselors are not relegated to only pushing paper, responding to crises, or providing discipline. As professional school counselors' job descriptions and roles as achievement advocates are developed and clarified, professional school counseling programs must publicize to internal and external publics their roles as academic leaders, advocates, team members and collaborators, users of data for assessment of academic success, counselors and coordinators, and vital members of the school possessing multicultural and technology competencies (Education Trust, 2000).

When school counseling programs put achievement advocacy for all students at the center of their work, they become invaluable to the mission of all schools. When professional school counselors are seen as leaders, change agents, and persons able to challenge systemic and institutional barriers to learning, and demonstrate how to use data to ensure that all students have the resources and high expectations to succeed in school through school counseling programs, everyone benefits from the refocused vision. Proactive professional school counselors who publicize their work in academic, career, college, emotional, personal, and social success for all students demonstrate how school counseling programs are successfully implementing *ASCA National Standards* (C. Campbell & Dahir, 1997; Dahir, Sheldon, & Valiga, 1998) and the *ASCA National Model* (ASCA, 2003a).

From Gatekeepers of the Status Quo to Promoting Advocacy for Systemic Change and Leadership in Schools

In the past, many professional school counselors and school counseling programs have been criticized for helping maintain the status quo in schools (Hart & Jacobi, 1992). Professional school counselors and school counseling programs have been criticized for neglecting or unfairly judging students, particularly if they were: (a) students of color, particularly African, African American, Caribbean, Latino/a, or Native American; (b) tracked in low- or middle-ability groups; (c) uninterested in or perceived as unable to handle college preparatory class material; (d) bilingual or spoke Black English or English with an accent or lacked fluency in English as a second language; (e) students with one or more developmental, emotional, physical, or learning disabilities; (f) girls seen as not needing college or careers; (g) boys seen as having too many discipline problems to be good students; (h) perceived as less than worthy of success due to being lesbian, bisexual, gay, transgendered, or gender variant; (i) from a nontraditional family; (j) an immigrant; (k) seen as having a nontraditional appearance, including being overweight; or (l) from a nondominant religious or spiritual belief system. In other words, professional school counselors used various forms of oppression to unfairly sort students based on biases toward children and youth with nondominant race, class, gender, sexual orientation, gender identity or expression, disability, language, family type, religion/spirituality, and other cultural identities (Chen–Hayes, 2000; Chen-Hayes et al., 2000; Herring, 1997b; R. Johnson, 1996, 2002; Nieto, 2004).

There is a significant body of literature that includes anecdotal evidence of similar patterns on the part of many professional school counselors (Gandara, 1995; R. Johnson, 1996; Nieto, 1996, 1999, 2004). It is after incidents such as these that public awareness and support for professional school counselors and school counseling programs takes on such urgency—challenging past practices and demonstrating how professional school counselors and school counseling programs have changed to include academic success for all students and achievement advocacy as the top priority (ASCA, 2003a, 2004b). So not only do professional school counselors and school counseling programs need to publicize their changing roles and the data-based results of their successes, but they must also recognize that

there is just as much work to be done with adults in schools and communities who had poor experiences with professional school counselors.

One way to overcome past difficulties is for professional school counselors and school counseling programs to take on advocacy roles for academic, career, and college success for all students. C. Lee and Walz (1998) and Lewis and Bradley (2000) defined the counselor's role as a social change agent and as an advocate in schools and communities. Information about counselor advocacy efforts to create academic success, high standards, and high aspirations for all students is welcome news to most parents, guardians, teachers, and principals. However, most remain unclear regarding the professional school counselor's role as academic success advocate for all students (R. Johnson, 1996) through a school counseling program (ASCA, 2003a).

Nieto's (1999, 2004) recent work about outstanding school reform efforts contains an excellent set of recommendations for professional school counselors interested in public relations and support from an advocacy perspective. She states that the best school reform promoted equity for all students through access to learning in five areas. According to Nieto (1999), positive school reform (a) is antiracist and antibias, (b) reflects that all students have talents and strengths that can enhance their education, (c) is based on the notion that those most intimately connected with students need to be meaningfully involved in their education, (d) is based on high expectations and rigorous standards for all learners, and (e) is empowering and just. This framework for equitable educational reform in all schools meshes with the school counseling program's advocacy role for all students' academic success and achievement in careers and college.

Savvy Ways to Send the Message of Professional School Counseling Programs as Achievement Advocates

Professional school counseling programs have a multitude of ways in which they can promote public support and awareness. R. Johnson (1996) and the *ASCA National Model* (ASCA, 2003a) discussed the importance of all schools' having a mission or vision statement focused on academic success and achievement for all students. School counseling programs should also have a mission statement aligned with the school's mission. The mission or vision statement then guides all functions of the school and school counseling program and is written specifically in terms of the results that all students will achieve based on participation in a school counseling program (ASCA, 2003a). Schmidt (2003) listed important ways to market and publicize the professional school counselor's role and function as part of a school counseling program, including (a) print and Web-based brochures, (b) a professional school counselor's column in the school or local newspaper, (c) use of Web sites and a school counseling program page, (d) speaking engagements at local events, and (e) classroom presentations. In addition, Schmidt (2003) advocated attention to (a) outreach in print formats such as newsletters, handouts, bulletin boards and disclosure statements; (b) uses of technology, including Web sites, interactive communications with parents and teachers via e-mail, and providing computer training for parents; (c) school counseling program advisory boards; and (d) building partnerships with other community members interested in the academic, career, and interpersonal success of children, youth, and families. Each of these ideas is an effective way of spreading the word about the professional school counselor's essential role as an academic success advocate.

Similarly, the ACA's Public Awareness and Support Committee developed a comprehensive set of guidelines for promoting public awareness and support for professional counselors. Attention to internal and external public relations, according to activities in the ACA public awareness and support packet, includes the need for professional school counselors to deliver speeches and presentations and to work with the media to get the word out about professional counseling programs in schools and communities. Specific suggestions that are applicable to professional school counselors include: (a) call or write TV, radio, cable, and newspapers in your area to promote the latest activities or awards for the school counseling program and the students it serves; (b) interview current and former students, parents, administrators, and teachers related to how professional school counseling programs made a difference in their lives; (c) create a school counseling program Web page to promote the school counseling program on the Internet; (d) create a school counseling program Listserv and encourage local media to have access to it for story ideas and questions related to referrals; (e) sponsor specific community or school events of a developmental nature and ask local media to cover them to publicize the school counseling program's role in prevention efforts; (f) request that professional school counselor license plates be offered by your state to promote the profession's visibility externally; and (g) advocate with local and state legislators to better fund and support school counseling programs (ACA, 2000b).

Professional school counselors and school counseling programs are a vital resource in the school for all persons. Using an academic achievement advocacy framework for all learners, coupled with the importance of addressing career, college, emotional, personal, and social issues, professional school counselors and school counseling programs have an important message to share in assisting students, their families, and educators in a successful learning process in schools. Using recent models of school counseling focused on ensuring academic success and high expectations for all students, professional school counselors can convey the importance and power of school counseling programs to internal and external publics (ASCA, 2003a, 2004b; Education Trust, 2005c). Using both traditional print and technological resources, as well as public speaking opportunities both inside the classroom and in community meetings far outside the school's walls, it is easier and more important than ever to effectively publicize and support the new focused mission of professional school counselors as academic achievement advocates for all students.

SUMMARY/CONCLUSION

Historically, the rhetoric has been that all kids can learn. Unfortunately, quality resources and opportunities are not allocated to all children in schools nor by all school counseling programs. Research substantiates that particular groups of children and adolescents in the United States are consistently provided fewer resources and substandard teachers and attend schools where administrators, teachers, and some politicians do not believe they can achieve at high levels, all resulting in achievement, opportunity, attainment, and funding gaps (Education Trust, 2005b; Education Watch, 1998). These children are often inappropriately labeled "at risk." Being at risk is often situational and too often based on poor practices used by educators that fail students, rather than students failing in schools on their own. School administrators, teachers, and communities can alleviate some risk by providing all students with qualified, well-trained teachers who affirm diversity (Nieto, 1999, 2004) and who truly believe that all students can achieve at high levels, transforming students "at risk" into students "at promise" (Swadener & Lubeck, 1995).

Professional school counselors and school counseling programs are in a critical position to initiate positive changes promoting high achievement because they have great opportunities to interface with all students, teachers, school administrators, and the community. Professional school counselors and the transformative school counseling program must be a link between schools and communities. They should be visible in schools and communities and recognized as achievement advocates for all students. To be achievement advocates, professional school counselors must have the requisite advocacy skills, consultation skills, commitment, and energy necessary to work with parents, teachers, administrators, civic organizations, agencies, and the community at large, and the ability to deliver these skills to students in measurable ways. To truly make a difference, professional school counselors and school counseling programs must be action-oriented risk takers whose actions demonstrate belief that all students can learn and all students deserve the academic, career-development, and college-development resources to access the very best educational opportunities beyond K–12 schooling.

Professional school counselors and school counseling programs recognize that nondominant ethnic/racial identity, socioeconomic status, disabilities, and English-learning status often are used unfairly by educators to create barriers to learning and achievement success on the part of all K–12 students (Nieto, 2004). Professional school counselors and school counseling programs advocate for the elimination of barriers faced by students from all nondominant cultural identity groups. Children attending some lower funded schools are excelling because these schools have removed barriers, expected all children to succeed, and provided the necessary opportunities for achieving excellence (Brennan, 1999).

Professional school counselors position themselves as achievement advocates for all students and an integral part of the school and the community. We challenge you to become facilitators of change, embracing the challenge inherent in becoming a risk taker as you create, develop, implement, and evaluate the results of your school counseling program. Furthermore, we challenge you to become exemplary role models of achievement advocacy for our colleagues in school counseling and other professions and to generate data showing how your school counseling program makes a difference for all students at your school.

Now go to our Companion Website at www.prenhall.com/erford to assess your understanding of chapter content with "Multiple-Choice Questions," apply comprehension with "Essay Questions," and broaden your knowledge of the school counseling profession with related "Web Links."

Case Study

Tyler and the Bully

Tyler is a 7-year-old first grader who has a growth disorder that makes him much smaller than even the smallest kindergartners. One night, Tyler told his mom that his privates hurt, and on investigation, his mom found a bruise on his penis. When she asked what happened, Tyler explained that a fourth grader had kicked him while he was waiting to get on the bus after school. His mom asked if this was the only time he had been kicked, and Tyler sadly said, "No, Mom, this kid punches me in the stomach or kicks me every day." His mom asked how long this had been going on, and Tyler replied, "I don't know, a long time—it's so long I can't remember when it started." When his mom asked if he had told a teacher, Tyler replied, "Momma, that would be tattling. I'm not a tattletale!" His mom asked if there were other kids around, and Tyler said there were, but they just watched. Tyler's mom was upset and called Tyler's teacher, who said she'd talk with the professional school counselor. Tyler's grades had been sinking for some time now, and his mom was very worried about his safety and his academics. When Tyler returned home from school the next day, his mom asked him if the kid had kicked or punched him. Tyler said, "No, he had to apologize to me, and he spent, like, the whole day in the principal's office."

1. Based on your knowledge regarding school counseling, in what way(s) did the professional school counselor and administrator demonstrate advocacy for Tyler?
2. What additional steps would you have taken to ensure Tyler's safety?
3. What specific policies and procedures should be in place to handle issues of bullying and school violence?
4. Should the "principal's office" be the only remediation for the bully?
5. What systemic advocacy approaches should you take if you discover that multiple students are being bullied throughout the school and there is no "bully-proofing" program being offered in the school?

CREATING A SYSTEMIC, DATA-DRIVEN SCHOOL COUNSELING PROGRAM

VIVIAN V. LEE AND GARY E. GOODNOUGH

Editor's Introduction: A systemic, data-driven school counseling program is an essential part of any K–12 education. It is responsible for supporting student achievement and forms the foundation for career and personal–social development. This chapter outlines systemic, data-driven procedures that, when coupled with the ASCA *National Standards* and *National Model,* address practical program implementation issues. A thorough understanding of a comprehensive developmental school counseling program sets the stage for comprehending the integration of the varied school counseling services presented in subsequent chapters.

The new vision of school counseling for the 21st century is to integrate the work of professional school counselors and programmatic interventions into the mission of schools. Today the mission of schools is driven by accountability mandates such as NCLB. Implicit in these mandates is an overarching belief that all students can achieve to high levels when provided with equitable access to rigorous academic preparation that readies them for college and other postsecondary opportunities. In the new vision, all students are taught by highly qualified professionals in a safe and drug-free learning environment that is both culturally responsive and inclusive to all diverse populations in the school community. This mission of schools is designed to close access, attainment, and achievement gaps between all student groups and the gap between achievement and academic standards set forth for all students. To be integral to the new mission, school counseling programs need to demonstrate the value-added role of counselors and their programs through measurable results directly linked to the achievement of all students, especially students from underrepresented populations. The *ASCA National Model* (ASCA, 2003a) supports the success of students from diverse populations through "closing the gap" activities. These activities can be most effective at closing achievement gaps when they emerge from an intentional systemic data-driven approach.

There is a real need for systemic data-driven school counseling programs. Citing the Education Trust (1997), the ASCA *National Model* (2003a) supports data-driven approaches as they create "urgency for change" and expose "evidence of access and equity issues for focused advocacy and interventions" (p. 49). The most critical point in developing and implementing effective systemic school counseling programs is that *the system* is as much the client as the individual student is (A. Green & Keys, 2001). This premise allows interventions to focus on transforming the system and all the subsystems to meet the needs of students, rather than maintaining the status quo and trying to transform or fix students.

Systemic transformation is achieved by placing the individual at the center of the system and examining the relations between, and expectations of, larger subsystems that impact the individual, such as school, family, community, and society. Additionally, because systemic approaches highlight the interconnectedness and interdependence of all subsystems within a school, they are more likely to address policy and procedural barriers to access, achievement, and attainment (Bemak, 2000; A. Green & Keys, 2001; Keys & Bemak, 1997; Keys & Lockhart, 1999). Moreover, when school counseling programs are developed and implemented using multilevel systemic approaches based on relevant data such as the data elements cited under NCLB, interventions become a focused and intentional response to students' academic, career, and personal–social needs. Finally, a systemic data-driven approach focuses on the structure of schools and supports embedding school counseling interventions across multiple levels of the educational program. The use of multilevel interventions across the school and community addresses complex social and cultural challenges in urban, suburban, and rural settings (A. Green & Keys, 2001; Sutton & Pearson, 2002). In this way, systemic data-driven school counseling programs enliven the transformed role of the professional school counselor

and provide a dynamic framework that is a reflection of the needs and goals of the entire school community. The main purpose of this chapter is to articulate the central components of a systemic data-driven program that reflects the new vision of school counseling.

A NEW VISION OF SCHOOL COUNSELING: PROGRAM DEFINITION

In the late 1990s, with the advent of the *ASCA National Standards* (C. Campbell & Dahir, 1997), a comprehensive school counseling program was defined as:

> . . . developmental in nature. It is systematic, sequential, clearly defined, and accountable. The foundation of the program is developmental psychology, educational philosophy, and counseling methodology. Proactive and preventive in focus, the school counseling program is integral to the educational program. It assists students in acquiring and using life-long skills through the development of academic, career, self-awareness, and interpersonal skills. The goal of the comprehensive school counseling program is to provide all students with life success skills. (p. 9)

The new vision of school counseling remains developmental, preventive, systematic, sequential, and clearly defined. While these concepts continue to guide the planning, implementation, and evaluation of a school counseling program, the new vision moves beyond this to a truly systemic data-driven school counseling program rooted in educational equity for all students, especially students from traditionally underserved populations. The difference in these two conceptualizations is that the new vision is grounded in the principles of systems theory described above. If a program is not grounded in these principles, it cannot be considered systemic. Additionally, it is important here to differentiate between systemic and systematic. Without attention to the principles of systems, school counseling programs can offer interventions in a systematic fashion that are not necessarily designed for systemic impact. Data-driven systemic programs impact the entire system and conduct interventions and services that are intentionally planned and delivered on a systemic level. All of those conditions are necessary for a school counseling program to be systemic. The new vision for all students is systemic in that it promotes holistic development, nurtures the uniqueness of each individual, and supports his or her aspirations and goals for the future. This vision is transformed into a specific mission based on the data and context of each individual school. The vision of a school counseling program concretizes the belief that all students not only can dream of success, but can achieve it as well. Table 7.1 demonstrates the development of a systemic data-driven school counseling program.

Commitment to Social Justice

A commitment to social justice and educational equity expands the awareness of all members of the school community, and thus increases the likelihood that all students will have equitable access to the school counseling program. Such a commitment is ensconced in the preamble of the ASCA *Code of Ethics* (2004a): The school counseling program

> . . . advocates for and affirms all students from diverse populations regardless of ethnic/racial status, age, economic status, special needs, English as a second language or other language

group, immigration status, sexual orientation, gender, gender identity/expression, family type, religious/spiritual identity and appearance.

Not only do systemic school counseling programs promote social justice through counseling services, but they extend attention to interventions that include the entire school community.

Mission of the Program

School counseling program mission statements address the overarching belief about all students and the global goals of the program. A school's or district's mission statement provides the foundation for the school counseling program and states the collective results desired for all students (S. Johnson & Johnson, 2003). As with goals, for the mission to become an integral part of the overall school mission, it must reflect and parallel basic tenets of belief and the purpose of the educational mission of the state, the district, and the school. Additionally, if the state and district have school counseling mission statements, the basic tenets and beliefs of these statements should also be reflected in the school's mission statement. A clear and concise mission statement impacts programmatic implementation and evaluation.

Mission statements can be written in a variety of ways. Some state a mission along with a programmatic philosophy and then state specific principles and objectives. Some include the role of the professional school counselor as advocate

TABLE 7.1
Data-driven systemic school counseling programs.

Vision	=	Social justice
Mission	=	Access and equity
Structure	=	Systemic
Goals	=	Data driven
Programs	=	Integrated with educational program
Implementation	=	Systemic, strategic, and systematic
Interventions	=	Multilevel and systemic
Evaluation	=	Accountability
Counselor skill	=	Transformed role
Result	=	Close the access, achievement, and attainment gaps

and collaborator focused on access to meet future societal needs. Others are longer and indicate within the statement their support of district and state mission statements. Yet others can be written to demonstrate the linkages with national and state school counseling associations and educational missions. Regardless of how a mission statement is written, the most critical point is that it sets the foundation for the program to serve all students. For example, the Newport News, Virginia (Newport News Public Schools, 2002), counseling program mission statement and program philosophy read as follows:

> The mission of the Newport News Public Schools Guidance and Counseling Department is to provide a structural comprehensive program that is preventative and proactive in nature and focuses on each student's potential within the context of his or her individual, family and multicultural perspective.
>
> *Program Philosophy:* The Guidance and Counseling Program of the Newport News Public Schools is dynamic, comprehensive, proactive, sequential and coordinated. It is an integral part of the total educational experience for all students and members of the school community.

The Richmond Public Schools (Virginia; n. d.) mission statement reads:

> The mission of the Richmond Public Schools counseling program is to provide a comprehensive, developmental counseling program addressing the academic, career and personal/social development of all students. School counselors are professional advocates who

provide support to maximize student potential and academic achievement. In partnership with other educators, parents, or guardians and the community, school counselors facilitate the support system to ensure all students in the Richmond City school district have access to and are prepared with the knowledge and skills to contribute at the highest level as productive members of society.

The development of the school counseling mission statement is one of the collaborative team initiatives of a school counseling advisory team. As this team has representatives from all of the diverse populations of the school community, the school counseling mission statement will be sure to serve the needs of all students. The Education Trust (1996b) provided a structured format for the process of creating a mission statement (adapted in Table 7.2).

Systemic Assessment

Creating programs that equitably serve the entire school community requires a systemic assessment. Systemic assessments identify the needs of students and the larger school community by reaching every subsystem of the school community to ensure that the needs of all diverse populations are included. Systemic assessments employ multiple methods to examine various data elements. For example, information can be gathered by examining school and district databases, and adequate yearly progress (AYP) reports. More qualitative methods such as surveys, focus groups, interviews, and observations can also be

TABLE 7.2
Creating a new mission statement.

Give careful consideration to the words that will convey the new program mission:

- What? What are the essential words that describe the major focus of a systemic data-driven school counseling program? What will the school counseling program do?
- Who? With whom/stakeholders? For what purpose?
- Where? What is the systemic scope of the school counseling program?
- To what end? What are the desired results/outcomes of implementing the systemic data-driven school counseling program? How are they measured? How will program accountability be demonstrated?

Source: Adapted from *National Institute for Transforming School Counseling,* Education Trust, 1996b, retrieved March 21, 2004, from www.edtrust.org.

TABLE 7.3
Rubric of data elements.

Student Demographic Data	*Student Safety/Conduct*
Enrollment data	Discipline infractions
Student group data; gender, race/ethnicity, ELL, and disability	Attendance patterns
	Violent incidents
Socio-economic data	Participation in enrichment activities
Mobility and stability of students and staff	Participation in extracurricular activities
AYP status	
Student Achievement	*Culture and Climate*
Passing classes	Staff to staff relationships
Grade Point Average	Student to student relationships
Scores on AP tests	Student to staff relationships
SAT, ACT, PSAT scores	Respect for diversity and equity agenda
Marking period, quarter, or semester grades	Leadership styles
Scores on required state assessments	Policies, practices and procedures; spoken and unspoken
Student Attainment	*School Community Life*
Promotion and retention rates	Parent involvement
Passing rates on all subjects	Family issues and configuration
Gifted and Talented Patterns	Neighborhood/community participation
Successful transitions to elementary, middle, high school and postsecondary options	Local business involvement and support
Enrollment patterns in: AP, IB college prep., and honors classes	Local employment patterns
	Environmental impact—deployments, layoffs, unemployment
Graduation rates	
Postsecondary patterns	Immigration
Dropout rates	Migrant communities

Source: V. V. Lee, Workshop Presentation Materials.

used to gather information. By examining these various data elements, school counselors can come to understand what influences access, attainment, and achievement. Because there are so many potential data elements, it can be helpful to group them for ease of use. Table 7.3 shows some rubrics that can provide invaluable information that is critical in conducting a systemic assessment. A comprehensive synthesis of these disaggregated data provides a clear picture of the needs of all students and the school community. Once the needs are identified, data-driven goals can be developed that will then drive the systemic school counseling program. This process ensures that the school counseling program is reflective of student need.

Goals

The goals of a systemic data-driven school counseling program represent not only the attempt to close the gaps between student groups but also the difference between established standards and the reality of the data for all students in a school or district. Additionally, goals are a synthesis of national, state, district, and local school goals. National goals (e.g., AYP requirements) provide key mandates such as closing the access, attainment, and achievements gaps; improving attendance and graduation rates; and ensuring safe and drug-free schools. States consider these national goals in developing their strategic plans and add issues specific to their states, such as promoting literacy or attending to the psychological repercussions of military deployments. School districts attend to these goals while adapting them to the specific needs of their districts. Individual schools then add additional goals to meet the needs of the students they serve. The progressive effect of goal formation from the national to the school level leads to similarities and differences among school counseling programs across the country. By being systemic and data driven, school counseling programs link to the goals of education and the mission of schools at the national, state, district, and building level.

Within the context of national, state, district, and schoolwide goals, professional school counselors apply the data collected from the systemic assessment to create the specific goals on which the school counseling program is developed. Goals are developed as general statements of a desired outcome based on the data. They give direction to the program while allowing flexibility and creativity in implementation. To ensure that goals are comprehensive and reflect the district needs, professional school counselors can team with counselors at feeder schools to develop goals that fortify students in transitions and identify potential trouble spots.

Goals need to be written so that the results can be linked to other schoolwide measures of student achievement and produce concrete measures. In this way, the results of the school counseling program can be used to demonstrate the value-added worth of professional school counselors and the school counseling program. Once goals are developed, they can be prioritized to reflect the most intense needs of the school community as identified by the data. As the school's goals exist in the context of district, state, and national goals, it is appropriate that the goals of each school counseling program reflect wider concerns such as the AYP

status of the school. School counseling programs that are not supportive of these broader needs, and fail to address them directly through their goals and interventions, are not integral to the mission of the school (i.e., are marginal goals). By creating such marginalized programs and services, professional school counselors and their programs do not serve the needs of all students.

Program Integration

The achievement of all students is a schoolwide issue and, therefore, the ethical and professional responsibility of all school personnel. This premise sets the stage for program integration, meaning that the educational program and the school counseling program do not stand alone. Rather, they are intertwined, sharing an overarching goal of equitable access, attainment, and achievement for all students to fully realize academic, career, and personal–social dreams and aspirations. It also means both programs are integrated through a similar or complementary structure in which content, delivery, and reporting of results are aligned. More specifically, the systemic data-driven school counseling program is integrated into the mission of schools by aligning program goals, development, implementation, and evaluation with the educational program. Alignment of the educational program and the school counseling program creates a collaborative commitment to serve all students through mutual goals and the development of interventions that highlight the specific value-added skills of counselors who facilitate school counseling programmatic interventions. Moreover, integration of the school counseling program with the educational program has the advantage of also integrating the school counseling program into school improvement plans and initiatives.

Driven by data, the school counseling program goals draw on the academic standards–based curriculum of district and state, as well as the school counseling standards of district, state, and *ASCA National Standards* (C. Campbell & Dahir, 1997). These standards are used to build the content and interventions of the school counseling program that reflect the goals of academic, career, and personal–social needs of all students as described by the data (see appendix C).

Understanding integration of the school counseling program with the educational program can be difficult. For successful integration that truly supports the educational program to occur, professional school counselors need to be familiar with the academic goals and standards of their district and state and any other established curriculum that is used in the school, such as reading programs and conflict resolution curricula. It is essential to understand how curricula are developed to achieve schoolwide goals, the multiple ways they are implemented, and how the results are measured and reported.

Structure/Delivery

To begin, it is essential to acknowledge that schools are systems (Rowley, Sink, & MacDonald, 2002) in which standards-based educational programs are delivered across the entire school community using multilevel initiatives. More specifically, each academic discipline has standards and competencies implemented in the school community, using multilevel initiatives. Standards and competencies are delivered in classrooms but also through other initiatives such as tutoring, clubs, service learning projects, sports, student buddies, mentoring projects, honor societies, band, chorus, and fine arts initiatives. Parent contacts, collaborations with businesses, and outreach programs are all part of the overall educational program.

Significantly, the educational program is also delivered through the policies, practices, and procedures of the school. These aspects of the educational program affect the culture and climate of a school and serve as long-term environmental instructors that either promote or hinder achievement. For example, policies that affect discipline, course enrollment patterns, attendance, and participation in co- or extracurricular activities systemically impact the educational program and therefore student outcomes. School counseling programs, central as they are to

schools' achieving their academic mission, need to have a structure/delivery process that mirrors this system-level reality.

Outcomes/Results

The outcomes or results of the educational program are collected and reported systemically. In the assessment climate fostered by NCLB, results are often reported at the following levels: individual, group/subgroup, [classroom] grade-level, and schoolwide. For example, Department of Education Web sites for individual states provide links to school districts and individual school performance report card data (Connecticut State Department of Education, 2004; Utah State Office of Education, 2004; Virginia Department of Education, 2004). A school counseling program that aligns with reporting categories provides a ready-made database to assist in conceptualizing and responding to the link between the educational program and the school counseling program. This linkage forms a collaborative and systemic integration in the accountability and results of both programs. When all school personnel team up and collaborate in these ways to reach collective goals, programs become integrated and all stakeholders share in the responsibility and results.

PROFESSIONAL FOUNDATIONS

The Transformed Role of the School Counselor

The transformed role of the professional school counselor delineates the knowledge and skill school counselors need to demonstrate their value-added role in the achievement of all students through concrete measures. Such knowledge and skills are essential to facilitate the development, implementation, and evaluation of a systemic data-driven school counseling program. In 1996, the Education Trust identified the following roles, each contextualized and required for professional school counselors to be culturally responsive: (a) leadership, (b) advocacy,

(c) assessment and use of data, (d) counseling and coordination, and (e) teaming and collaboration. ASCA also supports these roles and the associated knowledge and skills as essential to serving all students. School reform and accountability necessitates that professional school counselors participate in the educational leadership of schools (Bemak, 2000). This assumes that the professional school counselor, as both counselor and educator, holds the belief that all students can achieve high levels of academic success when provided with the opportunity and support to participate in rigorous academic curricula. To achieve this goal, the professional school counselor engages in program planning and delivery that addresses the access, attainment, and achievement gaps that exist between student groups and between standards and student achievement (Education Trust, 1996a). By internalizing this contemporary professional school counselor role, "the counselor can become the academic conscience of the school, insuring that the school remains focused on student achievement and accepts responsibility for student outcomes. [This vision] contributes to creating a climate of accountability within a school" (Hart & Jacobi, 1992, pp. 49–50).

Accountability is achieved when school counseling programs can provide concrete evidence of program accomplishments or student gains related to program goals (Hart & Jacobi, 1992). However, true systemic accountability cannot be demonstrated unless desired goals include identifying the diverse needs of the entire school community, as well as documenting that the program successfully addressed those needs. It is for that reason that professional school counselors need to internalize a contemporary role of emphasizing accountability, which is demonstrated through concrete measures such as disaggregated and longitudinal data (Education Trust, 1996a). This means breaking down and analyzing data by race, ethnicity, gender, socioeconomic groups, and other data elements to create multiple ways of understanding the needs of all students. This understanding paves the way to address access and equity issues for all students within a comprehensive school counseling program.

As stated earlier, leadership and advocacy are critical dimensions of the contemporary school counselor's role, as well as an ethical responsibility. Counselors operationalize these responsibilities when they

channel energy and skill into helping clients challenge institutional and social barriers that impede academic, career, or personal/social development . . . [and] act on behalf of marginalized or disenfranchised clients and actively challenge long-standing traditions, preconceived notions, or regressive policies and procedures that may stifle human development. (C. Lee & Walz, 1998, pp. 8–9)

Thus, in addition to serving as leaders in school policy revision, professional school counselors also facilitate programming that integrates environmental factors and school culture and climate with student development and academic achievement.

Many environmental factors impacting student development and achievement are beyond student control. Among these are family influences and systemic intolerance. Systemic intolerance is often manifested in phenomena such as racism, sexism, and homophobia in our culturally diverse society. These environmental factors may play a major role in shaping the attitudes, values, and behaviors of all members of a school community—factors that can insidiously affect student achievement. Consequently, professional school counselors need to address the negative effects of these environmental factors through the activities of the comprehensive school counseling program.

Ethical and Legal Directives

The doctrine of in loco parentis states that schools act in place of the parent, and therefore need to work in the best interest of the child. By addressing barriers, educators are acting in place of parents for the best interests of the child. Practicing ethically and legally guides the implementation of a systemic data-driven school counseling program. Federal, state, and district mandates as well as standards from professional organizations guide the development, implementation, and evaluation of the school counseling program. By appropriately implementing ethical and legal directives and practicing within these guidelines, the professional school counselor and the program interventions equitably serve all students and promote the overall educational mission of the school. As discussed earlier, the systemic approach views not only the student, but the entire system as the client. Therefore it is helpful to apply Kitchener's (1984) underlying ethical principles to systemic school counseling programs.

Autonomy

This principle is traditionally defined as honoring individual client decisions and promoting self-determination. In a systemic–ecological–developmental approach, counselors guided by the ethical principle of autonomy develop program interventions to remove systemic barriers that restrict student freedom of action within one's cultural context. These systemic barriers become evident through an analysis of disaggregated data.

Nonmaleficience

"All other things being equal, not harming others is generally a stronger ethical obligation than benefiting them" (Kitchener, 1984, p. 47). A systemic approach uses the information gleaned from disaggregated data to understand how the system perpetuates harmful policies, procedures, and strategies to students or groups of students and then develops strategies and interventions to counteract harm in the form of a lack of access and equity for all students.

Beneficence

Beneficence involves a responsibility to contribute to the welfare of students. Clearly the legal mandates of NCLB are primarily in place to promote public/collective good—the education of all children. Implicit is that systems promote what is best for all children: a sound and professionally designed education, delivered by highly qualified educators. Professional school counselors implementing systemic data-driven school counseling programs seek to do what contributes to the welfare of the students—not what is best or most expedient for staff, the teachers, or the community. A beneficence focus for school counseling programs promotes those aspects of the system that maximize the aspirations, development, and success of each.

Justice

Perhaps the largest change of priorities of a systemic data-driven school counseling program is its insistence that the school's program and interventions be fair for all groups of students. Typically in the educational history of the United States, the system supported and reinforced the biases of the wider culture. Thus, the achievement and outcomes for advantaged groups were advanced and those of less advantaged groups were not. Data-driven, systemic school counseling programs are motivated by the ethic of social justice, as described earlier in this chapter.

Fidelity

This principle is about keeping promises and telling the truth. This can be applied to systemic school counseling programs in that there are sometimes systemic forces that seek to obfuscate the truth about what schoolwide data suggest. Part of fidelity in this context is telling the truth about the data. This truth telling can lead to professional school counselor leadership and advocacy initiatives. When telling the truth, problematic information about diverse groups cannot be left out. Such an emphasis promotes counselor and programmatic integrity.

Policies, Ethical Codes, and Legal Mandates

Within the counseling profession, the ACA *Code of Ethics* (2005a) and the ASCA *Code of Ethics* (2004a) provide guidelines for appropriate school counseling practice. These guidelines outline the accepted values, beliefs, and assumptions of ethically competent practice for counseling professionals. However, school counseling practice is complicated as work with minors in a school setting is often gray and with few definite answers. To ensure that professional school counselors practice ethically and within the framework of the law, it is critical to routinely seek out consultation and supervision from supervisors and peers.

Federal mandates that impact school counseling programs include NCLB, IDEIA, FERPA, and Title IX. Each of these legal mandates can support and work in tandem with the values, beliefs, and assumptions of the ASCA *Code of Ethics* (2004a), which supports the rights and dignity of all individuals and their unique diversities and positions. (See chapter 4 for additional information on the topics of legal and ethical issues in school counseling.)

Although all educators involved in service delivery need to be aware of ethical guidelines and legal parameters, it is the professional school counselors' role to interpret and apply relevant ethical guidelines and laws for issues such as child abuse, school violence, and substance abuse. Other issues that need to be guided by ethical and legal parameters include confidentiality, privileged communication, informed consent, client rights, and parental and guardian rights (Salo & Shumate, 1993). Moreover, issues that can result in ethical dilemmas and legal complications center on issues of academic advising and college planning; NCAA regulations and scholarships; and more personal issues such as pregnancy, abortion, and various forms of abuse.

District and School Policies

District and school policies, both spoken and unspoken, govern and shape the day-to-day operations of a school district and individual schools. Policies are used to create a "way of doing things," set the tone for the culture and climate of the school, operationalize ethical and legal mandates, and implement goals. The practices and procedures used to implement policy, though assumed necessary and beneficial, can either advantage or disadvantage all or groups of students. For example, policies affecting attendance, discipline, tardiness, suspensions, makeup work due to illness, student recognition, club membership, release time from class for school-sponsored activities, promotion and retention, transitions from one level to another, decisions regarding placement in rigorous curricula, dissemination of academic and postsecondary information, college advising and application procedures, scholarships, testing practices, and communication with families and the community either promote access and equity for all students or may inadvertently create or maintain access, attainment, and achievement barriers. Since student and community demographics are dynamic, an ongoing analysis of policy is essential to ensure that policies, practices, and procedures promote access and equity for all students. Additionally, school policies, practices, and procedures can also be used to help or mitigate environmental influences that impact students, such as racism, classism, violence, and access to postsecondary opportunity.

District and school policies interface with the mission, goals, development, implementation, and evaluation of the systemic data-driven school counseling program. Since a data-driven school counseling program assists in the academic, personal–social, and career development of all students, effective program development and implementation needs to be infused with the examination and change of district and school policy (Ripley & Goodnough, 2001). Ongoing examination of school policy may point to needed revisions and change, and professional school counselors need to be aware of the impact of policy on the school community.

As part of the educational leadership teams in their schools, professional school counselors can be leaders and advocates who examine the impact of day-to-day interpretation and application of school policy. Impact on individuals, student groups, the entire student population, families, and the community at large is essential to ensure that all subsystems of the school are included. This process may identify inequities; however, identification alone is insufficient to effect change. Inequities may be the result of oversight; outdated rules; or the values, attitudes, and beliefs of the policy makers that are translated into school policy that creates barriers to educational access and equity. Although the role of the professional school counselor in the examination, influencing, and revision of school policy is new, it is a moral imperative as it is unethical for counselors, as part of the school community, to ignore aspects of the school or school counseling program that hinder academic achievement for all students.

THEORETICAL FOUNDATIONS

According to the definition of a comprehensive school counseling program presented at the beginning of the chapter, the theoretical foundation of the program comprises developmental psychology, educational philosophy, and counseling methodology. Integration of each of these theoretical categories provides a holistic foundation for the academic, career, and personal–social development of all students. However, to ensure appropriate application of any theory, attention to the culture-bound nature of many theories is essential. Careful contextual application of theory ensures responsive and sensitive understanding necessary to develop appropriate school counseling interventions. The above theoretical categories address aspects of growth and development, learning, and counseling strategies. Additionally, as described at the beginning of this chapter, the application of systems theories can articulate the way in which individuals and schools group and structure their environments and themselves as they grow and develop.

Developmental psychology or developmental theories describe various dimensions of human growth and development. These theories offer both stage and contextual perspectives and assist professional school counselors in conceptualizing the breadth of development students are likely to experience. They provide an understanding of the multiple other aspects of development, such as moral, psychosocial, racial, and ethnic identity development; gender issues; spiritual development; and sexual identity. Conceptualizing human growth and development as a multifaceted and complex process that requires a synthesis of various theoretical applications will provide a holistic view of development that recognizes the

environmental and societal influences that impact student lives and academic success.

In a systemic data-driven school counseling program, it is critical for all members of the school community to possess an understanding of the range of growth and development children and adolescents progress through during their K–12 educational experience. Data can point to aspects of development in which students require assistance. Additionally, assisting all members of the school community in understanding the wide range of diverse ways in which development is contextualized and expressed can assist them in becoming ambassadors for the positive growth and development of all students.

In addition to the above theories, professional school counselors need to know about Abraham Maslow's humanistic theory of development. Maslow (1987) posited that humans have needs for growth—and that humans won't develop past these needs until the lower level needs are met. These needs are, in order of most basic to most advanced:

1. Physiological
2. Safety
3. Belonging/acceptance
4. Competency/achievement
5. Actualization.

It is critical to note that school achievement is at Stage 4. This means that the first three have to be reasonably met; students must feel safe and accepted before they are free to focus on achievement and competence in school. The actualization of all of these needs is dependent not solely on the child, but on his environment as well. When this premise is applied to a systems approach and the system becomes the client, then school counseling interventions can take on a schoolwide perspective and ask the question, "Do the culture, climate, policies, practices, procedures, values, attitudes, and beliefs of the school provide safety and belonging for all students as a necessary condition for all students to achieve to high expectations?" This is an essential question as it is the ethical responsibility of the professional school counselor to advocate for a system that is likely to allow for the meeting of all children's

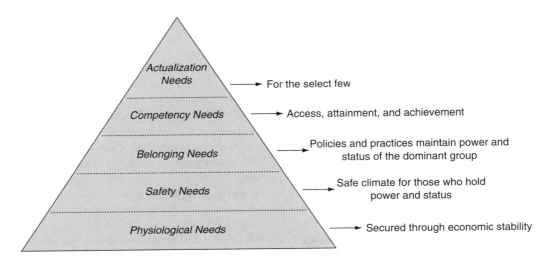

FIGURE 7.1

Maslow's hierarchy in a traditional school. Needs are met only for advantaged students.

needs. When professional school counselors and the programs and interventions they employ ignore these issues, one can see the barriers to learning in a school become the systemic negotiation of basic human needs. As is shown in Figures 7.1 and 7.2 needs can be met for all only when systems are imbued with social justice.

In addition to the educational philosophy of such luminaries as Dewey (1910) and Vygotsky (1978), professional school counselors in systemic data-driven school counseling programs need to know about the teaching theory of Bloom (n.d.). Counselors need to understand how higher order thinking skills are translated into a rigorous academic curriculum so they can identify and promote it—both in the wider instructional program and in the development of school counseling programs at all levels of intervention but particularly in classrooms. Counselors' ability to identify, promote, and use rigor is an essential element in closing gaps and ensuring readiness for substantial postsecondary options, including college.

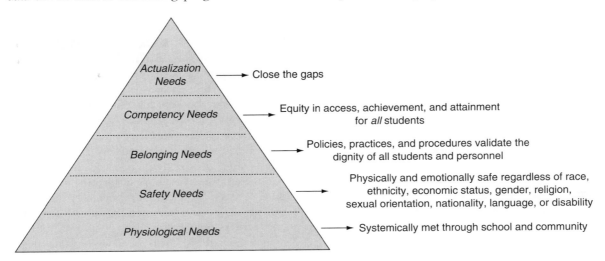

FIGURE 7.2

Maslow's hierarchy in a new vision school. All needs are met for all students.

CONTENT OF THE SCHOOL COUNSELING PROGRAM

As the *behavioral indicators of developmental theories*, student competencies form the bridge between theory and practice. The sequence of student competencies within a grade level as well as between grade levels outlines the desired student outcomes as a result of participating in the program. This specification of student competencies provides a holistic and sequential picture of student development within a school. Once student competencies are vertically articulated (i.e., expressed sequentially), they can be grouped within the three domains articulated in the *ASCA National Model* (2003a): academic, career, and personal–social development. These domains are not isolated, but connected and interdependent and focused on promoting students' growth and development. This means that the achievement of any developmental milestone likely will touch on all three domains.

While the national model conceptualizes school counseling interventions along the three domains, it is critical that these interventions be thoroughly integrated into the wider educational program. There are several ways the school counseling program does this. First, professional school counselors need to know what is being taught in the academic curriculum and when. Familiarity with the curriculum simplifies the process of integrating the school counseling program with the educational program. It does not mean that the professional school counselor teaches geometry and chemistry, but it does mean he or she knows the concepts and constructs that facilitate learning across the academic disciplines, such as critical thinking and problem solving. It also means that professional school counselors do assist teachers with the delivery of curriculum through collaborative classroom instruction in areas where counseling expertise can support and enhance student learning and development toward the achievement of goals.

For example, schoolwide goals under AYP may include an increase in student attendance. If this is true for the school as a whole, it is also appropriate for it to be a goal of the systemic data-driven school counseling program. Professional school counselors routinely assist students with attendance issues; when that assistance becomes part of the schoolwide intervention, the school counseling program shares the responsibility and results of collaborative efforts in the achievement of schoolwide goals. These types of collaborative efforts by all school personnel highlight individual expertise and targeted interrelated programmatic interventions delivered across the system.

Second, some states have goals and competencies without curricula that indicate what students should know and be able to do. As one of many possible examples, the Maryland State Department of Education (1998) proposed five *Skills for Success*. These skills have been identified as necessary for student success in school and to become a contributing member of society. Transferable skills used in all disciplines, the list includes: (a) learning skills, (b) thinking skills, (c) communication skills, (d) technology skills, and (e) interpersonal skills. School personnel are charged with facilitating the development of these skills as part of the overall educational and learning process. School counseling programs can also include the *Skills for Success* as programmatic goals to integrate with the academic program.

Third, professional school counselors can contribute to student learning and development in specific disciplines. For example, in civics, government, and history, issues of diversity, human rights, citizenship, conflict and war, oppression, and violence are prevalent. Professional school counselors do not have to be history experts to assist teachers with discussions and activities that help students explore these areas and relate them to their day-to-day lives. Additionally, language arts curricula often include topics of careers, resume writing, alternative points of view, conflict resolution, relationships, and a host of other types of human drama and triumph explored through literature. School counseling interventions that are integrated into the curriculum in these areas provide a holistic environment for learning. Finally, the health curriculum is often replete with topics in which professional school counselors possess expertise. Issues such as healthy relationships, alcohol and drug prevention, sexuality, personal safety, family relationships, and wellness are all areas where professional school counselors and teachers can team and collaborate to achieve curricular goals.

PLANNING THE SCHOOL COUNSELING PROGRAM

Strategic Planning and Program Development

A strategic plan begins with the vision, mission, data, and subsequent goals of the program. Once professional school counselors and other educational leaders have established goals, it is critical to set clearly defined programmatic priorities. Part of this process is to connect these priorities to others that the school has articulated. For example, AYP goals may include emphasis on attendance, graduation, promotion and retention, discipline, academic advising, and postsecondary transition. Because these goals are broad, it is important to involve various stakeholder groups such as parents, community members, teachers, administrators, and student representatives in the decision-making process. The achievement of each goal is monitored by the accomplishment of measurable objectives or competencies with a timeline and benchmarks and the articulation of each stakeholder's responsibility in the achievement of the goal. The plan should also be written and communicated to the school community to highlight the school counseling program. As goals are completed, data should be reviewed and evaluated and each success shared with the school community. In instances where goals are not accomplished, a review of strategies, implementation, skill levels of stakeholders, and any other contributing factor that may impact the accomplishment of goals should be followed by a revised plan. Strategic planning is often developed in cycles of 1, 3, and 5 years. Together

with administrators and other educational leaders, plans need to be reviewed and revised annually.

Creating a Calendar

A calendar for the school counseling program is an essential tool that serves a variety of purposes. First, the calendar format and structure demonstrate the systemic nature of the program in a monthly plan. Second, the calendar serves as a means of organizing interventions into a clear and intentional order. It is the written representation of the strategic plan and goals of the program. It defines the work of the counselor and presents a structure of professional activities similar to that of other educational professionals in the school.

Calendars are organized by months. The activities of each month are laid out using the same template for each month. This ensures consistency of interventions. While the type and volume of interventions may be different month to month, the use of a template further allows students, teachers, administrators, and parents to become familiar with the school counseling program. The template of the calendar reflects the seven levels of programmatic intervention. See Table 7.4 for an outline of a calendar.

A calendar also allows others to see the array of interventions and activities that professional school counselors engage in and removes any myths or misconceptions about how counselors spend their time or the integral nature of their work. The school counseling strategic plan as evidenced on the calendar is most effective and integrated into the school when it mirrors the academic curriculum calendar. For example, if one of the goals of the school counseling program is to address issues of citizenship and civic responsibility, it is advisable to coordinate those activities with civics and social studies teachers. In this way, students receive multiple opportunities to gain knowledge and skills in a variety of venues. The complex issues in today's schools require multidimensional interventions that impact the various contexts of students' lives to create a clear systemic expectation of achievement for all students.

TABLE 7.4
A content outline of activities for a school counseling calendar for a data-driven systemic school counseling program.

Each Month:	Service learning projects
Ongoing activities including individual	Career fairs
Team meetings	Open house
Staff planning meetings	Cultural events
Individual level	Conflict resolution programs
Referrals	School safety policies
IEP meetings	*Family Level:*
Section 504 meetings	Parent/Guardian groups
Crisis counseling	Information-/skill-building workshops
Group Level: (should indicate the grade level[s])	Advocacy activities for parents
Groups that are beginning, continuing, and/or ending this month	*Community Level:*
Any other targeted group activities	Task force for equity
Classroom: (collaborative classroom instruction)	Community advisory boards
Targeted interventions with classrooms in need	Collaborations to promote achievement
Grade Level:	Community educational and career mentors
Transitional interventions at a particular grade level	Special presenters
Grade-specific interventions—preventive, developmental, remedial—with students, teachers, or both	Business sponsors for student need
	School–community partnerships
	School-to-work initiatives
Schoolwide:	*Professional Development Activities:*
Data collection, analysis, presentation, planning, and revision of programs and policies	Conferences
Discipline policies	In-house trainings
Course enrollment patterns	School counselor building- and district-level meetings
Attendance policies	*Planning for Upcoming Events:*
Interventions with all teachers	List the activities that need to be accomplished to ensure timely and thorough planning for each upcoming intervention. This is essential so that school counselor work is professionally completed and seen as an intentionally and thoroughly planned program in response to the data, rather than a collection of random activities.
In-service on learning styles	
Interventions focused on schoolwide culture and climate	
Assemblies	

DELIVERY—IMPLEMENTATION AT MULTIPLE LEVELS OF PROGRAMMATIC INTERVENTION

A data-driven, systems approach requires that school counseling interventions be conceived as *levels of programmatic intervention*. This perspective focuses on seven levels of intervention: individual, group, classroom, grade-level, schoolwide, home/family, and community/ society. These levels of intervention can be viewed as concentric circles with individually based interventions in the middle. Each additional

FIGURE 7.3
Programmatic levels of
intervention intentionally use
the inherent interdependence
and interrelatedness of systems
to create an environment with
a consistent message of achievement throughout the multiple
subsystems that impact students'
lives and provide meaning within
a cultural context.

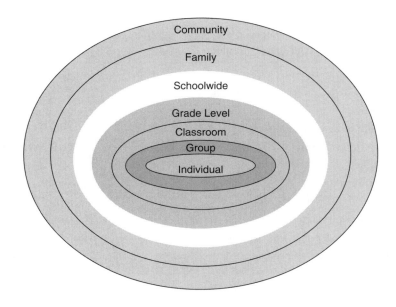

ring represents a larger and potentially more diverse population of the school community, including the larger society, as seen in Figure 7.3. The seven levels are intervention points into the structure of the school and community. The rationale behind this approach is that systemic transformation requires consistent and intentional intervention across all levels of a school. Additionally, these levels are basic structures in schools for collecting and reporting data at the elementary, middle, and high schools.

Levels of programmatic intervention are the structural framework of service delivery in a systemic, data-driven school counseling program. To deliver a program effectively, professional school counselors must possess the knowledge and skills to implement services in all levels of intervention. For example, group counseling is one method of service delivery. This method frequently emerges from recurring needs identified in individual sessions, needs assessment, and consultations with parents, teachers, or both. Planning and implementing group counseling services requires a cadre of knowledge and skills, such as teamwork, coordination, consultation, group skill building, and organizational skills, among all group leaders.

If any of these skills or knowledge bases is not developed, even the best-intended small-group counseling services might go awry. Therefore, in planning activities in each program component area, it is critical for professional school counselors to carefully inventory their knowledge and skills; deficits are opportunities for professional development. In this way, service delivery within the comprehensive school counseling program reflects student need and is not compromised by limited professional school counselor knowledge or skill.

Professional school counselor knowledge and skill development should not be limited to service delivery at any one level of programmatic intervention. The professional school counselor needs to possess knowledge and skills even in areas where the primary service to students is indirect and focused on classroom and academic performance. Consultation with teachers focused on issues of curriculum development, classroom management, and classroom assessment is critical even though professional school counselors' primary role is not teaching in the classroom all day. The counselors' knowledge and competence in these skill areas, applied through consultation services, deliver a direct service to teachers and an indirect service to students. They also broaden the counselors' skill base to facilitate delivery of curriculum in both the classroom and other large-group settings.

Each level of programmatic intervention provides a unique entry point into the system. Below is a description of how each level of intervention can be used to implement a data-driven program.

Schoolwide

The schoolwide level of intervention has the greatest potential for removing systemic barriers and creating the conditions for learning at all other levels (Hayes, Nelson, Tabin, Pearson, & Worthy 2002; R. M. House & Hayes, 2002). As far back as 1992, Gerler posited that the coordinating of systems-level interventions was the most important role of the professional school counselor. Now under accountability mandates, this level of intervention emphasizes the reform as a whole-school challenge in which all stakeholders must be actively involved because the achievement of AYP is a whole-school issue. School counseling programs that have a schoolwide perspective in managing data can impact all levels of the system.

The potential of this level of intervention lies in examining the interrelatedness and interdependence of schoolwide disaggregated data. This examination impacts learning and promotes culturally responsive practices and can alter school culture through program development and policy revision. Interventions at this level involve the entire school. They reflect the data profile and look at the interconnectedness of data. A review of policy and procedures that affect the entire school are often the focus of these interventions. These interventions can also reflect areas of growth and development that are important to the entire school. Schoolwide interventions can also involve corresponding interventions at all other levels of service to ensure that a comprehensive approach is achieved. For example, some of these may include activities that focus on culture and climate of the school. Culture and climate involve students, teachers, administrators, and all support staff as well as parents.

Grade Level

This level of intervention specifically attends to the context of grade-level experiences (e.g., sixth grade) and transitions at developmental benchmarks (e.g., entering and leaving kindergarten, middle school, and high school). An emphasis on examining policies that impact specific grade levels is also essential at this level of intervention. These interventions may also involve a number of other levels of service, such as schoolwide and community, and may require long-term planning such as transition events or postsecondary planning events. The ability to analyze and use disaggregated data such as postsecondary plans, promotions, course enrollment patterns, and retentions helps the professional school counselor discern the influence of grade level and transition points on these processes. Additionally, revision of grade-level policies that either support or hinder achievement is appropriate. Finally, grade-level data by subgroups (such as ethnicity, socioeconomic status, and English-speaking groups) are analyzed to develop interventions both within and between grade levels to promote achievement.

Examples of interventions at the grade level are transition activities—from elementary to middle school, from middle to high school, and from high school to postsecondary options. Others include senior activities such as postsecondary planning; resume writing; interview strategies; public relations and speaking skills; or the scholarship process, including letter to community, letter and information to parents, distribution to students, coordination policy with teachers, scholarship forms, application process, and awarding of local scholarships. Interventions at this level are grade-level assessments, academic advising, placement, assessment interpretation, course selection activities, parent nights, classroom information sessions, counselor coordination with feeder schools, actual scheduling, follow-up with parents, and final placement.

Classroom

Initiatives at this level of intervention reflect a wide variety of possibilities. This level of intervention is used in classrooms to align the school counseling program with the academic curriculum and calendar in *collaborative classroom instruction.* Whether initiatives are offered in one particular class or as part of an interdisciplinary team, classroom interventions require teaming and collaboration. The use of data to deliver developmental and preventive interventions to achieve specific student outcomes at this level is central. Data are also used to identify classrooms and teachers in need of specific and targeted assistance to transform the culture and climate of the learning environment. Specific collaborative classroom instruction interventions can focus on learning styles, healthy classroom relationships, or sharing responsibility or can be a supplement to an academic unit such as diversity in history, citizenship, careers in the curriculum, or any other area that impacts student performance and attainment.

Group

Efficacious use of group interventions requires examination of data elements gleaned from a systemswide assessment. This level of intervention responds to specific and targeted needs identified on the school's performance report card or through other types of needs assessment instruments. It allows professional school counselors to provide more intensive and in-depth work with individuals. These interventions can be either developmental or remedial.

This level of intervention provides equitable and accessible targeted assistance across all grade levels to identified student needs. Group interventions can focus on specific subgroups of students or can be offered across student groups depending on the identified needs of students. Additionally, group is a critical level of intervention because it provides social modeling and peer support and promotes learning through a developmentally appropriate forum. Because this level of intervention serves only a small population of students, it should be intentionally interrelated to corresponding services at other levels. When this intervention is used as small-group counseling, professional school counselors should consider:

1. Policies and procedures that govern small-group interventions and counseling (e.g., group ground rules, screening procedures, needs assessment form, information letter to faculty, parent/guardian permission form, sample group schedule).
2. Offering small groups annually, including both proactive and reactive formats (e.g., study skills, healthy relationships, diversity awareness, grief and loss, family breakups, substance abuse prevention, career, anger management, senior transitions).

Individual

This level of intervention is used to respond to crisis situations and issues particular to specific individual students. Importantly, individual counseling is not the key target of school counseling program interventions. Issues identified at this level provide insight into issues in the larger school that can then be further examined using specific data elements. Interventions at other levels of intervention can then be developed to address issues in a preventive, developmental, and even remedial fashion. Services under the individual level include personal and crisis counseling. Most often included in this area, referral represents collaborative interventions at the community level and therefore is not a singular intervention. Additionally, issues at the individual level also involve policies that are practiced schoolwide, such as policies around confidentiality, informed consent, duty to warn, and parental or guardian permission for counseling. Data around issues that necessitate the use of these policies, such as child abuse, substance abuse, and other self-injurious behaviors, can inform counselors about the health and wellness of the school population, which can also be addressed at other levels in a preventive fashion.

Family

This level of intervention uses data to intentionally involve parents and guardians in the school counseling program as equal partners in promoting student achievement. Intentional outreach to marginalized parent and guardian populations promotes access and equity and assists them in taking an active and empowered role in the school. Additionally, interventions at this level assist parents and guardians in learning skills to successfully navigate school and community services to gain access to resources for their children.

Community

This level of intervention is used to actively involve all community stakeholders in improving student achievement. Community involvement can increase the likelihood that students will experience consistent expectations across the multiple contexts of their lives. Connecting with community stakeholders (e.g., agencies, community mental health clinics, law enforcement, other health services, civic organizations, business leaders) is a critical element in creating broad-based partnerships for student achievement.

Additionally, the community level of intervention includes professional school counselors being advocates in the larger societal community, including professional organizations, state departments of education, and federal bodies that contribute to the creation of standards, policies, and laws that impact schools and school counseling programs and student achievement. Implementation of community-level interventions requires strategic planning. Successful and effective interventions at this level are often developed in phases over time. Careful planning, documentation, timely and clear communication, and shared decision making are essential. As with all other levels of intervention, using data to create urgency and drive decision making and using inquiry to continue to focus, evaluate, and revise interventions are essential and the hallmarks of a well-articulated data process. As each phase of an intervention is completed, presentations of the resulting data, regardless of the outcome, need to be made public as all stakeholders need to be responsible for student achievement. Administrative support and sanctioning (preferably codified in policy) of the collaborative efforts of the professional school counselor and program interventions can help prevent school counseling

programs from becoming marginalized and superfluous to the mission of schools (Bemak, 2000; Ripley & Goodnough, 2001). Examples of some of the types of community interventions that are possible include but are not limited to:

1. *Community outreach.* This includes activities that involve students, parents and guardians, teachers, and local community.
2. *Public relations.* This includes special one-time events, ongoing information events, and contact with local media to promote services and initiatives with local business, religious, and organizational personalities that promote school activities.
3. *Community advisory boards.* Counselor participation on such boards serves to connect the professional school counselor and the school counseling program to important communitywide efforts.

EVALUATING THE SYSTEMIC DATA-DRIVEN SCHOOL COUNSELING PROGRAM

Evaluating a systemic data-driven school counseling program serves several purposes. First, evaluation demonstrates accountability and establishes the credibility of professional school counselors and the school counseling program as a viable contributor to the achievement of all students. This occurs when concrete measures can demonstrate that established goals were met and allows counselors to assess the impact of the program and the levels of programmatic interventions that were most successful. It also allows counselors to determine combinations of interventions that proved successful in goal attainment.

Second, evaluation demonstrates where goals were not met. Determining when goals are not met is equally as important as determining success. Unachieved goals highlight the need for further examination of needs, assessment methods, strategic planning, and selected intervention as well as the skill level of all stakeholders involved in implementing the initiative. Regular evaluation and revision of the goal attainment process allows the school counseling program to remain dynamic and specifically tailored to the needs of the school and district it serves.

Third, evaluation based on concrete measures of goals aligned with the mission of the school demonstrates how the school counseling program contributes to the achievement of AYP, district, state, and national goals for the equitable achievement of all students.

IMPLICATIONS FOR PROFESSIONAL SCHOOL COUNSELORS

We believe that creating systemic data-driven school counseling programs is the ethical responsibility of all professional school counselors, including school-based directors of school counseling services and district directors of school counseling. It is especially important when individuals in these positions serve as mentors and supervisors for practicing school counselors, new

school counselors, and school counselor interns. While the knowledge and skills needed to develop and implement systemic data-driven programs are new to most practicing counselors and some preservice training programs have not yet adapted their training programs to include these competencies, it remains the responsibility of each individual, regardless of the stage they are at in their career, to attain the awareness, knowledge, and skills necessary to meet the needs of all students. Implicit in this statement is the recognition that professional school counselors are self-reflective practitioners who can assess and evaluate their own skill base and develop and implement an ongoing professional development plan that will ensure they remain relevant. Such a commitment ensures professional school counselors will develop the competence to implement the systemic data-driven programs that equitably meet the academic, career, and personal–social needs of all students. A real-life example of a systemic data-driven program goal is included in Figure 7.4.

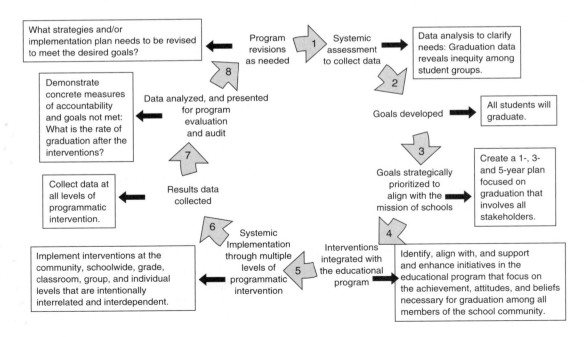

FIGURE 7.4

Vision: Social justice; Mission: Access and equity; Program: Data driven.

SUMMARY/CONCLUSION

This chapter has offered a rationale, description, and tools useful in creating a systemic data-driven school counseling program. To build this type of program, professional school counselors need to possess the values, attitudes, and beliefs implicit in the transformed role of the professional school counselor. Additionally, professional school counselors who possess the awareness, knowledge, and skills necessary to develop and implement such programs will also ensure that school counseling is integral to the mission of the school and demonstrate the value-added worth of school counseling through concrete measure of accountability. Most importantly, the implementation of systemic data-driven school counseling programs can form the bedrock from which the needs of all students are equitably met in a learning environment that encourages academic success with cultural integrity (Nieto, 1999).

Now go to our Companion Website at www.prenhall.com/erford to assess your understanding of chapter content with "Multiple-Choice Questions," apply comprehension with "Essay Questions," and broaden your knowledge of the school counseling profession with related "Web Links."

ACTIVITIES

1. Reflecting on your graduate training thus far, identify areas in which you need to develop greater levels of awareness, knowledge, and skill to begin the career-long process of becoming a transformed school counselor. Why? What do you need to do to improve those skills throughout the remainder of your training and after you graduate?

2. In which level(s) of program intervention do you feel most comfortable, and which level(s) are most challenging? Why? What do you need to do to improve those skills throughout the remainder of your training and after you graduate?

CHAPTER 8

DEVELOPMENTAL CLASSROOM GUIDANCE

*GARY E. GOODNOUGH, RACHELLE PÉRUSSE,
AND BRADLEY T. ERFORD*

Editor's Introduction: Whether conducted by the professional school counselor or classroom teacher, developmental classroom guidance is a common and efficient method for implementing the comprehensive developmental school counseling curriculum. Unfortunately, professional school counselors have not consistently focused on designing academically rigorous lesson plans, activities sensitive to diverse-learner needs, and assessment and follow-up procedures to determine the effectiveness and continuity of classroom guidance activities. The school reform movement, with its emphasis on academic performance, requires this of classroom teachers. The same is expected of the transformed professional school counselor.

In the past, professional school counselors were hired almost exclusively from the ranks of classroom teachers (Dudley & Ruff, 1970). It was implicitly assumed that these counselors, as former teachers, understood the role of teacher and could assume such a role. Beginning in the 1970s, states began to drop their requirements that professional school counselors be certified, experienced teachers (Randolph & Masker, 1997). It became clear to counselor educators and state officials that restricting entry into one profession (counseling) by requiring experience in a related profession (teaching) not only was a historical bias, but also served to lower the number of eligible and willing candidates for professional school counselor positions. Currently, only 13 states require professional school counselors to have experience as teachers (ASCA, 2005b). Most counselor educators suggest that this movement toward opening the ranks to nonteachers has had a beneficial result for the profession (S. B. Baker, 1994).

With the advent of comprehensive school counseling programs, professional school counselors at all levels are in the classroom. Most have responsibility to deliver their program directly, as well as indirectly, to students. Direct delivery of a school counseling curriculum means that professional school counselors have a significant role in teaching students in classrooms. Thus, professional school counselors, while increasingly not rooted in the teaching profession, nevertheless need to become knowledgeable of effective teaching methods. Clearly, this is a tall order. To become a teacher, one must receive an undergraduate degree, or in some cases a graduate degree, and then experience a teaching internship. In 37 states, many new school counselors do not have this background but will assume significant teaching responsibilities.

In this chapter, it is our intention to outline and discuss some pedagogically sound ways professional school counselors can provide for students' academic, career, and personal–social development. In so doing, it is our hope that professional school counselors will be able to better implement the classroom component of their comprehensive school counseling programs.

THE SCOPE AND RESPONSIBILITY OF THE PROFESSIONAL SCHOOL COUNSELOR AS DEVELOPMENTAL CLASSROOM GUIDANCE SPECIALIST

The *ASCA National Model* (2003a) charges professional school counselors with the responsibility of implementing programs to assist all students in their academic, career, and personal–social development. As discussed in the previous chapter, professional school counselors intervene at multiple levels, including the classroom. Gysbers and Henderson (2000) suggested that local districts inevitably determine the precise percentage of time spent in delivering classroom guidance. Nevertheless, Gysbers and Henderson provide general guidelines that describe how much time is typically devoted to curriculum implementation. Using Gysbers and Henderson as a guide, the *ASCA National Model* suggests that at the elementary school levels, approximately 35% to 45% of the counseling program be devoted to implementing the curriculum. At the middle school level, an appropriate amount of counselor time

devoted to curriculum is 25% to 35%; and at the high school level, the recommendation is that 15% to 25% of the program time be dedicated to guidance curriculum (ASCA, 2003a).

Although counselors are not the only professionals delivering the guidance curriculum, professional school counselors clearly commit significant resources to teaching. ASCA (1999d), in its position statement on comprehensive school counseling programs, supports the teaching role in stating that professional school counselors "teach skill development in academic, career and personal/social areas." With the decline in the number of counselors having backgrounds as teachers, professional school counselors must develop their teaching skills if they are to fulfill their roles within comprehensive, standards-based programs. Although many learn these important skills during their internship experiences (Olson & Allen, 1993), there is an undeniable need to address this potentially important skill during preservice training.

THE EFFECT OF CLASSROOM GUIDANCE ON STUDENT DEVELOPMENT

Lending credence to the discussion of the effect of classroom guidance on student achievement is a statewide study conducted in Missouri high schools by Lapan et al. (1997). They found that students who were in schools that had a fully implemented model guidance program including classroom guidance reported higher grades, better preparation and information for future goals, and a more positive school climate. According to Borders and Drury (1992), studies exist that demonstrate the positive effects of classroom guidance on specific outcome measures. In their review of the literature, they found studies that showed classroom guidance activities to be effective for a variety of student behaviors, including positive changes in classroom behaviors and attitudes, exam preparation, school attendance, career goals, college attendance, career planning skills, and coping skills.

With the advent of the accountability issues raised in the *ASCA National Model,* the Transforming the School Counseling Initiative, and the

NCLB Act of 2001, there is a necessity for professional school counselors to demonstrate that their interventions are effective. Such is also the case with classroom guidance interventions. There is a move away from simply counting how many times an intervention is used and toward a description of how effective an intervention is. One way to show effectiveness is to collect data both prior to the intervention and after the intervention, known as a pre–post test design. It is not enough to say that one has conducted a certain number of classroom guidance activities. Professional school counselors must demonstrate that they are effective and that students are different because of their intervention. There are many data points that can be used in a pre–post test design. For example, a professional school counselor might access school files to find out about grades, standardized test scores, and graduation rates; or, once data is already collected, disaggregate the data by gender, ethnicity, and socioeconomic status. For example, if one were conducting a classroom guidance unit on bullying behavior, one might count the number of bullying incidents on the playground or the number of referrals to the assistant principal.

Besides collecting pretest and posttest data, professional school counselors might also collect content evaluation data and process evaluation data from the students and teachers in the classroom. When conducting an evaluation based on the content of the classroom guidance activity, professional school counselors might use pretest and posttest measures resembling a quiz. For younger children, professional school counselors might use a Smiley–Frowny Form or a Feelometer (LaFountain & Garner, 1998). They might use multiple-choice and open-ended questions based on the unit. For example, D. S. Young (2005) conducted a classroom guidance activity based on the portrayal of Theodore Roosevelt. His content evaluation contained 10 multiple-choice questions asking students to identify facts presented during the activity.

A process evaluation is aimed at identifying which parts of the classroom guidance activity went well, and what parts can be improved on. Especially when a classroom intervention is new, it is important to get feedback from students and teachers about ways to improve the lesson the next time it is taught. A process evaluation might contain questions such as can be seen in Figure 8.1. Some classroom guidance curriculum materials have already been evaluated for effectiveness. The Web site for the Center for School Counseling Outcome Research (www.umass.edu/schoolcounseling/) located at the University of Massachusetts, Amherst, contains research briefs and monographs based on published works that show the effectiveness of school counseling interventions. Included among those evidence-based programs are: Second Step Violence prevention program (www.cfchildren.org/ssf/ssindex), Student Success Skills (www.studentsuccessskills.com), The Real Game (www.realgame.com), and Peacebuilders (www.peacebuilders.com).

DEVELOPMENTAL THEORY

It is relevant to stress the importance of a comprehensive developmental approach to classroom guidance. Within this framework, it has been argued that to be successful in implementing a classroom guidance curriculum, the professional school counselor must adhere to an overall theory of counseling. To this end, human development theories are most appropriate for professional school counselors to consider. Borders and Drury (1992) emphasized that developmental stages are the basis for effective counseling programs. They identified several human development theories, including those developed by Piaget, Erikson, Loevinger, Kohlberg, Gilligan, and Selman. In addition to these theorists, Myrick (1993) recommended the work of Havighurst and Super. The challenge for professional school counselors is how to translate developmental theory into practical ideas for classroom guidance. Table 8.1 contains examples of what professional school counselors might do in relation to the domains of cognitive, personal–social, and career development theory when presenting classroom guidance lessons.

Consistent among each of these developmental theories is the concept that developmental changes occur over the life span of the individual

FIGURE 8.1
Process evaluation.

Classroom Guidance Lesson: _____
Counselor: _____

1. I found this lesson to be: (Check one)

_____

Very   Somewhat   Not At All
Helpful   Helpful   Helpful

2. I especially enjoyed: _____
_____

3. I think the following could be done differently:
_____
_____

4. I found the counselor to be: (Check one)

_____

        Very   Somewhat   Not At All
        Helpful   Helpful   Helpful

5. Overall, I would rate this lesson: (Circle one)

        1_____2_____3_____4_____5_____6_____7_____8_____9_____10
        AWFUL   EXCELLENT

6. COMMENTS: _____
_____
_____
_____

---

and that achievement of each developmental task is dependent on the successful accomplishment of earlier tasks (Myrick, 1993). Thus, professional school counselors must ensure that relevant developmental changes be addressed in a sequential, orderly manner within a K–12 curriculum. Using this comprehensive developmental model, professional school counselors avoid delivering their services in isolated units. Instead, they build on previous efforts and successes toward a meaningful outcome. As an example of this hierarchical learning, Nicoll (1994) suggested a five-stage ramework, based in Adlerian psychology, for the implementation of classroom guidance programs. These five stages are: (a) understanding self and others, (b) empathy skill development, (c) communication

skills, (d) cooperation skills, and (e) responsibility skills. Nicoll noted that each of the five stages could be repeated throughout each grade and adapted to appropriate developmental levels. Thus, the framework would be applied with each year building on previous years.

ROLE OF THE PROFESSIONAL SCHOOL COUNSELOR IN DELIVERING THE CURRICULUM

Professional school counselors implement their curricular role in three ways—through consultation, collaboration, and direct teaching. While the most visible modality is through providing

TABLE 8.1
Classroom Applications for Cognitive, Personal–Social, and Career Development Theory

	Developmental Theorist	Key Concepts	How It Translates to Classroom Guidance
Cognitive	Piaget	Preoperational	Use props and visual aids. Use actions and words to give instructions. Use hands-on activities.
		Concrete operational	Use actions, props, and hands-on activities. Use brain teasers, mind twisters, and riddles.
		Formal operational	Set up hypothetical questions. Have students justify two opposite points of view. Use song lyrics to reflect on topics. Teach broad concepts that are open to discussion.
	Vygotsky	Sociocultural theory, coconstructed process, cultural tools, private speech, scaffolding	Provide examples, use prompts, give feedback. Encourage students to challenge themselves. Teach students to use tools such as homework planners and technology. Use peer tutoring.
Career Development	Super	Curiosity, exploration, career maturity	Plenty of materials with career-related information available. Career information integrated into all disciplines.
	Gottfredsen	Orientation to sex roles	Take care not to use gender-stereotyped materials.
		Orientation to social valuation	Help expand career areas outside of those typical of student's socioeconomic status.
Personal–social	Erikson	Initiative versus guilt	Allow students to choose an activity. Teach in small steps. Use costumes and props.
		Industry versus inferiority	Have students set and work toward goals. Delegate tasks to students to encourage responsibility. Use charts to keep track of progress.
		Identity versus role confusion	Invite guest speakers for career day. Include examples of women and people of color in your discussions.
	Kohlberg	Moral reasoning based on the ethic of justice	Conduct lessons on bullying, cheating, and peer relationships.
	Gilligan	Moral reasoning based on the ethic of care	Use themes of care as a basis to organize curriculum: Caring for self, Caring for family and friends, Caring for strangers and the world.

instruction directly to students and parents, professional school counselors also implement their curricular role in indirect ways (Goodnough & Dick, 1998). For instance, a professional school counselor might consult with a middle school team of teachers as they plan a unit on ecosystems. In working with the teachers, the professional school counselor can become a resource to help integrate guidance curriculum components into the unit. In this case, classroom teachers are teaching the school counseling curriculum and are helping promote the career maturity of students by providing world-of-work information as one of several important parts of the unit. By becoming involved with teachers as they plan, counselors educate the educators and are able to reach a wider audience more consistently.

A second way in which professional school counselors implement their curricular role is by working collaboratively not only in the planning phase, as in the previous example, but also in the implementation phase. In this case, a high school counselor might meet regularly with the physical education (PE) teachers to plan adventure-based education. The teachers and professional school counselor then implement the program together as a team, with each professional responsible for an area of expertise. For example, the PE teacher might attend primarily to the physical fitness components of a ropes course, and the professional school counselor would attend more directly to the team building and positive social interaction aspect of the program.

Although it is true that all members of a school community share responsibility for implementing a counseling curriculum, professional school counselors may still directly deliver a significant portion of it themselves. For instance, in this third service delivery method, counselors in an elementary school program might teach developmentally appropriate units on conflict resolution to multiple grade levels. At the high school level, they might administer interest inventories to sophomores and then follow up with interpretation and a series of carefully designed lessons to facilitate students' career growth.

Counselors, by virtue of their professional preparation, are the individuals best suited to teach the content, skills, and processes of conflict resolution. They understand the role of interests in career development and know how to foster the career maturity of high school students. For these reasons, it is not uncommon for professional school counselors to be directly involved in teaching students every day. Although it is vital to the ultimate success of the school counselors' curriculum to engage teachers and staff in supporting and reinforcing the program components, many counselors, particularly in elementary and middle schools, nevertheless spend a significant amount of time teaching.

SETTING UP AND MANAGING A CLASSROOM ENVIRONMENT

Arranging the Classroom

Classroom arrangement not only creates an atmosphere or climate for learning, but it also communicates the teaching philosophy and interaction expectations of the instructor. In a practical sense, how a professional school counselor chooses to physically set up a learning environment depends on the desired interaction strategies to be used during implementation of the lesson. For example, if the goal is to get students to explore an interpersonal issue in a deep and personally meaningful way, the professional school counselor might break the students into groups of two to four and have them cluster in small circles in several areas around the room or around small tables. On the other hand, if the goal is to simply impart information on how to fill out a college application, a typical classroom-style setup may suffice. The important point is that teaching style, learning style, instructional strategies, and participant seating should combine to form an effective learning atmosphere.

Figure 8.2 contains drawings of several typical seating arrangements used by professional school counselors. A lecture hall or classroom-style setup creates a formal, businesslike, and often cold and sterile atmosphere that leaves no question as to

FIGURE 8.2
Classroom arrangements.

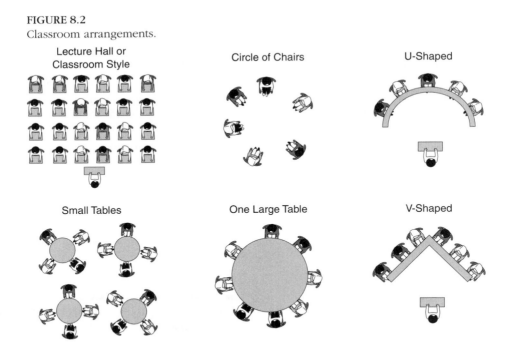

who is in charge. It sets the expectation that students are there to be taught and emphasizes one-way communication, with periodic pauses for questions. When discussion does occur, it is typically funneled through the instructor. The classroom-style setup lends itself to an authoritarian instructor style, relegating student participation to secondary status. Many students take a passive role or are minimally active and engaged.

The U-shaped or V-shaped arrangement with the instructor at the open end still creates a formal or instructor-centered atmosphere indicating the instructor is in command, but it also conveys that there will be opportunities for interaction. The philosophy conveyed by the U shape is that interaction can occur between participants, even though the instructor will still function as the primary source of information.

The small-tables arrangement presents a more relaxed, informal, student-centered atmosphere where all will have the opportunity to discuss, share, explore, and problem solve. In this arrangement, the instructor is more of a facilitator and serves as a catalyst and resource to all of the small groups. The small-tables environment sets an expectation of active participation

on the part of all students and is used primarily for small-group work and learning. Putting student desks into a circle or block is a modification of this arrangement.

The one-large-table (round or square) arrangement conveys the expectation of participation and free exchange of information. Generally, this arrangement is viewed as less formal, although the presence of a table often inhibits maximum expressiveness. Most important, the instructor's authority and status can be deemphasized, and he or she can be viewed as a participant in the group. This arrangement has a high potential for learning because a small-group environment can be a positive force in learning, and all students have the opportunity for significant involvement.

The circle-of-chairs arrangement presents a friendly, relaxed, warm atmosphere in which all participants are expected to be fully engaged. In many ways, interpersonal–social learning is dependent on the extent of participation, depth of cohesion, and quality of peer relationships. The instructor role must be conveyed as a group facilitator and participant who is also expected to learn from the group.

The arrangements of chairs, tables, desks, or even participants themselves will convey a learning atmosphere and instructor philosophy to all participants. The instructional objectives, strategies, and activities should lead the professional school counselor to an appropriate classroom arrangement choice.

Working with the Classroom Teacher's Rules

It is the rare professional school counselor who has his or her own classroom. More typically, counselors are in an itinerant role wherein they teach in different classrooms. As a result, professional school counselors usually present lessons to intact classroom groups. In the elementary school, these classroom groups often are taught by one teacher for the entire day. Certain norms are already established by the teacher and students relative to behavior and discipline. As a professional who "comes and goes," it is important to have an understanding of these norms so that students have some consistency and know what to expect. Typically, teachers appreciate it when professional school counselors follow the basic rules in the classroom as well. This is not to suggest that professional school counselors must rely solely on the teacher's rules for classroom management and discipline. In fact, professional school counselors usually augment and adapt some rules to meet their personal style and professional role. Nevertheless, it is best not to contravene basic classroom rules as this may serve to confuse students and annoy teachers.

One of the typical roles of professional school counselors is as a consultant to classroom teachers. Counselors sometimes provide help in classroom-management strategies and working effectively with children who provide teachers with significant challenges. It is important that professional school counselors themselves are able to deal effectively with the wide range of students present in classrooms and to prevent discipline problems from arising. When problems do arise, it is imperative that professional school counselors attend to the issues in effective ways that are respectful to the student and his or her classmates.

Preventing Discipline Issues in the Classroom

The best way to deal with discipline issues in the classroom is by preventing occurrences in the first place. A well-designed lesson is essential. This includes several components, including making sure that the work is neither too hard nor too easy, that the work is not boring, and that expectations and instructions are clear (Saphier & Gower, 1997). Further information about presenting clear, effective lessons will be discussed later in this chapter.

A good lesson is only part of the equation, however. Saphier and Gower (1997) suggested two classroom-management skills that are fundamentally important. The first is getting and keeping children's attention properly focused. Several strategies comprise getting and keeping children's attention. One is working to keep the whole group alert and on task through positive strategies such as encouragement, enthusiasm, praise, nonsarcastic humor, and being dramatic. Another strategy is enlisting student involvement in the lesson. Teachers and professional school counselors do this by using an interesting variety of voice tones, piquing students' curiosity, using suspense, and connecting with students' interests and fantasies.

A second general management component that prevents discipline issues from occurring is having a smooth flow to one's lessons, a quality Saphier and Gower (1997) referred to as momentum. Momentum is composed of several parts, two of which will be described. One facet involves the ready availability of sufficient quantities of materials that students will need during the lesson. Few occurrences are as distracting to the flow of a lesson as having too many students sharing a finite resource material. Second, professional school counselors need to be aware of several things going on simultaneously, what teachers refer to as having "eyes in the back of your head." Classroom educators know what most groups and individuals are doing at any given time; further, they know what comes next in the lesson and what potential stumbling blocks might exist for off-task behavior during transitions. Being aware and knowledgeable, they seek proactively to prevent problems from occurring.

Managing Disruptive Behaviors as a Counselor in the Classroom

Despite educators' best efforts at prevention, children sometimes behave in ways that educators find disruptive. Professional school counselors know that students often bring with them concerns from home or from peer relationships that have little to do with being in class. These matters can make it difficult for students to benefit from regular instruction. A discipline plan needs to take into account that there are sometimes quite understandable reasons for children's misbehavior. Counselors, as consultants, help teachers see this and provide advice on dealing with it. Professional school counselors working in classrooms need to have strategies to handle problems directly.

When discipline problems arise, professional school counselors must first decide if there is a need to deal with the problem. They need to know what behaviors require intervention. It is important that the teacher's rules be respected; still, professional school counselors need to have a sense of their comfort level with different types of student behavior. Professional school counselors need to behave in such a way as to help students understand that the responsibility for the classroom's environment belongs to students, and that professional school counselors are not police officers present to enforce oppressive rules. This being said, it is important to have strategies available to deal with difficult behaviors in respectful and effective ways. Having such strategies is particularly important for professional school counselors who, by virtue of being in the classroom, set up potentially conflicting dual relationships with students whom they may later counsel.

There are several approaches that professional school counselors can take in addressing discipline problems that arise in the classroom setting. Effective approaches are based on the notion that the professional school counselor not act in an authoritarian manner, but rather, embody democratic principles. As a result of their professional preparation and personal demeanor, most professional school counselors do not tend toward authoritarianism. A mistake often made, however, is to move toward the polar opposite of authoritarianism—that of passivity, of being a nondisciplining "nice guy." While all professional school counselors wish to be liked by students, being passive relative to student classroom misbehavior can both undermine the respect students have toward professional school counselors and render lessons ineffective. Of the several approaches toward discipline available to counselors, one developed by Driekurs will be discussed (for an in-depth discussion on classroom discipline, see Albert, 1996; Charles & Senter, 2005).

Driekurs and Cassell (1974) classified student misbehavior according to the goals toward which students strive. Their system is reflective of Driekurs's conceptions of misbehavior derived from his work with Alfred Adler. Driekurs noted that classroom misbehavior stems from one of four student goals: attention seeking, power, revenge, and showing inadequacy. Students who seek power or revenge often feel powerless or oppressed. It is particularly important to develop a healthy nonauthoritarian relationship with these students. As a result of their work in providing responsive services in the school, professional school counselors often know these students quite well and, indeed, have developed strong, healthy relationships with them. When professional school counselors have strong alliances with these students and the counselor's presence in the classroom is not authoritarian, then it is unlikely that misbehaviors stemming from the goals of power and revenge will be apparent in class. According to Driekurs, students who withdraw or show inadequacy are discouraged and need encouragement. Obviously, professional school counselors should provide such support.

Attention-seeking behavior is the most common form of classroom misbehavior and the one that is most amenable to the application of logical consequences. Logical consequences are based on the belief that "social reality" requires certain behaviors. It is not the power of the professional school counselor or teacher that requires students to behave in certain ways, but the requirements of a just social order. Punishment is not meted out by the authority, but rather, the professional school counselor, in conjunction with the class, makes it known that certain behaviors have certain consequences.

Professional school counselors using this discipline strategy do not get in power struggles with students. They refrain from judging students or thinking of them as bad, and in a caring manner, they help students realize that certain behaviors result in certain consequences. The consequences need to be logically related to the student misbehavior. It is important as well that consequences reflect the social order, not the authority of the professional school counselor or teacher. As such, professional school counselors do not imply any moral judgment toward the student and use a kind, but firm voice. Anger has no part in discipline (Saphier & Gower, 1997).

Professional school counselors seek to prevent discipline issues from arising by having well-designed lessons. They are aware of potential times during their lessons when children might tend toward off-task behavior, and they seek to mitigate such behavior proactively. Professional school counselors act in such a way as to be clearly perceived as being nonauthoritarian, yet neither are they passive. By embodying democratic, authoritative principles of classroom management and discipline, professional school counselors are able to enact their role as educator in a positive manner. Armed with such knowledge about the interpersonal role of the professional school counselor as educator, it is necessary to know how to go about creating and designing a curriculum to implement.

CRAFTING A CURRICULUM

The process of developing a school counseling curriculum, while unique in some ways, is similar to the development of curriculum in other subject areas. While some states have subject-area curriculum decisions made at the state level, educators in other states create the entire curriculum at the local level. Locally, curricula are often developed via committees having representatives from stakeholder groups such as parents, community members, administrators, and central office staff (L. S. Kaplan, 1996). Whether at the state or local level, social studies experts play a large role in the development of social studies

curriculum. In mathematics curriculum development, mathematicians and their professional organizations' contributions are central. Likewise, in the development of a school counseling curriculum, the professional school counselor and the extant professional literature play primary roles.

School counseling leadership teams (Dahir et al., 1998) or guidance advisory committees (Gysbers & Henderson, 2000) develop curricula that support the counseling program's vision and overall goals. Regardless of the name of the group that provides leadership to the curriculum-writing process, curriculum development is a schoolwide responsibility requiring the active commitment and involvement of administrators and teachers. Because of professional school counselors' knowledge of the subject matter, however, leadership for developing a comprehensive curriculum is often provided by, or at least shared with, the professional school counselor or guidance director. Questions such as "How do professional school counselors decide what will be taught in each grade level?" and "What factors determine the curriculum goals and priorities?" will be addressed in the next section.

The *ASCA National Model* (2003a) should be considered when crafting a curriculum. In addition to considering national standards, professional school counselors in some states also incorporate standards from their state guidance and counseling models. Twenty-four states now have their own comprehensive programs, which have been developed over the past 15 years (Sink & MacDonald, 1998). Regardless of whether a local counseling program is guided by national standards or a state program, a central component of these programs is a theoretical foundation of fostering the academic, career, and personal–social development of students.

Within a state or national program foundation, professional school counselors, working together with a steering committee or advisory group, assess students' guidance and counseling needs as perceived by important constituencies in the school and community. Comprehensive program professionals (Gysbers & Henderson, 2000) recommend a formal needs assessment be administered at the outset of a move to a comprehensive program, and then readminis-tered about every 3 years. In this way, the pro-gram consistently represents the perceived needs of the supporting community. During this formal needs assessment, students, parents, teachers, administrators, and the wider community are asked about their perceptions of student needs. In states where comprehensive programs exist, these formal needs assessments reflect the state's curricular priorities, thus incorporating local stakeholders' perceptions into the program.

Needs are also assessed on a regular basis in a less formal way. An example of informal needs assessment involves professional school coun-selors speaking regularly with teachers, students, and staff and responding to changing needs in a timely way. For instance, recently there has been an increased focus on bullying prevention and intervention. Some states (e.g., New Hampshire) have enacted legislation designed to foster systemwide prevention and intervention. Many professional school counselors assess student and staff concerns regarding bullying and assist the system and the students to create bully-free and safe environments. On a more local scale, profes-sional school counselors respond to myriad specific classroom and grade-level requests by teachers and administrators. These requests range from teaching social skills in a particularly difficult second-grade class to addressing sexual harass-ment with seventh graders. In sum, the substance of professional school counselors' classroom interventions reflects state and national standards. Professional school counselors broadly assess local stakeholders and also keep their curriculum current, responsive, and relevant.

After conducting the formal needs assessment, and in conjunction with national standards and state standards, the school counseling leadership team or advisory council decides on the student outcomes it deems appropriate for the locality (Dahir et al., 1998). These student outcomes reflect what students need to be able to know or do on graduating from high school. Many school systems will use the *National Standards for School Counseling Programs* (C. Campbell & Dahir, 1997) as their outcomes. In this case, the nine stan-dards, three each from the domains of academic, career, and personal–social development, are the

outcomes. These outcomes are further broken down into a series of competencies that, when accomplished, will lead to the outcome or stan-dard. Finally, methods of assessment are detailed. (See Figure 8.3 for a flowchart of this process.) It is important to have agreed-on methods by which to judge the attainment of competencies. This process of generating an integrated curricu-lum is often done in conjunction with a district's comprehensive strategic plan.

The next phase in curriculum development is deciding how to help students meet the competencies. Professional school counselors and teachers sometimes create their own cur-riculum materials or use commercially available curricula. As a result of the NCLB legislation, there has been a recent emphasis in schools on using commercial curricula for which research evidence of effectiveness exists. Using these "evidence-based" curricular materials supports the efficacy of professional school counselors' classroom interventions. When schools carefully adopt a commercial curriculum that matches their outcomes and implement it in a pedagogi-cally sound manner, students are then in a position to achieve the desired competency. In their study on the national trends of professional

FIGURE 8.3
Steps involved in crafting a curriculum.

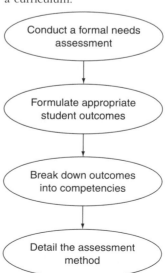

school counselors and curriculum materials, Rowley et al., (2005) surveyed school districts in 12 states about what type of curricular materials they use in implementing their guidance curriculum. Although this study does not suggest which are the best or most effective published curricular resources, the article does contain a table that lists over 20 curricular materials currently being used by those school counselors surveyed. For a description of several commonly used commercially available curricula, see Table 8.2. Classroom guidance lesson plans can also be found in journal articles,

books available from publishers, and on the Internet. Curriculum design and the creation of units and lessons will be discussed in the next section.

CREATING UNITS AND LESSONS

Scope and Sequence

To help students achieve the academic, career, and personal–social outcomes determined by leadership and advisory teams, professional

TABLE 8.2
Examples of commercially available curricula.

Second Step: Violence Prevention Curriculum. This program teaches social and emotional skills to prevent violence. The curriculum is easy to use and is unique in that it has parent education components. Research based, this program focuses on the three essential competencies that students need—empathy, impulse control and problem solving, and anger management. *Second Step* is a well-articulated curriculum spanning Grades Pre-K–9. It is one of the very few programs that meets the strict criteria of an "evidence-based" program (Poynton & Dimmit, 2004).

Student Success Skills. The *Student Success Skills (SSS),* designed for students in Grades 4–9, includes group counseling and a classroom guidance curriculum that helps students develop cognitive, social, and self-management skills. Also an evidence-based program, *SSS* has been shown in recent studies to improve math, reading, and social skills of students participating in the program (Brigman & Campbell, 2003).

DUSO (Developing Understanding of Self and Others). DUSO focuses on personal–social development. It is designed to help children in the primary grades understand social and emotional behavior.

Its goal is to assist children in developing positive self-images, in becoming more aware of the relationship between themselves and other people, and in recognizing their own needs and goals. *DUSO* uses listening, discussion, and dramatic play to help students focus on feelings, communication, and problem solving. Professional school counselors conduct activities with students that include stories, guided fantasies, puppetry, role play, and music.

Kelly Bear Programs:

Violence Prevention: A skills-based, video/DVD series for Grades Pre-K–3 that focuses on themes of bullying, resolving disputes, and controlling the self. *Drug Awareness (DAPP):* Also for Grades Pre-K–3, an eight-session program that promotes self-understanding, respect, empathy, positive behaviors, coping skills, resiliency, social competence, responsibility, problem-solving skills, refusal skills, and healthy-living habits.

Character and Resiliency Education Skills (CARES): This program seeks to prevent problem behaviors by promoting self-awareness, social competence, empathy and kindness toward others, problem-solving and anger-management skills, healthy-living choices, resiliency, refusal skills, and personal safety.

Educators for Social Responsibility (ESR) Programs:

Conflict Resolution in the Middle School presents developmentally appropriate classroom activities to help students effectively handle conflict. Skills are developed in areas such as active listening, perspective taking, negotiation, and mediation. Discussion, role-plays, and journal writing are employed to assist students in increasing their understanding of conflict, learning about conflict escalation and de-escalation, and exploring connections between diversity and conflicts.

(Continued)

TABLE 8.2 (Continued)

Creative Conflict Resolution provides elementary school teachers and counselors with ideas for responding to everyday classroom conflicts. A goal is to help teachers turn conflict into productive opportunity. Grounded in a theory of "peacemaking," ESR's programs are designed to help students deal nonviolently and constructively with anger, fear, aggression, and prejudice. ESR's elementary and middle school programs are focused on addressing conflict systemwide. In implementing these programs, professional school counselors work primarily as consultants to teachers and staff.

Here's Looking At You, 2000®. This program was designed to meet students' needs in drug education, is popular with counselors, and is often used in conjunction with Drug-Free Schools grants. The lessons in *Here's Looking At You, 2000®* seek to promote protective factors and to establish positive norms among students. A major thrust of the curriculum is to foster positive attitudes and behaviors among students and the school community. The curriculum features skills on self-control, how to resist pressure, making friends, and making and sticking to positive decisions. *Here's Looking At You, 2000®* makes use of cooperative learning teams. Cooperative learning fosters positive interdependence, individual accountability, and face-to-face interaction.

Skillstreaming. This psychoeducational program focuses on teaching students prosocial behavior through direct instruction in social skills. It uses the teaching procedures of modeling, role-playing, feedback, and transfer to help students develop these skills. Separate curricula have been developed for children of preschool age, elementary age, and adolescents. In contrast to some other programs, which seek broad, self-esteem-enhancing outcomes, *Skillstreaming* teaches specific skills such as asking permission, using self-control, accepting "no," and accepting a compliment (McGinnis & Goldstein, 1997; A. P. Goldstein & McGinnis, 1997).

The PASSPORT Program: A Journey Through Emotional, Social, Cognitive, and Self-Deveopment. This program, authored by Ann Vernon, is a prevention curriculum dedicated to helping students develop self-acceptance, build healthy relationships, solve problems, and make decisions effectively. This program integrates theory and a developmental understanding of school-age children, and uses them as a foundation to teach children how to act in their own and others' best interests (Hawes, 2000; Vernon, 1998).

National Education Association (NEA) (1–800–229–4200):

1. *Flirting or Hurting? A Teacher's Guide on Student-to-Student Sexual Harassment in Schools* (*Grades 6 Through 12*) by Nan Stein and Lisa Sjostrom.

2. *Bullyproof: A Teacher's Guide on Teasing and Bullying for Use with Fourth and Fifth Grade Students* by Nan Stein and Lisa Sjostrom.

school counselors must develop a comprehensive curriculum within their school or district. The breadth or content of the program provides its scope. Ideally, this is a K–12 effort; however, in districts, it is done by building level. In these cases, elementary counselors develop elementary curriculum, middle school counselors develop their curriculum, and high school counselors put together the secondary curriculum.

In curriculum design, it is important to ensure that grade-level learning is neither isolated from other grade levels nor redundant. This vertical articulation provides for a schoolwide or districtwide curriculum that builds skills and competencies sequentially (Kellough & Roberts, 2002). For professional school counselors, horizontal articulation is also important, particularly in schools where much of the curriculum is taught either solely by teachers or by professional school

counselors and teachers collaboratively. Horizontal articulation establishes the connection between the content of the counseling curriculum and content in other subject areas (Kellough & Roberts, 2002). For instance, social studies in the seventh grade might contain a unit on the medieval period, including the conflicts and battles of the time. Horizontal articulation suggests that professional school counselors weave their conflict resolution curriculum in with the social studies (and perhaps English and others) curriculum for a more integrated learning experience for students.

Conceptualizing a Unit

How professional school counselors conceptualize a curriculum unit depends on the model of curriculum implementation. As suggested, professional school counselors implement their curriculum either by direct teaching or by working collaboratively with teachers to present units and lessons together. A third model of implementation involves professional school counselors consulting with teachers and having teachers teach the lessons and units.

Professional school counselors who directly teach conflict resolution might choose to adopt a schoolwide approach to implementing this competency through using commercially available evidence-based curriculum materials. Professional school counselors using a locally developed approach for implementing a curriculum need to understand how to create and teach high-quality units and lessons. Many elementary counselors spend a set amount of time in different grade levels; it is not uncommon for professional school counselors to devise a curriculum unit that includes one lesson per week spanning 8 weeks. In this case, the professional school counselor would devise eight lessons in one general competency area, with one or more student outcomes being the anticipated result. The process of creating and teaching units and lessons is an important part of the role of the professional school counselor as educator.

In many schools, particularly at the elementary level, the professional school counselor's role in developmental classroom guidance includes itinerant, classroom-to-classroom teaching. It is important for professional school counselors to organize and present their units and lessons in classrooms in a manner that is coherent, clear, and effective. To achieve this, professional school counselors engage in a level of planning equivalent to that which teachers bring to their instructional planning.

Learning Considerations for Planning Units and Lessons

Professional school counselors see students as learners in a holistic sense. According to H. Gardner's (1999) theory of multiple intelligences, there are eight intelligences: linguistic, logical-mathematical, spatial, bodily-kinesthetic, naturalist, musical, intelligence about other people (interpersonal), and intelligence about ourselves (intrapersonal). Students may display

significant cognitive strengths and weaknesses in one or more of these intelligences (see Table 8.3). Understanding that students enter the learning environment with multiple cognitive strengths and weaknesses implies that instruction as well as assessment should be varied. At a minimum, this suggests that instruction should seek to help students develop in cognitive, affective, and psychomotor-kinesthetic-behavioral domains. Although these domains have much overlap and are not entirely discrete, the following discussion highlights their focus.

In the cognitive domain, there are six levels or categories of cognitive understanding (Bloom et al., as cited in Kellough & Roberts, 2002): knowledge, comprehension, application, analysis, synthesis, and evaluation. Within a lesson plan or unit, it is important to teach to and evaluate within several of the categories of the cognitive domain. In teaching conflict resolution, it might be helpful for students to have knowledge of the terms and words that describe the process of resolving conflict peaceably. Further, professional school counselors need to be sure that students show they understand the material. The domain of comprehension attends to this and is ascertained by having students explain or describe what they have learned. As an example of these first two levels, professional school counselors might devise a game-show activity to help students learn and show their understanding of terms such as *de-escalation* and *negotiation*. Applying the knowledge (application) can be taught by devising scenarios and having students be able to choose which particular conflict resolution strategy might best be applied in a given situation.

In other lessons in the unit, a professional school counselor might want students to analyze the relation among violence, bullying, and conflict by discussing and hypothesizing how to manage real conflicts that arise on the playground. A synthesis-level objective of a conflict resolution unit might have students combine knowledge learned about a specific conflict in social studies class—for example, the Revolutionary War—and have them act out a mediation session between the British and Americans. The final level of cognitive skill, evaluation, might be addressed by having a "courtroom" in which students sit on

TABLE 8.3
Gardner's multiple intelligences summarized.

Linguistic intelligence involves the ability to use language (native or otherwise) to express ideas and understand the ideas of others. Poets, writers, orators, speakers, and lawyers rely on linguistic intelligence.

Logical-mathematical intelligence requires an understanding of the underlying principles of some kind of causal system, or the manipulation of numbers, quantities, and operations. Scientists, logicians, engineers, and mathematicians rely on logical-mathematical intelligence.

Spatial intelligence involves the ability to represent the spatial world internally in your mind. It is important in the arts and sciences. For example, if you possess spatial intelligence and are artistic, you may gravitate toward painting, sculpture, or architecture. Surgeons, topologists, navigators, and chess players rely on spatial intelligence.

Musical intelligence involves the capacity to think musically—so much so that the music is omnipresent and free flowing. The musically intelligent are able to hear patterns, recognize them, remember them, and perhaps manipulate them.

Bodily-kinesthetic intelligence involves the ability to use the whole body or parts of your body (e.g., hands, fingers, arms) to solve complex motor problems. Such activities may involve making something or performing some action or production. Athletes, carpenters, dancers, and actors rely on bodily-kinesthetic intelligence.

Interpersonal intelligence involves understanding how to get along with other people, and how to solve problems of an interpersonal nature. Teachers, clinicians, salespersons, and politicians rely on interpersonal intelligence.

Intrapersonal intelligence involves having an understanding of oneself. People with intrapersonal intelligence know what they can and cannot do and when to ask for help. They can control impulses and are self-motivated.

Naturalist intelligence involves the human ability to discriminate among and classify living things (e.g., plants, animals) and features of the natural world (e.g., clouds, rock configurations). Hunters, farmers, botanists, and chefs rely on the naturalist intelligence. Children also frequently display these capabilities in classification hobbies.

panels as "judges" and evaluate the effectiveness of the mediation sessions using the knowledge they have learned. All of these cognitive levels of understanding might be included as a professional school counselor plans a unit on conflict resolution.

Cognitive learning is important, but it is not the sole means through which a holistic understanding of curricular areas occurs. The affective domain is also an important aspect of instruction. It focuses on using and developing intra- and interpersonal intelligences. While some consider teaching for affective understanding more difficult to conceptualize and assess, Krathwal, Bloom, and Masia (as cited in Kellough & Roberts, 2002) developed a system of affective understanding that is modeled after the cognitive levels of Bloom and colleagues described earlier. In this system, understanding is organized on a continuum that ranges from surface-level learning to those types

of affective understanding that reflect the personal internalization of values.

The five levels of affective learning are receiving, responding, valuing, organizing, and internalizing. At the receiving level, students might simply be aware of the affective aspect of a lesson. For instance, some students who were observing the courtroom scene might listen attentively to the proceedings; they are receiving affective instruction. At the responding level, we may ask the observing group to discuss how they believe the "actors" felt during their role-play. The valuing domain is critical in affective learning. Again, using the example of conflict resolution, professional school counselors might focus on valuing by asking students how they feel when they are called belittling names by their peers. As such, this group-brainstorming activity would be addressing students' values regarding respect. After several lessons, professional school counselors might ask students to monitor their own and others' behaviors regarding conflict, thus providing a gauge for ascertaining the depths to which affective learning (and ultimately behavioral change) has occurred.

The fourth and fifth levels in the affective domain are typically longer term goals and may, in fact, be ultimate standards or outcomes within a comprehensive program. Nevertheless, lessons often attend to them. For instance, in the organizing domain, teaching typically refers to conceptualizing and arranging values. In our example of the Revolutionary War and conflict resolution, professional school counselors and teachers can engage students in understanding and organizing their values relative to peaceful conflict resolution and notions of liberty and fairness. Finally, we want lessons to help students internalize their beliefs and help them develop consistency between their beliefs and their actions. This can be done by teachers and professional school counselors at regular class meetings wherein students discuss and process the events of the day. (For an in-depth discussion of a classroom and schoolwide approach to developing interpersonal values and respect, see Charney, 1992.)

The final broad area of learning is the psychomotor–kinesthetic–behavioral domain. Harrow (as cited in Kellough & Roberts, 2002) discussed four areas within this hierarchy: moving, manipulating, communicating, and creating. Because they concern skill development in areas of gross- and fine-motor coordination, moving and manipulating focus on areas of learning that are typically less relevant to the professional school counselor's curriculum. Communicating and creating are the domains that are the most salient. For instance, in a lesson on conflict resolution, students might improve their communication skills and be able to create solutions to problems that have led to conflict in the past.

In a well-designed unit, professional school counselors attend to learning and development in the cognitive, affective, and psychomotor–kinesthetic–behavioral domains. To ensure adequate attention to the levels of learning and development, professional school counselors create learning objectives.

Learning Objectives

When the counseling curriculum is competency based, it is necessary that the lessons result in measurable outcomes. One way to ensure attainment of outcomes is to write learning objectives for each lesson. Learning objectives focus the professional school counselor on the desired outcome of students' participation in the lesson. To address the holistic needs relative to student development, it is helpful for professional school counselors to write objectives that are reflective of the cognitive, affective, and psychomotor—kinesthetic—behavioral domains of instruction. With this focus in mind, consider the components of thoroughly conceived and written learning objectives.

There are four parts that comprise measurable learning objectives commonly referred to as the ABCDs of learning objectives (Erford & McKechnie, 2004; Kellough & Roberts, 2002). First, the audience (A) for whom the objective is intended needs to be stated. In most cases, this is the student, although it could be the learning group or the whole class. It is not uncommon for many learning objectives to include the phrase "The student will be able to. . . ." Second, the expected behavior (B) needs to be stated clearly. These behaviors are typically descriptive verbs that address the cognitive, affective, or psychomotor–kinesthetic–behavioral outcome around which the lesson is structured. Using the example of conflict resolution again, one cognitive domain outcome might read, in part, "The student will be able to identify behaviors that lead to conflict." A learning objective that addresses affective learning at the valuing level, yet is still written in behavioral terms, might state, "Students will voice their beliefs regarding. . . ." Finally, a learning objective might be more oriented toward psychomotor–kinesthetic–behavioral outcomes. An example of this might be, "The class will create a process allowing students to solve conflicts without teacher intervention."

In addition to denoting the audience and the expected measurable outcome, learning objectives also typically include the conditions (C) under which the learning will occur and be observed.

This third component specifies when or how the intended behavior will be measured. One of the examples with the inclusion of this third component might read, "After observing role-plays, the student will be able to identify behaviors that lead to conflict." The fourth and final component of a well-written learning objective is the degree (D) of the expected performance, or how frequently students will need to exhibit the behavior for the objective to be considered met. If there were three role-plays and students successfully identified the behaviors in two of the three, the professional school counselor needs to know whether that level of performance is considered successful. The inclusion of the level of expected performance would render the complete learning objective to read, "After observing three role-plays, the student will be able to identify behaviors that lead to conflict in at least two of the three scenarios." If students do not achieve the competency or do not achieve it at the specified rate, then the professional school counselor may decide to design a new learning activity to reach the desired outcome. See Table 8.4 for a summary table of the ABCDs of learning objectives with examples from cognitive, affective, and psychomotor–kinesthetic–behavioral domains.

CONSTRUCTING DEVELOPMENTAL LESSONS AND ACTIVITIES

Lessons can be conceptualized as having three distinct parts: an introduction, the developmental activities of the lesson, and the conclusion.

TABLE 8.4
Components of measurable learning objectives by learning domain.

	Cognitive Domain	Affective Domain	Psychomotor–Kinesthetic–Behavioral Domain
Component A **Audience:** Specify the audience for whom the objective is intended	The student will . . .	Students will . . .	The class will . . .
Component B **Behavior:** Specify the expected behaviors	The student will be able to identify behaviors that lead to conflict.	Students will voice their beliefs.	The class will create a process allowing students to solve conflicts without teacher intervention.
Component C **Conditions:** Specify the conditions under which learning will occur and be observed. How will the intended behavior be measured?	After observing role-plays, the student will be able to identify behaviors that lead to conflict.	After discussing the components of respect, students will voice their beliefs regarding respectful behavior.	At the end of four meetings on playground behavior, the class will create a process allowing students to solve conflicts without teacher intervention.
Component D **Degree:** Specify the expected degree of performance. Specify what is acceptable performance.	After observing three role-plays, the student will be able to identify behaviors that lead to conflict in at least two of the three scenarios.	After discussing the components of respect, at least two thirds of the students in the class will voice their beliefs regarding respectful behavior that includes both significant personal experience and considerable content from the discussion.	At the end of four meetings on playground behavior, the class will create a process allowing students to solve conflicts without teacher intervention. If it reduces the need for teacher intervention by 25%, it will be considered successful.

A well-designed lesson increases the likelihood that students will invest their energies in learning the material and will be more likely to learn what is being taught. Further, a pedagogically sound lesson captures students' interest and allows them to extend their knowledge and competency.

Introducing Lessons

There are two important aspects to introducing a lesson to students. One is to communicate with the student an overview and the overall objective of the lesson. When professional school counselors do this clearly, students develop an itinerary of their learning and know what the expected learning objectives will be. The second important aspect of lesson introduction is to help students understand that they already know something about the topic at hand and that, during the lesson, they will be working to extend their knowledge or skills (Saphier & Gower, 1997).

Typically, students already know some information about the areas being taught. For instance, a school counseling program may be working toward the outcome that "Students will acquire skills to investigate the world of work in relation to knowledge of self and to make informed career choices" (C. Campbell & Dahir, 1997, p. 25). Since this is a program outcome or standard, learning will have been developed at various checkpoints throughout previous grades. Therefore, it is likely that students will already have some knowledge of the required skills as well as how to go about making informed choices. In fact, if we have vertically articulated the curriculum properly, the counseling curriculum builds in a sequential and logical manner. Let us posit that the specific eighth-grade benchmark comprising the standard is that students will understand their interests, motivations, skills, and abilities. Prior to the eighth grade, students likely will have had some curricular and personal experiences supportive of the benchmark. Activating this previous knowledge helps provide the groundwork for a productive educational session.

Activating previous knowledge helps students orient themselves to the lesson. It shows them that they already know some important information and that the topic at hand is not entirely new. Done well, it also motivates students and provides a continued rationale for their efforts. There are several ways school counselors can activate students' previous knowledge and, in so doing, effectively introduce a lesson.

One method frequently used is semantic mapping (Saphier & Gower, 1997). In a semantic mapping exercise for the career development example, the professional school counselor might ask the class, "What motivates people to receive good grades or work hard?" The professional school counselor might list the students' responses in logical categories suggesting internal motivators (wanting to learn the material, being interested in it) and external motivators (making the honor roll, being rewarded by parents). The professional school counselor can show students what they already know on the topic and get them actively involved in the lesson.

Developmental Activities

Once students' previous knowledge has been activated and they have been oriented to the topic, they are ready to engage in the learning activity. Learning activities are student experiences that facilitate mastery of the lesson's objectives. It is essential to clearly delineate learning objectives because understanding what students are to learn not only helps professional school counselors design lessons most likely to accomplish that end, but also allows meaningful assessment. There are two broad areas of understanding that can help guide professional school counselors as they design learning activities: multiple intelligences and level of activity.

As discussed earlier, students can be considered to have multiple intelligences. Given this theory, professional school counselors make efforts to structure and implement their lessons to draw on the variety of cognitive strengths and weaknesses that students may have. Schools have traditionally focused on fostering linguistic or verbal learning. For instance, both traditional, teacher-led discussions and most writing assignments draw heavily on linguistic intelligence. Although professional school counselors will want to teach and assess students, using language and verbal skills, they have a broad understanding of intelligence and design lessons likely to draw on a variety of student strengths. For instance, learning can both occur and be expressed through music. Tapping students' musical intelligence might involve having students create a song, rap, or chant that describes the steps involved in problem solving or conflict resolution (Armstrong, 1994). Other activities can involve drawing on knowledge of self (intrapersonal intelligence). In a lesson on feelings, this intrapersonal approach might ask students to reflect on times they were sad. Interpersonal intelligence is activated when professional school counselors ask groups to work together to come up with a solution to a problem. Other avenues for learning include artistic, spatial, naturalist, logical-mathematical, and kinesthetic modalities. To access these avenues, professional school counselors often use role-plays and art during lessons. Professional school counselors design a variety of activities that draw on the multiple intelligences students may possess, to teach and assess the learning objectives.

In a similar vein, there are many types of teaching strategies relative to student activity level. These range from the teacher or expert at the front of the class to those strategies that keep all students actively involved in their learning. Generally, it is better pedagogically for the professional school counselor to keep students active as opposed to passive. This is not to suggest that professional school counselors never stand before a group of students and explain information. In fact, this may be an important aspect of some lessons. Still, this type of learning experience limits student participation to only one sense—auditory learning. Professional school counselors can increase the students' experience to two senses by adding visual activities (e.g., pictures, videos, and overheads) to their presentations (Kellough & Roberts, 2002). Although the addition of visual cues does not amount to what is considered active learning, it involves more of the student than merely listening to the teacher or counselor does. The more active levels of student involvement have students simulating or engaging in direct experiences.

Using an example of teaching conflict resolution, professional school counselors might have students role-play conflict de-escalation strategies to provide a simulated experience. In a lesson on connecting interests to career clusters, all students might take a computerized interest assessment individually and then work with a partner or in small groups to investigate several career clusters. Or, all students might play a classroom game such as the Real Game (Barry & Wright, 1996) or the Real Deal (Ad Council, 2000). Many teachers and professional school counselors use cooperative learning groups (CLGs) to foster students' active learning. In CLGs, students work together, each having a specific role within the group (Kellough & Roberts, 2002). Finally, when teachers and professional school counselors use peer mediators to help resolve conflict, the type of learning students experience is direct and reflects real life. Professional school counselors are aware of the various levels of learning and strive to help students be as active as possible during lessons and units.

Conclusion, Assessment, and Follow-up

On completing the planned developmental activities, it is important to reinforce and conclude the session's learning by summarizing the essential points of the lesson. An experienced classroom educator will usually plan for at least 2 to 5 minutes to successfully summarize and end the lesson. Many professional school counselors also prefer to have the students contribute to the summary as a way of promoting an additional learning experience and testing students' comprehension and knowledge of the day's lesson. It is generally most efficient to begin the summary by restating the lesson's objective(s) and briefly reviewing how the lesson built on previously developed skills and knowledge. Next, the professional school counselor should strive to encapsulate the content of the developmental activities, highlighting the important content and experiences. Finally, experienced professional school counselors attempt to get students to generalize the classroom experience to real-world experiences by asking students how the lessons learned can apply to life outside of the classroom or to their short- or long-term academic, career, or personal–social goals. Skilled classroom educators know that this generalization process, accompanied by real-life homework assignments, is the best way to get students to remember the classroom-based learning and transfer it to daily life.

Perhaps the most essential and overlooked part of guidance instruction is the assessment of learning objectives. For some reason, many professional school counselors develop the self-defeating perception or attitude that "What we do can't be measured or evaluated." Nothing could be further from the truth. In fact, it is this errant attitude that has put the profession in jeopardy in this age of educational accountability and reform. Can you imagine a math, science, reading, or social studies teacher explaining that he or she can't measure what children have learned or can do as a result of his or her instruction? It sounds equally ridiculous when principals or other stakeholders hear this from professional school counselors! Of course effective school counselors produce measurable gains in students' learning. The key, however, is to plan for assessment when the learning objectives are written, rather than after the lesson is taught.

Well-written learning objectives are the key to effective instruction and outcomes. If a learning objective is written in accordance with the model in Table 8.4, assessment is made simple because the audience, expected behavior, measurement parameters, and expected level of performance have already been specified. At this point, all the professional school counselor need do is collect the data as specified in the learning objective and apply the specified criterion. For example, consider the cognitive domain learning objective shown in Table 8.4: "After observing three role-plays, the student will be able to identify behaviors that lead to conflict in at least two of the three scenarios." To document that the learning objective has been met, the professional school counselor must design three role-plays and write out a list of behaviors leading to conflict that the student may observe. Then the scenarios are presented one at a time and the student is asked to write at least one observable behavior for each scenario that led to the conflict. If the student is able to discern behaviors that were on the list compiled by the professional school counselor for two of the three scenarios, the learning objective has been met.

Of course, the real value of assessment is that it helps to inform our practice. If assessment of learning objectives indicates student nonmastery, then it follows that the instructional process must be analyzed and improved. Were objectives clearly stated? Were the expectations too high? Were the activities ineffective? Were the assessment criteria and strategies inappropriate? Each of these steps in the process must be visited, analyzed, and, if necessary, refined or redesigned before the lesson is repeated. Too often in education—and school counseling—professionals continue to implement ineffective curricula and even blame the unsuccessful students. Professional school counselors, as educators, must look to the processes and strategies implemented and further tailor them to the needs of the students.

Chapter 12 discusses outcome assessment procedures and program evaluation in detail, stating that those types of programmatic assessments should be conducted systematically. The assessment of learning objectives at the classroom level is just as important. Logically, if a professional school counselor successfully implements a guidance curriculum as documented by assessments of learning objectives at the classroom level, and these objectives directly relate to the school counseling program's outcomes, then the evaluation of the program will also result in success.

Finally, follow-up is an essential part of the learning process frequently disregarded by professional school counselors. Why should busy professional school counselors "waste time" on follow-up? After all, when someone has been "fixed," that's the end of the story, isn't it? Not at all! Many children require booster sessions to review and extend on what they have learned. Regarding personal–social and mental health interventions, recidivism, or slipping back into old habits and behaviors, is a huge problem. If nothing else, simply checking back with students within a few days or weeks after a lesson or intervention can bolster their learning and behavioral change. Another part of follow-up may involve follow-up assessment procedures to ensure that changes in learning and behavior are continuing. Such valuable information helps the professional school counselor and classroom teacher to be responsive to potential recidivism and act accordingly.

Follow-up is a way of checking progress and shoring up support for students. It is arguably the most important, cost-effective step in the process because it prevents all previous instructional or intervention time and effort from being wasted! In other words, choosing not to spend a few minutes on follow-up could lead to hours of wasted instructional or intervention effort. Figure 8.4 presents a flowchart of the process for constructing developmental lessons and activities.

Professional school counselors as educators are knowledgeable about how students learn. They are aware of students' multiple intelligences and design learning activities that attend to the development of the whole student. Lessons featuring cognitive learning are commonly taught alongside lessons that address both affective and psychomotor–kinesthetic–behavioral domains of learning. Professional school counselors design units and lessons for students at all grade levels—they carefully plan the objectives for the lesson and how they will both teach and evaluate learning. Figure 8.5 shows a planning outline for professional school counselors to use as they prepare their lessons. Figures 8.6, 8.7, and 8.8 show lessons and examples of counseling curriculum at elementary, middle, and high school levels, respectively.

FIGURE 8.4
Constructing developmental lessons and activities.

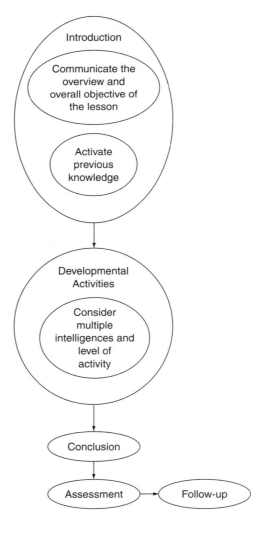

FIGURE 8.5
Outline for effective lesson plans.

Title of Lesson:

Outcome or Standard:

Competency:

Learning Objective(s):

Materials:

Developmental Learning Activities:

   Introduction:

   Activity:

   Conclusion:

Assessment/Evaluation:

Follow-up:

FIGURE 8.6
Example of an elementary school lesson.

Title of Lesson: Understanding your multiple intelligences

Outcome or Standard: Students will acquire the attitudes, knowledge, and skills that contribute to effective learning in school and across the life span. (C. Campbell & Dahir, 1997).

Competency: (a) Identify attitudes and behaviors that lead to successful learning; (b) Apply knowledge of learning styles to positively influence school performance.

Learning Objective: After completing the Teele Multiple Intelligences Inventory,* 90% of fifth-grade students will be able to identify their top three intelligence strengths as determined by personal ratings.

Materials: One copy of the Teele Multiple Intelligences Inventory and a pencil for each student.

Developmental Learning Activities:

   Introduction: Begin with a discussion of how every student has different learning strengths and weaknesses. For example, some students would rather work in groups, others alone. Some like to think out loud, others in silence. Some like to draw a picture of how something works, others would rather act it out. Then solicit several examples of learning strengths from students (thereby connecting the current objective to previous knowledge).

(Continued)

FIGURE 8.6 (Continued)

Activity: Pass out one copy of the Teele Multiple Intelligences Inventory to each student and read the directions for completing the inventory aloud. Because the inventory is pictorial, no reading or language skills are required. After the directions are completed, allow 15 minutes for students to complete the inventory. When time is up, explain how to transfer student responses to the scoring form and "score" the inventory. After students have scored their own inventories, have them write the titles of their top three categories (intelligences) on a sheet of paper. Use Table 8.3 of this text (Gardner's multiple intelligences) to explain to students the skills associated with their top three intelligences.

Conclusion: Next, lead students in a discussion of their interests and skills related to each intelligence on their list and challenge students to think about what they have done to develop these abilities, and what they could do to develop these abilities to even higher levels.

Assessment/Evaluation: At the end of the session, collect student papers containing their top three intelligences and determine the percentage of fifth-grade students who have determined their top three choices. If 90% of the students complied, the objective has been met.

Follow-up: In a future session, review Gardner's eight intelligences and ask students to share events when they were using these abilities to master academic content.

*Teele, S. (2000). *Rainbow of intelligence: Exploring how students learn.* Thousand Oaks, CA: Corwin Press.

FIGURE 8.7
Example of a middle school lesson.

Title: Understanding Sexual Harassment

Outcome or Standard: Students will understand safety and survival skills (ASCA National Standard C within "Personal/Social Development"; C. Campbell & Dahir, 1997).

Competency: Students will learn about the relation between rules, laws, safety, and the protection of individual rights.

Learning Objective(s):

1. After group discussion and counselor-led instruction, all students will be able to identify the correct definition of sexual harassment. (This is basic *knowledge* within the cognitive domain of understanding.)
2. Subsequent to group discussions, all students will describe incidences of sexual harassment they have seen or experienced and how these incidences made them feel. (This objective supports the development of the *responding* level of affective learning.)

(Continued)

FIGURE 8.7 (Continued)

Materials: Large-sized paper, markers.

Developmental Learning Activity:

Introduction: The professional school counselor begins by initiating a discussion with students about respectful behavior. (This serves as groundwork to connect the current learning objectives to previous knowledge.) The professional school counselor then asks the students to brainstorm in pairs about how respectful behavior is sometimes codified in rules and laws. Pairs then share ideas with the larger group and the counselor writes the ideas on the board. (Make a connection to previous knowledge, this time regarding social studies. The activity of having students work in pairs increases the level of student involvement and is called Think, Pair, Share [Saphier & Gower, 1997].)

Activity:
1. The counselor asks students to get into groups by gender, i.e., all male and all female groups. Their task is to brainstorm examples of disrespectful behavior they have seen or heard that is directed toward one gender or the other.
2. Groups write their experiences on large sheets of paper. Then representatives from the groups tape the sheets of paper on the walls.
3. The counselor discusses the students' experiences, paying particular attention to how it feels or might feel to be the recipient of such behavior.
4. Finally, using the concepts generated, the counselor shares with the students the definition of sexual harassment (unwanted behavior directed at a person based on his or her gender). The counselor can provide examples of sexual harassment that the students have not generated (for example, see Strauss, 1994, for a thorough listing of commonly reported types of student-to-student sexual harassment).

Conclusion: The professional school counselor asks students to share ideas about how the knowledge they have generated can be used to better their environment. (This is also a lead into the follow-up activity below.)

Assessment/Evaluation:
1. At the beginning of the next session when the professional school counselor meets with the group, he or she reads the students the three possible definitions of sexual harassment. Students vote by a show of hands which definition is correct. (This attends to the first learning objective and provides a time lapse so that the counselor can ascertain whether students retained the information.)
2. Accomplishment of the second learning objective is completed by the lesson itself. By observing the group's process and outcome (as demonstrated by students' verbal and written responses), the professional school counselor determines the degree to which the objective is met.

Follow-up:
In a subsequent session, the counselor has students work in mixed-gender groups to create a system of classroom and school norms regarding sexual harassment.

FIGURE 8.8
Example of a high school lesson.

Title: Career Exploration and Postsecondary Planning

Outcome or Standard: Students will acquire the skills to investigate the world of work in relation to knowledge of self and to make informed career decisions (ASCA National Standard A within "Career Development"; Campbell & Dahir, 1997).

Competencies:

1. Students will develop skills to locate, evaluate, and interpret career information.
2. Students will learn about the variety of traditional and nontraditional occupations.
3. Students will develop an awareness of personal abilities, skills, interests, and motivations.

Learning Objective(s):

Using the Internet, students will be able to locate self-assessments, career assessment materials, career information, and postsecondary options in sufficient quantity and quality so that they are able to write a paper about their postsecondary choices (knowledge, application, analysis, and synthesis).

Materials: Computer lab with access to the Internet, a list of Web sites.

Developmental Learning Activities:

Introduction: The counselor introduces the topic of postsecondary planning and the importance of self-assessment in career decision making. The counselor gives an overview of the use of assessment materials and their strengths and limitations in helping select appropriate postsecondary options.

Activity:

1. Students meet in groups of four to discuss the types of postsecondary options and career choices in which they may already be interested. Each student generates at least three postsecondary options.
2. In a computer lab at a computer, students begin by taking an interest inventory online. The counselor should provide students with some Web site addresses where they can access a career quiz.
3. Students identify 10–12 careers that seem interesting and look for other relevant Web sites to explore these occupations (such as Occupational Outlook Handbook: http://stats.bls.gov/oco/).

Conclusion: Students share their experience and relate what they found to be surprising, or what reinforced earlier beliefs about themselves.

Assessment/Evaluation: In collaboration with the English teacher, students are asked to prepare a paper about their postsecondary choices and the developmental steps they could take to reach their goals. (This analysis-synthesis-level assessment is in the cognitive domain. If students accomplish this higher level task, they will have shown that they also mastered the knowledge and application-level objectives.)

Follow-up: The professional school counselor meets with the English teacher to discuss future classroom guidance units to bolster student learning and decision making in the career domain. In addition, the professional school counselor offers groups based on postsecondary options (such as a 4-year college group, a 2-year college group, a job-entry group, a military group) that will meet on a regular basis and address barriers and other issues relevant to postsecondary and career options.

SUMMARY/CONCLUSION

Professional school counselors provide direct services to students through a number of roles, including that of classroom educator. Professional school counselors spend time in classrooms teaching developmental lessons to students. Through these lessons, counselors seek to implement a comprehensive developmental curriculum comprised of standards from academic, career, and personal–social domains. The ultimate goal of the professional school counselor in this role is for all students to achieve the developmental outcomes that the local school counseling leadership team deems essential.

To reach this important goal, professional school counselors work with teachers to integrate the counseling curriculum with other components in the school's curriculum. Professional school counselors ensure that all students receive instruction in the counseling curriculum either through teachers, by teacher–counselor teams, or by professional school counselors themselves. When professional school counselors deliver the curriculum themselves, they strive to maintain the high standards of the teaching profession. This means that they manage the classroom well and create positive learning environments for students. Most important, professional school counselors know how to design effective, interesting lessons for diverse groups of students. At times, this means starting from scratch and creating one's own unit or plan. Other times, counselors incorporate lesson elements from well-researched commerically available curricula. Whether they use their own or commercially available curricula, professional school counselors help students attain important cognitive, affective, and behavioral outcomes.

Now go to our Companion Website at www.prenhall.com/erford to assess your understanding of chapter content with "Multiple-Choice Questions," apply comprehension with "Essay Questions," and broaden your knowledge of the school counseling profession with related "Web Links."

ACTIVITIES

1. Think back to when you were in elementary, middle, or high school. Who was your favorite teacher? Why was he or she your favorite? How can you honor the memory of that teacher in your work as a developmental guidance classroom specialist?
2. Go to a local school and ask to observe a master teacher for a half day. Note the following:
   a. How does the teacher introduce lessons?
   b. What rules seem to be implicit in the classroom? Which are explicit?

   c. How do students treat each other? What is your sense of the teacher's role in this?
   d. How active are students? How does the teacher help them to learn?

3. Brainstorm five classroom guidance lessons that you could develop that would be appropriate for the education level you are interested in pursuing. For one of the five lessons, create a full lesson plan. Make sure to include appropriate headings and activities for the age group with which you are working.

CHAPTER 9

COUNSELING INDIVIDUALS AND GROUPS IN SCHOOL

DEBBIE W. NEWSOME AND SAMUEL T. GLADDING

Editor's Introduction: Individual and group counseling have long been effective tools in the professional school counselor's toolbox and will continue to be so in the transformed role. It is essential that professional school counselors have a strong background in developmental counseling theory as well as more specialized approaches, especially brief, solution-focused models. Such breadth of training reflects belief in both the developmental nature of many childhood struggles and the value of time-limited counseling interventions.

VIGNETTE 1

Meagan, age 6, is in Mrs. Hendrick's first-grade classroom. Recently, Meagan has been crying in class and withdrawing from activities. On talking with Meagan's mother, Mrs. Hendrick learns that Meagan's mother and father separated last month. Mrs. Hendrick wonders if it would be helpful for Meagan to talk with you, the professional school counselor.

VIGNETTE 2

Since starting 10th grade, 16-year-old Eric, an African American, has been skipping classes. Consequently, his grades have dropped from Bs and Cs to Ds and Fs. One of Eric's friends stops by your office and tells you that he thinks Eric has become involved with a gang and is thinking about dropping out of school.

VIGNETTE 3

This academic year has been especially difficult for several students on the sixth-grade team. Two students have experienced the death of a parent. One student had a sister killed in an automobile accident. Another sixth grader recently lost his grandmother, with whom he had a very close relationship. Mr. Tobias, the school principal, approaches you to see if there is anything you can do to help.

VIGNETTE 4

Andrea, age 10, is new to the school. She is Romanian and was adopted in July by an American family. She speaks limited English and has made very few friends. Andrea has heard that you are available to talk with students who are having difficulties, but she is embarrassed to approach you.

VIGNETTE 5

Stephen, a 15-year-old Caucasian boy, is questioning his sexual orientation. Last week, somebody defaced his locker by writing "gay" and "fag" on it. He comes to you distressed, angry, and hurt, stating, "Sometimes I think I'd be better off dead."

VIGNETTE 6

Mrs. Macon, the PE teacher, has noticed that one of her eighth-grade students, Abby, has lost several pounds over the course of the past quarter. She tires easily in gym class, refuses to shower afterward, and is wearing sweaters even though it is warm outside. "I'm worried that Abby has an eating disorder," Mrs. Macon tells you. "What can we do?"

Professional school counselors in elementary, middle, and high school settings are likely to face issues similar to these during the course of their work. When faced with such situations, it is important to know how to respond.

Comprehensive developmental school counseling programs provide the means for addressing students' immediate needs and concerns through the component called *responsive services*. Responsive services provide special help to students who are facing problems that interfere with their personal, social, career, or educational development. Specific interventions may be preventive, remedial, or crisis oriented. Individual and small group counseling are two activities that are classified as responsive services (ASCA, 2003a; Gysbers & Henderson, 2000). Other activities that are considered part of the responsive services component include crisis counseling, referrals, consultation and collaboration, and peer facilitation.

Although the amount of time allocated for responsive services differs from school to school, general guidelines (e.g., Gysbers & Henderson, 2000) suggest that professional school counselors in elementary and middle schools allocate 30% to 40% of their time to responsive services, and that high school counselors spend 25% to 35% of their time administering these services. In this chapter, we focus on the counseling component of responsive services by describing strategies for working with individuals and groups in schools. We also provide an overview of crisis counseling and crisis intervention in schools.

INDIVIDUAL COUNSELING IN SCHOOLS

Family changes, violence, poverty, chronic illness, and interpersonal difficulties, as well as typical developmental transitions, are just a few of the myriad issues that can interfere with students' personal, social, and academic growth. When these or other concerns negatively impact a student's development and progress, individual counseling may be warranted. Professional school counselors make decisions about how to administer individual counseling services, keeping in mind that those services need to closely align with the educational mission and philosophy of educating all students to high levels of academic, career, and personal–social success (ASCA, 2003a; Eschenauer & Chen–Hayes, 2005). In this section, we provide a definition of counseling in school settings. We then discuss developmental factors that affect the counseling process and provide a generic model for individual counseling in schools. Finally, we describe a model of brief counseling that has been used effectively in schools: solution-focused brief counseling (SFBC; Sklare, 1997, 2005).

COUNSELING IN SCHOOLS DEFINED

ASCA (2003a) defined counseling as "a special type of helping process implemented by a professionally trained and certified person, involving a variety of techniques and strategies that help students explore academic, career, and personal/social issues impeding healthy development or academic process" (p. 129). The ultimate goal of implementing counseling interventions is to promote students' personal and social growth and to foster their academic process. Some of the concerns that may be addressed in counseling include academic problems, relationship issues, grief and loss, family concerns, anger control, sexual issues, and stress management. Referrals for individual counseling may come from students, parents, teachers, or others who are involved with students. Although individual counseling cannot meet the needs of all students in K–12 schools (Eschenauer & Chen–Hayes, 2005), it represents a vital component of a comprehensive developmental school counseling program.

Individual counseling involves a confidential relationship between a student and the professional school counselor that can last from a single session to several sessions. Not all one-on-one meetings with students are considered individual counseling (D. B. Brown & Trusty, 2005; Schmidt, 2003). What distinguishes individual counseling from other forms of interaction is the close emotional contact between the student and the professional school counselor. Also, with

individual counseling, the focus is on the student's problem or concern, and the goal is to help the student make positive changes in coping, in adapting, or in specific behaviors that are problematic (D. B. Brown & Trusty, 2005).

Because professional school counselors are responsible for a wide range of services and because they typically serve a large number of students, teachers, and parents, it is critical for counselors to assess who will benefit from individual counseling relationships within the school setting. The *ASCA National Model* (2003a) clearly states that professional school counselors do not provide traditional therapy (p. 42). Instead, they work within a developmental framework on issues that have direct relevance to educational success (Borders & Drury, 1992). If more expanded counseling services are needed, it is appropriate to engage in referral and consultation practices with outside agencies and community resources.

Identifying which students will benefit the most from individual counseling services can pose a tremendous challenge for professional school counselors. Additional challenges include how to integrate these services into the school day, how to conduct the counseling process, and how to evaluate the effectiveness of the

The Case of Carlos

Carlos, an 8-year-old third grader, was referred to the professional school counselor by his teacher for being disruptive in class. The teacher feared that Carlos was having problems in the home that might be distracting him from his schoolwork. Assisted by a Spanish translator, the professional school counselor met with Carlos and his mother and discovered that Carlos had only been in the United States for 6 months, and that getting to the United States had been a very traumatic experience.

Six months earlier, Carlos was sitting in his school classroom in Mexico when his mother, who had abandoned the family 3 years earlier to move to the United States, showed up at his school and told him that they were leaving. That same day, they began their journey to the United States.

Because of the language barrier between the professional school counselor and the client's mother (the mother did not speak or understand

any English), the professional school counselor decided to refer the family to an agency in the community that offered bilingual counseling. Through counseling, Carlos was able to express his anxiety and stress over leaving his home for a foreign land, where people spoke a foreign language and looked very different from him. Family counseling at the agency also helped build family trust and cohesion between Carlos, his mother, and his two siblings.

As Carlos's language skills increased and his anxiety decreased, he began making friends at school. His behavior improved, as did his academic progress. Throughout the process, the professional school counselor served as a link between the school, the home, and the community counseling agency, which helped ensure that all systems were working together to facilitate Carlos's developmental and educational success.

interventions (Cobia & Henderson, 2003). Professional school counselors need to be proactive in making decisions about how to conduct individual counseling, with whom, at what time, and under what circumstances. As they make those decisions and deliver individual counseling services, professional school counselors will want to take into account the various developmental changes and challenges that influence the students with whom they work.

DEVELOPMENTAL CONSIDERATIONS

Counseling with children and adolescents differs in multiple ways from working with adults. Indeed, interventions that are appropriate for adult populations may be ineffective and even detrimental if applied to children. Knowledge of developmental theory can help professional school counselors make decisions about what approaches to use with students at different levels. Moreover, such knowledge helps professional school counselors make informed decisions about whether a particular behavior is developmentally appropriate or is out of the range of "normal" (Vernon, 2004).

Development is multidimensional and complex and is marked by qualitative changes that occur in many different domains (Gladding & Newsome, 2004). In this section, we provide an overview of some general developmental characteristics associated with students in elementary, middle, and high school. A more detailed summary of developmental theories and counseling implications is presented in Table 9.1. Readers also may wish to refer to texts that provide in-depth descriptions of child and adolescent development (e.g., Berk, 2001; Bjorklund, 2000; Thomas, 2000; Vernon, 2004).

Early Childhood

Counselors working in elementary schools may work with children in kindergarten or even preschool. Children between the ages of 2 and 6 are in the *early childhood* stage, sometimes called the *play years* (Berk, 2001). During this period, motor skills are refined, children begin to build ties with peers, and thought and language skills expand rapidly. To understand the way young children think and use language, it is helpful to refer to Jean Piaget's stage-constructed theory of cognitive development. Although current research indicates that the stages of cognitive development are not as discrete and clear-cut as Piaget hypothesized, his description of cognitive development provides a relatively accurate picture of how children think and reason at different ages (Bjorklund, 2000).

According to Piaget, children between 2 and 7 years of age are *preoperational*, which means they are developing the ability to represent objects and events through imitation, symbolic play, drawing, and spoken language. They are most likely egocentric, implying that they cannot see the viewpoint of another. Preoperational children may attribute lifelike qualities to inanimate objects and have difficulty with abstract nouns and concepts such as time and space (Vernon, 2004). They are likely to engage in magical thinking and may offer imaginative explanations for things they do not understand. As children progress through early childhood, they become better able to represent and recall their feelings. As they near the end of the preoperational stage, their emotional self-regulation improves.

Erik Erikson's psychosocial theory provides another way to understand children's development. Erikson described development as a series of psychological crises that occur at various stages. The manner in which each crisis is resolved, along a continuum from positive to negative, influences healthy or maladaptive outcomes at each stage (Berk, 2001). Young children are in the process of resolving the developmental crisis of *initiative versus guilt. Initiative* refers to being enterprising, energetic, and purposeful. Children in this stage are discovering what kinds of people they are, particularly in regard to gender. Because of their increased language and motor skills, they are capable of imagining and trying out many new things. To navigate this period successfully, children need to be given a variety of opportunities to explore, experiment, and ask questions. Understanding adults can be instrumental in helping young children develop self-confidence, self-direction, and emotional self-regulation.

TABLE 9.1
Developmental theories and emerging developmental trends.

Developmental Theories	Founder	Key Concepts	Implications for Counseling
Cognitive theory	Piaget, Elkind	Divided cognitive development into four stages: Sensorimotor (birth to 2), Preoperational (2 to 7), Concrete operations (7 to 11), Formal operations (begins after 11).	Counselors can adjust their approach and select interventions to match the child's level of cognitive functioning. For example, counselors working with young children will want to use some form of play media.
Theory of moral development	Kohlberg, Gilligan	Kohlberg identified three levels of moral development, beginning with a punishment and obedience orientation and progressing to higher stages of moral reasoning. Gilligan posited that feminine morality emphasizes an ethic of care, focusing on interpersonal relationships.	Counselors can use their understanding of moral reasoning to help children learn self-control and to help parents with discipline issues. Girls and boys may make moral judgments in different ways.
Psychosocial development	Erikson	Identified seven psychosocial stages and their associated developmental tasks (for example, from birth to 1 year of age, the central task is trust).	Counselors can help clients obtain the coping skills necessary to master developmental tasks so they can move forward in their development.
Developmental psychopathology	Kazden, Kovacs, and others	Study of child and adolescent psychopathology in the context of maturational and developmental processes.	The theory provides a framework for understanding child psychopathology as unique from adult psychopathology, aiding in accurate assessment.
The classic theories	Freud, Adler, and Jung	The theories of personality posited by the classic theorists emphasize the role of early life experiences on child and adolescent development.	The classic theories help counselors understand the dynamics of behavior *before* selecting counseling techniques to promote change.
Attachment theory	Ainsworth, Bowlby, and others	Focuses on the relationship between the parent/child emotional bond and the child's psychosocial development over the life span.	An understanding of attachment relationships can provide useful insights into how to move toward optimal psychosocial development.
Emotional intelligence	Salovey and Mayer	Focus is on the role that social emotions play in psychological functioning.	Counselors can help promote emotional intelligence through such activities as social skills training in groups.

Play is an extremely important activity for children in this age group. Through play, children find out about themselves and their world. Professional school counselors will want to use some form of play when working with young children. Play provides a way for children to express feelings, describe experiences, and disclose wishes. Although young children may not be able to articulate feelings, toys and other play media serve as the words they use to express emotions (Landreth, 1993, 2002). Materials used to facilitate play include puppets, art supplies, dolls and dollhouses, tools, and toy figures or animals.

Middle Childhood

Children between the ages of 7 and 11 are in *middle childhood*. During this time period, children develop literacy skills and logical thinking. Cognitively, they are in Piaget's *concrete operational* stage, meaning that they are capable of reasoning logically about concrete, tangible information. Concrete operational children are capable of mentally reversing actions, although they still can only generalize from concrete experiences. They grasp logical concepts more readily than before, but they typically have difficulty reasoning about abstract ideas. Children in this stage learn best through questioning, exploring, manipulating, and doing (Flavell, 1985). As a rule, their increased reasoning skills enable them to understand the concept of intentionality and to be more cooperative.

From a psychosocial perspective, children in middle childhood are in the process of resolving the crisis of *industry versus inferiority*. To maximize healthy development, they need opportunities to develop a sense of competence and capability. When adults provide manageable tasks, along with sufficient time and encouragement to complete the tasks, children are more likely to develop a strong sense of industry and efficacy (Thomas, 2000). Alternatively, children who do not experience feelings of competence and mastery may develop a sense of inadequacy and pessimism about their capabilities. Experiences with family, teachers, and peers all contribute to children's perceptions of efficacy and industry.

Negotiating relationships with peers is an important part of middle childhood. Acceptance in a peer group and having a "best friend" help children develop competence, self-esteem, and an understanding of others (Vernon, 2004). Some of the interpersonal skills children acquire during middle childhood include learning to get along with age mates, learning the skills of tolerance and patience, and developing positive attitudes toward social groups and institutions (Havighurst, 1972). Professional school counselors can help children develop their interpersonal skills through developmental guidance activities and group counseling, as well as through individual counseling.

Adolescence

Adolescence is the period when young people transition from childhood to adulthood. During adolescence, youth mature physically, develop an increased understanding of roles and relationships, and acquire and refine skills needed for performing successfully as adults (Crockett & Crouter, 1995). Puberty marks the beginning of adolescence, with girls typically reaching puberty earlier than boys. For most students, *early adolescence* (ages 11–14) begins in middle school, *midadolescence* (ages 15–18) begins in high school, and *late adolescence* (18 and over) occurs at the end of high school and continues beyond.

As young people enter adolescence, they begin to make the shift from concrete to formal operational thinking. The transition takes time and usually is not completed until at least age 15 (Schave & Schave, 1989). Adolescents moving into the formal operational stage are able to deal with abstractions, form hypotheses, engage in mental manipulation, and predict consequences. As formal operational skills develop, adolescents become capable of reflective abstraction, which refers to the ability to reflect on knowledge, rearrange thoughts, and discover alternative routes to solving problems (Bjorklund, 2000). Consequently, counseling approaches that provide opportunities to generate alternative solutions are more likely to be effective with adolescents than with younger children.

A new form of egocentrism often emerges during adolescence, characterized by a belief in one's uniqueness and invulnerability (Elkind, 1984). Egocentrism may be reflected in reckless behavior and grandiose ideas. Related to this heightened sense of uniqueness is the adolescent phenomenon of feeling constantly "on stage." It is not uncommon for adolescents to feel that everyone is looking at them, leading to increased anxiety and self-consciousness. These feelings tend to peak in early adolescence and then decline as formal operational skills improve (Bjorklund, 2000).

The onset of puberty often triggers the psychosocial crisis of *identity versus role confusion* (Erikson, 1968). A key challenge during adolescence is the formation of an identity, including self-definition and a commitment to goals, values, beliefs, and life purpose (Waterman, 1985). To master this challenge, adolescents need opportunities to explore options, try on various roles and responsibilities, and speculate about possibilities. Sometimes adolescents enter a period of role confusion, characterized in part by overidentification with heroes or cliques, before they develop a true sense of individuality and recognize that they are acceptable human beings (Thomas, 2000).

Spending time with peers continues to be important throughout adolescence. As adolescents develop self-confidence and sensitivity, they base their friendships on compatibility and shared experiences. Intimate friendships increase, as do dating and sexual experimentation. Counseling may involve helping these young people deal with issues of complex relationships and decision making about the future.

It is important to keep in mind that developmental generalizations may not be applicable to all ethnic or cultural groups. For example, the search for self-identity may be delayed, compounded by a search for ethnic identity, or even nonexistent among certain groups of adolescents (Herring, 1997a). Also, research on Piagetian tasks suggests that some forms of logic do not emerge spontaneously according to stages but are socially generated, based on cultural experiences (Berk, 2001). Developmental theories provide useful guides for understanding children and adolescents; however, no theory provides a complete explanation of development, nor does any theory take into account all cultural perspectives.

Developmental knowledge helps professional school counselors build relationships, assess concerns, and design effective interventions for students at all grade levels. By understanding developmental levels and their implications, professional school counselors are better prepared to meet the needs of the children and adolescents with whom they counsel and the parents and teachers with whom they consult.

A COUNSELING MODEL FOR CHILDREN AND ADOLESCENTS

Models of individual counseling can range anywhere from three to a multitude of stages (Schmidt, 2003). The model presented in this section is adapted from Orton (1997) and consists of the following phases: *building a counseling relationship, assessing specific counseling needs, designing and implementing interventions,* and *conducting evaluation and closure.* Generic and nonlinear in nature, the model can be applied to different theoretical orientations and situations, and certain phases can occur throughout the counseling process.

Building a Counseling Relationship

The key to any successful counseling experience is the development of an effective working relationship built on mutual trust and acceptance (Muro & Kottman, 1995). Developing a counseling relationship sometimes takes longer with children than with adults because children may need more time to believe that an adult can help them (Orton, 1997). Essential factors involved in establishing a counseling relationship include building rapport, clarifying the counseling role, and explaining confidentiality.

Establishing Rapport

To build relationships successfully, professional school counselors need to tailor their responses and interactions to fit the specific needs of each student, taking into account developmental experiences, sociocultural background, and reasons for referral (McClure & Teyber, 2003). Perhaps the most important first step is being willing to enter completely into that student's world, with no preconceptions, expectations, or agenda. It is important to be fully "with" student clients, accepting them for who they are at that moment. All judgment needs to be suspended so that the counselor can remain open to what the child is sharing, either verbally or nonverbally. As the relationship is being established, listening skills are more important than questioning skills (Erdman & Lampe, 1996). Professional school counselors can create bridges of trust and understanding by listening carefully to what young people have to say; giving them undivided attention; and responding sensitively to feelings, reactions, and cultural cues.

It helps to be knowledgeable about a variety of rapport-building approaches. For example, play and art media can help professional school counselors establish relationships with young children who have difficulty verbalizing. With older children, games like Jenga or "in-house" basketball can provide a nonthreatening introduction to the counseling process. Use a dry-erase white board and markers with children, inviting them to draw pictures or symbols that illustrate

things they would like you to know about them. As a variation, ask students to create an *About Me* collage by decoratively writing their names in the center of a piece of art paper. Then ask them to select magazine pictures that illustrate things about them, including strengths, interests, relationships, or other characteristics they want to reveal at that point. Their choices serve as a springboard for further discussion and provide a lens for glimpsing their subjective worlds. Other children may be eager to talk, and the professional school counselor can respond accordingly with reflective listening, summarizing, probing, and clarifying.

One of the factors that makes building a relationship with children different from building a relationship with adults is that children may have no idea what counseling is all about. They may be confused about the counseling process or reluctant to participate. In schools, students frequently are referred by teachers or parents, and it is these adults, not the child, who want change to occur. Consequently, the student may not be motivated to make changes. This is particularly true when children or adolescents are referred because of behavioral patterns that are troublesome to adults (Sommers-Flanagan & Sommers-Flanagan, 1997).

When children are "sent" to counseling rather than self-referred, they may be resistant to

Reflections of a First-Year Master's Student on Conducting Individual Counseling at an Alternative School During Practicum

I completed my practicum experience at the New School, which hosts students who have been referred from their home schools because of behavior problems. Problematic behaviors range from minor classroom disruptions and peer conflicts to aggressive and sometimes violent displays of anger. During the first 3 weeks of my practicum, I was regularly questioned by the school's administrators, teachers, and staff: "Do you know what you're getting yourself into with *these* students?" I spent the first month at the site building relationships with administrators, teachers, staff, and, most importantly, with the students.

I found it surprisingly easy to build rapport and empathize with the students. I expected to

have to work extremely hard to tear down barriers to trust and communication to establish a counseling relationship. Interestingly enough, a smiling face and an attentive ear were more than enough to gain the students' respect. Many of the students with whom I worked had rarely had an adult willing to spend time with them and listen to their opinions, fears, anger, and experiences. Teachers and administrators were shocked when students returned to classrooms or the office talking with me calmly after walking out of a classroom, yelling profanities at the teacher, and banging lockers. This was the turning point: I'd won the teachers over.

the counseling process. One professional middle school counselor in a local public school shared her strategy for working with students who have been referred by parents or teachers:

> If a child is ready to talk, I sit back, relax, and hear her story. If she is not, I'll generally do something temporarily diverting, such as say, "You know, I realize we're supposed to talk about whatever it is you've been sent here for, but do you mind if we do something else for a while? Do you see anything here that you'd like to do?" I keep lots of games and toys, art supplies, clay, etc. out and about, and almost always something will catch a child's interest. (Niedringhaus, 2000, p. 1)

When students are self-referred, resistance may not be an issue. However, in such situations the need to obtain parental consent for counseling services can become a concern. Many counselors will not counsel students without parental consent (Freeman, 2000). Professional school counselors need to be aware of state regulations, school policies, professional ethical codes, and limits of confidentiality as they make decisions about counseling individual students.

Clarifying the Counseling Role

Professional school counselors are responsible for explaining to students the purpose and nature of the counseling relationship (ASCA, 2004a). Providing an age-appropriate explanation of the counseling role can help establish structure and initiate the development of a collaborative relationship. With younger students, the professional school counselor might say something like, "My job is to help children with lots of different things. Sometimes people have unpleasant feelings they want to talk about. Other people might want help figuring out a problem. I wonder what I might be able to help you with?" With older students, it might be helpful to ask students to describe what they think individual counseling entails, after which the professional school counselor can provide clarification as needed.

Explaining Confidentiality

During the initial phase of counseling, it is necessary to clarify confidentiality and its limits. ASCA's

(2004a) ethical standards state that professional school counselors have a responsibility to protect information received through confidential counseling relationships with students. Confidentiality should not be abridged unless there is a clear and present danger to the student, other individuals, or both. Also, professional school counselors have the responsibility of explaining the limits of confidentiality to their students and of notifying them regarding the possible necessity of consulting with others. Moreover, professional school counselors recognize that although their primary obligation for confidentiality is to the student, that obligation must be balanced with "an understanding of the legal and inherent rights of parents/guardians to be the guiding voice in their children's lives" (ASCA, 2004a, p. 4).

The way a professional school counselor approaches the issue of confidentiality with students depends on the students' age. With young children, the counselor will want to use words that the child can understand. In many cases, professional school counselors will not counsel with students, especially young children, before obtaining parental permission. Also, it often is in the child's best interest to consult with parents or teachers during the process. Therefore, the counselor might say to the student, "Most of the things you and I talk about in here are between you and me, unless you tell me that you are planning to hurt yourself or someone else. If you tell me something that I think your mother (father, other caregiver, teacher) needs to know, you and I will talk about it before I tell anything."

Adolescents often have a heightened concern about privacy and confidentiality in the counseling relationship. Sommers-Flanagan and Sommers-Flanagan (1997) emphasized the importance of making sure that teenagers understand the counselor's explanation about how confidentiality will be maintained. They suggested that adolescents may respond to a modified or even humorous presentation of confidentiality information, such as the following:

> So if you're planning on doing something dangerous or destructive, such as dissecting your science teacher, it's likely that we'll need to have a meeting with your parents or school officials to talk that over, and it's the law that

I would need to warn your science teacher. But day to day stuff that you're trying to sort out, stuff that's bugging you, even if it's stuff about your parents or teachers or whoever—we can keep that private. (p. 40)

In addition to the ethical issue of confidentiality, a number of state and federal statutes affect the counselor–client relationship in school settings. Each state has its own laws that directly influence the practice of counseling in schools (S. B. Baker, 2000; Linde, 2003). For example, many states mandate privileged communication, which is a client's right to have prior confidences maintained during legal proceedings. If clients are under the age of 18, their parents maintain the right to privileged communication. Privilege is not absolute and several exceptions to privilege exist, including child abuse, with those exceptions varying from state to state (Glosoff, Herlihy, & Spence, 2000). It is the professional school counselor's responsibility to stay abreast of state statutes and exceptions to privilege.

Professional school counselors also need to be aware of federal statutes that affect their work with students and limits to confidentiality. In particular, FERPA, enacted in 1974, ensures that parents' rights to information about their children's education are honored (S. B. Baker, 2000). Part I of FERPA specifies that parents have the right to access school records about their children. Because this stipulation refers to the school's educational records, professional school counselors are advised to keep their counseling records separate from the official educational records (Anderson, 1996; Linde, 2003). Part II of FERPA requires parental consent for medical, psychiatric, or psychological evaluations of children under 18 as well as for participation in school programs designed to affect a student's personal behavior or values.

It is not unusual for professional school counselors to face dilemmas regarding the requirements of confidentiality; minor students' requests for information; and counselor responsibilities to parents, teachers, and colleagues. By keeping the lines of communication open and taking responsibility for knowing state and federal law, it may be possible to circumvent potential problems before they arise (Freeman, 2000).

Assessing Specific Counseling Needs

Assessment is an integral part of the counseling process that can, in and of itself, be therapeutic. The purposes of assessment are to gain a better understanding of the child's needs and to establish goals for meeting those needs (Orton, 1997). Assessment methods, which can be informal or formal, help the professional school counselor understand the student's current problems within the context of his or her unique developmental and contextual history.

The Case of Gabriella

Gabriella, a second-generation Latina student in the ninth grade, has been referred to you, the professional school counselor, because she has been falling asleep in class for the past 2 weeks. You know Gabriella but have not conducted individual counseling with her until now. During your initial meeting with Gabriella, she tells you that she is just tired because she has to stay up late to take care of her younger brother while her mother and stepfather are working. In a subsequent session, Gabriella reveals that the real reason she is so tired is because she is afraid to go to sleep at night. On further questioning, she reveals that her stepfather has been touching her in ways that make her uncomfortable and that during the past month he has been coming into her room at night. She insists that he has not done anything except touch her in "an embarrassing way." She now keeps her door locked at night and stays awake as long as she can, until she is sure that her stepfather has gone to bed.

- What are your responsibilities to Gabriella?
- What are your legal and ethical responsibilities in this situation?
- What would you do in this situation? What considerations should you keep in mind?
- What factors make this situation challenging?

Exploring Student Concerns

Whereas counselors in mental health settings conduct intake interviews to collect information about client concerns, counselors in school settings typically do not conduct formal intake interviews. Nonetheless, some form of early and ongoing assessment is warranted for accurate case conceptualization and effective intervention planning. Often, professional school counselors begin this process with an informal interview through which students' concerns are explored. Myrick (2002) suggested professional school counselors look for effective ways to collect information without turning the session into a fact-finding question-and-answer period. When exploring students' concerns, it is important to use active listening skills, be sensitive to nonverbal expressions, and probe gently and sensitively.

The type of information collected during early stages of assessment varies according to developmental levels and student concerns. If professional school counselors will be working with the student for more than just a few sessions, Orton (1997) suggested information be gathered in the following areas:

- *The student's specific concerns.* The manifestation, intensity, frequency, and duration of concerns should be explored. In what settings and around what individuals are the concerns evidenced? To what extent are the concerns developmentally appropriate?
- *Physical, cognitive, emotional, and social development.* Depending on the situation, it may be beneficial to consult with parents and teachers to get more information about the student's medical history, cognitive functioning, and ability to express and regulate emotions. It also is helpful to gather information about socioeconomic and sociocultural factors that have influenced the student's development.
- *Relationships between the student and his or her parents, siblings, classmates, and teachers.* Understanding the nature and quality of relationships the student has with family members and peers is a key component of assessment. The degree to which these areas are explored depends on the nature of the problem. For example, if a student is not turning in homework, the professional school counselor will want to gather information about what is going on at home and in the school that may be contributing to the problem.
- *The student's school experiences, including academics, attendance, and attitude.* Academic and social successes or failures play important roles in a student's overall development. Students who experience repeated failures often have poor self-esteem and may engage in disruptive behaviors to compensate (Orton, 1997). Also, school failure may signify a learning disorder that typically requires formal testing for diagnosis.
- *The student's strengths, talents, and support system.* Implementing a strengths-based approach to assessment can help take the focus off the problem so that it is possible to begin moving more toward solutions. SFBC, which is addressed later in the chapter, places particular emphasis on assessing students' strengths. Creative activities, checklists, and various qualitative assessment methods provide useful tools for evaluating strengths and supports.

Informal and Formal Assessment

Informal assessment includes observation and qualitative assessment activities. Observation can occur in counseling sessions or in the classroom. Qualitative assessment emphasizes a holistic study of students using methods that typically are not standardized and do not produce quantitative raw scores (Goldman, 1990). A variety of qualitative assessment methods can be used with children and adolescents, including informal checklists, unfinished sentence activities, writing activities, decision-making dilemmas, games, art activities, storytelling, self-monitoring techniques, role-play activities, and play therapy strategies (e.g., Myrick, 2002; J. Peterson, 2004; Vernon, 2004). Informal assessment procedures of this nature can reveal patterns of thoughts and behaviors relevant to concerns and issues. They can be especially helpful with young children, who may not know exactly what is bothering them or who lack the words to express their concerns verbally (Orton, 1997).

In some situations, professional school counselors may wish to obtain information through the use of formal assessment instruments, which require students to respond to standardized measurements. Formal instruments that have sound psychometric properties provide a way for professional school counselors to gain a somewhat more objective view of children's behaviors and attributes than do informal methods of assessment (Orton, 1997). Examples of formal assessment include standardized behavioral checklists, values scales, interest and skill inventories, self-concept measures, and personality inventories. Professional school counselors have been trained in appraisal procedures and have the ability to use these instruments effectively with students.

By evaluating counseling needs though interviews, informal assessment, and formal assessment, the professional school counselor can gain a better understanding of the student's concerns within his or her developmental and environmental context. This understanding can then be used to set goals, design and implement interventions, and evaluate the counseling process.

Designing and Implementing Interventions

After a relationship has been established and initial assessment conducted with a child, what is the next step? Vernon (1993) cautioned that counseling should not be a "fly by the seat of your pants" endeavor. Interventions should be developed and selected after carefully considering the student's developmental level, personality characteristics, and particular circumstances. Other considerations that need to be taken into account are time constraints, teacher and parental support, and the counselor's level of expertise. If, during the course of counseling, it becomes apparent that the student's problems are more serious and chronic, then the professional school counselor will want to refer him or her to mental health counselors or other helping professionals within the school or community (ASCA, 2003a; D. B. Brown & Trusty, 2005). When it is necessary to refer, professional school counselors can continue to play significant roles

by working collaboratively with clinical mental health counselors and other referral sources (Geroski, Rodgers, & Breen, 1997).

Intentionality and Flexibility

Being intentional implies taking steps to set goals for counseling collaboratively with the student. Being flexible refers to recognizing that no single counseling approach is best for all students or all problems. By designing interventions in ways that are both intentional and flexible, professional school counselors can personalize the intervention for the student within the context of a collaborative relationship.

One way professional school counselors can intentionally plan interventions is by asking specific questions related to the following areas (Vernon, 1993):

1. *Vision.* What could be different? How could things be better? What would be ideal?
2. *Goal setting.* What is going well? What needs to be worked on?
3. *Analysis.* What is enabling or interfering with achieving these goals? What is getting in the way of resolving the problem?
4. *Objective.* What specifically does the student want to change?
5. *Exploration of interventions.* What has already been tried and how did it work? How does the student learn best? Who will be involved in the helping process? What has research shown to be the most effective intervention for this type of concern?

In many ways, these guiding questions are similar to those that guide SFBC, an approach that we describe in further detail later in the chapter.

Selecting Interventions

In making decisions about which intervention to use, professional school counselors can select from a wide range of theoretical approaches. Although no single theoretical approach to counseling children and adolescents has been found to be more effective than another (e.g., Bergin, 1999; Sexton et al., 1997), some approaches are more suited to school settings than others are. D. B. Brown and Trusty (2005) outlined six aspects of counseling theory for professional school counselors to consider as they make decisions about interventions:

1. The degree to which the theory (or model) focuses on the **counseling relationship**, including the relationship between the counselor and students as a whole.
2. The degree to which the theory enhances **student empowerment.**
3. The amount of attention devoted to students' **overt behavior.**
4. The usefulness of the theory at students' various levels of **development.**
5. The **flexibility** of the theory to various student characteristics, student problems, and school counseling delivery formats.
6. The **time span** of counseling associated with the theory. (p. 292)

An additional consideration is the degree to which the theory or model takes into account issues related to diversity and cultural strengths.

Theoretical approaches that seem to be particularly effective in school settings include Adlerian counseling, reality therapy (RT), cognitive–behavioral counseling, and SFBC (D. B. Brown & Trusty, 2005; Schmidt, 2003). Other models and structures that are effective with school-aged children include multimodal counseling, Gestalt techniques, and family counseling approaches (D. B. Brown & Trusty, 2005). Also, a variety of expressive arts techniques, including art, music, clay, puppetry, storytelling, drama, bibliotherapy, sand play, and other forms of directive and nondirective play therapy can guide the counseling process and promote healing and growth (e.g., Bradley, Gould, & Hendricks, 2004; Gladding, 2005; Gladding & Newsome, 2004).

Professional school counselors need to select counseling approaches systematically (Schmidt, 2003), matching the approach and intervention with the presenting issue and taking developmental, cultural, and other contextual factors into account. For example, a professional school counselor working with a student with attention-deficit/hyperactivity disorder (ADHD) may find cognitive–behavioral approaches useful, with an emphasis on specific tasks related to organization, self-monitoring, and impulse control. For students who have difficulty completing

assignments, RT (Glasser, 2000b), which focuses on the present and future rather than the past, may be the treatment of choice. Professional school counselors using this approach ask students to evaluate their actions and determine whether they want to change. Together, the student and counselor design a plan for change that emphasizes personal control. For adolescents struggling with depression, cognitive theory (e.g., Beck & Weishaar, 2000), which focuses on recognizing automatic thoughts and their effects on emotions, may be the preferred approach.

Implementing Interventions

After the professional school counselor and student have collaboratively selected interventions, it is time to implement the plan. Professional school counselors can empower students by affirming their resilience, offering affirmation and encouragement, and providing acceptance and stability (J. Peterson, 2004). Depending on the situation, counselors should consult with other people in the school or family invested in the success of the intervention. It may be important to inform teachers and parents that the situation may get worse before it gets better. In some cases, it may be helpful to work with teachers on designing a behavior contract, recognizing that teachers are more likely to implement a plan they have helped create (Orton, 1997).

Conducting Evaluation and Closure

Implementation of interventions also includes working with the student to evaluate progress. Evaluation of the counseling relationship, interventions, and outcomes is an ongoing process. As with assessment, evaluation methods can be informal or formal. Informal evaluation involves observing changes in the student's thoughts, feelings, and behaviors. It also includes monitoring interactions during counseling sessions and being aware of personal responses to the child. Formal evaluation of counseling outcomes may include checklists completed by teachers and parents, grades in academic areas and in conduct, and self-reports completed by students related to the issues on which they are working (Orton, 1997). Measuring progress in counseling can be challenging because evaluation tends to be subjective and not all counseling goals are stated in measurable terms. Finding ways to demonstrate the effectiveness of counseling is important, however, and professional school counselors are encouraged to incorporate formal and informal methods of outcome evaluation into their work with students, teachers, and parents. Single-case study experimental designs provide one effective way to conduct outcome research evaluating the effectiveness of professional school counselors' interventions (Eschenauer & Chen-Hayes, 2005).

Closure, sometimes called termination, refers to the ending of the counseling relationship, either naturally or circumstantially (Schmidt, 2003). Gladding (2004) indicated that it is the least researched and most neglected aspect of counseling. In school counseling, the process of ending the helping relationship deserves particular attention (Henderson, 1987). As Schmidt (2003) pointed out, "Students who see counselors for individual sessions also interact with them in other ways during the day . . . Because these interactions are ongoing, closure of an individual counseling relationship must be planned and carried out gradually" (p. 143). Closure is facilitated when professional school counselors reinforce the progress students have made, encourage them to express their feelings about ending the helping relationship, and determine resources for continued support.

Solution-Focused Brief Counseling

Brief counseling approaches, including SFBC (e.g., Bonnington, 1993; de Shazer, 1985; Metcalf, 1995; J. J. Murphy, 1997; Sklare, 1997, 2005) and systematic problem solving (Myrick, 2002), are advocated in the school counseling literature and are particularly valuable in schools where time constraints are crucial. The successful brief counseling model is brief by design, not by accident (Bruce, 1995). Brief counseling models parallel the generic model for individual counseling presented in this chapter by encouraging students to (a) assess the problem in concrete terms; (b) examine previously attempted solutions; (c) establish a specific, short-term goal; and (d) implement the

intervention. Because of its utility in school settings, a particular form of brief counseling, SFBC (Sklare, 2005), is discussed next.

Overview of SFBC

SFBC is an approach that "has shown great promise and that allows counselors to provide effective counseling to students in less time" (Charlesworth & Jackson, 2004, p. 139). It emphasizes strengths, resources, successes, and hope and is a model that can be used with students from diverse backgrounds. Sklare (2005) attributed the SFBC model primarily to de Shazer (1985), though many other innovative practitioners have contributed to its evolution (e.g., Berg & Miller, 1992; Berg & Steiner, 2003; O'Hanlon & Weiner–Davis, 1989; Selekman, 1997; Walter & Peller, 1992). Charlesworth and Jackson (2004) cited numerous studies supporting the efficacy of SFBC in school settings. Sklare (2005) referred to research providing support for the use of SFBC with students from culturally diverse backgrounds.

Core Beliefs, Assumptions, and Concepts

The core beliefs on which SFBC is based were originally proposed by de Shazer (1985) and Berg and Miller (1992) and are summarized by Sklare (2005) as follows:

- "If it ain't broke, don't fix it." Do not make an issue out of something that is not an issue for the student.
- "Once you know what works, do more of it." Once successes are identified, professional school counselors have students replicate them.
- "If it doesn't work, don't do it again." Repeating ineffective strategies does not make sense; it is more productive to try out new strategies. (pp. 9–10)

In addition to these core beliefs, Sklare (2005) presented five assumptions and four concepts that guide the SFBC model:

- *Assumption 1.* Counselors should focus on solutions, rather than problems, for change to occur.
- *Assumption 2.* Every problem has identifiable exceptions that can be discovered and transformed into solutions.

- *Assumption 3.* Small changes have a ripple effect that leads to bigger changes.
- *Assumption 4.* Student clients have the necessary resources to solve their problems.
- *Assumption 5.* Constructing goals in positive terms (what clients want to happen) is more effective than stating them in negative terms (an absence of something). For example, "I want to get to class on time" represents a positive goal; "I don't want to get in trouble" represents a negative goal.
- *Concept 1.* Avoid problem analysis. SFBC addresses what is working for students rather than exploring the etiology of their problems.
- *Concept 2.* Be efficient with interventions. Because counseling in schools is time limited, professional school counselors want to get the most accomplished in the minimum amount of time.
- *Concept 3.* Focus on the present and the future, not the past. Past events are only highlighted in the process of finding exceptions to problems.
- *Concept 4.* Focus on actions rather than insights. Insight requires a level of cognitive development that young students may not have. Also, insight is not necessary for change to occur (Yalom, 1995).

Implementing the SFBC Model

Sklare (2005) suggested that professional school counselors begin the first session with students by explaining the SFBC approach. He provides the following as an example of what professional school counselors might say to students:

> I want to let you know how this is going to work. I am going to ask you a lot of questions, and some of them are going to sound kind of crazy and will be tough to answer [for some students, informing them that the questions will be hard to answer is intriguing and challenging]. Some of the answers you give I'm going to write down on my notepad, and I'm going to use these notes to write you a message. When I finish, I will tell you what I was thinking about and read the message to you. I will make a copy of the message so you can take one with you and I can keep one. What do you think about this? (p. 20)

After the process has been explained, the next step is to help the student formulate clear goals. As Assumption 5 indicates, goals need to be stated in positive rather than negative terms. Sklare (2005) classified goals as (a) positive, (b) negative, (c) harmful, and (d) "I don't know" goals. Skillful questioning on the part of the professional school counselor can help the student state positive goals that are observable, behaviorally specific, measurable, and attainable.

Professional school counselors can use a wide range of techniques to help students develop positive goals and envision solutions. Examples of those techniques include:

- *The miracle question.* With young children, the professional school counselor might ask, "Suppose I had a magic wand and waved it over your head and the problem was solved, what would be different? What would you see yourself doing differently?" (Sklare, 1997, p. 31). If students state wishes that are impossible (e.g., "I would not live here anymore"), the professional school counselor can ask questions like, "How would things be different for you if your miracle happened?" and "What would other people notice?"
- *Identifying instances and exceptions.* Following Assumption 2, professional school counselors ask students to think of a time when the miracle has already happened to some extent. For example, the professional school counselor might say, "Tell me about a time when you were getting along with your teacher. What was going on then?"
- *Mindmapping.* Mindmapping refers to identifying specific behaviors that led to success in the past. Identifying concrete steps that were beneficial in the past can help students create a mental road map to guide them in the future.
- *Cheerleading.* Supporting and encouraging students, acknowledging their accomplishments, and expressing excitement when a new behavior is successfully implemented is called cheerleading. Sklare (2005) pointed out that it is important to be genuine in cheerleading and to avoid patronizing.
- *Scaling.* Scaling can be used to establish baselines, set goals, and measure progress. For

example, the professional school counselor might ask the student, "On a scale of 0 to 10, with 10 being the day after the miracle has happened and the problem is solved, where are you right now?" Subsequent questions might be, "What would it take for you to move to a ——— on the scale?" and "How would you know when you were at a ———? What would be happening?"

- *Flagging the minefield.* Helping students anticipate obstacles that might impede their progress gives them an opportunity to consider ways to overcome those obstacles before they are encountered. Reviewing strategies in advance can help keep students from being caught off guard and can empower them to make positive choices.

SFBC is an example of one of several forms of brief counseling. Although this and other brief approaches may not be appropriate for every student in every situation, professional school counselors can incorporate models like SFBC as one way to effectively deliver individual counseling services. For a more in-depth description of the model, readers are encouraged to refer to Sklare's (2005) text, *Brief Counseling That Works: A Solution-Focused Approach for School Counselors and Administrators* (2nd ed.).

Individual counseling represents an essential responsive service in comprehensive developmental school counseling programs. Another powerful and effective means of helping students with situational and developmental concerns is group counseling. In school settings, group work, including group counseling, is often viewed as the intervention of choice.

GROUP COUNSELING IN SCHOOLS

Group counseling, in addition to individual counseling, represents a mode of delivering direct services to students and is an integral part of a comprehensive developmental school counseling program (ASCA, 2003a). From a developmental and a pedagogical perspective, students often learn best from each other (Goodnough & Lee, 2004); therefore, group settings are ideal

places to conduct both preventive psychoeducational work and remedial counseling. Groups provide a social environment in which members can learn and practice new behaviors, exchange feedback, and experience support. They allow students to develop insights into themselves and others, and provide an effective, efficient way of helping students deal with developmental and situational issues.

Group work is one of the professional school counselor's most specialized skills (Goodnough & Lee, 2004). It represents a central means of delivering services in a comprehensive developmental school counseling program. In this section, ways to set up and conduct group work in school settings are described. Before examining those activities, however, the types of groups that are most prevalent in school settings are discussed.

Types of Groups

Group work in schools can be classified in several different ways (e.g., Bergin, 2004; Cobia & Henderson, 2003; Goodnough & Lee, 2004; Greenberg, 2003; Myrick, 2002). The ASGW (2000) defined four types of group work: task group facilitation, group psychoeducation, group counseling, and group psychotherapy. Task groups, also called work groups, are made up of members working together on a particular assignment or task. Examples in a school setting include Student Assistance Teams, crisis response planning groups, and peer helpers orientation groups (Jacobs & Schimmel, 2005). Group psychotherapy, which is used with people who may be experiencing severe maladjustment, chronic maladjustment, or both, is usually conducted in community mental health settings, not schools.

Our focus in this section is on the two types of groups involving students led most frequently by professional school counselors: psychoeducational groups and counseling groups. In educational settings, psychoeducational groups include guidance groups, which typically are conducted in classrooms and are described in chapter 8, and smaller (usually fewer than 10 members), growth-oriented groups that help students learn new skills and develop an awareness of their values, priorities, and communities. Counseling groups, while also growth oriented, are designed to help individuals who are experiencing some form of stress in their lives, such as loss of a family member, family changes, or issues related to sexual identity.

Although psychoeducational and counseling groups are conceptualized here and elsewhere as two distinct entities, it is more accurate to consider them along a continuum, with psychoeducational groups tending to be more structured and content oriented and counseling groups being less structured and more process oriented. In reality, any number of topics (e.g., grief and loss, managing stress, school success) can be the focus of either a psychoeducational group or a counseling group. Goodnough and Lee (2004), who classify groups in schools as *developmental, remedial,* and *school climate* groups, point out that psychoeducation has a place in all types of group work, as does group processing, which refers to interpersonal interactions among members within the group (Gladding, 2003). The professional school counselor's role is to design groups intentionally and balance content and process appropriately.

Psychoeducational Groups

Psychoeducational groups use educational methods to help students gain knowledge and skills in several domains, such as personal identity, interpersonal interaction, developmental transitions, social maturity, academic achievement, and career planning (Bergin, 2004). When young people in psychoeducational groups face natural age and stage developmental tasks together, they frequently master more than the specifically targeted skills. Interaction within the group can promote an improved sense of well-being, leading to the prevention of future problems as group members develop new resources and coping skills. The goal of psychoeducational group work in schools is to "prevent future development of debilitating dysfunctions while strengthening coping skills and self-esteem" (Conyne, 1996, p. 157).

Psychoeducational groups tend to focus on central themes that correspond with students' developmental levels (Bergin, 2004). For example, young children may benefit from friendship groups or problem-solving groups. Older children and adolescents may respond well to groups that focus on managing stress, assertiveness training, or boy–girl relationships. Topics for psychoeducational groups come from several sources. In part, professional school counselors select topics based on the academic, career, and personal–social domains outlined in the planned scope and sequence of a comprehensive developmental school counseling program. In addition, professional school counselors can select topics based on the results of needs assessment surveys distributed to students, parents, teachers, and related school personnel.

Psychoeducational groups vary in format according to topic and the age of the students in the group. Regardless of the specific format selected, professional school counselors will want to take a number of factors into account as they prepare to lead psychoeducational groups, including students' developmental levels, multicultural issues, school climate, and the overall purpose of the school's counseling program (Akos, Goodnough, & Milsom, 2004). Furr (2000) outlined a six-step model for psychoeducational groups that moves from a statement of purpose to a session-by-session design that includes didactic, experiential, and processing components. The model includes the following sequential steps:

1. *Statement of purpose.* Psychoeducational groups should be guided by a clear statement of the reason for the group's existence that answers the following questions: (a) What is the primary content focus of the group? (b) What population is expected to benefit from participating in this group? (c) What is the purpose of the intervention (i.e., remediation, prevention, development)? and (d) What is the expected outcome of participating in the group (e.g., change in thoughts, affect, behavior, or values)?

2. *Establishing goals.* Clearly defined goals describe how a student may change as a result of the group experience. Goals need to be achievable, measurable, short term, and clearly articulated. For example, a goal for a psychoeducational group designed to help

students build self-esteem might be, "To develop an understanding of the relationship between self-talk and self-esteem and to learn to modify inappropriate self-talk" (Furr, 2000, p. 45).

3. *Setting objectives.* Objectives specify the steps needed to reach the group goals. To build on the previous example, an objective for reaching the goal of understanding the relationship between self-talk and self-esteem might read, "Participants will learn the definition of self-talk and be able to differentiate between positive, negative, and coping self-talk" (Furr, 2000, p. 45).

4. *Selecting content.* Group content includes didactic, experiential, and process components. *Didactic content* refers to the information that will be taught directly to group members, such as information about types of self-talk. *Experiential activities* help group members learn by doing rather than just by listening or discussing. To help students connect the experiential and didactic components, professional school counselors use the *process component.* It is important to plan processing questions in advance, first focusing on what happened during the activity and then moving to group members' reactions to and reflections on the experience.

5. *Designing exercises.* There are multiple resources professional school counselors can access that describe group exercises that can be adapted to meet the needs of a particular group. Group exercises can generate discussion and participation, help the group focus, promote experiential learning, provide the group leader with useful information, increase group comfort, and facilitate fun and relaxation (Jacobs, Masson, & Harvill, 2006). It is important to select theoretically grounded, developmentally appropriate exercises so as to enhance the group experience, not just fill time or provide entertainment. Role-playing, imagery, and creative arts are just a few examples of types of exercises that can be used effectively in psychoeducational groups. Furr (2000, p. 41) stated, "Without exercises, the psychoeducational group would become a vehicle that only conveys information rather than changes perceptions and behavior." As stated earlier, effective group leaders take steps to fully process the exercises with the participants.

6. *Evaluation.* Evaluation is an important component of any group activity. *Process evaluation* refers to ongoing, session-to-session evaluation of how the group members are perceiving their experiences, whereas *outcome evaluation* measures the overall effectiveness of the group experience, particularly in regard to individual change. Additional attention to evaluation is given later in this chapter.

Counseling Groups

In addition to psychoeducational groups, professional school counselors also offer counseling groups that are primarily remedial in nature. Group counseling is remedial "when it addresses topics or issues that impair the learning and development of specific groups of students" (Goodnough & Lee, 2004, p. 174). It is often employed with children who have special life-event concerns, such as death of a family member, family changes, teenage parenting, or school failure. Group counseling is also appropriate for children who have disruptive or acting-out behavioral problems such as violent outbursts, excessive fighting, defiance, maladjustment, and an inability to get along with peers and teachers (Brantley, Brantley, & Baer–Barkley, 1996; J. R. Nelson, Dykeman, Powell, & Petty, 1996). A large body of research supports the efficacy of group counseling in schools (e.g., C. A. Campbell & Brigman, 2005; Goodnough & Lee, 2004; Prout & Prout, 1998; Shechtman, 2002; Whiston & Sexton, 1998; see chapter 3). Group counseling can help reduce social isolation and negative emotions as well as increase positive peer relations and a sense of belonging (Arman, 2000).

In group counseling, the affective as well as the cognitive and behavioral domains of students are emphasized. The group creates a climate of trust, caring, understanding, and support that enables students to share their concerns with their peers and the counselor (Orton, 1997). Through group experiences, members maximize the opportunity to help themselves and others. Group counseling frequently takes one of three approaches to dealing with persons and problems: crisis centered, problem centered, and growth centered (Myrick, 2002).

Crisis-centered groups are formed due to some emergency such as conflict between student groups. These groups usually meet until the situation that caused them to form is resolved. Crisis-centered groups may also form as a result of crisis intervention for large-scale trauma that affects the school's population. For example, in the aftermath of the tragedy of a school shooting incident, crisis-centered groups can help students process their feelings and develop ways of coping. Sometimes, groups that were formed because of a crisis continue to meet after the crisis has passed and develop into either problem-centered or growth groups. For example, after a fight between fourth and fifth graders, students in one school formed a "peace group," whose initial purpose was to resolve problems among the children who had been in open conflict. As the group continued to develop, however, its purpose expanded to finding ways to identify problems in the school and to correct them in a productive way.

Problem-centered groups are small groups that are established to focus on one particular concern that is interfering with educational progress. This type of group is beneficial to students who have demands placed on them that are beyond their current ability to handle. Examples of problem-centered group topics include coping with stress, resolving conflicts, making career choices, getting better grades, and substance abuse. Like members of crisis-centered groups, students in problem-centered groups are often highly motivated and committed to working on their situations and themselves.

Growth-centered groups focus on the personal and social development of students. Their purpose is to enable children to explore their feelings, concerns, values, and behaviors about a number of everyday subjects such as social competence and making transitions. Through the sharing process, "students can learn effective social skills and acquire a greater concern and empathy for the needs and feelings of others" (Orton, 1997, p. 194). Often, growth-centered groups are formed after classroom guidance lessons have been presented on a particular topic, such as anger management. Students are identified who would benefit from additional focus on the topic through growth-centered counseling groups.

Setting Up Groups in Schools

Several factors need to be considered in planning for group work in schools. In particular, professional school counselors will want to give attention to each of the following areas:

- Collaborating with school staff and parents
- Determining group topics
- Logistics (e.g., group size, length of sessions, scheduling, group composition)
- Recruiting and screening group members
- Group guidelines and confidentiality

In this section, an overview of each of these important topics is provided. Readers are encouraged to refer to the sources cited for more in-depth information on each topic.

Collaborating with School Staff and Parents

For group work in schools to be effective, professional school counselors need to have the support of the school administration, teachers, and parents. To gain this support, professional school counselors work collaboratively with school faculty and parents to develop awareness of the centrality and importance of group counseling services in their schools (Ripley & Goodnough, 2001). Among the barriers to successful group work is the justifiable concern about the possibility of students missing class to participate in group sessions. Schools are held accountable for students' academic performance; consequently, it is important to demonstrate ways group counseling can enhance, rather than diminish, student performance.

Open, clear communication about the nature and purpose of a comprehensive developmental school counseling program is the key to successful group work in schools. Professional school counselors can lead in-school workshops early in the academic year. At this time, they can explain the overall comprehensive school counseling program, which includes group counseling, an example of responsive services. Similarly, professional school counselors can introduce the program to parents through an orientation at the first PTA or PTSA meeting (Greenberg, 2003). Other suggestions for communicating with faculty and parents include (Greenberg, 2003; Ripley & Goodnough, 2001):

- Distribute needs assessment surveys to obtain suggested topics for group counseling, suggestions for a schoolwide counseling focus, and specific parent or teacher concerns.
- Consult with teachers frequently and encourage them to let you know about particular student needs.
- Meet regularly with the principal to discuss program concerns and goals. Inform the principal of activities taking place within the program, including group work.
- Send notes to faculty announcing such things as the topics for groups that are being formed, dates of standardized testing, and general activities of the program.
- Visit classrooms to introduce yourself to students and inform them about all the services offered by the school counseling program as well as guidelines for participation.
- Share information about group goals and objectives and, when appropriate, written materials about group topics.
- Provide outcome data to faculty and parents regarding the effectiveness of the groups that you coordinate.
- Encourage faculty and parents to give you feedback about what they have observed.
- Have a clear process for establishing groups, selecting students, scheduling sessions, and obtaining parental or guardian permission.

Determining Group Topics

There are several ways to make decisions about which groups to offer. As discussed earlier, administering a needs assessment survey to students, parents, and teachers is an effective way to select group topics. One approach to the survey can ask respondents to develop a list of topics they think would be helpful to discuss in small groups. Another option is for the professional school counselor to list group topics and have the

respondents indicate whether they are interested (Jacobs & Schimmel, 2005). A third option is to use a confidential "counselor suggestion box" in which students place their ideas for group topics and other concerns (Stroh & Sink, 2002). Yet another way to make decisions about what groups to offer is to examine existing data. School databases about attendance, test scores, retention, and other information can provide additional sources of information about schoolwide needs (Jacobs & Schimmel, 2005).

Group topics are directly connected to the academic, career, and personal–social development of students. Whereas many topics are applicable across grade levels (e.g., building self-esteem, peer relationships), others are more developmentally specific (e.g., transitioning to high school, teenage pregnancy). Also, although general topics may be applicable across grade levels, the specific manner in which they are addressed differs according to developmental level. An example of sample group topics that might be offered at various grade levels is presented in Table 9.2.

Logistics: Group Size, Length of Sessions, Scheduling, Group Composition

Early in the planning process, professional school counselors will want to consider several factors related to the logistics of group formation. Generally speaking, the younger the child, the smaller the number of group members and the shorter the session (Gladding, 2003; Myrick, 2002). Children have shorter attention spans and tend to be easily distracted in a large group. With young elementary school children, it is advisable to limit the group to no more than five students (Gazda, Ginter, & Horne, 2001). When working with children as young as 5 or 6, groups may be limited to three or four members, with sessions lasting only 20 minutes (C. L. Thompson, Rudolph, & Henderson, 2004). With older elementary school children and preadolescents (ages 9–12), groups may consist of five to seven students and meet from 30 to 45 minutes (Gazda et al., 2001). Adolescents (ages 12–19) typically meet for one class period, which lasts between 40 and 50 minutes. Group size should be limited

TABLE 9.2
Sample group topics for elementary, middle, and high school students.

Elementary	Middle	High School
Dealing with feelings	Peer pressure	Assertiveness training
Friendship	Interpersonal relationships	Dating/relationships
Academic achievement	Organizational/study skills	Test-taking anxiety
Family changes	Body image	Teen parenting
Self-esteem	Transitioning to high school	Personal identity
Career awareness	Understanding interests and skills	Career exploration and planning
Social skills	Conflict management	Managing stress
Problem solving	Being new to the school	Transitioning to college or work
Valuing diversity	Multicultural issues/sensitivity training	Gay, lesbian, bisexual issues

to no more than eight members, with six being ideal (Jacobs et al., 2006). When groups get too large, it is difficult for all members to participate, and groups are more likely to lose focus. These are "rule of thumb" guidelines; group size and session length should be based on a number of factors, including students' developmental levels, the purpose of the group, and the nature of the problems with which students are dealing (D. B. Brown & Trusty, 2005).

Scheduling groups can be a challenging task, especially in middle and high schools. With the increased call for raising achievement on standardized testing, many teachers are understandably reluctant to release students from classes (Hines & Fields, 2002). Consequently, it is imperative to work collaboratively with teachers in designing group schedules. In some educational settings, group sessions are rotated so that students do not have to miss the same class more than once. Another option is for professional school counselors to consult with teachers to determine whether there is a time in the day that would have the lowest impact on teaching.

Another logistical consideration relates to the group's composition. Should the group be homogenous or heterogeneous in regard to such factors as gender, age, ethnicity, and other dimensions? Decision making about group composition is complex, and there are few definitive answers. First, there is considerable disagreement regarding whether to separate groups by gender. For example, Kulic, Dagley, and Horne

(2001) indicated that is helpful to separate younger children along gender lines, whereas C. L. Thompson et al. (2004) stated that most counselors prefer a balance of both sexes in a group unless the problem to be discussed is such that the presence of the opposite sex would hinder discussion (e.g., some sex education topics). In regard to age, it is generally agreed that groups should be composed of members who are relatively close in age, both developmentally and chronologically (Gladding, 2003; Kulic et al., 2001). Ethnic and cultural diversity in groups is desirable, unless the topic is specific to a particular group. For example, Villalba (2003) described group work with Latino/a children with limited English proficiency.

Some groups lend themselves to homogeneity in regard to the issues that are addressed. In such cases, the groups are homogenous in that the students are experiencing similar concerns, and being together can contribute to a sense of universality (Yalom, 1995). Examples of homogenous groups of this nature include groups for children whose parents are divorced and groups for adolescents questioning their sexual orientation (Stroh & Sink, 2002). However, there also are benefits to heterogeneity in membership. Group members can learn from each other about different ways of addressing problems (Goodnough & Lee, 2004). Also, heterogeneity may be desired in a group for social skills development or anger management so as to have role models in the group. In general, groups should possess some in-group heterogeneity but not so much that group members have nothing in common (Kulic et al., 2001).

Recruiting and Screening Group Members

Professional school counselors recruit potential group members in several ways. One way to recruit members is to provide parents, teachers, and students with an *information statement* that describes what the group is about and what is expected of its members (Ritchie & Huss, 2000). Flyers, bulletin boards, newsletters, and word of mouth also can be used to promote group participation. Professional school counselors often have special knowledge about students, gained through long-term relationships and through communication with teachers and parents, which may allow them to identify potential group members (Hines & Fields, 2002). Also, particularly when groups are topic specific, students may volunteer to participate.

Not all students who volunteer or are referred, however, are suitable for a group. Therefore, professional school counselors will want to conduct screening interviews to determine whether the student is a candidate for group participation and whether the student wants to participate. Screening potential group members is a practice endorsed by the ACA (2005a) and by the ASGW (2000). Corey and Corey (2002) recommended conducting individual interviews to screen students, although screening may also take place in small groups.

During screening interviews, the professional school counselor talks with students about the group, its purpose, and expectations of group members. Students are encouraged to ask questions about the group so that they can make informed decisions about joining (Corey & Corey, 2002). Through this interactive process, the professional school counselor can assess students' motivation and level of commitment. Issues to be taken into account in making decisions about whether a student is suitable for a group include emotional readiness, willingness and ability to participate interactively, willingness to accept the rules of the group (e.g., confidentiality), and desire to be helpful to other group members (Greenberg, 2003). If a student has been referred to the group (either self-referred or other referred) and it appears that he or she is not ready to be in a group, Greenberg (2003) suggested that the professional school counselor consider initiating individual counseling, with one of the goals being to get the student ready to become a member of a group.

If the professional school counselor and the particular student decide that the student is ready to participate, letters requesting permission for participation should be sent to parents or guardians, assuming that notification is appropriate. Notes should include information about the type of group, length and number of sessions, and activities that will take place in the group, as well as the professional school counselor's contact information. Some school systems or states may have a policy mandating or recommending notification and approval for students to participate in groups. The most recent ASCA ethical code (2004a) also states that parents and guardians should be notified if the counselor considers it appropriate and consistent with school board policy or practice (Section A.6.b). Professional school counselors will want to follow their school policy or state law in regard to parent notification (Bodenhorn, 2005; Sink, 2005). In addition to obtaining permission from parents, professional school counselors should ask students to sign consent forms so that everyone is in agreement about the purpose of the group and the procedures involved before the group begins (Gladding, 2003).

Group Guidelines and Confidentiality

Early in the process, professional school counselors will want to discuss group procedures and expectations with all group members. Corey and Corey (2002) recommended having a pregroup meeting designed to help members get acquainted and to prepare them for the group experience. During this time, students can be asked to sign informed consent forms. Group rules can be discussed and confidentiality clarified.

Group guidelines are needed to set the foundation for cooperative group relationships (Schmidt, 2003). In most cases, it is advisable to get students' input in establishing the ground rules so as to foster a sense of ownership and investment (Greenberg, 2003). Examples of ground rules, which can be adapted to match the developmental level of group members and purpose of the group, include being a good listener, participating in the group, sharing experiences and feelings, not interrupting, showing respect for group members, and confidentiality. The concept of confidentiality is especially important, as professional school counselors are bound by their professional code of ethics to protect the confidentiality of group members (Jacobs & Schimmel, 2005). Corey and Corey (2002) recommended having students sign contracts in which they agree to not discuss outside the group what happens in the group.

Professional school counselors also need to let students know that confidentiality in a group setting cannot be guaranteed. As sensitive matters are brought up during group discussion, professional school counselors can remind members about confidentiality and its limits.

Conducting Group Work

The reader may have already taken or will soon take a course in group counseling. In that course, one develops knowledge and skills about group dynamics, effective group leadership, group stages, ways to work with different populations, and legal and ethical aspects of group work, among other topics. It would be beyond the scope of this chapter to discuss each of those areas or to provide suggestions for group sessions on various topics, although many excellent sources address the scope and practice of group work. Instead, in this section, the role and functions of group leaders in schools are outlined and suggestions for planning, implementing, and evaluating groups in schools are provided.

Role and Functions of Group Leaders

"Effective group leadership is a process, never ending and cycling through stages" (DeLucia–Waack, 1999, p. 131). To be effective, group leaders must be able to function in a variety of ways at different times. Bergin (2004) described the professional

school counselor's role during the group process in this way:

> During the group process, the counselor concentrates on promoting the development of group interaction, establishing rapport among group members, leading the group progressively through all four stages, and encouraging individual members' self-exploration and personal decision making. The counselor guides the group as it discusses individual and joint concerns, models appropriate attending and responding behaviors, and reinforces members for supporting one another during their individual self-exploration. In addition, the counselor confronts resistance sensitively, redirects negative behavior, and encourages the group's efforts to become self-regulatory. The counselor safeguards the group's integrity by enforcing the rules the group establishes for itself. (p. 360)

Professional school counselors who lead groups need to develop knowledge and skills in several areas. Five noteworthy areas include the following (Corey, 2004; Jacobs & Schimmel, 2005; Shechtman, 2002):

1. *Be clear as to the purpose of the group.* Is the group primarily a psychoeducational group or a counseling group? What goals and outcomes are desired for students who participate in the group? Group leaders need to clarify the group's purpose and help members move in that direction.

2. *Know how to relate developmental theory and counseling theory to group work.* As stated earlier in this chapter, a strong grounding in developmental theory is essential for any type of counseling work with children. It also is important for professional school counselors to apply counseling theory to the group process so that they can feel confident about the strategies they are using (Goodnough & Lee, 2004). Cognitive therapy, RT, Adlerian therapy, and SFBC represent four theoretical approaches that have been shown to be effective in group work with students.

3. *Be knowledgeable about the topic or content being covered in the group.* Professional school counselors will want to acquire knowledge and information about a wide range of topics, including such things as

stress management, grief and loss, study skills, bullying, teenage parenting, divorce, stepfamilies, acculturation, and racial identity development. There are many resources available that contain a wealth of information about topics and about ways to present them at different developmental levels. It may be helpful for professional school counselors to create a portfolio that includes information about various topics, suggestions for group exercises related to those topics, and specific developmental and cultural considerations.

4. *Be creative and multisensory.* Children and adolescents respond well to activities that engage their minds and their senses. Professional school counselors can use art, drama, music, movies, and props to generate discussion and participation, help the group focus, and promote experiential learning (Jacobs et al., 2006). Moreover, employing a variety of creative methods provides a way to address students' different learning styles, thereby enhancing the overall group experience. Examples of creative, multisensory group activities are described in the "Introductory Group Activities" text box. For other examples, readers are referred to Gladding (2005), Greenberg (2003), and Jacobs et al. (2006).

5. *Possess multicultural understanding.* For group leaders to work effectively with all populations, they need to be culturally competent (Bemak & Chung, 2004). Multiculturally competent counselors have the self-awareness, knowledge, and skills needed to interact successfully with people from different cultural backgrounds. They recognize their own values, biases, and assumptions and are open to diverse value orientations and assumptions about human behavior (Corey, 2004). Multiculturally competent group leaders understand the different cultures of their group members, and they also recognize how different cultural backgrounds might affect members' participation in the group (Jacobs & Schimmel, 2005). A key aspect of multicultural group work is fostering "acceptance, respect, and tolerance for diversity within and between members" (Bemak &

Chung, 2004, p. 36). Professional school counselors can refer to the *ASGW Principles for Diversity-Competent Group Workers* (ASGW, 1999) for guidance in addressing issues of diversity with sensitivity and skill.

Planning, Implementing, and Evaluating Groups

To maximize the group experience, it is important for leaders to plan for sessions ahead of time (Furr, 2000; Jacobs & Schimmel, 2005). An example of a six-step model for psychoeducational groups was presented earlier in the chapter. As with individual counseling, group leaders will want to balance *intentionality* (planfulness) with *flexibility* (being responsive to the needs of the group at a given time). When groups are focused on specific topics such as stress management, study skills, or anger management, leaders can plan the content and activities for each session in advance (Jacobs & Schimmel, 2005). Planning a series of sessions in this way is a "big picture" reminder that helps the leader keep the group focused and goal oriented.

Some general suggestions for beginning, middle, and ending sessions include the following:

- During beginning sessions, group leaders strive to create a safe environment in which members feel free to share their experiences. The creation of cohesion and trust, which begins during the initial session, contributes to the overall success of the group. Some of the activities that take place during the initial group session (unless there has already been a "pregroup" meeting) include introducing members, discussing the group's purpose, establishing ground rules, explaining confidentiality, and discussing expectations. Suggestions of activities to include in an initial session are presented in the "Introductory Group Activities" box. Also, during the beginning sessions, leaders will want to take note of how group members relate to each other and how they relate to the purpose or content of the group (Jacobs & Schimmel, 2005).
- The format of subsequent sessions will vary according to the age of the group members and the purpose of the group. In general, it is helpful to establish a routine that is used in

Introductory Group Activities

Elementary School: *Coat of Arms*

Create a coat of arms by drawing a shield and dividing it into four equal sections. Explain to children that a coat of arms tells different things about a person. Ask group members to create a shield that illustrates things they would like other people to know about them. (The group leader might give specific suggestions such as, "In the first section, draw or write something about your family. In the second section, draw or write something that you are really good at. In the third section, draw or write about a good book or something that you have read recently. In the last section, draw or write what you have a lot of fun doing."

Middle School: *Decorating My Bag*

Ask group members to cut out pictures representing themselves from magazines or newspapers. Tape or paste these pictures, along with other symbols, on the outside of their bags. Also, as part of the exercise, students can put loose pictures and symbols that they are not yet ready to share inside their bags. The students can use the bags to introduce themselves to one another in relation to the pictures and symbols on the outside of the bags. During subsequent sessions, as trust develops, provide students with opportunities to share the material inside the bags, as they see fit (Gladding, 1997).

High School: *Empty Chair Introductions*

Ask group members to think of someone they trust and value. This person can be a friend or family member. Ask members to stand behind their chairs, one at a time, and pretend to be that friend or family member. Then ask the student how that person would introduce the student. Next, the student, speaking as the trusted individual, introduces the "empty chair" as though the student were sitting in it. After introductions have been made, encourage group members to share what they learned about each other.

---

all group sessions (Gilbert, 2003). Suggested elements to include in this routine are:

1. Welcoming members individually
2. Reviewing group rules
3. Summarizing what occurred during the previous session
4. Focusing on the current topic or issue
5. Leading an experiential exercise related to the topic
6. Processing the exercise
7. Leading a closing activity in which members describe what they have learned or how they experienced the session

During these "middle" sessions, general goals include moving to a deeper level where feelings are identified and shared and group cohesion, support, and awareness are increased.

- The final group session is a time of summary and termination. Goals for the final session include helping group members focus on the future, instilling hope, and helping members translate insights into behaviors (Corey & Corey, 2002). Termination of the group should be planned in advance, with leaders announcing two to three meetings before the final session that the group experience will be ending. Like the initial session, the final group session tends to be structured. Students discuss their feelings about the group ending and identify what they have learned from the group experience. There are a number of ways to conclude groups, many of which include a time of group celebration. Some of the tasks that may occur during the group's closing stage include:

1. Reviewing and summarizing the group experience
2. Assessing members' growth and change
3. Finishing business
4. Applying change to everyday life
5. Providing feedback
6. Handling good-byes
7. Planning for continued problem resolution (Jacobs et al., 2006, p. 362)

Giving group members an opportunity to evaluate the group experience takes place either during the final session or during a follow-up meeting. Evaluation is needed to determine the usefulness of the group and its effect on the members (Akos & Martin, 2003). Group evaluation can take several forms. Brief questionnaires or surveys with incomplete statements are two ways to evaluate students' perceptions and learning. Examples of incomplete statements include: The group helped me at school by ———, One thing I learned in this group was ———. The most helpful part about being in this group was ———, One thing I wish we had done differently was ———, and to improve the group, I suggest ———.

In addition to asking group members to evaluate the group, professional school counselors can design pretest and posttest surveys to evaluate outcomes (Akos & Martin, 2003). Professional school counselors may also want to ask teachers, parents, or both to evaluate the group based on their observations of students after the group sessions have ended. Such evaluations are particularly helpful when the group focus was improved behavior (e.g., anger management, study skills, social skills). Finally, following up with students approximately six to eight weeks after the group has ended can provide professional school counselors with additional information about the group's impact and effectiveness.

SUMMARY/CONCLUSION

Individual and group counseling are important components of a comprehensive developmental school counseling program. They represent responsive services and provide ways to address students' needs and concerns. In particular, individual and group counseling are ways to help students who are facing problems that interfere with their personal, social, career, or academic development.

The manner in which professional school counselors carry out individual counseling and group work is affected by a number of factors, including the developmental characteristics of students, personal philosophical orientations, and specific school demands. In this chapter, counseling in school settings was defined. Certain developmental characteristics of children and adolescents, particularly as they related to the counseling process, were described. A model of individual counseling was presented, which included building a counseling relationship, assessing specific counseling needs, designing and implementing interventions, and conducting evaluation and closure. Also, because of its utility in school settings, SFBC was described (Sklare, 2005). This approach allows professional school counselors to provide effective counseling to students in a brief amount of time.

Whereas some students have needs that warrant individual counseling, students are more likely to participate in psychoeducational or counseling groups in schools. Psychoeducational groups use educational methods to help students gain knowledge and skills in several domains. They help group members develop new resources and coping skills, which may prevent problems in the future. Counseling groups tend to be more remedial than psychoeducational groups are and may be crisis centered, problem centered, or growth oriented.

Regardless of the type of group offered, several issues need to be considered by professional school counselors as they plan for group work. Important factors associated with setting up groups include collaborating with school staff and parents, determining group topics, making decisions about group composition and scheduling, screening students, and establishing group guidelines. Factors related to conducting groups effectively include: demonstrating effective group leadership skills; planning for initial, middle, and final group sessions; and group evaluation. Professional school counselors can effectively use group work, as well as individual counseling, with students to enhance development and remediate problems.

Now go to our Companion Website at www.prenhall.com/erford to assess your understanding of chapter content with "Multiple-Choice Questions," apply comprehension with "Essay Questions," and broaden your knowledge of the school counseling profession with related "Web Links."

ACTIVITIES

1. Develop an interview for screening members for a group topic of your choice (e.g., children from changing families, social skills, study skills).

2. Develop a psychoeducational group for young children in a school setting using Furr's six-step model for psychoeducational groups.

PROMOTING EDUCATIONAL AND CAREER PLANNING IN SCHOOLS

PATRICK AKOS AND SPENCER G. NILES

Editor's Introduction: When professional school counselors provide career and educational guidance to students, they influence the future by helping clarify developmental decisions that often last a lifetime. Although educational and career planning have been responsibilities of professional school counselors for decades, the school reform movement has placed renewed emphasis on challenging students to pursue rigorous academic coursework, oftentimes regardless of future aspirations. In the future, professional school counselors must continue to challenge students academically while building support systems and contingencies for exploring diverse vocational and avocational opportunities. In other words, professional school counselors must help students pursue a rigorous academic path while supporting important developmental life-role decisions that will affect students long after high school.

BACKGROUND FOR EDUCATIONAL AND CAREER PLANNING INTERVENTIONS IN SCHOOLS

Providing career assistance to students has always been an integral part of the work performed by professional school counselors. During most of the 20th century, professional school counselors fostered their students' career decision making by administering and interpreting interest inventories and aptitude tests. In the 1950s, however, Donald

Super (1957) proposed a developmental perspective emphasizing career development as a lifelong process. Super's theory created a paradigm shift within the career development field. Specifically, the focus of career interventions shifted from a single-point-in-time event of making a career decision to the manifestation of career behaviors over time. Super outlined career development stages and tasks, proposing that development through the life stages could be guided "partly by facilitating the maturing of abilities and interests and partly by aiding in reality testing and in the development of self-concepts" (Super, 1990, p. 207).

In addition to Super's contributions to the field, changes in the economy in the past few decades have enhanced the need for professional school counselors to focus on the area of career development. Changes in population, sociology, economics, and technology have had the largest impact on the job market. Furthermore, an increase in the globalization of jobs has altered job titles, roles, and structure within the workplace (Feller, 2003). Of particular interest to the professional school counselor should be the shift toward jobs in technology. According to Feller, of the 30 jobs that are projected to grow the most quickly in the coming decade, one third of them are in the field of technology. Because of these advances, a focus on career planning is at an all-time high and will continue to grow.

EDUCATION AND CAREER PLANNING TODAY

Fostering career development in youth is a prominent component of the current standards for developmental school counseling programs established by the ASCA (C. Campbell & Dahir, 1997). ASCA standards identify three core areas of development as goals of comprehensive developmental school counseling programs: academic, career, and personal–social. All three areas are interrelated and occur together in multiple systems. The *National Standards for School Counseling Programs* specify three important areas of student career development:

- *Standard A.* Students will acquire the skills to investigate the world of work in relation to knowledge of self and to make informed career decisions.
- *Standard B.* Students will employ strategies to achieve future career success and satisfaction.
- *Standard C.* Students will understand the relationship between personal qualities, education and training, and the world of work. (p. 16)

A complete list of competencies for each of these three standards of the career development component of the developmental school counseling program can be found in appendix C. These competencies include the development of career awareness and employment readiness; the acquisition of career information; and the identification of, and skills to achieve, career goals.

Among the academic competencies in the *ASCA National Model* (2003a) are several statements on educational planning that are interconnected with those for career development. Through educational planning, the professional school counselor can accomplish goals for both the academic and the career development areas of the program. Trusty and Niles (2004) demonstrated the long-term impacts (e.g., completion of a bachelor's degree) of course taking in middle and high school. According to Hobson and Phillips (2005), an effective educational planning process eliminates making a career choice by chance because it creates a foundation for a student's career development and prosperity as a citizen. Others have promoted career development strengths that are needed by all. Lapan (2004) and Savickas (2004) created schema based on decades of career development research that contribute to positive career behaviors. Lapan highlighted positive expectations, identity development, person–environment fit, vocational interests, academic achievement, and social skills (work readiness behaviors). Similarly, Savickas proposed a structural model of career adaptability that includes a taxonomy of adaptive attitudes of concern, control, conviction, competence, commitment, and connection. Although a full description of these is beyond the scope of this chapter, these constructs are integrated into the programs and interventions later.

Finally, life-span, life-space theorists define *career* as the total constellation of life roles that people engage in over the course of a lifetime (Super, 1980). Career development tasks include developing the skills necessary not only for selecting and implementing an occupational choice, but also for selecting, adjusting to, and transitioning through a variety of life roles, with an emphasis on helping students develop life-role readiness (Niles, 1998). Counselors using this multisystemic approach to career development ask questions such as, "What skills are necessary for successful performance as a student, worker, citizen, and so forth?" "What types of awareness do students need to acquire to make effective personal, educational, and career decisions?" "What knowledge is essential for students to make informed choices about life-role participation?" and "What skills do I need to accomplish my desired life roles?" The ASCA *National Model* (2003a) supports this idea of life-role readiness by focusing on the holistic development of each student in the three core areas of academic, career, and personal–social development. These foci (ASCA *National Standards,* educational planning, career development strengths, life-role readiness) all encompass the content for a K–12 educational and career planning program.

IMPLEMENTING SYSTEMATIC AND WELL-COORDINATED EDUCATIONAL AND CAREER PLANNING PROGRAMS

To help students acquire the knowledge, skills, and awareness necessary for effectively managing their career development, counselors implement systematic and well-coordinated educational and career planning programs (Herr, Cramer, & Niles, 2004). Counselors recognize that the piecemeal implementation of such programs limits the degree to which they can positively influence students. Moreover, an unsystematic and poorly coordinated intervention program often creates confusion about the meaning and purpose of career programs by those not directly involved in their creation and implementation. The ASCA *National Model* (2003a) is one example of a comprehensive and systematic program that can be implemented.

Specific to career development and similar to the *ASCA National Model*, a five-stage planning model for implementing systematic educational and career intervention programs was recommended by Herr and Cramer (1996).

> Stage 1: Develop a program rationale and philosophy.
> Stage 2: State program goals and behavioral objectives.

> Stage 3: Select program processes.
> Stage 4: Develop an evaluation design.
> Stage 5: Identify program milestones. (p. 310)

An important component of Stage 1 involves conducting a needs assessment to determine appropriate program rationales, goals, and interventions (Herr & Cramer, 1996). The needs assessment provides benchmarks against which program outcomes can be assessed. Herr and Cramer emphasized the importance of incorporating teachers, students, parents, and community participants in the needs assessment to increase their understanding of, and involvement in, career development programs. Clearly, a properly conducted needs assessment provides a firm foundation on which effective educational and career intervention programs can be constructed.

An implicit theme in these recommendations is that program planners need to be sensitive to the political climate in which they operate. In some locations, not clearly connecting career development interventions to student academic achievement (e.g., educational planning) will significantly decrease the chances of program success. Also, not adequately communicating successful program outcomes will result in the program resources being vulnerable to funding cuts. If school personnel view the program as an additional burden to their already heavy workloads, then there is little chance that the program will succeed. Thus, the "marketing" of the program to all stakeholders and integration into current goals are important aspects of program development and implementation. Clearly defined behavioral objectives that address the specific needs of program participants will be useful in marketing the program and providing outcome data demonstrating program benefits.

Another theme implicit in these recommendations for implementing systematic educational and career planning programs is the importance of taking a team approach to service delivery. The *ASCA National Model* (2003a) emphasizes this team approach to service delivery in the stress it places on collaboration. Working with administration, professional and support staff, parents, and community members, the professional school counselor can add depth and variety of experience to the school's career development program. Counselors may, at times, provide classroom instruction, and teachers may, at times, perform more counseling-related functions. Although there is no one prescription for how the roles and responsibilities should be defined, it is logical that counselors take the lead role in developing and implementing the programs. For example, bringing together parents and professionals within the community for a career fair would provide a much wider base of knowledge and firsthand experience about various careers than would merely using the information that the counselor could locate.

To address career development within the traditional academic curriculum, professional school counselors integrate career development interventions into the classroom. For example, students in an English class can conduct research projects to explore a potential career path. In this format, academic development (via engaging in research) and career development (through gathering occupational information) are connected with a writing assignment. Students learning about government can be introduced to presidents and legislators not only as historical figures, but also as real people with job descriptions and salaries, and as possessing specific job qualifications. This type of integration or infusion of career and educational planning concepts into the curriculum enhances the academic and career development of students.

Professional school counselors are often the only professionals in the school system with specific training in career development; therefore, professional school counselors possess the knowledge of career development theory and practice necessary for formulating appropriate program interventions. Moreover, the processes typically used in program delivery relate to counselors' primary areas of expertise. These processes are: counseling, assessment, career information services, placement services, consultation procedures, and referrals (National Occupational Information Coordinating Committee [NOICC], 1992).

In addition to specific training in career development, the professional school counselor

is frequently the primary figure within the school to help students with educational planning. Throughout the middle and high school years, educational planning and career development are inextricably tied to one another because decisions that are made about class choice and high school pathways often correlate with the postsecondary options that are available. Hobson and Phillips (2004) suggested that the professional school counselor should discuss the following three areas with students and parents: the amount of postsecondary training the student is willing to attain, the career in which the student is currently interested, and the type of training or education that is required to attain that career.

Counselors can also play an important role in program delivery by helping teachers communicate to parents the ways in which systematic career development programs can enhance student achievement. Communicating clearly the value of programs to parents and incorporating parents into program interventions will increase the likelihood that the program will be successful. At the same time, professional school counselors can help students understand the connection between current academic activities and future careers. Again, Super's concept of career development as a lifelong process and ASCA's *National Model*'s multiple, interrelated competencies are essential.

Finally, the professional school counselor must use emerging technology to sustain an educational and career planning program. In the past, technology was used primarily for computer-assisted career guidance systems (CACGS), but more recently, the Internet has emerged as the primary way to use technology in career development programs. This includes career assessments, career exploration, and job information Web sites that are easy to access and inexpensive. For example, a classroom guidance lesson that focuses on career exploration could center on the use of technology. Students can use the Internet to take an inventory of their own career interests and then search for specific information on jobs that align with those interests. Additionally, the Internet can be used to gather information on creating cover letters and resumes when teaching students about employability skills and for coaching students on the job-search process.

Developing a systematic and coordinated educational and career planning program across Grades K–12 requires understanding the developmental tasks confronting students as they progress through school. Understanding these tasks prepares school personnel to work collaboratively in program development and implementation. A comprehensive understanding of the career development process also sets the stage for developing program interventions that are sequential and cohesive.

ELEMENTARY SCHOOL

During the elementary school years, children begin formulating a sense of competence and interests through greater interaction with the world beyond their immediate families. Interactions with peers, teachers, parents, and community members shape the child's self-perceptions. Through exposure to adult life patterns via observations in schools, community activities, home, and the media, children draw conclusions about their lives. The conclusions children draw include assumptions about their current and future place in the world.

Obviously, there is tremendous variability in the quality-of-life patterns to which children are exposed. Television, for example, often provides children with examples of men and women in gender-stereotyped roles and occupations (e.g., only women working as nurses, only men working as auto mechanics, and women taking primary responsibility for homemaking and parenting). It also may provide very limited perceptions of careers for people of color. Children use this information to draw conclusions about the life patterns that are appropriate for them. As children are increasingly exposed to stereotypical behaviors and expectations of majority groups, they begin to eliminate nontraditional life patterns and narrow occupations from further consideration. The *ASCA National Model* (2003a) addresses the discussion of traditional

and nontraditional career choices in several of the career development competencies.

Gottfredson (1996) contended that a gender-based elimination process begins as early as age 6. He also suggested that between the ages of 9 and 13, children begin to eliminate those occupations from further consideration that they perceive to be less prestigious for their social class. Variables such as race or gender typing and prestige rankings interact with self-perceptions of abilities and interests as well as family and community expectations. These influences shape the decisions young people make about potential occupational options. An additional variable that influences students' perceptions of certain careers is geography. Students who have resided in more rural locations may have been exposed to entirely different jobs than those who have grown up in urban areas.

Because elementary school children have not yet had the opportunity to fully explore their options, an important goal of career development interventions in elementary school is to counteract environmental factors that pressure students to prematurely commit to educational and occupational options (Marcia, 1989). The use of nontraditional models (e.g., male nurses and female engineers) and exposure to a broad range of occupational environments is encouraged during the elementary school years. Because gender stereotyping is prevalent in society, students in elementary school should be encouraged to examine beliefs about female and male roles in society and how the various life roles interact to shape the overall life experience. To help students develop the skills necessary for effective career planning, they are taught decision-making strategies.

Another goal of career development interventions with elementary school children is to provide an environment in which each student's natural sense of curiosity can flourish (Super, 1990). Curiosity provides the foundation for exploring; children naturally express curiosity through fantasy and play. Children often engage intensely in fantasy-based play related to occupations such as physician, firefighter, teacher, and nurse. Curiosity can be guided to help students learn accurate information about themselves and their environments. For example, field trips to occupational environments related to a child's fantasy-based interests reinforce the child's sense of curiosity and stimulate further exploring and the gradual crystallization of interests (Super, 1957).

Encouraging students to participate in activities relating to their interests nurtures a sense of autonomy, the anticipation of future opportunities for exploring, and the beginning of planful behaviors (Super, 1990). When interests connect with skills and capacities, a positive self-concept emerges, which, in turn, provides the foundation for coping with the career development tasks of adolescence (Super, 1990). As children move toward adolescence, they must accomplish four major career development tasks. Specifically, they must (a) become concerned about the future, (b) increase personal control over their lives, (c) convince themselves to achieve in school and at work, and (d) develop competent work habits and attitudes (Super, Savickas, & Super, 1996).

Career Development Guidelines in Elementary School

NOICC (1992) developed National Career Development Guidelines to help counselors identify developmentally appropriate goals and interventions across the life span. The specific career development competencies identified as appropriate for elementary school children fall within three categories: (a) self-knowledge, (b) educational and occupational exploration, and (c) career planning.

At the elementary school level, students develop a basic sense of self (e.g., the activities in which they enjoy participating, the things they like and do not like) that provides the foundation for career exploration activities. Students also learn how to interact effectively with others. They learn that as they grow and develop, they will take on additional responsibilities. By learning school rules, students develop a basic understanding of the importance of cooperative behavior within institutions. Erikson (1963) noted that developing a sense of initiative and industry during the elementary school experience provides children

with a solid foundation from which they clarify their identities during secondary school.

Students in the elementary grades also engage in educational and occupational exploration by developing an understanding of the importance of educational achievement. Developing a sense of personal competence and positive self-worth is an important goal for elementary school children to achieve. Erikson (1963) noted that children who do not achieve this goal will struggle as they attempt to move forward in educational and career planning.

Students also need assistance connecting the school activities to their future possibilities. By connecting school to work, teachers and professional school counselors help students appreciate the relevance of their learning in school to their future work experiences. Helping students understand that school is, in essence, their work helps students understand the importance of developing good work habits. Students are encouraged to engage in career exploration and to consider the ways in which various workers contribute to the day-to-day operation of society.

The primary focus of career development interventions in the elementary school is awareness. Children need to develop an awareness of important self-characteristics (e.g., values, interests, and capacities). According to the National Model (ASCA, 2003a), professional school counselors need to promote self-knowledge; academic self-concept; and awareness of skills, interests, and motivations in relation to careers. They also need to receive accurate information about educational and career options. Helping children learn about a variety of occupations and the educational requirements for entering different occupations reinforces the fact that current activities relate to future options. School personnel must also work to challenge the gender and racial occupational stereotypes that confront children. Teaching children about the importance of diversity helps children learn how to interact more effectively with others in the school and community. Collectively, these interventions provide the basis for effective educational and career planning during secondary school.

MIDDLE OR JUNIOR HIGH SCHOOL

Students at the middle or junior high school level are confronted with a more sophisticated set of developmental tasks than they experienced during their elementary school years. The stormy experience of transitioning from childhood to adolescence presents a challenge to the young person. Physiological and social development lead the early adolescent to take strides toward independence; these strides, however, are often accompanied by feelings of insecurity, conflict, fear, and anxiety. Dramatic changes in cognition and the intensification of affect contribute to a "fluctuating sense of self" (Vernon, 1998, p. 10). As a result of their advancing development, middle or junior high school students are preoccupied with belonging and are influenced significantly by same-gender peers. Thus, the personal and social developmental tasks experienced by middle school students influence the delivery of career development interventions. The primary focus of these interventions is to help students crystallize and articulate their identities. Counselors need to challenge students to become agenic in the career development process, while offering supportive assistance as students acquire additional information about self and career.

Middle school students demonstrate a growing understanding of the world of work. Often this progress is the result of students' participating in school activities, hobbies, and part-time work. Herr and Cramer (1996) reported several important facts pertaining to the career development of middle school students. For example, they noted that boys and girls at age 13 tend to be equally knowledgeable about highly visible occupations and can link at least one school subject to a job. Most students at this age indicate that they have at least started the process of thinking about a future job. Interestingly, their choices for future jobs tend to be occupations requiring college degrees or lengthy training periods beyond high school rather than jobs now held by the majority of the workforce. This is reason for a necessary focus on educational planning during the seventh and eighth grades. Hobson and Phillips (2004) addressed the notion

of balancing the high career aspirations of students with the influence of others. They suggest that the professional school counselor can play a role in coaching students as they make course selections while attempting to attend to both the dominance of their parents and the influence of their peers.

Variability in career development among middle school students points to the importance of being clear about the societal expectations placed on students in middle or junior high school. As these students transition between Super's (1980) growth and exploration stages, they encounter the task of crystallizing occupational preferences. They are expected to develop a realistic self-concept and to learn more about opportunities (Super, 1980). Specifically, middle or junior high school students are required to learn about themselves and the world of work and then translate this learning into an educational plan for the remainder of their secondary school education. Through educational planning, students make important choices about their career futures. For example, during the eighth grade, a student is expected to identify a specific pathway of academic classes that will lead to certain possibilities on graduation. To make an educational plan, it is important that he or she has developed some self and career awareness prior to this time. Without sufficient coursework or achievement, he or she may find that the post-secondary option that was desired is no longer available because requirements were not met early on in the educational planning process. Super, Savickas, and Super (1996) stated the following about the crystallization process:

> When habits of industriousness, achievement, and foresight coalesce, individuals turn to daydreaming about possible selves they may construct. Eventually, these occupational daydreams crystallize into a publicly recognized vocational identity with corresponding preferences for a group of occupations at a particular ability level. (p. 132)

Thus, to establish an appropriate course of action for high school and beyond, educational and career planning interventions during middle or junior high school must be directed toward helping students cope successfully with the tasks of crystallizing and specifying occupational preferences (Super et al., 1996). Although research has shown that career identity will change several times in the future, students take interests discovered in elementary school to career thinking in middle school.

Career Development Guidelines in Middle or Junior High School

Middle or junior high school students learn that a positive self-concept is crucial for effective career planning. Developing a positive self-concept is facilitated by increased competence. They develop more sophisticated interpersonal skills and gain a greater understanding of human growth and development.

Middle or junior high school students must also develop specific competencies in educational and occupational exploration to advance in their career development. For example, the link between school activities and future opportunities first developed during elementary school must continue to be strengthened. Guest speakers representing a variety of occupations can discuss the relationship between learning and work. Specific subject areas can be linked to occupational success. The importance of lifelong learning for occupational success can also be stressed. To reinforce the importance of academic achievement, professional school counselors can inform students about the positive correlation between level of academic attainment and the amount of income workers earn. Teaching students how to locate, understand, and use career information fosters independent activity in educational and career planning. To this end, students can be taught the Holland (1992) occupational codes as a means for developing self-understanding and organizing occupational information.

The primary focus of career development interventions during middle or junior high school is on exploration. Career exploration can take place in numerous ways. Through classroom guidance on self-exploration (e.g., using Holland's [1992] theory), students can use computers to take the Career Key (L. K. Jones, 2004) and learn more about their own personality types. On discovering their types, they may look through a list of correlating career options and begin to explore these options through activities such as career days, job shadowing, and Internet searches. Students can be encouraged to explore by learning more about themselves not only as that knowledge pertains to important characteristics (e.g., interests, skills, values), but also in terms of considering the life roles that are important now and that are likely to be important in the future. Moreover, students learn the skills necessary for accessing and using educational and occupational information. These competencies are essential for moving forward with educational and career planning in high school.

During the middle school years, an educational and career portfolio is started for every student. Included in this portfolio are interest inventories, career exploration information and activities, educational planning materials, results from Internet searches, resources acquired at career fairs or job shadowing, and any other information that will add to the student's career development process. Using this portfolio, the student and professional school counselor can meet throughout the year and discuss the career development process using easy-to-access information that is specific to the student. Although this portfolio is started during middle school, it should be passed on to the high school counselor and maintained throughout the high school years. It is during the high school years that items in the portfolio will become more specific toward certain career choices.

HIGH SCHOOL

As students transition from middle or junior high school to high school, they focus more directly on the task of identifying occupational preferences and clarifying career and lifestyle choices. According to Super (1957), the tasks of crystallizing, specifying, and implementing tentative career choices occur during early (ages 12–15), middle (ages 16–18), and late (ages 18–24) adolescence.

When adolescents complete the relevant training and preparatory experiences, they then implement their occupational choices by acquiring positions in their specified occupations. In today's dynamic job world, the ability to adapt to various work environments may be the most important people skill. Thus, the key elements to a successful school-to-work and school-to-school transition involve being able to implement and adjust to career choice(s).

It is important to note that the majority of secondary school students in the United States are those who enter work immediately on leaving high school or who do not finish college. Thus, a majority of adolescents must acquire workforce readiness to cope successfully with their school-to-work transition. The definition of *workforce readiness* changes with the times. Until recently, this term may have focused solely on helping adolescents acquire training for a specific job, but today, employers are more concerned with "finding youth who can read and write, have a good attitude, are motivated, are dependable, follow directions, and can be good team members" (Krumboltz & Worthington, 1999, p. 316). Obviously, academic skills, interpersonal skills, and engaging in lifelong learning have emerged as important skills for youth to acquire if they are to be successful workers. Most current job skills are transferable to other occupations and contexts.

Hansen (1999) argued for expanding school-to-work career development interventions to include student development in addition to the more traditional emphasis on workforce development. Hansen pointed to curricula such as the Missouri Life Career Development System, the Minnesota Career Development Curriculum, and a model developed by the Florida Department of Education titled, *A Framework for Developing Comprehensive Guidance and Counseling Programs for a School-to-Work System* as excellent examples of comprehensive career development interventions to help youth prepare for the transition from secondary school to work. The *ASCA National Model* (ASCA, 2003a) also reinforces many of these ideas through its career development competencies. In particular, several of the competencies emphasize the transition from school to work and the relation between learning and work (e.g., each student should demonstrate an understanding of the value of lifelong learning and have the skills necessary to adjust to career transitions).

S. B. Baker (2000) emphasized the importance of providing "transition enhancement" assistance to secondary school students as they progress toward further education, training, or employment. Baker recommended that because such transitions are a regular part of high school students' development, counselors view transitions as a process rather than as events or a sequence of events. The basic needs of students coping with the transition process can be classified into the categories of support, awareness, and skills. Because most adolescents have lived their lives primarily in the arenas of home and K–12 schools, postsecondary work, training, and education present new challenges and experiences. Professional school counselors can aid in normalizing the transition process by providing reassurance to students that, although somewhat frightening, these new opportunities will present them with normal challenges and that many of the competencies they have developed thus far will be useful to them as they move forward.

When conceptualized as a process, the skills required for coping with the school-to-work and school-to-school transition are linked to the elementary and middle school career development competencies discussed previously. That is, transition skills build on the self-awareness, occupational awareness, and decision-making skills students have developed throughout their educational experience. Transition skills also build on the basic educational competencies related to reading, writing, and arithmetic (S. B. Baker, 2000). For example, composing a resume and cover letter requires self- and occupational awareness and writing skills. Performing effectively in a job or college interview requires skill in oral communication and interpersonal communication. Acquiring information about jobs, colleges, and training programs requires research, technology, and reading skills. Transition skills can also be expanded to include skills related to stress and anxiety management. ASCA takes the position that counselors in the school must assume the primary (but not sole) responsibility for fostering these skills in students. Providing career guidance to students is one of the most important contributions professional school counselors make to a student's lifelong development. Thus, proactively bolstering students' readiness to cope with the career development tasks they are likely to encounter is a primary component of the professional school counselor's role. Likewise, counselors must be competent in developing and delivering strategies to help students who encounter difficulty in coping with career development tasks.

Much of Super's research focused on understanding how adolescents can develop their readiness to cope effectively with the various career development tasks confronting them. The term initially used by Super (1957) to describe this process was "career maturity." Because the career development tasks confronting adolescents emerge from expectations inherent in academic curricula and society (e.g., family and teachers), the career development process during this life stage is more homogeneous than in adulthood. That is, the school system expects students to make career decisions at specific points in the curriculum (e.g., eighth graders choose an academic program that they will study in high school). Because the timing of these tasks can be predicted, career development practitioners can provide a systematic set of interventions to foster adolescent career development.

Savickas (1999) noted the importance of orienting students to the tasks they will face and the decisions they will make during their secondary school years. Discussing the items on career development inventories such as the Career Maturity Inventory (Crites, 1978) or the Adult Career Concerns Inventory (Super, Thompson, & Lindeman, 1988) is one technique that Savickas suggested for helping secondary school students consider the career development tasks they will encounter as they move through high school. Students need to develop awareness of the choices they will make throughout high school and beyond. Additionally, Savickas suggested

that a positive attitude toward making educational and career plans, a willingness to become actively involved in the career development process, the relevant competencies and motivation to acquire information about the world of work, and decision-making abilities comprise some of the competencies high school students need to manage their career development effectively.

Other researchers such as Marcia (1989) have also identified important variables for adolescent career development. Marcia focused on two variables—crisis/exploration and commitment—as central to the career development process during adolescence. Crisis/exploration refers to the process of sorting through identity issues; questioning parentally defined goals, values, and beliefs; and identifying personally appropriate alternatives regarding career options, goals, values, and beliefs. Commitment refers to the extent that the individual is personally involved in, and expresses allegiance to, self-chosen aspirations, goals, values, beliefs, and career options (Muuss, 1998). The degree to which adolescents resolve the tasks associated with crisis/exploration and commitment provide the conceptual structure for Marcia's (1989) taxonomy of adolescent identity. This taxonomy comprises four identity statuses: (a) identity diffused or identity confused, (b) foreclosed, (c) moratorium, and (d) identity achieved.

The *identity-diffused* person has yet to experience an identity crisis or exploration and has not made any personal commitment to an occupation, as well as to a set of goals, values, and beliefs. The *foreclosed* person has yet to experience an identity crisis or exploration but has committed to an occupation and to a set of goals, values, and beliefs (usually due to indoctrination or social pressure by parents or significant others). This type of foreclosure is premature because it has occurred without exploring and struggling with the basic existential questions related to identifying one's values, beliefs, goals, and so on. The *moratorium* person is engaged in an active struggle to clarify personally meaningful values, goals, and beliefs. Committing to a particular set of values, goals, and beliefs has been placed "on hold" until the process of identity clarification is more complete. The *identity-achieved* person has sorted through the process of identity clarification and resolved these issues in a personally meaningful way. Moreover, as a result of exploring and resolving identity issues, the identify-achieved person commits to an occupation and a personal value system.

Rather than being a singular process of exploring and committing to a set of values, goals, and beliefs, identity formation occurs across several domains such as occupation, religion, politics, ethnicity, and sexuality, among others. In many respects, these domains parallel Super's (1980) notion of life-role self-concepts (e.g., worker, leisurite, student, and homemaker) and reinforce Hansen's (1999) call for holistic career development interventions in the schools. Additionally, the individual's identity status within each domain is not static, but rather an ongoing process involving back-and-forth movement across stages. Marcia (1989) noted that although any of the identity statuses can become terminal, the foreclosed person experiences the greatest risk of closed development. Thus, career development interventions for early adolescents and adolescents (who, by definition, enter into these life stages with a relatively diffused identity) shoule be carefully designed to foster exploration and identity development related to the career domain.

Career Development Guidelines in High School

The extensive body of literature related to adolescent career development helps professional school counselors identify appropriate career development goals and interventions for high school students. High school students continue the momentum gained in self-knowledge during the middle school years. They acquire a more sophisticated understanding of the importance of developing a positive self-concept that serves as a basis for career planning. They also continue developing more sophisticated interpersonal skills during the high school years.

High school students grow increasingly aware of the relation between educational achievement

and career planning as the need to choose post-secondary educational and career options moves from being a remote event to one that is more immediate. Through work and extracurricular experiences, high school students increase their understanding of the need for positive attitudes toward work and learning. They increase their skills in locating, evaluating, and interpreting career information, and they develop and begin to refine job search skills.

Throughout high school, adolescents also continue to develop and refine their decision-making skills. The approaching inevitability of participation in multiple life roles provides motivation for additional clarification of life-role salience. Life-role structure issues (Super et al., 1996) become more realistic topics of importance for adolescents. Finally, the need to consider the approaching end of high school requires secondary school students to continue being active participants in their own career planning.

In essence, high school provides the opportunity for adolescents to build on the career development competencies they acquired during middle or junior high school. As life after high school moves from being remote to more immediate, adolescents must learn to assume greater responsibility for their career planning. Participation in multiple life roles becomes a serious component of the career planning process. Some adolescents are relatively well prepared for the life roles they will assume after high school. Others need substantial assistance to prepare for life after secondary school.

MULTICULTURAL IMPLICATIONS

When designing a K–12 educational and career planning program, students' cultural backgrounds are salient and an important part of the process. Although within-group variance is an important factor, generally, cultural values are an important lens. For example, the impact of gender on career circumscription in elementary school was highlighted. Another example is the concept of decision making as an independent process. This may be typical of European Americans but is often not true of many other cultures. Others may make decisions in a more collective or linear manner.

Studying the cultural values of the client is a necessity. Specifically, having an understanding of the client's time orientation, problem-solving strategies, and view on social relationships becomes an essential factor in discussing careers. For example, an Asian American client may have interests and abilities in the education field, but his or her father may insist that the client enter the field of engineering. For this Asian American client, decisions may be made in accordance with the wishes of the father because of the culture's lineal view on relationships. The professional school counselor must be aware of how culture intersects and influences all aspects of career and educational planning in elementary, middle, and high school to promote development that is congruent to the client's culture. One example of this is the concept of life-role readiness and salience.

Developing Life-Role Readiness and Salience

An approach to addressing the academic, career, and personal–social development emphasizes the importance of developing students' life-role readiness. The life-role readiness concept is based on developmental approaches to school counseling (Myrick, 1997). According to Myrick, developmental approaches contain objectives and activities directed to the following eight content areas:

1. Understanding the school environment
2. Understanding self and others
3. Understanding attitudes and behavior
4. Decision making and problem solving
5. Interpersonal and communication skills
6. School success skills
7. Career awareness and educational planning
8. Community pride and involvement

Each of these content areas focuses on specific life roles. For example, "understanding the school environment" focuses on the life role

of student, "community pride and involvement" focuses on the life role of citizen, and "career awareness and educational planning" focuses on the life role of worker. Counseling activities within each content area are essentially intended to help students cope with the task of identity formation within the context of developing life-role readiness. "Life-role readiness" can be defined as the possession of the knowledge, attitudes, and skills necessary for effective life-role participation in a multicultural society. For example, among other things, effective parenting requires possessing basic knowledge about child development, a positive attitude toward parenting as a life role, and the skills necessary for providing basic child care. Likewise, life-role readiness related to the leisure role requires possessing basic knowledge about specific leisure activities, a positive attitude toward leisure as a life role, and the basic skills necessary for participation in specific leisure activities.

Developmental school counseling interventions should include learning opportunities that foster the development of the knowledge, attitudes, and skills necessary for effective life-role participation (i.e., life-role readiness). By providing these learning opportunities within a context that is sensitive to cultural diversity, professional school counselors help students avoid adherence to the cultural uniformity myth and cultural ethnocentrism. That is, students learn to appreciate and value cultural differences in life-role behavior. For example, the life role for a sibling may be different between a White and a Hispanic adolescent. Perhaps a student's ethnicity and family traditions will call for duties and responsibilities that are unique.

Encouraging students to discuss life-role salience is useful because life-role salience provides the motivating force behind the development of life-role readiness (Super et al., 1996). If a life role is important to someone, then it is likely that the individual will engage in the behaviors necessary to become prepared for taking on that life role. Likewise, when salience is low, there is often little motivation for developing the requisite behaviors for effective participation in that role.

Addressing the issue of life-role salience, Super (1980) noted that work is only one role among many that individuals play. He identified the primary roles of life (e.g., student, worker, citizen, homemaker) and noted that some roles are more important than others at particular points in time. For example, some adolescents attend high school, work in part-time jobs, and are also parents. For a majority of adolescents, the life role of peer is paramount in middle and high school. Others devote a majority of their time to leisure, student, and family-of-origin activities. Developing life-role readiness requires secondary school students to identify their salient life roles and to examine the relation between their goals and their current life-role activities.

Obviously, patterns of life-role salience are significantly influenced by immediate (e.g., family, cultural heritage, level of acculturation) and distal (e.g., economics, environmental opportunities for life-role participation) contextual factors. Contextual factors, therefore, contribute to patterns of life-role salience among secondary school students. However, many students lack an awareness of the ways in which contextual factors (such as the dominant culture and the student's culture of origin) interact with identity development to shape life-role salience (Blustein, 1994).

Often students simply "inherit" patterns of life-role salience that are passed on from the dominant culture. Such inheritances can be problematic when they are embedded with beliefs based on gender and racial stereotypes. For instance, researchers have consistently found gender differences that coincide with traditional gender-role expectations in life-role salience (e.g., women participating more in home and family and expecting more from this life role than men do [Niles & Goodnough, 1996]). Women who have high salience for the worker role are placed at an obvious disadvantage in the workforce by such traditional expectations. Also, men limit their opportunities for participating in the home and family when they adhere to traditional expectations for life-role salience. By raising students' awareness of the influence of the dominant culture on life-role salience, students will be less likely to allow beliefs reflecting racist and sexist attitudes to influence their beliefs about life-role salience.

To foster the development of life-role readiness, professional school counselors can encourage students to address several topics. First, counselors at the elementary school level can introduce students to the primary roles of life (e.g., student, worker, family member, citizen). After developing life-role awareness in the elementary school, middle school students can be encouraged to identify the life roles that are important to them (i.e., their life-role salience). Second, students can identify the contextual factors (e.g., family, culture, economics, new occupational options) influencing their life-role salience. Third, middle and high school students can be encouraged to participate in specific activities that foster the development of life-role readiness. Together, these topics provide a conceptual framework around which counseling interventions that facilitate life-role readiness in a multicultural society can be constructed.

Using a group guidance format, students can examine their current life-role salience by responding to such questions as, How do you spend your time during a typical week? How important are the different roles of life (e.g., student, worker, and citizen) to you? What do you like about participating in each of the life roles? What life roles do you think will be important to you in the future? What do you hope to accomplish in each of the life roles that will be important to you in the future? In which life roles do members of your family participate? What do your family members expect you to accomplish in each of the life roles?

Professional school counselors can also use a group guidance format to help students identify the life roles they are currently spending most of their time emotionally committed to and expect to be important to them in the future. With regard to the latter, counselors can help students construct strategies for preparing for their salient life roles. For example, if the life role of parent is expected to be salient in the future, students can discuss ways to plan and prepare for that role. Counselors can also encourage students to examine areas of potential role conflict and discuss strategies for coping with excessive demands from multiple life roles.

Discussions related to the influence of the dominant culture on life-role salience can also lead to discussions that focus on how students' cultural backgrounds influence their viewpoints on life-role salience. Professional school counselors can emphasize how different cultures often influence the values individuals seek to express in life roles (e.g., seeking to express self-actualization in work for the student from a Eurocentric cultural background or seeking to express cultural identity in work for the student from an Asian background). By discussing the ways in which culture influences life-role salience, students become aware of how their cultural backgrounds influence their life-role salience, and they learn about differing patterns in role salience across cultures.

Intervention

Through group guidance and classroom discussions, students can explore the various cultural prescriptions that are generally assigned to specific life roles. In these discussions, counselors can encourage students to identify how they perceive and interpret the role expectations emanating from their cultures of origin and how these expectations influence their decisions as to whether a particular life role is important. Particular attention can be paid to exploring how these expectations influence students' understandings of the behaviors required for effective role performance.

Borodovsky and Ponterotto (1994) suggested one specific activity that may provide opportunities for discussing these topics. They identified the family genogram as a useful tool for exploring the interaction among family background, cultural prescriptions, and career planning. The genogram provides a tool for tracking career decisions across generations and identifying sources of important career beliefs and life themes that students have acquired.

This technique can be expanded to address the same topics for other life roles. By using the genogram, professional school counselors can encourage students to identify the beliefs and life themes pertaining to specific life roles (e.g., parent and citizen) that they have acquired from members of their immediate

and extended families. Counselors can also use the information provided by the students to contrast the influences on life-role salience emanating from group-oriented cultures with influences from more individualistic cultures. Terms such as *cultural assimilation* and *cultural accommodation* can be introduced in these discussions. The effects of gender-role stereotyping on life-role salience can also be examined here and challenged in these discussions. The goal of these interventions is to increase student awareness of the factors influencing their beliefs about the primary roles of life.

Knowing which life roles are salient and how contextual factors influence one's life-role salience is a starting point for developing life-role readiness. Professional school counselors must also encourage students to participate in activities that foster further development of life-role readiness. Super's (1957, 1977) theory is also useful in this regard. Super suggested that by actively planning for career decisions, exploring occupational options, gathering occupational information, learning how to make occupational decisions, and reality testing tentative occupational choices, individuals develop their readiness for participating in the life role of worker.

These same behaviors can be applied to other life roles. To develop readiness for the life role of student, college-bound secondary school students must plan for the academic tasks they are likely to encounter (e.g., choosing a program of study, registering for college entrance examinations, knowing when to begin the process of college selection). They must also engage in thorough exploration of postsecondary school options. In the process of exploring, students must gather information relevant to the academic options they are considering. Once options are explored and information is gathered, students are then ready to make tentative academic plans and decisions. As students implement their decisions (e.g., entering an academic program intended to prepare them for college, narrowing a list of prospective colleges), they begin the process of reality testing their choices. The postimplementation feedback they receive (e.g., grades) informs them as to the appropriateness of their current plans and indicates ways in which their plans may need to be revised (e.g., a high school student who plans on majoring in engineering in college but earns poor grades in science may need to explore, gather information, make decisions, and reality-test options related to nonscience majors).

An effective tool for helping students engage in purposeful planning, exploring, information gathering, decision making, and reality testing related to the life roles of student and worker is an education and career planning portfolio. This can be expanded to a "life-role portfolio" by addressing students' readiness for life roles beyond those of student and worker. Students can be encouraged to plan, explore, and gather information, and so forth, for each of the major life roles.

For example, students who anticipate one day being a parent can plan for this role by considering how parenting interacts with other roles. Students can explore different styles of parenting by interviewing parents about their parenting practices and philosophies. Students can also gather information about the skills required for effective parenting (perhaps by taking a parenting class). Through these activities, students can learn about the factors that are important to consider in making decisions about parenting. Finally, students can reality-test their interest in parenting through participating in child care activities. Thus, the life-role portfolio stimulates counselor and student meetings focused on planning, exploring, information gathering, decision making, and reality testing vis-à-vis the major life roles. When the portfolio is used over successive years, it also provides developmental documentation of activities and decisions related to major life roles.

This expanded use of the planning portfolio is an example of a counseling activity that is intended to help students cope with the task of identity formation within the context of developing life-role readiness. It also provides additional opportunities for discussing contextual influences on life-role salience. Regardless of the life role, it is important that professional school counselors are sensitive to the cultural diversity among their students.

SUMMARY/CONCLUSION

According to the *ASCA National Model* (ASCA, 2003a), one of the primary roles of any professional school counselor is to facilitate a career development program. A major goal of professional school counseling programs is to facilitate student development toward effective life-role participation. Professional school counselors must initiate appropriate developmental guidance activities in elementary school (self-awareness, curiosity, etc.) and facilitate culmination of this process with assistance in the transition to school, work, and a variety of life roles. Professional school counselors can enhance students' life-role readiness by helping students develop life-role awareness and by encouraging students to examine their life-role salience and the contextual factors influencing their role salience. To foster the continued development of life-role readiness, professional school counselors can encourage students to engage in planning, exploring, information gathering, decision making, and reality testing vis-à-vis the major roles of life. In addition, the program should anticipate adaptations to various cultural backgrounds and the utilization of technology. By systematically addressing these topics throughout Grades K–12, professional school counselors facilitate the development of life-role readiness in their students and increase the probability that students will cope successfully with life-role tasks in school and beyond.

Now go to our Companion Website at www.prenhall.com/erford to assess your understanding of chapter content with "Multiple-Choice Questions," apply comprehension with "Essay Questions," and broaden your knowledge of the school counseling profession with related "Web Links."

ACTIVITIES

1. Develop a career exploration activity for the grade level of your choice using technology.
2. Plan a classroom guidance session for elementary students that discusses traditional and nontraditional occupations.

3. Plan a career development group for high school students that focuses on employability skills.

CONSULTATION, COLLABORATION, AND PARENT INVOLVEMENT

BRADLEY T. ERFORD*

Editor's Introduction: Consultation and collaboration are efficient interventions that not only allow professional school counselors to address the issue at hand, but also provide a model for consultees and collaboratees to take responsibility for solving their own problems in the future. The collaborative model encompasses the establishment of partnerships with parents and community organizations to solve systemic problems and remove barriers to student performance. The practices of collaboration and partnering hold tremendous potential for the transformation of the school counseling profession. Professional school counselors are in a wonderful position to build bridges between students who are in need and needed community resources, be they human or material. Students whose parents are involved in and supportive of their educational journey achieve higher levels of performance and are better adjusted socially and emotionally. Collaboration, outreach, and school–community partnering are processes meant to get parents and the community involved in the educational enterprise. Although these processes may diverge from a traditional role, the transformed role of the professional school counselor makes such initiatives crucial. While no one is expected to "do it all," this chapter presents some ideas to get the professional school counselor to start thinking about the possibilities. The discerning professional school counselor will also note that

---

*In the first edition of this text, portions of this chapter were written by Susan G. Keys, Alan Green, Estes Lockhart, Peter F. Luongo, Gayle Cicero, and Pat Barton.

many of the suggestions may require only an initial impetus followed by delegation of responsibilities to colleagues and volunteers, thus preventing professional school counselors from perpetually investing valuable time and resources over the long term.

THE COUNSELOR AS CONSULTANT: CASE EXAMPLES

Samantha is a kindergarten student in Mrs. Miller's class at River Falls Elementary School. Samantha has few friends and limited social skills. She is often bossy and frequently demands to have things her own way. Mrs. Miller has met with little success in helping Samantha respond more appropriately. Running short of ideas for how to intervene, she refers Samantha to the professional school counselor.

Alberto is a ninth-grade student who is having difficulty with math class and is in danger of failing the course. Although his other courses are challenging, he is managing passing grades. Mr. Long, Alberto's math teacher, feels Alberto's behavior contributes to his problem with math. According to Mr. Long, Alberto interrupts him and his classmates frequently. Alberto is rude in class, generally making sarcastic comments to Mr. Long and the other students. Most of his classmates consider him to be a big annoyance. Alberto has started to cut class. On the surface, Alberto exhibits an "I don't care" attitude. Mr. Long recently referred Alberto to the school's Student Support Team. Alberto's professional school counselor is a team member.

Westwood Middle School is located in a culturally diverse urban area. A recent increase in discipline referrals for aggressive behavior has prompted Westwood's School Improvement Team to make the promotion of school safety an important goal for the year. Westwood's principal, Ms. Johnson, has charged the school's four professional school counselors with taking the lead in developing a comprehensive school violence prevention program.

Each of these cases represents typical referrals that a professional school counselor at the elementary, middle, or high school level might receive in the normal course of the school day. Professional school counselors represent an important resource for teachers who are confronted by students for whom the usual methods of instruction and discipline are often less than successful. Parents and family members also seek support from the professional school counselor when confused or uncertain about what is normal development or expected behavior, and how to help their child when personal, interpersonal, or academic difficulties arise. Administrators also use the professional school counselor's expertise when looking to solve problems involving individual students, as well as problems that affect larger groups of students, family members, and staff. In each of these cases, the professional school counselor may respond from a number of different roles—counselor, consultant, program developer and coordinator, or classroom educator—and in all likelihood will use a combination of roles to provide assistance to teachers, staff, families, and students.

This chapter looks in detail at one of these roles: the counselor's consultant role. ASCA's *National Model* (2003a) points to the importance of consultation and collaboration services in a comprehensive developmental school counseling program. Collaboration and consultation are effective methods for intervening in developmental student issues by working with essential people in the student's life (e.g., parents, teachers). Furthermore, consultation and collaboration have been important services provided by counselors for decades, across many settings (Brown, Pryzwansky, & Schultz, 2000; Dinkmeyer & Carlson, 2001; Kahn, 2000; Kampwirth, 2002). In schools, the collaborative approach to consultation currently predominates because it allows the professional school counselor to become an active agent of change even after a course of action has been agreed to by all parties (Dinkmeyer & Carlson, 2001; Dougherty, 1999; Kampwirth, 2002). How might professional school counselors, as collaborators and consultants, approach the problem-solving process in each of the above cases? What models of consultation might professional school counselors draw on? How do professional school counselors integrate their expertise with the skills and knowledge of other problem solvers? This chapter explores these and other questions as a way of discovering more about the professional school counselor's very important consultant role.

BACKGROUND

Gilbert Wrenn's (1962) landmark report on the condition of school counseling, *The Counselor in a Changing World,* strongly urged that consultation with teachers, parents, and administrators be considered an essential element of the professional school counselor's role and function. With the emergence of the developmental guidance and counseling movement in the 1970s, consultation became a widely accepted function (Schmidt, 2003). The professional school counselor's responsibility for large numbers of students added impetus to the adoption of a consultation focus. Although the ASCA recommends 100:1 as the ideal student-to-counselor ratio, with 300:1 as a maximum ratio (ASCA, 1993), all but a few school systems have been able to maintain this standard. Providing individual counseling services becomes prohibitive when faced with unrealistic student-to-counselor ratios. Through consultation, professional school counselors can assist more students by working directly with those individuals who have frequent contact with students—teachers and family members. Professional school counselors as consultants also work with other professionals and family members when planning broad-based prevention and intervention programs.

CONSULTATION MODELS

Keys et al. (1998) noted that models of consultation can be distinguished by the type of interaction that occurs between the consultant and the person or persons seeking the consultant's help. They described three types of interaction as triadic-dependent, collaborative-dependent, and collaborative-interdependent.

Triadic-Dependent

Traditionally, consultation is thought of as a problem-solving process that involves a helpseeker, referred to as a consultee (teacher, administrator, family member); a helpgiver (consultant); and a third person who is the focus of concern (client or student). This three-party relationship is referred to as triadic. In this type of relationship, the consultant provides services indirectly to the client through the consultant's work with the consultee (see Figure 11.1).

Counseling, in contrast, is considered a direct student service since the professional school counselor works in direct contact with the student. In some situations, the professional school counselor may combine different types of services; in effect, the counselor may consult

FIGURE 11.1
Consultation as indirect service to the client.

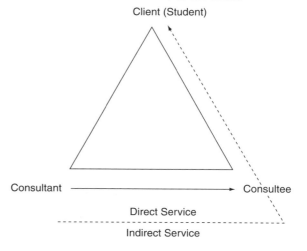

with teachers or family members (indirect service to the student) and provide the same student with one-on-one or group counseling services (direct service to the student).

In the triadic-dependent model, the consultant is viewed as the expert from whom the consultee seeks assistance to remediate a problem with the client (see Figure 11.2). In effect, the consultee is dependent on the consultant's advice and recommendations. The consultant works through the consultee to bring about change for the client. Although the expectation is that the consultation ultimately ends in improved achievement, affect, attitude, or behavior for the student, the immediate recipient of this service is the administrator, teacher, or family member, not the student. The immediate goal of the consultation might be increasing the skills, knowledge, and objectivity of the consultee so that the consultee is better able to implement an intervention plan designed to achieve change for the client.

Many consultations that professional school counselors conduct with teachers and family members fall under the triadic-dependent relationship category. Using this model, the professional school counselor would meet with a teacher or family member (or both) to assess their perspectives on the student's problem. The professional school counselor may collect additional data through observations, consultations with other

teachers or professionals, and meetings with the student. As a consultant, the professional school counselor makes recommendations to the consultee, with the consultee being the one responsible for implementing the prescribed plan. The consultant's recommendations may include interventions that focus on change for the client, the consultee, and the system. R. Parsons (1996) referred to this as client-focused, consultee-focused, and system-focused consultation. In actuality, a consultation could result in recommendations for changes in all three areas.

Bergan's (1977) and Bergan and Kratochwill's (1990) behavioral consultation is an example of a triadic-dependent consultation model. Within this model, the consultant, as a behavioral expert, draws on principles of behaviorism to help define the problem, identify environmental conditions that maintain the problem, generate solutions that result in changes in behavior for the client or the consultee, and change the social context within which the client or consultee functions. Professional school counselors who help teachers and family members acquire the skills and knowledge necessary to implement a behavior management plan draw on this particular consultation model (Sterling–Turner, Watson, & Moore, 2002; Sterling–Turner, Watson, Wildmon, Watkins, & Little, 2001). Behavior consultation has also been reported to be quite effective (Sheridan, Welch, & Orme, 1996), with 89% of all studies reporting

FIGURE 11.2
Consultation as a triadic-dependent relationship.

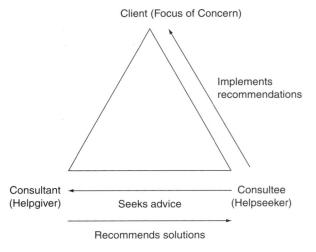

TABLE 11.1
Suggestions for conducting effective triadic-dependent consultation.

Make sure the environment for the consultation is comfortable and professional.

Quickly establish the purpose of the consultation, identifying the client (usually the student) and defining the problems or issues of concern.

Try to minimize anxiety and maximize cooperation quickly. Maintain a friendly, professional demeanor even in the face of angry or emotional consultees. Do not become defensive.

Give the consultee the opportunity to "tell his or her story." Be supportive, help as necessary, and listen actively.

Get to the point efficiently and avoid educational or psychological jargon.

Establish clear boundaries for the consultee (usually the parent or teacher) so that the student becomes the focus of problem identification and intervention, not the consultee.

Probe for any factors or conditions that may be relevant to effective treatment planning, including what the consultee has tried previously and any condition that may contraindicate a potential intervention.

Focus on the student's behavior, not the student. Reframe the presenting behaviors in terms of student needs to provide alternative perspectives to consider in treatment. Often, understanding the goal of behavior helps adults to better help the student meet those needs.

Classroom observation can be a helpful way of collecting additional information about the context surrounding student behavior and performance.

Dougherty (1999) suggested four questions that must be addressed for interventions to be understood and effective: (a) What are we going to do? (b) How are we going to do it? (c) When and where are we going to do it? and (d) How well did we do?

Be sure to develop a working relationship with the consultee as an equal partner in the endeavor. Try to have the consultee suggest potential interventions and evaluation plans.

Provide resources (e.g., books, handouts, Web sites) that can help the consultee better understand the issues and interventions.

Be sure to schedule follow-up procedures during the initial consultation. All interventions must be tracked and evaluated. When consultees fail to achieve desired results, they may assume either they are incompetent or the consultant is incompetent. Follow-up and evaluation ensure an atmosphere of cooperation and continued addressing of issues until a successful resolution is reached. Most counseling interventions require adjustments or even a completely different approach.

Document in writing contacts with consultees or others involved with the issue.

positive results. Watson, Butler, Weaver, & Foster (2004) proposed a four-step behavioral consultation model that is similar to other models of collaboration and consultation: (a) problem identification, (b) problem analysis, (c) plan implementation, and (d) plan evaluation. During plan implementation, behavioral contracting, positive reinforcement, and response cost are strategies that might be implemented. Each of these strategies would result in client-focused change. However, if the consultant needed to spend time educating the teacher or family member about how to implement these procedures, then the consultation would include both client-focused

and consultee-focused interventions. Table 11.1 includes helpful suggestions for conducting effective triadic-dependent consultations with parents and teachers.

Case Example: Samantha

How might a professional school counselor who functions as a consultant within the triadic-dependent model respond to Mrs. Miller in the case of Samantha? After receiving Mrs. Miller's initial referral, the counselor–consultant will take several steps to develop a more thorough understanding of Samantha and Mrs. Miller's concerns. This could include:

- An initial consultation session with Mrs. Miller to better define the problem and assess how the teacher and the other students typically respond to Samantha when she is disruptive and demanding.
- Observation of Samantha in Mrs. Miller's classroom to further identify occasions when Samantha is disruptive and demanding, and to see firsthand patterns that may exist in how others respond to Samantha. The consultant may also spend time observing Samantha in less structured situations such as the lunchroom and playground to determine if the same behaviors exist in these contexts.
- A meeting with Samantha to determine her perception of the problem and further assess her social skills development.

The consultant integrates all information and in a subsequent consultation session (or sessions) with Mrs. Miller recommends strategies Mrs. Miller might use to encourage Samantha to exhibit more positive behavior in the classroom. These strategies may include teaching Mrs. Miller new techniques for positive reinforcement, and the use of modeling to teach Samantha new social skills. The consultant may also recommend that Samantha participate in small-group counseling sessions (with the consultant then functioning as counselor) focused on social skill development. Because follow-up and accountability are essential to successful outcomes, the consultant monitors the student's progress and maintains contact with Mrs. Miller to determine the intervention's effectiveness.

Collaborative-Dependent

In a collaborative-dependent relationship, the helping process departs from a view of the consultant as a solitary expert. The consultee continues to depend on the consultant's (a) problem-solving expertise, (b) knowledge of normal and abnormal development, and (c) skills for effecting client and systemic change.

In a collaborative-dependent relationship, the consultant also recognizes and engages the knowledge and expertise of the consultee about both the client's and the system's strengths and weaknesses, contextual factors that influence the client, and the client's reaction to previously attempted interventions (see Figure 11.3).

Creating a partnership relationship is important to this process. Consultants who work within a collaborative-dependent relationship may educate consultees about the problem-solving process itself, as well as facilitate how the actual problem-solving process unfolds. Importantly, and in some ways in contrast to a triadic-dependent model, the collaborative professional school counselor is not seen as an expert, but as a partner in defining the problem, implementing interventions, and providing evaluation and follow-up services. Together, the consultant and consultee establish mutual goals and objectives for the client and develop an intervention plan. The consultee is responsible for implementing the intervention plan with either the client and the classroom system (if the consultee is a teacher) or the client and the family system (if the consultee is a family member). The consultant and the consultee depend on the knowledge and skills each person brings to the problem-solving process.

A collaborative-dependent consultation relationship may focus on help for a specific client (client-focused consultation), help for the consultee (consultee-focused consultation), or more broadly on change within the organizational context or system (system-focused consultation). Schein's (1969) process model illustrates system-focused consultation. As a process consultant, the professional school counselor, using Schein's (1969) model, approaches problem solving by examining six different variables critical to the organizational system: (a) communication patterns, (b) group members' roles and functions, (c) processes and procedures for group problem solving and decision making, (d) group norms and group growth, (e) leadership and authority, and (f) intergroup cooperation and competition. Within a process consultation model, the focus of change is the organizational system, with the consultant contributing expertise on assessment and interventions related to system

FIGURE 11.3

Consultation as a collaborative-dependent relationship.

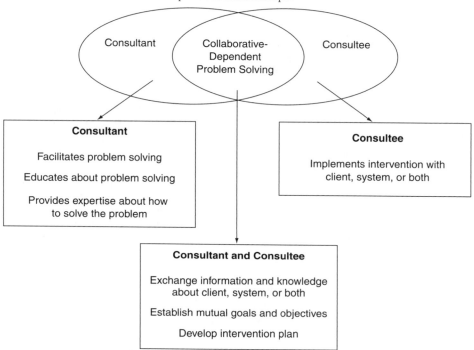

change. These variables are also relevant for the consultant who wants to bring about change in a family system.

Case Example: Alberto

As a member of the school's Student Support Team, the professional school counselor participates in the initial review meeting for Alberto's case. Other participants include the referring teacher, Mr. Long; the school's assistant principal; a special education resource teacher; the school psychologist; the school nurse; and the school social worker. Alberto's academic record indicates that math has been a consistent area of weakness for Alberto; however, he has always managed passing grades. No special education services have been provided in the past, and the team does not feel a referral for such services is warranted. After reviewing case information, the team makes two recommendations: (a) that Alberto

be invited to participate in an after-school math tutoring session, and (b) that Mr. Long and the professional school counselor work on helping Alberto develop a more positive classroom demeanor.

After meeting with Mr. Long and visiting his class during math time, the professional school counselor, functioning as a consultant, meets with Mr. Long again to establish mutual goals and to develop an intervention plan. Mr. Long is well recognized in the school for his expertise as a math teacher. The consultant is careful to convey respect for Mr. Long's expertise and to support his interest in helping Alberto to be successful in his classroom. The consultant stresses the need for the two of them to agree on a mutual goal and plan for helping Alberto.

When visiting in Mr. Long's classroom, the consultant observes that Mr. Long has the students compete as teams in weekly math quizzes. The team that scores the most points earns a homework pass for one night. This competition seems to make Alberto uncomfortable, with a noticeably higher rate of disruptive behavior occurring at these times. During the consultation session, the consultant shares this observation about Alberto with Mr. Long. Together they devise a plan for how students can practice their math skills (the reason for the competition) in a way that supports cooperative learning and minimizes stress for Alberto as well as the other students. This system-focused intervention will be implemented by Mr. Long, the consultee. The consultant will remain in contact with Mr. Long in an assessment or accountability role to ascertain if the solution is bringing about a change in Alberto's behavior.

Collaborative-Interdependent

Keys et al. (1998) suggested that triadic-dependent and collaborative-dependent consultation models are helpful when seeking change for an individual client, family, or single organizational system related to normal developmental problems. When problems are more complex, especially the multi-causal and multicontextual problems of youth who are at risk, these more traditional models are too limited in scope to provide comprehensive solutions. A collaborative-interdependent relationship is a useful alternative.

Collaboration is "an interactive process that enables groups of people with diverse expertise to generate creative solutions to mutually defined problems" (Idol, Nevin, & Paolucci-Whitcomb, 1994, p. 1). This model emphasizes an interdependent problem-solving process in which family members, educators, counselors, youth, and members of the broader community contribute as equal participants (see Figure 11.4). Unlike previously discussed models that rely heavily on the counselor–consultant as an expert, a collaborative-interdependent model does not presume that any one person has sufficient knowledge or information to understand the problem and develop and implement solutions. Ultimately, it is the sharing and transferring of knowledge and information among all problem solvers that enables the group to determine and implement a more comprehensive plan (Keys et al., 1998). The plan may include change for an individual client,

FIGURE 11.4
Consultation as a collaborative, interdependent relationship.

new knowledge and skills for team members (including the consultant), and change for the organizational system. Each person in the group is interdependent on the expertise of the other group members in formulating and executing the problem-solving plan.

Friend and Cook (1996) described consultation as a process and collaboration as the style of interaction within the process. Collaboration refers to how people interact during the problem-solving process. Professional school counselors who use collaboration work within a team framework. To have convened a team, however, does not necessarily mean that the team functions collaboratively. Keys et al. (1998) cautioned that although family members, teachers, and other professionals and community members may share information about a problem and may have knowledge of what each is doing to solve the problem, they are not necessarily functioning collaboratively unless they actively involve each other in carrying out their functions. The interdependence of a collaborative style extends to all phases of the problem-solving process—problem identification, goal setting, strategy development and implementation, and evaluation.

Friend and Cook (1996) defined several distinguishing features of a collaborative style of interaction:

- Collaboration is *voluntary*. People who come together to solve complex problems must want to collaborate for a collaborative style of interaction to occur. Collaboration cannot occur merely because it has been mandated by an administrator.
- Collaboration requires *parity* among all participants. Parity suggests that each participant has an equal voice in decision making and that all team members value equally each member's input. This characteristic is often the most difficult to support in the school setting. Administrative oversight in some schools precludes parity. In some schools, the school-based professionals often decide outcomes before the team even assembles, with the team more of a rubber stamp of what the "school experts" feel should be done, rather than an interactive body that values the expertise of family and community members. Attitudes and assumptions by some school professionals about those who are economically disadvantaged or culturally diverse may also prohibit parity. Professional school counselors–consultants need to pay particular attention to issues of parity and seek to provide balance in the crucial dialogue between teachers, administrators, and students and their families.
- Collaboration depends on *shared responsibility* for decision making. In a school context, shared responsibility suggests that it is not the school (e.g., teachers) alone or family members alone or the community alone that is responsible for "fixing the problem." Each participant has a role in identifying the problem, setting objectives, implementing solutions, and evaluating outcome. Not all team members necessarily contribute equally to the implemented solution, nor is the division of labor necessarily equal across all members. The degree to which any team member contributes is directly dependent on the need for that individual's skills and expertise.
- Collaboration is based on *mutual goals* and a *shared accountability* for outcomes. All participants must agree on what the team is to accomplish. Commitment from each member is critical. Each member may contribute a different expertise to achieve the desired outcome, but the desired end result must be supported by all partners. Responsibility for outcomes—successes as well as disappointments—is shared by all members.
- Individuals who collaborate *share their resources* without dictating how these resources are to be used. How to best use resources becomes a part of the collaborative decision-making process.

What is the consultant's role in helping professionals and family members function collaboratively? First, the consultant can model a collaborative style when interacting with teachers and family members. Engaging others as equals in the problem-solving process sends a clear message that the consultant does not perceive himself or herself as "the expert." Additionally, the consultant encourages a collaborative process by (a) seeking other's perspectives, (b) being open to new ways of conceptualizing problems, (c) integrating others' suggestions in intervention plans, (d) reinforcing others' ideas, (e) being flexible with how he or she defines and executes his or her own role, and (f) assisting a team in establishing group norms that reflect collaboration.

Case Example: Westwood Middle School

To address the needs of the Westwood Middle School, the four professional school counselors develop a violence prevention work group consisting of local higher education institution partners, relevant community resource agencies, family members, and school staff—including administrators, teachers, and student support personnel. The purpose of the group is to develop a useful and comprehensive solution to the violence and aggressive behavior problems at Westwood Middle School.

Since the discipline referral problem at Westwood Middle is an ongoing issue, the work group develops a violence prevention initiative that includes primary and secondary prevention strategies. After reviewing data and collaboratively brainstorming, the group finds that the students need to develop positive social, problem-solving, and anger-management skills. Skill development will occur through (a) classroom guidance lessons, jointly planned and delivered by the professional school counselors and teachers; (b) activities integrated within the broader educational curriculum, delivered by classroom teachers; (c) small-group counseling sessions, led by the professional school counselors and other student services personnel, including the school psychologist, social worker, and school-based mental health clinicians; and (d) educational classes for students and family members provided at the local community center, with community center staff coleading evening training sessions with the school counseling staff.

The work group also recommends staff development on school safety, including the integration of skill training into the broader curriculum, strategies for responding to volatile students, and skills for classroom management. Staff development sessions will be jointly planned and implemented by a professional school counselor, teacher, student support staff, and community representatives from the work group. A school newsletter for family members will highlight all prevention efforts. Family members who participate in the work group will advise about how best to disseminate program information to families and how to engage family members in training and workshop opportunities. The work group invites community leaders to join them in developing employment opportunities for youth.

The work group consults with the school's administrative staff on redesigning the school's discipline referral process so that a student referred for a discipline problem is automatically involved in identifying more productive ways of behaving. This process also ensures that a student referred for a discipline problem is referred to the student support team for further evaluation and an intervention plan is designed specifically for that student. Intensive counseling sessions with the professional school counselor or a school-based mental health clinician may be part of the intervention plan.

Each member of the work group is involved in all phases of the problem-solving process—from problem and need identification through evaluation. Each member assumes multiple roles based on his or her particular area of expertise. Communication among work group members, role sharing, and shared accountability for outcomes underscore the group's interdependence and collaborative nature. For example:

- In addition to the previously mentioned skills training and counseling services, *professional school counselors* provide leadership within the work group by coordinating the group's work, establishing norms for a collaborative group process, modeling collaborative behavior, and recommending program evaluation procedures.
- The *school-based mental health clinician* and other *community mental health practitioners* help the group identify contributing mental health problems and facilitate the referral of students and family members who are in need of more intensive services to community-based services. These clinicians also participate with professional school counselors and student support staff members in providing training for school staff about risk factors and warning signs for mental health problems.
- *Faculty members* in the departments of counseling, social work, and school psychology at a nearby university provide the work group with information about theoretical models and "best practices" for primary and secondary intervention. These professionals also provide leadership for the work group in exploring grant funding to support prevention initiatives and to ensure linkage of this smaller program with broader partnership initiatives between the school system and their respective departments.
- *Teacher* representatives team with professional school counselors and mental health clinicians to implement staff development workshops. The teacher work group representatives also provide leadership to the group on how best to integrate school violence prevention skill training within the broader curriculum.

- *Family members* of the group will serve as liaisons between the work group and other parents to communicate the goals and strategies of this initiative to the broader community. Family members will also help identify neighborhood leaders who could provide the work group with information about community needs.

Through this team process, the professional school counselor functions as one of many "collaborative consultants." Each member of the team joins his or her expertise with the expertise of other members to develop and implement a comprehensive prevention plan. Work group members function interdependently, both during the team process itself and when enacting their roles during the implementation of the comprehensive prevention plan.

CONSULTATION PROCESS

As indicated in the previous discussion of consultation models, effective consultation in a school setting requires skill in problem solving and an ability to form collaborative relationships

with other experts, including family members. A consultant who works within a school setting must also be astute about the systemic issues that affect the consultant's ability to fully implement his or her role and function. This section describes these issues through a six-step system-based process model for school consultation (see Table 11.2). Although each step is presented sequentially, the process is not linear and may involve repeated patterns and cycles.

Step 1: Entering the System

In addition to having physically entered the school building, the professional school counselor as consultant needs to be psychologically ready to enter the organizational system that exists within the building. Both the professional school counselor who is new to the building and the seasoned professional school counselor need to enter the school's system with a mind-set that is (a) flexible in its approach to problem solving, (b) committed to establishing collaborative relationships, and (c) motivated to encourage the types of systemic changes that may be needed to promote student learning.

TABLE 11.2
System-based process model for school consultation.

Enter	Join	Initiate Problem Solving	Frame Change	Evaluate Change	Facilitate Closure
Enter the system physically and psychologically	Learn system rules and metarules	Create group norms based on:	Identify goals	Monitor progress	Debrief
Clarify role perceptions	Observe positions of power	• parity • mutual goals • shared decision making • shared resources • shared expertise	Determine outcome measures	Assess outcomes	Terminate consultation services for identified student
Perceive self as direct and indirect service provider	Build alliances	Facilitate collaborative group process	Empower participants as change agents	If no progress occurs or if change is in an undesired direction, assess reasons	Maintain relationships with other professionals
Understand goals of the school system	Establish communication with subsystems	Assess problems	Think multisystemically	Decide whether to continue the intervention	Reinitiate consultation process for new students and problems
	Maintain objectivity	Identify strengths	Encourage flexible roles and permeable boundaries		
	Stay one down		Protect change		

Many professional school counselors enter the building ready to provide direct counseling services to students most in need. Counseling is an important role for the professional school counselor. In fact, many professional school counselors would probably view counseling as their most important role. The problems confronting many student-clients, however, may require a more comprehensive plan that engages the multiple systems (school, classroom, peer, family, neighborhood–community) that are a part of the student's life. Consultation provides a means through which the professional school counselor can access the range of systems necessary for long-term change. Hence, it is important for professional school counselors to perceive their role broadly—a role that includes both direct counseling services as well as the indirect services of consultation. Being ready to enter the school system and encouraging system-focused changes presupposes an indirect service orientation.

As the consultant enters the school's system, it is important to understand the goals of the system and how these goals relate to the consultant's role. Schools exist to support the academic achievement of students. Test scores and other measures of academic success drive what happens in schools. The consultant who can directly link his or her program to the school's mission will have an easier time gaining support from faculty and administrators. It is also important for the consultant to have a clear understanding of the school's perception of his or her role. A misperception of role by the consultant, school adminstrator, faculty, or family member can create expectations for different types of services. Failure to meet these unrecognized expectations can place the consultant at a disadvantage. Clarifying these expectations, therefore, is an important step in the entry process.

Step 2: Joining the System

Leaving at the school door all expectations that faculty and administrators "should" recognize how much the consultant has to offer is an important part of joining the school system. Schools are very busy places. Teachers are under enormous pressure to produce "educated" students. Earning the respect of teachers, administrators, and family members is an important part of joining the system. Consultants can begin to acquire this respect, can in effect "join with the school system," by attending to the six points that follow:

Learn the System Rules and Metarules

Knowing the policies and procedures that govern professional behavior within the system is essential. The consultant will need to know (a) the larger school system's policies and procedures related to a number of issues, including confidentiality, reporting of abuse, and parental notification about service delivery, as well as (b) the specific school's interpretation of how these policies and procedures are implemented at the school level. For example, it might be school board policy that parents be notified of a change to the student's educational plan, including the addition of counseling services, before instituting the changes. How that policy is carried out at the school level could differ from school to school. One school might ask the student to deliver a written message to the parents, another school might notify the parents in writing by mail, and still another school might allow a brief grace period before notifying parents.

It would be easy for the consultant if all of the school rules were written in a manual that the consultant could read. Many are, but as is apparent from the previous discussion, having a written policy or rule does not mean it is interpreted and executed similarly across all schools. Many unwritten and unspoken rules, or *metarules,* also exist that can be learned only through interaction with the system. Metarules exist in how teachers manage their classrooms, and these rules can differ from teacher to teacher. Some teachers resent interruptions, preferring not to have students leave the classroom for counseling services or have other professionals enter the room during class time. Other teachers may be more open to the ebb and flow of students' movement, more willing to excuse students from their classes, and quite comfortable with other professionals entering the room to speak with them or observe a student.

Observe Explicit and Implicit Positions of Power

Nothing, be it an academic program or a counseling and consultation service, works well in a school without the principal's support. It is important for the consultant to join with, and maintain sufficient contact with, the school principal. Demonstrating how the consultant's work directly relates to the principal's agenda is an important avenue for gaining acceptance and support from the principal. Allotting ample consultation time with the principal allows the consultant to maintain lines of communication and act as a support to the principal. This will often involve learning the principal's schedule and putting in extra time to be able to catch up with the principal when he or she is available. Valuing the principal's contributions and recognizing the principal as an essential collaborator is an important part of joining the school system.

Not all people in a school who occupy a position of power have an accompanying title that suggests such status. All experienced school professionals know that most school secretaries occupy an implicit power position within the school. Some control who has access to the principal, and others are an important communication link between teachers and parents, and possibly the consultant and parents. In some schools, other professionals in the building may hold a certain teacher or teachers in high esteem. Such teachers can enhance or jeopardize change, depending on whether or not they support the initiative. The consultant who is not accepted by these power figures may find it difficult to accomplish his or her mission.

Build Alliances Through Shared Agendas, Recognition of Individual Strengths, and Supportive Actions

To have the principal's support does not necessarily mean the consultant will have the support of others in the building. As suggested earlier, the need for others to perceive a common agenda between themselves and the consultant is critical to the consultant's acceptance. Forming an alliance with those who hold explicit and implicit positions of power is an important strategy. Taking the time to get to know others, to offer assistance that may make the other person's job easier or help him or her be more successful, and to explicitly recognize the other person's strengths are helpful ways of offering support and building alliances. Such actions must be conveyed and perceived as sincere and genuine.

Some alignments can be a serious hidden danger for consultants. For example, certain teachers might be in conflict with the school principal over any number of issues. If the principal sees the consultant aligning with these individuals, then the consultant unknowingly can experience resistance from the principal and those aligned with the principal. Being aware of staff alignments around issues affecting counseling and consultation services is an important part of the joining process.

In general, the consultant must be sensitive to giving the impression of aligning with any one group against another. In some instances, the school could perceive the consultant and family to be aligned against the school. If the consultant and family meet and make school-related decisions that are then conveyed to the teacher or administrator, the rest of the school understandably could feel left out. It is important for the consultant to be cautious about forming alignments with families that position the consultant and family against the school. It is important for the consultant to work toward collaboration with staff and families rather than fragmentation.

Establish Communication with Members of All Relevant Subsystems

The school as a system is made up of several subsystems—administrative, staff, faculty, parental, student-peer, and community. Each of these subsystems may also be composed of smaller subsystems. For example, special education faculty and regular education faculty could be subunits within the larger faculty subsystem. When working with students with complex needs, interventions may need to involve several, or even many, layers of subsystems. Getting to know and be known by members of these different subsystems can be an important first step in establishing a working relationship. Face-to-face contact through consultation services; attendance at staff, parent–teacher, and community meetings;

participation in classroom activities; and announcements about services provided by the consultant in the school newsletter can provide avenues for connecting with subsystems. Developing an awareness of the types of issues that might create friction between subsystems is also important. Special education and regular education teachers will need to work together when implementing inclusive procedures for students. Collaboration may be hindered, however, by territorial issues and role rigidity. The consultant can provide a neutral perspective as subsystems strive to overcome the barriers that prohibit problem solving.

Maintain Objectivity

Joining with a system can take time. Acceptance by a few may precede acceptance by many. The consultant may do everything right, and still some members of the system may resist accepting the consultant as a team member and may impede full implementation of the consultant's services at the school. This can be frustrating and discouraging. The consultant may begin to resent the challenges presented by the school. Reframing challenges as opportunities and seeing resistance as a systemic reaction to change rather than a personal affront are important if the consultant is to maintain objectivity. A loss of objectivity as the consultant is in the process of joining with the system could threaten the consultant's ability to eventually effect client, consultee, and systemic change.

Stay One Down

Teachers, administrators, and the consultant all act as helpers in the school setting. Many schools have a number of individuals in addition to the professional school counselor who deliver some type of mental health services. These might include social workers, school health nurses, crisis intervention counselors, and school psychologists. To work effectively, the consultant needs to work in a way that is not threatening to anyone's territory. Also, the consultant who is trying to acquire acceptance by a system has a harder time gaining acceptance if other professionals perceive his or her interactions as intimidating. Consultants who

seek acceptance by the faculty or family subsystem need to minimize status differences between themselves and teachers and family members (Cherniss, 1997). Acknowledging the expertise of the other person, seeking advice, asking for assistance, and being open to trying new approaches are all ways the consultant can overtly recognize another person's skills and knowledge, and covertly maintain a "one-down" position.

Step 3: Initiating Problem Solving

After entering and joining the school system, the consultant is in a position to initiate problem solving. This begins the working stage of the process model. The stages of problem solving remain the same regardless of whether the consultant is implementing a triadic-dependent, collaborative-dependent, or collaborative-interdependent type of relationship. As indicated, problem complexity often determines which consultation model the consultant uses.

The consultant begins the problem-solving phase of the consultation process by collecting information to assist in identifying the problem. This could mean working directly with the client, meeting with teachers and family members, and participating as part of a problem-solving team. Collecting and integrating available data about the client and the broader system occurs at this stage of the process. The focus of problem solving could be an individual student, such as Samantha from our earlier example; or the consultee, such as Mrs. Miller, who needed to learn new skills; or a classroom system, as in Mr. Long's math class; or the broader systemic issue of increased violence and aggression at Westwood Middle School. Regardless of the focus, a thorough understanding of the client, consultee, or system's needs, including strengths and weaknesses, is an important part of a comprehensive assessment of the problem.

The opportunity to function as a consultant within a team context occurs frequently in today's schools. In addition to specific content knowledge about a particular problem, the consultant also brings to the team knowledge of group dynamics and an ability to facilitate group process. Most school teams are task oriented;

group process issues, so central to the ability of a team to function collaboratively, are often unnoticed or ignored. Without an attention to process, it will be difficult for a collaborative dynamic to emerge. Without strong process skills, it will be difficult for the consultant to become an integrated part of the school system and difficult for the consultant to establish a collaborative identity.

The consultant can use his or her expertise to facilitate a team's movement through the developmental stages of group process. The consultant can work to (a) establish collaborative group norms, (b) encourage cooperative rather than competitive behavior, (c) explicitly recognize the expertise of all participants, and (d) create communication patterns that allow all to participate equally in the problem-solving process. Establishing a collaborative team process might also require educating the school administrator about collaboration and acquiring the administrator's support prior to initiating this type of team process.

Step 4: Framing Change

During this fourth step of the process, the consultant works with others to set goals and shape an action plan for accomplishing goals that is realistic and able to be executed reasonably by those involved. A collaborative style of interaction continues as team members (if the consultant is working in a group context) or individuals (if the consultant is working with an individual teacher or family member) ascertain their roles in supporting client change. When framing change, the consultant may find the following points helpful.

1. *Identify goals.* After a thorough assessment of the problem in the initial problem-solving phase, appropriate goals are identified. These could include outcomes for the client, the consultee, and the system. Establishing concrete objectives further refines and defines each goal statement. Goals and objectives for students will need to be connected to academic achievement to be consistent with the school's larger mission.

2. *Determine outcome measures.* The measures and methods to be used in the evaluation process need to be considered prior to conducting the actual evaluation (D. Brown, 1993). Clarifying how outcomes will be measured at this point in the process also helps ensure that goals have been appropriately operationalized.

3. *Empower participants as change agents.* Some teachers and family members may feel less able or less committed to being part of a solution. Family members may blame the school for the problem, while some teachers may feel that the student's problems are a result of poor parenting. The consultant needs to reframe problems so that the emphasis is on common goals and how each person can help rather than who is at fault. Affirm teacher and family strengths and use these strengths as part of the change process. Create hope that change can be accomplished. When the consultation is student focused, it is important for the consultant to remember that while client change may be the explicit outcome, change in the consultee or system might be a first step toward change for the client.

4. *Think multisystemically.* Many of the students with whom the consultant will work have very complex problems, with no single easy solution. Change for the individual is often predicated on change in the systems within which the individual is embedded. This would suggest that to be comprehensive, an action plan would need to include more than interventions targeting the individual. A word of caution is important here: A school that is open to viewing the student as the identified problem may not be open to examining staff or family actions that affect the student. Such a change in focus could result in a great deal of resistance. The consultant will need to proceed prudently, being careful to offer suggestions tentatively. Earlier work in forming alliances and building a collaborative ethic will help support such efforts. In some cases, the consultant may work separately with a particular teacher or parent to help shape a change in the classroom and family subsystems.

5. *Encourage flexible roles and permeable boundaries.* When people assemble to problem solve, quite often they bring with them a particular notion of how change should occur and what their role is or is not in that process. Creative solutions often reside in being able to step outside of such preconceived notions. Initially, the professional counselor may have viewed his or her role primarily as one of direct service. To redefine that role to include consultation—using a variety of models—suggests flexibility. In another instance, a teacher may see himself or herself primarily as someone who conveys academic material within a specific discipline. Asking the teacher to conduct or colead classroom activities focused on social–emotional issues would encourage role flexibility. As people begin to collaborate, the boundaries that often separate and restrict professionals and families can become more permeable and less rigid.

6. *Plan to protect change.* Creating expectations about what might happen once participants enact the plan for change is a way to protect the change effort from failure. The wise consultant lets participants know ahead of time what they might expect; for instance, things might get worse before they improve. Strategize about what to do if the unexpected happens. Protect change by creating a system of shared accountability; make sure the action plan identifies who is responsible for what and describes benchmarks for evaluating progress. Recognize persistence, and remember the importance of linking student change to academic achievement. Creating mechanisms for ongoing communication and sources of support is also important.

Step 5: Evaluating Change

Monitoring progress and determining whether goals have been accomplished are tasks that are part of the evaluation process. Consistent with the shared accountability ethic of collaboration, those involved in the intervention are potential participants in the evaluation. Collecting data, summarizing and recording information, and developing mechanisms for sharing data are all tasks that can be shared.

The evaluation should assess if change has occurred, and if so, to what degree? If no change is noted or if undesired change has occurred, the consultant can help assess the reason for a lack of progress and make recommendations for revising the intervention. Decisions about continuing the intervention are also made at this time.

Step 6: Facilitating Closure

Bringing the consultation relationship to closure can be a very different process for the school-based consultant who remains in the school than for a consultant who physically leaves the building at the end of the consultation. Although the intervention for a particular client may have ended, the consultant remains in relationships with the professionals in the building. Debriefing with consultees allows an opportunity to reflect on not only achieved outcomes, but also the process of working together. Debriefing provides an opportunity for the consultant and other team members to assess how well they collaborated as a group.

SCHOOL CONSULTATION AND COLLABORATION WITH DIVERSE POPULATIONS

While substantial attention has been given to issues of multicultural diversity in the counseling profession in general, infusion of multicultural research and practices into the area of collaboration and consultation has been slow in coming. During the 1990s, only a few studies explored cultural influences in the consultation process, exploring such essential factors as acculturation, ethnicity, and socioeconomic status (Duncan, 1995; Edens, 1997; Henning-Stout, 1994; Tarver-Behring & Gelinas, 1996). In spite of a lack of research and even a lack of emphasis on cross-cultural consultation in training programs, most educational professionals perceived that they had the necessary skills and training to work effectively with culturally and linguistically diverse students (Roache, Shore, Gouleta, & de Obaaldia Butkevich, 2003). But within the literature, some approaches and modified consultation strategies have emerged that may help professional school counselors to even more effectively address the needs of culturally diverse youth, their families and teachers.

Tarver-Behring and Ingraham (1998) defined multicultural consultation as "a culturally sensitive, indirect service in which the consultant adjusts the consultation services to address the needs and cultural values of the consultee, the client, or both" (p. 58). Ingraham (2000) further defined cross-cultural consultation as a facet of multicultural consultation in which the consultant and consultee share dissimilar ethnic, socioeconomic, or linguistic characteristics. So even though the professional school counselor and parent may speak the same language and be of the same ethnicity, socioeconomic differences may indicate that cross-cultural modifications may be necessary for effective consultation to occur.

While the basic process of multicultural collaboration or consultation are virtually identical to the processes discussed above, the framework or lens of the professional school counselor must account for cross-cultural issues that may impede the effectiveness of interventions. Ingraham (2000) has proposed a multicultural school consultation framework to focus school professionals on the important facets of effective cross-cultural consultation. Her model consists of five components.

1. *Domains of consultant learning and development* involve knowledge and skill requirements in eight competence domains, including:

> Understanding one's own culture . . . Understanding the impact of one's own culture on others . . . Respecting and valuing other cultures . . . Understanding individual differences within cultural groups and multiple cultural identities . . . Cross-cultural communication/ multicultural consultation approaches for rapport development & maintenance . . . Understanding cultural saliency and how to build bridges across salient differences . . . Understanding the cultural context for consultation . . . [and] Multicultural consultation and interventions appropriate for the consultee(s) and client(s). (p. 327)

2. *Domains of consultee learning and development* involve the knowledge, skills, confidence, and objectivity to deal with diverse circumstances.
3. *Cultural variations in the consultation constellation* involve cultural similarity between and among the consultant, consultee, and client.
4. *Contextual and power infleunces* involve societal influences, balance of power issues, and "cultural similarity within a differing cultural system" (p. 327).
5. *Hypothesized methods for supporting consultee and client success* involve knowledge, skills, and strategies of various supportive interventions in areas such as how to frame problems. This component also encompasses the professional school counselor's commitment to professional development.

Competence in the area of multicultural consultation is essential to the effective functioning of the professional school counselor in a diverse society. Increasingly, the literature is addressing the importance of understanding the consultation process through a multicultural lens (Ingraham, 2000; Sheridan, 2000), immigration (Maital, 2000), acculturation and bilingual educational services (B.S.C. Goldstein & Harris, 2000), and bicultural educational issues (Lopez, 2000). From time to time, professional school counselors may need to work with interpreters, and schools need to be proactive in locating, collaborating with, and training interpreters to better meet the needs of linguistically diverse students and their families (Lopez, 2000; Rogers et al., 1999).

In general, the effectiveness of collaboration and consultation approaches relies on the consultant and consultee participating as equal partners (Conoley & Conoley, 1992). But one should not expect the approaches discussed in this chapter to be equally effective with consultees from all cultures. Indeed, D. R. Atkinson and Lowe (1995) concluded that more directive styles of consultation, as opposed to more indirect collaboration styles, may be more effective with consultees from some cultures, such as Asian Americans. As great diversity exists in society and in the school population, great diversity must exist in the professional school counselor's intervention approaches to collaboration and consultation.

COLLABORATIVE CONSULTATION: REACHING OUT TO THE BROADER COMMUNITY

Students with complex problems are typically involved in the broader community of core social institutions. Core social institutions are those enduring structures whose mission is to provide the basic level, the core, of public services. These services for children include child welfare services, to protect children, and the juvenile justice system, to protect the public from children's misdeeds (Luongo, 2000).

The collaborative consultation model has to engage and be responsive to this context and advocate for the integration of basic services. When children simultaneously appear in multiple systems, and the evidence is that there is a 30% to 40% overlap in population among core social institutions serving children (Loeber & Stouthamer-Loeber, 1998; Stroul & Friedman, 1996), simply connecting the different professionals in the system is insufficient. Collaborative consultation supports an integrative approach that demands a shared responsibility for defining, planning, and moving with good intent for the student. This is an outcomes focus and places a premium on collaboration across systems of care. Helping professionals, no matter what core social institution they represent (public education, by definition, is a core social institution), need to be unburdened of the routine administrative responses to children's needs so that they can concentrate on creative and joint responses to complex needs. Through collaborative consultation, the definition of "helping" moves away from the narrow confines of any one core social institution to the focus of "what can we do together for this child?"

To create an effective integrated network of community–school professionals, professional school counselors (as collaborative consultants) need to be familiar with other core social institutions—how they function and who in these systems represent potential partners. Bringing

these potential partners together to create positive outcomes for students expands the consultant's role to include a community liaison function. While partnering with community resources is essential to effective school counseling programs, it is perhaps even more vital that educators partner with parents and involve them deeply in their children's education. It is this essential topic that becomes the focus of the remainder of this chapter.

INVOLVING PARENTS IN EDUCATION

Today, schools harbor a population of students with academic, personal, and social problems that create barriers to academic success (Keys & Bemak, 1997). Complex and multifaceted issues are forcing professional school counselors to assess and redefine their current roles. While schools have traditionally stood alone in their mission to educate children, this isolation is no longer possible or desirable (Hobbs & Collison, 1995). Children are arriving in the classroom with needs that far exceed traditional educational methods (Payzant, 1992). As health-care organizations continue to limit services offered, including mental health services, it has become critical for professional school counselors to work with other human service professionals to meet their students' wide-ranging needs (Ponec et al., 1998).

Professional school counselors are well positioned to act as proactive change agents in the school setting. Training in group processes, as well as the understanding of the cycle of change, are necessary skills acquired in counselor training. School reform has redefined the roles of many school professionals, including professional school counselors. All must become actively engaged in strengthening relationships among schools, families, and communities (Colbert, 1996).

A primary obstacle to creating voluntary collaboration among local programs is the belief that federal and state policies will not permit it. While *cooperation* and *collaboration* have become operative words over the last several years, little progress has been made in establishing collaborative relationships.

True collaboration includes jointly agreeing to identify and address specific problems and areas of service (Payzant, 1992). This description goes far beyond talking about problems, learning about resources, and coordinating service delivery. When true collaboration exists, all parties equally share the outcomes. In his book *Thinking Collaboratively,* C. Bruner (1991) defined collaboration as a process to reach goals that cannot be achieved acting singly, shared responsibility for obtaining goals, and working together to achieve goals using the expertise of each collaborator. Bruner acknowledged that his process requires consensus building and may not be imposed hierarchically. Collaborators must learn about each other's roles and explain their own. Expertise in the process of goal setting is critical.

Through collaboration, professional school counselors will gain a clearer understanding of what other agencies can contribute and how they function (resources and procedures). By developing personal relationships, people will become more willing to respond and work together for all children (Hobbs & Collison, 1995). They must remind themselves that their leadership efforts will improve the academic achievement of students.

Schools are in the business of education, and this generation of professional school counselors must be trained to work effectively with others to meet the needs of students and their families. It is critical to understand the system in which one works to be accepted and meet with success. Professional school counselors need to collect and analyze data when identifying needs and creating partnerships.

Braback, Walsh, Kenny, and Comilang (1997) described schools as conservative, with many gatekeepers, rules, regulations, and structures that make collaboration difficult. They further stated that staff members are often threatened by the appearance of other professionals. Professional school counselors need to help staff members recognize the benefits of developing relationships with other agencies and service providers. Because it is necessary for families and outside agencies to know the rules and regulations with a special sensitivity to hierarchy and the structure of the system, professional school counselors are positioned best to facilitate collaborative efforts (Ponec et al., 1998).

A number of studies have underscored the challenges to school–agency collaboration, as well as curative factors. For example, Ponec et al. (1998) conducted a study to explore, understand, and describe the therapeutic relationship shared among professional school and community counselors engaged in collaborative relationships. Although mutual concerns focused on confidentiality and the responsibility of financial obligations, community counselors expressed the value of personal interaction and identified time (specifically, a 9-month cyclical school calendar) as an impediment to those interactions. The authors of this study concluded that it is only through the enhancement of communication that the ability to be effective helping professionals can be advanced. Personal knowledge, interaction, a perception of professionalism, and teamwork will develop and enhance the collaborative effort.

SCHOOL OUTREACH AND CHANGING FAMILY NEEDS

Schools have traditionally engaged in outreach strategies such as the fall open house and parent–teacher conferences. Other strategies such as parent resource centers, home visits, and positive phone calls are less common. Doing a better job of making schools more family-friendly is within the reach of all educators. In particular, professional school counselors are in a key position to increase opportunities for parents to be involved and supportive of their child's education.

Today's parents seem to fall into one of three categories:

1. Parents who are able to, and do, prepare their children for success in school on their own. They initiate contact with the school and take the steps to maintain a continuous line of communication with the school.

Working with such parents requires little effort on the part of the professional school counselor and school officials.

2. Parents who want to help their children be successful in the school setting, yet do not take the steps necessary to do so. Sometimes the reticence may be due to a lack of knowledge of what to do; sometimes it may be due to a lack of resources. These are the parents to reach out to and continuously encourage. Often, professional school counselors encounter parents with no health insurance, no transportation, or rigid work schedules and demands. Counselors must use their listening skills to hear and respond to these parents' needs.

3. Parents (a small percentage) who do not have the skills or interest necessary for involvement in their child's school success. These are the truly challenging families who are often living at the subsistence level and who may be involved with multiple agencies and organizations, all attempting to intervene to assist the family toward independence. Counselors' consultation, coordination, and collaborative skills are put to the test with these families.

The great majority of parents, however, care about their children's education (USDE OERI, 1996). They understand that an education is their child's ticket to success in the job market and the avenue to a better lifestyle than, perhaps, they were able to provide. Job and family demands, however, engage much of parents' time, often to the exclusion of school involvement. Parents in low socioeconomic groups and those who speak English as a second language also tend to shy away from school involvement. Professional school counselors should view such families as a welcome challenge to their communication skills and creative thought processes, and invite parents to become involved in the school. Table 11.3 suggests some ways in which parent involvement in school and community activities can be accomplished.

Parent involvement initiatives around the world have been effective in improving achievement and a wide variety of childhood adjustment difficulties (Jordan, Snow, & Porche, 2000; Shaver & Walls, 1998; Westat & Policy Studies Associates, 2001). Parent involvement in the home makes an even greater difference in achievement than parent involvement at school (Christenson & Sheridan, 2001; Izzo, Weissberg, Kasprow, & Fendrich, 1999; Trusty, 1999). Thus, the challenge and impetus for professional school counselors and educators in general must be to actively engage parents and guardians in the academic lives of their children.

TABLE 11.3
Possible types of parental involvement.

Type of Involvement	Sample Activities
1. Parenting	Parent education workshops Home visits at transition points
2. Communicating	Yearly conference with every parent Weekly folder of student work sent home
3. Volunteering	Parent room or family center Class parent
4. Learning at home	Information on homework policies Summer learning packets or activities
5. Decision making	Active PTA or PTO District-level councils and committees
6. Collaborating with community	Service to community Service integration through partnerships

Correlative studies have indicated that parental involvement predicts student achievement (Fantuzzo, Davis, & Ginsberg, 1995; Jimerson, Engeland, & Teo, 1999; Keith et al., 1998), student attendance (Stevenson & Baker, 1987), drop outs (Carnegie Council on Adolescent Development, 1996; K. Wright & Stegelin, 2003), and student attitudes and behaviors (R. M. Clark, 1993; Comer, 1984). As a more specific example, when parents are trained to help increase their children's achievement at home, significant improvements have been documented. Darling and Westberg (2004) reported that parents who were trained to teach their children how to read using guided exercises and questioning produced significantly better results than parents who simply listened to their children read—which most do.

The research on parental involvement indicates that most involved parents are mothers (Henry, 1996), White, and married (Griffith, 1998; T. Klein, Thornburg, & Kilmer, 1993) and have higher levels of education and socioeconomic status (Griffith, 1998; Grolnick, Benjet, Kuriwski, & Apostoleris, 1997). Parent involvement is far more common in elementary schools than high schools (Eccles & Harold, 1996), with the transition from elementary to middle school resulting in an average decline in parent participation of nearly 50% (Manning, 2000). However, some research indicates that when educators deliberately seek out, encourage, and invite parent involvement, factors such as educational and socioeconomic levels are eliminated as differentiating factors. Many studies have explored what motivates parents to become involved in schools and student achievement (e.g., Aronson, 1996; Benson, 2004). Table 11.4 provides some suggestions for increasing parent involvement in student achievement and the schools. Of course, a major benefit of parent involvement is frequently greater parental satisfaction with the quality of education their children are receiving (Applequist & Bailey, 2000).

TABLE 11.4
A dozen strategies for increasing parent involvement.

1. Focus on student achievement (academic and otherwise) as a school and extended community.

2. Acknowledge parent contributions at school or community events as well as through print and personalized expressions of gratitude.

3. Be specific in giving directions so that parents understand exactly what you expect them to do.

4. Use varied and repeated types of communications to solicit volunteers. These may include personal, phone, or written contacts by educators, other parent volunteers, and even students. Recruitment must be a continuous process.

5. Include parents in the planning and decision-making stages of programs to enhance feelings of ownership.

6. Find out what parents are interested and skilled in doing so that volunteer activities will match parent needs, interests, and skills.

7. Develop a school climate that is positive, inviting, and interactive. Make the school a place that parents want to be.

8. Provide (at least) monthly opportunities for parents to visit the school and interact with the educators and parent volunteers.

9. Provide parents with resources and information that help them help their children learn at home.

10. Encourage the rest of the family (e.g., grandparents, aunts, uncles, siblings), neighbors, employers, and community leaders to get involved.

11. Select a coordinator of volunteer activities to keep everyone moving in sync. This can be a parent volunteer.

12. Provide niceties (e.g., refreshments, name tags) and remove barriers to participation (e.g., transportation, baby-sitting).

Not surprisingly, all of the research literature does not back the effectiveness of parent involvement on academic achievement. For example, Mattingley, Prislin, McKenzie, Rodriquez, and Kayzar (2002) conducted a meta-analysis of more than 40 studies evaluating parent involvement, finding little empirical support for such claims. However, it is important to note that flaws/overgeneralizations in research methodologies (e.g., the studies were primarily correlational studies rather than causative-comparative studies) of the 40-plus studies led to this conclusion, not necessarily ineffective results. Henderson's (1987) study is often cited as conclusive evidence of the effectiveness of parent involvement in student achievement, but Mattingly et al. correctly point out that less than half of the studies Henderson reviewed explored the effect of interventions, and only one out of every five of the reviewed studies was published in a refereed journal. Likewise, White, Taylor, and Moss (1992), reviewing 172 research studies, also found the evidence of effectiveness of parent involvement unconvincing. Much better research is needed in this area before conclusive results can be stated with confidence. Better research is likely to occur soon, given that parent involvement was one of six targeted and funded areas in the NCLB Act.

Opportunities for parent involvement in the school (and school counseling program) include serving on an advisory committee; staffing registration or special events tables; presenting at career fairs or career programs; providing character education or social skills training (after brief training by the professional school counselor; Cuthbert, 2001); grandparents day; coffee or tea gatherings with teachers, counselors, or administrators; computer training days; parent visitation days; special events days (e.g., field day, cookout, talent show); awards assembly; ice cream social; community fund-raising dinner; parent workshops; field trips; and parent–child events (e.g., father–son, mother–daughter, father–daughter, mother–son, grandparent, etc.)—among many others. The limits to parent involvement are primarily the limits of creativity and time.

COMMUNICATING EFFECTIVELY WITH PARENTS AND GUARDIANS

Although parents and school personnel often seem to have similar goals, both can set up road-blocks to effective communication. Berger (2000) identified six parental roles that inhibit their ability to communicate with schools, albeit often unintentionally: Protector, Inadequate-me, Avoidance, Indifferent parent, Don't make waves, and Club-waving advocate. These roles can potentially become roadblocks to successful communication. Likewise, schools often unintentionally install roadblocks to successful communication. Berger also identified five roles that hamper communication between home and school: Authority figure, Sympathizing-counselor, Pass-the-buck, Protect-the-empire, and Busy teacher. School staff must treat parents and guardians as partners in education, involving each to maximize the potential of all students. The bottom line is that educators must adopt what Blue-Banning, Summers, Frankland, Nelson, and Beegle (2004) called the six themes of collaborative family–professional partnerships: communication, commitment, equality, skills, trust, and respect.

Although job and family demands, as well as cultural and socioeconomic backgrounds, pose a temporary roadblock to school involvement, most parents want guidance from schools on ways to support their children's learning (Epstein, 1986). The professional school counselor is often the first contact toward making parents feel welcome in the school during student registration, back-to-school nights, new-families gatherings, and so on. In addition, contact with parents can often be made by letter, e-mail, phone call, or home visit.

Most schools today are concerned about communicating with parents. Many schools provide newsletters and flyers to distribute information to families. This one-way communication is quite common. Ideally, schools will consider some methods of two-way communication, allowing parents an opportunity to express ideas and concerns, give feedback, and interact with school personnel. Some examples of two-way communication are phone calls; e-mail; home visits; conferences; breakfast with a grade-level team, professional school counselor, or administrator; and community meetings to discuss a particular topic or concern.

One of the national education goals challenges every school to promote partnerships and increase parent participation in the growth of children. If we are to achieve the high standards of the Goals 2000: Educate America Act as we move into the 21st century, it is imperative that all parents and families become involved in their children's learning process. Educators cannot wait for parents to make the first contact, but must communicate with all families about school programs and procedures, individual student progress, and ways parents can help their children at home.

Demanding work schedules often make setting and keeping appointments with school staff difficult (J. E. Evans & Hines, 1997). Why not visit parents instead? An innovative program, Lunch with School Counselors, involves professional school counselors regularly visiting targeted work sites to provide resources and information to parents. This type of approach requires flexibility and commitment, but it is a great public relations initiative for professional school counselors to improve existing parent–school–community relationships.

Although teachers remain the first line of defense in the communication effort, professional school counselors continue to be critical in maintaining ongoing dialogue with families. They may inform parents of special concerns regarding their child, provide updates on their child's progress with modifications and interventions, coordinate workshops to increase parents' skills, or assist in connecting families to needed community-based services.

Through parent workshops, parents learn the importance of two-way communication. If families are to be truly involved as partners in their child's education, they must learn the skills of listening to their child as well as expressing their concerns regarding their child's learning success. Teachers, as well, need to learn good listening and communicating skills to effectively convey their students' progress. Together, teachers,

parents, and professional school counselors make an effective team to support children's learning success.

Many of the following strategies for communicating with families are outlined in the U.S. Department of Education publication *Reaching All Families* (USDE OERI, 1996). They may be used by professional counselors to open lines of communication with parents and clarify the counselor's role in the school setting:

- *Welcome letter.* Generally sent home by teachers at the beginning of the school year, this letter is also a good opportunity for the counselor's introduction as well as to underscore the partnership of parent, teacher, and counselor in meeting the needs of the whole child.
- *Home–school handbook.* Most schools publish a handbook of general school policies and procedures. This is another forum for defining the professional school counselor's role and function.
- *Information packets.* These packets provide more detailed information about the role of the counselor in the school setting. The packets may include information on school policy and procedures as well as services offered by the school. By adding pertinent telephone numbers, this packet becomes an easy reference for parents to access needed people, programs, and services.
- *Calendars.* Weekly, monthly, or annual calendars highlight counselor planned or coordinated meetings and events for parents. They may also include encouraging and informative parenting tips, upcoming community events, family resources, and appropriate television shows and movies. They should be simply designed, only one page in length, and posted on the refrigerator door or family bulletin board for easy reference.
- *School newsletter.* Counselors often maintain a regular column in the school newsletter. This is another opportunity to connect with parents by providing parenting and child development tips from a variety of resources. It is important to use clear, simple language

that avoids educational or counseling jargon in these articles, and to address the needs of the audience.

- *Open house.* Publicity, planning, and preparation are keys to the success of this annual school event. Counselors can help market the event during other contacts with parents. They should plan to greet the families as they arrive and prepare a formal presentation to explain their role in the school. Counselors will want to encourage parents to contact them and to participate in planned activities for parents held throughout the year. In addition, the counselor may want to have a display table of parent and community resource brochures and other items of interest to families.

- *New-families meeting.* Most new families have registered their children prior to the first day of school. Holding a new-families meeting during the week before school begins will enable the counselor to connect with these families on a personal basis. The counselor might also give the families a tour of the school, introduce the families to the students' teachers, and answer other questions regarding school procedures and practices. This meeting can serve as a prelude to new

student group sessions held after the start of school.

- *School–parent compacts.* These are voluntary agreements between the home and school to define goals, expectations, and shared responsibilities of schools and parents as partners. Although this is a requirement of schools receiving federal Title I funds, it is a good practice for all schools to build partnerships that help students achieve high standards. Compacts need to be used in combination with other family involvement activities, not as the only way schools communicate with parents. The USDE produces a booklet on compacts with examples from schools around the country.

- *Positive phone calls.* Traditionally, parents have received a phone call from the school when there was a problem. Imagine the impact of a telephone call from the school that carries information that is positive! This kind of call opens lines of communication, helps parents feel hopeful, and encourages everyone to believe that all children can learn. To be most beneficial, parents need to receive at least two to three positive phone calls over the course of the school year. Counselors can assist and support teachers and administrators in this important effort.

SUMMARY/CONCLUSION

It is unlikely that school resources are going to increase over time to the extent necessary to provide optimal professional school counselor-to-student ratios. The challenges facing counselors are many, with too many students to serve and too few resources. Through consultation, professional school counselors effect positive growth for students by working directly with teachers and family members and the systems within which these groups live and work. By helping to expand the skills and knowledge of these significant others, professional school counselors, as consultants, extend the reach of their services. Consultation efforts that focus on changing the nature and functioning of a system— be it a school or family system—provide the most promising prevention potential for large numbers of students because "changing the system's goals, framework, and method of operation is a better predictor of lasting change than is the practice of changing people" (Kurpius, 1985, p. 369).

Many professional school counselors have been trained primarily as direct service providers. Changing the mind-set—getting ready to enter the system as an agent of change—presupposes a change in orientation from direct to indirect service provider. A professional school counselor's primary focus is prevention, which can be accomplished most effectively by maximizing the consultation function.

Connecting school, family, and community continues to be a nationwide challenge. Professional school counselors are uniquely positioned to provide both traditional and innovative services to meet the needs of children and families. As we move forward in the 21st century, professional school counselors' use of technology and other innovative approaches will provide new opportunities and forums for schools and parents to connect and communicate.

ACTIVITIES

1. Spend some time in a school setting. What examples of consultation and collaboration do you witness? How effective do they appear to be?
2. Imagine you are a professional school counselor and a teacher comes to you with concerns regarding one of her students, who has been acting out in class. Perform a consultation role-play to come up with a plan of action for this teacher. What model of collaboration did you use? Why?
3. Pretend you are a new professional school counselor. Create a list of steps you would take to acclimate to your new school. Who would you attempt to build relationships with? Compare lists with another member of your class. What similarities and differences are evident between your lists? Discuss these with your partner.

CHAPTER 12

ACCOUNTABILITY

BRADLEY T. ERFORD*

Editor's Introduction: Educational reform movements have made accountability a central responsibility of all educators, including professional school counselors. But accountability is not just tallying the number of students seen for individual or group counseling, or how much time has been spent in direct or indirect services. At its core, accountability addresses several issues: needs assessment, program evaluation, service assessment, outcome studies, and performance appraisal. This chapter addresses each of these important facets of accountability.

One of the cornerstones of the ASCA *National Model* (2003a) is accountability. Accountability involves responsibility for professional actions; in other words, the effectiveness of one's actions. Cobia and Henderson (2003) indicated that accountability involved three facets: (a) Having a set of duties or responsibilities that are well-defined, (b) assessment or evaluation of performance on those duties and responsibilities must be conducted, and (c) the results of this evaluation must be reported to stakeholders. In the more specific context of school counseling program accountability, this may involve

- Identifying and collaborating with stakeholder groups (e.g., a school counseling program advisory committee, parent, teacher, students)
- Collecting data and assessing needs of students, staff, and community
- Setting goals and establishing objectives based on data and determined need
- Implementing effective interventions to address the goals and objectives
- Measuring the outcomes or results of these interventions
- Using these results for program improvement

*The author would like to acknowledge the previous contribution of Dr. Mary Guindon for a portion of a section in this chapter, "Managing a Schoolwide Testing Program."

- Sharing results with major stakeholder groups such as administration, teachers and staff, parents and guardians, students, school boards, community and business leaders, school counselors, and supervisors (Isaacs 2003; Loesch & Ritchie, 2004; Myrick, 2003)

It is undeniable that accountability and assessment have, in general, been given greater visibility in both the extant counseling literature and the day-to-day functioning of the average professional school counselor over the past 10 years. Indeed, calls for greater accountability from professional school counselors have been occurring since at least the mid-1970s (Nims, James, & Hughey, 1998). This increased focus on assessment is due to numerous contemporary factors, including the educational reform movement, the rise in high stakes and other standardized testing programs, federal and state legislation (e.g., NCLB, Title I, IDEIA, Section 504), data-driven transformative initiatives, and outcomes-driven practice emphases. Professional school counselors are often called on to take a leadership role in a school's testing and program evaluation efforts. In addition, it is the professional and ethical responsibility of professional school counselors to ensure that the comprehensive school counseling services offered to stakeholder groups are truly effective. Given the impetus of school reform, the time is right for professional school counselors to partner with administration and key stakeholders to promote accountability and provide effective services to ensure the academic success of all students (C. B. Stone & Clark, 2001).

The focus of this chapter is on the wide-ranging accountability functions of the professional school counselor, including needs assessment, program evaluation, test program management, and interpretation of assessment results. The content of this chapter is among the most important in terms of understanding the needs of a school community and a school counseling program's effectiveness (i.e., answering that critical question, "Why do we need school counselors?"). This information will also allow professional school counselors to speak the language of decision makers, thus allowing social

and academic advocacy for children with special needs or those encountering systemic barriers to academic, career, or personal–social success. Finally, every professional school counselor should be constantly asking and gathering information to answer the question, "Is what I'm doing working with this student?" As with nearly every counselor function, conducting accountability studies has its advantages and disadvantages. Table 12.1 lists some of these. Consider these and others as you peruse the remainder of this chapter.

More to the point, accountability in the school counseling program must address five primary questions: (a) Is a comprehensive, standards-based program in place? (program evaluation or audit), (b) What are the needs of the school's student population when compared to these standards? (needs assessment), (c) What services were implemented to address the identified needs and standards? (service assessment), (d) What was the result of the implemented services? (results or outcomes studies), and (e) How well is the professional school counselor performing? (performance evaluation/appraisal). Each of these questions will be focused on in this chapter. But first, an essential facet of a school counseling program must be introduced: the school counseling program advisory committee (SCPAC).

THE SCPAC

Composition

An SCPAC serves as a sounding board and steering committee. The most important factor to consider when composing an SCPAC is influence. The professional school counselor must seek to include individuals who can influence and hold the confidence of school and school system decision makers, generally the principal and central office administrators. Including influential members on the SCPAC will ease the way for necessary programmatic changes as well as resources.

From a personnel perspective, it is essential for the principal to be a member of the SCPAC. The principal can hear firsthand the ideas and

TABLE 12.1
Advantages and disadvantages of accountability studies.

Advantages

1. Data is almost always better than perception when it comes to guiding decision making about programs, practices, and interventions.

2. Accountability studies help demonstrate necessity, efficiency, and effectiveness of counseling services.

3. Accountability studies can help identify professional development and staff development needs.

4. Professional school counselors can network to share program results, thereby spreading the word about effective practices.

5. Conducting accountability studies is a professional responsibility and demonstrates one's commitment to personal and professional improvement.

6. Accountability results can serve a public relations function by informing educators and the public of a school counseling program's accomplishments.

Disadvantages

1. Outcome measures and surveys take some training and skill (sometimes including consultation with experts) to develop.

2. It takes time and resources to do quality outcomes research and evaluation, time and resources that could be dedicated to additional service delivery.

3. Many do not understand the nature and purpose of accountability (e.g., impact of school counseling program on student outcome data) because of misperceptions or previous "bad" experiences (e.g., evaluations by principals or others not skilled in counseling, having to "count" every minute or service).

4. Data is sometimes "overinterpreted" or given undue meaning (e.g., the facts may not support the conclusion). All studies have limitations that must be considered when arriving at conclusions.

5. Comprehensive evaluations are seldom conducted. More often, bits and pieces of evaluative information are collected and the "big picture" is often incomplete.

---

planning that go into recommendations for improvement, as well as the rationale behind why additional funding may be needed. In addition to the professional school counselor(s), at least several influential teachers and parents should be included as well. Political linkages to parent–teacher organizations often play to the advantage of a professional school counselor as these members can serve as conduits to and from the organizations. The members can inform the SCPAC of various constituencies' concerns and provide information back to those constituencies regarding actions recommended by the SCPAC, or the blockage of the recommended actions.

To round out the committee, an influential school resource person (e.g., school psychologist, special education teacher, reading specialist, etc.) and influential community organization and business leaders should be included. Individuals from the community and businesses are useful for providing an external perspective, as well as partnerships and external funding and resources.

Role of the SCPAC

The SCPAC should convene at least twice annually, more frequently if the program is new or undergoing major changes. The primary role of the SCPAC is to review the results of the needs assessment, make recommendations for program development, review accountability data and outcomes research generated by staff, and locate internal and external funding sources for program development. Locating funding sources often requires the cooperation of the building principal; this is where it pays off to include the principal on the committee, as well as other individuals who can influence the principal's decision making. Thus, the SCPAC can serve a practical and political function, making it a top priority on the professional school counselor's agenda.

NEEDS ASSESSMENT

At least two primary purposes underlie the use of a needs assessment in school counseling programs. First, needs assessment helps professional school counselors understand the needs of various subpopulations of a school community. These subpopulations may include teachers, parents, students, administrators, community organizations, local businesses, and the general citizenry. Subpopulations may also include groups of students experiencing achievement gaps or differential access to rigorous academic programming. Each of these groups holds a stake in the success of the total educational enterprise. Second, needs assessment helps establish the priorities that guide the construction of a comprehensive developmental school counseling program, as well as continuous quality improvement of the program (D. W. Cook, 1989). "The emphasis in a needs assessment is not so much on what presently exists, but rather on what the present condition is compared to identified goals and objectives" (Wiles & Bondi, 1984). Assessing the needs of a school community provides a trajectory for addressing what the community values and desires to pursue.

Data-Driven Needs Assessment

Data-driven decision making deals with real needs and impact, not perceived needs. It begins with an analysis of school-based performance data. Given the prominence of high-stakes testing and large-scale testing programs required under NCLB, schools are frequently provided with aggregated and disaggregated performance results. *Aggregated* means that all student results are lumped together to show total grade-level or schoolwide (average) results. Aggregated data is helpful in understanding how the average students perform in a given class, grade, or school,

but tells very little about the diversity of learner performance or needs, and nothing about how various subgroups or subpopulations performed. In Table 12.2, the aggregated results are represented by the "Total Grade" line at the top for a school with 100 fifth graders.

To fully understand how to use school performance data, professional school counselors must become proficient in understanding norm-referenced and criterion-referenced score interpretation. While a comprehensive explanation of score interpretation is beyond the scope of the book and typically encountered by counselors in an assessment or testing course, what follows can be considered a very basic primer on interpretation of norm-referenced scores. For an understanding of the necessary assessment competencies expected of professional school counselors, please see the ASCA/AACE Competencies in Assessment and Evaluation for School Counselors in Appendix D.

Note that in the example in Table 12.2, the mean national percentile rank was 50. A percentile rank is most easily understood if one visualizes a lineup of 100 individuals all with certain characteristics in common—in this case, they are all fifth-grade math students. Importantly, when interpreting percentile ranks, the first student on the line is the lowest performing student and the 100th student is the highest performing student. A student's place indicates his or her relative standing compared to other fifth-grade math students across the country (thus the term *national percentile rank*). For example, a student scoring at the 79th percentile performed better than 79% of the fifth graders in the national norm group, or was the 79th student standing in the line. Likewise, a student performing at the 5th percentile would be standing in the fifth place in line and has outperformed only 5% of the fifth graders in the nationwide norming group. A quartile is a commonly used interpretive statistic that divides the percentile rank distribution into four segments. The first quartile includes percentile ranks ranging from 0 to 25, the lowest quarter of a distribution and designated Q_1. The second quartile (Q_2) includes percentile ranks ranging from 26 to 50. The third quartile (Q_3) includes percentile ranks ranging from 51 to 75. The fourth quartile (Q_4)

TABLE 12.2
Aggregated and disaggregated results from a typical large-scale math achievement test for a total-school fifth-grade level.

	n	NPR	Q_1	Q_2	Q_3	Q_4
Total Grade	100	50	19	31	26	24
Male	48	45	22	34	26	18
Female	52	56	10	31	31	28
Asian	8	72	0	25	38	38
Black	31	37	29	52	13	6
Hispanic	8	43	25	50	25	0
White	52	58	9	30	33	28
Other	1	44	0	100	0	0
Low SES	48	31	36	38	23	3
Non Low SES	52	71	5	24	36	35
English (second language)	3	43	0	67	33	0
English (primary language)	97	51	19	30	27	24
Special Education	10	25	60	20	20	0
Non Special Education	90	58	11	31	32	26

Note. n = number of students in sample; NPR = national percentile rank; "% in Quartile" means the percentage of the sample that performed in a given quartile; SES = Socioeconomic Status.

includes percentile ranks ranging from 76 to 100, the highest quarter of the distribution. Some test publishers also use an interpretive statistic known as stanines. Stanines, short for "standard nine," divide a normal distribution into nine segments; however, in a manner quite different from quartiles. Stanines actually represent one-half standard deviation units. So while each quartile represents 25% of the population, stanines may be comprised of varying percentages of the population. The first stanine represents the lowest level of performance, and the ninth stanine represents the highest level of performance. Importantly, parents, teachers, and students will understand performance easiest and most accurately when using percentile ranks. Other standardized scores can require some sophistication and may lead to errors in interpretation. Figure 12.1 provides a graphic of the normal curve and commonly used standardized scores the professional school counselor may encounter. Note that each of these standardized scores can be

converted into percentile ranks for easy explanation to parents, teachers, and students.

Disaggregated means the data has been broken down by subpopulations so that performance differences between and among groups can be analyzed. Usually, this analysis involves intergroup differences (e.g., male vs. female, race, ethnicity, special education vs. regular education status). Most test publishers can provide this information on request, broken down by school, grade level, and even by individual classes. Differences can be determined using statistical methods or by informal comparison. Seeing differences in disaggregated data helps to provide hard evidence of gaps in student performance, rather than relying on perceptions. It also provides direction for the types of strategies and interventions needed to close these achievement gaps. Returning to the data provided in Table 12.2, one can see several noticeable gaps in achievement. First, students

FIGURE 12.1
The normal curve and related standardized scores.

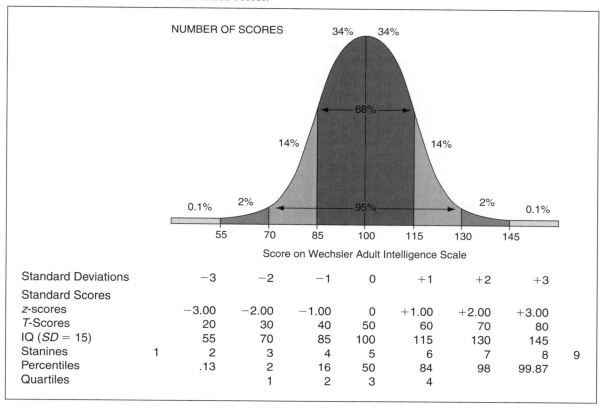

Standard Deviations		−3	−2	−1	0	+1	+2	+3
Standard Scores								
z-scores		−3.00	−2.00	−1.00	0	+1.00	+2.00	+3.00
T-Scores		20	30	40	50	60	70	80
IQ (SD = 15)		55	70	85	100	115	130	145
Stanines	1	2	3	4	5	6	7	8	9
Percentiles		.13	2	16	50	84	98	99.87
Quartiles			1	2	3	4		

from the low SES group performed at the 31st percentile rank, on average, while students from the non low SES group performed at the 71st percentile rank, on average. Second, there is a noticeable difference between the average math performance for Black and Hispanic students (37th & 43rd percentile ranks, respectively) as compared to Asian and White students (72nd & 58th percentile ranks, respectively). Third, females outperformed males, on average, 56th to 45th percentile rank. From these comparisons of disaggregated data, discussions can ensue and strategies developed to lower the math performance gap. But importantly, it all starts with the data, thus the name data driven. In this way, data provides the impetus and drive behind school improvement plans and responsive school counseling programs.

Perceptions-Based Needs Assessments

In contrast to a data-driven needs assessment, a traditional needs assessment process is more content and perception driven. Professional school counselors are often interested in what teachers, parents, and students perceive as primary needs to be addressed in a developmental way.

Frequency of Conducting a Needs Assessment

While it may seem tempting to design and conduct a global needs assessment on an annual basis, such an endeavor would be a massive administrative undertaking, likely resulting in findings being outdated by the time changes are made to the total program. It is probably best to follow a continuous cycle of assessing programmatic needs. This will allow ample time for program development and improvements over the course of the cycle. For example, the ASCA *National Standards* (C. Campbell & Dahir, 1997) and *National Model* (ASCA, 2003a) designate the areas of academic, career, and personal–social development as cornerstones of a comprehensive developmental guidance program; therefore, it makes sense that school community needs can be assessed according to these components on a rotating basis. For a new program or one undergoing tremendous renovations, years 1 and 2 of a 6-year cycle can be spent conducting needs assessment and implementing programmatic changes to address horizontal and vertical articulation issues surrounding student academic development. Years 3 and 4 can be spent on student career development needs; years 5 and 6 can focus on student personal–social issues. On the other hand, the 6-year cycle could alternate between the three domains, addressing half of the domain issues every 3 years (i.e., Year 1: academic, Year 2: career, Year 3: personal–social, Year 4: academic, Year 5: career, Year 6: personal–social). A program in good condition requiring only fine-tuning may be put on a 3-year continuous improvement cycle. The main point here is that assessing needs is part of a much bigger endeavor—that of implementing curricular changes to continuously improve the comprehensive developmental counseling program. Implementing curricular changes can be quite time intensive and simply a waste of time if not guided by accurate needs assessments and program outcomes research. An effective program uses this information to fine-tune its efforts in data-driven decision making.

Populations to Be Assessed

In the broadest sense, any stakeholder group can provide helpful information about the needs of a school community. However, it is most practical and efficient to seek out those who are informed and likely to respond. Teachers, administrators, students, and parents are the most likely to be informed of school issues and needs and, under most circumstances, will be the primary stakeholder groups surveyed during a needs assessment. Valuable information can be garnered from community organizations, local businesses, and the general citizenry as well. It is just more difficult to obtain a large response sampling from these groups. Information from these stakeholders is probably best obtained through personal contacts and interviews.

Return rate is another factor in the needs assessment process. Return rate is the percent of returned surveys out of those sent out. As in any research sampling procedure, the higher the return rate, the lower the sampling error; this leads to greater confidence in the accuracy of the results. Return rate is generally maximized when the participants are a "captured audience." For example, if a social skills needs assessment of fourth-grade students is conducted in the classroom, the response rate should be nearly 100%. On the other hand, if a needs assessment for parents is sent home, the professional school counselor may be lucky to receive 25% to 50% of the surveys back. Whenever possible, surveys should be distributed and collected immediately during faculty meetings, class meetings, and parent gatherings.

Triangulation of needs across populations should be attempted when possible; that is, the highest priority needs should be those agreed to by all or most populations assessed. This ensures that the school community's needs, not an individual's agenda, drive the developmental guidance curriculum. For instance, if a principal has decided to place a high priority on social skills, but teachers, parents, and students indicate this is a low priority, and far below other issues such as school safety, substance abuse, and study skills, the triangulated responses of the teachers, parents, and students can provide compelling, data-driven evidence to guide the program's focus.

Design Issues in an Efficient Needs Assessment

Designing an efficient needs assessment is essential to meaningful results. While some advocate for a comprehensive needs assessment simultaneously assessing all goals and topics associated with a comprehensive developmental guidance program, others have found it more helpful to focus the assessment on specifically defined topics or issues that are being updated or altered. This chapter will focus on the latter method.

L. A. Stone and Bradley (1994) recommended seven methods for determining needs: questionnaires and inventories, analysis of records, personal interviews, counseling statistics, classroom visits, use of outside consultants, and systematic evaluation of the guidance program. Perhaps what is most important is that the needs assessment uses objective methods for data gathering and analysis (Wiles & Bondi, 1984). It is essential to understand that some questions are addressed by different methodologies. Although all of these methods are important and useful, questionnaires (formal or informal surveys) are most commonly used (Schmidt, 2003) and will be focused on here. Importantly, while open-ended questionnaires are generally easier to design and yield rich and diverse information, such questionnaires are usually more difficult to interpret and translate into goals and objectives. Also, consider that the younger a student is, the lower the demands must be for reading comprehension and written responses.

From a return-rate perspective, it is good practice to try to design a needs assessment that is only one page in length (a maximum of two pages) and can be completed in only 2 to 3 minutes. The content of the needs assessment should be topical (e.g., social skills, changing families, substance abuse, college application procedures) rather than service related (e.g., individual counseling, group counseling, consultation, etc.). As will be explained later, the professional school counselor should keep in mind that services are simply methods for meeting needs, not needs in themselves. Of course, the topics should be related to the program goals as described in the ASCA *National Standards* (C. Campbell & Dahir, 1997), ASCA *National Model* (ASCA, 2003a), and local or state standards so that priority status can be placed on addressing the most pressing needs of the school in comparison to these standards. A good needs assessment directly translates into program development.

In general, the following steps form the basis of an efficient needs assessment:

1. Decide what you need to know.
2. Decide on the best approach to derive what you need to know.
3. Develop the needs assessment instrument or method.
4. Enlist the support of colleagues and a few individuals from the target groups to review and try out items for understanding.
5. Implement the final version on the target groups.
6. Tabulate, analyze, and interpret the results.
7. Translate the results into programmatic goals and objectives.

The design of the scale itself deserves some mention. The survey should ask for the name of the individual completing the form (unless the form is to be completed anonymously). Teacher surveys may ask for the grade level, the number of students in class, or other pertinent information. Parent surveys should ask for the names of the parent's children in case their response to the survey requires contact by the counselor. Student surveys should ask for the student's grade and homeroom teacher's name. Questions or response stems should be short, to the point, and easily understood. The reading level of the items should also be appropriate for the target audience. Figures 12.2, 12.3, and 12.4 show examples of topic-focused needs assessments for teachers (student interpersonal skills), students (academic development), and parents (student tolerance for diversity of sexual orientation), respectively.

Substantial consideration also should be given to the response format. If the purpose of the survey is to determine the importance or frequency of a potential problem, it is generally best to use a multipoint scale with three to five choices. For example, Figure 12.2 asks about the frequency of display of interpersonal skills, so the response choices "Rarely," "Sometimes," "Frequently," "Most of the time," and "Almost always" are appropriate. Note that the response choices "Never" and "Always" do not appear. It is rare that behaviors never or always occur; to include these descriptors may force responses to the center of the distribution and truncate the range of results. Also notice how each category has a descriptor. Thankfully, gone are the days in survey construction when a survey listed the response categories of 0, "Rarely," and 4, "Almost always," and then

FIGURE 12.2
Elementary teacher needs assessment of interpersonal skills.

Grade you teach _____   Number of students in your homeroom _____   Teacher's name _____
Please place an X in the boxes that you agree with. Do the students in your class:

	Rarely	Sometimes	Frequently	Most of the time	Almost always	About how many of your students need help in this area?
1. Complain of others teasing them?						
2. Complain about problems on the playground?						
3. Complain about problems with others during less structured class time?						
4. Work well in cooperative groups?						
5. Show respect for other students?						
6. Show respect for adults?						
7. Identify feelings of frustration with other students?						
8. Express feelings of frustration with other students?						
9. Have trouble making friends?						
10. Have trouble keeping friends?						

Thank you for taking the time to complete this!

provided the center points of 1, 2, and 3 with no accompanying descriptor. The reliability problems of such a scale are obvious: Will all respondents agree on what a 1, 2, and 3 represent? Certainly not! All choice categories must be accompanied by a verbal descriptor.

Figure 12.4 asks parents to rate the importance of seven sexual orientation tolerance items. Notice that the scale responses move from "Not important" (because in this case it is possible that a parent may perceive a total absence of importance) to "Very important." Such a scaling

FIGURE 12.3

Secondary-level student needs assessment for academic development.

Student Name and Grade: _____

Below is a series of questions. Answer these questions by placing a check mark in the appropriate boxes.

	Almost never	Seldom	Sometimes	Often	Almost always	I need help with this	
						Yes	No
Are you an active participant in class discussions and activities?							
Do you look forward to going to class every day?							
Do you double-check assignments before turning them in for a grade?							
Do you complete lengthy assignments on time?							
Do you ask for help as soon as you don't understand an assignment?							
Do you use a variety of learning strategies when performing school tasks?							
Do you take immediate responsibility for your actions, whether positive or negative?							
Do you enjoy working independently in class?							
Do you enjoy working in cooperative groups in class?							
Do you willingly share what you have learned with your peers when they don't seem to know or understand?							

Thanks for your help!

FIGURE 12.4
Parent needs assessment of tolerance for diversity of sexual orientation in the student body. (Targeted group: parents of sophomore students.)

My child is in (check one) □ 9th grade □ 10th grade □ 11th grade □ 12th grade	Very important	Important	Somewhat important	A little important	Not important
1. How important is it to be aware of the school's mission statement as it pertains to tolerance for students who are gay or lesbian?					
2. How important is it for students to exhibit tolerance for students who are gay or lesbian?					
3. How important is it that diversity in sexual orientation not be a cause of verbal conflict in the school?					
4. How important is it that diversity in sexual orientation not be a cause of physical conflict in the school?					
5. How important is it that "jokes" regarding sexual orientation be eliminated from the school community?					
6. How important is it that slang words and other inappropriate references to students who are gay or lesbian be eliminated in the school community?					
7. How important is it that students who are gay or lesbian feel safe and secure in the school community?					
8. I believe my child could benefit from a program on this topic.			Yes _____	No _____	
9. I believe other students could benefit from a program on this topic.			Yes _____	No _____	
10. I believe parents could benefit from a program on this topic.			Yes _____	No _____	

choice format allows parents to register incremental perceptions of importance. Alternatively, the scaling choice format could have simply stated "Yes" or "No," but to do so would have significantly truncated parent perceptions and forced an all-or-nothing response, thus complicating rather than simplifying the interpretation of the needs assessment.

Another important response component of a needs assessment is a frequency count. Suppose a professional school counselor would want to not only assess the importance of an issue, but also determine how many students were likely in need of services to address the problems stemming from the issue. When possible, the needs assessment should be designed to include an indication of whether the student should be targeted for intervention. In Figure 12.3, notice how the far right-hand column asks for a yes or no answer to the statement, "I need help with this." An affirmative response targets the student for intervention to address a self-perceived weakness.

Figure 12.2 asks teachers, "About how many of your students need help in this area?" The teachers' responses will indicate the type of intervention required. For example, if the teacher determines that 25 out of 26 students require intervention, the professional school counselor may decide to implement a series of group guidance lessons or consult with the teacher in this regard. If only a handful of students in each of several classes require intervention, the counselor may opt for a small-group counseling program to address the needs. If only one or a few individuals are identified, the counselor may attempt to address the difficulties through teacher or parent consultation or through time-limited individual counseling services.

Finally, Figure 12.4 asks for a frequency count of those students parents believe could benefit from a program dealing with tolerance for diversity of sexual orientation. Such information gives impetus for a schoolwide program that is either developmental or preventive in nature.

Tallying or computing the information from a needs assessment is simple and has been alluded to in the preceding paragraphs. Tallying simply involves counting the number of students who may benefit from intervention. Computing the

results of a needs assessment is probably best accomplished by assigning a number value to each response category and averaging all responses for a given item. In Figure 12.3, assume that the response categories are assigned the following values: "Almost never" = 0, "Seldom" = 1, "Sometimes" = 2, "Often" = 3, and "Almost always" = 4. For Item 1, "Are you an active participant in class discussions and activities?" simply add all student response values and divide by the number of responses. Therefore, if 25 students completed the needs assessment and 2 students marked "Almost never" ($2 \times 0 = 0$), 4 students marked "Seldom" ($4 \times 1 = 4$), 10 students marked "Sometimes" ($10 \times 2 = 20$), 5 students marked "Often" ($5 \times 3 = 15$), and 4 students marked "Almost always" ($4 \times 4 = 16$), simply sum the points ($0 + 4 + 20 + 15 + 16 = 55$) and divide by the number of student responses (sum of 55 divided by 25 students = 2.20) to compute the average frequency rating (2.20). Although this assumes a ratio scale and is somewhat nebulous from a statistical interpretation perspective (i.e., what does a 2.20 really mean?), it does offer a reasonable estimate of the average frequency of a behavior, or importance of an issue, in comparison with the other issues under study.

Converting Needs to Program Goals and Objectives

If the needs assessment was designed correctly, translating the results into goals and learning objectives is relatively easy. The first step is to prioritize the needs in order of importance and their relation to existing components of the program. Prioritization can be accomplished most easily by using the tallying, computing, and triangulation strategies mentioned. Next, the needs must be matched with, or translated into, the goals included in the national standards (C. Campbell & Dahir, 1997) or state and local standards. Finally, the goals are operationalized through development of learning objectives. (See chapter 8 for an excellent nuts-and-bolts discussion of how to write learning objectives.)

A reasonable goal stemming from the needs assessment shown in Figure 12.2, would be

"To increase students' interpersonal and friend-ship skills." Notice how the wording of a goal is nebulous and not amenable to measurement as stated. In developing learning objectives related to goals, particular emphasis is given to specific actions that are measurable. For example, a pos-sible objective stemming from this goal could be, "After reading *Frog and Toad* by Arnold Lobel and answering discussion questions, 80% of the students will be able to recognize at least two qualities (describing words) to look for in a friend." Another possible objective might be, "After reading *Frog and Toad* by Arnold Lobel and answering discussion questions, 80% of the students will be able to identify at least one issue that may cause problems among friends." Notice how the objectives designate the audience, the stated behavior, how the behavior will be meas-ured, and the level of expected performance.

A reasonable goal from the assessment shown in Figure 12.4 might be, "To create a school environment that is tolerant of gay and lesbian students." A possible learning objective stemming from this goal might be, "After partici-pating in a series of class sessions focusing on school policies and respect for sexual diversity, 85% of the students will recognize that tolerance toward gay and lesbian students is an integral part of a school's mission and essential to harassment-free life at school." Again, notice how the objec-tive designates the audience, the stated behavior, how the behavior will be measured, and the level of expected performance.

ACCOUNTABILITY: EVALUATING PROGRAMS AND ASSESSING OUTCOMES

In this age of school reform and accountability, program evaluation is more important than ever. Traditionally, however, professional school coun-selors for many reasons have failed to hold their programs and services accountable or to provide evidence that activities undertaken were achiev-ing intended results (Lombana, 1985). Some com-plained that the nature of what school counselors do is so abstract and complicated as to render the services and results unmeasurable. Others are so busy attempting to meet the needs of students that they shift time that should be spent in evalu-ation to responsive interventions. Some lack an understanding of how to conduct accountability studies—the methods and procedures. Still others are unsure of the effectiveness of the services provided and shy away from accountability unless forced to do so by supervisors.

Whatever the reason, the end result is a glar-ing lack of accountability that poses dangers for the future of the profession. Each contributes to a shirking of professional and ethical responsibility to ensure that the services provided to students, school personnel, and parents are of high quality and effective in meeting intended needs. Think about it from a business perspective. How long would a business last if it continued to engage in indiscernible or ineffective activities, the value of which was unknown to the business's con-sumers, managers, or employees? Such busi-nesses are selected out for extinction! The same may hold true for professional school counselors. Without accountability data to back up service provision, school counseling services are often among the first "nonessential services" to go during budget cutbacks.

L. A. Stone and Bradley (1994) suggested six purposes of evaluation:

(1) To measure the effectiveness of the total guidance program as well as each of the activities included in it . . . (2) To collect data that, after interpretation, will be meaningful in determining what program modifications are indicated . . . (3) To determine the level of program acceptance and support from students, staff, parents, and the community as a whole . . . (4) To obtain information that can be used to inform the public about the guidance program . . . (5) To collect data that will become an important part of the counselor's evaluation . . . [and] . . . (6) To analyze the program budget and compare expenditures to future program needs. (p.229)

The key, then, is to document and determine the worth of all aspects of the comprehensive school counseling program.

The evaluation of a comprehensive school counseling program is conducted on many levels. Baruth and Robinson (1987) described process and outcome evaluation. Gysbers and Henderson

(2000) expanded on these to highlight the importance of program evaluation (process), results (outcomes) evaluation, and added personnel evaluation. Each component is essential in holding school counseling programs accountable. In addition to describing these techniques, an explanation of service assessments follows as well.

Program Evaluation

Program evaluation (also sometimes called process evaluation or program audit) as defined by Gysbers and Henderson (2000) is akin to the measurement concept of content validity, which is a systematic examination of a test's (in this case, program's) content. In this context, "Program evaluation asks two questions: Does the school district have a written comprehensive guidance program? Is the written program of the district being implemented fully in the school buildings of the district?" (p. 262). In short, the audit or evaluation of a program involves determining whether there is written program documentation, and whether the program is being implemented appropriately in various locales. A program audit frequently provides an analysis of each facet of the comprehensive school counseling program (Bowers & Colonna, 2001; C. D. Johnson & Johnson, 2003). Auditing the program will often point to areas of programmatic strengths and weaknesses. The ASCA (2003a) *National Model* provided a sample program audit aligning with model components. For example, sample criteria included "a statement of philosophy has been written for the school counseling program" and "addresses every student's right to a school counseling program" (p. 66). ASCA suggested that program criteria be evaluated on the following response choices: "None: meaning not in place; In progress: perhaps begun, but not completed; Completed: but perhaps not implemented; Implemented: fully implemented; Not Applicable: for situations where the criteria does not apply" (p. 66). In practice, a program audit should be conducted near the end of each academic year. Reports derived from the audit should address program strengths, areas in need of improvement, and long- and short-term improvement goals (ASCA, 2003a). These goals then drive program development procedures and activities during subsequent years.

Service Assessment

Service assessments are often requested by guidance supervisors and demanded by superintendents and school boards to document how counselors are spending their time. Two types of service assessments are commonly used: event-topic counts and time logs. Event-topic counts involve the professional school counselor's documenting each time an individual is contacted or provided with a counseling service and the nature of the topic addressed. In this way, professional school counselors can keep a weekly or monthly tally of the number of students seen not only for global individual counseling, but specifically for individual counseling for depression, anxiety, behavior, changing family, social skills, anger-management, or conflict resolution issues. Such data are quite impressive when aggregated and presented to a school board to indicate that "38,961 individual counseling sessions were held with students last year."

A time log is sometimes kept by professional school counselors to document the amount of time spent in various counseling and non-counseling-related activities. For example, some administrators may wish to know the percentage of time counselors actually spend doing group counseling or teacher consultation at the high school level. Time logs require professional school counselors to document and categorize their activities for every minute of the workday. In states with mandates for providing direct service activities (e.g., elementary professional counselors must spend at least 50% of their time in the direct service activities of individual counseling, group counseling, and group guidance), time logs are necessary to document compliance for funding purposes.

While service assessments do a wonderful job of telling what or how much a professional school counselor is doing, such assessments give no information about the quality or effectiveness of counselor interventions. The important question becomes, "What good things happen as a result of professional school counselors choosing to use their time this way?" After all, what will a professional school counselor who spends 80%

TABLE 12.3
The "is" and "isn't" of assessment.

Assessment of school counseling programs is

- A way to answer important program-related questions
- The responsibility of an accountable professional school counselor
- A cooperative endeavor with other SCPAC members and stakeholders
- Ongoing and evolving
- A means to a better end—better education for *all* students

Assessment of school counseling programs isn't

- The evaluation of an individual professional school counselor
- An assault on the professional school counselor's freedom
- A mandate for standardized tests or curricula
- All figured out

of his or her time doing group and individual counseling, but has ineffective counseling skills, really accomplish? For this kind of information, we must conduct outcome studies.

Results or Outcomes Evaluation

Results evaluation (sometimes called outcomes evaluation) answers the question, "How are students different as a result of the program?" (S. Johnson & Johnson, 2003). There is much confusion in the field regarding what program assessment is and what it isn't. Table 12.3 shows a list of some of these issues.

Most important among these is the ongoing, cyclical nature of evaluation. The assessment loop shown in Figure 12.5 provides a helpful way to visually conceptualize program evaluation and how outcome studies can be used to improve programs.

Many educators view assessment as a discrete component, but it is actually an integrated part of a continuous process for program improvement. All assessment procedures must have the institution's mission in mind because the institutional values and needs will determine the focus of study. Questions of worth and effectiveness are derived from a confluence of values, needs, goals, and mission, and these questions lead to the determination of what evidence must

be collected. Evidence may exist in many places, but it is typically derived using preplanned measures or from the performances or products students engage in during program activities. Once information has been gathered, it must then be interpreted, and conclusions must be drawn from it regarding the program's or activity's worth, strengths, and weaknesses. Finally, the interpretations and conclusions must be used to change the program or parts of the program to improve it.

Notice how the loop in Figure 12.5 never stops—it represents a continuous process in which assessment results are interpreted and

FIGURE 12.5
The assessment cycle.

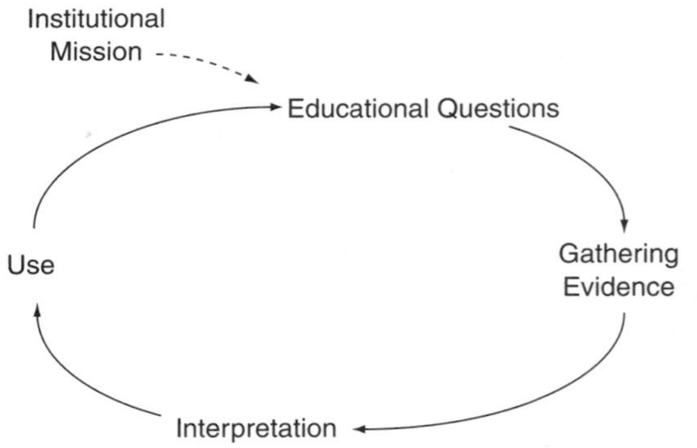

fed back into the improvement process. As assessment information is used to prompt programmatic changes, so goal setting and the posing of new questions about the revised program begin anew. Most professional school counselors fail in the assessment loop because they gather evidence and then stop, believing that the program has been evaluated and the job finished. Why spend valuable time collecting evidence and not use it to improve what you are doing?

Important Assessment Terms

A number of terms associated with research and evaluation are important to understand. *Evaluation* is the measurement of worth and indicates that a judgment will be made regarding the effectiveness of a program (Cronbach, 1983). This is one major reason why professional school counselors avoid accountability procedures and outcome studies—they perceive the results may reflect poorly on their performance. The experienced researcher knows that being very specific about what you are measuring and how you are measuring it is the key to successful results. This is made clear in the section on writing learning objectives in chapter 8. Too often, professional school counselors are not specific about what they are trying to accomplish and become frustrated when they fail to measure what they may or may not have achieved. If a person doesn't know where she is heading, she must either get specific directions (write a specific, measurable objective) or be satisfied with wherever she ends up (perhaps an ineffective program)!

Evidence is any data that will help make judgments or decisions and can be quantitatively or qualitatively derived. *Formative evaluation* is evaluative feedback that occurs during the implementation of a program, whereas *summative evaluation* is feedback collected at a specified endpoint in an evaluation process (Worthen, Sanders, & Fitzpatrick, 1997). Although summative evaluation is conducted most frequently, formative evaluation has the advantage of allowing corrective action to occur if an implemented program is shown to

be off course. This makes sense when you consider that some programs are expensive (in time and money) to implement. If you know after one third of the program has been implemented that desired results are not occurring, then midcourse corrections can be made to tailor the program to the audience and desired outcomes.

A *stakeholder* is anyone involved in or potentially benefiting from the school counseling program (Worthen et al., 1997). Stakeholders may include students, parents, teachers, professional school counselors, administrators, community organizations, and local businesses, among others. A *baseline* is any data gathered to establish a starting point. It is essential to know where students are so you can tailor interventions to help facilitate their development. *Inputs* are any resources (e.g., personnel, material) that go into a program; *outcomes* are what stakeholders can do as a result of the program.

A *pretest* is a measure administered before a program is implemented, and a *posttest* is a measure administered after the program or intervention has been completed. If a study calls for both a pretest and a posttest, usually there is tremendous overlap in their content because the goal is to determine changes in the individual or group as a result of participating in the program. Any changes that occur in the examinee between administration of the pretest and posttest are usually attributed to the program activities (Worthen et al., 1997).

An interesting recent addition to evaluation procedures is the concept of value-added assessment. *Value-added assessment* generally utilizes a pretest–posttest design, but the question posed is, "How much value has been added to the individual's performance as a result of participating in the program?" This is an interesting question to ask because it focuses attention on both the timing of interventions and the final yield of an intervention. For example, if 80% of the targeted students have already met a given criterion, why reintroduce the concept to the entire group at this time? Would it have been more appropriately introduced earlier in the vertically articulated curriculum? Value-added assessments also focus on the improvements (yield) of the products of a program. For example, elite schools are famous for their desire to produce "creative thinkers and problem solvers," but if students entering the school are selected because of their higher levels of creative thinking and problem-solving capacities, what improvements are the schools really making? Value-added assessment seeks to answer that question by establishing a baseline and evaluating the students' progress over time.

Sources of Evidence

Both people and products merit discussion as potential sources of evidence. Almost anyone can serve as a helpful source of evidence: students, teachers, staff, administration, parents, employers, graduates, community resource people, and so on. Numerous products from data collection methods can also be used. A short list includes portfolios, performances, use of ratings from external judges or examiners, observations, local tests, purchased tests, student self-assessments, surveys, interviews, focus groups, and student work. Each of these sources or products can produce helpful evaluative data, but what is collected will result from the specific question to be answered.

Practical Program Evaluation Considerations

A number of researchers have provided practical guidelines for conducting accountability studies (D. R. Atkinson, Furlong, & Janoff, 1979; Fairchild, 1986; Krumboltz, 1974). To be of practical value, assessment must be connected to real program concerns as well as the core values of the school or program. Avoid overwhelming the data collectors, focus on only one or several important questions at a time, and always select measures that will yield reliable and valid scores for the purposes under study. Oftentimes, ineffective program outcomes stem from poor or inappropriate measurement rather than faulty programming. Be sure to involve the relevant stakeholders and use a variety of approaches. Perhaps most important, do not reinvent the wheel—use what you are already doing to generate useful data about program effectiveness. Also, don't be afraid to call

on outside experts to consult on the development and evaluation of a program (Schmidt, 2003; Vacc, Rhyne-Winkler, & Poidevant, 1993).

It is good advice to start small and build on what is found to work; the methods and goals of individual programs are celebrated, and successes can be shared across programs. This often leads to a cross-pollination effect that yields both diversity of approach and homogeneity of results. In other words, over time, counselors will learn from each other what works and implement these strategies with their own populations after necessary refinements based on the needs of a differing school community. Different can still be effective!

Aggregated Outcomes

As mentioned earlier, aggregation is the combining of results to provide a more global or generalized picture of group performance. While such a practice may deemphasize subgroup or individual performance, aggregation can also be a valuable tool when it comes to evaluating how well school counseling programs meet higher level standards, such as the ASCA *National Standards* (C. Campbell & Dahir, 1997). Due to their more abstract or generalized wording, standards (sometimes called goals) are difficult, if not impossible, to directly measure. This is why curriculum development begins with a statement of standards (goals) that are then further described through a series of outcomes (sometimes called competencies). While more specific and well defined, these outcomes are still ordinarily not amenable to direct measurement in the classic sense. Instead, educators rely on educational objectives, such as those discussed in chapter 8. Objectives are written in such specific, measurable terms that everyone (e.g., teacher, student, parent, professional school counselor) can tell when an objective has been met. The use of objectives, outcomes, and standards comprises an aggregated hierarchical model and is an important way that professional school counselors can demonstrate the effectiveness of a school counseling program. Figure 12.6 provides as example of this aggregated hierarchical model.

FIGURE 12.6
Aggregated hierarchical model for evaluating the effectiveness of a school counseling program.

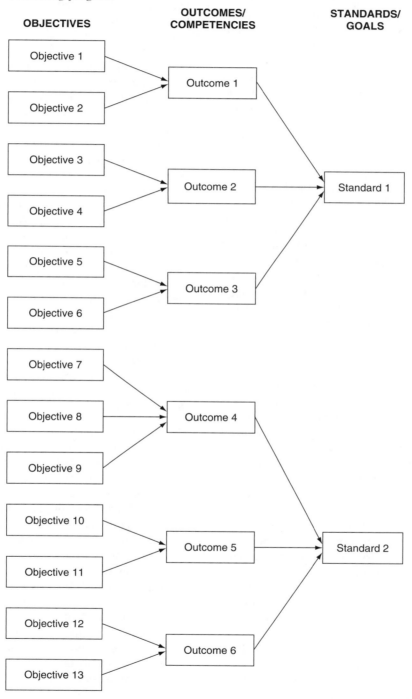

In Figure 12.6, note the alignment of objectives to outcomes to standards. Objective 1 measures Outcome 1, which is aligned with Standard 1. Likewise, Objective 13 measures Outcome 6, which is aligned with Standard 2. Such a hierarchical structure allows the professional school counselor to conclude that meeting the lower order objectives provides evidence that higher order outcomes and standards have been successfully met. For example, assume the professional school counselor provides evidence that Objectives 1 through 6 have been met. By extension, if Objectives 1 and 2 were met, then Outcome 1 was met. If Objectives 3 and 4 were met, then Outcome 2 was met. If Objectives 5 and 6 were met, then Outcome 3 was met. Because Outcomes 1 through 3 were met, the professional school counselor has provided evidence that Standard 1 was met. Success! In addition, areas of curricular strength have been identified.

Again referring to Figure 12.6, now consider a second example in which Objectives 7 through 10 were met, but Objectives 11 through 13 were not met. By extension, if Objectives 7 through 9 were met, then Outcome 4 was met. If Objective 10 was met, but Objective 11 was not met, then Outcome 5 was either not met or, more accurately, was only partially met. If Objectives 12 and 13 were not met, then Outcome 6 was not met. Now, because of some inconsistent results, interpretation is a bit cloudier. It is most appropriate to conclude that Standard 2 was only partially met, because Outcome 4 was met, Outcome 5 was partially met, and Outcome 6 was not met. Given the inconsistency of the outcomes, it would be inappropriate to conclude that Standard 2 had been met; it would be equally inappropriate to conclude that Standard 2 had not been met. A conclusion of "partially met" identifies the hierarchical set of standard, outcomes, and objectives as a curricular area in need of improvement, additional attention to or revision of the criteria for successful performance, or both. From these examples one can see that an aggregated hierarchical model can be a valuable curriculum evaluation method. It also underscores the importance of a measurable objective as the building block of an effective developmental curriculum (see chapter 8).

Designing Outcome Studies

While any data collected on counselor effectiveness can be helpful, in most instances, professional school counselors should measure outcomes or results by designing a research-type study. Importantly, a bit of forethought and planning can lead to much more meaningful conclusions. Research studies are typically empirical in nature and involve providing some control over how students are assigned to counseling interventions and the timing and circumstances under which data is collected. D. T. Campbell and Stanley (1963) explored helpful, easy-to-implement designs, and several of these designs that may be particularly useful to professional school counselors have been included in Table 12.4. Although a comprehensive treatise of this topic is beyond the scope of this book, the following are some of the relevant points professional school counselors should consider when designing outcome studies. Counselors generally receive an entire course in research that can be useful in this context. The interested reader should consult Erford (in press) for a helpful source on research methodology and statistical analysis written specifically for counselors.

Answering several questions can help the professional counselor determine which research design to use:

1. *Has the treatment already been implemented?* So much for planning ahead! If the intervention has not already occurred, one has many possible options. If the intervention has already occurred, one is relegated to a nonexperimental design, probably a case study or static-group comparison design. It is critical to think about outcomes assessment in the early stages of planning for an intervention and certainly before the intervention has begun!

2. *Can I randomly assign participants to treatment conditions?* If the answer is yes, outstanding! Control over the random assignment of participants is critical to implementing true experimental designs. If one does not have control over assignment of participants, the professional school counselor must choose a quasi-experimental or nonexperimental design.

TABLE 12.4
Common designs used for outcomes research.

Nonexperimental Designs		
1. Pretest–posttest single group design		O I O
2. Case study		I O
3. Static-group comparison	group 1	O
	group 2	I O
Quasi-Experimental Designs		
4. Two-sample pretest–posttest design		R O
		R I O
5. Nonequivalent control group design		O I O
		O O
6. Time series design		O O O I O O O
True Experimental Designs		
7. Randomized pretest–posttest control group design		R O I O
		R O O
8. Randomized posttest only control group design		R I O
		R O

Note. R = participants are randomly assigned to groups; I = intervention (implemented treatment or program); O = observation or other data collection method.

3. *Can I conduct (one or several) pretests, posttests, or both?* Usually, measuring the dependent variable both before (pretest) and after (posttest) is desirable, although not always essential.

The answers to each of these questions will help the professional school counselor choose the most useful and powerful design. For example, if the answers to the three questions are no, yes, and yes, respectively, the professional school counselor may opt for an experimental design (i. e., designs 7 or 8 in Table 12.4). If the answers are yes, no, and posttest only, one is relegated to a nonexperiment design (designs 2 or 3 in Table 12.4). As one can no doubt surmise, outcome studies require some level of planning early on in program development.

Most true experimental designs involve randomization of participants, which also randomizes various sources of error allowing for the control of numerous threats to validity. True experimental designs allow causative

conclusions to be reached. This is a big advantage when the professional school counselor wants to know conclusively if his or her interventions caused significant improvements in students. For example, if a professional school counselor wants to know if a group intervention designed to improve study skills and academic performance was effective, he or she could use the randomized pretest–posttest control group design (design 7 in Table 12.4). He or she would begin by randomly assigning his or her students into two optimal-sized groups, designated control and treatment, and determining a data collection method (e.g., test, survey, or observation) to measure an outcome of interest (e. g., academic achievement, study skills, social skills). He or she would begin by administering the "test" (called the pretest) to all participants in both the control and treatment conditions. Next, he or she would implement the intervention (e. g., group counseling experience) to the treatment group, but not to the control group. (*Note:* the control group would either experience nothing or may undergo a group counseling experience for some issue other than academic performance, study skills, social skills, etc.) On conclusion of the treatment (program, intervention) the professional school counselor would again administer the test (this time called the posttest) to participants in both groups. It would be expected that no change in the control group participants' scores would be observed (i.e., no statistically significant difference between pretest and posttest scores). However, if the group counseling experience was successful, it would be expected that a significant change would be observed in the treatment group (e.g., posttest scores are higher than pretest scores, higher grades at end of group than at the beginning). Of course the other designs in Table 12.4 also could be used with this or other examples. However, quasi-experimental and nonexperimental designs do not allow the professional school counselor to conclude that the treatment was the "cause" of the changes noted in the participants. Thus, in many ways, results or outcomes from studies with experimental designs are more valuable and powerful.

A lot of thought must be given to the design of the outcome measure used. Often, nonsignificant results are not due to the intervention, but to the selection of an outcome measure not sensitive enough to demonstrate the effect of the treatment. Some outcome measures can be easily obtained because they are a matter of record (e.g., grade point average, percentage grade in math class, number of days absent, number of homework assignments completed) or already exist in published form (e.g., Conners Parent Rating Scale–Revised [CPRS–R], Achenbach System of Empirically Based Assessment [ASEBA], Beck Depression Inventory [BDI–II], Children's Depression Inventory [CDI]). The number of available outcome measures may be limitless. Still, sometimes professional school counselors need to design an outcome measure with sufficient sensitivity and direct applicability to the issue being studied (e.g., adjustment to a divorce, body image, social skills, math self-efficacy). When professional school counselors need to develop an outcome measure from scratch, the basics of scale development covered above in the discussion of

needs assessments can be helpful. In addition, Weiss (1998) provided a dozen principles the assessor should consider:

1. Use simple language.
2. Ask only about things that the respondent can be expected to know.
3. Make the question specific.
4. Define terms that are in any way unclear.
5. Avoid yes–no questions.
6. Avoid double negatives.
7. Don't ask double-barreled questions [e.g., two questions in one].
8. Use wording that has been adopted in the field.
9. Include enough information to jog people's memories or to make them aware of features of a phenomenon they might otherwise overlook.
10. Look for secondhand opinions or ratings only when firsthand information is unavailable.
11. Be sensitive to cultural differences.
12. Learn how to deal with difficult respondent groups. (pp. 140–142)

These principles apply to most types of data collection procedures. Professional school counselors can use a wide range of procedures, each with advantages and disadvantages. Table 12.5 presents descriptions of several of the most common methods of data collection used by professional school counselors.

Reporting the Results

Although professional school counselors, or perhaps an outside consultant, may write the majority of a report, the SCPAC should be involved at every step of the process. A comprehensive report may be helpful for SCPAC analysis purposes; however, a one- to two-page executive summary should also be prepared for release to building administrators, system administrators, and the school community. Loesch and Ritchie (2004) suggested that dissemination of school counseling program results could occur through a written report, a verbal presentation, a multimedia presentation, journal articles, a Web page, television, a videotape, posters, e-mail, or a newspaper article.

Regardless of the vehicle for dissemination, results of the program outcomes should be

TABLE 12.5
Common data-collection methods.

1. *Interviews* of the professional school counselor, key personnel, or members of stakeholder groups can provide valuable data. Interviews can be structured, semistructured, or unstructured. Structured interviews present a formal sequence of questions to interviewees, with no variation in administration, thus generating clear evidence of strengths and weaknesses. Unstructured formats allow for follow-up deeper exploration and are commonly used in qualitative studies. Usually, multiple respondents are required for patterns and conclusions to emerge. Face-to-face interviews are generally better than phone interviews, although usually more costly and inconvenient. Careful consideration must be given to question development, and interviewers must guard against introducing bias.

2. *Observations* can also be classified as informal or formal. Informal observations tend to yield anecdotal data through a "look-and-see" approach. Formal or structured observations usually involve a protocol and predetermined procedures for collecting specific types of data during a specified time period. Structured procedures tend to minimize bias. As an example of observation, professional school counselors can be observed implementing a developmental guidance lesson by a supervisor or peer.

3. *Written questionnaires, surveys, and rating scales* are usually paper-and-pencil instruments asking a broad range of questions (open ended, closed ended, or both). Questionnaires and rating scales typically ask for factual responses while surveys generally solicit participant perceptions. By far the greatest weakness of this data collection method is that many participants do not complete or return the instrument (i.e., low return rate). It also requires a certain level of literacy. Few respondents take the time to write lengthy responses, so it is usually best to keep the questions simple and closed ended with the opportunity for participants to expand a response if needed. Multiscaled response formats (e.g., Likert scales) often provide more helpful results than yes–no questions. E-mailed or online versions of these instruments are becoming more commonly used.

4. *Program records and schedules* are a naturally occurring and helpful source of evaluation data. If stored on a computer in a database format, this kind of data is particularly accessible, and a professional school counselor is well advised to consider this ahead of time when determining how best to maintain electronic records and schedules. Archives should also be kept in good order to facilitate record searches. In particular, professional school counselors should keep previous program improvement documents and outcome study reports.

5. *Standardized and educator-made tests* provide objective sources of measurable student performance and progress in the academic, career, and personal–social domains. Individual, classroom, and schoolwide tests can be extremely helpful and powerful measures. Tests exist that measure academic achievement, depression, anxiety, substance use, distractibility, career indecision, and myriad other student behaviors. Likewise, professional school counselors can design and develop tests to measure student behaviors and characteristics, much like teachers design tests to measure academic achievement.

6. *Academic performance indicators* may include a student's grade point average or classroom grade but also includes daily work behaviors and habits (e.g., attendance, homework completion, disruptions) and attitudes (e.g., academic self-efficacy, attitude toward school).

7. *Products and portfolios* are real-life examples of performance. A product is anything created by a student (or the professional school counselor) that stemmed from a program standard (e.g., artwork, composition, poster). A portfolio is a collection of exemplar products that can be evaluated to determine the quality of an individual's performance.

released to relevant stakeholder groups at regular intervals after the results have been reviewed by the SCPAC, professional school counselors, and administration. As general guidelines for report writing, Heppner, Kivlighan, and Wampold (1992) suggested, "(1) Be informative, (2) be forthright, (3) do not overstate or exaggerate, (4) be logical and organized, (5) have some style, (6) write and rewrite, and (7) when all else fails, just write!" (p. 376). While the last guideline may have been intended to be humorous, the important point is that results must be circulated for accountability to occur.

As mentioned, the results of the outcome studies are used to make substantive program improvements that then prompt more questions to be studied—and the process cycles again and again. This cycle is essential to the transformation and continuous quality improvement of any comprehensive developmental school counseling program.

Performance Appraisal

The effectiveness of a school counseling program often relies on the competence and efficiency of its implementers. While an entire book could be written on procedures for assessing the performance of professional school counselors, this section will provide but a few guiding principles. It is not an exaggeration to say that the services provided by, and responsibilities of, the professional school counselor are among the most complex of any school employee. The advanced, specialized training certainly demands that individuals placed in a position to evaluate the counselor must also have equivalent training and advanced supervision skills. Thus, while the experiences and training of principals often provide a useful vantage point from which to evaluate teachers and secretarial staff, principals seldom have the training and counseling supervision experience to evaluate counselors effectively. That is not to say that principals lack the ability to provide helpful information regarding counselor performance. It is a better practice, however, to have counselor supervisors coordinate or at least participate in the appraisal of counselor performance. One facet of a professional school counselor's performance appraisal that a principal or other noncounselor administrator may be able to contribute to is evaluation of the professional school counselor's skill when providing a classroom-based developmental guidance lesson. The criteria for any evaluation always should be available well in advance. Figure 12.7 provides a sample instructional evaluation adapted for the purpose of assessing a professional school counselor's skill in the classroom.

Most professional school counselor performance appraisals are composed of a rating system that aggregates or averages responses across a variety of categories of work-related responsibilities. Generally, these rating schemes involve some indication of "Satisfactory" or "Unsatisfactory" performance in each of the targeted skill categories. Some performance appraisal forms allow greater differentiation in ratings; for example, "Unsatisfactory," "Inconsistently meets expectations," "Consistently meets expectations," and "Consistently exceeds expectations." This latter differentiation is particularly useful when incentives such as merit pay are in effect.

Numerous formats are used for professional school counselor performance appraisal. In fact, nearly all school systems tailor forms and criteria to their specifications and needs. Some are particularly comprehensive models, using a multipoint rating system (see Gysbers & Henderson, 2000). Figures 12.8 and 12.9 are actual performance-appraisal documents from public school systems. Although briefly stated and somewhat open to interpretation, notice how the indicators and competencies serve as discussion points for an ongoing professional development dialogue between counselor and supervisor. Such discussions are meant to highlight a professional school counselor's strengths and weaknesses and guide him or her in the direction of needed improvement. This dialogue eventually results in a rating of "Satisfactory" or "Unsatisfactory" in each category under investigation; then an overall rating is determined, generally for retention purposes. While performance appraisals do sometimes affect retention and dismissal of counselors, the truth is that the number dismissed for unsatisfactory performance is very small. Thus, the primary focus of the appraisal system should be, and in most instances is, to enhance the quality and competence of all those evaluated.

The ASCA *National Model* (2003a) provided 13 school counselor performance standards, each with several subcomponents. These standards are presented in an adaptive format in Figure 12.10, with a response format similar to those discussed above. It is essential that professional school counselors held to performance standards such as these provide additional evidence and comments to give an appropriate context for those supervisors ultimately making evaluative decisions. Regardless of the evaluation system used, it is critical that the focus be on development of higher levels of counselor skills.

FIGURE 12.7
Instructional evaluation of a developmental guidance lesson.

Observee: _____ Observer: _____ Date: _____					

Directions: Circle the number for each statement corresponding with your observation. Please write in any additional comments. *Key:* NA = not applicable; NI = needs improvement; S = satisfactory; VS = very satisfactory.

Presentation of Introductory Material

	NA	NI	S	VS
1. Indicated the purpose of the presentation.	NA	NI	S	VS
2. Provided preview/overview of presentation.	NA	NI	S	VS
3. Connected today's content to previous presentations or experiences.	NA	NI	S	VS

Body of Presentation

	NA	NI	S	VS
4. Content was arranged in a logical order.	NA	NI	S	VS
5. Assessed throughout presentation to determine if information was understood.	NA	NI	S	VS
6. Gave examples to help students understand ideas and/or to tie subject to prior knowledge that students possessed.	NA	NI	S	VS
7. Summarized important ideas throughout presentation.	NA	NI	S	VS

Conclusion of Presentation

	NA	NI	S	VS
8. Asked questions to see what students understood/learned, any misconceptions they might have, and what needed to be retaught/covered again.	NA	NI	S	VS
9. Summarized main concepts in presentation.	NA	NI	S	VS
10. Dealt effectively with any problems/questions that came up in the presentation.	NA	NI	S	VS
11. Previewed what will be covered next time, linking it to the current presentation.	NA	NI	S	VS
12. Evaluated what students learned to see if objectives were met.	NA	NI	S	VS

Overall Instructional Presentation

	NA	NI	S	VS
13. The material presented was important and aligned with content standards/competencies.	NA	NI	S	VS
14. Distinctions were made between fact and opinion, as appropriate.	NA	NI	S	VS
15. Statements were supported with reference to authoritative sources, as appropriate.	NA	NI	S	VS
16. Presented and encouraged divergent viewpoints.	NA	NI	S	VS
17. Included an appropriate amount of content for the available time period.	NA	NI	S	VS
18. All materials were ready.	NA	NI	S	VS
19. Presentation began on time.	NA	NI	S	VS
20. Presentation ended on time.	NA	NI	S	VS
21. Presentation time was used efficiently.	NA	NI	S	VS

Clarity of Presentation

	NA	NI	S	VS
22. Defined any new items, concepts, and/or principles.	NA	NI	S	VS
23. Explained why problems are solved using certain processes or techniques.	NA	NI	S	VS
24. Used clear and relevant examples to explain major ideas and connect them to students' prior knowledge.	NA	NI	S	VS

(Continued)

259

FIGURE 12.7 (Continued)

Verbal Communication				
25. Spoke clearly and could be easily heard.	NA	NI	S	VS
26. Raised and lowered voice to emphasize points and provide variety.	NA	NI	S	VS
27. Minimized use of speech distracters (e.g., ahh, OK).	NA	NI	S	VS
28. Speech rate was appropriate (neither too fast nor too slow.)	NA	NI	S	VS
29. Invited participants to share.	NA	NI	S	VS
30. Answers and asks questions clearly.	NA	NI	S	VS
31. Gives students feedback when appropriate.	NA	NI	S	VS
Nonverbal Communication				
32. Kept appropriate eye contact with students throughout presentation and when listening to student questions and responses.	NA	NI	S	VS
33. Mannerisms were comfortable and inviting, allowed students to participate (not too formal or casual).	NA	NI	S	VS
34. Facial and body movements matched speech and/or expressed intentions.	NA	NI	S	VS
35. Listened attentively to students' questions and comments.	NA	NI	S	VS
Classroom Management				
36. Kept participants' attention.	NA	NI	S	VS
37. Encouraged everyone to participate.	NA	NI	S	VS
38. Was able to keep control of the group.	NA	NI	S	VS
39. Respected and valued all members of the group and differences between members.	NA	NI	S	VS

MANAGING A SCHOOLWIDE TESTING PROGRAM

Frequently, professional school counselors have some role in the schoolwide testing programs. Sometimes, a professional school counselor may coordinate the entire program. Schoolwide testing programs have several primary purposes. First, schoolwide testing programs provide quality control and public accountability. Taxpayers have the right to know what affect their tax dollars have on the education of students. Parents also want to know if their children are receiving a "quality education," and quite frankly, educators want some validation that they are providing one. Second, the results of schoolwide testing programs help to provide curricular and program evaluation. School system administrators are keenly interested in the results of schoolwide testing programs because their results often inform decisions about the rigorous nature of the curriculum. Curriculum and special program strengths and weaknesses can frequently be

identified (or at least hypothesized). Often schools are interested in tracking average grade-level performance from year to year to see if gains are being made in primary academic subjects. Curriculum- or standards-based tests are particularly helpful in this regard. Finally, test results can help assess individual student performance, identify student strengths and weaknesses, and facilitate screening and diagnostic services for general instructional purposes for children with special needs (e. g., gifted and talented, section 504, IDEIA, academically at-risk, achievement groupings).

Managing a schoolwide testing program is a time-consuming endeavor that requires a great deal of organizational skill, dedication, and personal responsibility. In this era of large-scale and high-stakes testing, it is not unusual for a school system's calendar to have some form of assessment schedules for up to half of the total school days. Not counting in-class teacher-made tests, students in Grades 3–8 can spend more than

Last Name _____ First Name _____ Initial _____ Social Security Number _____

	Yes	No
Certified		
Tenure		

School _____

Assignment _____

School Year _____
Date of Last Evaluation _____
Total Years Counseling Experience _____
Years in Baltimore County _____
Years in Present Assignment _____

I. PROFESSIONAL COMPETENCIES	Meets Standards	Does Not Meet Standards
A. Knowledge of the Students		
B. Developmental Guidance		
C. Clinical Counseling Skills		
D. Program Planning		
E. Program Implementation		
F. Evidence of Professional Growth		
G. Communication Skills		
H. Ethical Behavior		
I. Assessment of Student Learning		

Overall Rating for Professional Competencies
___ Satisfactory   ___ Unsatisfactory

Comments Mandatory:

II. HUMAN RELATIONS COMPETENCIES	Meets Standards	Does Not Meet Standards
A. Group Relationships		
B. Relationships with Students		
C. Relationships with Management Personnel		

Overall Rating for Human Relations
___ Satisfactory   ___ Unsatisfactory

Comments Mandatory:

FIGURE 12.8
Evaluation of school counselor progress.

	Meets Standards	Does Not Meet Standards
D. Relationships with Parents		
E. Relationships with Co-workers		
F. Contributions to Total School		

III. MANAGEMENT COMPETENCIES

	Meets Standards	Does Not Meet Standards
A. Availability to Students		
B. Pupil Management		
C. Maintenance of Routine Procedures		
D. Appearance/Organization of Guidance and Counseling Area		
E. Dependability		

Overall Rating for Management Competencies

___ Satisfactory   ___ Unsatisfactory

Comments Mandatory:

IV. OVERALL EFFECTIVENESS OF COUNSELING
SUMMARY COMMENTS MANDATORY:

___ Satisfactory   ___ Unsatisfactory

_____ _____   _____ _____   _____ _____
Signature of Counselor   Date   Signature of Principal   Date   Other Evaluator   Date

(The signature indicates the school counselor has read the report and a conference was held. This does not necessarily indicate agreement with this evaluation.)

_____ _____
Other Evaluator   Date

_____ _____
Other Evaluator   Date

SCHOOL COUNSELOR'S COMMENTS (Optional) May include special contributions to education on a local, countywide, state, and/or national level, if not cited elsewhere in this report.

Evaluation of Professional/Clinical Competencies for School Counselors
(Supervisory Worksheet)

Last Name	First Name	Initial	School	Date

	Meets Standards	Does Not Meet Standards
A. KNOWLEDGE OF STUDENTS		
• Assists students to recognize their developmental patterns and potential for growth		
• Identifies and assists students with unique needs, e.g., social, emotional, educational		
• Demonstrates sensitivity to the various stages of the emotional and physical development of students		
• Works from an awareness of family and community needs that impact upon students		
• Consults with school personnel and parents to assist them in understanding students		
B. DEVELOPMENTAL GUIDANCE	**Meets Standards**	**Does Not Meet Standards**
• Demonstrates knowledge of developmental needs of students		
• Provides a variety of programs which nurture developmental growth of students		
• Uses varied and age-appropriate instructional strategies		
C. CLINICAL COUNSELING SKILLS	**Meets Standards**	**Does Not Meet Standards**
• Identifies students' counseling needs and the issues within		
• Sets appropriate counseling goals and related student indicators		
• Uses a variety of counseling theories and strategies to assist students		
• Understands and appropriately applies crisis counseling interventions		

FIGURE 12.8 (Continued)

	Meets Standards	Does Not Meet Standards
• Incorporates group counseling theory and techniques to meet students' needs		
• Demonstrates effective consultation skills with parents, school staff members, and school teams		
• Makes appropriate referrals		

D. SCHOOL COUNSELING PROGRAM PLANNING

	Meets Standards	Does Not Meet Standards
• Develops a school counseling program plan based on assessed needs of students		
• Uses student indicators to identify targeted student learnings to be attained and skills to be developed		
• Includes significant personnel in planning process		

E. SCHOOL COUNSELING PROGRAM IMPLEMENTATION

	Meets Standards	Does Not Meet Standards
• Delivers a program of services corresponding to the school's counseling program plan		
• Manages time to realize both planned services and crisis intervention needs		
• Utilizes resources necessary for success of plan		
• Assesses impact of program's services on students		

F. EVIDENCE OF PROFESSIONAL GROWTH

	Meets Standards	Does Not Meet Standards
• Takes inservice and graduate courses in counseling and related fields		
• Participates in county-level and state professional meetings		
• Utilizes creative strategies from professional journals and books		
• Holds membership or participates in professional counseling organizations		

	Meets Standards	Does Not Meet Standards
• Shares professional competencies with other counselors		
• Uses current ideas and materials to adapt and supplement school counseling program		
• Serves as a mentor to other school counselors		
G. COMMUNICATION SKILLS		
• Presents ideas clearly and at the appropriate level for each individual or audience		
• Communicates successfully with individual students, small groups, and large groups		
• Responds to questions and comments in a manner which helps others achieve greater self-awareness		
• Models appropriate social and mediation skills		
H. ADHERENCE TO PROFESSIONAL ETHICAL STANDARDS		
• Adheres to the Ethical Standards of the American Counseling Association and the American School Counselors' Association		
• Respects the confidentiality of counselees and understands the privacy of student records		
• Understands and follows principles of ethical practices related to "duty to warn"		
• Conducts oneself as a professional school counselor		
• Avoids dual relationships in counseling commitments to counselees		
• Seeks feedback from supervisory personnel on ethical practices		

FIGURE 12.8 (Continued)

I. ASSESSMENT OF STUDENT LEARNING	Meets Standards	Does Not Meet Standards
• Assesses the learning of students		
• Assesses impact of counseling interventions on students' attainment of targeted indicators		
• Provides for assessments in program plan		
• Adjusts plan as indicated from assessment results		

_____   _____   _____
Evaluator   Title   Date

DISTRIBUTION: 1 copy to school counselor, 1 copy to principal, 1 copy to area office, 1 copy to Office of Guidance and Counseling Services

Source: Reprinted by permission of the Baltimore County Public School System, Towson, MD, 21204. Reproduction or use of this document without the express written permission of Baltimore County Public Schools is expressly prohibited.

FIGURE 12.8 (Continued)

FIGURE 12.9
Howard County Public School System school counselors evaluation form.

_____   _____
            Name   Professional Assignment

A complete description of the teacher evaluation process of the Howard County Public Schools is provided in the Guide to Teacher Evaluation and Professional Development.

Please place the appropriate letter   Circle either **Tenured** or **Nontenured**
Symbol in the box next to the objective:

S - Satisfactory
U - Unsatisfactory

School counselors and administrators must note that staff members selecting a differentiated supervision option as part of the professional development and evaluation process will receive a final overall evaluation rating of SATISFACTORY unless the staff member and administrator rewrite the Professional Development and Evaluation Objectives form prior to January 31.

☐ 1. **INTERPERSONAL SKILLS**
        Relates Effectively with Students
        Develops Collaborative Relationships with Administrative, Teaching,
        and Support Staff
        Fosters Positive Relationships with Families and Community Members
        Comments:

☐ 2. **PLANNING AND PREPARATION/MANAGEMENT**
        Demonstrates Knowledge of Guidance and Counseling Theory and Strategies
        Demonstrates Knowledge of Students
        Selects Appropriate Counseling/Instructional Goals
        Demonstrates Knowledge of Resources
        Designs Coherent Counseling/Instruction
        Assesses Students' Needs Effectively
        Comments:

☐ 3. **THE CLASSROOM ENVIRONMENT/SCHOOL ENVIRONMENT**
        Establishes a Culture for Learning
        Manages Counseling/Classroom Procedures Effectively
        Manages Student Behavior Effectively
        Organizes Physical Space Appropriately
        Comments:

(Continued)

267

FIGURE 12.9 (Continued)

[ ] 4. **DELIVERY OF INSTRUCTION/PROGRAM IMPLEMENTATION**
Communicates Clearly and Accurately
Uses Questioning and Discussion Techniques Effectively
Engages Students in Learning Activities Directed to Guidance Goals (Comar 13A05050) and Student Needs
Provides Effective Feedback to Students
Demonstrates Flexibility and Responsiveness
Comments:

[ ] 5. **PROFESSIONAL RESPONSIBILITIES**
Reflects on Guidance and Counseling
Supports and Maintains Accurate Records
Communicates with Families
Shows Professionalism
Grows and Develops Professionally
Comments:

[ ] Overall Rating   [ ] See attachments (Attachments are required for all overall ratings of unsatisfactory.)

_____   _____
Counselor's Signature & Date   **Designated Evaluator's Signature & Date**

                                    _____
                                    Principal's Signature & Date

Note: Must be given to counselor within five school days after it is signed by the principal and no later than the last duty day.

Distribution: Principal, Employee, Personnel File

FIGURE 12.9 (Continued)

HOWARD COUNTY PUBLIC SCHOOL SYSTEM
Framework for Excellence in Guidance and Counseling

DOMAIN 1   **INTERPERSONAL SKILLS**

INDICATOR 1A   RELATES EFFECTIVELY WITH STUDENTS
Knowledge of students
Interactions with students
Communication skills

INDICATOR 1B   DEVELOPS COLLABORATIVE RELATIONSHIPS WITH ADMINISTRATIVE, TEACHING, AND SUPPORT STAFF
Respect and rapport
Communication skills
Conflict resolution

INDICATOR 1C   FOSTERS POSITIVE RELATIONSHIPS WITH FAMILIES AND COMMUNITY MEMBERS
Respect and rapport
Communication skills
Conflict resolution

DOMAIN 2   **PLANNING AND PREPARATION/MANAGEMENT**

INDICATOR 2A   DEMONSTRATES KNOWLEDGE OF GUIDANCE AND COUNSELING THEORY AND STRATEGIES
Content
Application in a school setting

INDICATOR 2B   DEMONSTRATES KNOWLEDGE OF STUDENTS
Developmental needs of students and characteristics of age groups
Students' varied approaches to learning
Students' skills and knowledge
Students' interests and cultural heritage

INDICATOR 2C   SELECTS APPROPRIATE COUNSELING/INSTRUCTIONAL GOALS
Value
Clarity

Indicator 2D   DEMONSTRATES KNOWLEDGE OF RESOURCES
Resources for counseling
Resources for student support

INDICATOR 2E   DESIGNS COHERENT COUNSELING/INSTRUCTION
Long/short term planning
Integrated with individual school improvement planning
Learning/informational activities
Counseling/instructional groups
Counseling/instructional materials and resources

(Continued)

FIGURE 12.9 (Continued)

INDICATOR 2F	ASSESSES STUDENTS' NEEDS EFFECTIVELY Prevention and intervention appropriate to specific grade levels Use in designing or modifying guidance program appropriately

DOMAIN 3	THE CLASSROOM ENVIRONMENT/SCHOOL ENVIRONMENT
INDICATOR 3A	ESTABLISHES A CULTURE FOR LEARNING Development of life skills and career connections Expectations for learning and achievement
INDICATOR 3B	MANAGES COUNSELING/CLASSROOM PROCEDURES EFFECTIVELY Managing counseling/instructional groups Managing materials and supplies Performing non-instructional duties Supervising volunteers and paraprofessionals
INDICATOR 3C	MANAGES STUDENT BEHAVIOR EFFECTIVELY Expectations Monitoring student behavior Response to student misbehavior
INDICATOR 3D	ORGANIZES PHYSICAL SPACE APPROPRIATELY Safety and accessibility Respect for confidentiality Welcoming and inviting environment

DOMAIN 4	DELIVERY OF INSTRUCTION/PROGRAM IMPLEMENTATION
INDICATOR 4A	COMMUNICATES CLEARLY AND ACCURATELY Directions and procedures Oral and written language
INDICATOR 4B	USES QUESTIONING AND DISCUSSION TECHNIQUES EFFECTIVELY Quality of questions Discussion techniques Student participation
INDICATOR 4C	ENGAGES STUDENTS IN LEARNING ACTIVITIES DIRECTED TO GUIDANCE GOALS (Comar 13A05050) AND STUDENT NEEDS Variety of guidance interventions Materials, activities, technology, and assignments Relevant and thoughtful applications Counseling/instructional groups Lesson/unit structure and pacing Transitions across grades/schools/community

270

FIGURE 12.9 (Continued)

INDICATOR 4D	PROVIDES EFFECTIVE FEEDBACK TO STUDENTS
	Quality: accurate, substantive, constructive, and specific
	Equitability
	Timeliness

INDICATOR 4E	DEMONSTRATES FLEXIBILITY AND RESPONSIVENESS
	Adjustment of counseling strategies
	Response to students
	Persistence

| DOMAIN 5 | PROFESSIONAL RESPONSIBILITIES |

INDICATOR 5A	REFLECTS ON GUIDANCE AND COUNSELING
	Accuracy
	Use in future guidance and counseling planning

INDICATOR 5B	SUPPORTS AND MAINTAINS ACCURATE RECORDS
	Record keeping
	Standards of confidentiality/security

INDICATOR 5C	COMMUNICATES WITH FAMILIES
	Information about the counseling/instructional program
	Information about individual students
	Opportunities for involvement in the counseling/instructional program
	School and community resources

INDICATOR 5D	SHOWS PROFESSIONALISM
	Student advocacy
	Collaborative problem solving
	Relationships with business and community
	Following federal, state, and local policies and procedures
	Adherence to the Code of Ethics of the American Counseling Association

INDICATOR 5E	GROWS AND DEVELOPS PROFESSIONALLY
	Enhancement of content knowledge and counseling skills
	Service to the school, district, and profession

Source: Reprinted by permission of the Howard County Public School System, Ellicott City, MD, 21042. Reproduction or use of this document without the written permission of Howard County Public Schools is expressly prohibited.

FIGURE 12.10
A sample performance appraisal using the ASCA School Counselor Performance Standards.

	Does Not Meet	Does Meet	Exceeds
Standard 1: The professional school counselor plans, organizes, and delivers the school counseling program.			
1.1 A program is designed to meet the needs of the school.			
1.2 The professional school counselor demonstrates interpersonal relationships with students.			
1.3 The professional school counselor demonstrates positive interpersonal relationships with educational staff.			
1.4 The professional school counselor demonstrates positive interpersonal relationships with parents or guardians.			
Standard 2: The professional school counselor implements the school guidance curriculum through the use of effective instructional skills and careful planning of structured group sessions for all students.			
2.1 The professional school counselor teaches school guidance units effectively.			
2.2 The professional school counselor develops materials and instructional strategies to meet student needs and school goals.			
2.3 The professional school counselor encourages staff involvement to ensure the effective implementation of the school guidance curriculum.			
Standard 3: The professional school counselor implements the individual planning component by guiding individuals and groups of students and their parents or guardians through the development of educational and career plans.			
3.1 The professional school counselor, in collaboration with parents or guardians, helps students establish goals and develop and use planning skills.			
3.2 The professional school counselor demonstrates accurate and appropriate interpretation of assessment data and the presentation of relevant, unbiased information.			
Standard 4: The professional school counselor provides responsive services through the effective use of individual and small-group counseling, consultation, and referral skills.			
4.1 The professional school counselor counsels individual students and small groups of students with identified needs and concerns.			
4.2 The professional school counselor consults effectively with parents or guardians, teachers, administrators, and other relevant individuals.			
4.3 The professional school counselor implements an effective referral process with administrators, teachers, and other school personnel.			

FIGURE 12.10 (Continued)

Standard 5: The professional school counselor provides system support through effective school counseling program management and support for other educational programs.			
5.1 The professional school counselor provides a comprehensive and balanced school counseling program in collaboration with school staff.			
5.2 The professional school counselor provides support for other school programs.			
Standard 6: The professional school counselor discusses the counseling department management system and the program action plans with the school administrator.			
6.1 The professional school counselor discusses the qualities of the school counselor management system with the other members of the counseling staff and has agreement.			
6.2 The professional school counselor discusses the program results anticipated when implementing the action plans for the school year.			
Standard 7: The professional school counselor is responsible for establishing and convening an advisory council for the school counseling program.			
7.1 The professional school counselor meets with the advisory committee.			
7.2 The professional school counselor reviews the school counseling program audit with the council.			
7.3 The professional school counselor records meeting information.			
Standard 8: The professional school counselor collects and analyzes data to guide program direction and emphasis.			
8.1 The professional school counselor uses school data to make decisions regarding student choice of classes and special programs.			
8.2 The professional school counselor uses data from the counseling program to make decisions regarding program revisions.			
8.3 The professional school counselor analyzes data to ensure every student has equity and access to a rigorous academic curriculum.			
8.4 The professional school counselor understands and uses data to establish goals and activities to close the gap.			

(Continued)

FIGURE 12.10 (Continued)

Standard 9: The professional school counselor monitors the students on a regular basis as they progress in school.			
9.1 The professional school counselor is accountable for monitoring every student's progress.			
9.2 The professional school counselor implements monitoring systems appropriate to the individual school.			
9.3 The professional school counselor develops appropriate interventions for students as needed and monitors their progress.			
Standard 10: The professional school counselor uses time and calendars to implement an efficient program.			
10.1 The professional school counselor uses a master calendar to plan activities throughout the year.			
10.2 The professional school counselor distributes the master calendar to parents or guardians, staff and students.			
10.3 The professional school counselor posts a weekly or monthly calendar.			
10.4 The professional school counselor analyzes time spent providing direct service to students.			
Standard 11: The professional school counselor develops a results evaluation for the program.			
11.1 The professional school counselor measures results attained from school guidance curriculum and closing the gap activities.			
11.2 The professional school counselor works with members of the counseling team and with the principal to clarify how programs are evaluated and how results are shared.			
11.3 The professional school counselor knows how to collect process, perception, and results data.			
Standard 12: The professional school counselor conducts a yearly program audit.			
12.1 The professional school counselor completes a program audit to determine the degrees to which the school counseling program is being implemented.			
12.2 The professional school counselor shares the results of the program audit with the advisory council.			
12.3 The professional school counselor uses the yearly audit to make changes in the school counseling program and calendar for the following year.			

FIGURE 12.10 (Continued)

Standard 13: The professional school counselor is a student advocate, leader, and collaborator and a systems change agent. 13.1 The professional school counselor promotes academic success of every student.			
13.2 The professional school counselor promotes equity and access for every student.			
13.3 The professional school counselor takes a leadership role within the counseling department, the school setting, and the community.			
13.4 The professional school counselor understands reform issues and works to close the achievement gap.			
13.5 The professional school counselor collaborates with teachers, parents, and the community to promote academic success of students.			
13.6 The professional school counselor builds effective teams by encouraging collaboration among all school staff.			
13.7 The professional school counselor uses data to recommend systemic change in policy and procedures that limit or inhibit academic achievement.			

Source: Adapted with permission from the American School Counselor Association. Further reproduction prohibited.

2 weeks each year taking several different standardized tests. Professional school counselors who manage schoolwide testing programs may hold any number of responsibilities, including:

- Prepare and monitor the schedule for test administration
- Keep the tests in a secure location
- Receive and return test protocols to the publisher for scoring
- Distribute and collect test protocols from the teachers or other test administrators
- Receive and disseminate student, class, and schoolwide score reports to stakeholder groups
- Ensure that standardized test administration procedures are adhered to
- Provide in-service training to teachers for test administration and interpretation
- Consult with administrators, teachers, parents, and students to interpret test scores

Professional school counselors also have the expertise to develop interviews, surveys, questionnaires, and needs assessments to fulfill a wide range of potential school information needs. They frequently serve as a communication coordinator between the school and community to ensure that accurate, understandable information is distributed. Counselors must follow ethical standards (see section E of the ACA *Code of Ethics* [2005a]) and fair testing practices, including the *Code of Fair Testing Practices* (2nd ed.; Joint Committee on Testing Practices, 2004) and *Responsibilities of Users of Standardized Tests* (RUST; AACE, 2004). Also, given the prominent role high-stakes testing plays in today's educational decision making, professional school counselors should be very familiar with the *ACA Position Statement on High Stakes Testing* (ACA, 2005b). In-depth understanding of each of these documents will prepare one to be a proactive advocate for students.

Several factors should be considered when launching or implementing a testing program. First, professional school counselors need to be clear about the purpose of all aspects of testing and understand the goals of their school's testing program. What information is needed about individual students or groups of students and how that information is to be used throughout the school and district will influence the choice of assessment instruments.

Second, it is good practice to create an advisory council to help establish policies and guidelines, interface with the public over controversial testing issues, and ethically oversee the use of assessment instruments. Constituents representing the school community and testing professionals may participate as council members.

Third, professional school counselors must adhere to the ethical standards of their profession. They must keep testing materials secure; monitor test use; and follow confidentiality, informed consent, and invasion of privacy guidelines. They should be aware of their own competence in the use of specific tests and not administer or interpret assessments beyond their level of training and knowledge. In addition, the use of computers presents unique challenges. Professional school counselors should be familiar with ethical considerations related to computer administration. Issues such as test scoring and reporting, interpretation, and access to tests available on the Internet need to be carefully weighed.

Fourth, monetary concerns must be considered. Developing an appropriate budget for purchasing assessment instruments is a key activity. Professional school counselors and administrators should have a consistent and routine system for purchasing and replenishing needed items.

Fifth, when deciding on assessment methods, professional school counselors should follow some basic steps in determining the appropriateness of a test for any particular situation. The following steps offer a useful guideline:

- *Study the technical manual.* When choosing any standardized instrument, the professional school counselor needs to evaluate its utility and the reliability and validity of scores. This means it is important to consider how the test developer has defined the construct it purports to test (achievement, aptitude, etc.) and to use the assessment only within that context. Does this instrument actually measure what it says it measures? Does it have strong empirical support for its validity?
- *Read test reviews.* Reviews of available instruments can be found in professional literature such as *Test Critiques, Tests in Print*, and Buros's *Mental Measurements Yearbook.*
- *Continually ask relevant questions.* Whether making decisions about quantitative or qualitative appraisal, the professional school counselor should always ask these questions: Does this instrument measure what I need to know about this student? Is it normed on a population appropriate for this client? Does the instrument measure the general or specific trait or characteristic in question? Does it have utility? Can its results be used to indicate a direction for intervention?

Effective management of the school testing program ensures the integration of assessment and program evaluation data into program decision making within the counseling program or throughout the school. It provides appropriate, responsible appraisal to meet student needs.

SUMMARY/CONCLUSION

Accountability involves the demonstration of responsibility for professional actions. An SCPAC is a diverse group of stakeholders and can be helpful in guiding the program in positive directions to understand and meet the needs of the school community. The SCPAC can also play an important role in securing resources and demonstrating accountability. Professional school counselors demonstrate accountability by providing evidence that answers five primary questions.

First, is a comprehensive, standards-based program in place? A program evaluation (or audit) should be conducted annually near the end of the school year to determine whether a written school counseling program is being fully implemented.

Second, what are the needs of the school's student population when compared to these standards? A needs assessment can be implemented using one of two primary methods. A data-driven needs assessment evaluates real needs demonstrated through derived information. Aggregated results are broken down (disaggregated) so they can be examined on the subgroup level. Such analysis is critical to demonstrate whether all students are given access to rigorous academic coursework and are benefiting from the curriculum. A perceptions-based needs assessment assesses what primary stakeholder groups (e.g., teachers, parents, students) perceive as needs. These perceptions can be gathered through a variety of methods, but some form of quantifiable result is preferred so that various perceived needs can be compared and prioritized.

Third, what services were implemented to address the identified needs and standards? A service assessment provides an accounting of who did what, how much, and for how long. This type of evidence is helpful in demonstrating that professional school counselors are using their time to provide valuable (or even not so valuable) services and is often requested by administration and school boards. Unfortunately, service assessment is more of a process evaluation (i.e., how one spends one's time) rather than an outcomes evaluation (i.e., what valuable result has occurred by spending one's time that way). In other words, time is a process variable. Results stem from the actions one performs given the precious commodity of time.

Fourth, what was the result of the implemented services? Some argue that results or outcomes studies are the most valuable facet of accountability. The assessment loop shows that the purpose of evaluation is continuous quality improvement. Data is collected to evaluate actions and interventions so that judgments can be made on the worth or value of services and programs. Often, traditional research designs can yield the most helpful and authoritative information about program or event quality. Because of the broad-ranging nature of standards and competencies, professional school counselors attempting to demonstrate the effectiveness of a developmental curriculum should use an aggregated hierarchical model in which evidence is collected at the objectives level to demonstrate whether higher order competencies and standards have been met.

Fifth, how well is the professional school counselor performing? As a condition of employment, professional school counselors undergo periodic performance evaluation or performance appraisal. The purpose of this process is to determine the performance of the individual rather than that of the program. Of course, if there is only one professional school counselor in the school, the individual appraisal often also reflects program quality. Professional school counselors should be aware of the evaluation criteria well in advance of any assessment, and such processes should be aimed at developing higher level counseling skills and competencies.

Accountability applies to every facet of a school counseling program. The better prepared a professional school counselor is to engage in accountability activities, continuously collect evidence, and report on program performance, the more valuable one is to the school, system, and profession. Being responsible for one's actions and the quality of services provided is an important ethical and professional responsibility.

ACTIVITIES

1. Develop a preliminary needs assessment for a school in your community. What type of method did you use (questionnaire, classroom visits, etc.)? What types of needs were addressed in your assessment?

How will this assessment influence the development of your program?

2. Interview a professional school counselor regarding the use of needs assessment. Ask to view a needs assessment recently given

and what learning objectives were derived from student responses.

3. Conduct a role-play with a partner in which you are the school counselor and your partner is an administrator. Using

assessment and accountability, convince the administrator that your school counseling program is an important aspect of student academic success.

COUNSELING YOUTH AT RISK

*BRADLEY T. ERFORD, DEBBIE W. NEWSOME, AND ELANA ROCK**

Editor's Introduction: Youth at risk for academic failure and personal–social problems present a substantial dilemma for schools, families, and communities. This dilemma also presents an extraordinary example of how the transformed professional school counselor can collaborate with and coordinate school and community organizations and resources to benefit these students in need. After a brief introduction recapping the state of affairs for youth at risk in America, a case is made for professional school counselors as "coordinators of interdisciplinary resources" to collaborate and develop partnerships with community agencies and organizations providing overlapping services with school personnel. Specialized issues in working with specific high-risk populations of students also will be introduced. Perhaps most important, professional school counselors must help educators support, rather than blame and punish, youth at risk.

THE CHANGING NEEDS OF STUDENTS AND FAMILIES

American society and the world in general have changed so much in the past few decades that educators at all levels have struggled to keep pace. While technological innovations and socially progressive movements have yielded many positive and exciting outcomes, the unintended consequences at times seem overwhelming. Rising levels of poverty, substance abuse, and domestic and community violence are but a few of the major problems affecting mental health during the latter half of the 20th century (Dryfoos, 1994; Lockhart & Keys, 1998; National Institutes of Health, 2005).

---

*The first edition chapter, "A New Perspective on Counseling At-Risk Youth," was written by Fred Bemak, Rita Chi-Ying Chung, and C. Sally Murphy. Much of their outstanding work on systemic approaches to working with at-risk youth was continued in this revised chapter.

Society's fast-paced changes have resulted in myriad mental health dilemmas. Consider but a few of the staggering statistics. The SAMHSA (1998) reported that 15% to 22% of all children and adolescents have significant emotional impairment requiring treatment, but only about one out of five of these affected children and adolescents actually receives treatment. This is a particularly critical statistic given that almost half of all students with emotional problems drop out of school (Institute of Medicine, 1997). The American Psychiatric Association (2000) estimated that clinical depression afflicts 3 to 6 million children, contributing to widespread social and emotional problems, including suicide. Suicide continues to be the third leading cause of death among American adolescents. More than 2,000 adolescents kill themselves each year, and approximately 10,000 to 20,000 adolescents attempt suicide annually (D. Brown, 1996). Finally, about 30% to 50% of school-aged children referred to community mental health agencies experience conduct problems and behavior disorders, the most common of which is ADHD, which is estimated to exist in 3% to 5% of school-aged children (APA, 2000). Many children with ADHD are served in the public schools either through special education or Section 504 of the U.S. Rehabilitation Act of 1973; they comprise a large subgroup of the more than 5 million students who annually receive special education services (Kupper, 1999; USDE, 2005).

All in all, there is an increasing trend toward mental and emotional problems among American students, perhaps stemming from rapid societal and technological changes. These problems have been compounded by government funding procedural changes and shortages of affordable community-based mental health services (Keys & Bemak, 1997; Luongo, 2000; NIMH, 2005). As so often has been the case, governments and citizens have turned to the schools to help resolve societal difficulties. Fortunately, professional school counselors can play an essential role in the amelioration of many of these mental health concerns.

Twenty-first-century society has the potential to learn from the past and improve on what has been done in previous centuries. This is especially true given technological innovations, globalization, dramatic improvements in health care, economic prosperity, and increased consciousness about cultural diversity. Yet, U.S. reports continue to show increasing numbers of youth who are alienated and disconnected from the positive aspects and opportunities of society and have difficult and negative experiences in schools, communities, and families. The result is an increasing quantity of youth who are struggling to mature and develop into contributing members of society.

In previous decades, youth at risk in the United States were identified as socially and culturally deprived, with a focus on impoverished and minority youth who were labeled as disadvantaged. As the realization dawned on policy makers and professionals working with youth, families, communities, and schools that children and adolescents at risk came from all socioeconomic classes and ethnic and racial backgrounds, the characterization of this population changed to include those youth identified as disengaged and not connected to mainstream institutions and society at large. They were not just the minority or urban poor students, but originated in urban, suburban, and rural neighborhoods, were rich and poor, were immigrants and native born, had one or two parents living at home, and came from any racial and ethnic background. They came from the best schools and communities that the United States had to offer, as well as the poorest, most decayed neighborhoods, which resembled war-torn zones in the most impoverished countries in the world. Anyone could be exposed to community, school, and family violence; family dysfunction; drugs and alcohol; teenage suicide; or problems with peers. It is critical to understand that in America, at-risk youth have no boundaries. Given the growing numbers of these youth, despite numerous programs to address their problems, it is clear that overall intervention and prevention strategies have been limited in their success.

The ASCA (2003a) *National Model* proposes that the academic, career, and personal–social needs of all children be addressed through comprehensive school counseling programs that focus on systemic change, advocacy, leadership, and collaboration. Helping to address the needs of children at risk requires sound foundational skills in each of these primary areas. This chapter begins by defining *at risk,* followed by a review of demographics and a presentation of current perspectives and policy implications. The chapter goes on to review some new, innovative, and culturally responsive strategies for working with at-risk youth, and it examines reasons why the needs of this population have not been fully addressed, discusses the accountability for program failure, and provides systemic recommendations for professional school counselors working with at-risk youth. Finally, the chapter provides information for working with specific subpopulations of youth at risk, multicultural implications, and transition issues across grade levels.

WHO ARE YOUTH AT RISK?

Although attempts to address at-risk youth have been long-standing, remarkably as we begin the 21st century, there is still ongoing debate and controversy over defining this population. Professionals view the term *at risk* differently. For example, mental health professionals identify *at risk* with adjustment and emotional problems, medical professionals view it in terms of health issues, law enforcement officials describe it as crime related, educators relate the term to dropouts and failing students, businesses see at-risk youth as youth without the requisite skills for successful job performance, and sociologists and public health workers link the term to deteriorating communities. The dictionary defines *at risk* as someone "in a dangerous situation or status; in jeopardy" (*Random House Dictionary,* 1987, p. 1660). Educators, mental health workers, and government agencies relate the term more specifically to children who have a high probability of failing in school due to multiple risk factors (Kagan & Gall, 1998).

Dryfoos (1990, 1998) broadened the definition of *at risk* to attribute the more serious problems of youth to harmful social conditions such as high levels of poverty, career limitations, racial hatred and discrimination, urban chaos, and increasing alienation in rural communities, claiming that specific problems of at-risk youth are interrelated rather than distinctly separate. This definition has been substantiated and elaborated to include

behaviors such as violence, gang membership, and substance abuse, as well as the issues of crime, school dropouts, and poor academic performance (Morley & Rossman, 1998). A different dimension was added by McWhirter, McWhirter, McWhirter, and McWhirter (1998), who proposed that being at risk involves past events that lead to problematic future behaviors. Hazler and Denham (2002) even went so far as to define at-risk youth as those young people who feel isolated from their culture, society, school, family, and peers.

The Improving America's Schools Act (U.S. House of Representatives, 1994) expanded the definition of *at-risk youth* beyond schools, stating,

> [S]chool-aged youth who are at-risk of academic failure, have drug or alcohol problems, are pregnant or are parents, have come into contact with the juvenile justice system in the past, are at least one year behind the expected grade level for the age of the youth, have limited-English proficiency, are gang members, have dropped out of school in the past, or have high absenteeism rates at school. (H. R. 6, Sec. 1434, p. 2)

This definition includes youth both inside and outside of the school environment. Compatible with this definition, Dryfoos (1996) found that one third of our teenagers are at extremely high risk due to participation in multiple at-risk behaviors, and suggested an examination of common antecedents or at-risk factors to determine a child's risk level. The six categories of common antecedents provide a framework for addressing the issues of at-risk youth and include: parental effects, school experience, peer influences, mental health, poverty neighborhood, and race and ethnicity (Dryfoos, 1996). Although a framework for understanding at-risk youth has been proposed, there is still no one definition inclusive enough to consider all the parameters necessary for a culturally responsive approach to addressing the needs of children at risk. Since the definition of *at risk* has a significant bearing on when and how the term is used, hence the type of services provided, the following guidelines are offered rather than a definition.

Youth are considered at risk when they lack the familial, community, cultural, institutional, and societal supports necessary to develop and grow in an environment that is safe, positive, healthy, and conducive to personal, social, cultural, intellectual, spiritual, economic, and physical development. The absence of these supports inhibits the potential for development as a person, and the potential for choices and opportunities necessary to contribute as a productive member of society. Healthy growth and development for youth must include the context of the family and other social networks; environment; health and nutrition; opportunities for spiritual development; and a positive interaction with the surrounding community, society, and culture within which one lives. The quality of a child's or adolescent's physical, mental, emotional, social, spiritual, and economic health significantly correlates to being at risk; therefore, prevention and intervention program design and implementation must include a holistic framework.

PROBLEMS CATEGORIZING AT-RISK YOUTH

Five potential problem areas are identified when categorizing youth at risk. First, when using this term, there is a danger of discounting resiliency. Potential strengths, coping abilities, and strategies for handling the variables that constitute being at risk are disregarded with the shift in focus to pathology, problems, and weaknesses. Second, the label "at risk" has strong negative associations and stigmatizes youth. Chances of moving out of at-risk status are nominal, leaving many youth labeled for their entire childhood and adolescence. Third, when youth are identified as being at risk during adolescence, the prospect of being at risk is no longer a question but becomes a fact. This leaves far less opportunity for designing prevention programs that would impact on the youths' future, given the permanency associated with the label being designated during adolescence. It determines that being at risk, in essence, means "deep trouble," which has implications for how we regard, treat, and conceive of this population. A fourth problem with categorizing youth at risk is that the term has been used as a catchall phrase that does not differentiate the risk level one is facing or the conditions, causes, or problem

behaviors associated with that risk. This generalization of the term does not help in defining the problems or the strategies best employed to address them. Fifth, there is no sensitivity to or awareness of cultural differences related to at-risk behavior. For example, some cultures (including various cultural minorities in the United States) have far greater tolerance for youth behaviors than other cultures do. This has been differentiated as "broad socialization" or more open and tolerant practices that minimize social constraints, versus "narrow socialization," where obedience and conformity to community norms are demanded, thus reducing experimentation and sensation-seeking behaviors (Arnett & Balle-Jensen, 1993).

Cultures were further differentiated as child centered and not child centered by Rohner (as cited in Bretherton, 1985). In child-centered cultures, there is greater acceptance of children and support in developing personal, family, and community social skills within a social context, resulting in youth demonstrating higher levels of achievement and greater self-reliance. In contrast, non-child-centered cultures prioritize individuality over the family and community at large and have less tolerance for children. In non-child-centered cultures, children are shown to be more aggressive, to feel rejected and disengaged more often, and, subsequently, to be more independent. In turn, the adults in non-child-centered cultures exhibit greater hostility and less compassion for people in need, and their response to problems is in a reactive crisis mode that many of the schools, communities, and families in the United States face today. These problems contribute to confusion in characterizing and identifying at-risk youth and are reflected in the lack of effective programming to reduce problems such as teenage pregnancy, substance abuse, violence, juvenile delinquency, gangs, school dropout, and school failure.

APPROACHES TO WORKING WITH AT-RISK YOUTH

Historically, the definition of at risk has been based on one of four approaches: predictive, descriptive, unilateral, or school factors, with each approach having its flaws (Hixson & Tinzmann, 1990). For example, the predictive approach is based on a deficit model that emphasizes what is wrong or missing in the individual student, family, or community. The descriptive method focuses on after-the-fact reporting and, therefore, addresses the issue after the behavior has occurred. The unilateral technique assumes that all students are at risk by virtue of living in today's society. Finally, the school factors approach states that schools are solely accountable and therefore absolves parents of any responsibility.

To further illustrate inherent problems in defining youth at risk, look more closely at the categorization of individuals at risk solely by the criteria of academic achievement and success. When considering the large and growing number of immigrant and refugee students entering the United States, it is increasingly apparent that psychosocial adjustment, acculturation, and psychological well-being are not reflected solely by academic performance. Yet when "at-riskedness" is standardized and measured by academic success, it is not reflective of the complex and demanding issues faced by this population (Bemak & Chung, 2002). Designating immigrant and refugee students or any students at risk by virtue of their academic success automatically limits the area of concern to schools, neglecting other aspects of the student's life, rather than examining the issues within a social context that would include collaboration with parents, community agencies, businesses, and government agencies. This, in turn, places the onus of responsibility for intervention and prevention strictly on school personnel, leading to the conclusion that being at risk is related only to the confines of the brick and mortar of a school building. These assumptions are not only misleading, but also egregiously incorrect.

DEMOGRAPHICS AND RISK

Demographic data confirm the current status of youth at risk. For example, recent data show the powerful impact of peers on these youth (National Center for Chronic Disease Prevention

and Health Promotion, 2000; National Institute of Mental Health [NIMH], 1999). Data from the NIMH (1999) National Youth Survey demonstrate that association with delinquent peers precedes the initiation and progression of serious violent offenses for all ethnic minority groups. The results revealed that more than 50% of the participants exhibited violent behavior that began between the ages of 14 and 17, with a substantial number beginning as young as age 12.

The National Center for Chronic Disease Prevention and Health Promotion (2000) reported behavioral trends for at-risk youth, providing data from 1991 to 1999 on the evolution of risk behaviors. The number of children using tobacco, some on a daily basis, rose nearly 5% from 1993 to 1999. The continued use of alcohol or other drugs among youth is also on the rise. For example, lifetime marijuana use rose from over 30% in 1991 to more than 47% in 1999. Students using cocaine went from under 2% in 1991 to 4% in 1999. Males (57%) were more likely than females (47%) to drink alcohol or smoke marijuana (42% vs. 33%, respectively), while African American (33%) and Hispanic (50%) high school seniors reported a lower rate of drug and alcohol use than European Americans (58%). Thirty percent of African American youth reported using marijuana compared to 40% of their White counterparts (Juvenile Offenders and Victims National Report, 1999). It is obvious from this data that increasing numbers of youth are purchasing, using, and under the influence of drugs and seeking drug-related forms of diversion, evidence that current programs are not reaching large numbers of youth.

Although the data suggest that some risk behaviors are increasing, other risk behaviors are on the decline. For instance, the percentage of students who reported riding with a drunk driver declined from 40% to 33%. The number of students who reported carrying a gun to school also declined from just under 8% to nearly 5%. Students who carried a weapon onto school property declined from just under 12% in 1993 to less than 7% in 1999. Even with the improvements, these statistics still present a significant problem: 7% of a school with 1,500 students means that 105 students may harbor weapons on school grounds. The same holds true for the 7% of high school students who reported being threatened or injured with a weapon at school (Juvenile Offenders and Victims National Report, 1999).

Risk behaviors outside of school remain a serious problem that affects school performance. Underage and premarital sex remains a high-risk behavior. In 1991, just over 50% of youth under the age of 18 reported they had had sexual intercourse. Additionally, 16% of these adolescents had four or more sexual partners. Other data point toward a substantial number of youth who are considering suicide. Although the percentage of adolescents who admitted they considered suicide declined from 29% in 1991 to just over 19% in 1999, the figure still hovers at around one fifth of the youth population. Of particular concern are female Hispanic adolescents, who in 1995 reported suicide attempt rates at 15%, compared to less than 8% of the total high school student population (Centers for Disease Control and Prevention, 1999).

Statistics show that most juvenile crime takes place between the hours of 2:00 p.m. and 8:00 p.m. Aggravated assaults by juveniles are most common around 3:00 p.m., directly after school; adolescents are at greater risk of being victims during after-school hours as well. Robberies perpetrated by juveniles peak at 9:00 p.m. Statistics also show that one in five violent crimes involving juvenile victims occurs between the hours of 3:00 p.m. and 7:00 p.m. on school days (Office of Juvenile Justice and Delinquency Prevention, 1999).

WORKING WITH ALL YOUTH

Working with at-risk youth cuts across several disciplines, including mental health, education, public health, substance abuse, business, social services, juvenile justice, and child and family services. Many professionals working within these various systems are disheartened by failures to reach at-risk youth. They are frustrated, burned-out, and even angry at the lack of responsiveness to honest intervention attempts. These attitudes frequently result in schools, programs, and society giving up on those youth in

most need and in trouble. In fact, a culture has emerged that blames the child in more subtle and sophisticated ways and molds itself into a 21st-century version of "blaming the victim." This defeatist attitude is observed in principals and other educators who want certain children out of their school, programs that identify children and adolescents as "too difficult" to benefit from their good services, families that are labeled and stigmatized as "unreachable," and neglected communities that are considered dangerous and "too far gone."

These negative attitudes toward at-risk youth are fueling the trend toward containment, punishment, and banishment rather than treatment and prevention. The emphasis is on a "quick fix" rather than an in-depth examination of the problem from family, community, and societal perspectives. For example, Americans are more concerned with metal detectors than community prevention models, as demonstrated after the flurry of public school shootings in different parts of the United States (Keys & Bemak, 1997). The emphasis on punishment not only results in resentment and disregard toward the disenfranchised youth of today, but also marginalizes and segregates youth for whom there is little hope and on whom society has essentially given up. This is a dangerous proposition and will ultimately result in disenfranchised youth who are at risk of leading difficult and frustrating lives and who lack the skills and knowledge to participate in society in healthy, positive ways. Even more alarming is that a significant number of these youth will contribute to growing social problems and become an economic and social burden in the country.

Contrary to this subtle but growing movement, is the contention that all children can be reached (Bemak, 1997). But, this requires a dramatic step in redefining the programs to fit the changing needs of youth in trouble. Rather than reject and abandon youth who do not respond to traditional programs, it is critical that professionals develop new and innovative strategies for working with families, communities, and schools to reach those children now regarded as unreachable. This requires support on multiple levels: new ways of training professionals at the university level to work with at-risk youth; innovative programming that goes beyond what we currently propose; policy changes; an emphasis on prevention and intervention rather than crisis management; interdisciplinary cooperation to address the complexity of the problems that at-risk youth face (Bemak & Keys, 2000); and a shift in attitude from control and punishment to intervention and prevention. Underlying this support is the firm belief and hope in the dignity and possibility of each child and adolescent.

SYSTEMS FAILURES: WHO IS TO BLAME?

There are a large number of facilities in the United States that have the potential to effectively serve at-risk youth. For example, there are 85,000 public and 25,000 private elementary and secondary schools; 400 national organizations (e.g., Boy Scouts, 4H, YMCA, etc.); 17,000 community-based programs; and 6,000 libraries, recreational centers, and police departments that provide programs for youth (Dryfoos, 1998). Even so, schools today, despite valiant efforts to prevent school dropout, still encounter a 6% dropout rate in urban areas and a 4% rate in suburban areas (U.S. Bureau of Census, 1999). The inability to reach these students reflects the inadequacy of programming strategies rather than a belief that these students are hopeless and won't respond to programming.

For a number of years, at-risk youth have been blamed for their problems, whether done consciously or more subtly. The general consensus has been that youth fail our programs rather than programs fail our youth. This has perpetuated a system of hopelessness and acceptance of failure and directly contradicts a reevaluation of current prevention and intervention methodologies that have a substantial rate of failure yet continue to be funded. We contend that youth do not fail, but that programs and systems have a long-standing record of failing at-risk youth. By blaming children and adolescents who are already powerless, programs are not only negligent in protecting our youth, but also add to and perpetuate the existing problems faced by this population. If we truly want to help our youth

engage in future opportunities, we can no longer blame the youth but must critically evaluate our intervention strategies and admit that they may not be effective; at the same time, we must move beyond the blame and work to redesign successful interventions.

To address the complexity of problems that interrelate with youth, peer groups, family, school, and community, it is critical that we not only reexamine our current strategies, but also redesign and develop new workable interventions. Advocates have strongly argued for service integration (e.g., Bemak, 1998; Bemak, 2000; Keys & Bemak, 1997; Keys, Bemak, & Lockhart, 1998; Lerner, 1995; Taylor & Adelman, 2000), given the complexity of interrelated problems facing at-risk youth, rather than addressing discrete problem areas. Many programs and interventions with at-risk youth focus on problem areas that are categorized by distinct behaviors. This results in intensive and expensive programs that are aimed at specific issues such as substance abuse, teenage pregnancy, anger management, juvenile delinquency, school failure, or suicide risk.

Programs that are narrow in focus and aim to address isolated problems fail the youth in need of services. It is important to adapt intervention strategies to the complex needs of the target population from the perspective of an interagency response that is not limited to schools. Furthermore, professional school counselors are in a pivotal position to lead this endeavor, given that they are based in schools. Schools have the potential to be the focal point for all youth during childhood and adolescence.

WHY HAVEN'T NEEDS OF AT-RISK STUDENTS BEEN ADDRESSED?

There are five major reasons for the lack of commitment to the needs of at-risk youth. First, funding priorities have not been focused on this population within the broader context of multiple problems. Funding of intervention and prevention programs must be reevaluated, and cross-disciplinary, research-based, interagency funding must be supported. Simplifying the problems of at-risk youth into discrete categories is insufficient, yet many funding initiatives remain limited in scope or breadth. Second, it is difficult to change systems. Professional school counselors and other professionals should study systems change theory and practice, learning how to move resistant systems that are set in their ways. Third, the nation does not have a consensual moral commitment to working with this population. As discussed previously, the current national trend in the United States emphasizes punishment and excommunication from one's community or society rather than intervention strategies that aim to reengage youth into mainstream cultures.

A fourth reason for the lack of commitment to at-risk youth is the absence of societal, institutional, and community commitment to address these problems for a disengaged and essentially powerless population. Neither is there a true commitment reflected in school, state, and federal policies. For example, schools that are measured by student performance on standardized tests may prefer that problem students in jeopardy of failing those exams transfer to another school or leave school entirely. Essentially, this translates into education for some of our students, not all. Finally, graduate-level university training of professionals often lacks innovation and responsiveness to addressing modern-day concerns with at-risk youth as part of the curriculum. This can be seen in training for professional school counselors, which rarely focuses specifically on the at-risk population in courses such as career counseling, group counseling, individual counseling, family counseling, and human growth and development, or during practicum and internships when counselors in training have the opportunity to work in agencies that serve this population.

POLICY IMPLICATIONS

Federal and state policies often define the work that is done with children who are at risk. In turn, policies are instituted with program initiatives at the federal and state levels, such as through the federal or state departments of education or the NIMH or state departments of mental health. Although many policies affect youth at risk, we will discuss only a few that affect this population.

One example of major federal legislation was passed in 1965—the ESEA. The ESEA, which is renewed every 5 years, is the primary law that supports continuing public education (kindergarten through Grade 12) in the United States, with a specific focus on the war on poverty. The first amendment to that bill, Title I: Helping Disadvantaged Children Meet High Standards, provides the authority needed to address the issues surrounding children who are at risk of failing to learn, and Title IV speaks directly to the issues of safe and drug-free schools. A subsection of Title X ensures that children are adequately cared for before and after school hours. All of these policies have direct implications for youth at risk.

Another example of government intervention focused on the need to provide support personnel within the academic environment. Only a few states had established school counseling programs as part of their school system by the mid-1950s (Aubrey, 1977). In reaction to the Soviet *Sputnik* launch, the U.S. government passed the 1958 NDEA to authorize school counseling jobs nationwide. Historically, professional school counselors had been directed to help students focus on vocational training. After the launch of *Sputnik*, the United States instituted school counseling jobs to help guide students to math and science fields to keep up with the Soviets (Baker, 2000). NDEA directed a total of $1.5 million a year for secondary school counseling programs to encourage students to develop their aptitudes and attend college or postsecondary training, while providing funding to colleges and universities to train new professional school counselors. Today, professional school counselors are embedded in the U.S. educational system and have the potential to assume leadership roles in working with at-risk youth.

Forty years later, in 1999, Senator Tom Harkin (D-Iowa) introduced to the Senate the Elementary and Secondary Counseling Improvement Act [S. 1443], aimed at designing model school counseling programs to reduce the risk of academic, social, and emotional problems among elementary and secondary school children. This bill proposed authorization of $100 million to hire and train professional school counselors. It listed research findings that addressed the societal stress under which children now live, including fragmentation of the family, drug and alcohol abuse, violence, child abuse, and poverty. Additionally, the bill recommended a reduced ratio of professional school counselors to students of 1:250, which is dramatically lower than current figures cited in the bill, where national averages were 1:531 for elementary and secondary schools. The 106th U.S. Congress closed with no action taken on this bill. However, it is noteworthy that as the United States entered the new millennium, a proposed policy was under discussion illuminating the potential dangers for children at risk.

WORKING WITH SPECIFIC AT-RISK POPULATIONS

There are many issues that lead students to struggle academically or emotionally. This section identifies and addresses several of the more prominent issues that professional school counselors must prepare themselves to address, including crisis intervention, suicide, school violence, substance abuse, divorce, teen pregnancy, and delinquency. This list is by no means comprehensive, nor is the treatment given to each topic in this chapter. What follows is meant to educate and provide some strategies for assessing or intervening with students experiencing these issues.

Responding to Crisis Situations

During the past 2 decades, there has been a heightened awareness of the need for crisis intervention in schools. Crises in schools can affect a single student, a small group of students, or the entire school. Experiences of violence, disaster, and any form of trauma can leave students without the sufficient resources needed to cope. Crises that may affect the school community include suicide, loss, medical emergencies, family trauma, school shootings, gang activities, abuse, and natural disasters (e.g., hurricanes, floods, earthquakes, tornadoes). Professional school

counselors play a key role in planning and implementing crisis response in schools. Consequently, professional school counselors need to understand what constitutes a crisis, know how to intervene effectively, and be able to help implement a response plan to schoolwide crises (ASCA, 2000; D. B. Brown & Trusty, 2005).

Definition of Crisis

The term *crisis* has been defined in many ways (e.g., James & Gilliland, 2001). The Chinese characters that represent *crisis* mean both "danger" and "opportunity." A crisis represents danger because it initially is experienced as an intolerable difficulty that threatens to overwhelm the individual. Unless the person obtains relief, the crisis potentially can cause severe psychological, cognitive, physical, and behavioral consequences (James & Gilliland, 2001). In contrast, the term represents opportunity because during times of crisis, individuals are usually more receptive to help. Prompt, skillful interventions not only may prevent the development of sustained problems, but also may help individuals develop new coping patterns, thereby increasing their ability to adapt and function in the future.

The concept of crisis is not simple or straightforward. With all crises, stress is a major component (Steigerwald, 2004a). However, individuals experience stress in different ways, with some students having stronger coping skills, resources, and support systems than others. An event that is perceived as relatively minor by one student, such as failing an exam or being "dumped" by a girlfriend, may be perceived as a crisis by another student. Also, the timing and intensity of the crisis, as well as the number of other stressors the student is experiencing, can impact the complexity of the crisis situation (Gladding & Newsome, 2004).

Crisis Intervention

Crisis intervention differs from counseling in several ways. Crisis intervention refers to the immediate action a professional school counselor takes to "provide the support and direction that the student in crisis cannot provide for him or herself"

(Steigerwald, 2004a, pp. 830–831). It is an action-oriented approach designed to help students cope with a particular life situation that has thrown them off course. Goals of crisis intervention include helping the student to defuse emotions, organize, and interpret what has happened; to integrate the traumatic event into his or her life story; and to interpret the event in a way that is meaningful (Bauer et al., 2000). Crisis intervention is time limited and should not be confused with more long-term postcrisis counseling, which may be needed and which usually necessitates referral to other helping professionals.

Trusty and Brown (2005, pp. 312–313) and Steigerwald (2004b, p. 840) suggested several guidelines for school counselors to follow in crisis counseling. These are summarized in Table 13.1.

Crisis Response Plans

At times, a crisis affects a large number of students, and a systematic response from the school is required (ASCA, 2000; Trusty & Brown, 2005). Examples of crises that may dictate a systemic response include student homicide or suicide, unexpected death, and natural disasters. Although crises are, unfortunately, an uncontrollable aspect of school life, the manner in which school professionals respond to crisis can be controlled. Professional school counselors often play leadership roles in helping schools develop and implement a systemic crisis plan, which is comprehensive, well planned, mobilizes resources, and operates quickly (Steigerwald, 2004b).

Crisis response plans should exist on both a district level and on an individual-school level. Professional school counselors may be members

TABLE 13.1
Crisis counseling guidelines.

1. *Respond immediately.* The longer students wait for counseling to occur, the more difficult it is to cope with the crisis.

2. *Be directive at first.* Environmental interventions may be necessary, especially when there are safety concerns. Being directive and caring provides structure, predictability, safety, and comfort to the students.

3. *Listen actively and nonjudgmentally as students tell their stories.* Attempt to view the crisis from their perspective. Pay close attention to feelings and help normalize them. Emotions typically associated with crisis include confusion, sadness, loss of control, loss of self-worth, stigma, loneliness, fear of mortality, guilt, and anger.

4. *Follow a holistic approach.* Observe and assess the physical, behavioral, emotional, and cognitive domains of the student in crisis.

5. *Begin work where the student is experiencing the most impairment.*

6. *Get the facts surrounding the crisis.* The counselor needs to understand the situation to assess the student's reactions.

7. *Sustain relationships and resources.* Help students keep lines of communication open and use family, peer, school, and community resources for support. Watch for isolation behavior.

8. *Keep a multicultural awareness of the student's expressions of emotions, perspectives, and behaviors.*

9. *Do not offer false reassurance.* Students who have experienced crises face difficult tasks. Work toward generating realistic hope.

10. *Help students take action.* Helping students move from the victim role to the actor role is a key component of crisis counseling.

11. *Determine whether the effects are long-lasting and whether a referral for further assessment and counseling is needed.*

12. *Do not work in isolation.* Involve the student's support system and work with a consultant or supervisor.

13. *Continue to develop knowledge and skills in crisis intervention by reading current literature about the topic and by participating in crisis training workshops.* Such workshops are sponsored by the American Red Cross and the National Organization for Victim Assistance (NOVA).

of the district and school critical response teams or solely members of the school-level response team. In either case, the professional school counselor takes a leadership role in the prevention, intervention, and postincident support of school critical responses (ASCA, 2000). In this role, professional school counselors provide individual and group counseling; consult with administrators, teachers, parents, and professionals; and coordinate services within the school and the community (ASCA, 2000; Allen et al., 2002).

Crisis plans need to be put in place before a crisis occurs. Crisis response planning committees and crisis response teams (CRTs) are instrumental in planning for, coordinating, and implementing a systemic crisis response. Gilliland and James (2004) recommended the following minimum requirements for a school crisis plan:

- *Physical requirements:* Identify locations for temporary counseling offices. An operations/communications center should be identified where crisis intervention procedures are monitored, needs are assessed, and information for the media is disseminated. Also suggested are a break room, a first-aid room, and an information center designed to handle media personnel and to facilitate parent communication.
- *Logistics:* Address specific areas that need consideration as an intervention plan is implemented. For example, attention needs to be given to the manner in which on-site and off-site communication will take place. Other logistics that need attention include providing (a) procedural checklists to ensure that the intervention plan is being followed, (b) building plans for emergency personnel, and (c) food and drink for crisis personnel.
- *Crisis response:* A sequential plan for crisis response includes gathering and verifying the facts, assessing the impact of the crisis to determine what assistance is needed, providing triage assessment to determine who is most in need of immediate attention, providing psychological first aid as a first-order response, having a model in place, providing crisis intervention, and following through by briefing, debriefing, and demobilizing. (pp. 553–558)

It is essential for professional school counselors to be familiar with their district and school

crisis response plan. If no such plan is in place, professional school counselors will want to work with administrators and other school personnel to create and implement a plan to respond to crisis. Moreover, professional school counselors can be instrumental in leading workshops in the school and community to communicate the plan to others. A helpful resource that provides information and guidance for crisis planning is the *Crisis Communications Guide and Toolkit* (www.nea.org/crisis), produced by the National Education Association (NEA, 2002).

Suicide

Suicide is a real problem in schools, particularly high schools, and professional school counselors need to be prepared to assess suicidal ideation, behaviors, and risk as well as be ready to intervene decisively. As discussed in chapter 4, some states and many school systems require that professional school counselors inform parents or guardians of students demonstrating suicidal thoughts or behaviors. One is well advised to take all threats seriously and be very familiar with state laws and regulations as well as local school system policies and procedures. Although the next section focuses on assessment of suicidal threat, a comprehensive explanation of how to intervene in cases of student suicidal threat is well beyond the scope of this book. While the student is in the school, it is common practice to be sure the student is in the company of an adult at all times and that contact is made with a parent or guardian as soon as possible. Many school systems require that the parent pick the child up from school. Professional counselors can be valuable consultants to parents, facilitating transitions to treatment with mental health professionals, community agencies, or psychiatric inpatient facilities. Professional school counselors are well advised to find out the scope of avilable community services available to students in crisis to develop a referral network that can be acted on instantaneously.

Assessing Suicidal Ideation and Behaviors

Professional school counselors should pay close attention to student suicidal ideation and behaviors during an initial interview and revisit the issue periodically during the course of treatment. Nearly all suicides are avoidable. A current and thorough understanding of the prevalence statistics across population demographics is essential to effective practice. A brief presentation can be found in Table 13.2, and professional counselors are encouraged to delve more deeply into this area of the literature.

Predicting who will attempt suicide is extremely difficult, which is why experienced professional school counselors take every client with suicidal ideation very seriously. Depressed, suicidal students may appear at minimal risk one day and the next day may experience a situational, environmental stressor or a frustrating, negative interpersonal encounter that leads to an attempted suicide. D. C. Clark and Fawcett (1992) reported that 57% to 86% of suicides are related to depression and alcoholism, so pay particularly close attention to students with these conditions, with expressions of hopelessness and helplessness being key indicators.

In addition to assessing risk of suicide, professional school counselors should also assess for resiliency and protective factors, activities, or people in a student's life that provide responsibilities, meaning, and hope for the student (Sanchez, 2001). Such factors may include significant supportive relationships (e.g., parents or relatives, friends, coworkers) or purpose (e.g., work or school, caregiving responsibilities).

When assessing suicidal risk, it is essential to determine both the existence and intensity of suicidal thoughts and behaviors and respond quickly and decisively with a treatment plan to immediately address student needs and safety. Table 13.3 presents the seven areas Stelmacher (1995) recommended as the focus during an interview for determining suicidal risk.

Several instruments have been published that professional school counselors may find useful adjuncts to the interview when assessing suicidal ideation and behaviors. These include the Suicide Probability Scale (SPS, Cull & Gill, 1992), Beck

TABLE 13.2
Demographic parameters, clinical conditions, and suicide risk.

Suicide is the 11th leading cause of death in the United States.

Suicide is the 3rd leading cause of death in the 15–24-year-old range and the 7th leading cause of death in the 5–14-year-old range.

Females are more likely to attempt suicide; males are more likely to complete a suicide attempt, generally because they choose more lethal means (e.g., guns).

73% of all suicides are completed by White males. Of these, the highest prevalence occurs in the over-85-year-old category.

Married clients are at lower risk of suicide than single, divorced, or widowed clients.

Parents responsible for minor children are at lower risk.

Individuals who have attempted suicide are more likely to make future attempts.

Clients with depression who have experienced a recent loss (e.g., divorce, separation) are at greater risk of suicide.

Certain personality factors may increase risk (e.g., perfectionism, impulsivity, pessimism, aloofness, dependency).

Clients with personality disorders (e.g., Borderline PD, Antisocial PD) account for about one third of completed suicides.

Firearms account for nearly one half of all suicides. Hanging, strangulation, and suffocation are the next three most lethal means. Taking most poisons and medications have low levels of lethality.

Of counselors in professional practice, about 70% have treated a client who attempted suicide, and 28% had a client who committed suicide.

Source: Statistics from "America's Children: Parents Report Estimated 2.7 Million Children with Emotional and Behavioral Problems," by the National Institute of Mental Health, 2005, retrieved on September 2, 2005, from www.nimh.nih.gov/healthinformation/childhood_indicators.cfm

TABLE 13.3
Seven facets of suicidal risk determination and some related brief, important queries.

1. *Verbal communication.* Has the student verbalized suicidal thoughts overtly or subtly? Are there themes of escape, self-mutilation, or self-punishment? Has the student ever thought of hurting herself?

2. *Plan.* Does the student have a plan or idea about how he may kill himself? Is the plan concrete, detailed, and specific? Is it feasible? Does it contain provisions to prevent rescue?

3. *Method.* Has the student chosen a specific method of self-harm? Firearms are the most lethal and commonly used method by students who complete suicide.

4. *Preparation.* Has the student obtained the means to carry out the plan? Has he written a note or contacted others to resolve old business, put finances in order, given away possessions, or "said good-bye"? Preparation is a good index of the seriousness of a suicidal attempt.

5. *Stressors.* What are the student's past, present, and future stressors (e.g., loss, employment, illness)? What are important loss-related anniversary dates?

6. *Mental state.* What is the student's degree of hopelessness? Is the student impulsive, using alcohol, or both? Is the student despondent, angry, or distraught? Particular concern is warranted during periods of remission (e.g., uplifted spirits) because this may indicate a decision to commit suicide was made and the plan is progressing.

7. *Hopelessness.* What is the student's level of perceived hopelessness? To what degree is death viewed as the only way to relieve pain? This area is particularly important to assess when students do not verbalize suicidal thoughts.

Source: Based on "Assessing Suicidal Clients," by Z. T. Stelmacher, in *Clinical Personality Assessment: Practical Approaches,* edited by J. N. Butcher, 1995, New York: Oxford University Press, pp. 336–379.

Scale for Suicide Ideation (BSSI; Beck & Steer, 1991), Beck Hopelessness Scale (BHS; Beck & Steer, 1993), and Suicide Ideation Questionnaire (SIQ; Reynolds, 1988). The SIQ was specifically designed for use with school-aged youth. Professional school counselors who use these instruments must use caution because of the potential for clients to underreport the severity of suicidal thoughts and behaviors. In addition, checklists and rating scales rarely differentially weight suicide risks. Thus, at most, scores should be used as helpful guidelines. As with most psychological tests, students who respond openly and honestly generally yield accurate scores and interpretations; those who respond in a guarded or deceitful manner do not.

Violence and Threat Assessment

Several highly publicized school shootings over the past decade have heightened public interest, and fears, related to school safety. Thankfully, such instances are rare, but unfortunately, other types of school violence are not rare. Compared with a generation ago, students today are more likely to bring a weapon to school, fight on school grounds, and bully or harass other students.

Bullying, Harassment, Abuse, and Dating Violence

Hazler and Denham (2002) noted that at-risk status stemmed from isolation from societal, cultural, school, family, or peer interactions and institutions. Such isolation may lead to victimization and perpetuation of violence in the forms of bullying and harassment, abuse and neglect, and suicide. A form of peer-on-peer abuse, bullying and harassment occur throughout American society (Hazler, 1998) and the world (P. K. Smith et al., 1999) and may serve as a contributing factor to homicide (Heide, 1999) and suicide (J. V. Carney, 2000; Rigby & Slee, 1999). While these potentially devastating results have been infrequently observed, the more insidious long- and short-term influences of bullying and harassment may impact not only victims, but also perpetrators and bystanders (Janson, 2000).

Bullying and harassment are caused when an imbalance of power (e.g., social, physical, emotional) is created. It is maintained when others, including adults or peer bystanders, do not act to balance the inequalities (Hazler, Miller, Carney, & Green, 2001). Failure of adults and bystanders to act encourages perpetuation of abusers' reputation as strong individuals and victims' reputation as weak (J. C. Wright, Zakriski, & Fisher, 1996). The quickest way to interrupt the cycle of bullying or harassment is for adults and peers to intervene. Thus, teaching adults and peers the importance of intervening and how to effectively intervene is a critical role the professional school counselor can undertake. Bullying and harassment have become so problematic in schools that a number of states have passed antibullying and antiharassment legislation or regulations prohibiting these behaviors—accompanied by stiff consequences for school system employees who do not intervene appropriately. This area of prevention and intervention becomes a huge opportunity for teaching advocacy skills. Importantly, this includes "indirect" forms of harassment and bullying, such as spreading vicious, hurtful rumors or socially excluding a victim (Randall, 1997).

Physical and sexual abuse and neglect are also widespread problems in society, often resulting in devastating long-term emotional problems, including anxiety, depression, substance abuse, and other serious psychiatric disturbances (McCauley et al., 1997). Emotional and social isolation is particularly problematic with individuals who have been abused or neglected—a result of the embarrassment and secrecy endemic to the acts. This social and emotional isolation is not restricted only to children who are directly abused; children who witness domesticated abuse, such as occurs when their mother is battered, have similar isolative reactions (Forte, Franks, Forte, & Rigsby, 1996; Weitzman, 1998). But violence in significant or intimate relationships is no longer related only to the home and behind closed doors.

Dating violence has experienced an unfortunate rise over the past decade and affects many teenagers. Howard and Wang (2003) reported that about 10% of high school girls reported dating violence, with the occurrence increasing to more than 15% in seniors. The Centers for Disease Control and Prevention's (2000) estimates ranged from 9% to 65%, depending on definitions and methodologies used; likely estimates of prevalence were 22% of high school seniors and 32% of college students. Victims of dating violence displayed increased risks of suicidal thoughts and actions, substance use, depression, and risky sexual behavior (Howard & Wang, 2003; Silverman, Raj, Mucci, & Hathaway, 2001).

Threat Assessment

Violent acts committed on school property increased sharply during the 1980s but, contrary to popular opinion, have been steadily declining since 1993 (Borum, 2000; Rollin, Kaiser-Ulrey, Potts, & Creason, 2003). Sensationalized school shootings in various parts of the United States have created a quite different public perception. One of the benefits of this attention is an increased research focus on the topic, both scholarly and governmental, particularly by the Federal Bureau of Investigation (FBI) and the U.S. Secret Service. Both of these agencies have developed protocols and procedures that have been used by school crisis management and public safety specialists. Their reports can be accessed, respectively, at www.fbi.gov/publications/school/school2.pdf and www.ustreas.gov/USSS/. While much of what follows was developed to understand school shooters, much of the information generalizes to less drastic forms of school violence.

From the outset, it is important for professional school counselors to understand that there is no foolproof profile of violent youth or list of risk factors that allows certain identification of youth as violent. Indeed, the research is clear that the majority of youth who display multiple risk factors never become violent offenders. Likewise, many violent offenders do not display many of the risk factors commonly considered by experts to indicate increased risk. Violence, by its nature, is unpredictable. Also, an exclusive focus on identification, to the exclusion of prevention and intervention, is misguided. Threat assessment, developmental programming, prevention, and intervention are all part of a comprehensive school safety program. Threat assessment is an important facet that will be expounded on below. The developmental, prevention, and intervention facets will be addressed at the end of this section and in chapter 14, which deals with conflict resolution and peer mediation.

Historically, mental health practitioners have been no better at predicting violent behavior in clients than informed nonprofessionals, but recent innovations have improved predictability somewhat, although the accuracy is very far from perfect. Importantly, violence is brought on by multiple factors, not just one.

Most violent students are not planful, although exceptions certainly exist. Violent students often feel desperate and panic stricken, fearing that others want to hurt them. Striking out violently is a means of defense and, at times, retribution. In general, males aged 15 to 24 years have a higher risk of violence. Race is not ordinarily associated with violence risk, but students with lower socioeconomic status have higher associated risks. Students with thought disorders (e.g., hallucinations, delusions) and disorders of impulse (e.g., ADHD, conduct disorder) present with higher degrees of risk. Of course, those with a history of violent acts are at greater risk for future violent acts (F. R. Wilson, 2004). Environmental risk factors include unstable family and peer relationships, association with criminal or sexual predators, association with antisocial peers, educational problems, and living in an urban environment.

Specific to school shooting incidences, motivation includes revenge for social isolation and bullying. The FBI reported that attackers frequently engage in "behaviors of concern," although not necessarily aberrant behaviors, prior to the incident. Most of the time, the attacker revealed his plan to at least one other person not involved in the attack, and most had access to guns and previous experience using guns. Finally, although the notion of a school shooter as a loner is often true, this is certainly not always the case.

The FBI defines a threat as intent to do harm or act out violently against someone or something. They classify threats of violence into four categories.

1. *Indirect threats* are ambiguous and vague but with implied violence. The phrasing of an indirect threat ordinarily suggests that a violent act may occur, not necessarily that it will occur.
2. *Veiled threats* do not specifically threaten violence but strongly infer the possibility.

3. *Conditional threats* warn of violence if certain conditions or demands are not met (e.g., extortion).
4. *Direct threats* are clear, straightforward, and explicit warnings of a specific act against a specific target.

The FBI also presented guidelines for determining the seriousness of a threat. *Low-level threats* are vague and indirect, lack realism, and pose minimal risks to the victim or public. The specific content of a low-level threat ordinarily leads to the conclusion that the student is unlikely to carry out the threatened act of violence. *Medium-level threats* are somewhat more direct, concrete, and plausible than low-level threats are, but frequently they do not appear entirely realistic. Some evidence of rudimentary planning is often apparent (e.g., place, time, method), but the plan lacks detail, and preparations to fulfill the plan are absent. Often students making a medium-level threat will state "I mean it," to convey a seriousness to the threat. A *high-level threat* is direct, specific, and plausible, with a serious and imminent danger to the safety of the victim or public. Plans have been made and concrete steps have been taken to prepare for the act (e.g., obtaining weapon). High-level threats almost always require the involvement of law enforcement officials.

When assessing threat, the FBI suggests a "four-pronged assessment model" involving attention to the student's personality, family dynamics, school dynamics, and social dynamics. Table 13.4 provides specific facets of each of these areas that the professional school counselor should attend to during a threat assessment.

The literature is replete with suggestions for helping to mitigate and minimize violence. Table 13.5 provides a short list. This topic will be dealt with in even greater detail in chapter 14.

The U.S. surgeon general reported that commitment to school, intelligence, intolerance toward deviance, and a positive social orientation were important protective factors (U.S. Public Health Service Office of Surgeon General, 2001). Adult mentoring programs have also had positive effects (Catalano, Loeber, & McKinney, 1999), as have programs designed to enhance positive social interaction, decision making, and problem solving

TABLE 13.4
The FBI's "Four-Pronged Assessment Model" for conducting a threat assessment.

Prong 1: Personality of the Student
- Leakage (intentional or unintentional revelation of clues to an impending violent act)
- Low tolerance for frustration
- Poor coping skills
- Lack of resiliency
- Failed love relationship
- "Injustice collector" (resentment over real or perceived injustices)
- Signs of depression
- Narcissism (self-centeredness)
- Alienation
- Dehumanizes others
- Lack of empathy
- Exaggerated sense of entitlement
- Attitude of superiority
- Exaggerated or pathological need for attention
- Externalizes blame
- Masks low self-esteem
- Anger-management problems
- Intolerance
- Inappropriate humor
- Seeks to manipulate others
- Lack of trust
- Closed social group
- Change in behavior
- Rigid and opinionated
- Unusual interest in sensationalized violence
- Fascination with violence-filled entertainment
- Negative role models
- Behavior appears relevant to carrying out a threat

Prong 2: Family Dynamics
- Turbulent parent–child relationship
- Acceptance of pathological behavior
- Access to weapons
- Lack of intimacy
- Student "rules the roost"
- No limits or monitoring of TV and Internet

Prong 3: School Dynamics (from the student's perspective)
- Student's attachment to school
- Tolerance for disrespectful behavior (bullying)

- Inequitable discipline
- Inflexible culture
- Pecking order among students
- Code of silence
- Unsupervised computer access

Prong 4: Social Dynamics

- Media, entertainment, technology
- Peer groups
- Drugs and alcohol
- Outside interests
- The copycat effect

Source: From "The School Shooter: A Threat Assessment Perspective," by the Federal Bureau of Investigation, 2005, retrieved September 2, 2005, from www.fbi.gov/publications/school/school2.pdf.

(Dwyer, Osher, & Wargar, 1998). Finally, one cannot overemphasize the essential impact that a hopeful and rewarding future career can play in bolstering the motivations and attitudes of adolescents. Constantine, Erickson, Banks, and Timberlake (as cited in Rollin et al., 2003):

> identified the following critical factors for vocational development in youth at-risk for violence: (a) control over career choices, (b) confidence in academic ability, (c) close relationship with a teacher, (d) academic/

vocational planning initiated by the end of middle school, (e) role models or mentors in careers of interest, and (f) parental influence through support. (p. 405)

Substance Abuse

Substance abuse is a substantial problem in society and has reached an alarming level among children and adolescents. The U.S. Department of Health and Human Services (USDHHS, 2001)

TABLE 13.5
Suggestions for preventing violence and intervening with at-risk youth.

1. Increase the quality and frequency of peer contacts.
2. Create a sense of hope and feelings of togetherness in the school and community.
3. Teach and role-play interpersonal and social skills in real-life situations.
4. Establish a clear districtwide policy for exploring and dealing with allegations of violence, bullying, harassment, abuse, and neglect.
5. Encourage participation in mentoring programs (e.g., Big Brother, Big Sister).
6. Develop and train a threat assessment team in each school.
7. Establish a peer mentoring program in the school to address needs of new and socially isolated students.
8. Collaborate with law enforcement, faith leaders, and representatives of social service agencies.
9. Create a school climate of trust between adults and students.
10. Help parents, guardians, and other adults in the life of the child make systematic connections in the community. Socially and emotionally isolated students often have socially and emotionally isolated caretakers.
11. Above all, provide supportive intervention services to potential offenders. This connection with a caring professional school counselor may make all the difference!

estimated than nearly one third of youth aged 12 to 20 drank alcohol in the previous month and as many as 10% of youth in this age group abused, or were dependent on, alcohol. Clients with substance abuse problems ranged between 12% and 30%, depending on the treatment setting. While substance abuse counselors receive specialized training in the assessment, diagnosis, and treatment of substance disorders, and professional school counselors may serve more as a referral source than as providers of actual treatment in the school context, professional school counselors must, at the very least, become proficient in substance abuse assessment to ensure that students get much-needed services. Similar to the assessment of suicidal thoughts and behaviors, assessment of substance abuse is best conducted early in the counseling process so that a comprehensive treatment program can be implemented.

Fortunately, self-reports of substance use are pretty reliable (Oetting & Beavais, 1990), although certainly not with all clients. During an initial interview, it is important to explore with the student any and all medications and substances being taken, including over-the-counter, prescription, alcohol, and illegal substances. Such a survey of substances helps the professional school counselor to understand potential for abuse, as well as whether use of such substances may cause side effects of concern. The *Physician's Desk Reference* is an excellent source of information on drugs and side effects.

Because self-report of substance use is fairly reliable, professional school counselors often use a straightforward interviewing approach. Table 13.6 includes some commonly asked questions that professional school counselors can include in an initial interview to directly assess for substance use and abuse. Another brief interview method designed for alcohol abuse screening, but which can be easily adapted to other substances, uses the acronym CAGE (Mayfield, McLeod, & Hall, 1974):

C – Have you ever felt you need to **Cut down** on your drinking?

A – Have people **Annoyed** you by criticizing your drinking?

G – Have you ever felt bad or **Guilty** about drinking?

E – Have you ever had a drink first thing in the morning to steady your nerves or get rid of a hangover (**Eye opener**)?

Client responses to a brief screening device such as CAGE can lead the professional counselor to suspect alcohol or other drug abuse and use more formalized or systematic data collection procedures. While there are a number of tests designed to assess for substance abuse issues, the most popular for use with adolescents is the

TABLE 13.6
Useful questions when screening for potential substance abuse.

1. Do you take any over-the-counter medications? If yes . . . What is it called? What do you take it for? How much? How often? Side effects?

2. Do you take any prescription medications? If yes . . . What is it called? What do you take it for? How much? How often? Side effects?

3. Do you take any other drug or substances? If yes . . . What is it called? What effect does it have on you? How much? How often? Side effects? When did you start?

4. Do you drink alcohol? If yes . . . What kind? How much? How often? How does it affect you? When did you start?

5. With whom do you drink (take drugs)?

6. Has drinking (taking drugs) caused you problems (financial, legal, family, friends, at work)?

7. Has anyone ever suggested you have a problem with drinking (taking drugs)? Who? What makes them say this?

8. Have you ever tried to quit? Successful for how long? What happened (withdrawal, symptoms, relapse)?

Substance Abuse Subtle Screening Inventory–Adolescent 2 (SASSI–A2; F. G. Miller, 2001).

Grief Work and Children from Changing Families

Any time you experience a loss, you grieve. Sometimes the grief passes in a few moments, such as when a student gets an unexpected poor grade on an exam or when a teenage girl is informed she will not be allowed to carouse with her friends at the mall because Grandma is coming for a visit. Other times, the loss is so profound that recovery may take months, years, or longer. For example, when a parent or sibling dies or when parents separate or divorce, children and adolescents often experience a long emotional road before accepting the loss and moving on. Sometimes, these youngsters never do recover properly. Professional school counselors encounter children with grief reactions quite frequently, so some mention of strategies and interventions is appropriate. Most grief reactions share commonalities. This section will focus on helping mitigate grief reactions in youth from changing families, the grief-inducing circumstance most commonly encountered by school-aged youth. First a review of relevant extant literature will be presented, then strategies and interventions. Importantly, most of the interventions are applicable to work with groups or individuals.

Understanding the Effects of Divorce

There is a large, rich literature base on children of divorce. A generally accepted conclusion of this research is that most children adjust well to divorce, although, on average, older children experience more negative outcomes (Amato, 2000). Importantly, Amato (1994, 2000) and Heatherington (1999) reported that the majority of children from divorced families are emotionally well adjusted, contrary to popular cultural mythology. However, there are a number of risk and resiliency factors that play into the mix. Grych and Fincham (2001) and Whiteside and Becker (2000) identified interparental conflict as the primary risk factor associated with negative outcome. Heatherington (1993, 1999) found gender, poor-quality parenting, and lack of contact with father

to be additional risk factors. It is essential to understand from the outset that these factors are family process variables, not family structure variables (Demo & Acock, 1996; Voydanoff & Donnelly, 1998). That is, negative emotional and social outcomes can be expected of children from nondivorced families if many of these risk factors are evident. In other words, it is not difficult to imagine or conclude that many children growing up in an intact family in which the parents are in conflict, provide low-quality parenting, or have an uninvolved father, would be at a disadvantage. Still, when compared to nondivorced peers, adolescents from divorced families demonstrate, on average, more depression, greater conflict with parents, poorer school performance, and higher levels of aggression and disruptive behavior (Amato, 1993; Demo & Acock, 1996).

Numerous resiliency and protective factors have been observed to ameliorate the potential negative effects of divorce. Resiliency is "the process of, capacity for, or outcome of successful adaptation despite challenging or threatening circumstances" (Masten, Best, & Garmezy, 1991, p. 426). Protective factors are characteristics or environmental facets that serve as buffers against stressors and harmful forces. In some ways, protective factors are on the opposite end of the spectrum from risk factors. Researchers have identified a number of resiliency or protective factors associated with positive outcomes for children of divorce, including interparental cooperation and diminished conflict following the divorce (Whiteside & Becker, 2000), competent parenting from custodial parents (Amato, 2000; Emery, Kitzman, & Waldron, 1999; Heatherington, 1999; Krishnakumer & Buehler, 2000), and contact with and competent parenting from nonresidential parents (Amato & Gilbreth, 1999; Bauserman, 2002; Stewart, Copeland, Chester, Malley, & Barenbaum, 1997). Relationships and activities outside of the family also frequently serve as important buffers. Having a trusting relationship with a nonparental adult (Masten & Coatworth, 1998) and peers (Heatherington, 1989) and having positive school experiences (Masten et al., 1991; Werner, 1992) may all play a protective role.

While divorce continues to be a troubling societal issue and its effects on children can be grief inducing, emotionally draining, and even at times traumatic, it is critical for professional school counselors to understand that 75% to 80% of children and young adults from divorced families do not experience major psychological problems (e.g., depression), aspire to and achieve career or higher educational goals, and enjoy intimate relationships as adults (Amato, 2000; Larmann-Billings & Emery, 2000; McLanahan, 1999). Indeed, some researchers (J. B. Kelly & Emery, 2003) have concluded that factors prior to the divorce, such as the degree of marital conflict or the child's ability to adjust to emotional and social circumstances, may be more indicative of long-term social adjustment and mental health.

A Primer on Grief Work

Various researchers and authors have discussed reactions to grief as a development process proceeding through stages such as:

- *Stage 1: Shock and denial*—the individual is in disbelief that the event has occurred. Anxiety is heightened but ordinarily decreases as fears are pinpointed.
- *State 2: Anger*—a period of rage, generally accompanied by an awareness of unfair treatment. Individuals often ask questions such as "Why me?" or "What did I do to deserve this?"
- *Stage 3: Guilt*—feelings that the individual may have contributed to the situation or done something to deserve it. Some may try to bargain with others (including God) to change what has happened. Generally, fear and anger decrease as fewer conditions for forgiveness are set.
- *Stage 4: Hopelessness/Depression*—individuals experience loneliness and feelings of sadness and hopelessness. This is often the longest stage and ordinarily becomes so uncomfortable that the individual becomes motivated to move on.
- *Stage 5: Acceptance*—involves moving on from the event and readjusting to one's new life situation. Fears and anxieties are frequently harnessed and used as energy to propel the individual in new directions.

Many of the physical symptoms associated with grief reactions are similar to those of

depression: fatigue, loss or increase in appetite, loss of concentration, feelings of hopelessness and isolation, frequent sighing or breathlessness, aches and pains. The intensity of the grief experience is usually determined by a combination of factors, including one's relationship to a person (e.g., parent, spouse, cousin, neighbor), the intensity of or ambivalence to that relationship, the dependency or security provided by that relationship, how the loss occurred (e.g., single vs. multiple events, knowledge ahead of time), one's personality (e.g., hardiness, resilience, mental illness), history of dealing with grief experiences, and individual characteristics (e.g., sex, age, cultural determinants). A number of obstacles to effective grieving have been identified, including sudden loss (e.g., no warning, no chance to say good-bye), lack of finality or uncertain loss (possibility that things may still work out), lack of support, and developing the perception that grief is a weakness and should be avoided or denied.

Helping students deal with grief is a common service provided by professional school counselors. If the student is experiencing "complicated grief," specialized counseling services are usually required and an immediate referral should be made. But in the context of developmental grief reactions, the professional school counselor should continuously remind the student that the symptoms and reactions are normal and life and emotional health will get better in time. Professional school counselors can help students resolve the four primary tasks of grieving (Worden, 1991). The first task is to accept the reality of the loss, usually by talking about the loss and integrating the reality of the situation on both the intellectual and emotional levels. The second task is to experience (not avoid) the pain of the grief. Worden referred to this task as the "bleeding stage" of grief, when the student must experience the pain of the grief reaction internally and externally. The third task is adjusting to life without the lost object or condition. This usually involves accepting help from others, acknowledging limitations, and performing new coping skills and activities on one's own. The final task involves emotionally relocating the loss and moving on with life. This requires students to reinvest energy from the lost relationship into new relationships or activities, as well as to find an appropriate place for the loss inside one's emotional psyche.

While helping students to resolve these tasks of grieving, professional school counselors should use good listening and communication skills, use questions sparingly, and honor silence when possible. Try to adjust to and connect with the person's mood or emotional state and be fully attentive to them. Help them to talk about the loss at a pace comfortable to them. Provide a safe place for and encourage emotional release (e.g., crying, raging, ranting, complaining) and offer assistance in practical as well as emotionally supportive ways. Help students to maintain helpful routines and encourage them to find a way to resolve the loss. Encourage social support (e.g., peers, caring adults), bibliotherapy, and journal writing. Also help the students keep busy in meaningful activities (including volunteering) and take care of their physical health. Finally, professional school counselors should always be alert for signs of complicated grief or other sings of trouble (e.g., extreme behavior changes, suicidal or homicidal ideation, changes in eating or sleeping habits, substance abuse). Refer these students to community mental health practices as appropriate.

Dropout Prevention

Because students at risk for academic failure drop out at significantly higher rates than peers do, a large part of successful programming is dropout prevention. Recent research has identified a number of factors that contribute to or reduce dropout risk in students (Lehr, Johnson, Bremer, Cosio, & Thompson, 2004). Some risk factors are fixed and not subject to change. However, many of the factors associated with dropout risk are alterable, including high rates of absenteeism and tardiness, low grades, a history of course failure, limited parental support, low participation in extracurricular activities, alcohol or drug problems, negative attitudes toward school, high levels of mobility, and grade retention. In addition, there are factors that provide protection to students with other risk factors; these preventive factors relate to increased likelihood of persisting in school despite difficulties. Some preventive factors include

more time in general education for students with disabilities, provision of tutoring services, training for competitive employment and independent living, and attending schools that maintain high expectations for all students. In addition, at-risk students who remained in school reported participating in a "relevant" high school curriculum, receiving significant support from teachers, perceiving positive attitudes from teachers and administrators, and benefiting from improvements in curriculum and instruction (e.g., additional assistance, better teaching, more interesting classes, better textbooks).

Taking risk factors and preventive factors into account, most dropout interventions seek to enhance students' sense of belonging in school; foster the development of relationships with teachers, administrators, and peers; improve academic success; address personal problems through counseling; and provide skill-building opportunities in behavior and social skills. Reviews of effective dropout intervention programs found that most of these interventions could be categorized according to the following types (Lehr, Hansen, Sinclair, & Christenson, 2003).

- Personal/affective (e.g., retreats designed to enhance self-esteem, regularly scheduled classroom-based discussion, individual counseling, participation in an interpersonal relations class)
- Academic (e.g., provision of special academic courses, individualized methods of instruction, tutoring)
- Family outreach (e.g., strategies that include increased feedback to parents or home visits)
- School structure (e.g., implementation of school within a school, redefinition of the role of the homeroom teacher, reducing class size, creation of an alternative school)
- Work related (e.g., vocational training, participation in volunteer or service programs)

Professional school counselors can help develop and implement schoolwide dropout prevention programs, using risk screenings to identify students at highest risk, and promoting some of the key components related to school completion. Table 13.7 lists key intervention components

TABLE 13.7
Key dropout prevention interventions.

Environmental support:

- Help provide a structured environment that includes clear and equitably enforced behavioral expectations.

- Monitor the occurrence of risk behaviors, regularly collect data, and measure effects of timely interventions.

Counseling support:

- Provide individual behavioral assistance.

- Help students address personal and family issues through counseling and access to social services.

- Help students with personal problems (e.g., on-site health care, availability of individual and group counseling).

- Develop students' problem-solving skills and enhance skills to meet the demands of the school environment.

- Provide conflict resolution and violence prevention programs to enhance effective interpersonal skills.

Enhancing relationships and affiliation:

- Incorporate personalization by creating meaningful and supportive bonds between students and teachers and among students.

- Create a caring and supportive environment (e.g., use of adult mentors, expanding role of homeroom teachers, organizing extracurricular activities).

- Promote additional opportunities for the student to form bonding relationships and include tutoring, service learning, alternative schooling, and out-of-school enhancement programs.

- Foster students' connections to school and sense of belonging to the community of students and staff (e.g., clubs, teams activities, intraschool competition, retreats).

Providing/supporting vocational programming:

- Provide vocational education that has an occupational concentration.

- Provide career counseling and life-skills instruction.

- Coordinate the academic and vocational components of participants' high school programs.

- Communicate the relevance of education to future endeavors (e.g., offer vocational and career counseling, flexible scheduling, and work-study programs).

Bolster outside influences:

- Recognize the importance of families in the success of their children's school achievement and school completion.

- Link with the wider community through systemic renewal, community collaboration, career education, and school-to-work programs.

synthesized from the research on dropout prevention and increasing school completion (Lehr et al., 2004) that are particularly appropriate for initiation or support by professional school counselors.

RECOMMENDATIONS FOR PROFESSIONAL SCHOOL COUNSELORS: GENERATING EFFECTIVE PROGRAMS

Schools alone no longer have the capacity to handle the multileveled problems facing today's at-risk children and adolescents. The extent and degree of problems presented by this troubled population require a multidisciplinary and multi-leveled response that goes far beyond isolated school interventions and professional school counselors (Bemak, 2000; Hobbs & Collison, 1995; Lerner, 1995). A problem of this nature requires a redefined role for the professional school counselor, one that allows counselors to reach out to other resources in the community and in homes. We would term this aspect of the new role for the professional school counselor the coordinator of interdisciplinary resources (CIR), and shift the focus of the position from a primary intervention specialist to a facilitator of multiple resources.

There are nine key recommendations for shifting the role and responsibilities of the professional school counselor to ensure effective counseling of at-risk youth:

1. *Develop authentic partnerships.* Although fostering partnerships with community agencies, businesses, families, universities, police departments, recreational centers, and so on is important, it oftentimes does not truly address the problems of at-risk youth. Partnerships have become fairly stable components of school outreach programs but are frequently established merely for the sake of saying that schools have collaborative relationships. In fact, many of the partnership relationships retain the status quo rather than develop new and innovative strategies to address the complex problems presented by youth at risk. Therefore, partnerships must be forged without traditional institutional boundaries and examine unique ways that multiple partners can cooperatively address the difficulties of children and adolescents who are experiencing problems.

2. *Facilitate interdisciplinary collaboration.* The modern-day problems of at-risk youth are far too complex to be addressed in any one system. Thus, to expand on the first recommendation, professional school counselors should assume the role of CIR to facilitate interdisciplinary school collaboration with community agencies, government, businesses, and families to generate comprehensive approaches to multifaceted problems. This requires moving beyond partnerships with one institutional or parental body and fostering cross-disciplinary collaboration.

3. *Maintain a strong multicultural focus.* Racial and ethnic demographics are changing in the United States, creating a growing ethnic minority population (Aponte & Crouch, 2000); therefore, problems manifested by youth must be considered from a cultural perspective. Too often, at-risk youth populations are defined and addressed by the nature of their problems, without considering the cultural distinctions among the youth when designing prevention and intervention programs. It is important to underscore the need for a concerted awareness of cultural differences in worldviews, especially when working with youth at risk.

4. *Be a systems change agent.* To better serve the needs of youth at risk, professional school counselors must assume the role of change agents (Bemak, 1998; Lee, 1998). Professional school counselors are in an ideal position to understand what needs to change to provide successful support and educational services for youth with problems. Rather than simply "hearing" about those problems from students and parents, we recommend that professional school counselors take an active role in challenging inequities, injustices, and harmful practices within the school context.

5. *Empower clients.* Truly empowering students means giving up power (Bemak, 2000). This is particularly important within the school setting when working with children and adolescents who are facing obstacles. Thus, professional school counselors should help empower students at risk and their families while modeling and promoting collaboration.

6. *Look for short-term successes.* One way to ensure failure with students who face myriad problems is to demand unrealistic goals. This is done regularly in schools where students who are angry are told not to be angry, students who are not studying are told simply to study, and students with low grades are commanded to work harder and improve their grades. We argue that professional school counselors must pave the way in establishing short-term realistic goals as measures of success, particularly when working with at-risk youth. Building on these short-term positive experiences will provide a building block to longer-term success.

7. *Become an advocate.* Advocacy is a key ingredient in working with youth at risk. Traditionally, many of the disenfranchised youth are without anyone to fight for their rights and dreams. The professional school counselor is in a unique position to intimately know the child or adolescent and the system. Furthermore, the professional school

counselor has access to important systemic information regarding the child. Given their unique position, professional school counselors must assume the role of advocate, challenging policies, practices, and procedures that perpetuate failure for the at-risk population.

8. *Research and document outcomes.* It is not sufficient to justify the success of prevention and intervention programs with anecdotal reports. Professional school counselors must assume a leadership role in documenting and disseminating the efficacy of programs through publishing and presenting their findings, both within the school system and externally at state and national forums (Bemak, 2000). Clear outcomes and dissemination of findings will help tailor successful program strategies, create a base for future funding, and facilitate better job descriptions and responsibilities for professional school counselors.

9. *Assume responsibility for successes and failures.* It is important that professionals model the demands made on youth at risk to assume responsibility for their lives. Professional school counselors, institutions, agencies, and other professionals must become more accountable for their work with these youth. It is important to acknowledge and accept when intervention strategies are flawed, and therefore discontinue using such interventions. At the same time, professional school counselors need to recognize and implement effective intervention strategies. Although this sounds straightforward, there is a history of systems blaming the at-risk child or adolescent for failures and creating a culture of victimization rather than assuming responsibility for ineffective interventions.

SUMMARY/CONCLUSION

It is clear that the issues encountered by youth at risk in the United States continue to present serious problems for schools, families, and communities. It is essential that professional school counselors design innovative service systems to effectively address the complex and multifaceted needs of the at-risk population. It is clear that many of the existing prevention and intervention programs are ineffective and unsuccessful, given the high numbers of disengaged and marginalized youth. Therefore, a new approach to working with this population is critical.

The professional school counselor is in a unique position to assume a leadership role in more effectively working with at-risk children and adolescents. As a CIR, advocate, social change agent, multicultural expert, and documenter of successful programs, the professional school counselor is well positioned to make a difference. Professional school counselors must shift the blame from the youth to ensure that the service system and programs assume responsibility and that youth are supported rather than punished. These paradigm shifts will be critical in changing the trajectory of at-risk youths' lives. It is an opportune time to change the course of a growing number of youth at risk in the United States, and the professional school counselor is an ideal professional to become a leader in this process.

ACTIVITIES

1. Developing an accurate definition of at-risk youth has been a challenge throughout the years. Based on your own experiences and what you have read in this chapter, write your own definition of what it means to be an at-risk youth. Compare your definition with a partner. What similarities and differences in definitions do you identify? Why is it difficult to establish one definition for the term *at risk*?

2. Interview a high school counselor regarding his or her approach to working with at-risk students. How does he or she identify students who are at risk? What techniques does he or she find to be helpful in dealing with these students?

3. Create a program for use in either a primary or secondary school to reach at-risk youth. How would you define the population? How do you plan to reach your desired population? What messages would you try to convey to them? Why would such a program be important to implement in schools and communities?

CHAPTER 14

CONFLICT RESOLUTION AND PEER MEDIATION IN SCHOOLS

VIVIAN V. LEE AND AMBER THROCKMORTON

Editor's Introduction: Violence and interpersonal conflict appear to be on the rise in schools. The system response has been more detentions, suspensions, and expulsions. However, many professional school counselors around the world have implemented developmental conflict resolution curricula and peer mediation programs to stem the tide of violence and conflict—with remarkable results that include dramatic reductions in discipline referrals and suspensions. Although not a part of the traditional school counselor role, this aspect of curriculum and collaboration is accommodated by the transformative professional school counselor quite adeptly. This chapter introduces conflict resolution and peer mediation programs to address the developmental needs of students and help students take the lead in making schools safe for all.

Today's children and youth often face confusing and contradictory messages about violence. While the United States is considered a highly civilized country, it is one of the most punitive, with the highest rate of incarceration in the world (T. S. Jones & Compton, 2003). Issues of gang violence, domestic violence, fear of terrorism, and war permeate our culture and yet we continue to glorify and romanticize violence as a way to solve problems and resolve conflict. Moreover, school shootings in rural Red Lake, Minnesota, in 2005 and in Columbine High School in suburban Littleton, Colorado, in 1999 and ongoing violence in urban school settings remind us that violence is not limited to any one sector of society but is an ever-present threat to schools in diverse communities all across the country. Community leaders, school personnel, and families are left struggling to cope with the tragic acts of violence that are killing and physically and psychologically scarring our youth. In response to increasing school and societal violence, federal legislation such as NCLB and the Safe and Drug-Free Schools Act is an attempt to provide states, districts, and schools with guidelines and standards to ensure students have a safe learning environment in which all students can achieve. When school counseling initiatives address conflict resolution and violence prevention, they link school counseling to the larger mission of schools. This chapter will examine the prevalence of violence in schools and offer an understanding of conflict, multicultural considerations, and programs and strategies for nonviolent conflict resolution.

VIOLENCE AMONG TODAY'S YOUTH

There are conflicting reports about the extent and scope of youth and school violence. Despite reports suggesting that youth and school violence are on the decline (DeVoe et al., 2004; USDHHS, 2001), it is nonetheless a significant area of concern, especially for school personnel (Smith, Daunic, Miller, & Robinson, 2002). Moreover, changing trends reported in youth aggression and school violence over the past 20 years evidence significantly more serious, "proactive" aggression and an increasing occurrence of aggression among younger children (McAdams & Lambie, 2003, p. 125). A 1998 study reported 43 of every 1,000 students (4.3%) were the victims of a nonfatal violent crime at school or on their way to or from school (K. E. Miller, 2003). In a study of urban elementary school students, 25% indicated they did not feel safe going to or from school, and 23% to 43% worried about being physically attacked in or around school (Price, Telljohann, Dake, Marsico, & Zyla, 2002). An NCES survey of middle and high school students reported that "more than one in three did not feel safe in school" (Fields, 2004, p. 108). A 2001 Rand report indicated that during one school year, about half of public middle and high schools reported at least one incident of physical attacks, fights without a weapon, theft, larceny, or vandalism (Juvonen, 2001). DeVoe et al. (2004) reported that:

- From July 1, 1999 through June 30, 2000, there were 32 school-associated violent deaths in the United States.
- Twenty-four of the 32 were homicides, while eight were suicides.

- Sixteen of the 24 homicides involved school-aged children.
- In 2002, students ages 18–24 years were more likely than students age 15–18 to be victims of crime at school.
- In 2003, 5% of students ages 12–18 years reported being victims of nonfatal crimes, 4% reported being victims of theft, and 1% reported being victims of violent incidents.
- From 1993 to 2003, 7% to 9% of students reported being threatened or injured with a weapon such as gun, knife, or club on school property in the preceding year.
- In 2003, 7% of students ages 12–18 years reported having been bullied at school.
- In 1999, 20% of all public schools experienced one or more serious crimes such as rape, sexual assault, robbery, and aggravated assault. Of public schools, 71% reported one or more violent incidents, while 46% reported one or more thefts.
- In 2003, 4% of students ages 12–18 years reported that they had avoided one or more places at school.
- In 2003, 12% of students ages 12–18 years reported that hate-related words (derogatory word related to race, religion, ethnicity, disability, gender, or sexual orientation) had been used against them by someone at school.
- In 2003, 21% of students ages 12–18 years reported street gangs being present at their school.
- In 1999–2000, 29% of public school principals reported student bullying had occurred on a daily or weekly basis, 19% reported disrespectful acts by students toward their teachers and 13% reported student verbal abuse of teachers, 3% reported occurrences of student racial tensions, and 3% reported widespread disorder in classrooms. (pp. 6–48)

According to the USDHHS (2001), youth violence is an ongoing national problem. It has become, however, a problem that is substantially hidden from the public view. Confidential surveys conducted with students between 1993 and 1998 revealed that 13% to 15% of high school seniors reported having committed a serious violent act in recent years. These types of acts do not typically come to the attention of the police, in part because they are less likely to involve firearms. Therefore, official reports, which essentially determine the extent of youth violence via arrest data, do not indicate the entire scope of the problem. Thus, while the official reports are indicating a decline in youth violence, the confidential, self-reports from students are providing evidence to the contrary. According to the USDHHS, neither the incident rate nor the proportion of high school seniors involved in violence has declined since 1993; rather, it has remained at peak levels. Over the past 20 years, in fact, the number of violent acts committed by high school seniors has actually increased by almost 50%.

School violence can be seen in the classroom, hallways, lunchroom, and on the playground (Leff, Power, Manz, Costigan, & Nabors, 2001). It takes many forms, including pushing, bullying, shoving, grabbing, slapping, and verbal insults and threats (Bucher & Manning, 2003). Thus, it is no surprise that serious conflicts among students and between students and faculty have become more common-place in today's public and private schools. This alarming reality points to the need for schools to implement conflict resolution programs that help students seek alternatives to violence.

Among the most common types of conflicts in schools today are verbal harassment (e.g., name-calling, insults), verbal arguments, rumors and gossip, physical fights, and dating/relationship issues (D. W. Johnson & Johnson, 2002; Theberge & Karan, 2004). Traditional punitive discipline alone has proven ineffective; however, the inclusion of well-planned violence prevention and conflict resolution programs and strategies can offer alternatives to the violent resolution of conflict. These strategies can include increasing understanding of one's own and others' feelings and teaching students the necessary "personal and interpersonal" (social) skills to avoid violence (Peterson & Skiba, 2001).

Conflict Resolution and Peer Mediation Programs

Conflict resolution and peer mediation appeared on the educational horizon in the 20th century, but only recently has each enjoyed widespread acceptance in American schools. With increased awareness of social injustice during the 1960s and 1970s, peer mediation has become the fastest-growing type of conflict resolution program implemented in schools today (CRENet, 2000; Shepherd, 1994). Following the founding of the National Association for Mediation in Education (NAME) in 1984, conflict resolution programs increased dramatically to approximately 10,000 school- and community-based programs in the last decade (Michlowski, 1999; Vail, 1998).

As a microcosm of society, schools reflect a rapidly changing and diverse society. The complex nature of conflict affects the growth and development and achievement of youngsters and presents a potential for violence. Consequently, it is appropriate to conceptualize conflict resolution and peer mediation programs from a systemic perspective as part of a systemic data-driven school counseling program. A systemic approach has the potential to reach the needs of all students through multilevel interventions (see chapter 7). A vertical articulation of interventions can build on cognitive, affective, and moral development as students progress through their school experience to become responsible citizens in a pluralistic society.

Within the personal–social domain of the *ASCA National Model* (2003a), the standards outline competencies that students should know and be able to do to develop healthy and safe interpersonal relationships, manage stress, cope with life events, and find healthy resolutions to conflict. In addition, when students apply these skills in the contextual settings of home, school, and community, students further learn and demonstrate a respect and appreciation for individual and cultural differences. The goal of conflict resolution skills is to assist students in processing conflict in safe and healthy ways. These skills become key in light of recent and increasing violence in the schools.

CONCEPTS AND CONSTRUCTS

Conflict is an inevitable part of life, occurring naturally in various settings (George, Dagnese, Halpin, Halpin, & Keiter, 1996; D. W. Johnson &

Johnson, 2002). It consists of a disagreement within the self or between two or more parties. Conflict can be resolved in either constructive or destructive ways; therefore, conflict need not be perceived as undesirable. Rather, conflict can be seen as desirable and necessary, presenting individuals with the potential for positive outcomes that can foster insight and growth. According to D. W. Johnson & Johnson (2002), "as long as conflicts are managed constructively, they should be sought out and enjoyed" (p. 4). Constructive conflict can gain and hold students' attention, increase their motivation to learn, incite their intellectual curiosity, and improve their problem-solving skills and abilities (D. W. Johnson & Johnson, 1995a; also see chapter 1). Thus, conflict is not only desirable, but beneficial and healthy.

Understanding Conflict

To understand conflict, it is helpful to understand the context in which it occurs. Perlstein and Thrall (1996) identified four kinds of conflict: (a) within the self (intrapersonal), (b) between two or more parties (interpersonal), (c) between two or more parties within a group (intragroup), and (d) between two or more groups (intergroup). In schools, conflict can occur between students, between student and teacher, inside the classroom, or off school grounds (G. R. Carter, 2004). Conflict in any of these contexts may escalate to involve more than one type. For example, interpersonal conflict can escalate into intragroup or intergroup conflict, as often happens in schools with cliques. Many professional school counselors have experienced a minor dispute between two students at the start of the school day that escalates into a group-against-group dispute by the end of the day.

Conflicts have several characteristics that are commonly seen in schools or other venues where human interaction occurs. In general, conflicts may stem from incongruence with the self or others, incomplete information as a result of not hearing the whole story, inaccurate information, stress overload, different viewpoints based on varying values and beliefs, limited resources, and unmet needs (Glasser, 1984; Maslow, 1968; Perlstein & Thrall, 1996; Vatalaro, 1999). These

characteristics of conflict are manifested within the social structure and climate of a school and delve deep into the underlying attitudes, values, and beliefs operating in a school. Large schools may lack a sense of personalization behaviors such as respect and may have strained teacher–student relationships; poor support at the administrative level; inconsistent policies, practices, and procedures; rigidity in thought and treatment of staff and students; valuing of the status quo; and a sense of disconnectedness (Christle, Jolivette, & Nelson, 2000; Flaherty, 2001).

Types of Conflict

Implicit within these factors is that conflicts can be conceptualized as either tractable or intractable (i.e., resolution resistant). Tractable conflicts are minor disputes in which a simple misunderstanding occurred. This type of conflict is usually easily resolved through mediation strategies. Intractable conflicts, on the other hand, are deeply rooted in contrasting values and worldviews, such as those held by various religious or racial or ethnic groups. Intractable conflicts could also be domination conflicts involving a disproportionate distribution of wealth, power, and status. Although tractable conflicts may be temporarily resolved, if there are underlying core differences or intractable conflicts, the conflict will inevitably resurface. Therefore, if underlying intractable issues are not addressed, mediation strategies become suspect at best (Burgess & Burgess, 1996). In a school setting, this may suggest a twofold process of conflict resolution: an immediate process for tractable conflict resolution using typical mediation strategies, and a preventive, educational process for addressing the issues that fuel intractable conflicts. Thus, a comprehensive approach to conflict can assist students by offering alternatives that challenge destructive expressions of conflict in favor of positive outcomes. These learned conflict resolution strategies can have more desirable positive outcomes such as:

- increased achievement and long-term retention of academic material;
- increased use of higher-level cognitive and moral reasoning;

- increased healthy cognitive and social development;
- focused attention on problems and increased energy dedicated to solving them;
- identified areas in need of change;
- released anger, anxiety, insecurity, and sadness that, if kept inside, may contribute to mental distress and illness; and
- strengthened relationships by increasing individuals' confidence in their ability to resolve their disagreements and minimizing irritations and resentments so that positive feelings can be expressed fully. (D. W. Johnson & Johnson, 1996, p. 324)

When students learn how to negotiate their own disputes and mediate their peers' conflicts, they have the tools necessary to self-regulate their own behavior, determine what is appropriate given the situation and another person's perspective, and change the way they behave or act accordingly (D. W. Johnson & Johnson, 2002).

Conflict Resolution in the Larger School Structure

Conflict resolution strategies do not replace traditional discipline approaches. Instead, they expand the parameters and enhance discipline methods to allow individuals to interact with one another to resolve their differences nonviolently (Bucher & Manning, 2003; Stomfay-Stitz, 1994; Sweeney & Carruthers, 1996). Thus, conflict resolution teaches students alternatives by focusing on understanding conflict, negotiation skills (Peterson & Skiba, 2001), and how to control one's own behavior (Bucher & Manning, 2003). Students are empowered to resolve disputes on their own, without requiring the attention of a teacher, professional school counselor, administrator, or other adult (Close & Lechman, 1997; D. W. Johnson & Johnson, 2002). Conflict resolution strategies also enhance resiliency and help students preserve their relationships (Bucher & Manning, 2003). According to D. W. Johnson and Johnson (2002), the foundational principle of conflict resolution training is teaching students how to negotiate constructive resolutions to their own disputes. Conflict resolution most often

occurs as part of a broader program, typically through peer mediation programs in schools (Peterson & Skiba, 2001). Mediation is a process whereby a neutral third party (either an individual or a team) known as the mediator assists two or more individuals experiencing a conflict. The goal of mediation is to confidentially assist disputants in finding their own solutions through collaborative and equitable means to reach a win–win resolution. Skills such as critical thinking, problem solving, and self-discipline are employed (D. W. Johnson, Johnson, Dudley, Ward, & Magnuson, 1995; Lane & McWhirter, 1992; Leviton & Greenstone, 1997; Morse & Andrea, 1994; Sweeney & Carruthers, 1996). In schools, mediation is generally called for when disputants cannot (a) move beyond the disagreement, (b) see beyond their own perspective, (c) negotiate due to a lack of skills, (d) find a way to maintain the relationship after the conflict, and (e) find a solution that will benefit both parties (Leviton & Greenstone, 1997). The underlying goal is to encourage socially appropriate, self-regulatory behavior in the absence of an adult authority figure (Lane & McWhirter, 1992).

Peer mediation can be used in conjunction with traditional disciplinary measures (Lane & McWhirter, 1992; Perlstein & Thrall, 1996). However, there are situations in schools in which peer mediation is not advised; for example, when disputants (a) have committed a crime, (b) are not rational, (c) are using illegal drugs and alcohol, and (d) engage in violent acts. Use of peer mediation programs is not advised in conflicts involving weapons and issues of child abuse (Wilburn & Bates, 1997). Mediation is advised when disputants have relational conflicts that interfere with classroom functioning. Typical conflicts appropriate for the intervention of peer mediators include: (a) spreading rumors, (b) gossiping, (c) name-calling, (d) racial put-downs, (e) bullying, and (f) disputes over property. Recognizing that any of these disputes can escalate to more serious acts, early attention combined with peer mediation offers an alternative to violence. Mediation should not be seen as an escape from other disciplinary sanctions (Lane & McWhirter, 1992). Rather, it should be seen as a means to empower students to connect with each other to solve problems in age-appropriate ways, with common language and frames of reference and without fear of adult judgment (Angaran & Beckwith, 1999; Bodine, 1996; Morse & Andrea, 1994).

Despite the benefits, programmatic efforts to incorporate conflict resolution and peer mediation into the core curriculum can be met with resistance. Teachers, administrators, students, and parents may question the value and relevance of such programs to educational theory and practice.

Multicultural Implications

According to the USDHHS (2001), African American and Hispanic males who attend large inner-city schools that serve very poor neighborhoods are at the greatest risk of becoming victims or perpetrators of school violence. These youths become more familiar with violence as it is socially constructed (Williams, 2001). Generally, racial minority youth not only represent families from the lowest socioeconomic level, but they also live in lower income communities. Thus, these youth are much more vulnerable to the oppressions and negative afflictions plaguing society today. This can escalate the potential for these youth to adopt self-destructive, especially violent, attitudes and behaviors (Brinson, Kottler, & Fisher, 2004). But suburban and rural youth are no longer immune to school violence either. An incisive look into American culture punctuates some disturbing realities that influence youth, including poverty, disintegrating families, child abuse, romanticized violence, materialism, and pressure to achieve (Long, Fabricus, Musheno, & Palumbo, 1998). These social injustices in our society are believed to be the antecedents of most forms of school violence (Casella, 2001; Coleman & Deutsch, 2000; Nieto, 1999). Moreover, Casella (2001) suggested race, gender, social status, sexual identity, prejudice, and fear are also central to varying forms of violence. Alcohol and drug abuse (Peterson & Skiba, 2001; Sandhu, 2000) and gang affiliation (Sandhu, 2000) also contribute to youth violence.

Some authors believe that to be truly effective, conflict resolution and violence prevention efforts must "adjust" to the diverse cultural, ethnic, and socioeconomic influences of society and involve every segment of society (e.g., families, neighborhoods, civic and social organizations, government and private institutions, businesses, cities, states, schools, justice systems, health professionals; L. A. Stone, 1996). Within the school setting, that translates into emphasizing the need to educate students in a global context and use education to bridge the divides between groups of people (Carter, 2004). Carter (2004) stated that "bridging the divides" between groups of people "requires attention not only to teaching about differences, such as language, culture, and religion, but also to exploring areas of deep cultural understanding" (p. 2). Brinson et al. (2004) asserted that there is also a lack of emphasis on cross-cultural conflict resolution, particularly within peer mediation and process curriculum approaches to conflict resolution. Therefore, schools must not only implement programs that educate and promote violence prevention, but also they must teach students how to manage and resolve conflicts through multiple contexts that move beyond merely tolerating diversity to seeking out and celebrating the rich dimensions of multiple diversities. All students need to learn alternatives to using violence for resolving their disputes (Bucher & Manning, 2003; D. W. Johnson & Johnson, 1995a) and to learn to become peacemakers (D. W. Johnson & Johnson, 2002) in a pluralistic society.

CONFLICT RESOLUTION PROGRAM FORMAT

Conflict resolution initiatives are operationalized through various programmatic and pedagogical venues in the schools. Four basic approaches to conflict resolution education in schools will be addressed in this section. These venues are similar across the literature: (a) the process curriculum approach, (b) the mediation program approach, (c) the peaceable classroom approach, and (d) the peaceable school approach (Bodine & Crawford, 1998). These approaches can be used as stand-alone initiatives or in a variety of multilevel interventions across subsystems of the school and school community. Multilevel interventions may consist of specific courses; integrating core concepts and skills into a variety of academic disciplines; creating multidisciplinary teaching teams; infusing conflict resolution concepts, skills, and values into the day-to-day activities of the classroom (e.g., teaching strategies, teachable moments, classroom rituals); and institutionalizing the practices and principles of conflict resolution, social and emotional learning, and intergroup relations into the culture and policies of the school (Compton, 2000). The basic training principles of conflict resolution and peer mediation remain the same regardless of the mode of implementation. The following section briefly describes these four possible approaches: the process curriculum approach, the mediation program approach, the peaceable classroom approach, and the peaceable school approach.

Process Curriculum Approach

The process curriculum approach to conflict resolution is characterized by a separate course, often referred to as a stand-alone course. This course includes a distinct curriculum, or daily or weekly lesson plan, in which a specific time is dedicated to teaching the basic foundational principles, abilities, and problem-solving processes of conflict resolution. Typically, courses teach negotiation or mediation over a semester-long period or in a series of workshops. Daily or weekly lessons are typically taught as part of the unified scope and sequence of the content and skills of the conflict resolution processes (Bodine & Crawford, 1998). Most learning occurs via structured activities such as simulations, role-plays, group discussions, and cooperative learning activities. This method is very useful in both the middle and high school. In middle school, a conflict resolution course can be used as part of an exploratory elective, or it could be a required course elective. At the high school, the same format can be used to implement a stand-alone course. This course can be taught by teachers, with regular visits from the professional school counselor for collaborative classroom instruction. Professional school counselors can also serve in a consultative role to assist teachers in developing and implementing strategies and techniques. Either way, the role of the counselor in

implementing the course is an important function of a systemic school counseling program.

Mediation Program Approach

The mediation program approach trains selected individuals (students or adults) in the principles and basic foundational abilities of conflict resolution and in the mediation process so that they may act as a neutral third party to assist individuals in resolving disputes. This approach can be used in the classroom and as a schoolwide strategy for resolving conflicts between students, between students and adults, or even between adults. Teachers, administrators, and other school personnel are ideal candidates to serve as mediators helping adults in resolving conflicts such as work problems between faculty members, disciplinary actions disputed by parents, and development of appropriate programs for children with special needs. Students are ideal mediators for conflicts among and between peers involving jealousy, rumors, misunderstandings, bullying, harassment, threats, fights, personal property, and damaged friendships. Adults and students may also serve together as comediators to resolve disputes between students and teachers involving clashing personalities, respect issues, behavior issues, and other conflicts that negatively impact the potential for positive student–teacher relationships (Bodine & Crawford, 1998). This format is used in the middle and high school with options to train older students to serve as mediators at the elementary level. Professional school counselors are more likely to be the coordinator or cocoordinator of this level of intervention than to teach a semester course as discussed earlier. See below for diversity considerations in revising an existing program or building a new peer mediation program.

Peaceable Classroom Approach

The peaceable classroom approach is a whole-classroom approach that integrates conflict resolution education into the core curriculum subject areas and into classroom management strategies using cooperative learning and academic controversy. This approach is considered the foundation for the peaceable school approach and is typically initiated teacher by teacher (Bodine & Crawford, 1998). This approach is applicable for grades K–12. Careful examination of curricula from various academic and fine arts disciplines reveals a plethora of opportunities to incorporate conflict resolution into the core curriculum and daily life of each and every classroom in a school. This type of integration into the educational program sets the foundation for a schoolwide expectation of constructive conflict resolution. Professional school counselors can work with teams of teachers to incorporate these strategies into their lessons as well as leading activities to supplement curricular initiatives.

Peaceable School Approach

The peaceable school approach is a comprehensive, whole-school approach that builds on the peaceable classroom approach and incorporates cooperative learning environments, direct instruction and practice of conflict resolution skills and processes, noncoercive school and classroom management systems, and integration of conflict resolution principles and abilities into the curriculum. This approach uses conflict resolution as a total operational system for managing both the school and classroom. Conflict resolution principles and skills are learned by everyone within the school community to create and promote a culture and climate of caring, honesty, cooperation, and appreciation of diversity (Bodine & Crawford, 1998).

Schools implementing this approach create a system where diversity is valued and encouraged and in which peacemaking is the standard behavior among all students and adults. Peacemaking involves applying basic foundational abilities and problem-solving processes to address the interpersonal and intergroup problems and issues facing students, school personnel, and parents. The objectives of peacemaking are to achieve personal, group, and institutional goals and to maintain cooperative relationships. Training in basic foundational abilities and problem-solving processes is offered to the entire school community. Consensus decision making and negotiation are used by all members of the school community to help resolve conflicts peacefully and fairly for all, with peer mediation being used both as a schoolwide and classroom strategy (Bodine & Crawford, 1998).

When individual school districts incorporate multiple conflict resolution strategies in Grades K–12, it becomes a developmental and sequential learning opportunity throughout students' educational experience. Cutrona and Guerin (1994) suggested a stage process for Grades K–12. Grades K–3 emphasize sharing feelings, self-affirmation, and cooperation. Grades 4–6 focus on anger management, creative problem solving, and negotiating. Grades 7–12 address violence prevention and peer mediation models. Learning these abilities, processes, skills, and strategies is a lifelong process of reinforcement and reeducation. Moreover, Bodine and Crawford (1998) emphasize the need for, and value of, diverse age-appropriate opportunities to transfer what is learned and insist that students "need to be taught the intellectual framework, provided the tools to think systematically about conflict, and given the opportunity to practice these skills and employ these tools within a real-life context" (p. 118).

For K–12 core curricular infusion, a shift in traditional pedagogical practices is required, underscoring the need for teacher training in diverse learning styles. For instance, role-playing utilizes dramatization by re-creating historical figures, applying conflict resolution principles to the scenarios, and analyzing alternative solutions to the story or event. Students discuss how the course of history may have been altered by constructive nonviolent solutions to historical events. Role-playing can also teach "perspective taking," which encourages bias awareness. Using perspective-taking strategies, students rewrite and discuss stories from various characters' perspectives. Perspective taking, using various framing devices, allows students to see only limited physical views of dramatizations, highlighting the importance of information gathering before drawing conclusions to dispel stereotypes that lead to biases. Additionally, the use of games, plays, puppets, or even service learning in the school and community involves a wide variety of strategies.

Examples of Effective Conflict Resolution Programs

Teaching Students to be Peacemakers

The Teaching Students to Be Peacemakers program is designed for students in Grades K–12 and teaches students negotiation and other conflict resolution processes (Druliner & Prichard, 2003). It focuses on teaching all students in a school to be peacemakers (D. W. Johnson & Johnson, 2002) and assists them in developing the skills necessary to effectively manage their own disputes (Druliner & Prichard, 2003). The program involves a 12-year instructional track starting in kindergarten so that students can understand and build on those lessons each subsequent school year (Druliner & Prichard, 2003). The six steps to the program (D. W. Johnson & Johnson, 2002) focus on creating a cooperative climate and teaching students that conflict can be a useful and normal part of life (Druliner & Prichard, 2003). After students learn the basic principles of the program, they are taught negotiation and mediation procedures, with the level of sophistication increasing every year from kindergarten through the 12th grade (Druliner & Prichard, 2003). Research has suggested that when the negotiation and mediation training is integrated into other coursework, students' academic achievement is positively impacted (Druliner & Prichard, 2003).

We Can Work It Out! Problem Solving Through Mediation

The We Can Work It Out! program (as cited in Bodine & Crawford, 1998) has both elementary school and secondary school editions. The elementary school program has a step-by-step design that teaches personal conflict management skills and the mediation process. Lessons cover analytical reasoning, active listening, patience, empathy, and generating options. Key terms and concepts are reviewed, terminology is made appropriate for elementary school students, and skills are learned via scenarios (fairy tales, cartoons, interpersonal conflicts) acted out through role-plays (disputant and mediator). The secondary school program is almost identical except that the terminology and scenarios are made appropriate for middle school and high school students (Bodine & Crawford, 1998).

The Conflict Zoo

The Conflict Zoo (as cited in Bodine & Crawford, 1998) is a curriculum designed to teach third- and fourth-grade students the foundational principles and skills of conflict resolution and the concepts of justice and fairness. Lessons are taught at the beginning of the school year and begin with the story of a junior zoo, where baby animals play together. As the story goes, in order for the baby animals to play together, they must resolve their conflicts nonviolently and build a sense of togetherness. Through the lessons, students experience these conflicts through the animals' perspectives and move from helping the animals resolve their conflicts to resolving their own conflicts. Students learn important terms, create journals, and apply what they have learned to their own life. Role-plays, art, and journals keeping are used (Bodine & Crawford, 1998).

Program for Young Negotiators

The Program for Young Negotiators (as cited in Bodine & Crawford, 1998) operates on the belief that the best violence prevention method is teaching individuals how to achieve their goals without resorting to violence (Bodine & Crawford, 1998). This program is designed for middle school and high school students and uses a negotiation curriculum that teaches students the skills necessary to solve their normal, everyday problems (Druliner & Prichard, 2003). The approach emphasizes self-empowerment and enables students to resolve their disputes in such a way that both sides are satisfied with the outcome and achieve their goals (Bodine & Crawford, 1998). The curriculum is made up of 10 interactive sessions that utilize role-plays, games, group discussion, and reflection exercises to teach students the skills. Sessions are approximately 90 minutes, or 15 classroom hours (Druliner & Prichard, 2003). While the program was designed as a stand-alone program, lessons can be incorporated into regular coursework. The program has four primary components: "(1) teacher training and community involvement,

(2) negotiation curricula, (3) follow-up opportunities, and (4) ongoing curriculum development and innovations" (Bodine & Crawford, 1998, p. 63).

PROGRAM DEVELOPMENT

The development of any conflict resolution or peer mediation program or intervention should reflect the unique contextual needs of the school or district to be served. Climate assessment and strategies for systemic change are integral to program development.

Assessing Climate

Prior to proposing a conflict resolution–peer mediation program, careful assessment of school culture and climate is essential. It is particularly relevant to gain an understanding of the atmosphere of competition versus collaboration that characterizes most schools, as well as the systemic patterns, policies, and procedures that sustain and promote imbalances in power, and prejudice and discrimination of any disenfranchised population. It is also necessary to understand the structure of competition in the school. The ultimate goal of competition is to win, thus creating a loser. Winning rarely results in maintaining good relationships, understanding each others' perspectives, or understanding the legitimacy of others' needs and feelings. Conversely, in a cooperative win–win environment, there exists a commitment to developing mutual goals beneficial to all while preserving positive relationships that honor and respect multiple perspectives (D. W. Johnson & Johnson, 1995b).

The implementation of a cooperative school environment in which to manage conflict seems appropriate given the positive effects of cooperative learning on cognitive and social development. However, opponents of school conflict resolution programs believe that these programs cover the real causes of conflict without focusing on the policies and practices of the adults who hold power. Essentially, the opponents of peer mediation and conflict resolution programs seem to be advocating attention to the issues that create

intractable conflict. These issues are woven into the fabric of educational practices and contribute to the inequity that fuels the inevitable conflict of differing attitudes, values, and beliefs. For example, academic tracking and inconsistent policies and practices in attendance, discipline, and entrance into extracurricular activities can create inequities for students from low-income and underserved populations, based on policies that sort and select students, often diminishing access and equity to educational opportunity. Student and parent awareness of these inequities causes conflict as students and parents strive to meet their needs satisfactorily.

Using Maslow's need theory, conflict theorists suggest that need is a motivating factor in intractable conflict and will go on indefinitely, as human needs are not negotiable (Conflict Research Consortium, 2000c). Most relevant to schools is conflict over the need for identity, a salient factor in racial, ethnic, gender, and family conflicts (Conflict Research Consortium, 2000a). Of additional concern are issues of dominance that reflect a power structure and hierarchy of "one up, one down" or "one group up, one group down." Students are keenly aware of inequities in power. When conflict arises and is peer mediated, the two disputants may come to an agreement to fight no more, but the underlying unmet needs have not been addressed. Unless students believe their needs can be met satisfactorily, the conflict will continue (Conflict Research Consortium, 2000b). However, if the issues that undergird intractable conflict are brought to light by a peer mediation program and are addressed from an institutional perspective, then the program takes an active role in institutional change, and the process becomes part of the framework of a transformed school climate and culture. This affords students a venue for meeting their needs while saving face (Conflict Research Consortium, 2000d). This process suggests the need for conflict resolution training for all members of the school community. Teachers cannot impart feelings and principles of empowerment to their students if they feel estranged from their colleagues and the school in which they work. Transformation of school culture and climate is a slow process that

requires careful assessment of the unique structure and assumptions of a school, but it is well
worth the effort.

Systemic Change

Resolving conflicts and preventing violence are
interrelated (D. W. Johnson & Johnson, 1995a).
The relation between initiatives addressing conflict resolution and youth violence reduction war-
rants attention to a systemic change model that
targets youth violence. Hazler (1998) suggested
that successful school programs recognize violence as a developmental issue, with various
grade-level interventions that are both preventative and remedial. Then, efforts to create a high
level of personal and community awareness and
participation in conflict resolution and peer mediation programs can stimulate collective power
and share information about similarities and differences that is useful in formulating solutions.
Efforts of the collective whole lead to change in
daily patterns of the majority of the school rather
than isolated changes for only a few. Given that
change is difficult, invitational strategies that
involve all concerned stakeholders in planning
and implementing change, address formal and
informal policies, give attention to the needs of
diverse constituents, and personalize and maintain involvement of all parties are essential. Student involvement in the change process broadens
role expectation beyond the classroom setting.
These opportunities encourage more genuine
renegotiated relationships and roles between students and school personnel. As teachers broaden
their roles in systemic change initiatives, they
become empowered and actively involved in
redefining the school culture and climate.

Administrative support is vital to systemic
change efforts as principals are responsible for
promoting the overall school mission through the
efforts of school personnel. Therefore, administrators need to trust that change efforts will be carried
out appropriately through a process defined by
clear goals and objectives that foster and complement existing efforts and priorities (Hazler, 1998).
Because multilevel interventions reach beyond the
school, the inclusion of families and the school
community is essential.

Diversity Considerations in Recruitment, Selection, and Training of Peer Mediators

Peer mediation programs are utilized in many
schools either as stand-alone programs or in
conjunction with other initiatives. Because these
programs put students in leadership roles, it is
essential that peer mediators represent the multiple diversities of the school. In this way, programs demonstrate an appreciation for the
dynamic worldview and cultural complexity of
students and school personnel (Graham &
Pulvino, 2000). In this way, initiatives are inclusive and contribute to a balance in power as
both an institutional and programmatic objective
(Day-Vines, Day-Hairston, Carruthers, Wall, &
Lupton-Smith, 1996; Graham & Pulvino, 2000;
Opffer, 1997; Ponterotto, Casas, Suzuki, &
Alexander, 1995; Sweeney & Carruthers, 1996).
Specifically, when developing new programs
and revising existing peer mediation programs to
reflect the pluralistic composition of schools,
examination of three factors is necessary: recruitment, selection, and training. The diverse populations of schools—differentiated by age, race or
ethnicity, disability, socioeconomic status, and
academic ability—need to be reflected in programming. The basic goal in addressing difference is to assist students and school personnel in
recognizing diversity as a resource, not a point
of contention (Tyrrell, Scully, & Halligan, 1998).

Day-Vines et al. (1996) supported the paral-
lels between peer mediation and multiculturalism,
suggesting that the potential exists to:

> (a) promote intercultural sensitivity among
> participants by including diverse segments of the
> student population in the program as mediators;
> (b) stimulate in mediators an openness,
> appreciation, and consciousness of the difference
> that can be generalized to other aspects of their
> lives; and (c) make the mediation program more
> responsive to the needs of the entire student
> body. (p. 401)

Recruitment

Empowering students to be leaders and role models is essential toward creating and maintaining a
school environment that prevents harassment and

violence (Wessler & Preble, 2003). Some groups of students who feel disenfranchised from the school community distance themselves from participation in extracurricular activities. As a result, traditional methods of recruitment prove unsatisfactory. Individual solicitations to students with low participation in school activities are advisable. Individual solicitation communicates interest in a particular student or group and may be helpful coming from a teacher who has a close relationship with a student or group, or from a teacher whom students respect (Day-Vines et al., 1996). Moreover, enlisting the assistance of teachers helps to enlighten teachers on the institutional issues that prevent some students from participating in school activities. On a cautionary note, only students who are likely to be selected should be encouraged because creating hopeless situations can be as detrimental as exclusion.

Selection

Selection of student mediators should reflect a cross section of the student population. Multiple criteria of student attributes are suggested, including leadership skills, maturity, communication skills, responsibility, perspective taking, empathy, and problem-solving skills. High academic achievement is not necessarily a prerequisite for selection. Students with average grades and some who are considered at risk may well possess the desirable skills. A heterogeneous configuration of mediators makes the service more approachable.

The varying levels of racial or ethnic identity development among students is another salient factor to consider. It is critical that program coordinators are familiar with the stages of racial or ethnic identity development for students of color and White students. Day-Vines et al. (1996) stated:

> Racial or ethnic factors are only one aspect of the diversity that needs to be considered. Representation of students from various neighborhoods and socio-economic levels also should be sought, as well as student representatives with physical and academic disabilities and students challenged by medical issues. At the same time, students with

disabilities should not be just from racial or ethnic populations because it further reinforces stereotypes. Some students experiencing academic difficulties may require pretraining prior to selection. However, as with all students, school personnel must avoid encouraging those who are likely not to be selected because they may create or magnify feelings of rejection. (p. 397)

Coordinators need to be aware of and understand the impact of their own racial or ethnic identity development and the potential challenges that selecting for diversity may present to them and other members of the school community.

Training

Throughout the literature, training is equated to the acquisition of lifelong skills that can be generalized beyond the school environment. Multicultural sensitivity should be integrated throughout the training process as students will not always, nor should they, mediate conflicts between students from only their own racial or ethnic background (Day-Vines et al., 1996). Training for awareness of ways members of different groups view conflict and mediation within a cultural, family, and community context is essential to understanding the pattern of behavior and avoiding inaccurate assumptions and conclusions. Additionally, patterns of speech and issues specific to the special needs of non-English-speaking students or students for whom English is a second language must be considered in peer mediation training to avoid bias and discrimination, as well as to encourage the use of mediation services by all students.

PROGRAM IMPLEMENTATION

Regardless of the initiative or combinations of initiatives, implementation that is strategically planned, artfully carried out, and well documented is essential. This is especially important as the results of conflict resolution initiatives and peer mediation programs can be directly linked to schoolwide data as initiatives that assist in creating a safe school environment for learning. The specifics of implementation may vary from school to school and district to district, depending on who coordinates the initiatives. The professional school counselor may or may not coordinate the initiatives. Either way, program implementation can be conceptualized as a cyclical process including development of a mission statement, the collection of data used to set goals, the prioritizing of goals, training for skill development, an implementation schedule, evaluation, and follow-up. Additionally, careful examination of policies, practices, and procedures that impact the development, implementation, and access to these initiatives is important to ensure they reflect the spirit of the initiatives under construction. For example, inconsistencies in discipline referrals and patterns of punishments can undermine even carefully planned efforts to build peaceable schools and peer mediation programs.

Throughout every step of program revision or development, it is essential to enlist the input of all stakeholders. The use of multiple levels of input in a variety of venues that move beyond a onetime newsletter sent home, a community speaker, or several morning announcements can increase the level of ownership a school community feels in conflict resolution and peer mediation initiatives.

Training for Program Coordinators

As with any important role in the school, the responsibility of coordinating peer mediation programs and conflict resolution initiatives requires specific training. A study of Safe and Drug-Free School coordinators revealed a desire for strategies and information that are practical, easy to use, and able to be directly applied (K. A. King, Wagner, & Hedrick, 2001). Some of these strategies include improving student success; preventing alcohol, tobacco, and other drug use; building school–community–parent partnerships; and resolving conflicts safely. Well-trained coordinators can take a leadership role and provide the school community with this practical information, as well as initiate appreciation of cultural diversity and challenge the beliefs of disenfranchised students.

Student Access to Services

As with other programs, careful examination of policies that govern program access helps ensure that programs serve the entire school community. For example, schoolwide policies establishing when and how mediation takes place should be publicized to all members of the school community. Individual teachers or staff members should not deny students access to the mediation process. Administrative support in establishing policy lends credibility to peer mediation as an integral part of the total school program and creates consistent student access. Moreover, it sends a message of the shared values, attitudes, and beliefs that form the foundation of the school culture and climate.

Research on Conflict Resolution and Peer Mediation Programs

"Although their number is growing, few reliable studies of the effects of violence prevention and conflict resolution education programs have yet appeared" (Burstyn & Stevens, 2001, p. 146). A review of earlier studies provides unreliable and inconsistent findings because of poor methodology, poor theorizing, and lack of generalizability (Carruthers, Sweeney, Kmitta, & Harris, 1996; D. W. Johnson, Johnson, & Dudley, 1992; Long et al., 1998). D. W. Johnson et al. (1992) noted two recurring problems in peer mediation research studies: (a) Many studies do not emphasize systematic sampling of students in schools, and (b) many studies do not "relate their findings to the theoretical frameworks in the field of conflict resolution" (p. 830). An exception is the comprehensive conflict resolution program study by DeCecco and Richards (as cited in Johnson et al., 1992). Carruthers et al. (1996) concluded:

> [A]lthough the evidence is encouraging, we cannot say with assurance that training in conflict resolution curriculum or experience with peer mediation programs increases academic achievement, decreases the incidences of conflict and violence at school, translates into other settings or situations, or affects school climate.... On the other hand, principals, counselors, and teachers are being told that implementing these programs has many benefits for students and staff. (p. 15)

Program Evaluation

The lack of sound empirical data is problematic in schools where limited funds mandate programmatic outcomes such as student achievement (Stevahn, Johnson, Johnson, Laginski, & O'Coin, 1996). As the focus of accountability through concrete measure increases, it is incumbent on school-based peer mediation and conflict resolution coordinators to document results.

The importance of conducting evaluations for conflict resolution and peer mediation programs cannot be overstated. As professional school counselors work to link school counseling programs to the mission of schools, evidence of concrete measures that contribute to creating a safe leaning environment is essential.

Regular program evaluation reports should be completed and presented to all school personnel. Program evaluations should specify the impact conflict and violence within the school have on the culture and climate of the school and student academic achievement (e.g., AYP). Program evaluation reports should be completed regularly and presented to all school personnel to keep them up to date and informed.

SUMMARY/CONCLUSION

Conflict resolution and peer mediation programs have become an accepted part of the educational arena and valuable tools in creating a culture and climate of safety in schools. The rapid demands of our pluralistic society punctuate the need for peer mediation programs that focus on systemic integration as part of a systemic data-driven school counseling program designed to meet the complex needs of all students. All members of the school community are essential participants, as stakeholders strive to create schools that are dynamic yet peaceful environments where students learn to be productive, lifelong learners and members of a self-governing democratic society. To reach this ambitious goal, effective programming, supported by research and evaluation and grounded in theory, is essential. Contemporary professional school counselors are in a unique position to help facilitate the development and implementation of peer mediation programs as part of a comprehensive school counseling program.

ACTIVITIES

1. Design an outline for a violence prevention program for an elementary, middle, or high school. What message would you attempt to convey to the students? What programs and activities would you ask the students to participate in?

2. Observe a school cafeteria during lunch hour. What types of conflicts do you notice? How are these conflicts resolved?

3. Conduct a role-play involving a professional school counselor and two students who are involved in a conflict. What conflict resolution strategy was used? How well did it work?

THE PROFESSIONAL SCHOOL COUNSELOR AND STUDENTS WITH DISABILITIES

*ELANA ROCK AND ERIN H. LEFF**

Editor's Introduction: Advocating for the needs of *all* students is a primary responsibility of the transformed professional school counselor. For too long, students with special needs have been identified and served through special programs without appropriate attention given to their developmental academic, career, and personal–social needs. This chapter focuses on what professional school counselors can do to effectively advocate for and serve students with special needs.

Each person has the right to receive the information and support needed to move toward self-direction and self-development and affirmation within one's group identities, with special care being given to students who have historically not received adequate educational services: students of color, low socio-economic students, students with disabilities and students with nondominant language backgrounds. (ASCA, 2004a)

POOR OUTCOMES FOR STUDENTS WITH DISABILITIES

Considered a population requiring "special care," students with disabilities face a number of barriers to successful school and postschool outcomes. According to recent national data, the most common disabilities affecting more than 90% of school-aged students are learning

---

*The authors acknowledge the significant contribution of Estes J. Lockhart to the previous edition of this text chapter. May he rest in peace.

disabilities, emotional/behavioral disorders, mild mental retardation, language disorders, and other health impairments, including ADHD (USDE, 2003a). These disorders interfere with learning and behavior in school and cause students to struggle with academic achievement, most commonly in the areas of reading and math. In addition to the effects of the disorders themselves, students with disabilities have not always received adequate educational services.

As a result, students with disabilities have significant problems attaining academic progress in schools. They earn lower grades, are retained more often, and often fail to graduate with a diploma. In addition, they drop out at significantly higher rates than students without disabilities do. Currently, the dropout rates range from 34% of students with mental retardation to 65% of students with emotional/behavioral disorders (USDE, 2003a). Regarding adult outcomes, adults who were students with disabilities have lower rates of postsecondary educational involvement (including vocational training) and higher rates of unemployment and underemployment (National Council on Disability, 2004).

These poor outcomes are particularly disheartening when considering the fact that approximately 90% of students receiving special education services have "mild" or high-prevalence disabilities (USDE, 2003a). Many of these students have average cognitive ability and lack significant physical or sensory impairments that might further interfere with functioning. In effect, these students are capable of positive school and adult outcomes, including college and competitive employment, despite a long history of poor outcomes in these areas.

The USDE has recognized the poor outcomes for students with disabilities and articulated requirements in an effort to ensure improved progress. In its 2004 reauthorization of the IDEIA, Congress noted that:

> [d]isability is a natural part of the human experience and in no way diminishes the right of individuals to participate in or contribute to society. Improving educational results for children with disabilities is an essential element of our national policy of ensuring equality of opportunity, full participation, independent

living, and economic self-sufficiency for individuals with disabilities. (IDEIA, 2004)

Students with disabilities are capable of becoming, and are expected to become, contributing members of society, providing they receive the appropriate supports necessary for positive school and adult outcomes. To achieve these ends, Congress has mandated the delivery of special education and related services in the IDEIA (2004) and has required accountability measures for students with disabilities through the NCLB Act of 2002.

IDEIA (2004) states that 30 years of research and experience has demonstrated that the education of children with disabilities can be made more effective by:

> having high expectations for such children and ensuring their access to the general education curriculum in the regular classroom, to the maximum extent possible, in order to . . . meet developmental goals and, to the maximum extent possible, the challenging expectations that have been established for all children; and . . . be prepared to lead productive and independent adult lives, to the maximum extent possible.

SERVING STUDENTS WITH DISABILITIES

According to IDEIA, educational programming for a child with a disability requires an individualized approach to all identified needs. To identify and serve each student with a disability, a multidisciplinary team is constituted. Each team includes the parent(s), at least one general educator (if the child may be participating in general education), at least one special educator, related service providers, transition services participants (for students age 16 and older), and the student whenever appropriate. In addition, the parent or school may bring in other individuals who have knowledge or special expertise regarding the student. For example, a child with a learning disability may have a multidisciplinary team consisting of the student, parent, school principal, general educator, special educator, professional school counselor, speech pathologist, psychologist, and occupational therapist.

The team is initially responsible for determining whether a newly referred student requires assessment. If assessment is warranted, the team determines what assessments are needed, orders the assessments, reviews the findings, and determines whether the student is eligible for special education services because he or she meets the criteria for "a child with a disability." Once the student is found eligible for special education and related services, the team is responsible for developing the student's IEP, identifying all necessary services and supports required to meet areas of identified need, determining the student's placement, and implementing the IEP.

As a member of the multidisciplinary team, the professional school counselor may have many roles and potential responsibilities associated with programming and delivering services for children with disabilities. These responsibilities may be to the team (e.g., for assessment, development of the IEP, and implementation planning); directly to the child (e.g., counseling services, career development); or indirectly to the child, supporting him or her through others on the team (e.g., parent training, consultation with educators, clinical support).

ASCA, in its (2004b) position paper, described various roles of the professional school counselor regarding students with special needs:

When appropriate, interventions in which the professional school counselor participates may include but are not limited to:

- Leading school counseling activities as a part of the comprehensive school counseling program
- Providing collaborative services consistent with those services provided to students through the comprehensive school counseling program
- Serving on the school's multidisciplinary team that identifies students who may need assessments to determine special needs within the scope and practice of the professional school counselor
- Collaborating with other student support specialists in the delivery of services
- Providing group and individual counseling

- Advocating for students with special needs in the school and in the community
- Assisting with the establishment and implementation of plans for accommodations and modifications
- Providing assistance with transitions from grade to grade as well as post-secondary options
- Consulting and collaborating with staff and parents to understand the special needs of these students
- Making referrals to appropriate specialists within the school system and in the community.

It is clear that there are many roles in which professional school counselors support students with disabilities. Table 15.1 lists the most frequent roles reported by professional school counselors working with students with disabilities.

Despite clear expectations for the delivery of services by professional school counselors and counselors' involvement in the multidisciplinary team process, many master's-level school counseling programs do not adequately prepare counselors for these responsibilities. Many professional school counselors report having little if any coursework dealing with the needs of students with disabilities (McEachern, 2003). In addition, even professional school counselors who have taken coursework on programming for students with disabilities often report feeling underprepared or unprepared for the delivery of services to the children in their schools (Dunn & Baker, 2002; Milsom, 2002).

This chapter discusses the legal mandates involving the delivery of counseling-related services to children with disabilities. It then examines the roles of professional school counselors, including review of relevant responsibilities, service delivery options, and description of best practices in delivering services in areas associated with the needs of school-aged students with disabilities. Since many of the professional school counselors' responsibilities to students with disabilities are the same as or similar to their responsibilities to students without disabilities, emphasis in this chapter will be placed on those processes not discussed elsewhere in this text.

TABLE 15.1
Frequent roles for counselors working with students with disabilities.

From 75% to 83% of professional school counselors reported involvement in each of these roles:

- Provide individual/group counseling
- Make referrals
- Serve on multidisciplinary team
- Counsel parents and families
- Advocate for students
- Assist with behavior modification plans
- Provide feedback for team

From 40% to 60% of counselors reported involvement in these roles:

- Provide self-esteem activities
- Serve as consultant to parents/staff
- Provide social skills training
- Assist with transition plans

Source: "Students with Disabilities: School Counselor Involvement and Preparation," by A. S. Milsom, 2002, *Professional School Counseling, 5,* 331–339.

FEDERAL LEGISLATION

The federal laws that articulate and protect the rights of students with disabilities can be grouped into one of two categories: education laws or civil rights laws. The special education law most widely applied in schools is the IDEIA (2004). It was originally entitled the Education for All Handicapped Children Act when it was first enacted in 1975. IDEIA provides federal funding and requires states to guarantee a free appropriate public education (FAPE) to students who need special education and related services because of an eligible disability. There are other education laws that also impact the delivery of special education programs and services. Among them are Title I of the ESEA and the recent NCLB Act (USDE, 2002).

The most widely applied civil rights law is Section 504 of the Vocational Rehabilitation Act of 1973 (commonly referred to as Section 504). Although it provides no federal funding, it mandates that programs receiving federal funding under other laws may not exclude an otherwise qualified individual with a disability from participation in the program. It also requires that individuals with disabilities be provided reasonable accommodations that will allow them to access these programs. The Americans with Disabilities Act (ADA) of 1990 is another civil rights act whose school-related provisions are nearly identical to Section 504 of the Vocational Rehabilitation Act. The ADA extends the protection from discrimination because of disabilities to all public and private schools, except for religious schools, whether or not they receive federal financial assistance.

Understanding the differences between IDEIA and Section 504 is of practical importance for the professional school counselor. Professional school counselors often act as consultants for school staff, family, and outside agency representatives to help them understand how the legal rights of a student with a disability are appropriately addressed within an educational setting. As Bowen and Glenn (1998) stated, "In order to provide appropriate remedial and preventative services, counselors must more fully understand the present legislative requirements, characteristics, terminology and related counseling needs associated with exceptional learners" (p. 17).

The major difference between IDEIA and Section 504 is one of focus. IDEIA focuses on educational remediation whereas Section 504 focuses on prevention of discrimination. IDEIA attempts to address gaps in skills or abilities by ensuring the provision of appropriate services and modified instruction for students in need of special education. Section 504, on the other hand, attempts to level the playing field for those students whose disabilities may not directly affect their academic abilities but who may require accommodation to achieve at their ability levels.

For example, a student with a learning disability served under IDEIA may require special instruction in reading as well as related services such as speech therapy or counseling to learn. In contrast, a student with cerebral palsy qualified under Section 504 may be achieving at grade level in all academics but still need accommodations such as being allowed to dictate responses rather than write them, due to having limited fine motor skills.

IDEIA

IDEIA is the major special education law governing identification, evaluation, program, placement, and the provision of a FAPE for school-aged students determined to have one of 13 identified disabilities. This law provides that eligible students receive "special education," which is defined as "specially designed instruction, at no cost to parents, to meet the unique needs of a child with a disability, including instruction conducted in the classroom, in the home, in hospitals and institutions, and in other settings. . . ." (IDEIA, 2004). Table 15.2 includes the definitions of each of the categories of disabilities that may entitle a child to receive special education under IDEIA. As can be seen from the definitions in Table 15.2, IDEIA requires that nearly all disabilities affect educational performance. While a student with a disability may need, or at least benefit from, some interventions or special instruction, if the disability has minimal or no negative effect on learning, the student would not qualify as eligible for special education under IDEIA. However, he or she might be eligible for reasonable accommodations or supports under Section 504.

When a student is determined to be eligible for services under IDEIA, the school system is required to provide him a FAPE. It is important to remember that the law specifically states that the education be "appropriate." This standard has been adopted by most states. *Appropriate* does not mean *best*, and loosely using the term *best* when the school team means appropriate can cause significant problems. While professional school counselors and other professionals will try to do their best in providing services, they will not always provide the maximum or most beneficial services to an individual student. When the word *best* is used, it can lead to parental expectations of a range of services that are not required under the law or necessary for the student to learn. This increased level of services might be helpful in assisting the student to reach optimal performance if there were no limits; however, IDEIA does not require optimal programming, only appropriate programming that enables a child to make reasonable educational progress. In addition, the professional school counselor needs to be clear that the requirement under the law for school systems is to educate students, not to rehabilitate them. Rehabilitation services sometimes are provided, but only for the purpose of educating or helping students make a transition from secondary school to a useful career path, not for rehabilitation in and of itself.

The provision of FAPE generally involves two types of services, special education and related services. Special education is provided by special educators, as well as general educators and paraprofessionals in consultation with special educators. IDEIA identifies a continuum of placements where students may receive their instructional services, related services, or both. They range from full-time regular class placement to part-time regular class placement to services provided in residential schools and hospitals. Most students with disabilities are primarily educated in regular education classes for a majority of the school day (USDE, 2003a).

Once found eligible for special education, students are also entitled to receive special education instruction, related services, accommodations, and supports that meet their needs and enable them to benefit from their educational program. In a few statutorily specified instances, some related services, for example, speech, can be considered

TABLE 15.2
Handicapping conditions under IDEIA.

Autism means a developmental disability significantly affecting verbal and nonverbal communication and social interaction, generally evident before age 3, that adversely affects a child's educational performance. Other characteristics often associated with autism are engagement in repetitive activities and stereotyped movements, resistance to environmental change or change in daily routines, and unusual responses to sensory experiences. The term does not apply if a child's educational performance is adversely affected primarily because the child has an emotional disturbance, as defined below. A child who manifests the characteristics of autism after age 3 could be diagnosed as having autism if the criteria above are satisfied.

Deaf-blindness means concomitant hearing and visual impairments, the combination of which causes such severe communication and other developmental and educational needs that they cannot be accommodated in special education programs solely for children with deafness or children with blindness.

Deafness means a hearing impairment that is so severe that the child is impaired in processing linguistic information through hearing, with or without amplification, that adversely affects a child's educational performance.

Developmental delay means a significant cognitive delay in a child age 3 to 9 not accounted for by another handicapping condition.

Emotional disturbance means a condition exhibiting one or more of the following characteristics over a long period and to a marked degree that adversely affects a child's educational performance:

(A) An inability to learn that cannot be explained by intellectual, sensory, or health factors.

(B) An inability to build or maintain satisfactory interpersonal relationships with peers and teachers.

(C) Inappropriate types of behavior or feelings under normal circumstances.

(D) A general pervasive mood of unhappiness or depression.

(E) A tendency to develop physical symptoms or fears associated with personal or school problems.

The term includes schizophrenia. The term does not apply to children who are socially maladjusted, unless it is determined that they have an emotional disturbance.

Hearing impairment means an impairment in hearing, whether permanent or fluctuating, that adversely affects a child's educational performance but that is not included under the definition of deafness in this section.

Mental retardation means significantly subaverage general intellectual functioning, existing concurrently with deficits in adaptive behavior and manifested during the developmental period, that adversely affects a child's educational performance.

Multiple disabilities means concomitant impairments (such as mental retardation–blindness, mental retardation–orthopedic impairment, etc.), the combination of which causes such severe educational needs that they cannot be accommodated in special education programs solely for one of the impairments. The term does not include deaf-blindness.

Orthopedic impairment means a severe orthopedic impairment that adversely affects a child's educational performance. The term includes impairments caused by congenital anomaly (e.g., clubfoot, absence of some member, etc.), impairments caused by disease (e.g., poliomyelitis, bone tuberculosis, etc.), and impairments from other causes (e.g., cerebral palsy, amputations, and fractures or burns that cause contractures).

Other health impairment means having limited strength, vitality, or alertness, including heightened alertness to environmental stimuli, that results in limited alertness with respect to the educational environment, that is due to chronic or acute health problems such as asthma, ADD or ADHD, diabetes, epilepsy, a heart condition, hemophilia, lead poisoning, leukemia, nephritis, rheumatic fever, or sickle cell anemia and adversely affects a child's educational performance.

Specific learning disability means a disorder in one or more of the basic psychological processes involved in understanding or in using language, spoken or written, that may manifest itself in an imperfect ability to listen, think, speak, read, write, spell, or do mathematical calculations, including conditions such as perceptual

(Continued)

TABLE 15.2 (Continued)

disabilities, brain injury, minimal brain dysfunction, dyslexia, and developmental aphasia. The term does not include learning problems that are primarily the result of visual, hearing, or motor disabilities; of mental retardation; of emotional disturbance; or of environmental, cultural, or economic disadvantage.

Speech or language impairment means a communication disorder such as stuttering, impaired articulation, a language impairment, or a voice impairment that adversely affects a child's educational performance.

Traumatic brain injury means an acquired injury to the brain caused by an external physical force, resulting in total or partial functional disability or psychological impairment, or both, that adversely affects a child's educational performance. The term applies to open or closed head injuries resulting in impairments in one or more areas such as cognition; language; memory; attention; reasoning; abstract thinking; judgment; problem solving; sensory, perceptual, and motor abilities; psychosocial behavior; physical functions; information processing; and speech. The term does not apply to brain injuries that are congenital or degenerative, or to brain injuries induced by birth trauma.

Visual impairment including blindness means an impairment in vision that, even with correction, adversely affects a child's educational performance. The term includes both partial sight and blindness.

Source: Adapted with permission from the National Dissemination Center for Handicapped Children and Youth with Disabilities (NICHCY, 2002).

special education instruction. In these circumstances, the child can receive an IEP that includes only the related services. In general, however, a child must need special education instruction to be found eligible under IDEIA. For a child to receive special education and related services under IDEIA, a multidisciplinary team must complete a multistep process. The process involves a series of statutorily defined steps, including identification, screening, notification and consent, assessment, eligibility determination, IEP development, and implementation. Table 15.3 provides an outline of the special education process.

Section 504 and the ADA

The ADA builds on the original disability civil rights legislation, the Vocational Rehabilitation Act of 1973. Section 504 specifically focuses on students with disabilities in school and their right to access all services and programs available to students without disabilities (USDE/OCR, 2005). A student is eligible under Section 504 if the student has a physical or mental impairment that substantially limits one or more major life activities. Major life activities include caring for oneself, walking, talking, seeing, hearing, performing manual tasks, breathing, learning, or working. Thus,

for example, students who are educationally able but physically disabled, such as typically achieving students with asthma or cerebral palsy, would be qualified individuals under Section 504. All students found eligible for services under IDEIA, then, are also qualified individuals under Section 504 because they have a substantial impairment of a major life function—learning. This is important because this means that special education students may not be excluded from school activities such as assemblies, field trips, vocational programs, sports teams, or clubs simply because they have disabilities.

A student is also qualified under Section 504 if he or she has a record of having such an impairment or is regarded as having such an impairment. To "have a record of having, or be regarded as having such an impairment" means that the student has had a disability or has been believed to have a disability for a significant period of time even though the student did not, in fact, have a disability or no longer has a disability. An example would be someone who does not meet the criteria for autism but has been classified as having autism in the past. However, if a person not qualified to diagnose physical or mental disorders tells a parent or some other person that the student has a disability, the student is not considered as "having

TABLE 15.3
Outline of steps in the special education process.

Identification. A parent, guardian, state educational agency, other state agency, or local school system may initiate a request for initial evaluation for eligibility for special education (referral).

- Referral must be made to the IEP team of the child's "home" school (public school to which child is zoned), even if he or she attends a public or private school.
- Referral should be in writing and clearly specify that it is a "referral for special education services." It should provide parents' and child's names, address, and phone number.
- Referral should include area(s) of concern, for example, problems with reading, problems attending and learning, and so forth.

Screening. A multidisciplinary team (e.g., parent, guardian, regular educator, special educator, administrator) reviews the records and history of the child's learning problem(s) to determine if there is a need for individualized assessment.

- Parent will be asked to provide basic and historical information to determine possible areas of impairment.
- Parent will be asked to allow review of records (e.g., medical, school) and sign consents to obtain any needed information.
- Parent will be asked to complete screening interviews or data forms.
- The evaluation team will determine if assessments are needed and in what areas.
- If the team does not believe assessment is necessary, parent may request mediation or due process.

Notification and consent. If screening identifies a need for further assessment, the team notifies parents and requests written consent for all areas to be assessed.

- Parents must be notified in advance of any possible assessments.
- Parents must sign written consent for all assessments.
- Parents must receive 10 days' notice of all meetings.

Assessment. Professionals (e.g., special educators, psychologists, audiologists) administer tests individually to the student in a nondiscriminatory manner (considering dominant language, etc.).

- Assessments should be completed in every area of suspected problem(s).
- Assessments typically include educational and other areas (e.g., psychological, related health, visual acuity).
- For each area of suspected disability, particular assessments are usually required, and these assessments are performed by assessment-specific evaluators. For example, a suspected learning disability requires at least an educational assessment and a psychological (cognitive) assessment, with the possible need for a speech/language or other assessments. The required evaluators are a special educator, psychologist, and speech/language pathologist.
- If parent disagrees with results of assessment, the parent may request that the school fund an independent evaluation.
- Initial assessments are to be completed within 60 days of receipt of parental consent.

Eligibility determination. The multidisciplinary team considers all assessment results and determines if the child meets the criteria for a disability under one of the eligible categories.

- Team (including parent) reviews all assessment results.
- With parent input, team determines whether the child meets eligibility criteria for one (or more) disability areas.
- If team determines that the child does not meet eligibility requirements and parent disagrees, the parents can request mediation or due process.

(Continued)

TABLE 15.3 (Continued)

IEP development. The team (including the parent) collaboratively (a) develops goals to meet the student's needs and (b) determines all required services and supports needed to provide FAPE. IEPs must include:

- Present levels of performance in academic and functional areas.
- A statement of measurable annual goals.
- A description of how the child's progress toward meeting the goals will be measured.
- A statement of the special education and related service and supplementary aids and services to be provided.
- An explanation of the extent, if any, to which the child will not participate with nondisabled children in regular classes and activities.
- A statement of any appropriate accommodations.
- Start date for services.
- Anticipated frequency, location, and duration of services and modifications.
- Beginning not later than age 16, transition goals.

Implementation. The team, including the parent, determines the least restrictive environment (LRE) in which the student's IEP can be implemented.

- Occurs only after all the components of the IEP, described above, have been developed.
- Need to justify each successive removal from a less restrictive placement to a more restrictive placement (e.g., from full-time regular class placement to part-time resource room).
- Placement in LRE includes placing the student, if at all possible, in the home school. It also means placement with age-appropriate peers.
- Students need not be assigned to a particular placement to obtain a service. Any service can be provided in any placement.
- LRE is individually determined for each child—not by disability type, severity, program availability, or cost.

a record of, or as being regarded as having, an impairment." These phrases protect students who otherwise might be excluded from services under subsequent changes in the qualifying criteria despite having received accommodations or services as a person with a disability in the past.

To determine whether a student is protected under Section 504, an evaluation is conducted or existing records are reviewed. Public elementary and secondary school districts receiving federal financial assistance are required by Section 504 regulations to provide a FAPE, parallel to the IDEIA requirement, to students with disabilities in their jurisdiction (IDEIA, 2004). A FAPE under Section 504 consists of "regular or special education and related aids and services that . . . are designed to meet individual educational needs of handicapped persons as adequately as the needs of nonhandicapped persons are met" and are provided in accordance with Section 504

requirements relevant to educational setting, evaluation and placement, and procedural safeguards (IDEIA, 2004). While there is a clear overlap regarding the use of the words "special education" in both IDEIA and Section 504, in practice, students who require special education are served under IDEIA, and students who require only accommodations and support are typically served under Section 504.

Decisions about what educational and related services are appropriate for a child under Section 504 must be made by a placement group including persons knowledgeable about the child, the meaning of evaluation data, and placement options (IDEIA, 2004). Students who are found eligible under Section 504 receive a 504 Plan. A 504 Plan is frequently patterned after an IEP, although it tends to contain less detail. The 504 Plan describes the services the student is to receive under Section 504, along with the accommodations the student needs in order to access education. The services that may be provided under Section 504 include:

> counseling services, physical recreational athletics, transportation, health services, recreational activities, special interest groups or clubs sponsored by the recipients, referrals to agencies which provide assistance to handicapped persons, and employment of students, including both employment by the recipient and assistance in making available outside employment. (IDEIA, 2004)

Schools are also required to provide "reasonable accommodations" under Section 504. Just as IDEIA (2004) requires the provision of "appropriate" but not necessarily the best services, 504 requires schools to provide only "reasonable" accommodations. Some examples of the types of accommodations that schools are typically required to provide include "auxiliary aids" such as

> taped texts, interpreters or other effective methods of making orally delivered materials available to students with hearing impairments, readers in libraries for students with visual impairments, classroom equipment adapted for use by students with manual impairments, and other similar services and actions. (IDEIA, 2004)

In addition, the eligible student does not have to provide one's own "attendants, individually prescribed devices, readers for personal use or study, or other devices or services of a personal nature" (IDEIA, 2004).

Section 504 is a civil rights statute that addresses discrimination in access to programs and services, not remediation of learning. Eligibility under Section 504 is not limited to a specific list of disabilities as is IDEIA eligibility, nor is there a defined list of educational requirements and related services. In this sense, Section 504 provides more flexibility in that any physical or mental impairment could potentially create eligibility. Impairments frequently resulting in eligibility under Section 504 are ADHD (the most often cited diagnosis in schools under Section 504), temporary medical conditions, physical impairments, behavioral or emotional disorders, addictions, communicable diseases, chronic medical conditions, and dyslexia. Examples of students who are covered under Section 504 but not

IDEIA include students with alcohol or drug problems who are not currently using or abusing substances, allergies or asthma, environmental illnesses, temporary disabilities such as those from accidents, communicable diseases, and conduct disorders. A comprehensive compliance guide for elementary and secondary schools regarding Section 504 is available online at www.edlaw.net/service/guidcont.html.

FERPA

In the role of case manager, professional school counselors are likely to encounter issues regarding confidentiality of records and other communications referred to them. A federal law, FERPA, defines access to and confidentiality of student educational records. FERPA also is sometimes referred to as the Buckley Amendment, in honor of its sponsor, Senator James Buckley. Under FERPA, parents have rights to control access to academic records until the student is 18, at which time the rights are transferred to the student. Thus, under FERPA, an 18-year-old student must sign a release of information for a professional school counselor to share written records with anyone, including a service provider outside the system.

For the professional school counselor serving students with disabilities, four issues in FERPA are of particular importance:

1. Parents have a right to inspect and review all educational records of the student. Essentially, once a written document from any source is placed in the school file, parents have a right to inspect it. Further, they have a right to decide if the school may share the report in the future. In general, written permission must be obtained before an educational record can be shared.

2. FERPA defines what an educational record is and what a professional school counselor or anyone else may call a personal confidential file. Virtually every piece of paper, including all professional mental health reports, relating to a student in a school is an educational record. For professional school counselors to call any written documents in their possession personal confidential notes, they must not

have shared the information with anyone at any time. For example, if a professional school counselor at a multidisciplinary meeting pulls out his or her notes and reads from them, the notes become educational records and cease to be confidential counselor notes.

3. Under FERPA, the parent has a right to challenge what is in the school records and to have any information that can be proven to be inaccurate or misleading removed.

4. While FERPA doesn't address destruction of the educational records of students with disabilities, IDEIA does. The records must be retained for a minimum of 3 to 5 years, depending on the specific situation, following the students' graduation from secondary school. Also, there must be an attempt to contact the parents prior to destroying the records. One very good reason for maintaining the records is that they might be needed to avoid additional evaluations for students who may be seeking services through an agency such as a department of rehabilitation services or accommodations in college after leaving secondary education.

Another issue of confidentiality facing professional school counselors who keep records on students with disabilities is that of safekeeping the confidential files. Most counselors may believe that the files are safe in their office. It is important, however, that the counselor ensures the records are locked up and that only the counselor (and supervisor) has keys that will allow access to the records. A good Web site that provides access and additional information on all of the disability/education laws, regulations, and resources is available at www.edlaw.net/service/specialaw.html.

RELATED SERVICES FOR STUDENTS WITH DISABILITIES UNDER IDEIA AND SECTION 504

Students may receive related services under both Section 504 and IDEIA. Related services are non-instructional, ancillary services that are not part of the regular instructional program but may be required for the successful implementation of a student's instructional program under IDEIA or Section 504. The IDEIA (2004) definition of related services is, "transportation, and such developmental, corrective, and other supportive services . . . as may be required to assist a child with a disability to benefit from special education." These services include audiology, counseling, early identification and assessment, interpreting services, medical services (for diagnostic and evaluation purposes only), occupational therapy, orientation and mobility services, parent counseling and training, physical therapy, psychological services, recreation, rehabilitation counseling, school nurse services, social work services, speech language services, and transportation (IDEIA, 2004). In some instances, individual aides also are provided to assist students with school functioning.

School counseling services, when provided under IDEIA, are listed on the IEP or 504 Plan as a related service. Related services can be provided on a direct basis, or they may be delivered indirectly using a consultation model with a teacher or family member. For example, the professional school counselor might instruct the teacher in how to reinforce social skills in class rather than hold social skills training sessions individually with the student. The professional school counselor also might consult with the classroom teacher on how best to preempt or defuse the angry outbursts of a student with disabilities.

Recent data indicate that one in five students receiving special education has mental health services, an increase of nearly seven percentage points over the number 15 years earlier (Wagner, Newman, & Cameto, 2004). While mental health service may be provided by a number of different professionals in schools (e.g., psychologists, social workers, professional school counselors, mental health assistance, behavioral specialists), professional school counselors are increasingly being considered important resources in the delivery of services to students with emotional, behavioral, or social needs affecting their learning.

IDEIA specifically includes as related services for students with disabilities the following three service areas that are often performed by professional school counselors: counseling services, parent counseling and training, and rehabilitation counseling services (IDEIA, 2004).

The following information on these three related service areas is provided by the National Dissemination Center for Children with Disabilities (2001) in collaboration with the Office of Special Education Programs, USDE.

Counseling Services

Counseling services, according to ASCA (2004b), focus on the needs, interests, and issues related to various stages of student growth. Professional school counselors may help students with personal and social concerns such as developing self-knowledge, making effective decisions, learning health choices, and improving responsibility. Counselors may also help students with future planning related to setting and reaching academic goals, developing a positive attitude toward learning, and recognizing and utilizing academic strengths. Other counseling services may include parent counseling and training and rehabilitation counseling (i.e., counseling specific to career development and employment preparation). Counseling services are services provided by qualified social workers, psychologists, professional school counselors, or other qualified personnel (IDEIA, 2004).

Parent Counseling and Training

Parent counseling and training is an important related service that can help parents enhance the vital role they play in the lives of their children. When necessary to help an eligible student with a disability benefit from the educational program, parent counseling and training can include "assisting parents in understanding the special needs of their child, providing parents with information about child development, and helping parents to acquire the necessary skills that will allow them to support the implementation of their child's IEP or IFSP [individualized family service plan]" (IDEIA, 2004).

Rehabilitation Counseling Services

Rehabilitation counseling services are:

. . . services provided by qualified personnel in individual or group sessions that focus specifically on career development, employment preparation, achieving independence, and integration in the workplace and community. . . . The term also includes vocational rehabilitation services provided to a student with disabilities by vocational rehabilitation programs funded under the Rehabilitation Act of 1973, as amended. (IDEIA, 2004)

According to the Council on Rehabilitation Education (2003–2004), a rehabilitation counselor is a counselor who possesses the specialized knowledge, skills, and attitudes needed to collaborate in a professional relationship with people who have disabilities to achieve their personal, social, psychological, and vocational goals. To this end, rehabilitation counseling services generally may include: assessment of a student's attitudes, abilities, and needs; vocational counseling and guidance; vocational training; and identifying job placements.

TRANSITION SERVICES UNDER IDEIA 2004

The professional school counselor may have a variety of responsibilities in providing transition services to students with disabilities. According to IDEIA, the term *transition services* means a coordinated set of activities for a child with a disability that:

1. Is designed to be within a results-oriented process, that is focused on improving the academic and functional achievement of the child with a disability to factilitate the child's movement from school to postschool activities, including postsecondary education, vocational education, integrated employment (including supported employment), continuing and adult education, adult services, independent living, or community participation
2. Is based on the individual child's needs, taking into account the child's strengths, preferences, and interests
3. Includes instruction, related services, community experienes, the development of employment and other postschool adult living objectives, and when appropriate, acquisition of daily living skills and functional vocational evaluation

TABLE 15.4
Definitions of typical services performed by professional school counselors for children
with disabilities as required under IDEIA.

Advocacy. Actively supporting the rights of individual children with disabilities, including referral, active participation in team processes, promoting the rights and needs of students, and support for service delivery by self and others.

Assessment. Determining current performance and identifying areas of need for social or emotional functioning in school; evaluation in other areas, including substance abuse, social skills, self-determination, self-esteem, and career development.

Career counseling. The process of assisting individuals in the development of a life-career with focus on the definition of the worker role and how that role interacts with other life roles (National Career Development Association [NCDA], 1997).

Clinical case management. Coordinating counseling and delivery of other services for students with disabilities. In its 2004 position statement, ASCA (2004b) recommended against serving as case manager for students for whom a counselor is not delivering direct services.

Clinical support. Providing supervision and support of certified or trained assistants who are assisting in the delivery of related services, including mental health associates, interns, special educators, paraprofessionals, assistants, or others.

Collaboration. Working with other team members (e.g., educators, parents, other related service personnel) to deliver required services and supports to students with disabilities.

Crisis intervention. Providing intervention for emergent situations including acting out behavior, suicide risk, panic attacks, or other urgent needs.

Decision making. Contributing to team consensus on the eligibility of a child for special education services under the current federal definitions of disability categories. Determination of required services and supports or accommodations as well as LRE where the student can receive an appropriate education.

Discipline and manifestation determination. Responding to serious discipline issues warranting possible suspension and explusion. In cooperation with the multidisciplinary team, determining whether the behavior at issue was a manifestation of the disability and the need for alternative placement or supports.

Dropout prevention. Identifying students at high risk for dropping out and providing interventions aimed at engaging these students in school activities, promoting attendance, improving school functioning, and accessing other supports (e.g., mentors) as appropriate.

Direct services. Providing counseling to individuals or groups of students to address specific behavioral or emotional needs. May include social skills training, self-determination, career development, clinical support, grief work, and brief family counseling.

IEP development. Participating in designing measurable goals and identifying services and supports to address each area of need that interferes with functioning in school.

IEP team membership. Participating in screening, assessment, eligibility determination, IEP development, and progress monitoring for students with disabilities. Attending IEP meetings or providing written recommendations concerning the nature, frequency, and amount of counseling service to be provided to the child.

Parent counseling and training. Helping families access services in the school and community providing information on disability and disability management, and supporting the implementation of their child's IEP. This may also involve helping the parent gain skills needed to support IEP goals and objectives at home.

Positive behavioral support. Collecting data on a student's interfering behaviors to determine patterns of occurrence and to identify the function of the behavior. Generation of strategies designed to replace inappropriate behavior with more appropriate behaviors meeting the same function. Devising a system of prevention and intervention emphasizing positive behavior change methods.

Referral. Completing screening or other identification procedures to help identify students in need of special education. Referring individual children, as needed, to the multidisciplinary special education team for eligibility determination.

TABLE 15.4 (Continued)

Safekeeping confidential records. Ensuring compliance with IDEIA and other laws (e.g., FERPA) concerning access to and contents of confidential records of students receiving special education.

Self-determination training. Helping students acquire the skills necessary to direct their own lives. Skills in this area include: self-awareness; identification of strengths, limitations, and interests; identifying and programming goals; self-advocacy; and goal-directed activity.

Transition program planning. Developing and implementing a transition plan for all students with disabilities who are 14 years old or older, including an individual's and family's postschool goals specific to postsecondary education, employment, and independent living. Providing linkages to adult services, supported employment, independent living options, and postsecondary education supports as appropriate.

Beginning not later than the first IEP to be in effect when the child is 16 years old, and updated annually thereafter, each student's IEP must include:

1. Appropriate measurable postsecondary goals based on age-appropriate transition assessments related to training, education, employment, and, where appropriate, independent living skills
2. The transition services (including courses of study) needed to assist the child in reaching those goals
3. Beginning not later than 1 year before the child reaches the age of majority under state law, a statement that the child has been informed of the child's rights under this title, if any, that will transfer to the child on reaching the age of majority

In addition to programming for transition services and the provision of related services areas as described above, there are other support services required for students with disabilities that may involve the professional school counselor. These areas include some types of assessment, interpretation of assessments, positive behavioral support services, case management, advocacy, collaborating with other pupil support specialists, providing social skills training, leading activities to improve self-esteem, support for high school completion, dropout prevention, self-determination training, vocational programming, career development, evaluating college options, and referral to outside agencies. These

support services and other IEP responsibilities are defined briefly in Table 15.4.

PROVIDING SERVICES TO SUPPORT STUDENTS WITH DISABILITIES

Professional school counselors have many responsibilities, which can be roughly divided into three categories. First, are the counselor's responsibilities to the multidisciplinary team, in providing assessments, collaborating on the eligibility decision-making process, and developing counseling goals and objectives. Second, are the counselor's responsibilities to the child, in the provision of direct services, including counseling services, vocational guidance, and transition programming. Third, professional school counselors have indirect responsibilities to support the child by providing case management, consulting with teachers, training parents, or developing community-based resources that can assist the child after his or her graduation.

Multidisciplinary Team Responsibilities

Assessing Students with Disabilities

Professional school counselors serving students with disabilities often provide wide-ranging assessment services (see Table 15.5). In addition, professional school counselors may be asked to explain the assessments of others rather than conducting the assessments themselves. Usually,

TABLE 15.5
Assessment functions of professional school counselors serving students with disabilities.

1. Carry out and/or interpret functional behavioral assessments.

2. Interpret educational skill assessments.

3. Carry out and/or interpret curriculum-based assessments.

4. Explain psychological testing, including cognitive ability, emotional status, and behavior measures.

5. Carry out and/or interpret counseling assessments, including social skill, emotional status, and behavioral measures.

6. Carry out structured observations of the student.

7. Carry out a student records review.

8. Help stress the need for assessing student strengths.

9. Assess peer attitudes toward students with disabilities.

10. Collaborate with others using portfolio-, performance-, and curriculum-based assessments.

the reason professional school counselors are asked to review the assessment reports of others is because of time conflicts preventing the assessor from attending meetings. The professional school counselor can prepare for this eventuality through training or by asking the report writer, usually the school psychologist or educational diagnostician, for a briefing on the specific report prior to the day of the multidisciplinary meeting. The key guideline for the professional school counselor to consider while carrying out this function is to review only what is written in the report and never attempt to add to the interpretation of data stemming from someone else's report.

Professional school counselors sometimes perform a complete assessment or a portion of an assessment. The professional school counselor must be trained in the administration of any assessment instruments used. Whenever assessing a student, the professional school counselor will need signed permission to assess. Professional school counselors also need to be aware that in school systems, disagreements over who may use a testing instrument may arise among professionals who do assessments. Professional school counselors who find themselves in such conflicts will have to determine whether administering a specific assessment instrument is worth being in conflict with a colleague.

Professional school counselors often do assessments of social skills and career skills

and frequently deliver or consult on the delivery of these skills. In assessing social skills, most programs have a preintervention screening measure, or pretest. Using the pretest along with implementing the social skills program provides an indicator of the treatment success.

In particular, the professional school counselor may be asked to assess a student's social, emotional, or behavioral functioning in school. One method is to use a behavior checklist that has parent, teacher, and student forms. The results of the assessment are the answers given by the parent, teacher, and student that the professional school counselor may then interpret, report, or both.

An example of this type of assessment instrument is the Child Behavior Checklist (CBCL), part of the Achenbach System of Empirically Based Assessment (ASEBA) by Achenbach and Rescorla (2001). The CBCL has become one of the most widely used instruments for assessing children's behavior, with separate norms for males and females and for different age groups from age 6 to 18. A direct observation form, teacher rating form, semistructured interview form, and youth self-report are also available. The CBCL has six *DSM*-oriented scales: Affective Problems, Anxiety Problems, Somatic Problems, Attention Deficit/Hyperactivity Problems, Oppositional Defiant Problems, and Conduct Problems. In addition, the CBCL provides descriptive measures in nine observable behavioral areas. Other instruments are available to address more specific areas of social, emotional, or behavioral functioning. For example, there are substance abuse, depression, social skills, self-esteem, and anxiety surveys available. Most of these survey instruments, as long as they are not being used to evaluate or diagnose but rather to describe how the student perceives the situation or how others perceive the student's situation, require only training on the instrument for the professional school counselor to become adept with using them.

Another form of assessment the professional school counselor may find useful is that of measuring the attitudes of students without disabilities toward students with disabilities. Students who do not have disabilities are found, in general, to have less than desirable attitudes toward students with disabilities, and these attitudes can affect how much cooperative and beneficial interaction they have with students with disabilities (Salend, 1994). Professional school counselors can play a key role in helping the peers of students with disabilities develop a positive attitude toward these students.

There are two other assessments that are seeing increased usage because of 1997 IDEA changes. When disciplinary actions by school personnel will result in extended periods of removal from school for a student (after the first removal beyond 10 cumulative school days in a school year or after a removal that constitutes a change in placement), IDEIA requires that the IEP team meet within 10 days to formulate a functional behavioral assessment (FBA) plan for developing an intervention plan. If a behavior intervention plan already exists, the team must review and revise it as necessary, to ensure that it addresses the behavior on which disciplinary action is predicated. FBA and the development of BIPs are discussed in detail later.

Positive Behavioral Support

A significant percentage of students identified as having emotional disturbance, behavioral disorders, or ADHD demonstrate behaviors that interfere with their learning or the learning of their peers. Under IDEIA, the IEP team is charged with specific responsibilities to support such

students and others with similarly disruptive or problematic behaviors (e.g., students with autism, traumatic brain injury, mental retardation, learning disabilities, etc.).

There are three primary occasions that require the provision of "positive behavioral supports" (PBSs) under IDEIA. They are (a) the development of schoolwide systems of support, (b) PBS to individual students, and (c) PBS after a serious behavior (IDEIA, 2004). The professional school counselor has roles in each area. In the creation of schoolwide systems of PBS, the counselor can serve on the school improvement team, help provide staff development activities, or otherwise provide assistance in general school programming for student well-being. By taking a leadership role in developing systems of schoolwide support, the school counselor can facilitate improvement for all students in the building in areas of appropriate behavior and reduction of problem behaviors (e.g., substance abuse, vandalism, bullying), and can help support increased learning for all.

In the second two areas for providing PBS, the counselor is likely to be more directly involved in the collection of information for FBA and the development of the BIP. In some schools, psychologists or behavior specialists typically conduct FBAs; in other systems, a behavioral support team collaboratively conducts them. This team is usually composed of a special education teacher, a regular teacher, a professional school counselor, a school psychologist, and an administrator. Sometimes professional school counselors are given the role of carrying out or interpreting FBAs. In these cases, the professional school counselor will want to attend training on the process. Most school systems provide their own training and have a required process for carrying out assessments. A general description of the process is provided below.

Schoolwide Systems of PBS. The first approach for providing PBSs is in the establishment of general, schoolwide policies and procedures that promote positive behavior among all students, commonly referred to as school-wide positive behavior support (SWPBS; Osher, Dwyer, & Jackson, 2004; Sprague & Golly, 2004;

Sugai, Horner, & Gresham, 2002). According to the National Technical Assistance Center on Positive Behavioral Interventions and Supports (Office of Special Education Programs [OSEP], 2005), the SWPBS process emphasizes the creation of systems that support the adoption and durable implementation of evidence-based practices and procedures that fit within ongoing school reform efforts.

Comprehensive behavior management systems are very effective at improving school climate, decreasing instances of office referral by 50%, and preventing 80% of problematic student behaviors, including antisocial behavior; vandalism; aggression; later delinquency; and alcohol, tobacco, and other drug use. In addition, positive changes in academic achievement and school engagement have been documented using an SWPBS approach in concert with other prevention interventions (Sprague & Walker, 2004).

There are several major components in the development of effective schoolwide systems. These crucial elements are often constructed in a staff development program or incorporated into a model system that is developed, implemented, evaluated, and modified on a regular basis by school staff. Data are collected regularly and used to evaluate progress and monitor system implementation. The seven components are:

1. An agreed-on and common approach to discipline.
2. A positive statement of purpose.
3. A small number of positively stated expectations for all students and staff.
4. Procedures for teaching these expectations to students.
5. A continuum of procedures for encouraging displays and maintenance of these expectations.
6. A continuum of procedures for discouraging displays of rule-violating behavior.
7. Procedures for monitoring and evaluating the effectiveness of the discipline system on a regular and frequent basis (OSEP, 2005).

One example of a process-based model for comprehensive behavior management systems is the PAR model (Rosenberg & Jackman, 2003). In this model, collaborative teams of teachers,

school administrators, related service personnel, and parents work together within a prescriptive workshop format to come to consensus on an individualized schoolwide, comprehensive approach to discipline. They collaboratively develop, implement, and evaluate plans and strategies to prevent the occurrence of troubling behavior, respond to instances of rule compliance and noncompliance in a consistent fashion, and resolve many of the issues that underlie or cause troubling behavior.

Another system, the Best Behavior Program (Sprague & Golly, 2004), provides a standardized staff development training program aimed at improving school and classroom discipline and associated outcomes. The Best Behavior Program addresses whole-school, classroom, individual student, and family collaboration practices and is intended to be used in combination with other evidence-based prevention programs such as the *Second Step Violence Prevention Curriculum* (Committee for Children, 2002a). Representative school team members are trained to develop and implement positive school rules, direct teaching of rules, positive reinforcement systems, data-based decision making at the school level, effective classroom management methods, curriculum adaptation to prevent problem behavior, and functional behavioral assessment and positive behavioral intervention plans.

PBS to Individual Students. The second area in which PBSs are used is when a student's behavior interferes with his or her learning or that of others. The IEP team must consider the need for a targeted intervention comprised of strategies and support systems to address disruptive or problematic behavior in children with disabilities (Quinn, Gable, Rutherford, Nelson, & Howell, 1998). This targeted intervention involves the completion of an FBA and the development of a BIP to address the specific target behaviors. The rationale for an FBA is that identifying the function of a student's behavior, specifically what the student seeks to receive or avoid by engaging in the behavior, helps the IEP team develop proactive instructional strategies (such as a positive behavior management program or strategies) that address behaviors interfering with learning. The use of BIPs has wide applicability to individuals with serious challenging behaviors and has been demonstrated to reduce problem behavior by 80% in two thirds of the cases. The FBA/BIP process has also been used to successfully reduce disruptive classroom behaviors in students with mild disabilities in a general education classroom (e.g., Roberts, Marshall, Nelson, & Albers, 2001).

Unlike other types of assessment, the goal of an FBA is the identification of the function of a student's misbehavior and the development of information on the conditions that give rise to the behavior as well as the conditions likely to sustain or decrease the behavior. This information is directly applicable to the generation of strategies to prevent the occurrence of the behavior and to subsitute more appropriate behaviors when similar conditions arise. The steps in the FBA process include (a) the clear identification and description of the problematic behavior, (b) the identification of the conditions and settings in which the behavior does and does not occur, (c) the generation of a hypothesis regarding the "function" of the behavior to the child, and (d) testing the hypothesized function of the behavior by manipulating the environmental antecedents and consequences. An excellent overview of the FBA process, including completed samples, is available on the

Multimodal Functional Behavioral Assessment Web site (http://mfba.net).

To identify the target behavior, team members first collect data on the occurrences of the behavior in a variety of environments and under a number of differing conditions. Data need to be collected on the situation in which the behavior is demonstrated, such as the setting, time of day, environmental conditions, and group membership (situation demands). Data also need to be collected on the specific requirements expected of the child at that point in time (setting demands). Data are typically collected via an ABC log, which is a narrative listing of antecedents (what occurs immediately before the target behavior), the description of the behavior, and consequences (what occurs immediately after the behavior). When conducting ABC observations, it is important to identify class or setting demands, describe what is occurring, describe student behavior, describe the response (from teacher or environment), identify next antecedent (and repeat), and take copious anecdotal notes. It also helps to compute percent of time on task or percentage of work completed, if possible. An example of an ABC log is presented in Table 15.6.

The ABC data allow for the clear examination of the student's behavior. The ABC reveals that some of Kerri's problematic behavior can be

TABLE 15.6
ABC log for Kerri, a student with disruptive classroom behaviors.

Time:	9:30 a.m.
Setting:	Social studies class with Mr. Pepper
Setting demands:	Group discussion with teacher-directed questioning
Participants:	Class of 28 students in Grade 4

Antecedent	Behavior	Consequence
Teacher (T) asks question.	Kerri says, "Ooh, ooh" and waves hand.	T calls on Kerri.
T asks another question.	Kerri calls out answer.	T says, "Raise your hand" and says answer is correct.
Jon (student) asks question.	Kerri calls out answer.	T says, "Kerri that is incorrect."
T says, "Kerri that is incorrect."	Kerri argues with T that she read it in a book.	T says, "You are wrong." The correct answer is _____.
T says, "The correct answer is _____."	Kerri says sarcastically, "Like you know anything, Pepper!"	T says, "You've disrupted class one too many times. Go to the principal's office!"

described as "calling out answers" and "arguing with teacher," both more objective targets than "disruptive behavior." Other data to collect include amount of work turned in, discipline referrals, grade report, frequency of time-outs or direct intervention, and educational history regarding the demonstration of similar behaviors.

In addition to the ABC data collection, a variety of individuals are asked to complete an interview regarding the possible behavioral targets. Parents, teachers, and other school staff would be asked questions about problematic behavior that occur in their interaction with the student, the conditions under which it occurs, and what the individual has done to address the behavior in the past. In addition, the student should be interviewed to examine his or her perception of the behavior and its benefit to him or her. Interview data should include a description of the behavior, settings where it occurs, frequency, intensity, duration, previous interventions used, and effect on the student. The Center for Effective Collaboration and Practice (www.air.org/cecp/fba) has copyright-free samples of interview instruments available for FBAs, along with ABC charts and scatterplots to record frequency of behavior. Additional forms and completed FBA samples are available from the Center for Evidence-Based Practice (http://challengingbehavior.fmhi.usf.edu/fba.htm) and Special Connections, at the University of Kansas (www.specialconnections.ku.edu).

To select a specific target behavior to address, the team considers the existing problems that were revealed from the interviews and ABC data. Potential target behaviors must be described objectively and must be repeatable, controllable, and measurable. These elements are essential for verifying that the behavior is within the conscious control of the student, as well as quantifiable by the observer. To be measurable, a behavior typically must have a clear beginning and end point, contain movement, or produce a product that can be measured. Therefore, "throwing objects" would be an appropriate target behavior, whereas "aggressive behavior" would not. Similarly, "laziness, off-task behavior, and daydreaming" are not measurable targets, but "failure to complete work" can be measured. Only one or two behaviors are targeted at any

one time. If necessary, the team can generate a list of behaviors and ask members to rank order them by priority level. A useful hierarchy is Severity Level I: Physically dangerous to self or others; Severity Level II: Interfering with work or learning of self or others; and Severity Level III: Inappropriate for age or grade placement or likely to cause increasing problems in the future.

Next, by examining situations where the target behavior does and does not occur, team members can identify variables that may predict the behavior (e.g., from Kerri's example in Table 15.6, the teacher asking a general question to the class) or consequences that may sustain it (e.g., the teacher paying attention to Kerri's call-outs and arguing with her). In addition, by seeing where the behavior does *not* occur, the team can explore possible functions for the student. For example, in other data collections conducted with different teachers and in different instructional settings, it became obvious that Kerri did not call out in class activities that included cooperative learning groups (but did actively assume a group leadership role).

The next step is to synthesize the available data to determine the possible function of the behavior for the student. Functions of behavior may relate to involvement with others ("interactive functions"), such as requests for attention (e.g., social interaction, play interactions, affection, permission to engage in an activity, action by receiver, assistance, information/clarifications, objects, food); negations/protest (e.g., cessation, refusal); declarations/comments about events or actions (e.g., about objects/persons, about errors/mistakes, affirmation, greeting, humor); or declarations about feelings/anticipation (e.g., boredom, confusion, fear, frustration, hurt feelings, pain, pleasure). Functions of behavior also may be "noninteractive" in that they provide internalized effects. For example, noninteractive functions can be habitual or for self-regulation, rehearsal, pleasure, or relaxation or tension release.

In our example, interview data were collected from Kerri as well as from her divorced parents. Her mother reported extreme difficulty getting Kerri to follow directions without a struggle. Her father reported no difficulty, as he "laid down the law" with no room for negotiation or discussion. He reported that he was surprised her male teacher had problems with her, as she should respond immediately to him as she does her father. Based on the synthesis of all of the available data, the team hypothesized that the function of her behavior may be to seek power or control.

Once the function of the behavior is hypothesized, the next step is to manipulate the environment to test the hypothesis. For example, if a student's behavior was hypothesized as seeking attention from peers, the team might construct a strategy to collect data in times where peer response was or was not forthcoming and to determine if the hypothesis was supported.

Once the function of the behavior is identified, the team can begin to craft a BIP. This document is used to provide information to educators and parents to address the student's target behavior. Typically, problematic behavior is addressed by (a) identifying ways to prevent or minimize the occurrence of the behavior, (b) providing appropriate methods to change the behavior, and (c) assisting the student in building more appropriate behaviors to meet the same function as the inappropriate behaviors did.

To reduce instances or prevent the occurrence of the behavior, strategies may be provided to help teachers and parents restructure the setting demands where the behavior occurs. For example, a teacher may use "Every Student Responds" (whole class response) techniques to reduce the times when he or she calls on a single student for a response. Similarly, a parent may be advised to tell a child, "Come to the table now," instead of asking, "Are you ready for dinner?"

Next, the BIP often includes a specific behavior change plan to address problem behavior as it occurs. For example, Kerri's BIP might include the use of extinction procedures for call-outs to be combined with a DRL (differential reinforcement of lower rates of behavior) strategy. By ignoring the call-outs, Kerri's teacher stops reinforcing problem behavior, and the DRL provides reinforcement to Kerri as she meets preset (and increasingly lower) goals for number of call-outs per time period.

Finally, the BIP typically includes strategies to help the student learn more appropriate ways

to achieve the same objective. For example, a student like Kerri who seeks control or power may be provided with choices and opportunities for appropriate leadership within the classroom or in other school activities.

Sugai et al. (2000) provided an excellent resource for school staff and administrators in the procedures for implementing the FBA process in schools. To implement the FBA and BIP processes effectively in schools, teams typically follow a series of steps:

1. Identify the case manager responsible for the overall management of the plan.
2. Describe the expected outcomes and goals for the plan.
3. Identify the problem.
4. Conduct the FBA.
5. Identify expected outcomes and goals.
6. Develop interventions.
7. Identify barriers to plan implementation.
8. Specify the interventions used to achieve the goals.
9. Specify person or people responsible for specific interventions.
10. Specify a review date.
11. Implement BIP.
12. Collect follow-up data on the effects of the BIP.
13. Review data and modify the plan as necessary.

PBS After a Serious Behavior. The third situation requiring PBS is when a student has been suspended or expelled because of problem behavior. According to IDEIA, FBAs and BIPs are required in connection with disciplinary removals for drugs and weapons offenses, for offenses involving serious bodily injury, or for any combination of school removals totaling 10 days. The IEP team must meet within 10 days to conduct the FBA and formulate a BIP. If a BIP already exists, the team must review and revise it as necessary to ensure that it addresses the behavior on which disciplinary action is predicated. This process follows the same series of steps described earlier, but it is obviously less preventive in nature, as the student has already demonstrated seriously problematic behavior, warranting the school removal.

Collaboration and Group Decision Making

Professional school counselors often will serve on multidisciplinary teams for determining eligibility and planning programs for students with disabilities. While the laws are different with regard to the formation, membership, and responsibilities of multidisciplinary teams under IDEIA and Section 504, the professional school counselor's role is the same whether at a meeting operating under IDEIA or under Section 504. The professional school counselor must be a supportive member of a group decision-making process whose goal is to enable a student with a disability to learn. A primary task of the professional school counselor is to help the multidisciplinary team understand the whole student, especially the individual assets of the student that are sometimes not readily apparent in paper reviews. Assets such as good character, perseverance, mood, gross- or fine-motor coordination, special talents, desire to help others, motivation, sports skills, leadership qualities, unique experiences, supportive relationships, enriching hobbies, vocational experiences, close family ties, and membership in organizations need to be brought before the multidisciplinary group planning an individualized program for the student.

All professional school counselors should consider whether peer tutoring or other generally available services would address the student's needs without the student's having to be labeled as having a disability. Most schools use some type of prereferral team process that attempts to address the student's performance problems prior to seeking eligibility for special services. On the other hand, no student may be refused the opportunity to receive special education under IDEIA when qualified. Professional school counselors should always keep in focus the fact that the student's learning needs are the main purpose of the multidisciplinary meeting.

Once a student has been deemed eligible, the IEP team will determine the appropriate constellation of services to address the student's needs. If a student needs counseling services, this responsibility sometimes will be assigned to the professional school counselor. In other situations, a psychologist or social worker will provide the services. Sometimes the goals are written so that any one of these three professionals can provide the service, and the professionals determine among themselves who will take the responsibility. It is important that the provider of the service have the necessary training and availability.

Manifestation Meetings

Manifestation hearings are multidisciplinary team meetings convened because a student has been excluded for disciplinary reasons from his educational program for 10 or more days during 1 school year. The meeting must occur within 10 days of the student's removal from school. The purpose of the manifestation meeting is for the team to determine whether the student's behavior was caused by, or had a direct and substantial relation to, the student's disability. It is important to remember that the student's competency is not at issue in a manifestation meeting. In other words, manifestation is not a determination of whether the student understood if his actions were right or wrong; rather, the meeting is purely intended to determine whether there was a causal connection between the student's disability and the behavior.

If the team decides that the behavior was caused by, or was directly related to, the student's disability, the student is reinstated with all information related to the disciplinary issue removed from the discipline record and cumulative file. If the team determines that the student's disability did not cause the behavior, the student may be suspended or expelled unless the team finds one of two situations occurred. If the student's IEP was not implemented or the team determines that the IEP did not provide the student with a FAPE (and additional or different services should be included in the IEP), the student may not be suspended or expelled.

Under IDEIA, if a student with a disability is removed from school for more than 10 days, he or she must continue to receive programs and services that will allow him or her to progress toward meeting the goals on the IEP and in the general curriculum. These programs and services may be provided through home teaching or may be provided at a different location such as an alternative education setting. Under Section 504, if the problem behavior is not a result of the student's handicapping condition, then the student may be excluded, and there is no requirement for additional educational services.

In some instances, a student's behavior may relate to a disability and still result in a removal from school for 45 school days. This can occur if (a) the student is involved in a drug offense, (b) the student is involved in a weapons offense, or (c) the student's behavior inflicted serious bodily injury.

The professional school counselor can be an important player in the manifestation hearing, particularly when the student's disability is emotionally based or has strong emotional or behavioral aspects (e.g., ADHD, emotional disturbance, or autism). The team may look to the professional school counselor to help it better understand the nature of the emotionally or behaviorally based disability. This can place the professional school counselor in a difficult position if other staff members disagree with his or her perspective. For example, the student might have physically or verbally assaulted a staff member in a fairly serious manner. When this happens, the counselor can lose the trust or respect of staff by simply focusing on the manifestation issue without acknowledging the effect of the assault on the staff member, whether or not it was a manifestation of the student's disability.

Determining Need for Counseling Services for Students with Disabilities

When considering individual counseling for a student, the professional school counselor should work with the family and staff to construct a list of the social, emotional, or behavioral issues and concerns affecting the student's educational performance. Information from assessments (including the FBA if available) and interviews can provide important information on the extent and nature of the problems. A review and prioritization of this data can help the team to clarify the problem, identify ways to involve parents and other staff (e.g., teachers, other related service providers), recognize the need for implementation in multiple settings, and reveal the extent of

the needs and the impact on types and amounts of services needed.

It is important for the professional school counselor to help the team remain focused on the purpose of school counseling as a related service for children with disabilities, that is, to enable the student to learn. It is easy to slip into discussing counseling interventions that might be helpful for the student but are not required for the student to learn. For example, the parents of a child with a learning or emotional disability might feel that counseling could reduce the child's anxiety. However, unless such a reduction in anxiety is needed for the child to be able to learn, it should not be included in the IEP.

Counseling goals usually fall under the areas of social–emotional or behavioral needs, though they may include transition goals as mandated by law for students over age 16. Typical areas addressed by counseling goals include: anger management, stress/anxiety management, respecting authority, following school rules, self-determination/life planning, career awareness/vocational development, coping skills/frustration tolerance, interpersonal skills, family issues regarding postschool outcomes, and self-esteem.

Counselor Concerns About Providing IEP Services

The IEP team, as a group, determines what services the student is to receive, the frequency of the service, and who is to provide the service. No one individual can change the components of an IEP. Sometimes the professional school counselor may feel this is not the appropriate time to provide the service, these are not the appropriate services to provide, or the training to carry out the task appropriately is lacking. Any of these issues could produce an ethical dilemma for the professional school counselor. In these situations, the professional school counselor must follow the IEP as written until it is changed. At a meeting to revise the IEP, the concerns can be raised and the team will have the opportunity to revise the IEP to appropriately address them. Under the 2004 provisions of IDEIA, nonsubstantive changes can be made to the IEP without another meeting. For example, a new goal may be added to existing services on the IEP when a previous goal has been met.

It is also important that the professional school counselor remain cognizant of the limits of his or her role and ensure that he or she does not perform activities outside his or her area of qualification. In particular, counselors should be careful not to assume responsibilities typically within the purview of psychologists or social workers or that are specifically assigned to others by the IEP. In some instances, IEP counseling goals will indicate that the counselor, psychologist, or social worker may provide the service. In that situation, the providers can decide who will implement the IEP. If a student's IEP calls for counseling services and the professional school counselor is unable to provide them, the school may contract with another counselor to provide the services or may rewrite the IEP so that a psychologist can provide the services.

IEP Development

Writing Counseling IEP Goals. Goals are the core components of an IEP. They are intended to estabilish what the IEP team, including the parent and child when appropriate, thinks the student should accomplish in a year. These goals are based on the needs of the student as determined by relevant assessments and on the student's present levels of academic achievement and functional performance. IDEIA requires goals to address all areas of identified needs in academic and functional skill areas. Functional skills may include adaptive skills, classroom behavior, social–interpersonal skills, self-determination, and vocational skills. In developing goals, IDEIA specifically requires that the IEP team consider the strengths of the child; the concerns of the parents for enhancing the education of their child; the results of the initial evaluation or most recent evaluation of the child; and the academic, developmental, and functional needs of the child. The goals are to be designed to enable the student to be involved in and make progress in the general education curriculum and to address all of the student's other educationally related needs that result from the disability. Since goals are

focused on the student's expected achievement in 1 year's time, goals are generally written in broad but measurable terms.

For each area of identified need, at least one goal should be written. If there are multiple areas, the team may decide to prioritize the issues and first address those issues it considers most important. The following are provided as guidelines on how to develop effective goals.

Each annual goal should include five components: (a) *direction* of change desired, (b) *deficit* or *excess*, (c) *present* level, (d) *expected* level, and (e) *resources* needed. The direction of change is one of the following: (a) *increase* (e.g., social skills, impulse control, self-determination), (b) *decrease* (e.g., hitting, temper tantrums, call-outs, days absent), or (c) *maintain* (e.g., attention span, attendance).

The deficit or excess is the general area that is identified as needing special attention. Examples of areas in which deficits may occur include work completion, following staff directions, frustration tolerance, coping, impulse control, and peer relationships. Examples of areas in which excesses may occur include physical aggression, activity level, talking out, and anxiety level.

The present level ("from" _____) is a description of what the student does now in the area of deficit or excess; it is his or her present performance level. Examples of present level include ability to work with a peer for 2 minutes, completing 40% of class work, arguing with teacher when corrected, ability to remain on task with direct adult supervision, and following directions with repeated prompts.

The expected level ("to" _____) is where the student can reasonably be expected to be, or what he can reasonably be expected to attain, at the end of 1 year, if the needed resources are provided. Each expected level must be specific to the individual student and must be based on where the student is at present and what is realistic to expect from him or her in a year's time if the needed resources are provided. Examples of expected level include working with a peer cooperatively for 10 minutes, following teacher directions the first time given, responding appropriately to redirection/correction, remaining on task for 15 minutes with no reminders, using appropriate language in school, asking for help or a break when needed.

The resources needed describe the special methods, techniques, materials, situations, equipment, and so forth that will be needed to enable the student to reach the expected levels of performance. Examples of resources include positive reinforcement, a point system, individual counseling, parent training, and job coaching. Table 15.7 provides sample goals with all essential components.

Evaluation Procedures. IEPs must include evaluation procedures and schedules for determining, at least on an annual basis, whether the goals and objectives are being achieved. The evaluation procedure selected must be appropriate for the behavior or skill in question. Put another way, not every behavior or skill can be evaluated through "teacher or therapist observation." Some of the evaluation procedures that might be used for different objectives include direct observation, formal or informal assessments, or permanent products.

Direct observation by counselors and teachers provides a continuous and potentially valuable source of assessment information regarding student performance and may be used in all areas of instruction, including academic and social behavior. Observation can vary in its degree of

formality and specificity, but when used to evaluate student progress, it must be objective. Observational methods that are both objective and structured include event recording (e.g., number of call-outs), duration recording (e.g., time on task), interval recording (e.g., whether student kept hands to self for each 15-minute period), and time sampling (e.g., whether student was in seat each time the timer went off). Evaluation methods may also use formal and informal tests (e.g., the ARC's Self-Determination Scale) or permanent products (e.g., a point sheet, percent work completed, homework returned, attendance record).

The frequency of data collection should be determined by (a) the importance of the objective in question and (b) the amount of additional staff time that it takes. As a guideline, evaluative data should generally be collected at least every week. It is this data that must be reported on regular IEP report cards. Table 15.8 provides examples of objectives that include the three required parts as well as the evaluation procedure and schedule.

Specifying IEP Services. IDEIA further requires that the IEP include a statement of the special education and related services and supplementary aids and services, based on scientifically based practices, to the extent practicable, to be provided to or on behalf of the child. In addition, the IEP must describe the student's participation

TABLE 15.7
Sample goal statements.

1. Jon will decrease destructive behavior from an average of five incidents per week to no destructive acts through reinforcement of positive behavior and individual counseling.

2. Chandra will increase vocational skills from ability to recognize basic kitchen utensils to ability to function as a cook's helper through community-based instruction.

3. Lin will increase self-control from overreacting emotionally to normal events to ability to function with limited supervision in classroom settings through individual counseling and reinforcement of positive, appropriate behaviors.

4. Keon will increase peer relationships from total rejection by peer group members to inclusion in group activities through the use of group contingencies and social skills training.

5. Davon will increase employability skills from ability to follow simple instructions and use simple psychomotor skills to ability to use hand tools in designated work situations through individual instruction in a sheltered workshop setting.

6. Keisha will increase social behavior from daily hitting, kicking, and throwing objects to no hitting, kicking, or throwing objects through positive reinforcement for appropriate social behaviors and small-group interaction.

TABLE 15.8
Sample objectives.

1. Given a 10-minute cooperative learning activity, Rodney will participate with peers without leaving the group in two of three trials. Evaluation: Peer group log, daily

2. Given a verbal direction from the teacher, Jay will comply within 1 minute 80% of the time. Evaluation: Event recording, weekly

3. When included in a small group of peers, Julie will exhibit consideration for others by taking turns, sharing, and refraining from physical aggression in three of four opportunities. Evaluation: Teacher observation, weekly

4. Given bus tokens, Jose will arrive for school on time 95% of school days. Evaluation: Attendance records, weekly

in regular education programs, a list of the projected dates for the initiation of services, and the anticipated duration of services.

The frequency and intensity of counseling sessions are determined at the IEP meeting. Services will range significantly according to an individual child's needs. Sometimes, for example, a student's needs require weekly sessions, either to help a student learn a new coping skill or to help a student stay emotionally stable and support his or her access to education. In other situations, the student may need to be seen less frequently, for monitoring only. In any counseling relationship, there also may be situations requiring that the counselor see the student when in crisis in addition to the time allotted on the IEP. A counselor is able to provide more services than the IEP dictates, but not less.

With the professional school counselor's input, the IEP team may also determine whether required services are provided individually or in group sessions. In other situations, the team will leave that decision to the judgment of the service provider. Also, the IEP team determines whether the service is delivered directly or via consultation with another staff member or parent.

Individualized Transition Program Planning

As noted above, IDEIA requires the IEP team to create a transition plan for a student with a disability by the time the student is 16 years old. Section 504 has no transition requirements. Students must be invited to IEP meetings when their transition plans are discussed. Representatives of programs,

such as vocational rehabilitation services, also are to be invited to transition planning meetings. Sometimes, a department of rehabilitation services representative can provide diagnostic services while the student is in school, and can then offer training for a career, money to assist in obtaining educational or support services, or linkages to adult services as needed after graduation.

The transition plan is intended to address all areas of the student's post high school life, including postsecondary education, career, independent living, recreation, and community involvement. Counselors can help the team by assessing student career interests, developing appropriate transition goals, and providing resources and connections to adult services as needed, and by helping the student with personal adjustment, self-concept development, self-determination training, career exploration, and job coaching. Professional school counselors might also help plan and implement a school-to-work program or internship for the student.

Since a transition plan focuses on the individual's present needs and stated preferences, assessment is required. Typically, the assessment includes interest inventories, interviews of the student and parents (to determine expectations regarding employment, education, and living arrangements after high school), review of work history and work habits, review of progress toward graduation and postsecondary acceptance, self-determination assessment, and other information specific to the individual student as needed (e.g., assessment of functional living skills, vocational assessment, interpersonal skill assessment). In many schools, the professional school counselor provides some or most of this assessment information to the team.

The individualized transition plan (ITP) is developed after information is collected on the student's and family's hopes and expectations for the future and synthesized with assessment results as described earlier. For example, the goals and needs addressed in a transition plan for Ryan, a 16-year-old 11th-grade student with learning and behavioral disorders, might include:

- Obtaining a part-time paid job in the community
- Selecting and applying to a 2-year college or vocational program
- Shadowing workers in three areas of career interest: elevator maintenance, cable installation, and computer networking
- Identifying community-based counseling agencies to assist in addressing the life stresses after high school
- Participating in church-related youth activities on a monthly basis

Transition planning also includes goals relating to personal development, independence, self-determination, social skill development, or other needs for adult independent functioning (e.g., self-care, accepting criticism, cooking, resume development). For example, if a student plans to live independently in an apartment, then he or she may need goals in some or all of the following areas:

- Identify living options in the community
- Describe processes and requirements for renting an apartment
- Secure employment to financially support the goal
- Budget for the cost of living by oneself
- Demonstrate skills for maintaining an apartment
- Identify and access needed community resources

Secondary Transition Programming

In addition to the development of an ITP for each student with an IEP over age 16, IDEIA requires transition programming to support the needs of the students and enable them to meet their specific goals. Research has documented many "best practices" in transition. The following list of recommended practices is synthesized from the literature and is intended to be integrated into secondary programs serving students with disabilities (Sitlington, Clark, & Kolstoe, 2000): vocational training, parent involvement, interagency collaboration, social skills training, paid work experience, follow-up employment services, integrated settings, community-based instruction, vocational assessment, community-referenced curriculum, career education curricula and experience, employability skills training, and academic skills training.

While not every school can or will provide all of the recommended transition practices, there are a number of strategies that can be incorporated into any school program and that often involve the secondary school counselor. Hughes et al. (1997) identified the following socially validated transition support strategies: identify and provide social support, identify environmental support and provide environmental changes, promote acceptance, observe the student's opportunities for choice, provide choice-making opportunities, identify the student's strengths and areas needing support, teach self-management, and provide opportunities to learn and practice social skills.

An excellent resource for schools and professionals serving secondary students with disabilities is the National Alliance for Secondary Education and Transition (NASET). NASET is a voluntary coalition of 30 national organizations representing general education, special education, career and technical education, youth development, postsecondary education, workforce development, and families. NASET was formed specifically to promote high quality and effective secondary education and transition services by identifying what youth need in order to achieve successful participation in postsecondary education and training, civic engagement, meaningful employment, and adult life. NASET has identified benchmarks that reflect quality secondary education and transition services for all students in its Standards for Secondary Education and Transition. The standards focus on five areas relating to the transition of students with disabilities to adult living: schooling, career preparatory experiences, youth development and youth leadership, family involvement, and connecting activities and service coordination. These standards are available online at www.ncset.org/teleconferences/docs/TransitionToolkit.pdf.

High School Programming

The professional school counselor has an essential role in providing support for appropriate curricular programming for secondary students with disabilities. Recent data indicate that students with disabilities have increased significantly the number of academic courses they are taking in mathematics, science, and foreign language (Wagner et al., 2004). This is likely a positive effect of the increased requirements for access to the general curriculum under NCLB. It is unknown whether this access, in and of itself, will be sufficient to enable students with disabilities to pass high-stakes testing for graduation, now required in virtually every state. It will be essential to monitor student progress carefully over the next few years to determine what additional supports and services are required to enable students with disabilities to graduate with a standard diploma.

Another concern recently noted has been the significant decrease in the numbers of students taking vocational courses (Wagner et al., 2004). This is likely a fallout of the increase in courses taken in the general curriculum by students with disabilities. This is a large concern, however, as vocational programming can significantly increase positive postsecondary outcomes (Wagner, Blackorby, Cameto, & Newman, 1993).

As Wagner et al. (2004) noted, "An overriding emphasis on academics, to the exclusion of vocational and other kinds of nonacademic instruction, could be mismatched to the goals of some students with disabilities." Professional school counselors should advocate for curricular programming to address individual student needs and help families to realistically determine whether goals should relate primarily to postsecondary education or to employment and independent living.

Postsecondary Educational Programming

As noted above, students with disabilities attend college and other postsecondary educational programs at rates far below those of their nondisabled peers. One of the greatest needs for these students is to have others hold high expectations for their continued education, including attendance at 4-year universities, 2-year colleges, technical schools, and community colleges. There are excellent resources available to help students identify appropriate colleges, seek reasonable accommodations, and access support services (e.g., mental health services) during their postsecondary educational programs. Some examples include:

1. DO-IT (Disabilities, Opportunities, Internetworking, and Technology), at the University of Washington (www.washington.edu/doit/Resources/postsec.html)
2. Post-ITT (Postsecondary Innovative Transition Technology), supported by the USDE Office of Special Education and Rehabilitation Services (www.postitt.org/indexs.html)
3. HEATH Resource Center (Higher Education and Adult Training for People with Disabilities), national clearinghouse on postsecondary education for individuals with disabilities (www.heath.gwu.edu)

Professional school counselors can help students significantly by providing specialized information to students with disabilities and their parents regarding readiness for college, including accommodations for the SAT-I or ACT exams, information on disability disclosure during the application process, methods to interview effectively, ways to document a disability at the postsecondary level, information on how to identify available accommodations in various colleges, and tips for finding a "good match" for a specific student's special needs.

General tips on supporting transition to college for students with learning disabilities (Skinner & Lindstrom, 2003) include:

1. Teach students about their disability and compensatory strategies. Students should understand the nature of their learning problems. Specifically, they should be aware of their academic strengths and weaknesses, accommodations that allow

them to circumvent their learning problems, and other study skills and learning strategies.

2. Teach students to self-advocate. Students become self-advocates when they (a) demonstrate an understanding of their disability, (b) are aware of their legal rights, and (c) can competently and tactfully advocate for their rights and needs to those in positions of authority.

3. Teach students about the law. After high school, students with disabilities are no longer entitled to special services, only equal access. Students need to know that it is their responsibility to self-identify and provide documentation supporting their need for accommodations that is sufficient to meet their school's criteria. They must request necessary accommodations, be familiar with college requirements, make programming decisions with the assistance of an adviser, monitor their own progress, request assistance when needed, and meet the same academic standards as all other students.

4. Help students select postsecondary schools wisely. Although choosing the right college is important for any student, it takes on added significance when the student has a learning disability.

Career Counseling

Career counseling for students with disabilities requires the professional school counselor to understand the implications of the disability on a potential career. The school counselor must encourage and support while remaining realistic. Computerized career programs can easily be used with assistive technology like screen readers to enable students with disabilities to explore various career possibilities and requirements independently. The professional school counselor knowledgeable about training opportunities through private and public agencies and about resources in general, including financial resources, can be helpful to students with disabilities. There are excellent resources for career exploration online, including:

1. *Kids & Youth Pages* from the U.S. Department of Labor at www.dol.gov/dol/audience/aud-kidsyouth.htm
2. *Occupational Outlook Handbook* at www.bls.gov/oco
3. *Teenager's Guide to the Real World Careers* at www.bygpub.com/books/tg2rw/careers.htm
4. *Job and Career Resources for Teenagers* at www.quintcareers.com/teen_jobs.html

In addition to the Web sites intended for the general population, there are a number of excellent resources specifically developed for students with disabilities. Partners in Employment is a free online course designed to help people with developmental disabilities find meaningful jobs and plan a career. In this course, available at www.partnersinpolicymaking.com/employment/index.html, participants create a resume or portfolio of their strengths, skills, and interests; learn how to network and identify potential employers; prepare for an interview; and understand the hiring process.

An additional resource is a comprehensive course, complete with lesson plans, entitled Life Skills for Vocational Success, available at www.workshopsinc.com/manual/TOC.html. This course includes lessons intended for students with disabilities, on wide-ranging competencies including listening skills, avoiding destructive behaviors, getting along with coworkers, good attitude, and sexual behavior in the workplace.

Vocational/Career Planning. In many school systems today, online programs and software are used to assist students in career planning. Typically, they include interest inventories and career-trait surveys. In addition, some programs provide decision-making support to students to help them identify job values, personal strengths, and coursework related to professions of interest (e.g., the Career Decision-Making System [CDM]).

In addition to computerized testing for vocational interests, there are typically either school system staff or local agency staff trained to do vocational aptitude testing of students with disabilities. In fact, in many school systems, all secondary students with IEPs complete a lengthy vocational assessment at a vocational school or center.

Other information necessary for vocational/career planning includes interview data from parents regarding their expectations and dreams for their child, the student's stated career goal, history of work expeience, reports of work habits and behaviors, and observation of the student's functioning on the work site.

The involvement of staff from the Division of Rehabilitative Services is essential in obtaining linkages to adult services, determining funding for postsecondary educational or vocational programs, and assisting families with ongoing transition needs beyond high school. For some students (including even those who are high functioning), providing information on how to access Social Security Insurance and Social Security Disability Insurance (www.ssa.gov) can allow students with disabilities to obtain adult vocational training programs, access job coaching and other adult services (e.g., Ticket to Work Program), pay for college, or defer income to pay for disability-related expenses (e.g., Plan for Achieving Self-Support [PASS]).

Vocational Training

Another strategy employed to improve post high school outcomes for individuals with disabilities is vocational training. The School-to-Work Opportunities Act, passed in 1994, focuses on coordinated efforts between schools and the community to design and provide an appropriate, individualized education for individuals with disabilities, including those with emotional and behavior disorders, that smoothly and successfully moves them from the school environment to the work environment. This act and other school efforts focus on providing students with the skills that employers seek. Thus, while still in school, students are provided with specific job training and experiences through vocational work placements, job coaching, and other related activities.

Self-Determination

The Division of Career Development and Transition of the Council for Exceptional Children defines self-determination as a combination of skills, knowledge, and beliefs that enable a person to engage in goal-directed, self-regulated, autonomous behavior. These skills enhance individuals' abilities to take control of their lives and assume the role of successful adults. Research has found that helping students acquire and exercise self-determination skills is a strategy that leads to more positive educational outcomes, including higher rates of employment, postsecondary education, and independent living (S. Field, Martin, Miller, Ward, & Wehmeyer, n.d.).

Elements of self-determination include self-awareness, self-evaluation, choice and decision making, goal setting and attainment, problem solving, self-advocacy, and IEP planning. Professional school counselors can utilize some of the strategies below to assist students in their development of self-determination skills:

- Use a structured curriculum to directly teach skills and attitudes. (See the curriculum descriptions on the Self-Determination Synthesis Project Web site at www.uncc.edu/sdsp/sd_curricula.asp.)
- Use assessments to determine student needs (e.g., the ARC's Self-Determination Scale is available free online at the Beach Center on Disability of the University of Kansas, at www.beachcenter.org).
- Prepare students for the IEP planning and implementation process. Expect and support active student participation and leadership of their IEPs. (Resources for student participation in the IEP process are available through the National Dissemination Center for Children with Disabilities at www.nichcy.org.)
- Meet with students weekly to discuss student goal attainment and help students implement strategies.
- Provide the student with information on his or her disability. Help the student to describe his or her needs to others and appropriately request needed accommodations.
- Help the student access available resources, especially online, to assist with college, career, leisure, and living planning. (See, e.g., the National Center on Secondary Education and Transition at www.youthhood.org.)

- Help students adjust strategies, schedules, or supports in collaboration with their teachers or family members to help attain their goals.
- Encourage families to promote choice and decision making.
- Allow for student selection of course electives and program of study.

There are excellent resources, including staff development materials, curricula, and lesson plans available online to promote self-determination in students with disabilities. Some examples of electronic resources include:

- The Person-Centered Planning Education Site (PCPES), at www.ilr.cornell.edu/ped/tsal/pcp, was developed by the Employment and Disability Institute at Cornell University. The PCPES provides coursework and staff development activities in such areas as transition planning, community membership, and self-determination.
- The Self-Advocacy Synthesis Project (www.uncc.edu/sdsp), at the University of North Carolina, provides information on exemplar programs, reviews existing research on self-advocacy models for students with disabilities, and develops and disseminates an array of products, including a directory of self-advocacy model programs.
- The Council for Exceptional Children and the University of Minnesota Institute on Community Integration collaboratively developed

Student-Led IEPs: A Guide for Student Involvement, a 2001 publication useful for working with secondary students with disabilities (available at www.cec.sped.org/bk/catalog2/student-led_ieps.pdf).

INFORMATION ABOUT THE SPECIAL EDUCATION PROCESS AND THE RIGHT OF APPEAL

Many families seek information about special education services for students with disabilities. For instance, parents may want to know what will happen to their child during an evaluation, what will happen with the evaluation results, or what information is included in the IEP. Parents may question whether they should seek their own evaluations, worry about going to a meeting without their own legal representatives, or want to know if there are any safeguards or appeals if they disagree with the process.

Many excellent organizations provide assistance to families, educators, agency workers, and professional school counselors seeking additional information. Four national organizations are listed in Table 15.9.

States also have parent advocacy groups and public law organizations that are focused on providing parents a range of assistance.

TABLE 15.9
Organizations assisting parents and guardians with appeals.

1. The National Association of State Directors of Special Education (NASDSE; www.nasdse.org) facilitates state agency efforts to maximize educational outcomes for individuals with disabilities.

2. The Council for Exceptional Children (CEC; www.cec.sped.org) is the professional organization for special education with divisions and councils that address many aspects involved in educating students with disabilities. Professional school counselors will probably find subdivisions such as the Council for Children with Behavioral Disorders, the Division of Career Development and Transition, the Division for Culturally and Linguistically Diverse Exceptional Learners, and the Division for Research most helpful.

3. The National Dissemination Center for Children and Youth with Disabilities (NICHCY; www.nichcy.org) is a national information and referral center that provides information and fact sheets on disabilities and disability-related issues for families, educators, and other professionals.

4. The ERIC Clearinghouse on Disabilities and Gifted Education (http://ericec.org; the searchable database is now at www.eric.ed.gov) provides research and publications related to individuals with disabilities. ERIC also maintains a National Parent Information Network.

The professional school counselor can identify these organizations in a local area, but for a listing of parent resources by state, go to www.taalliance.org/centers.

IDEIA and Section 504 require that families be given a statement of their rights and means of appeal, if the parent has a disagreement with the identification, classification, program, or services developed for or provided to the student. At multidisciplinary team meetings, families are given a booklet on these rights and asked to sign a paper saying they have received such a booklet. In some instances the parents may resolve their concerns without using these dispute resolution processes by appealing directly to the school principal or district supervisory personnel. However, IDEIA and Section 504 have more formal processes to resolve disagreements.

Under IDEIA, the first step in the dispute resolution process is the resolution session. The resolution session provides an opportunity to resolve issues without having to use the due process system. Parties may agree not to conduct the resolution session. Parents' other approaches to dispute resolution are mediation and due process. Due process is a hearing process where parents and the school district present their disagreement to an impartial hearing officer, who then issues a legal decision resolving the matter. Appeals from the hearing officer's decision can go to state or federal court. There are similar processes under Section 504.

In addition to these processes, IDEIA and Section 504 include complaint investigation processes. In these situations, state or federal offices assign investigators who determine whether appropriate laws and regulations have been followed, and if not, they order that corrective actions be taken.

GENERAL ISSUES FOR PROFESSIONAL SCHOOL COUNSELORS SERVING STUDENTS WITH DISABILITIES

Clearly, there are numerous ways in which professional school counselors will come into contact with students with disabilities. Although there are

significant similarities in serving students with and without disabilities in schools, there are a few areas where special sensitivity is required or where special considerations are necessary in serving youth with disabilities.

Cultural Considerations

High stress can be felt by the parents of a child with a disability in families from all cultural backgrounds. However, the professional school counselor needs to be sensitive to cultural considerations because families from different cultures may approach identification of a child with a disability differently, particularly regarding the level of protection and independence afforded.

In some cultures, the disability of a family member is too private to share, and some families feel that discussion about the disability with anyone outside the family would be shameful. In other cultures, a high value on learning and achievement may create added pressure on a student. In still other cultures, those identified by mainstream society as having disabilities are not seen as disabled. Sometimes, attempting to physically help a child with a disability can present a challenge, because in some cultures, the degree of physical touch implies respect or disrespect.

When collaborating with or counseling families of students from different cultures, the professional school counselor must consider the language differences and the cultural views of those involved. This process can be improved with the help of a friend of the family who is from the same culture, who can be an interpreter of both the language and the culture. It is critical for the professional school counselor to hear the "real" needs and priorities of the family and attempt to address them. To the extent possible, professional school counselors must place themselves in the position of the families. Before the professional can begin to meet the needs of families and children with disabilities, he or she must understand how family needs are shaped by the context of their subculture (Seligman & Darling, 1989). Among groups where there is a strong religious presence, a clergy member can provide support for a student with a disability, and this aid may be more readily accepted than assistance offered by the counselor would be.

The professional school counselor can help the family of diverse students cope with the maze of bureaucracy that public education may present to someone from another culture. For parents of a student with a disability, fears often exist because of language issues; those in the school system may not understand the

needs of their child, and the parents may not understand how best to acquire services for their child. The CEC (www.cec.sped.org) has a Division for Culturally and Linguistically Diverse Exceptional Learners that can be a resource for the professional school counselor addressing the needs of a student with a disability from another culture. The ACA maintains a division of multicultural counseling, the AMCD, referred to in chapter 5, which could also provide resources.

SUMMARY/CONCLUSION

The professional school counselor's role with the student who has a disability is still emerging, even though the laws addressing students with disabilities have been around since the early to mid-1970s. Professional school counselors have always served students with disabilities; however, it was usually with services similar to those given regular-education students who might be experiencing a problem. When professional school counselors addressed the clinical needs of students with disabilities, it was most often to provide appropriate referral sources. Today, professional school counselors are being called on to play a major role in delivering a broad array of counseling services to students with disabilities. Thus, professional school counselors must have a clear understanding of the laws that govern eligibility and service delivery to those students.

Professional school counselors are well trained to provide counseling services to students with disabilities and their families—in part because professional school counselors have a strong tradition of training in developmental counseling. Professional school counselors have traditionally focused on integrating social and academic skills, and prefer working collaboratively rather than in isolation. Increasingly, counselors are seeking additional training and taking on greater mental health and case management roles. ASCA has responded by issuing a position paper (ASCA, 2004b) on appropriate and inappropriate roles for professional school counselors serving students with disabilities. One of the main concerns of ASCA is that counselors not be put in positions that will harm their counseling relationships and thus their effectiveness. ASCA leaves open the opportunity for professional school counselors to address any issue that falls in the counselor's arena, and seeks to promote a role for the school counseling profession that works collaboratively and in a transdisciplinary mode when serving students with disabilities. It is possible that a new subspecialty in school counseling could develop in response to the increasing needs of students with disabilities. For example, perhaps special education and student services may jointly fund positions providing a school team with a professional school counselor specially trained in the areas discussed in this chapter.

The number of students with disabilities has grown, and counseling services will be essential for many of them. Contracting outside mental health services can be expensive, but it may be necessary for schools to address these needs. How this will affect the school counseling profession is unclear, but those school counselors today who seek additional training in clinical counseling and collaborative team problem solving to better serve students with disabilities may be blazing a path for future professional school counselors.

ACTIVITIES

1. Interview a school administrator regarding how the IDEIA and NCLB acts have affected his or her school policies. What changes were made to accommodate students with special needs? How effective have these adjustments been?
2. Create an example of an SWPBS system. What positive expectations would you convey to all students and staff? How would you encourage positive behaviors and discourage negative behaviors? How would you monitor and evaluate the effectiveness of your program?
3. Bobby is a fourth-grade student identified with a serious emotional disturbance. He is aggressive and having difficulty getting along with peers. Create three sample goal statements that could be included on his IEP.

HELPING STUDENTS WITH MENTAL AND EMOTIONAL DISORDERS

CAROL J. KAFFENBERGER AND LINDA SELIGMAN

Editor's Introduction: Whereas the historical roots of professional school counseling lie in developmental counseling theories, societal changes are contributing to substantial increases in psychopathology among school-aged children. A professional school counselor's ability to treat students with emotional disorders depends on education, training, and experience, as well as local school board policies and procedures; however, all future professional school counselors living the transformed role must know the characteristics and diagnostic criteria for common disorders of childhood and adolescence. Such knowledge is essential to one's ability to make timely and appropriate referrals, as well as to facilitate school-based services to supplement mental health treatment. This chapter introduces the vast array of mental disorders that professional school counselors may encounter in their work with students. In addition, each section addresses common treatment interventions and discusses their relevance to the professional school counselor. Whether referring, treating, collaborating, or advocating, professional school counselors must be aware of this information to interface with and make appropriate referrals to the medical and mental health communities and help the students achieve academic and social success at school.

The professional school counselor's primary responsibility is to support the educational mission of schools—to help all students be academically successful. The NCLB Act of 2001 and the school reform movement have increased the pressure on schools to focus on academic performance and achievement for *all* students (USDE, 2001). Unfortunately, a number of factors interfere with the achievement of that goal. Environmental and mental health issues impact children and make it difficult for schools to provide an appropriate education for each child. As a result, schools are increasingly expected to deal with emotional and mental health concerns of students.

This chapter will briefly review the history of the professional school counselor's role in serving students with mental and emotional disorders, the role professional school counselors can play in the diagnosis and treatment of these mental disorders in light of the transformation of the school counseling profession, the nature and prevalence of mental disorders most often diagnosed in students, and the implications for the future.

PREVALENCE OF MENTAL DISORDERS AND MENTAL HEALTH ISSUES IN CHILDREN AND ADOLESCENTS

The prevalence of mental health issues in children and adolescents is increasing and is considered a mental health crisis in the United States (APA, 2004). One in five children and adolescents has a mild to moderate mental health issue, and 1 in 20 has a serious mental or emotional illness (USDHHS, 2000). Of the approximately 4 million children, ages 9 to 17, who have a serious emotional illness (SAMHSA, 1998), only 20% receive mental health services (Hoagwood, 1999; Kataoka, Zhang, & Wells, 2002; USDHHS, 2000). In addition to the increased prevalence of mental illness, children are presenting with mental health concerns at a younger age. The rate of unmet needs among Latino youth and uninsured children is even greater than among White and publicly insured youth (Kataoka et al., 2002).

Adolescent suicide rates are another indicator of the severity of mental health concerns. Suicide is the third leading cause of death for adolescents after accidents and homicide (NIMH, 2000; Shaffer & Pfeffer, 2001). Furthermore, it is estimated that 7% of adolescents who develop a major depressive disorder will commit suicide (NIMH, 2000) and that 90% of teens who commit suicide have a mental disorder (Shaffer & Pfeffer, 2001). Adolescents who use alcohol or illicit

drugs are three times more likely than nonusing adolescents to attempt suicide (SAMSHA, 2002).

The high incidence of violent, aggressive, and disruptive behavior in children is another reflection of children's emotional difficulties (Luongo, 2000). Approximately one third to one half of referrals of young people to mental health agencies are for behavioral and conduct problems primarily occurring in school (Atkins et al., 1998). One of the most common and increasingly diagnosed disorders seen in children and adolescents is ADHD. Approximately 3% to 5% of children are thought to have ADHD (APA, 2000).

FACTORS CONTRIBUTING TO HIGH INCIDENCE OF EMOTIONAL DISTURBANCE

Environmental factors such as the breakdown of the family, homelessness, poverty, and violence in the community place increased stress on families and contribute to an increase in mental health needs (Dryfoos, 1994, 1998; Keys, Bemak, & Lockhart, 1998; Lockhart & Keys, 1998). During the 1970s and 1980s, the number of children living in poverty steadily increased (Dryfoos, 1994). Poverty, as well as exposure to violence and substance use in the community, puts children at greater risk for developing mental disorders and experiencing emotional difficulties, thus making it more difficult for them to attend school regularly and succeed academically (Dryfoos, 1994; Kirst, 1991; Weist, 1997).

Particularly at risk are children from diverse ethnic and cultural groups, who have a higher incidence of mental disorders and are overrepresented in special education programs (Coulter, 1996; Hoberman, 1992). Children and adolescents of color have been unserved or underserved and have had their emotional difficulties overlooked or misdiagnosed (Kress, Erikson, Rayle, & Ford, 2005). Diagnostic tools and procedures that have been developed for Euro-American populations may not be appropriate for diagnosing emotional difficulties in children from other cultures (Kress et al., 2005; Mezzich et al., 1999).

Low-cost mental health services available in the community are limited, thereby putting added pressure on schools to provide those services (Dryfoos, 1994; Henggeler, 1994; Keys & Bemak, 1997; Luongo, 2000). Additionally, lack of transportation, poor insurance coverage, limited after-school office hours, and understaffing at mental health agencies all serve as barriers to young people receiving mental health services (Weist, 1997). Services that are available often are fragmented, and typically no one agency takes responsibility for providing or coordinating care.

Changes in the way special education services are provided to students have increased the number of students receiving services. Mainstreaming and the inclusion movement have meant that, after years of students being served in self-contained special education classrooms, students with a variety of mental health and learning problems, no matter how severe, are being returned to the regular education classroom (Green et al., 1994; Lockhart & Keys, 1998). Federal special education legislation and Section 504 regulations have increased the type and range of services provided to students with special education needs. The Individuals with Disabilities Education Act (IDEA) of 1990 prohibited discrimination on the basis of disabilities and required that schools provide mental health services when needed to enable students to succeed in school (Gibson & Mitchell, 1999; Maag & Katsiyannis, 1996). Professional school counselors are often members of the school's special education team (Green et al., 1994). Recent legislation, designed to provide appropriate educational opportunities to children and adolescents, also requires that counselors be well versed in the nature of, and requirements for, psychological assessment and services. The 1997 amendments to the IDEA require that FBAs and positive behavioral improvement goals be included in the IEPs (Douglas, 1997; Flaherty et al., 1998).

Section 504 of the Rehabilitation Act of 1973 protects students who have a physical or mental disability that substantially limits a major life activity (USDHHS, 2004). Section 504 provides program modifications that are different from special education services. This legislation, too, has increased professional school counselors'

involvement with students' mental health needs. Students who are eligible for 504 accommodations require modifications to their learning environment so that they will have access to educational opportunity. Examples of students who might be eligible for 504 services include a student with leukemia who requires a shorter school day and homebound instruction; a student with ADHD who might benefit from modifications to assignments, special seating, and permission to take frequent breaks; and a child with dysgraphia who requires special testing accommodations. In some school districts, professional school counselors chair the 504 committee and are responsible for working with parents, teachers, and students to develop and implement appropriate accommodations.

Failure to address the emotional and mental health concerns of students has a cost. An increasing number of adolescents will drop out of school (Dryfoos, 1998; Institute of Medicine, 1997). Estimates suggest that 48% of students with emotional problems drop out of school and that students with severe emotional problems miss more days of school than those in any other disability category.

THE PROFESSIONAL SCHOOL COUNSELOR'S ROLE

The role of professional school counselors is in a period of transformation (ASCA, 2003a; Bemak, 2000; Paisley & Borders, 1995). Part of the ongoing debate focuses on how professional school counselors should address the mental health and emotional issues of students and how that role fits into a comprehensive school counseling program as framed by the *ASCA National Model: A Framework for School Counseling Programs* (ASCA, 2003a). The mental health needs of students have not always been the concern of professional school counselors. School counseling in the 1950s and 1960s emphasized a personal growth model that promoted individual development (Keys, Bemak, & Lockhart, 1998; Paisley & Borders, 1995). Currently, most school counseling programs are based on a comprehensive developmental model that focuses on prevention and meeting the needs of the whole child and emphasizes the educational goals of counseling services and programs.

While many professional school counselors, influenced by the work of ASCA and the National Center for Transforming School Counseling at the Education Trust, affirm the educational goal of their school counseling programs, others argue that professional school counselors are not doing enough to meet the complex needs of children who are at risk (Keys, Bemak, & Lockhart, 1998). They claim that professional school counselors are not allowing sufficient individualization of services and are focused on student competencies rather than individual mental health needs (Gysbers & Henderson, 1994). Leaders in the counseling field argue that the role of school counselors is still evolving (Bemak, 2000; Paisley & Borders, 1995). Others (Dryfoos, 1994; Keys, Bemak, & Lockhart, 1998) believe that new delivery systems for providing school-based mental health services are required (Bemak, Murphy, & Kaffenberger, 2005). For example, Dryfoos (1994) envisioned *full-service* schools where community mental health resources combine forces with schools and other agencies to provide adequate mental health services for students.

Barriers to Providing Mental Health Services in Schools

The ability of professional school counselors to meet the needs of students with mental health issues is limited by several factors, including workload and other responsibilities, ratio of students to counselors, local policy, fragmented programs, and lack of expertise (Bemak, 2000; Keys & Bemak, 1997). The first barrier is the number of noncounseling duties that professional school counselors are asked to shoulder (ASCA, 2003a). Overworked professional school counselors with a host of other school responsibilities, both of a counseling and a noncounseling nature, are unable to provide adequate counseling services or consult with parents and mental health professionals to serve students with chronic and serious mental health needs.

The second barrier that interferes with a counselor's ability to serve the mental health needs of students is the fragmentation and duplication of services and programs (Bemak, 2000; Bemak et al., 2005; Collins & Collins, 1994; Henggeler, 1994). School- and community-based services and programs often have been developed in isolation, without consideration of existing services and programs. Lacking knowledge and awareness of collaborative opportunities, both school and community settings miss the opportunity to provide comprehensive and coordinated services.

The third barrier is the discrepancy that exists between professional school counselors' need to understand mental disorders and their knowledge base (Lockhart & Keys, 1998; Seligman, 2004). Not all professional school counselors possess the knowledge, experience, and expertise needed to recognize and address the mental health needs of students. Counselor education programs have typically prepared professional school counselors to understand the developmental needs of students but have not provided the training required to recognize and treat mental disorders affecting children, adolescents, and their families.

Current and Future Trends in the Way Services Are Provided

If schools are to achieve their educational mission, new service models will be required of professional school counselors (Bemak, 2000; Bemak et al., 2005; Keys, Bemak, & Lockhart, 1998). The way mental health services are provided for children and the role of the professional school counselor are beginning to change (Flaherty et al., 1998). Professional school counselors have tried to be responsive to the needs of students by adapting service delivery models that were effective in the 1970s. But these models no longer meet students' mental health needs (S. B. Baker, 1994). The USDE, the USDHHS, and private managed health-care organizations are encouraging preventive health care as a way of ultimately reducing the need for future costly care, remediation, and intervention (Power, DuPaul, Shapiro, & Parrish, 1998). Schools are the logical place for programs that seek to both prevent and ameliorate mental health problems in students and their families. As a growing number of public schools privatize, various counseling service models have been developed (Dykeman, 1995). Some schools have increased their use of community and private resources by hiring psychiatrists and using outside consultants to provide direct treatment, psychotherapy, and psychopharmacology to students (Bostic & Rauch, 1999). In increasing numbers of schools, the counseling functions are either shared between the professional school counselor and outside agencies or are contracted out completely.

Flaherty et al. (1998) described an ideal service model in which professionals from different disciplines collaborate to promote mental health in children and adolescents. The team would be composed of professionals representing school health, mental health, and education. Most schools already have child study teams charged with managing the special education evaluation process. The collaborative interdisciplinary teams proposed by Flaherty et al., would expand the membership of special education teams to include professionals from community agencies who would develop and implement programs for individuals and for schools. Interdisciplinary teams could also provide a vehicle for educating staff and students about mental health issues (Weist, 1997). High levels of collaboration and coordination will be required to effect necessary systems-level change (Bemak, 2000; Henggeler, 1994).

The effectiveness of new community-based mental health services and comprehensive guidance programs is being assessed. One study evaluated the effectiveness of high school counseling programs statewide and found that students who attend schools with fully implemented mental health programs are more academically successful and have a greater sense of belonging and safety than those who do not (Lapan et al., 1997). Another study showed that comprehensive community-based services to children cut state hospital admissions and inpatient bed days by between 39% and 79% and reduced average days of detention by 40% (SAMHSA, 1995).

The discussion of how best to provide services to students is ongoing. What is clear is that, to efficiently and effectively use the limited resources available to meet the needs of students, a high level of collaboration will be required (Bemak et al., 2005). Collaboration among mental health professionals is even more important when fiscal concerns threaten to reduce services to students (Allen, 1994; Gibelman, 1993). To maximize their effectiveness, professional school counselors need to develop interdisciplinary and interagency relationships and practices (Bemak, 2000; Bemak et al., 2005). Professional school counselors must abandon traditional roles in favor of a more collaborative relationship with other professionals. For this to occur, professional school counselors must acquire a working knowledge of the role and function of the other mental health professions in schools and in the community (Flaherty et al., 1998).

Professional school counselors must increase their knowledge, skills, and expertise regarding mental health issues of students to assume a more collaborative role (Bemak, 2000; Lockhart & Keys, 1998). They must be knowledgeable about the *Diagnostic and Statistical Manual of Mental Disorders* (DSM; APA, 2000) criteria, the symptoms of mental disorders, and the appropriate treatment recommendations (Seligman, 2004). They must understand psychological evaluation processes, be able to explain them to school staff, and communicate with other mental health professionals.

WHAT PROFESSIONAL SCHOOL COUNSELORS NEED TO KNOW ABOUT MENTAL AND EMOTIONAL DISORDERS

With the increased prevalence of mental health and emotional issues in children and adolescents, professional school counselors need to take an increasingly active role in understanding these disorders and facilitating services. The professional school counselor is often the first person contacted by parents or teachers when concerns about children arise. Professional school counselors must understand normal social, emotional, cognitive, and physical development. In addition, it is essential that they possess a working knowledge of the range of mental disorders and mental health issues affecting young people. Professional school counselors need to be familiar with the diagnostic criteria for those mental disorders that are commonly found in young people, even though professional school counselors may not be responsible for diagnosing mental disorders. Professional school counselors can play a pivotal role in raising awareness concerning mental disorders, identifying students who are experiencing significant emotional difficulties, interpreting diagnostic information, recommending school-based interventions, and making referrals. Counselors' awareness of diagnostic information also will be invaluable to parents, teachers, and administrators as initial treatment decisions are being made.

Mental health professionals, including psychologists, psychiatrists, social workers, and licensed professional counselors, regularly use the *DSM–IV–TR* (APA, 2000) to diagnose emotional, behavioral, and mental disorders in children and adolescents. In general, school psychologists did not use the *DSM* until the 1987 publication of the *DSM-III-R*, but for the last 10 to 15 years, they have viewed diagnosis as one of their essential skills (House, 1999). By 1994, when the fourth edition of the *DSM* was published, the expectations of the school's role in the diagnostic process had increased, and many professional school counselors recognized that they, too, needed to be familiar with the diagnostic criteria for mental disorders in young people. Changes in the way mental health services were provided to children and increased pressure to provide special education services to children required that schools develop more sophisticated ways of diagnosing educational and behavioral disorders. *DSM* criteria are now accepted as the standard, and workshops, training, and textbooks guiding the use of *DSM* criteria proliferate (House, 1999).

While the *DSM* is gaining greater credibility among mental health professionals, a debate about the relevance of *DSM* criteria to people of other cultures and ethnicities is increasing (Dana, 2001; Gardner & Miranda, 2001; Good, 1996; Kress et al., 2005; Mezzich et al., 1999). Beginning in the late 1980s, researchers began the discussion of the relevance of *DSM* criteria to

people of other cultures and ethnicities. In spite of goodwill efforts on the part of *DSM*, working groups, collaborative task forces, and independent researchers found the most recent *DSM–IV–TR* does not reflect "cultural or racial difference in symptoms, syndromes" (Dana, 2001, p. 31). The *DSM–IV–TR* (APA, 2000) addressed ethnic and cultural considerations and warned that *DSM* diagnostic criteria may not be appropriately assessed unless the cultural frame of reference is considered. In this edition of the *DSM*, APA provided three types of information related to cultural considerations. The first is a discussion within the text description of each disorder of known cultural variance. The second is a discussion in Appendix I of culture-bound syndromes. And the third is an outline (also contained in appendix I) of cultural formation.

Professional school counselors are not expected to, nor have most of them been trained to, make diagnoses using the *DSM* criteria. While professional school counselors may not make formal diagnoses and will probably not provide primary services to students diagnosed with a mental disorder, they often are expected to identify young people in need of mental health services; to consult with other school-based mental health professionals such as school psychologists and social workers; to make referrals to outside community agency resources such as psychiatrists, psychologists, social workers, and mental health counselors; and to decipher mental health reports for school personnel and parents. Once an outside referral has been made, professional school counselors, with the parents' permission, may be asked to provide input from the school, including observations, behavioral checklists, and sample schoolwork. When parents, professional school counselors, teachers, and mental health therapists work together successfully, the results can be very beneficial for children. Although professional school counselors typically will not provide therapeutic services to students with severe mental disorders, having a working knowledge of the diagnosis of mental disorders, and understanding ways that diagnostic criteria may not be relevant to students from other cultures or students of color, can greatly enhance the effectiveness of professional school counselors' interactions with students, teachers, and parents (Gardner & Miranda, 2001; Good, 1996; Lockhart & Keys, 1998).

Diagnosis and Treatment Planning

The *DSM–IV–TR* (APA, 2000) includes a multiaxial system of diagnosis that involves an assessment of a person on five different axes or areas. Each of these axes refers to a different domain of information that aids the clinician in planning treatment for the person being assessed. Axis I, Clinical Disorders and Other Conditions that May Be the Focus of Clinical Attention, describes clinical disorders such as conduct disorders, eating disorders, anxiety disorders, and mood disorders. Axis II, Mental Retardation and Personality Disorders, encompasses mental retardation and enduring, maladaptive personality disorders. Axis III, General Medical Conditions, includes general medical conditions or physical symptoms. Axis IV, Psychosocial and Environmental Problems, pertains to psychosocial and environmental problems such as educational, family, and occupational stressors. Axis V, Global Assessment of Functioning, indicates a person's global assessment of functioning by assigning a number on a scale of 1 to 100, with 100 indicating superior functioning and 1 indicating persistent and severe danger of hurting self or others.

A multiaxial approach to assessment is used to facilitate a comprehensive and systematic evaluation of a person. Professional school counselors usually will not be involved in the assessment process but will benefit from understanding how the multiaxial system is used in the diagnosis of an emotional or mental disorder. For example, when assessing an adolescent for depression, the clinician should know about all areas of this young person's life. This adolescent might have a medical condition such as cancer, or the adolescent's parents may have recently been divorced. It is helpful to be able to assess the child or adolescent for various issues other than the primary diagnosis to create a treatment plan that is tailored for the individual's issues and experiences rather than just for "depression." A sample DSM multiaxial diagnosis is presented in Table 16.1.

According to the *DSM–IV–TR* (APA, 2000), 13 types of disorders are often diagnosed in infancy, childhood, or adolescence. What follows is a description of those disorders. A description of disorders more likely to be diagnosed in adulthood but also frequently diagnosed in children and adolescents is also included. Specific characteristics of each disorder, intervention strategies, prognosis, and relevance to the professional school counselor are presented.

TABLE 16.1
Case example: Demonstrating a DSM–IV–TR multiaxial diagnosis.

Anna, a 7-year-old girl, was evaluated for an episode of depressed mood, sleeping problems, irritability, loss of weight, and reduced energy level. Anna's symptoms had been present for nearly 2 months. Her parents could hardly get her to wake up in the morning. She refused to dress or bathe and had been absent from school for 2 weeks. On further evaluation, it was discovered that Anna's dog, Max, was killed about 2 months ago, right around the time that Anna's symptoms began. Recently, Anna had begun to tell her parents that she wished the car could have hit her also so that she could be with Max.

Anna's multiaxial diagnosis is:

Axis I	296.22 Major Depressive Disorder, Single Episode, With Melancholic Features
Axis II	V71.09 No diagnosis on axis II
Axis III	None reported
Axis IV	Death of family pet
Axis V	50

MENTAL DISORDERS USUALLY FIRST DIAGNOSED IN INFANTS, CHILDREN, OR ADOLESCENTS

Mental Retardation

Mental retardation typically is described in terms of a person's failure to demonstrate skills that are age-, culturally-, and situation-appropriate reflected by an intelligence quotient (IQ) that is much lower than found in the normal population (Baumeister & Baumeister, 2000). Mental retardation has a pervasive impact on cognitive, emotional, and social development (Seligman, 1998). It is diagnosed from results of individual intelligence tests, such as the Wechsler Intelligence Scales for Children, Fourth Edition (WISC–IV; Wechsler, 2001) or the Stanford–Binet Intelligence Scale, Fifth Edition (SBIS–5; Roid, 2003). According to *DSM–IV–TR,* the criteria for diagnosis of mental retardation include onset prior to age 18; subaverage intellectual functioning reflected by an IQ of two standard deviations below the mean (WISC–IV or SBIS–5 Full Scale IQ of 70 or less); and impaired adaptive functioning in at least two areas, such as communication, social skills, interpersonal skills, self-direction, leisure, functional academic skills, safety, and work (House, 1999). Although people with an IQ that is in the 71–84 range are not typically diagnosed with mental retardation, they, too, are likely to have academic and other difficulties related to their below-average intellectual abilities. The *DSM-IV-TR* describes people in this group as having a condition called borderline intellectual functioning.

The impact of mental retardation is directly related to the degree of intellectual impairment. Four degrees of retardation are defined by the *DSM* as follows: mild retardation is diagnosed when the IQ score is in the range of 50–55 to 70; moderate retardation is diagnosed when the IQ score is in the range of 35–40 to 50–55; severe retardation is diagnosed when the IQ score is in the range of 20–25 to 35–40; and profound retardation is diagnosed when the IQ score is below 20–25.

According to Baumeister and Baumeister (2000), the American Association of Mental Retardation (AAMR) has recently modified the classification of mental retardation. The new system advocates a multidimensional approach: intellectual functioning and adaptive skills, psychological and emotional considerations, etiology, as well as environmental considerations.

Mental retardation is usually diagnosed in infancy or early childhood, although mild retardation may not be identified until the child reaches school age. It is estimated that 1% to 2% of the general population can be diagnosed with mental retardation, although estimates can vary depending on definitions and populations studied (APA, 2000; NIMH, 2000). Of those people meeting the criteria for mental retardation, 85% are diagnosed with mild retardation (Rapoport & Ismond, 1996). Boys are three times more likely than girls to be diagnosed with this disorder (Dulmus & Wodaraski, 1996).

Recent advances in knowledge have been made concerning the genetic, physiological, and neurological bases of mental retardation (State, King, & Dykens, 1997), which may have implications for the future diagnosis and treatment of this disorder. Approximately 25% to 30% of people with mental retardation have identifiable biological causes of the disorder, such as genetic and chromosomal abnormalities, prenatal and perinatal difficulties, or acquired childhood diseases (King & Noshpitz, 1991). Down syndrome is the most widely known genetic type of mild or moderate retardation. Severe and profound retardation commonly have a neurological origin and may be associated with more than 200 physical disorders, including cerebral palsy, epilepsy, and sensory disorders. When mental retardation lacks identifiable biological causes, it is thought to be the result of some combination of inherited cognitive impairment and environmental deprivation (Baumeister & Baumeister, 2000).

Children and adolescents diagnosed with mental retardation usually receive special education services under IDEA (MacMillan, Gresham, Spierstein, & Bocian, 1996). Prior to the passage of Public Law 94–142 in the 1970s (the precursor to IDEA in 1990), children who had previously been categorized as trainable and custodial were excluded from free public education (Hardman, Drew, & Egan, 1996). Today, public education is available to all children, regardless of the nature and degree of their impairment; thus, many children with mild mental retardation are found in the public schools.

The characteristics of children, adolescents, and adults with mental retardation vary greatly, depending on their level of impairment and on their environment. These clients often present with aggressive, overactive, or self-injurious behaviors (Kronenberger & Meyer, 1996). Although children with Down syndrome display fewer behavior problems overall than other children with mental retardation, these children still exhibit maladaptive behaviors, particularly stubbornness (Ly & Hodapp, 2002). Because of their cognitive limitations, they tend to be concrete in their thinking, reasoning, and problem solving. Developmental delays are common, with such milestones as walking and talking generally appearing later than average. Learning new tasks requires more practice and guidance for people with mental retardation than for their chronological counterparts (Seligman, 1998).

Children with mild disabilities sometimes are not accepted by their peers, and they often lack the social skills needed to interact with peers and adults. Categorizing these students and removing them from the mainstream may cause parents, teachers, and the students to lower their expectations and to lose confidence in the students' abilities. Therefore, this has led to the *inclusion approach*, which is defined as educating children with disabilities in regular education classrooms for much or all of the school day (Elias, Blum, Gager, Hunter, & Kress, 1998).

Intervention Strategies

Early intervention is essential for treatment of children with mental retardation (Seligman, 1998). Early intervention includes systems, services, and supports designed to enhance the development of young children, minimize the potential of developmental delays and need for special education services, and enhance the capacities of families as caregivers (B. L. Baker & Feinfield, 2003). Family, group, and individual counseling can be effective in promoting the child or adolescent's positive self-regard and

improving social, academic, and occupational skills (King & Noshpitz, 1991). Behavior modification has long been the treatment modality of choice for people with mental retardation (Baumeister & Baumeister, 2000).

Prognosis

Mental retardation has implications for a person's entire life span (Seligman, 1998). Adults with a mild level of retardation often live independently and maintain a job with minimal supervision. People with a moderate level of retardation may be able to live independently in group-home settings and gain employment in sheltered workshops. Those with severe and profound retardation often reside in public and private institutions.

Relevance to School Counselors

Professional school counselors are often members of multidisciplinary teams that attempt to develop appropriate educational plans for students with mild retardation. In so doing, they may engage in advocacy, consultation, diagnosis, assessment, development of a delivery system, and provision of support services for students, parents, and teachers (Wood Dunn & Baker, 2002). Professional school counselors may play a role in helping families understand and accept the diagnosis and make the transition to an appropriate school program. Professional school counselors may be asked to provide social skills training for students with mental retardation in special education programs housed in public schools. Professional school counselors may also be asked to facilitate mainstreaming so that high-functioning students can be part of the regular school program where appropriate, such as in physical education classes, art classes, or the cafeteria. It also is important for the professional school counselor to help educate the other students about mental retardation to promote their understanding and tolerance. It is suggested that professional school counselors be familiar with the overall procedural safeguards of IDEA and characteristics unique to students with disabilities. Professional school counselors who are more able to understand the challenges for students with disabilities are also able to provide the students, parents, and teachers with accurate information (Wood Dunn & Baker, 2002).

Learning, Motor Skills, and Communication Disorders

Learning, motor skills, and communication disorders are diagnosed in children when they are functioning significantly below expectations in a specific area, based on their age, cognitive abilities, and education, and when their level of functioning is interfering with daily achievement and functioning (Seligman, 1998). Significant discrepancies between functioning and performance are typified by achievement in a given area that is 20 to 30 standard score points below the child's intelligence as measured by standardized achievement tests and intelligence tests. Diagnosis of these disorders also requires that other factors that may be primary contributors to the learning problems, such as lack of educational opportunity, poor teaching, impaired vision or hearing, and mental retardation, be ruled out (Young & Beitchman, 2002). Specific learning disabilities (SLD) reflect a disorder in one or more of the basic learning processes, which may manifest itself in an impaired ability to listen, think, speak, read, write, spell, or do mathematical calculations (Federal Register; as cited in Young & Beitchman, 2002). SLDs, referred to as learning disorders in the *DSM–IV–TR*, are believed to affect approximately 10% of the population but are diagnosed in only about 5% of students in public schools in the United States (Rapoport & Ismond, 1996). The *DSM–IV–TR* identified three types of learning disorders: mathematics disorder, reading disorder, and disorder of written expression, characterized by significant difficulties in academic functioning in each of those areas. Reading disorder is diagnosed in approximately 4% of the school-aged population; 60% to 80% are boys. Children with reading disorder have difficulty decoding unknown words, memorizing sight-word vocabulary lists, and comprehending written passages. Estimates of the prevalence of mathematics disorder range from 1% to 6% of the population (APA, 2000; Maxman & Ward, 1995). Children

with mathematics disorder have difficulty with problem solving, calculations, or both (Seligman, 1998). Disorder of written expression is rarely found in isolation; in most cases, another learning disorder is also present (APA, 2000; Silver, 1992). Children with disorder of written expression have difficulty with handwriting, spelling, grammar, and the creation of prose (Seligman, 1998). Care must be taken to distinguish these disorders from underachievement, poor teaching, lack of opportunity, and cultural factors.

Communication disorders are defined in the educational category of speech and language impairment. This category is narrowly defined as impairments in language, voice, fluency, or articulation that are not a result of sensory impairment or developmental delay (C. R. Johnson & Slomka, 2000). Four communication disorders are identified in the *DSM–IV–TR*: expressive language disorder, mixed receptive-expressive language disorder, phonological disorder, and stuttering. Like nearly all sections in the *DSM–IV–TR*, this section also includes a not otherwise specified (NOS) diagnosis for disorders that belong in this category but do not fully meet the diagnostic criteria for any of the specific disorders (C. R. Johnson & Slomka, 2000). Expressive language disorder and mixed receptive-expressive language disorder are diagnosed when language skills are significantly below expectations based on nonverbal ability and interfere with academic progress. Phonological disorder involves "failure to use developmentally expected speech sounds that are appropriate for the individual's age and dialect" (APA, 2000, p. 65). Stuttering is diagnosed when speech fluency interferes with the child's ability to communicate or make good academic progress. Characteristic errors include repetitions of sounds, syllables, words, broken words, and production of words with excessive tension (C. R. Johnson & Slomka, 2000). Professional school counselors should be sure that an unusual speech pattern is not primarily the result of an inadequate education or a family or cultural environment before diagnosing a communication disorder. A referral to a speech and language specialist can facilitate this discrimination.

Learning, motor skills, and communication disorders are currently thought to involve perinatal or neonatal causes (D. Johnson, 1995).

Other causes for these disorders are being investigated. Changes in the communication skills of individuals with the human immunodeficiency virus (HIV) and the resultant disease, the acquired immunodeficiency syndrome (AIDS), are being recognized and studied (McCabe, Sheard, & Code, 2002). Lead poisoning or head trauma in childhood may also contribute to learning disorders. Silver (1991) reported a correlation between learning disorders and low birth weight, maternal smoking or alcohol use during pregnancy, and exposure to other toxins. Specific infections, such as a particular type of meningitis, have also been related to later learning difficulties (C. R. Johnson & Slomka, 2000). Approximately 35% to 40% of boys with learning disorders have at least one parent who had similar learning problems (Snowling, 2002; Young & Beitchman, 2002). Learning disorders are also associated with low socioeconomic status, poor self-esteem, depression, and perceptual deficiencies (Silver, 1992).

Children with these disorders often are unhappy in school, have negative self-images and social difficulties, and show increased likelihood of dropping out of school (Seligman, 1998). High school students with learning disabilities are reported to have lower educational and career aspirations than their peers (Young & Beitchman, 2002). Depression, anxiety, ADHD, and disruptive behavior disorders often coexist with learning disorders. In addition, a wide assortment of social skill deficits has been found in children with learning and communication disorders (Barnes, Friehe, & Radd, 2003; Young & Beitchman, 2002).

Intervention Strategies

The primary strategies for these disorders that occur at school (Seligman, 1998) include behavioral, cognitive-behavioral, and psychoeducational interventions (C. R. Johnson & Slomka, 2000). Children who demonstrate a significant discrepancy between intelligence and achievement, with achievement usually being 20 to 30 standard score points below measured intelligence, may be eligible to receive special education services. An IEP is developed by the school according to the requirements of the IDEA Amendments of 1997 (USDE, 1999). The IEP specifies areas of weakness, strategies for addressing the deficit areas, measurable behavioral goals, and criteria for determining whether goals have been successfully met. Young and Beitchman (2002) suggested teaching strategies that include attention to sequencing; drill-repetition-practice; segmenting information into parts or units for later synthesis; controlling task difficulty using prompts and cues; making use of technology (e.g., computers); systematically modeling problem-solving steps; and using small, interactive groups (Young & Beitchman, 2002). Frequently, social and emotional goals such as improved interpersonal relations and increases in motor or attention on-task behaviors are included in the IEP. Interventions, including counseling, individualized teaching strategies, and accommodations, and social skills training can lead to positive outcomes (Silver, 1995).

Prognosis

Learning disorders continue to have an impact on people's lives throughout adolescence and adulthood (Seligman, 1998; Young & Beitchman, 2002). When learning disorders are undiagnosed and untreated, they can lead to extreme frustration, loss of self-esteem, inadequate education, underemployment, and more serious mental disorders (Silver, 1995). Functioning of the family affects the prognosis of a child with learning problems. A "healthy" family may cope adequately in parenting a child with a learning disorder; however, families described as "disorganized" and "blaming" have more difficulty responding to the child's needs and providing appropriate support and intervention (C. R. Johnson & Slomka, 2000).

Relevance to Professional School Counselors

Professional school counselors frequently serve on child study and special education committees tasked with screening children for learning disorders. Through their contact with children, teachers, and parents, professional school counselors are often the first to be aware of how learning problems are impacting the child's performance in the classroom, in the home, and with peers. Professional school counselors may be required by the IEP to provide some individual or small-group counseling to the child, to help parents and children understand and cope with the diagnosis of a learning disorder, and to implement accommodations. Because children with learning disorders frequently have coexisting issues such as poor social skills, low self-esteem, negative attitudes toward school, behavioral difficulties, and family problems, professional school counselors can expect to be involved with students, teachers, and parents in a collaborative role.

Collaboration between professional school counselors and speech and language pathologists (SLPs) is important when helping students with communication disorders. It is suggested that the professional school counselor and SLP work together to make appropriate accommodations, such as in materials, activities, and instructional discourse, for these students during classroom group guidance lessons. In addition, it is usually important to include a classroom enrichment unit regarding disabilities. Professional school counselors can also coordinate support groups for students with communication disorders as well as see these students individually and meet with families (Barnes et al., 2003).

Pervasive Developmental Disorders

The increase in the diagnosis of pervasive developmental disorders (PDDs) is attributed to many factors. Some of these factors include more sensitive diagnostic procedures, a rise in appropriate referrals, ambiguity in diagnostic criteria, administrative mandates to use psychiatric diagnoses to ensure reimbursement for professional services in medical settings, categorical funding for children with autism by state and county health and social service agencies, educational placement in categorical programs, as well as changing biological and environmental influences on etiology of developmental disorders (Mulick & Butter, 2002). PDD is diagnosed in approximately 10 to 20 people per 10,000 (Lord & Rutter, 1994), although the addition of Asperger's disorder will likely substantially increase this rate. Males with

these disorders outnumber females by a ratio of approximately 2.5:1 (J. C. Harris, 1995; Sigman & Capps, 1997). Five subtypes of PDD included in the *DSM–IV–TR* are the following: (a) autistic disorder, (b) Asperger's disorder, (c) childhood disintegrative disorder, (d) Rett's disorder (Rapin, 1999), and (e) PDD–NOS.

Children with PDD are characterized by impaired social behavior and impaired communication as well as abnormalities of routine behavior (S. L. Harris, 2000). They usually exhibit a flat affect (lack of facial expression; emotionless), poor eye contact, and minimal social speech. Additionally, these children often show repetitive, stereotyped body movements such as rocking, waving, or head banging (Harris, 2000). They generally do not seek parental attention or involvement with peers and rarely engage in imitative or interactive play (J. C. Harris, 1995). Language impairment is present in most people with PDD.

Autistic disorder is present in 2 to 20 of every 10,000 people and causes significant deficits in socialization, communication, and behavior (APA, 2000; Sigman & Capps, 1997). The symptoms of autistic disorder are evident by age 3. Mental retardation accompanies this diagnosis 75% of the time. The ability to communicate varies widely in children diagnosed with autistic disorder. Some are mute, whereas others do eventually develop near-age-appropriate language skills. Generally, they do not form close relationships with others, preferring to engage in repetitive interactions with inanimate objects.

Rett's disorder and childhood disintegrative disorder are less prevalent than autistic disorder. Both are characterized by normal development in early childhood (for a period of 5 months to 4 years for Rett's disorder and for 2 to 10 years for childhood disintegrative disorder), followed by a steady deterioration. In the case of Rett's disorder, the result is ultimately severe or profound retardation. Rett's disorder is diagnosed only in females (M. Campbell, Cueva, & Hallin, 1996; S. L. Harris, 2000). Childhood disintegrative disorder results in significant regression in at least two of the following areas: language, social skills, elimination, play, and motor skills. Asperger's disorder is generally the mildest of the PDDs, which often makes it particularly difficult to diagnose. Like autistic disorder, Asperger's disorder is characterized by impaired social skills and repetitive or stereotypical behaviors, but it is not characterized by the delayed language development and impairment in communication skills found in people with other PDDs. Typically, children with Asperger's disorder have average to above-average intelligence, whereas in other forms of PDD, there is often mental retardation (S. L. Harris, 2000). Boys are diagnosed with Asperger's disorder five times more frequently than girls (APA, 2000).

Prognosis

For most children, the PDDs will last a lifetime. Although early intervention for many young children with autistic disorder, Asperger's disorder, and PDD–NOS has produced major developmental changes, the technology and knowledge of effective treatment approaches have not yet reached the point where the majority of children diagnosed with PDD make the degree of change that allows them to blend imperceptibly into their peer group (S. L. Harris, 2000). One review of outcome studies of autistic disorder (Gillberg, 1991) found that some children went on to lead independent lives. However, two thirds of the children required care throughout their lives. Those with Asperger's disorder have the best prognosis; many succeed in becoming self-sufficient (Seligman, 1998). Children with Rett's disorder and childhood disintegrative disorder will most likely be placed in residential treatment facilities due to the progressive nature of these disorders. Early intervention seems to be the most important factor for a positive outcome (Campbell, Schopler, Cueva, & Hallin, 1996).

Intervention Strategies

Children with a PDD will need a combination of special education services that may include speech and language therapy as well as physical therapy. These children may also require the services of neurologists, medical specialists, and behavioral therapists. The therapeutic goals suggested by Lord and Rutter (1994) are to foster the development of social and communication skills, enhance learning, and help the family cope. However, C. Smith (2001) stated that there are some difficulties in having children with PDD in social skills groups. For example, there are the anxieties intrinsic in group learning situations, the natural difficulty of the subject matter (i.e., social interaction and social understanding), and the typically high oral language load in social skills group work, compounded by the difficulties that the children have in generalizing their new skills into their real-life experiences (C. Smith, 2001). Instead, C. Smith (2001) suggested using Social Stories, a short story form (20–150 words), to inform and advise the child about a social situation. Some of the benefits of Social Stories are that they focus on immediate social difficulties, they can be more personalized than a traditional social skills group, they are easily produced and shared by those involved with the child, and they focus on real-life situations (C. Smith, 2001). Behavioral treatments have been found to be particularly effective in helping children with autistic disorders (Campbell, Schopler, et al., 1996). Social skills and social communication training have been beneficial for children with autistic disorder and Asperger's disorder.

Relevance to Professional School Counselors

Having a child with PDD in the family places a considerable strain on every family member (Bagenholm & Gillberg, 1991). Siblings typically have problems with friends, feel lonely, and worry about their sibling. Marital problems in the parents are also common. Most children with PDD will receive special education services; however, the professional school counselor may play an important role in helping siblings cope, as well as helping parents access supportive resources. Parents may also benefit from structured behavioral training programs that help them learn how to help their child (Lord & Rutter, 1994). Counselors need to become knowledgeable about such resources.

Additionally, professional school counselors may need to provide educators with resources as the expectation that students with PPD are included in regular education classrooms increases. In-service training for teachers can provide time for learning about the nature of the PDDs; discovering the preferences, priorities, and concerns of the children with PDD; and time for adapting curriculum and instruction to match learning strengths, needs, and interests of these students (Dow & Mehring, 2001).

Attention-Deficit Disorders and Disruptive Behavior Disorders

Attention-deficit disorders and disruptive behavior disorders include ADHD, conduct disorder (CD), and oppositional defiant disorder (ODD), as well as disruptive behavior disorder NOS. Children with ADHD or CD also often have learning disorders. Children with ODD or CD often have ADHD. Recent studies (Eaves et al., 2000) have investigated the genetic correlation between ODD and CD but so far have not supported a genetic correlation between ADHD and the disruptive behavior disorders.

ADHD

ADHD is found in as many as 50% of children seen for counseling or psychotherapy (Cantwell, 1996). The national public school systems spent in excess of $3 billion in 1995 to provide services for children with this prevalent disorder (National Institutes of Health, 1998). The *DSM–IV–TR* divides ADHD into three types: predominately hyperactive-impulsive type, predominately inattentive type, and combined type. By definition, ADHD has an onset prior to age 7; is present in two or more settings (such as home and school); and interferes with social, academic, or occupational functioning. For a diagnosis of ADHD, symptoms need to be present for at least 6 months (APA, 2000) and may include failure to give close attention to details, difficulty sustaining attention, poor follow-through on instructions, failure to finish work, difficulty organizing tasks, misplacement of things, distraction by extraneous stimuli, and forgetfulness. Children with hyperactive and impulsive symptoms are usually diagnosed at a younger age than are children with symptoms of the inattentive type of ADHD. The diagnosis of ADHD is made through medical,

cognitive, and academic assessments, as well as parents' and teachers' input on behavioral rating scales (Cantwell, 1996) such as the Conners' Rating Scales–Revised (Conners, 1997).

The current prevalence rates for ADHD range from 3% to 7% of children (APA, 2000; Cantwell, 1996; Jensen et al., 1999; National Institutes of Health, 1998; Wolraich, Hannah, Pinnock, Baumgaertel, & Brown, 1996). ADHD is diagnosed in boys two to nine times more frequently than in girls (APA, 2000). ADHD is diagnosed in 44% of children receiving special education services (Bussing, Zima, Perwien, Belin, & Widawski, 1998). Recent meta-analyses of gender differences have also pointed to diagnostic differences. Girls with ADHD had lower ratings on hyperactivity, inattention, impulsivity, and externalizing problems and greater intellectual impairment and internalizing problems than boys did (Gershon, 2002). However, more research is needed to clarify gender and ethnic differences in students with ADHD.

The diagnosis and treatment of ADHD remains controversial (National Institutes of Health, 1998). Dramatic increases in diagnostic rates of ADHD have raised questions about the accuracy of the diagnoses and have led to particular concern that lively and active boys may often be misdiagnosed with this disorder (Seligman, 1998). Correspondingly, concerns have been raised as to whether stimulant medication prescribed for treatment of this disorder is overused. One study of children diagnosed with ADHD in four communities concluded that of the 5.1% of the population of children meeting the ADHD criteria, only 12.5% of those children were being treated with psychostimulant medication (Jensen et al., 1999). However, this study also found that a number of children not meeting the ADHD criteria were being inappropriately treated with medication. This study supports the conclusion that children are both undermedicated and overmedicated for ADHD. Adding further support to this view is a recent study by Hoagwood, Kelleher, Feil, and Comer (2000) that found that only 50% of the children diagnosed with ADHD were receiving adequate and appropriate care.

Prognosis

The prognosis for improvement of ADHD via treatment is good (Pelham et al., 1993). Studies by DuPaul, Guevremont, and Barkley (1992) and Whalen and Henker (1991) indicated that behavioral interventions allowed most children with ADHD to reduce off-task and distractible behaviors. The effectiveness of psychostimulant medications such as methylphenidate (Ritalin or Concerta), Adderall, Strattera, and dextroamphetamine (Dexadrine) continue to be supported by research despite an ongoing debate concerning the use of these medications.

Intervention Strategies

The most commonly used interventions with children diagnosed with ADHD are behavioral strategies and the use of stimulant medication (National Institutes of Health, 1998; Seligman, 1998). Treatment most often addresses the behaviors of staying on task, completing work, and following directions (Rapport, 1995). Cognitive-behavioral strategies have been used to improve social skills in children with ADHD and to provide training for parents (Cousins & Weiss, 1993; Rapport, 1995). Social skills training programs focus on such skills as improving awareness of appropriate interpersonal distance, starting and maintaining a conversation, identifying the main idea of a conversation, and accepting and giving compliments (Seligman, 1998). Group therapy has also been used effectively to help children with ADHD improve self-esteem and communication and social skill development.

Training for parents involves helping them recognize and encourage socially competent behaviors, teach self-evaluation strategies, model good communication skills, establish appropriate limits, and provide consistent rewards and consequences (Anastopoulos, Shelton, DuPaul, & Guevremont, 1993; Cousins & Weiss, 1993). Programs like Systematic Training for Effective Parenting (STEP; Dinkmeyer, 1975) and support groups like Children and Adults with Attention-Deficit/Hyperactivity Disorder (CHADD) may also be useful (Seligman, 1998). Multifaceted approaches such as school-based community support programs (Hussey & Guo, 2003) that target elementary-aged students and aim to increase family involvement and support of the school and improve social and behavioral functioning as well as attendance and academic achievement also seem to be effective in reducing ADHD behaviors. Ultimately, the goal for children with ADHD is to learn self-monitoring behaviors (Seligman, 1998). Self-monitoring is encouraged through behavioral strategies such as praise to reinforce desirable behaviors, proximity (standing near the student), and the use of token economies. Token economies consist of providing children with tokens or points for appropriate behaviors that can be exchanged later for rewards (DuPaul et al., 1992).

One of the most controversial strategies for treating ADHD is the use of psychostimulant medication. Researchers continue to investigate the benefits and risks of using this medication to treat ADHD (National Institutes of Health, 1998). Effective medications are thought to stimulate the production of the neurochemicals that facilitate brain functioning (Seligman, 1998). Contrary to the misconception that these children are hypersensitive or hyperattentive, neurodevelopmental research suggests that ADHD is actually a problem of underarousal (Barkley, 1996). Methylphenidate (Ritalin) and dextroamphetamine (Dexadrine) are the most frequently prescribed medications. New medications such as Adderall, which is long acting and has less drop-off action; a sustained release version of methylphenidate (Concerta); and a stimulant-free medication, Strattera, are also being used. Approximately 75% of children with ADHD will respond positively to one of these drugs (Cantwell, 1996; King & Noshpitz, 1991). Meta-analyses of research on psychostimulant medication have consistently found that hyperactive, restless, and impulsive behaviors, as well as disruptive, aggressive, and socially inappropriate actions, diminish in response to psychostimulant treatment (R. G. Klein, 1993). The National Institutes of Health's (1998) *Consensus Statement on AD/HD* reviewed the major studies of medication use and concluded that stimulant medication was more effective than psychosocial interventions in reducing the symptoms of this disorder.

Disruptive Behavior Disorders

The *DSM–IV–TR* describes two disruptive behavior disorders: CD and ODD. Prevalence rates for CD are 6% to 16% of males under the age of 18, and 2% to 9% of females (APA, 2000). Prevalence rates for ODD are 2% to 16% for males and females.

A diagnosis of CD requires the presence of repeated and persistent violations of the basic rights of others or violations of major age-appropriate societal norms or rules (Seligman, 1998). CD is diagnosed when 3 of 15 criteria grouped into the following four categories are present: aggression against people and animals, destruction of property, deceitfulness or theft, and serious violation of rules. CD is divided into childhood-onset and adolescent-onset types. Adolescent-onset type is diagnosed when no symptoms are present before the age of 10, whereas the childhood-onset type is diagnosed if symptoms appear before that age. The prognosis for the childhood-onset type is worse than for the adolescent-onset type (Webster-Stratton & Dahl, 1995). Many children with a diagnosis of ODD experience a worsening of symptoms as they move into adolescence and develop CDs. If the symptoms of CD have not remitted by age 18, the diagnosis of CD is usually replaced with the diagnosis of antisocial personality disorder. Between 45% and 70% of children with CD are also diagnosed with ADHD (Kazdin, 1997). Mood disorders (D. E. Arredondo & Butler, 1994), anxiety disorders (Walker et al., 1991), substance use (Lavin & Rifkin, 1993), low verbal intelligence, learning disorders, school drop-out, delinquency, and violent behavior are common in young people with CDs (Snyder, 2001).

ODD is described as a pattern of negativistic, hostile, and defiant behaviors lasting at least 6 months. According to the *DSM–IV–TR*, characteristic behaviors include losing one's temper, arguing with adults, defying or refusing to comply with adults' requests, deliberately annoying people, being angry and resentful, being easily annoyed by others, blaming others for one's own negative behavior, and being vindictive (see Table 16.2). Younger children may have temper tantrums, power struggles, low tolerance for frustration, and be disobedient (Rey, 1993; Webster-Stratton & Taylor, 2001). Older children will argue, threaten, show disrespect for adults, destroy property in a rage, and refuse to cooperate. The presence of ODD is positively correlated with low socioeconomic status and growing up in an urban location. Generally, the symptoms of ODD first appear around the age of 8 (Maxman & Ward, 1995). During childhood, ODD is more prevalent in boys than in girls, but by puberty, equal numbers of boys and girls are diagnosed with ODD (APA, 2000).

Prognosis

Disruptive behavior disorders are sometimes thought to have no cure (Diamond, Serrano, Dickey, & Sonis, 1996) or a poor prognosis (Maxman & Ward, 1995). However, the prognosis for ODD is more promising than for CDs. Prognoses for disruptive behavior disorders appear to be best when there has been late onset, early intervention (Kendall, 1993), and long-term intervention (Diamond et al., 1996; Webster-Stratton & Taylor, 2001). The most critical element of successful treatment is parents' support and participation.

TABLE 16.2
Case illustration 1.

A 15-year-old female was brought to counseling by her parents. They reported that over the past year or so, she had changed; she has a quick temper and is hostile and argumentative, she has disobeyed her parents repeatedly to meet her boyfriend at a local shopping mall, she blames her teachers for her poor grades in some subjects but will not ask them for help, and she has even been teasing her 4-year-old sister, whom she used to adore. Family, as well as teachers, report that she is difficult and uncooperative but cannot provide an explanation for the change. A physical examination revealed no medical problems.

Principal Diagnosis: Oppositional defiant disorder

Intervention Strategies

Intervention for children with disruptive behavior disorders should be multifaceted. Four types of intervention strategies are suggested: individual counseling, family interventions, school-based interventions, and community interventions (Offord & Bennett, 1994). Residential or day treatment programs may be recommended when the child or adolescent poses a danger to self or others. School-based interventions include early education, classroom guidance units, classroom instruction, home visits, and regular meetings with parents.

Relevance to Professional School Counselors

Of all the categories of mental disorders, professional school counselors will have the greatest need to be knowledgeable about ADHD and disruptive behavior disorders. Classroom teachers and other school personnel as well as parents may look to the professional school counselor for guidance concerning how to effectively work with children diagnosed with these disorders. In fact, Jensen et al. (1999) found that children with ADHD were more likely to receive mental health counseling and school-based interventions than medication. Children are not usually diagnosed with ADHD and disruptive behavior disorders until they enter school. Teachers and professional school counselors will want to work closely with parents to help them understand these disorders and make appropriate referrals to medical and mental health professionals who can make the diagnosis. Since ADHD and disruptive behavior disorders frequently coexist, the diagnosis and decisions about interventions will require a high degree of collaboration among physicians, psychologists, classroom and special education teachers, professional school counselors, and parents. Children with disruptive behavior disorders may qualify for special education or Section 504 services.

Recent studies have examined the relation between low reading achievement and the development of CD in young children (Bennett, Brown, Boyle, Racine, & Offord, 2003); and the relation of perceived school culture, self-esteem, attachment to learning, and peer approval

(DeWit et al., 2000) to the development of disruptive behavior problems in adolescents. This research is encouraging the development of a range of school-based and family-focused prevention programs targeting young children (Webster-Stratton & Taylor, 2001). There are two approaches to early prevention. One is to provide social skills, problem-solving, and anger-management training to the entire school population through a developmental curriculum. *Second Step: A Violence Prevention Curriculum* (Committee for Children, 2002b) is an example of such a developmental program. The second approach to prevention is to identify high-risk students and provide a small-group curriculum for them. Fast Track (Bierman et al., 2002) is an example of a research-based program delivered to identified high-risk first graders. By the end of the third grade, 37% of the program participants were free of serious conduct-problem dysfunctions. The efficacy of both of these approaches will continue to be evaluated, but the implications for professional school counselors are clear. Using either approach, the professional school counselor will play a central role in the delivery of such programs.

Eating Disorders in Children and Adolescents

Feeding and eating disorders of early childhood include two disorders that can interfere with a child's development, social functioning, or nutritional health: pica and rumination disorder. Pica and rumination disorder are especially likely to be diagnosed in children with mental retardation and are often associated with PDD. Typically, these disorders will be diagnosed before a child enters school, but professional school counselors should be aware of them nonetheless.

Pica is characterized by the ingestion of non-food substances (House, 1999). Mouthing and eating nonnutritive substances is not uncommon in children under the age of 2; therefore, the diagnosis of pica should not be made before that age unless the behavior is judged to be problematic (Motta & Basile, 1998). Rumination disorder is characterized by persistent regurgitation and rechewing of food (House, 1999). Typically, rumination disorder is diagnosed in infants and very young children after a period in which a normal eating pattern has been established. Prevalence rates and risk factor assessments have been established based on Caucasian samples of adolescents and, therefore, do not accurately reflect the nature of eating disorders in other ethnic populations (Jacobi, Hayward, de Zwaan, Kraemer, & Agras, 2004).

Anorexia nervosa (AN) and bulimia nervosa (BN) are eating disorders that are diagnosed in adults as well as in children and adolescents. Prevalence rates of 0.5% to 2% have been reported for AN and 1% to 3% for BN (Roth & Fonagy, 1996) in late adolescent and young adult populations. Prevalence rates for AN and BN have increased during the last 50 years (Wakeling, 1996), and the incidence of eating disorders among elementary-aged children is also increasing. The most common risk factors for eating disorders in adolescence include early childhood eating and gastrointestinal problems, body dissatisfaction, depression or anxiety, and low self-esteem (Jacobi et al., 2004; Polivy & Herman, 2002). Other factors sometimes associated with eating disorders are environmental stressors, cognitive distortions such as obsessive thoughts, and weak identity formation. Caution must be used in the application of these risk factors to diverse cultural groups. For instance, body dissatisfaction is not a risk factor for females in many cultures (Katzman & Lee, 1997). The causes of eating disorders and the role culture plays in the manifestation of eating disorders are being debated. Recently, researchers (Keel & Klump, 2003) have challenged the belief that eating disorders are culture-bound syndromes, concluding that a strong genetic link exists. Eating disorders in both males and females are associated with sports or occupational choice (Carlat, Carmago, & Herzog, 1997); people in occupational or avocational roles that require low weight, such as ballet, theater, and many sports, are at an elevated risk of developing an eating disorder.

AN, according to the *DSM–IV–TR*, involves a person's refusal to maintain normal body weight or failure to gain weight at what would be an expected rate. For adolescents diagnosed with AN, the *DSM–IV–TR* criteria specify a body weight that is 85% or less than the normal weight for the person's age and size. Other symptoms include great fear of becoming overweight, a disturbed body image, dread of loss of control, and, in females, the cessation of menstrual cycles. In prepubescent girls, the disorder may be associated with apprehension about puberty. Two types of AN have been identified: restricting type (more common) and binge-eating/purging type (APA, 2000). Restricting type is associated with dieting, fasting, or excessive exercise. Binge-eating/purging type is associated with binge eating, purging, or both, accompanied by a very low weight.

Purging is accomplished through self-induced vomiting or the misuse of laxatives, diuretics, or enemas. The onset of AN is commonly between the ages of 10 and 30. However, 85% of the people with this disorder first meet the diagnostic criteria for the disorder between the ages of 13 and 20 (Kaplan, Sadock, & Grebb, 1994). Physiological consequences of AN include dry skin, edema, low blood pressure, metabolic changes, potassium loss, and cardiac damage that can result in death (Agras, 1987; Maxman & Ward, 1995).

Individuals diagnosed with BN engage in behaviors similar to those with binge-eating/purging type AN but do not meet the full criteria for that disorder, usually because their weight is more than 85% of normal. According to the *DSM–IV–TR*, BN involves an average of two episodes a week of binge eating (usually accompanied by compensatory behavior such as vomiting, fasting, laxative use, or extreme exercise), for at least 3 months. Physiological reactions to purging include dental cavities and enamel loss, electrolyte imbalance, cardiac and renal problems, and esophageal tears (Agras, 1987). Bingeing is associated with dysphoric mood, stress, and unstructured time. People usually binge alone and can consume 3,000 calories in a single binge (Maxman & Ward, 1995).

Prognosis

The prognosis for women with AN is mixed (Löwe et al., 2001). Maxman and Ward (1995) reported that 44% of people with AN recover completely

TABLE 16.3
Case illustration 2.

Marie, age 11, aspired to be a model. She exercised daily and ate very little. Her weight had dropped from 120 lb to 95 lb; at 5ft 5in. She looked gaunt and tired. Nevertheless, she continued to perform well at school and at home and was never disobedient. She had few friends but reported that she was so busy studying that she had little time for socializing. Part of her reluctance to socialize with others stemmed from some unusual behaviors she manifested. She would often wave her arm as though she were swatting flies. She also emitted sounds and words, including obscenities. Marie reported that she could not control these behaviors. Marie was in a special class because of severe difficulty with reading; her reading ability was nearly 2 standard deviations below the norm for her age. Diagnoses: Anorexia nervosa, Tourette's disorder, and a reading disorder

through treatment, 28% are significantly improved, and 24% are not helped or deteriorate. Approximately 5% of people with AN die as a result of the disorder (Maxman & Ward, 1995; Morrison, 1995). The prognosis for BN is somewhat better (Kaplan et al., 1994). Treatment that follows recommended guidelines can have a positive impact on eating patterns, typically reducing binge-eating and purging by a rate of at least 75% (Seligman, 1998). Positive prognosis is associated with the following factors: good functioning prior to occurrence of the disorder, a positive family environment, the client's acknowledgment of hunger, greater maturity, higher self-esteem, higher educational level, earlier age of onset, lower weight loss, shorter duration of the disease, little denial of the disorder, and absence of coexisting mental disorders.

Intervention Strategies

Primary intervention strategies for eating disorders involve a complete medical assessment and multifaceted therapy (Seligman, 1998). Behavioral therapy has been effective in promoting healthy eating and eliminating purging and other destructive behaviors. Cognitive therapy can help the individual gain an understanding of the disorder, improve self-esteem, and gain a sense of control. Group therapy has been used effec-

tively to treat people diagnosed with AN and BN, with family therapy included as an important component of the treatment plan, especially for children and adolescents.

Relevance to Professional School Counselors

Professional school counselors will need to have knowledge of the risk factors and symptoms of eating disorders and will need to consider how culture may influence the development of an eating disorder (Krentz & Arthur, 2001). Research (Leon, Fulkerson, Perry, Keel, & Klump, 1999) indicates that prevention programs and early detection in elementary and middle school may be the best defense against the development of an eating disorder during adolescence. Professional school counselors can enlist the help of classroom teachers by increasing their knowledge of eating disorder risk factors and encouraging strategies that promote healthy behaviors (Piran, 2004). Schoolwide antibullying programs can go a long way in protecting students' self-esteem, body image, and identity development.

Professional school counselors may become aware of students who are regularly eating little or no lunch, engaging in ritualized eating patterns, or purging. It is not uncommon in schools to have other students, influenced by the weight loss of youth with AN or BN, begin to experiment with restricted eating patterns. Working with the classroom teacher, the school nurse, and the parents, professional school counselors can help students and their families become aware of dangerous eating patterns and the long-term consequences of eating disorders. Children and adolescents who are diagnosed with eating disorders will need to have long-term medical and mental health interventions. However, professional school counselors can assist these students in school, support the efforts of their mental health counselors, and help parents and families find resources.

Tic Disorders

The *DSM–IV–TR* identifies four tic disorders: Tourette's disorder, chronic tic disorder, transient tic disorder, and tic disorder NOS. Tics are defined as recurrent, nonrhythmic series of movements and sounds (of a nonvoluntary nature) in one or several muscle groups. Tics are usually divided into simple and complex tics of a motor, sensory, or vocal nature (APA, 2000). Examples of motor tics are eye blinking, neck jerking, facial grimacing, or shrugging. Vocal tics include coughing, clearing one's throat, grunting, sniffing, or barking. Tic symptoms are typically worse under stress, less noticeable when the child is distracted, and diminish entirely during sleep (Seligman, 1998). Tic disorders are more common in boys and have an elevated incidence in children with other disorders such as ADHD, learning disorders, PDD, anxiety disorders, and obsessive-compulsive disorder (Coffey et al., 2000; Gadow, Nolan, Sprafkin, & Schwartz, 2002; Kadesjo & Gillberg, 2000; Kurlan et al., 2002).

Tourette's disorder is characterized by a combination of multiple motor tics and one or more vocal tics that have been present for at least 1 year. These involuntary movements have been reported to occur as frequently as 100 or more times per minute (Leckman & Cohen, 1994). Tourette's disorder often begins with simple eye blinking. Over time, the tic behaviors become persistent and occur at multiple sites in the body. These tics commonly interfere with academic performance and social relationships. Tourette's is diagnosed in 4 or 5 children per 10,000 and tends to run in families.

Budman, Bruun, Park, Lesser, and Olson (2000) reported sudden, explosive outbursts of behavior in children and adolescents with Tourette's disorder. These explosive outbursts are recognizable by their stereotypic features, which include the abrupt onset of unpredictable and primitive displays of physical aggression, verbal aggression, or both that are grossly out of proportion to any provoking stimuli, often threatening serious self-injury or harm to others. Explosive outbursts in children can be distinguished from the more common "temper tantrum" by their magnitude and intensity. These outbursts occur at an age when such symptoms are no longer regarded as age-appropriate (Budman et al., 2000).

Transient tic disorder, which includes symptoms of motor tics, vocal tics, or both, that have been present for at least 4 weeks but less than a year, is often associated with emotional stress (R. A. King & Noshpitz, 1991). Chronic tic disorder is diagnosed if the symptoms of either motor or vocal tics (not both) have been present for over 1 year. The prevalence of chronic and transient tic disorders is not known since many children with these disorders never come to the attention of medical or mental health professionals (Seligman, 1998).

Prognosis

Tic severity peaks at approximately 10 to 11 years and declines in early adolescence (Coffey et al., 2004). One study of the treatment of tic disorders compared the effectiveness of behavioral interventions with the use of medication (Peterson, Campise, & Azrin, 1994). Habit-reversal techniques showed a 90% reduction in tics as compared to medication, which showed only a 50% to 60% reduction. Coffey et al. (2004) conducted a study examining whether a substantial decline in the prevalence rate of tic disorders occurs from childhood to adulthood, suggesting that tic disorders may follow a remitting course. Results of this study found that early adolescence is the time of remission of tics and Tourette's disorder–associated impairment.

Intervention Strategies

The treatment of tic disorders currently includes identification of any underlying stressors; cognitive-behavioral methods for stress management; education of children and families about the disorder; advocacy with education professionals; and collaborative work with physicians, if pharmacological interventions are necessary (Towbin, Cohen, & Lechman, 1995). The first steps include gathering enough information about the symptoms to make an accurate diagnosis and educating the parents and the child about the course of the disorder and the influence of stress (R. A. King & Noshpitz, 1991; Towbin et al., 1995). Behavioral strategies such as self-monitoring, relaxation training, and habit-reversal training may be recommended after baseline data concerning the nature and frequency of the tic are collected (Azrin & Peterson, 1990; Kronenberger & Meyer, 1996). The current

HELPING STUDENTS WITH MENTAL AND EMOTIONAL DISORDERS

371

psychological treatment of choice for tics is habit reversal, which essentially addresses the tic as a behavior. The principal stages in habit reversal involve relaxation and introduction of a competing response (O'Connor, 2001). Social skills training has also been used successfully to offset the negative impact of tic disorders on peer relationships. While behavioral interventions may sometimes attenuate frequency and severity of the above-mentioned explosive outbursts, these symptoms often increase relentlessly without medication intervention (Budman et al., 2000). Pharmacological treatment is used only for children who do not respond to behavioral strategies (Towbin & Cohen, 1996).

Relevance to Professional School Counselors

The professional school counselor may be the first professional consulted about the development of tic behaviors in a child. A counselor who is knowledgeable about this disorder will be able to provide sources of referral and information to parents and teachers during the diagnostic period. Once the diagnosis has been made, professional school counselors can provide suggestions concerning classroom modifications to reduce stress, rewards for behavioral control, and adjustment of academic expectations. Professional school counselors may also be able to provide the social skills training to help children deal with the peer relationship problems that frequently result from tic disorders.

Elimination Disorders: Encopresis and Enuresis

Encopresis and enuresis are characterized by inadequate bowel or bladder control in children whose age and intellectual level suggest they can be expected to have adequate control of these functions. Many children diagnosed with these disorders have no coexisting mental disorders (Rapoport & Ismond, 1996). For the diagnosis to be made, the encopresis or enuresis cannot be associated with a general medical condition, with the exception of constipation (Mikkelsen, 2001; Seligman, 1998).

Encopresis is the voluntary or involuntary passage of feces in inappropriate places (S. Murphy & Carney, 2004). This diagnosis would not be made in a child younger than 4 years (Mikkelsen, 2001). "Antisocial or psychopathological processes may be behind deliberate incontinence" (Rapoport & Ismond, 1996, p. 172). There sometimes is an association between encopresis and ODD or CD. Sexual abuse and family pressure have also been associated with this disorder. The most effective treatment strategies involve medical, educational, and therapeutic interventions. Encopresis with constipation responds to treatment more quickly than does encopresis without constipation (Rockney, McQuade, Days, Linn, & Alario, 1996). Encopresis may continue for some time, but it is rarely chronic (Shaffer & Waslick, 1995). According to Mikkelsen (2001), the long-standing conventional treatment regimen, which encompasses educational, behavioral, dietary, and physiological components, has not been surpassed as a primary treatment modality.

Enuresis is the involuntary or intentional inappropriate voiding of urine, occurring in children over the age of 5 (Butler, 2004; Rapoport & Ismond, 1996). The subtype, nocturnal only, is the most common type of this disorder. Nocturnal enuresis can be caused by high fluid intake at night before bedtime, urinary tract infection, emotional stress, sexual abuse, chronic constipation, and a family history of enuresis (Silverstein, 2004). Traumatic events during a sensitive stage in the development of bladder control (2 to 3 years of age) have been found to be related to the later development of nocturnal enuresis (Butler, 2004; Mikkelsen, 2001). Behavioral interventions are the most successful (Seligman, 1998). Behavioral treatment in the form of bell-and-pad method of conditioning is usually considered the first line of intervention (Mikkelsen, 2001). Spontaneous remission occurs in many children.

Relevance to Professional School Counselors

Parents are likely to consult professional school counselors about their child's enuresis, most often manifested as "bedwetting." Parents will need information and education about the nature of this disorder and how to deal with it. Education may help alleviate parents' anxiety about the course of the disorder (Seligman, 1998). Parents should be encouraged to rule out medical causes of the bed-wetting; if a diagnosis of enuresis is made, professional school counselors can help parents cope. Encopresis is a less common but often more serious disorder than enuresis. Counselors suspecting this diagnosis in a student should recommend a medical evaluation as the first step in treatment.

Separation Anxiety Disorder

Separation anxiety disorder (SAD) is diagnosed in 4% to 5% of children and young adolescents (House, 1999; Masi, Mucci, & Millepiedi, 2001). SAD is the sole *DSM–IV–TR* anxiety disorder diagnosed only in children and adolescents under the age of 18 (House, 1999). This disorder is characterized by excessive distress on separation from primary attachment figures. Children diagnosed with SAD must have three or more of the following symptoms present for at least 4 weeks prior to age 18: worry about caregivers' safety, reluctance or refusal to go to school or be separated from caregivers, fear about being alone, repeated nightmares involving separation themes, and somatic complaints. SAD is more common in girls than boys (Masi et al., 2001), and 50% to 75% of children diagnosed with SAD come from low socioeconomic status homes. Children with SAD typically spend a great deal of time in the school clinic complaining of minor illnesses, will ask to go home (Popper & Gherardi, 1996), and have more negative thoughts and lower estimations of their ability to cope than do children without this disorder (Bögels, Snieder, & Kindt, 2003). School refusal is a prominent symptom in 75% of children diagnosed with the disorder (Masi et al., 2001). Adolescents exposed to domestic violence and living in abusive homes are at particular risk for developing SAD (Pelcovitz, Kaplan, DeRosa, Mandel, & Salziner, 2000). Children with a history of SAD are at a 20% increased risk of developing adolescent panic attacks (Hayward, Wilson, Lagle, Killen, & Taylor, 2004).

Prognosis

A study conducted by Last, Perrin, Hersen, and Kazdin (1992) reported a high rate (96%) of recovery from SAD with treatment. A history of the disorder is reported by many adults being treated for other disorders. Childhood SAD may be a precursor to early-onset panic disorder (Goodwin, Lipsitz, Chapman, Mannuzza, & Fyer, 2001), adult anxiety disorders (King & Noshpitz, 1991; Klein, 1994), and mood disorders (Popper & Gherardi, 1996). Additionally, a family history of emotional disorders seems to be related to a poor prognosis for children with SAD (Kearney, Sims, Pursell, & Tillotson, 2003).

Intervention Strategies

Treatment strategies can best be determined when the underlying cause of the disorder is understood, particularly whether it stems from insecurity and change in the home environment or is linked to negative experiences in the school setting. The first treatment strategy should be psychoeducational, involving the education of the parents and child (if he or she is old enough) about the symptoms, the consequences, and management strategies (Masi et al., 2001). Encouraging the child to face new situations and being positive may be enough to allow the child to return to school and participate in anxiety-producing situations.

SAD is considered a type of phobia; therefore, behavioral strategies such as systematic desensitization may be the most effective treatment (Seligman, 1998). Systematic desensitization, which is a cognitive-behavioral approach, involves rewards being given for successive approximations toward the goal (Weems & Carrion, 2003). Since getting the child back in school is frequently the goal, this strategy would involve rewarding the child for being driven to the school, then entering the school, and finally going into the classroom. Working closely with the parents and school personnel on consistent strategies will be essential. Family therapy may also be necessary, especially when family enmeshment is present.

Relevance to Professional School Counselors

Professional school counselors will most likely encounter children with SAD through referrals from the school nurse or other personnel in the school clinic. Parents also may be aware of the symptoms of this disorder and may seek the counselor's help. Children are more likely to demonstrate symptoms of the disorder during the first few weeks of school and particularly in the early years of school (kindergarten and primary grades). Professional school counselors can help parents distinguish between mild and transient symptoms associated with difficulty adjusting to school and true SAD. When SAD, the symptoms of school refusal, or both are present, professional school counselors can play an important role in helping to plan and implement systematic desensitization. Professional school counselors can also provide parents with encouragement and support to leave their children at school, and provide children with the help they need to stay in school.

Selective Mutism

Selective mutism is a disorder characterized by a person's consistently not speaking in selected social contexts, such as at school (House, 1999), but speaking in other situations, such as at home (Popper & Gherardi, 1996). The symptoms of selective mutism are not usually related to other communication difficulties such as lack of familiarity with the language, as would be the case for immigrant students (Krysanski, 2003). Selective mutism usually begins before age 5 and occurs in 30 to 80 people per 100,000 (Popper & Gherardi, 1996). Family dysfunction is often implicated in this disorder (Seligman, 1998). Approximately 97% of children diagnosed with selective mutism also had symptoms of an anxiety disorder, usually social phobia (Black & Udhe, 1995; Krysanski, 2003). The child with this disorder is often lonely and depressed, and the mother is often overinvolved or enmeshed (Silver, 1989).

Prognosis

The prognosis for successful treatment of selective mutism is excellent. Popper and Gherardi (1996) reported that half the children treated are able to speak in public by age 10. The prognosis is especially good for young children; however, the prognosis for children over the age of 10 who still exhibit symptoms of this disorder is

less hopeful. Older children are often teased by peers or inappropriately managed by teachers and therefore inadvertently encouraged to maintain the behaviors (Krysanski, 2003).

Intervention Strategies

The most effective treatment strategies are behavioral interventions designed to increase communication and teach social skills that help the child overcome feelings of fear and shyness (Kehle, Madaus, Baratta, & Bray, 1998; Krysanski, 2003), such as the use of reinforcements, shaping or prompting, self-modeling, and response initiation procedures. Play therapy can be used to help children overcome the symptoms and to provide a nonverbal way of communicating. Family therapy is also helpful in addressing the role families might play in perpetuating or reinforcing the symptoms.

Relevance to Professional School Counselors

Professional school counselors will want to understand the characteristics of this disorder and may be helpful to parents and school personnel in deciding whether a referral to an outside agency is necessary. Because of the impact selective mutism has on school performance and because school is often the place where children with this disorder choose not to speak, selective mutism will often come to the attention of school personnel before parents or others notice it. Professional school counselors may be part of the treatment team once selective mutism is diagnosed, may facilitate treatment by providing a safe environment in which the child can begin to speak in school, and can help teachers to use effective behavioral strategies to encourage speech.

Reactive Attachment Disorder

Reactive attachment disorder (RAD) is an uncommon disorder that begins before the age of 5 years and is characterized by children manifesting severe disturbances in social relatedness (Seligman, 1998). The style of social relating among children with RAD typically occurs in one of two extremes: (a) indiscriminate and excessive attempts to receive comfort and affection from any available adult, even relative strangers, or (b) extreme reluctance to initiate or accept comfort and affection, even from familiar adults and especially when distressed (Haugaard & Hazan, 2004). Children with this disorder are those whose attachments to their primary caregivers have been disrupted, leading to impairment of future relationships. Neglect, abuse, or grossly inadequate parenting, otherwise known as pathogenic care, is thought to cause this disorder (Coleman, 2003; Hanson & Spratt, 2000; Haugaard & Hazan, 2004; Sheperis, Renfro-Michel, & Doggett, 2003). Studies have considered the relation between RAD and behavioral problems among preschool children; RAD may reflect the roots of ODD and CD (Lyons-Ruth, Zeanah, & Benoit, 1996). In older children and adolescents, the behaviors associated with RAD present as withdrawing from others, acting out aggressively toward peers, social awkwardness, and sexual promiscuity, as well as being the frequent victim of bullying (Haugaard & Hazan, 2004). According to Sheperis et al. (2003), some additional symptoms of RAD include low self-esteem; lack of self-control; antisocial attitudes and behaviors; aggression and violence; and a lack of ability to trust, show affection, or develop intimacy. Behaviorally, these children are often self-destructive, suicidal, self-mutilative, and self-defeating (Sheperis et al., 2003). Coleman (2003) also suggested that behaviors such as tantrums, recklessness, risk taking, bullying, stealing, abuse of pets, hoarding of food, and deception are also believed to be associated with RAD; however, these problem behaviors are not currently considered a part of the *DSM–IV–TR* criteria.

Intervention Strategies

Early intervention is the key to treating RAD. Recent research based on Bowlby's theory of attachment has focused on the ways in which secure and insecure attachment patterns evolve and affect children (Seligman, 1998). Bowlby and others have found that without treatment, failure to achieve a secure and rewarding attachment during the early years can impair people's ability to form rewarding relationships throughout their lives.

Once the medical needs of the child are addressed, behavioral programs to improve feeding, eating, and caregiving routines can be implemented (Seligman, 1998). It will be important to provide caregivers with training so that they know how to provide infants and children with a nurturing environment. Speltz (1990), for example, developed a parental training program based on behavioral and attachment theory that might be useful to parents of children with RAD. Beneficial treatments of RAD should include (a) proper diagnosis at an early age; (b) placement in a secure and nurturing environment; (c) instruction for the parents in empirically based parenting skills; (d) emphasis on family functioning, copying skills, and interaction; and (e) working within the child's and family's more naturalistic environments as opposed to more restrictive and intrusive settings (Hanson & Spratt, 2000; Sheperis et al., 2003).

Relevance to Professional School Counselors

Professional school counselors will need to be aware of the diagnostic criteria for RAD because a connection has been found between insecure attachment and both subsequent behavior and impulse-control problems and poor peer relationships in young children (Zeanah & Emde, 1994). RAD may be associated with eating problems; developmental delays; and abuse, neglect, and other parent–child problems. In addition, it is important to distinguish RAD from other diagnoses with related symptoms, such as CD and depression, because effective treatment for RAD and these other disorders can be quite different (Haugaard & Hazan, 2004).

OTHER DISORDERS DIAGNOSED IN CHILDREN AND ADOLESCENTS

Mental disorders reviewed up to this point in this chapter are those that typically begin during the early years and are diagnosed primarily or exclusively in young clients. However, many other mental disorders, more likely to be diagnosed in adults, can also be found in children and adolescents. The most common of these include mood disorders, substance-related disorders, psychotic disorders, and several anxiety disorders (obsessive-compulsive disorder [OCD], posttraumatic stress disorder [PTSD], generalized anxiety disorder [GAD], and adjustment disorders. These disorders will be reviewed next.

Mood Disorders

Although the diagnostic criteria for mood disorders in adults and children are the same, children and adolescents diagnosed with mood disorders typically have symptoms that differ from those of adults (Emslie & Mayes, 2001; Seligman, 1998). Rather than manifesting the classic symptoms of depression, children tend to externalize their feelings and may be irritable, often presenting with somatic complaints. Adolescents are more likely to present with the more familiar symptoms of depression, similar to those of adults, including feelings of sadness and guilt, social withdrawal, and perhaps even thoughts of suicide.

Suicide is rare in children but increases in prevalence through adolescence (Shaffer & Pfeffer, 2001), with current estimates as high as one out of five students seriously considering taking his or her own life (Kann, Kinchen, & Williams, 2000). The rate of suicide in African Americans has always been lower than that in Whites but has been increasing in adolescent males. Attempted suicide is greater in Hispanic adolescents than in African Americans and Whites. Native American adolescents have a very high rate of suicide. Mood disorders, disruptive behavior disorders, and anxiety disorders increase the risk of suicidal ideation and attempts in both sexes. Approximately 90% of adolescents who commit suicide had been diagnosed with a psychiatric disorder for at least 2 years. Given the high correlation of mood disorders and suicide attempts, it is important to identify young people with mood disorders and begin treatment. Yet it is estimated that 70% of children and adolescents with serious mood disorders are either undiagnosed or inadequately treated (Lewinsohn, Rohde, Seeley, Klein, & Gotlib, 2000).

Major depressive disorder, characterized by at least 2 weeks of severe depression, is diagnosed in 0.4% to 2.5% of children and 0.4% to 8.3% of adolescents (Birmaher, Ryan, Williamson, Brent, & Kaufman, 1996). Major and minor depression have been reported in 14% of adolescents ages 15 to 18 (Kessler & Walters, 1998). Dysthymic disorder, a milder but more pervasive form of depression that lasts for at least 1 year, is diagnosed in 0.6% to 1.7% of children and 1.6% to 8% of adolescents. Bipolar disorder, characterized by episodes of depression and episodes of mania or hypomania, is difficult to diagnose in children and adolescents (Emslie & Mayes, 2001). Prevalence rates for adolescents are thought to be as high as 1%, but the estimates for young children are likely lower (Coyle et al., 2003).

Prognosis

Psychotherapy and psychoeducational interventions have been shown to be effective in treating depression in children. One study of children with dysthymic disorder demonstrated that children given a psychoeducational program were unlikely to develop a major depressive disorder in adulthood (Kovacs, Akiskal, Gatsonis, & Parrone, 1994). A meta-analysis conducted by Weisz, Weiss, Han, Grander, and Morton (1995) found that psychotherapy was effective in alleviating the symptoms of 77% of children diagnosed

TABLE 16.4
Case illustration 3.

A 17-year old girl was evaluated for an episode of depressed mood, sleeping problems, irritability, loss of weight, and reduced energy level. Symptoms had been present for nearly a month, since her best friend was killed by a car. Her parents could hardly get her up in the morning. She refused to dress or bathe and had been absent from school for 2 weeks. She repeatedly told her parents that she wished she could die so that she could be with her friend. No previous emotional difficulties were reported.

Principal Diagnosis: Major depressive disorder, single episode with depression. However, a less optimistic outlook offered by one longitudinal study demonstrated that early-onset depression often persists and is associated with mental illness in adulthood (Weissman et al., 1999).

Intervention Strategies

Treatment of children and adolescents with mood disorders is similar to that of adults; cognitive and behavioral interventions are emphasized. Psycho-educational programs (Evans, Van Velsor, & Schumacher, 2002; Kovacs et al., 1994; Lewinsohn, Clarke, Hops, & Andrews, 1990) focus on improving social skills and encouraging rewarding activities. Although medications are used successfully to treat depression in adults, the effective and safe use of antidepressant medications with children and adolescents has not been established (Coyle et al., 2003; Emslie & Mayes, 2001). Nevertheless, medication is often used with children and adolescents to relieve depression.

Relevance to Professional School Counselors

Professional school counselors will encounter many sad children and adolescents. It will be particularly important for counselors to understand the diagnostic criteria for mood disorders so they can distinguish situational sadness from a mental disorder, especially given the differences between adult and childhood depression. Mood disorders in children are frequently overlooked and mis-diagnosed (J. R. Evans et al., 2002). Given the increased risk of suicide behavior linked to mood disorders, this is a diagnosis that professional school counselors will need to be educated about. Professional school counselors will want to consult with parents, teachers, and other mental health professionals if a diagnosis of a mood disorder is suspected, given the evidence that early diagnosis and treatment are associated with better outcomes.

Substance-Related Disorders

Professional school counselors and other mental health professionals generally have considerable concern about the use of alcohol, tobacco, and other harmful substances by children and adolescents. Children who live with parents with substance-related disorders are at particularly high risk of developing these disorders themselves (Rapoport & Ismond, 1996). Professional school counselors need to have current and accurate information about substance use, abuse, and dependence to work effectively with students, teachers, and parents.

Substance-use disorders are unlike most other mental disorders in at least two ways. First, drug abuse and dependence rely on an external agent (the drug) and vary depending on the availability of drugs. Second, substance-use disorders always involve a willing host (the user), who is an active instigator and participant in creating the disorder (Newcomb & Richardson, 2000). Substance-related disorders, according to the *DSM–IV–TR*, include two substance-use disorders (substance dependence and substance abuse) as well as a variety of substance-induced disorders that stem from substance abuse or dependence. It is important to differentiate among the types of substance-related disorders (Rapoport & Ismond, 1996). Substance abuse is characterized by maladaptive use of substances, leading to significant impairment or distress. People may fail to fulfill their obligations or may have social or legal problems related to their substance use. Substance dependence is more severe than substance abuse and often includes not only distress and impairment, but also the development of tolerance and symptoms of withdrawal.

Determining whether a young person is using substances is often difficult. Children and adolescents commonly deny substance use for fear of punishment. Substance-use disorders have a high comorbidity with other mental disorders, such as mood disorders, impulse control disorders, and learning disorders in children and adolescents (House, 1999). Consequently, diagnosing substance-related disorders in young people may be complicated by a pre- or coexisting condition (Rapoport & Ismond, 1996).

Prognosis

Many factors are related to a good prognosis for substance-related disorders (Seligman, 1998). A stable family situation, early intervention, the lack of accompanying antisocial behavior, and no family history of alcohol use are indicators of a positive outcome (Frances & Allen, 1986). However, Newcomb and Richardson (2000) suggested several areas that work together to influence drug use and abuse. These areas are the cultural, societal environment (i.e., school, peers, and family); psychobehavioral factors (i.e., personality, attitudes, and activities); and biogenetic factors. Furthermore, Lambie and Rokutani (2002, p. 355) proposed 10 risk factors that predict or precipitate substance-related disorders, including (a) poor parent–child relationships; (b) mental disorders, especially depression; (c) a tendency to seek novel experiences or take risks; (d) family members or peers who use substances; (e) low academic motivation; (f) absence of religion/religiosity; (g) early cigarette use; (h) low self-esteem; (i) being raised in a single-parent or blended family; and (j) engaging in health-compromising behaviors. It has been found that adolescents who concurrently possess five or more of these qualities are at an extremely high risk for developing substance-use problems. Childhood anxiety disorders and depression have also been identified as potential risk factors affecting the development and course of substance-use disorders (Kendall, Safford, Flannery-Schroeder, & Webb, 2004). According to Wu et al. (2004), there is a strong association between alcohol abuse and suicide attempts. This relation may involve the disinhibitory effects of acute alcohol intoxication, the increase in vulnerability for depression resulting from chronic alcohol abuse, as well as possible use of drugs or alcohol as self-medication for depressive symptoms (Wu et al., 2004). Abusing substances poses significant health risks such as overdose, suicide, aggression, violent behavior, and other psychopathology (McClelland, Elkington, Teplin, & Abram, 2004).

Intervention Strategies

Prevention through substance-abuse education, recognition of risk factors, and early detection and treatment are the most important strategies for dealing with substance-use disorders in children and adolescents (Newcomb & Richardson, 2000). Accurate screening for substance use is the first step in intervention. Home drug-test kits are available to parents who wish to assess their child's drug use. The presence of other mental disorders should be assessed as part of any intervention (House, 1999). Treatment models vary and may be distinguished by their duration, intensity, goals, degree of restrictiveness, and participant membership. Contemporary treatments may be viewed on a continuum that ranges from brief outpatient therapy to intensive inpatient treatment (Newcomb & Richardson, 2000). Treatment may include detoxification, contracting, behavior therapy, self-help groups, family therapy, change in a person's social context, social skills training, and nutritional and recreational counseling (Newcomb & Richardson, 2000). Specific treatment strategies recommended for adolescents by A. B. Bruner and Fishman (1998) include family intervention, remedial education, career counseling, and community outreach. Additionally, McClelland et al. (2004) suggested that treatment programs for youth must target the specific needs of adolescents: level of cognitive development, family situation, and educational needs. Treatment programs must target all substances of abuse, especially marijuana, and address comorbid mental disorders. Unfortunately, appropriate drug treatment resources and facilities for children and adolescents who are economically disadvantaged are scarce (Bruner & Fishman, 1998).

Relevance to Professional School Counselors

Professional school counselors have an important role to play in the prevention of substance use. A survey conducted by the National Center on Addiction and Substance Abuse (Califano & Booth, 1998) concluded that the turning-point year, marking the most dramatic increase in exposure and drug use, is 12 to 13. The survey also concluded that there is a large gap between students' and school principals' perception of the prevalence of drug use. Students say drugs are everywhere, whereas principals say the problem is virtually nonexistent. Another study concluded that parents are largely unaware of the extent to which their adolescents are involved in major risk behaviors such as use of alcohol, LSD (lysergic acid diethylamide), cocaine, and marijuana (Young & Zimmerman, 1998). These findings indicate a need for continued proactive substance-use educational programs at the elementary and middle school levels, as well as an aggressive parent education component in these programs. To serve as a resource to school personnel and parents in the detection and treatment of substance use, and to be a credible resource to students, professional school counselors will need to obtain accurate and up-to-date information about levels of substance use in their community, detection of substance use, and available community resources.

Lambie and Rokutani (2002) suggested that professional school counselors can be the first line of defense in detecting student troubles that may require specialized treatment not offered in the school setting. Some visible indicators of possible substance-related problems are deterioration of academic performance, increased absenteeism and truancy, fighting, verbal abuse, defiance, or withdrawal (Lambie & Rokutani, 2002). Professional school counselors have four functions in working with students with possible substance-abuse issues: (a) identify the possible warning signs of student substance abuse; (b) work with the youth to establish a therapeutic relationship; (c) support the family system to promote change; and (d) be a resource and liaison between the student, the family, the school, and community agencies and treatment programs (Lambie & Rokutani, 2002).

Psychotic Disorders

Psychotic disorders in children are rare (Seligman, 1998). Approximately 1 child in 10,000 is diagnosed with schizophrenia. These disorders have both internalizing (e.g., flat affect, social withdrawal) and externalizing (e.g., impulsivity, inattention) features (S. R. Smith, Reddy, & Wingenfeld, 2002). The symptoms of psychotic disorders in children are the same as for adults: hallucinations, delusions, loose associations, and illogical thinking. The most common symptoms of

schizophrenia in childhood are auditory hallucinations and delusions, along with illogical conversation and thought patterns (McClellan, McCurry, Speltz, & Jones, 2002). Schizophrenia in children and adolescents is difficult to diagnose because of the comorbidity with other disorders such as mood and cognitive (organic) mental disorders. Given the complexities of psychotic disorders, children and adolescents with these disorders are often difficult to identify, leading to possible delays in treatment (S. R. Smith, Reddy, et al., 2002). Psychotic disorders are commonly misdiagnosed in youths, due in part to clinicians not following the diagnostic criteria and to the relative rarity of these disorders in children (Kumra et al., 2001; McClellan et al., 2002).

Prognosis

Bellack and Mueser (1993) reported a fairly positive prognosis for young people diagnosed with psychotic disorders when they are treated with a combination of family therapy and medication. Seventeen percent of children who received both family therapy and medication relapsed, as compared to 83% of children receiving only medication. Biederman, Petty, Faraone, and Seidman (2004) found that, within one sample, psychotic symptoms lasted an average of 3 years and were present during an average of 27% of the children's and adolescents' lives.

Intervention Strategies

Asarnow, Tompson, and McGrath (2004) suggested two phases within the treatment process: (a) acute and (b) stabilization and maintenance. The acute phase emphasizes pharmacological treatment. The stabilization and maintenance phase emphasizes the continuation of medication management supplemented with psychosocial and community treatment strategies. These include family psychoeducational interventions, individual psychotherapy, social skills training, and cognitive remediation (Asarnow et al., 2004). Treatment for children and adolescents with psychotic disorders should include family therapy, medication, counseling, and special education (Seligman, 1998). Social skills training, including the teaching of appropriate behaviors, interpersonal interactions, playing with peers, and effective communication should be included as part of treatment. Working with the family will also be important to promote a positive attitude, make modifications to the home environment, and teach parents effective coping skills. A positive and encouraging home environment can reduce the likelihood that a psychotic disorder will recur.

Relevance to Professional School Counselors

Due to the small number of children diagnosed with psychotic disorders, it is unlikely that professional school counselors will encounter many children with these disorders. It is important for professional school counselors to remember that loose associations in speech and illogical thinking are not unusual before the age of 7 and probably are not indicative of the symptoms of psychosis. However, professional school counselors do need to be aware that the frequency of schizophrenia increases from age 11 to late adolescence, when it reaches adult prevalence rates (Volkmar, 1996). Professional school counselors may be involved in the implementation and delivery of special education services as part of an IEP for young people with psychotic disorders that may include social and emotional goals.

Obsessive-Compulsive Disorder

Approximately 1 in 200 children and adolescents meet the criteria for obsessive-compulsive disorder (OCD; March & Leonard, 1996). OCD is more common in children than in adults (Gothelf, Aharonovsky, Horesh, Carty, & Apter, 2004). The symptoms for children are the same as for adults; most children with OCD present with obsessions about germs, external threats, or disease and exhibit rituals of washing or checking. Other common compulsions include touching, counting, hoarding, and repeating. A high rate of comorbidity between OCD and tic disorders (Rapoport, Leonard, Swedo, & Lenane, 1993), anxiety disorders, and bipolar disorder (Masi et al., 2004) has been reported. The most frequent age of onset among young patients treated for OCD at NIMH

was 7 years; the average age at onset was 10.2 years (March & Leonard, 1996).

Intervention Strategies

Children with OCD respond to cognitive-behavioral interventions. The primary intervention strategy is exposure to obsessions, with accompanying prevention of compulsions, to promote systematic desensitization (March & Leonard, 1996). Medication also is often used as part of the treatment plan. The family should be included in treatment because the family may have developed maladaptive coping strategies for dealing with the distressed child (Rapoport et al., 1993).

Relevance to Professional School Counselors

Professional school counselors may be the first consulted by teachers and parents concerning the symptoms of OCD. Counselors can provide information about the disorder and may be instrumental in helping parents determine whether a referral is warranted. When a diagnosis of OCD is made, professional school counselors can help structure the school modifications and interventions.

Posttraumatic Stress Disorder

The criteria for posttraumatic stress disorder (PTSD) are the same for children as for adults, although the disorder may be manifested differently due to differences in cognitive and emotional functioning (Seligman, 1998). The essential feature of PTSD is symptom development following direct personal experience of a traumatic event, witnessing a traumatic event, or learning of such an experience with someone interpersonally close (Cook-Cottone, 2004). The DSM–IV–TR describes the following criteria for a diagnosis of PTSD: great fear and helplessness in response to the event; persistent reexperiencing of the event; loss of general responsiveness; and symptoms of arousal and anxiety, such as sleep disturbances, anger, or irritability. Children might have nightmares, present with a flat affect, or act withdrawn. It is often difficult for children to express their feelings about the traumatic experience except through play (Kronenberger & Meyer, 1996).

Traumatic stressors can be naturally occurring (e.g., a hurricane) or man-made (e.g., terrorism). Trauma can occur in intimate physical and emotional proximity; occur physically distant and strike emotionally close (e.g., *Challenger* tragedy, September 11); or occur physically close and emotionally distal (witnessing the fatal accident of a stranger). The stress can be acute, as in a rape, or chronic, such as through years of repeated sexual abuse (Cook-Cottone, 2004).

In the past, children were thought to be resilient to the impact of traumatic events. Much has been learned about PTSD in the last 10 years through research focused on children who have been victims of natural disasters, war, violent crime, community violence, and sexual abuse (Cooley-Quille, Boyd, Frantz, & Walsh, 2001; Green et al., 1994; Nader, Pynoos, Fairbanks, al-Ajeel, & al-Asfour, 1993; Thabet, Abed, & Vostanis, 2004; Wolfe, Sas, & Wekerle, 1994). Although adolescents exhibit symptoms of PTSD similar to those of adults, including depression, anxiety, and emotional disturbance, children's symptoms are more likely to be behavioral or physical (Cook-Cottone, 2004; Green et al., 1994). Children who have experienced sexual abuse often exhibit inappropriate sexual behaviors (Deblinger, McLeer, Atkins, Ralphe, & Foa, 1989). According to Cook-Cottone (2004), preschoolers' PTSD symptoms are expressed in nonverbal channels, which include acting out or internalized behaviors, nightmares and disturbed sleep patterns, developmental regression, and clinging behavior. In school-age children, symptoms continue to be expressed behaviorally and may include regressions, anxious attachment, school refusal, weak emotional regulation, and an increase in externalizing or internalizing behavioral expression (e.g., fighting with peers, withdrawal from friends, poor attention, decline in academic performance). Physiological complaints such as stomachaches and headaches are also common in children. Adolescents often present with a sense of foreshortened future, self-injurious behaviors, suicidal ideation, conduct problems, dissociation, depersonalization, and possibly substance abuse (Cook-Cottone, 2004).

Prognosis

Symptoms of trauma-related disorders often decrease without treatment within 3 months of the event (Seligman, 1998). With treatment, the prognosis usually is also very good for recovery from symptoms that have not spontaneously remitted, especially for people whose functioning was positive before exposure to trauma, whose onset of symptoms was rapid, whose symptoms have lasted less than 6 months, whose social supports are strong, and who have received early treatment (Kaplan et al., 1994). According to Ozer and Weinstein (2004), children who perceive that they have strong social support, are able to talk about the traumatic event and feelings associated with the event, and who have safe schools and cohesive family environments have a better chance at decreasing their PTSD symptoms more quickly. Kaplan et al. (1994) reported that overall, 30% of those with trauma-related disorders recover completely, 40% have mild symptoms, 20% have moderate symptoms, and 10% do not improve through treatment.

Intervention Strategies

Effective treatment for children and adolescents is similar to treatment for adults diagnosed with PTSD. Treatment should begin as soon as possible after the event (Seligman, 1998). Preventive treatment, even before symptoms emerge, is recommended. When treatment for PTSD is required, a multifaceted approach emphasizing cognitive-behavioral strategies seems to work best. The goal of treatment is to help the person process the trauma, express feelings, increase coping and control over memories, reduce cognitive distortions and self-blame, and restore self-concept and previous levels of functioning. Group therapy involving people who have had similar traumatic experiences can be especially helpful in reducing feelings of isolation and feeling different. However, the group leader should ensure that the sharing of memories does not have a retraumatizing effect. Additionally, therapeutic interventions should be based within the school setting only when (a) comprehensive assessment has been completed; (b) it is determined that school-based support is the appropriate, least restrictive level of intervention; (c) parents have been informed of all treatment options; (d) the child is experiencing adequate adjustment and academic success with intervention; and (e) consultation, supervision, and referral are readily utilized by the professional school counselor (Cook-Cottone, 2004).

Relevance to Professional School Counselors

Professional school counselors will be called on to provide support to students, staff, and parents in the event of a trauma that affects individuals and school communities. When a student, teacher, or parent dies; when there is a natural disaster in the community; or when a violent crime has been committed, professional school counselors will be called on to provide group and individual interventions that offer accurate information, give people a place to ask questions and talk about the trauma, and screen for symptoms of PTSD. Professional school counselors will need to be aware of the differences between unhealthy and healthy responses to traumatic events, and be able to provide resources to students and families when a therapeutic intervention is deemed necessary or is requested. Professional school counselors should encourage and lead school administrators to develop crisis intervention plans to deal with traumatic events affecting school communities. The professional school counselor should have a solid working knowledge of etiological and diagnostic implications of PTSD, the therapeutic options, and, when needed, ways to facilitate school reintegration of a child who has suffered a traumatic event (Cook-Cottone, 2004).

Generalized Anxiety Disorder

The diagnosis, formerly known as overanxious disorder of childhood, is now included in the diagnosis of generalized anxiety disorder (GAD) because the symptoms of pervasive anxiety are the same, regardless of the person's age. GAD is characterized by feelings of worry or anxiety about many aspects of the person's life and is reflected in related physical symptoms such as

shortness of breath and muscle tension that are difficult to control (Wicks-Nelson & Israel, 2003). To meet the diagnostic criteria, symptoms of this disorder must persist for a minimum of 6 months (APA, 2000) and must have a significant impact on the person's functioning. Comorbidity of GAD with other disorders is common. SAD is present in 70% of children who had been diagnosed with GAD, while 35% met the criteria for both GAD and ADHD (Last, Strauss, & Francis, 1987). A child with GAD usually experiences anticipatory anxiety that is generalized to include situations requiring appraisal or performance but is not associated with a specific stimulus. GAD is the most common anxiety disorder in adolescents (Clark, Smith, Neighbors, Skerlec, & Randall, 1994).

Prognosis

People who receive cognitive-behavioral therapy for GAD frequently show significant and consistent improvement, although few will be free of all symptoms. Roth and Fonagy (1996) found that 60% maintained their improvement at a 6-month follow-up.

Intervention Strategies

As with other anxiety disorders, cognitive-behavioral strategies are the most effective treatments (Ollendick & King, 1998). The goal of treatment is to lessen the extent of the anxiety and the overarousal that accompanies it (T. A. Brown, O'Leary, & Barlow, 1993) by teaching children to cope with anxiety using a variety of strategies such as identification and modification of anxious self-talk, modeling, education about emotions, relaxation techniques, and homework (Kendall, Chu, Pimentel, & Choudhury, 2000).

Relevance to Professional School Counselors

Professional school counselors will undoubtedly encounter students exhibiting symptoms of GAD. Professional school counselors may be able to suggest stress-management strategies to students and can help parents understand this disorder. Professional school counselors can offer guidance units and small-group counseling sessions to students coping with anxiety as well as workshops to help their parents. Working in collaboration with mental health professionals, these psychoeducational strategies may afford considerable ongoing help to students coping with GAD.

Adjustment Disorders

Adjustment disorders are fairly common in adults as well as in young people (Rapoport & Ismond, 1996). Adjustment disorders are characterized by a relatively mild maladaptive response to a stressor that occurs within 3 months of that event. Stressors may include experiences such as changing schools, parental separation, or illness in the family. The maladaptive response may include anxiety or depression as well as behavioral changes. This diagnosis can be maintained only for 6 months beyond the termination of the stressor or its consequences. If symptoms remain after that time, the diagnosis must be changed.

Prognosis

The short-term and long-term prognosis for an adjustment disorder is quite good if the disorder stands alone. When other disorders are also diagnosed, the prognosis is less optimistic.

Intervention Strategies

Most adjustment disorders improve spontaneously without treatment when the stressor is removed or attenuated. However, counseling can facilitate recovery (Seligman, 1998). Treatment should focus on teaching coping skills and adaptive strategies to help people avert future crises and minimize poor choices and self-destructive behaviors (Maxman & Ward, 1995). A crisis-intervention model is most effective. This model focuses on relieving the acute symptoms first and then promoting adaptation and coping. A typical crisis-intervention model includes the following steps: understand the problem, view the problem in context, contract with the client for change, apply interventions, reinforce gains, and terminate treatment (Wells & Giannetti, 1990).

Relevance to Professional School Counselors

Professional school counselors are in an excellent position to provide students with the supportive strategies required to cope with the symptoms of an adjustment disorder. Professional school counselors regularly are asked to provide crisis intervention to students dealing with the death of a loved one, a divorce, or some other family crisis. Professional school counselors can also help parents understand the effect the stressor is having on their children.

SUMMARY/CONCLUSION

Clearly, professional school counselors need to increase their knowledge of the symptoms, diagnosis, and treatment of mental disorders to meet the needs of their students. Requirements of special education legislation and Section 504 regulations, an increased number of students with mental health concerns, and the reform movement calling for full-service schools demand that professional school counselors expand their repertoire of diagnostic skills and knowledge and work collaboratively with other educational and mental health professionals in schools and the community (ASCA, 2003a; Bemak, 2000; Green et al., 1995; Lockhart & Keys, 1998). Additional training in special education procedures, including Section 504 regulations, diagnostic assessment, multiculturalism, and the *ASCA National Model* will enhance professional school counselors' clinical knowledge and skills (ASCA, 2003a; Dana, 2001; Green et al., 1994; Wicks-Nelson & Israel, 2003). Currently, to qualify for endorsement by the CACREP, counselor education programs must include coursework that covers issues related to the development and functioning of children and adolescents, such as eating disorders, abuse, and attention-deficit disorders (CACREP, 2001).

The role of the professional school counselor is changing. Counselor education programs as well as school districts need to continue to be responsive to the changing nature of school counseling programs and the clinical challenges professional school counselors face. For professional school counselors to expand their role to include greater application of clinical knowledge and skills and increased collaboration with community and other mental health treatment programs, school districts may need to reconceptualize the role of the professional school counselor (Bemak, 2000; Maag & Katsiyannis, 1996). Recognition of the importance of the clinical aspect of the professional school counselor's role may necessitate realignment of duties, affording counselors the opportunity to use their clinical skills to more effectively help their students and families. In addition, professional school counselors must continue their role in making appropriate referrals to medical and mental health practitioners and working with teachers, parents, and students to help students achieve and develop in spite of clinical issues.

FURTHER READINGS

House, A. E. (1999). *DSM-IV diagnosis in the schools.* New York: Guilford.

Jones, W. P. (1997). *Deciphering the diagnostic codes: A guide for school counselors.* Thousand Oaks, CA: Corwin.

Morrison, J., & Anders, J. F. (2000). *Interviewing children and adolescents: Skills and strategies for effective DSM–IV diagnosis.* New York: Guilford.

Rapoport, J. J., & Ismond, D. R. (1996). *DSM–IV training guide for diagnosis of childhood disorders.* Levittown, PA: Brunner/Mazel.

Seligman, L. (1998). *Selecting effective treatments* (Rev. ed.): *A comprehensive, systematic guide to treating mental disorders.* San Francisco: Jossey-Bass.

Wicks-Nelson, R., & Israel, A. C. (2003). *Behavior disorders of childhood.* Upper Saddle River, NJ: Prentice Hall.

ACTIVITIES

1. Choose one of the mental or emotional disorders found in the *DSM–IV–TR* and find several current research articles that describe the school's role in helping students who have this disorder.

2. Interview a school psychologist or special educator in a local school. Find out the percentage of students in the school that have been diagnosed with mental or emotional disorders. Also inquire about how these students are handled within the system (i.e., inclusion, separate classes all day).

3. Home drug-testing kits are often easy to locate. Examine a home drug-testing kit and determine if it would be a simple procedure to use by parents who suspect their child of using drugs.

ACA CODE OF ETHICS

As approved by the ACA Governing Council 2005

AMERICAN COUNSELING ASSOCIATION
www.counseling.org

MISSION

The mission of the American Counseling Association is to enhance the quality of life in society by promoting the development of professional counselors, advancing the counseling profession, and using the profession and practice of counseling to promote respect for human dignity and diversity.

ACA CODE OF ETHICS PREAMBLE

The American Counseling Association is an educational, scientific, and professional organization whose members work in a variety of settings and serve in multiple capacities. ACA members are dedicated to the enhancement of human development throughout the life span. Association members recognize diversity and embrace a cross-cultural approach in support of the worth, dignity, potential, and uniqueness of people within their social and cultural contexts.

Professional values are an important way of living out an ethical commitment. Values inform principles. Inherently held values that guide our behaviors or exceed prescribed behaviors are deeply ingrained in the counselor and developed out of personal dedication, rather than the mandatory requirement of an external organization.

ACA CODE OF ETHICS PURPOSE

The *ACA Code of Ethics* serves five main purposes:

1. The *Code* enables the association to clarify to current and future members, and to those served by members, the nature of the ethical responsibilities held in common by its members.
2. The *Code* helps support the mission of the association.
3. The *Code* establishes principles that define ethical behavior and best practices of association members.

---

4. The *Code* serves as an ethical guide designed to assist members in constructing a professional course of action that best serves those utilizing counseling services and best promotes the values of the counseling profession.
5. The *Code* serves as the basis for processing of ethical complaints and inquiries initiated against members of the association.

The *ACA Code of Ethics* contains eight main sections that address the following areas:

Section A: The Counseling Relationship
Section B: Confidentiality, Privileged Communication, and Privacy
Section C: Professional Responsibility
Section D: Relationships With Other Professionals
Section E: Evaluation, Assessment, and Interpretation
Section F: Supervision, Training, and Teaching
Section G: Research and Publication
Section H: Resolving Ethical Issues

Each section of the *ACA Code of Ethics* begins with an Introduction. The introductions to each section discuss what counselors should aspire to with regard to ethical behavior and responsibility. The Introduction helps set the tone for that particular section and provides a starting point that invites reflection on the ethical mandates contained in each part of the *ACA Code of Ethics*.

When counselors are faced with ethical dilemmas that are difficult to resolve, they are expected to engage in a carefully considered ethical decision-making process. Reasonable differences of opinion can and do exist among counselors with respect to the ways in which values, ethical principles, and ethical standards would be applied when they conflict. While there is no specific ethical decision-making model that is most effective, counselors are expected to be familiar with a credible model of decision making that can bear public scrutiny and its application.

Through a chosen ethical decision-making process and evaluation of the context of the situation, counselors are empowered to make decisions that help expand the capacity of people to grow and develop.

A brief glossary is given to provide readers with a concise description of some of the terms used in the *ACA Code of Ethics*.

SECTION A THE COUNSELING RELATIONSHIP

Introduction

Counselors encourage client growth and development in ways that foster the interest and welfare of clients and promote formation of healthy relationships. Counselors actively attempt to understand the diverse cultural backgrounds of the clients they serve. Counselors also explore their own cultural identities and how these affect their values and beliefs about the counseling process.

Counselors are encouraged to contribute to society by devoting a portion of their professional activity to services for which there is little or no financial return (pro bono publico).

A.1. Welfare of Those Served by Counselors

A.1.a. Primary Responsibility

The primary responsibility of counselors is to respect the dignity and to promote the welfare of clients.

A.1.b. Records

Counselors maintain records necessary for rendering professional services to their clients and as required by laws, regulations, or agency or institution procedures. Counselors include sufficient and timely documentation in their client records to facilitate the delivery and continuity of needed services. Counselors take reasonable steps to ensure that documentation in records accurately reflects client progress and services provided. If errors are made in client records, counselors take steps to properly note the correction of such errors according to agency or institutional policies. (*See A.12.g.7., B.6., B.6.g., G.2.j.*)

A.1.c. Counseling Plans

Counselors and their clients work jointly in devising integrated counseling plans that offer reasonable promise of success and are consistent with abilities and circumstances of clients. Counselors and clients regularly review counseling plans to assess their continued viability and effectiveness, respecting the freedom of choice of clients. (*See A.2.a., A.2.d., A.12.g.*)

A.1.d. Support Network Involvement

Counselors recognize that support networks hold various meanings in the lives of clients and consider enlisting the support, understanding, and involvement of others (e.g., religious/ spiritual/community leaders, family members, friends) as positive resources, when appropriate, with client consent.

A.1.e. Employment Needs

Counselors work with their clients considering employment in jobs that are consistent with the overall abilities, vocational limitations, physical restrictions, general temperament, interest and aptitude patterns, social skills, education, general qualifications, and other relevant characteristics and needs of clients. When appropriate, counselors appropriately trained in career development will assist in the placement of clients in positions that are consistent with the interest, culture, and the welfare of clients, employers, and/or the public.

A.2. Informed Consent in the Counseling Relationship
(*See A.12.g., B.5., B.6.b., E.3., E.13.b., F.1.c., G.2.a.*)

A.2.a. Informed Consent

Clients have the freedom to choose whether to enter into or remain in a counseling relationship and need adequate information about the counseling process and the counselor. Counselors have an obligation to review in writing and verbally with clients the rights and responsibilities of both the counselor and the client. Informed consent is an ongoing part of the counseling process, and counselors appropriately document discussions of informed consent throughout the counseling relationship.

A.2.b. Types of Information Needed

Counselors explicitly explain to clients the nature of all services provided. They inform clients about issues such as, but not limited to, the following: the purposes, goals, techniques, procedures, limitations, potential risks, and benefits of services; the counselor's qualifications, credentials, and relevant experience; continuation of services upon the incapacitation or death of a counselor; and other pertinent information. Counselors take steps to ensure that clients understand the implications of diagnosis, the intended use of tests and reports, fees, and billing arrangements. Clients have the right to confidentiality and to be provided with an explanation of its limitations (including how supervisors and/or treatment team professionals are involved); to obtain clear information about their records; to participate in the ongoing counseling plans; and to refuse any services or modality change and to be advised of the consequences of such refusal.

A.2.c. Developmental and Cultural Sensitivity

Counselors communicate information in ways that are both developmentally and culturally appropriate. Counselors use clear and understandable language when discussing issues related to informed consent. When clients have difficulty understanding the language used by counselors, they provide necessary services (e.g., arranging for a qualified interpreter or translator) to ensure comprehension by clients. In collaboration with clients, counselors consider cultural implications of informed consent procedures and, where possible, counselors adjust their practices accordingly.

A.2.d. Inability to Give Consent

When counseling minors or persons unable to give voluntary consent, counselors seek the assent of clients to services, and include them in decision making as appropriate. Counselors recognize the need to balance the ethical rights of clients to make choices, their capacity to give consent or assent to receive services, and parental or familial legal rights and responsibilities to protect these clients and make decisions on their behalf.

A.3. Clients Served by Others

When counselors learn that their clients are in a professional relationship with another mental health professional, they request release from clients to inform the other professionals and strive to establish positive and collaborative professional relationships.

A.4. Avoiding Harm and Imposing Values

A.4.a. Avoiding Harm

Counselors act to avoid harming their clients, trainees, and research participants and to minimize or to remedy unavoidable or unanticipated harm.

A.4.b. Personal Values

Counselors are aware of their own values, attitudes, beliefs, and behaviors and avoid imposing values that are inconsistent with counseling goals. Counselors respect the diversity of clients, trainees, and research participants.

A.5. Roles and Relationships With Clients
(See F.3., F.10., G.3.)

A.5.a. Current Clients

Sexual or romantic counselor–client interactions or relationships with current clients, their romantic partners, or their family members are prohibited.

A.5.b. Former Clients

Sexual or romantic counselor–client interactions or relationships with former clients, their romantic partners, or their family members are prohibited for a period of 5 years following the last professional contact. Counselors, before engaging in sexual or romantic interactions or relationships with clients, their romantic partners, or client family members after 5 years following the last professional contact, demonstrate forethought and document (in written form) whether the interactions or relationship can be viewed as exploitive in some way and/or whether there is still potential to harm the former client; in cases of potential exploitation and/or harm, the counselor avoids entering such an interaction or relationship.

A.5.c. Nonprofessional Interactions or Relationships (Other Than Sexual or Romantic Interactions or Relationships)

Counselor–client nonprofessional relationships with clients, former clients, their romantic partners, or their family members should be avoided, except when the interaction is potentially beneficial to the client. (See A.5.d.)

A.5.d. Potentially Beneficial Interactions

When a counselor–client nonprofessional interaction with a client or former client may be potentially beneficial to the client or former client, the counselor must document in case records, prior to the interaction (when feasible), the rationale for such an interaction, the potential benefit, and anticipated consequences for the client or former client and other individuals significantly involved with the client or former client. Such interactions should be initiated with appropriate client consent. Where unintentional harm occurs to the client or former client, or to an individual significantly involved with the client or former client, due to the nonprofessional interaction, the counselor must show evidence of an attempt to remedy such harm. Examples of potentially beneficial interactions include, but are not limited to, attending a formal ceremony (e.g., a wedding/commitment ceremony or graduation); purchasing a service or product provided by a client or former client (excepting unrestricted bartering); hospital visits to an ill family member; mutual membership in a professional association, organization, or community. (See A.5.c.)

A.5.e. Role Changes in the Professional Relationship

When a counselor changes a role from the original or most recent contracted relationship, he or she obtains informed consent from the client and explains the right of the client to refuse services related to the change. Examples of role changes include

1. changing from individual to relationship or family counseling, or vice versa;
2. changing from a nonforensic evaluative role to a therapeutic role, or vice versa;

3. changing from a counselor to a researcher role (i.e., enlisting clients as research participants), or vice versa; and

4. changing from a counselor to a mediator role, or vice versa.

Clients must be fully informed of any anticipated consequences (e.g., financial, legal, personal, or therapeutic) of counselor role changes.

A.6. Roles and Relationships at Individual, Group, Institutional, and Societal Levels

A.6.a. Advocacy

When appropriate, counselors advocate at individual, group, institutional, and societal levels to examine potential barriers and obstacles that inhibit access and/or the growth and development of clients.

A.6.b. Confidentiality and Advocacy

Counselors obtain client consent prior to engaging in advocacy efforts on behalf of an identifiable client to improve the provision of services and to work toward removal of systemic barriers or obstacles that inhibit client access, growth, and development.

A.7. Multiple Clients

When a counselor agrees to provide counseling services to two or more persons who have a relationship, the counselor clarifies at the outset which person or persons are clients and the nature of the relationships the counselor will have with each involved person. If it becomes apparent that the counselor may be called upon to perform potentially conflicting roles, the counselor will clarify, adjust, or withdraw from roles appropriately. (*See A.8.a., B.4.*)

A.8. Group Work
(*See B.4.a.*)

A.8.a. Screening

Counselors screen prospective group counseling/therapy participants. To the extent possible, counselors select members whose needs and goals are compatible with goals of the group, who will not impede the group process, and whose well-being will not be jeopardized by the group experience.

A.8.b. Protecting Clients

In a group setting, counselors take reasonable precautions to protect clients from physical, emotional, or psychological trauma.

A.9. End-of-Life Care for Terminally Ill Clients

A.9.a. Quality of Care

Counselors strive to take measures that enable clients

1. to obtain high quality end-of-life care for their physical, emotional, social, and spiritual needs;
2. to exercise the highest degree of self-determination possible;
3. to be given every opportunity possible to engage in informed decision making regarding their end-of-life care; and
4. to receive complete and adequate assessment regarding their ability to make competent, rational decisions on their own behalf from a mental health professional who is experienced in end-of-life care practice.

A.9.b. Counselor Competence, Choice, and Referral

Recognizing the personal, moral, and competence issues related to end-of-life decisions, counselors may choose to work or not work with terminally ill clients who wish to explore their end-of-life options. Counselors provide appropriate referral information to ensure that clients receive the necessary help.

A.9.c. Confidentiality

Counselors who provide services to terminally ill individuals who are considering hastening their own deaths have the option of breaking or not breaking confidentiality, depending on applicable laws and the specific circumstances of the situation and after seeking consultation or supervision from appropriate professional and legal parties. (*See B.5.c., B.7.c.*)

A.10. Fees and Bartering

A.10.a. Accepting Fees From Agency Clients

Counselors refuse a private fee or other remuneration for rendering services to persons who are entitled to such services through the counselor's employing agency or institution. The policies of a particular agency may make explicit provisions for agency clients to receive counseling services from members of its staff in private practice. In such instances, the clients must be informed of other options open to them should they seek private counseling services.

A.10.b. Establishing Fees

In establishing fees for professional counseling services, counselors consider the financial status of clients and locality. In the event that the established fee structure is inappropriate for a client, counselors assist clients in attempting to find comparable services of acceptable cost.

A.10.c. Nonpayment of Fees

If counselors intend to use collection agencies or take legal measures to collect fees from clients who do not pay for services as agreed upon, they first inform clients of intended actions and offer clients the opportunity to make payment.

A.10.d. Bartering

Counselors may barter only if the relationship is not exploitive or harmful and does not place the counselor in an unfair advantage, if the client requests it, and if such arrangements are an accepted practice among professionals in the community. Counselors consider the cultural implications of bartering and discuss relevant concerns with clients and document such agreements in a clear written contract.

A.10.e. Receiving Gifts

Counselors understand the challenges of accepting gifts from clients and recognize that in some cultures, small gifts are a token of respect and showing gratitude. When determining whether or not to accept a gift from clients, counselors take into account the therapeutic relationship, the monetary value of the gift, a client's motivation for giving the gift, and the counselor's motivation for wanting or declining the gift.

A.11. Termination and Referral

A.11.a. Abandonment Prohibited

Counselors do not abandon or neglect clients in counseling. Counselors assist in making appropriate arrangements for the continuation of treatment, when necessary, during interruptions such as vacations, illness, and following termination.

A.11.b. Inability to Assist Clients

If counselors determine an inability to be of professional assistance to clients, they avoid entering or continuing counseling relationships. Counselors are knowledgeable about culturally and clinically appropriate referral resources and suggest these alternatives. If clients decline the suggested referrals, counselors should discontinue the relationship.

A.11.c. Appropriate Termination

Counselors terminate a counseling relationship when it becomes reasonably apparent that the client no longer needs assistance, is not likely to benefit, or is being harmed by continued counseling. Counselors may terminate counseling when in jeopardy of harm by the client, or another person with whom the client has a relationship, or when clients do not pay fees as agreed upon. Counselors provide pretermination counseling and recommend other service providers when necessary.

A.11.d. Appropriate Transfer of Services

When counselors transfer or refer clients to other practitioners, they ensure that appropriate clinical and administrative processes are completed and open communication is maintained with both clients and practitioners.

A.12. Technology Applications

A.12.a. Benefits and Limitations

Counselors inform clients of the benefits and limitations of using information technology applications in the counseling process and in business/billing procedures. Such technologies include but are not limited to computer hardware and software, telephones, the World Wide Web, the Internet, online assessment instruments and other communication devices.

A.12.b. Technology-Assisted Services

When providing technology-assisted distance counseling services, counselors determine that clients are intellectually, emotionally, and physically capable of using the application and that the application is appropriate for the needs of clients.

A.12.c. Inappropriate Services

When technology-assisted distance counseling services are deemed inappropriate by the counselor or client, counselors consider delivering services face to face.

A.12.d. Access

Counselors provide reasonable access to computer applications when providing technology-assisted distance counseling services.

A.12.e. Laws and Statutes

Counselors ensure that the use of technology does not violate the laws of any local, state, national, or international entity and observe all relevant statutes.

A.12.f. Assistance

Counselors seek business, legal, and technical assistance when using technology applications, particularly when the use of such applications crosses state or national boundaries.

A.12.g. Technology and Informed Consent

As part of the process of establishing informed consent, counselors do the following:

1. Address issues related to the difficulty of maintaining the confidentiality of electronically transmitted communications.
2. Inform clients of all colleagues, supervisors, and employees, such as Informational Technology (IT) administrators, who might have authorized or unauthorized access to electronic transmissions.
3. Urge clients to be aware of all authorized or unauthorized users including family members and fellow employees who have access to any technology clients may use in the counseling process.
4. Inform clients of pertinent legal rights and limitations governing the practice of a profession over state lines or international boundaries.
5. Use encrypted Web sites and e-mail communications to help ensure confidentiality when possible.
6. When the use of encryption is not possible, counselors notify clients of this fact and limit electronic transmissions to general communications that are not client specific.
7. Inform clients if and for how long archival storage of transaction records are maintained.
8. Discuss the possibility of technology failure and alternate methods of service delivery.
9. Inform clients of emergency procedures, such as calling 911 or a local crisis hotline, when the counselor is not available.
10. Discuss time zone differences, local customs, and cultural or language differences that might impact service delivery.
11. Inform clients when technology-assisted distance counseling services are not covered by insurance. (See A.2.)

A.12.h. Sites on the World Wide Web

Counselors maintaining sites on the World Wide Web (the Internet) do the following:

1. Regularly check that electronic links are working and professionally appropriate.
2. Establish ways clients can contact the counselor in case of technology failure.
3. Provide electronic links to relevant state licensure and professional certification boards to protect consumer rights and facilitate addressing ethical concerns.
4. Establish a method for verifying client identity.
5. Obtain the written consent of the legal guardian or other authorized legal representative prior to rendering services in the event the client is a minor child, an adult who is

legally incompetent, or an adult incapable of giving informed consent.

6. Strive to provide a site that is accessible to persons with disabilities.

7. Strive to provide translation capabilities for clients who have a different primary language while also addressing the imperfect nature of such translations.

8. Assist clients in determining the validity and reliability of information found on the World Wide Web and other technology applications.

SECTION B CONFIDENTIALITY, PRIVILEGED COMMUNICATION, AND PRIVACY

Introduction

Counselors recognize that trust is a cornerstone of the counseling relationship. Counselors aspire to earn the trust of clients by creating an ongoing partnership, establishing and upholding appropriate boundaries, and maintaining confidentiality. Counselors communicate the parameters of confidentiality in a culturally competent manner.

B.1. Respecting Client Rights

B.1.a. Multicultural/Diversity Considerations

Counselors maintain awareness and sensitivity regarding cultural meanings of confidentiality and privacy. Counselors respect differing views toward disclosure of information. Counselors hold ongoing discussions with clients as to how, when, and with whom information is to be shared.

B.1.b. Respect for Privacy

Counselors respect client rights to privacy. Counselors solicit private information from clients only when it is beneficial to the counseling process.

B.1.c. Respect for Confidentiality

Counselors do not share confidential information without client consent or without sound legal or ethical justification.

B.1.d. Explanation of Limitations

At initiation and throughout the counseling process, counselors inform clients of the limitations of confidentiality and seek to identify foreseeable situations in which confidentiality must be breached. (See A.2.b.)

B.2. Exceptions

B.2.a. Danger and Legal Requirements

The general requirement that counselors keep information confidential does not apply when disclosure is required to protect clients or identified others from serious and foreseeable harm or when legal requirements demand that confidential information must be revealed. Counselors consult with other professionals when in doubt as to the validity of an exception. Additional considerations apply when addressing end-of-life issues. (See A.9.c.)

B.2.b. Contagious, Life-Threatening Diseases

When clients disclose that they have a disease commonly known to be both communicable and life threatening, counselors may be justified in disclosing information to identifiable third parties, if they are known to be at demonstrable and high risk of contracting the disease. Prior to making a disclosure, counselors confirm that there is such a diagnosis and assess the intent of clients to inform the third parties about their disease or to engage in any behaviors that may be harmful to an identifiable third party.

B.2.c. Court-Ordered Disclosure

When subpoenaed to release confidential or privileged information without a client's permission, counselors obtain written, informed consent from the client or take steps to prohibit the disclosure or have it limited as narrowly as possible due to potential harm to the client or counseling relationship.

B.2.d. Minimal Disclosure

To the extent possible, clients are informed before confidential information is disclosed and are involved in the disclosure decision-making process. When circumstances require the disclosure of confidential information, only essential information is revealed.

B.3. Information Shared With Others

B.3.a. Subordinates

Counselors make every effort to ensure that privacy and confidentiality of clients are maintained by subordinates, including employees, supervisees, students, clerical assistants, and volunteers. (See F.1.c.)

B.3.b. Treatment Teams

When client treatment involves a continued review or participation by a treatment team, the client will be informed of the team's existence and composition, information being shared, and the purposes of sharing such information.

B.3.c. Confidential Settings

Counselors discuss confidential information only in settings in which they can reasonably ensure client privacy.

B.3.d. Third-Party Payers

Counselors disclose information to third-party payers only when clients have authorized such disclosure.

B.3.e. Transmitting Confidential Information

Counselors take precautions to ensure the confidentiality of information transmitted through the use of computers, electronic mail, facsimile machines, telephones, voicemail, answering machines, and other electronic or computer technology. (See A.12.g.)

B.3.f. Deceased Clients

Counselors protect the confidentiality of deceased clients, consistent with legal requirements and agency or setting policies.

B.4. Groups and Families

B.4.a. Group Work

In group work, counselors clearly explain the importance and parameters of confidentiality for the specific group being entered.

B.4.b. Couples and Family Counseling

In couples and family counseling, counselors clearly define who is considered "the client" and discuss expectations and limitations of confidentiality. Counselors seek agreement and document in writing such agreement among all involved parties having capacity to give consent concerning each individual's right to confidentiality and any obligation to preserve the confidentiality of information known.

B.5. Clients Lacking Capacity to Give Informed Consent

B.5.a. Responsibility to Clients

When counseling minor clients or adult clients who lack the capacity to give voluntary, informed consent, counselors protect the confidentiality of information received in the counseling relationship as specified by federal and state laws, written policies, and applicable ethical standards.

B.5.b. Responsibility to Parents and Legal Guardians

Counselors inform parents and legal guardians about the role of counselors and the confidential nature of the counseling relationship. Counselors are sensitive to the cultural diversity of families and respect the inherent rights and responsibilities of parents/guardians over the welfare of their children/charges according to law. Counselors work to establish, as appropriate, collaborative relationships with parents/guardians to best serve clients.

B.5.c. Release of Confidential Information

When counseling minor clients or adult clients who lack the capacity to give voluntary consent to release confidential information, counselors seek permission from an appropriate third party to disclose information. In such instances, counselors inform clients consistent with their level of understanding and take culturally appropriate measures to safeguard client confidentiality.

B.6. Records

B.6.a. Confidentiality of Records

Counselors ensure that records are kept in a secure location and that only authorized persons have access to records.

B.6.b. Permission to Record

Counselors obtain permission from clients prior to recording sessions through electronic or other means.

B.6.c. Permission to Observe

Counselors obtain permission from clients prior to observing counseling sessions, reviewing session transcripts, or viewing recordings of sessions with supervisors, faculty, peers, or others within the training environment.

B.6.d. Client Access

Counselors provide reasonable access to records and copies of records when requested by competent clients. Counselors limit the access of clients to their records, or portions of their records, only when there is compelling evidence that such access would cause harm to the client. Counselors document the request of clients and the rationale for withholding some or all of the record in the files of clients. In situations involving multiple clients, counselors provide individual clients with only those parts of records that related directly to them and do not include confidential information related to any other client.

B.6.e. Assistance With Records

When clients request access to their records, counselors provide assistance and consultation in interpreting counseling records.

B.6.f. Disclosure or Transfer

Unless exceptions to confidentiality exist, counselors obtain written permission from clients to disclose or transfer records to legitimate third parties. Steps are taken to ensure that receivers of counseling records are sensitive to their confidential nature. (See A.3., E.4.)

B.6.g. Storage and Disposal After Termination

Counselors store records following termination of services to ensure reasonable future access, maintain records in accordance with state and federal statutes governing records, and dispose of client records and other sensitive materials in a manner that protects client confidentiality. When records are of an artistic nature, counselors obtain client (or guardian) consent with regards to handling of such records or documents. (See A.1.b.)

B.6.h. Reasonable Precautions

Counselors take reasonable precautions to protect client confidentiality in the event of the counselor's termination of practice, incapacity, or death. (See C.2.h.)

B.7. Research and Training

B.7.a. Institutional Approval

When institutional approval is required, counselors provide accurate information about their research proposals and obtain approval prior to conducting their research. They conduct research in accordance with the approved research protocol.

B.7.b. Adherence to Guidelines

Counselors are responsible for understanding and adhering to state, federal, agency, or institutional policies or applicable guidelines regarding confidentiality in their research practices.

B.7.c. Confidentiality of Information Obtained in Research

Violations of participant privacy and confidentiality are risks of participation in research involving human participants. Investigators maintain all research records in a secure manner. They explain to participants the risks of violations of privacy and confidentiality and disclose to participants any limits of confidentiality that reasonably can be expected. Regardless of the degree to which confidentiality will be maintained, investigators must disclose to participants any limits of confidentiality that reasonably can be expected. (*See G.2.e.*)

B.7.d. Disclosure of Research Information

Counselors do not disclose confidential information that reasonably could lead to the identification of a research participant unless they have obtained the prior consent of the person. Use of data derived from counseling relationships for purposes of training, research, or publication is confined to content that is disguised to ensure the anonymity of the individuals involved. (*See G.2.a., G.2.d.*)

B.7.e. Agreement for Identification

Identification of clients, students, or supervisees in a presentation or publication is permissible only when they have reviewed the material and agreed to its presentation or publication. (*See G.4.d.*)

B.8. Consultation

B.8.a. Agreements

When acting as consultants, counselors seek agreements among all parties involved concerning each individual's rights to confidentiality, the obligation of each individual to preserve confidential information, and the limits of confidentiality of information shared by others.

B.8.b. Respect for Privacy

Information obtained in a consulting relationship is discussed for professional purposes only with persons directly involved with the case. Written and oral reports present only data germane to the purposes of the consultation, and every effort is made to protect client identity and to avoid undue invasion of privacy.

B.8.c. Disclosure of Confidential Information

When consulting with colleagues, counselors do not disclose confidential information that reasonably could lead to the identification of a client or other person or organization with whom they have a confidential relationship unless they have obtained the prior consent of the person or organization or the disclosure cannot be avoided. They disclose information only to the extent necessary to achieve the purposes of the consultation. (*See D.2.d.*)

SECTION C   PROFESSIONAL RESPONSIBILITY

Introduction

Counselors aspire to open, honest, and accurate communication in dealing with the public and other professionals. They practice in a non-discriminatory manner within the boundaries of professional and personal competence and have a responsibility to abide by the *ACA Code of Ethics*. Counselors actively participate in local, state, and national associations that foster the development and improvement of counseling. Counselors advocate to promote change at the individual, group, institutional, and societal levels that improve the quality of life for individuals and groups and remove potential barriers to the provision or access of appropriate services being offered. Counselors have a responsibility to the public to engage in counseling practices that are based on rigorous research methodologies. In addition, counselors engage in self-care activities to maintain and promote their emotional, physical, mental, and spiritual well-being to best meet their professional responsibilities.

C.1. Knowledge of Standards

Counselors have a responsibility to read, understand, and follow the *ACA Code of Ethics* and adhere to applicable laws and regulations.

C.2. Professional Competence

C.2.a. Boundaries of Competence

Counselors practice only within the boundaries of their competence, based on their education, training, supervised experience, state and national professional credentials, and appropriate professional experience. Counselors gain knowledge, personal awareness, sensitivity, and skills pertinent to working with a diverse client population. (*See A.9.b., C.4.e., E.2., F.2., F.11.b.*)

C.2.b. New Specialty Areas of Practice

Counselors practice in specialty areas new to them only after appropriate education, training, and supervised experience. While developing skills in new specialty areas, counselors take steps to ensure the competence of their work and to protect others from possible harm. (*See F.6.f.*)

C.2.c. Qualified for Employment

Counselors accept employment only for positions for which they are qualified by education, training, supervised experience, state and national professional credentials, and appropriate professional experience. Counselors hire for professional counseling positions only individuals who are qualified and competent for those positions.

C.2.d. Monitor Effectiveness

Counselors continually monitor their effectiveness as professionals and take steps to improve when necessary. Counselors in private practice take reasonable steps to seek peer supervision as needed to evaluate their efficacy as counselors.

C.2.e. Consultation on Ethical Obligations

Counselors take reasonable steps to consult with other counselors or related professionals when they have questions regarding their ethical obligations or professional practice.

C.2.f. Continuing Education

Counselors recognize the need for continuing education to acquire and maintain a reasonable level of awareness of current scientific and professional information in their fields of activity. They take steps to maintain competence in the skills they use, are open to new procedures, and keep current with the diverse populations and specific populations with whom they work.

C.2.g. Impairment

Counselors are alert to the signs of impairment from their own physical, mental, or emotional problems and refrain from offering or providing professional services when such impairment is likely to harm a client or others. They seek assistance for problems that reach the level of professional impairment, and, if necessary, they limit, suspend, or terminate their professional responsibilities until such time it is determined that they may safely resume their work. Counselors assist colleagues or supervisors in recognizing their own professional impairment and provide consultation and assistance when warranted with colleagues or supervisors showing signs of impairment and intervene as appropriate to prevent imminent harm to clients. (*See A.11.b., F.8.b.*)

C.2.h. Counselor Incapacitation or Termination of Practice

When counselors leave a practice, they follow a prepared plan for transfer of clients and files. Counselors prepare and disseminate to an identified colleague or "records custodian" a plan for the transfer of clients and files in the case of their incapacitation, death, or termination of practice.

C.3. Advertising and Soliciting Clients

C.3.a. Accurate Advertising

When advertising or otherwise representing their services to the public, counselors identify their credentials in an accurate manner that is not false, misleading, deceptive, or fraudulent.

C.3.b. Testimonials

Counselors who use testimonials do not solicit them from current clients nor former clients nor any other persons who may be vulnerable to undue influence.

C.3.c. Statements by Others

Counselors make reasonable efforts to ensure that statements made by others about them or the profession of counseling are accurate.

C.3.d. Recruiting Through Employment

Counselors do not use their places of employment or institutional affiliation to recruit or gain clients, supervisees, or consultees for their private practices.

C.3.e. Products and Training Advertisements

Counselors who develop products related to their profession or conduct workshops or training events ensure that the advertisements concerning these products or events are accurate and disclose adequate information for consumers to make informed choices. (*See C.6.d.*)

C.3.f. Promoting to Those Served

Counselors do not use counseling, teaching, training, or supervisory relationships to promote their products or training events in a manner that is deceptive or would exert undue influence on individuals who may be vulnerable. However, counselor educators may adopt textbooks they have authored for instructional purposes.

C.4. Professional Qualifications

C.4.a. Accurate Representation

Counselors claim or imply only professional qualifications actually completed and correct any known misrepresentations of their qualifications by others. Counselors truthfully represent the qualifications of their professional colleagues. Counselors clearly distinguish between paid and volunteer work experience and accurately describe their continuing education and specialized training. (*See C.2.a.*)

C.4.b. Credentials

Counselors claim only licenses or certifications that are current and in good standing.

C.4.c. Educational Degrees

Counselors clearly differentiate between earned and honorary degrees.

C.4.d. Implying Doctoral-Level Competence

Counselors clearly state their highest earned degree in counseling or closely related field. Counselors do not imply doctoral-level competence when only possessing a master's degree in counseling or a related field by referring to themselves as "Dr." in a counseling context when their doctorate is not in counseling or related field.

C.4.e. Program Accreditation Status

Counselors clearly state the accreditation status of their degree programs at the time the degree was earned.

C.4.f. Professional Membership

Counselors clearly differentiate between current, active memberships and former memberships in associations. Members of the American Counseling Association must clearly differentiate between professional membership, which implies the possession of at least a master's degree in counseling, and regular membership, which is open to individuals whose interests and activities are consistent with those of ACA but are not qualified for professional membership.

C.5. Nondiscrimination

Counselors do not condone or engage in discrimination based on age, culture, disability, ethnicity, race, religion/spirituality, gender, gender identity, sexual orientation, marital status/partnership, language preference, socioeconomic status, or any basis proscribed by law. Counselors do not discriminate against clients, students, employees, supervisees, or research participants in a manner that has a negative impact on these persons.

C.6. Public Responsibility

C.6.a. Sexual Harassment

Counselors do not engage in or condone sexual harassment. Sexual harassment is defined as sexual solicitation, physical advances, or verbal or nonverbal conduct that is sexual in nature, that occurs in connection with professional activities or roles, and that either

1. is unwelcome, is offensive, or creates a hostile workplace or learning environment, and counselors know or are told this; or
2. is sufficiently severe or intense to be perceived as harassment to a reasonable person in the context in which the behavior occurred.

Sexual harassment can consist of a single intense or severe act or multiple persistent or pervasive acts.

C.6.b. Reports to Third Parties

Counselors are accurate, honest, and objective in reporting their professional activities and judgments to appropriate third parties, including courts, health insurance companies, those who are the recipients of evaluation reports, and others. (See B.3., E.4.)

C.6.c. Media Presentations

When counselors provide advice or comment by means of public lectures, demonstrations, radio or television programs, prerecorded tapes, technology-based applications, printed articles, mailed material, or other media, they take reasonable precautions to ensure that

1. the statements are based on appropriate professional counseling literature and practice,
2. the statements are otherwise consistent with the ACA Code of Ethics, and
3. the recipients of the information are not encouraged to infer that a professional counseling relationship has been established.

C.6.d. Exploitation of Others

Counselors do not exploit others in their professional relationships. (See C.3.e.)

C.6.e. Scientific Bases for Treatment Modalities

Counselors use techniques/procedures/modalities that are grounded in theory and/or have an empirical or scientific foundation. Counselors who do not must define the techniques/procedures as

"unproven" or "developing" and explain the potential risks and ethical considerations of using such techniques/procedures and take steps to protect clients from possible harm. (See A.4.a., E.5.c., E.5.d.)

C.7. Responsibility to Other Professionals

C.7.a. Personal Public Statements

When making personal statements in a public context, counselors clarify that they are speaking from their personal perspectives and that they are not speaking on behalf of all counselors or the profession.

SECTION D RELATIONSHIPS WITH OTHER PROFESSIONALS

Introduction

Professional counselors recognize that the quality of their interactions with colleagues can influence the quality of services provided to clients. They work to become knowledgeable about colleagues within and outside the field of counseling. Counselors develop positive working relationships and systems of communication with colleagues to enhance services to clients.

D.1. Relationships With Colleagues, Employers, and Employees

D.1.a. Different Approaches

Counselors are respectful of approaches to counseling services that differ from their own. Counselors are respectful of traditions and practices of other professional groups with which they work.

D.1.b. Forming Relationships

Counselors work to develop and strengthen interdisciplinary relations with colleagues from other disciplines to best serve clients.

D.1.c. Interdisciplinary Teamwork

Counselors who are members of interdisciplinary teams delivering multifaceted services to clients, keep the focus on how to best serve the clients. They participate in and contribute to decisions that affect the well-being of clients by drawing on the perspectives, values, and experiences of the counseling profession and those of colleagues from other disciplines. (*See A.1.a.*)

D.1.d. Confidentiality

When counselors are required by law, institutional policy, or extraordinary circumstances to serve in more than one role in judicial or administrative proceedings, they clarify role expectations and the parameters of confidentiality with their colleagues. (*See B.1.c., B.1.d., B.2.c., B.2.d., B.3.b.*)

D.1.e. Establishing Professional and Ethical Obligations

Counselors who are members of interdisciplinary teams clarify professional and ethical obligations of the team as a whole and of its individual members. When a team decision raises ethical concerns, counselors first attempt to resolve the concern within the team. If they cannot reach resolution among team members, counselors pursue other avenues to address their concerns consistent with client well-being.

D.1.f. Personnel Selection and Assignment

Counselors select competent staff and assign responsibilities compatible with their skills and experiences.

D.1.g. Employer Policies

The acceptance of employment in an agency or institution implies that counselors are in agreement with its general policies and principles. Counselors strive to reach agreement with employers as to acceptable standards of conduct that allow for changes in institutional policy conducive to the growth and development of clients.

D.1.h. Negative Conditions

Counselors alert their employers of inappropriate policies and practices. They attempt to effect changes in such policies or procedures through constructive action within the organization. When

such policies are potentially disruptive or damaging to clients or may limit the effectiveness of services provided and change cannot be effected, counselors take appropriate further action. Such action may include referral to appropriate certification, accreditation, or state licensure organizations, or voluntary termination of employment.

D.1.i. Protection From Punitive Action

Counselors take care not to harass or dismiss an employee who has acted in a responsible and ethical manner to expose inappropriate employer policies or practices.

D.2. Consultation

D.2.a. Consultant Competency

Counselors take reasonable steps to ensure that they have the appropriate resources and competencies when providing consultation services. Counselors provide appropriate referral resources when requested or needed. (*See C.2.a.*)

D.2.b. Understanding Consultees

When providing consultation, counselors attempt to develop with their consultees a clear understanding of problem definition, goals for change, and predicted consequences of interventions selected.

D.2.c. Consultant Goals

The consulting relationship is one in which consultee adaptability and growth toward self-direction are consistently encouraged and cultivated.

D.2.d. Informed Consent in Consultation

When providing consultation, counselors have an obligation to review, in writing and verbally, the rights and responsibilities of both counselors and consultees. Counselors use clear and understandable language to inform all parties involved about the purpose of the services to be provided, relevant costs, potential risks and benefits, and the limits of confidentiality. Working in conjunction with the consultee, counselors attempt to develop a clear definition of the problem, goals for change, and predicted consequences of interventions that are culturally responsive and appropriate to the needs of consultees. (*See A.2.a., A.2.b.*)

SECTION E EVALUATION, ASSESSMENT, AND INTERPRETATION

Introduction

Counselors use assessment instruments as one component of the counseling process, taking into account the client personal and cultural context. Counselors promote the well-being of individual clients or groups of clients by developing and using appropriate educational, psychological, and career assessment instruments.

E.1. General

E.1.a. Assessment

The primary purpose of educational, psychological, and career assessment is to provide measurements that are valid and reliable in either comparative or absolute terms. These include, but are not limited to, measurements of ability, personality, interest, intelligence, achievement, and performance. Counselors recognize the need to interpret the statements in this section as applying to both quantitative and qualitative assessments.

E.1.b. Client Welfare

Counselors do not misuse assessment results and interpretations, and they take reasonable steps to prevent others from misusing the information these techniques provide. They respect the client's right to know the results, the interpretations made, and the bases for counselors' conclusions and recommendations.

E.2. Competence to Use and Interpret Assessment Instruments

E.2.a. Limits of Competence

Counselors utilize only those testing and assessment services for which they have been trained and are competent. Counselors using technology

assisted test interpretations are trained in the construct being measured and the specific instrument being used prior to using its technology based application. Counselors take reasonable measures to ensure the proper use of psychological and career assessment techniques by persons under their supervision. (*See A.12.*)

E.2.b. Appropriate Use

Counselors are responsible for the appropriate application, scoring, interpretation, and use of assessment instruments relevant to the needs of the client, whether they score and interpret such assessments themselves or use technology or other services.

E.2.c. Decisions Based on Results

Counselors responsible for decisions involving individuals or policies that are based on assessment results have a thorough understanding of educational, psychological, and career measurement, including validation criteria, assessment research, and guidelines for assessment development and use.

E.3. Informed Consent in Assessment

E.3.a. Explanation to Clients

Prior to assessment, counselors explain the nature and purposes of assessment and the specific use of results by potential recipients. The explanation will be given in the language of the client (or other legally authorized person on behalf of the client), unless an explicit exception has been agreed upon in advance. Counselors consider the client's personal or cultural context, the level of the client's understanding of the results, and the impact of the results on the client. (*See A.2., A.12.g., F.1.c.*)

E.3.b. Recipients of Results

Counselors consider the examinee's welfare, explicit understandings, and prior agreements in determining who receives the assessment results. Counselors include accurate and appropriate interpretations with any release of individual or group assessment results. (*See B.2.c., B.5.*)

E.4. Release of Data to Qualified Professionals

Counselors release assessment data in which the client is identified only with the consent of the client or the client's legal representative. Such data are released only to persons recognized by counselors as qualified to interpret the data. (*See B.1., B.3., B.6.b.*)

E.5. Diagnosis of Mental Disorders

E.5.a. Proper Diagnosis

Counselors take special care to provide proper diagnosis of mental disorders. Assessment techniques (including personal interview) used to determine client care (e.g., locus of treatment, type of treatment, or recommended follow-up) are carefully selected and appropriately used.

E.5.b. Cultural Sensitivity

Counselors recognize that culture affects the manner in which clients' problems are defined. Clients' socioeconomic and cultural experiences are considered when diagnosing mental disorders. (*See A.2.c.*)

E.5.c. Historical and Social Prejudices in the Diagnosis of Pathology

Counselors recognize historical and social prejudices in the misdiagnosis and pathologizing of certain individuals and groups and the role of mental health professionals in perpetuating these prejudices through diagnosis and treatment.

E.5.d. Refraining From Diagnosis

Counselors may refrain from making and/or reporting a diagnosis if they believe it would cause harm to the client or others.

E.6. Instrument Selection

E.6.a. Appropriateness of Instruments

Counselors carefully consider the validity, reliability, psychometric limitations, and appropriateness of instruments when selecting assessments.

E.6.b. Referral Information

If a client is referred to a third party for assessment, the counselor provides specific referral questions and sufficient objective data about the client to ensure that appropriate assessment instruments are utilized. (*See A.9.b., B.3.*)

E.6.c. Culturally Diverse Populations

Counselors are cautious when selecting assessments for culturally diverse populations to avoid the use of instruments that lack appropriate psychometric properties for the client population. (*See A.2.c., E.5.b.*)

E.7. Conditions of Assessment Administration
(*See A.12.b., A.12.d.*)

E.7.a. Administration Conditions

Counselors administer assessments under the same conditions that were established in their standardization. When assessments are not administered under standard conditions, as may be necessary to accommodate clients with disabilities, or when unusual behavior or irregularities occur during the administration, those conditions are noted in interpretation, and the results may be designated as invalid or of questionable validity.

E.7.b. Technological Administration

Counselors ensure that administration programs function properly and provide clients with accurate results when technological or other electronic methods are used for assessment administration.

E.7.c. Unsupervised Assessments

Unless the assessment instrument is designed, intended, and validated for self-administration and/or scoring, counselors do not permit inadequately supervised use.

E.7.d. Disclosure of Favorable Conditions

Prior to administration of assessments, conditions that produce most favorable assessment results are made known to the examinee.

E.8. Multicultural Issues/Diversity in Assessment

Counselors use with caution assessment techniques that were normed on populations other than that of the client. Counselors recognize the effects of age, color, culture, disability, ethnic group, gender, race, language preference, religion, spirituality, sexual orientation, and socioeconomic status on test administration and interpretation, and place test results in proper perspective with other relevant factors. (*See A.2.c., E.5.b.*)

E.9. Scoring and Interpretation of Assessments

E.9.a. Reporting

In reporting assessment results, counselors indicate reservations that exist regarding validity or reliability due to circumstances of the assessment or the inappropriateness of the norms for the person tested.

E.9.b. Research Instruments

Counselors exercise caution when interpreting the results of research instruments not having sufficient technical data to support respondent results. The specific purposes for the use of such instruments are stated explicitly to the examinee.

E.9.c. Assessment Services

Counselors who provide assessment scoring and interpretation services to support the assessment process confirm the validity of such interpretations. They accurately describe the purpose, norms, validity, reliability, and applications of the procedures and any special qualifications applicable to their use. The public offering of an automated test interpretations service is considered a professional-to-professional consultation. The formal responsibility of the consultant is to the consultee, but the ultimate and overriding responsibility is to the client. (*See D.2.*)

E.10. Assessment Security

Counselors maintain the integrity and security of tests and other assessment techniques consistent with legal and contractual obligations. Counselors do not appropriate, reproduce, or modify published assessments or parts thereof without acknowledgment and permission from the publisher.

E.11. Obsolete Assessments and Outdated Results

Counselors do not use data or results from assessments that are obsolete or outdated for the current purpose. Counselors make every effort to prevent the misuse of obsolete measures and assessment data by others.

E.12. Assessment Construction

Counselors use established scientific procedures, relevant standards, and current professional knowledge for assessment design in the development, publication, and utilization of educational and psychological assessment techniques.

E.13. Forensic Evaluation: Evaluation for Legal Proceedings

E.13.a. Primary Obligations

When providing forensic evaluations, the primary obligation of counselors is to produce objective findings that can be substantiated based on information and techniques appropriate to the evaluation, which may include examination of the individual and/or review of records. Counselors are entitled to form professional opinions based on their professional knowledge and expertise that can be supported by the data gathered in evaluations. Counselors will define the limits of their reports or testimony, especially when an examination of the individual has not been conducted.

E.13.b. Consent for Evaluation

Individuals being evaluated are informed in writing that the relationship is for the purposes of an evaluation and is not counseling in nature, and entities or individuals who will receive the evaluation report are identified. Written consent to be evaluated is obtained from those being evaluated unless a court orders evaluations to be conducted without the written consent of individuals being evaluated. When children or vulnerable adults are being evaluated, informed written consent is obtained from a parent or guardian.

E.13.c. Client Evaluation Prohibited

Counselors do not evaluate individuals for forensic purposes they currently counsel or individuals they have counseled in the past. Counselors do not accept as counseling clients individuals they are evaluating or individuals they have evaluated in the past for forensic purposes.

E.13.d. Avoid Potentially Harmful Relationships

Counselors who provide forensic evaluations avoid potentially harmful professional or personal relationships with family members, romantic partners, and close friends of individuals they are evaluating or have evaluated in the past.

SECTION F SUPERVISION, TRAINING, AND TEACHING

Introduction

Counselors aspire to foster meaningful and respectful professional relationships and to maintain appropriate boundaries with supervisees and students. Counselors have theoretical and pedagogical foundations for their work and aim to be fair, accurate, and honest in their assessments of counselors-in-training.

F.1. Counselor Supervision and Client Welfare

F.1.a. Client Welfare

A primary obligation of counseling supervisors is to monitor the services provided by other counselors or counselors-in-training. Counseling supervisors monitor client welfare and supervisee clinical performance and professional development. To fulfill these obligations, supervisors meet regularly with supervisees to review case notes, samples of clinical work, or live observations. Supervisees have a responsibility to understand and follow the *ACA Code of Ethics*.

F.1.b. Counselor Credentials

Counseling supervisors work to ensure that clients are aware of the qualifications of the supervisees who render services to the clients. (*See A.2.b.*)

F.1.c. Informed Consent and Client Rights

Supervisors make supervisees aware of client rights including the protection of client privacy and confidentiality in the counseling relationship. Supervisees provide clients with professional disclosure information and inform them of how the supervision process influences the limits of confidentiality. Supervisees make clients aware of who will have access to records of the counseling relationship and how these records will be used. (*See A.2.b., B.1.d.*)

F.2. Counselor Supervision Competence

F.2.a. Supervisor Preparation

Prior to offering clinical supervision services, counselors are trained in supervision methods and techniques. Counselors who offer clinical supervision services regularly pursue continuing education activities including both counseling and supervision topics and skills. (*See C.2.a., C.2.f.*)

F.2.b. Multicultural Issues/Diversity in Supervision

Counseling supervisors are aware of and address the role of multiculturalism/diversity in the supervisory relationship.

F.3. Supervisory Relationships

F.3.a. Relationship Boundaries With Supervisees

Counseling supervisors clearly define and maintain ethical professional, personal, and social relationships with their supervisees. Counseling supervisors avoid nonprofessional relationships with current supervisees. If supervisors must assume other professional roles (e.g., clinical and administrative supervisor, instructor) with supervisees, they work to minimize potential conflicts and explain to supervisees the expectations and responsibilities associated with each role. They do not engage in any form of nonprofessional interaction that may compromise the supervisory relationship.

F.3.b. Sexual Relationships

Sexual or romantic interactions or relationships with current supervisees are prohibited.

F.3.c. Sexual Harassment

Counseling supervisors do not condone or subject supervisees to sexual harassment. (*See C.6.a.*)

F.3.d. Close Relatives and Friends

Counseling supervisors avoid accepting close relatives, romantic partners, or friends as supervisees.

F.3.e. Potentially Beneficial Relationships

Counseling supervisors are aware of the power differential in their relationships with supervisees. If they believe nonprofessional relationships with a supervisee may be potentially beneficial to the supervisee, they take precautions similar to those taken by counselors when working with clients. Examples of potentially beneficial interactions or relationships include attending a formal ceremony; hospital visits; providing support during a stressful event; or mutual membership in a professional association, organization, or community. Counseling supervisors engage in open discussions with supervisees when they consider entering into relationships with them outside of their roles as clinical and/or administrative supervisors. Before engaging in nonprofessional relationships, supervisors discuss with supervisees and document the rationale for such interactions, potential benefits or drawbacks, and anticipated consequences for the supervisee. Supervisors clarify the specific nature and limitations of the additional role(s) they will have with the supervisee.

F.4. Supervisor Responsibilities

F.4.a. Informed Consent for Supervision

Supervisors are responsible for incorporating into their supervision the principles of informed consent and participation. Supervisors inform supervisees of the policies and procedures to which they are to adhere and the mechanisms for due process appeal of individual supervisory actions.

F.4.b. Emergencies and Absences

Supervisors establish and communicate to supervisees procedures for contacting them or, in their absence, alternative on-call supervisors to assist in handling crises.

F.4.c. Standards for Supervisees

Supervisors make their supervisees aware of professional and ethical standards and legal responsibilities. Supervisors of postdegree counselors encourage these counselors to adhere to professional standards of practice. (*See C.1.*)

F.4.d. Termination of the Supervisory Relationship

Supervisors or supervisees have the right to terminate the supervisory relationship with adequate notice. Reasons for withdrawal are provided to the other party. When cultural, clinical, or professional issues are crucial to the viability of the supervisory relationship, both parties make efforts to resolve differences. When termination is warranted, supervisors make appropriate referrals to possible alternative supervisors.

F.5. Counseling Supervision Evaluation, Remediation, and Endorsement

F.5.a. Evaluation

Supervisors document and provide supervisees with ongoing performance appraisal and evaluation feedback and schedule periodic formal evaluative sessions throughout the supervisory relationship.

F.5.b. Limitations

Through ongoing evaluation and appraisal, supervisors are aware of the limitations of supervisees that might impede performance. Supervisors assist supervisees in securing remedial assistance when needed. They recommend dismissal from training programs, applied counseling settings, or state or voluntary professional credentialing processes when those supervisees are unable to provide competent professional services. Supervisors seek consultation and document their decisions to dismiss or refer supervisees for assistance. They ensure that supervisees are aware of options available to them to address such decisions. (*See C.2.g.*)

F.5.c. Counseling for Supervisees

If supervisees request counseling, supervisors provide them with acceptable referrals. Counselors do not provide counseling services to supervisees. Supervisors address interpersonal competencies in terms of the impact of these issues on clients, the supervisory relationship, and professional functioning. (*See F.3.a.*)

F.5.d. Endorsement

Supervisors endorse supervisees for certification, licensure, employment, or completion of an academic or training program only when they believe supervisees are qualified for the endorsement. Regardless of qualifications, supervisors do not endorse supervisees whom they believe to be impaired in any way that would interfere with the performance of the duties associated with the endorsement.

F.6. Responsibilities of Counselor Educators

F.6.a. Counselor Educators

Counselor educators who are responsible for developing, implementing, and supervising educational programs are skilled as teachers and practitioners. They are knowledgeable regarding the ethical, legal, and regulatory aspects of the profession, are skilled in applying that knowledge, and make students and supervisees aware of their responsibilities. Counselor educators conduct counselor education and training programs in an ethical manner and serve as role models for professional behavior. (*See C.1., C.2.a., C.2.c.*)

F.6.b. Infusing Multicultural Issues/Diversity

Counselor educators infuse material related to multiculturalism/diversity into all courses and workshops for the development of professional counselors.

F.6.c. Integration of Study and Practice

Counselor educators establish education and training programs that integrate academic study and supervised practice.

F.6.d. Teaching Ethics

Counselor educators make students and supervisees aware of the ethical responsibilities and standards of the profession and the ethical responsibilities of students to the profession. Counselor educators infuse ethical considerations throughout the curriculum. (*See C.1.*)

F.6.e. Peer Relationships

Counselor educators make every effort to ensure that the rights of peers are not compromised when students or supervisees lead counseling groups or provide clinical supervision. Counselor educators take steps to ensure that students and supervisees understand they have the same ethical obligations as counselor educators, trainers, and supervisors.

F.6.f. Innovative Theories and Techniques

When counselor educators teach counseling techniques/procedures that are innovative, without an empirical foundation, or without a well-grounded theoretical foundation, they define the counseling techniques/procedures as "unproven" or "developing" and explain to students the potential risks and ethical considerations of using such techniques/procedures.

F.6.g. Field Placements

Counselor educators develop clear policies within their training programs regarding field placement and other clinical experiences. Counselor educators provide clearly stated roles and responsibilities for the student or supervisee, the site supervisor, and the program supervisor. They confirm that site supervisors are qualified to provide supervision and inform site supervisors of their professional and ethical responsibilities in this role.

F.6.b. Professional Disclosure

Before initiating counseling services, counselors-in-training disclose their status as students and explain how this status affects the limits of confidentiality. Counselor educators ensure that the clients at field placements are aware of the services rendered and the qualifications of the students and supervisees rendering those services. Students and supervisees obtain client permission before they use any information concerning the counseling relationship in the training process. (*See A.2.b.*)

F.7. Student Welfare

F.7.a. Orientation

Counselor educators recognize that orientation is a developmental process that continues throughout the educational and clinical training of students. Counseling faculty provide prospective students with information about the counselor education program's expectations:

1. the type and level of skill and knowledge acquisition required for successful completion of the training;
2. program training goals, objectives, and mission, and subject matter to be covered;
3. bases for evaluation;
4. training components that encourage self-growth or self-disclosure as part of the training process;
5. the type of supervision setting and requirements of the sites for required clinical field experiences;
6. student and supervisee evaluation and dismissal policies and procedures; and
7. up-to-date employment prospects for graduates.

F.7.b. Self-Growth Experiences

Counselor education programs delineate requirements for self-disclosure or self-growth experiences in their admission and program materials. Counselor educators use professional judgment when designing training experiences they conduct that require student and supervisee self-growth or self-disclosure. Students

and supervisees are made aware of the ramifications their self-disclosure may have when counselors whose primary role as teacher, trainer, or supervisor requires acting on ethical obligations to the profession. Evaluative components of experiential training experiences explicitly delineate predetermined academic standards that are separate and do not depend on the student's level of self-disclosure. Counselor educators may require trainees to seek professional help to address any personal concerns that may be affecting their competency.

F.8. Student Responsibilities

F.8.a. Standards for Students

Counselors-in-training have a responsibility to understand and follow the *ACA Code of Ethics* and adhere to applicable laws, regulatory policies, and rules and policies governing professional staff behavior at the agency or placement setting. Students have the same obligation to clients as those required of professional counselors. (*See C.1., H.1.*)

F.8.b. Impairment

Counselors-in-training refrain from offering or providing counseling services when their physical, mental, or emotional problems are likely to harm a client or others. They are alert to the signs of impairment, seek assistance for problems, and notify their program supervisors when they are aware that they are unable to effectively provide services. In addition, they seek appropriate professional services for themselves to remediate the problems that are interfering with their ability to provide services to others. (*See A.1., C.2.d., C.2.g.*)

F.9. Evaluation and Remediation of Students

F.9.a. Evaluation

Counselors clearly state to students, prior to and throughout the training program, the levels of competency expected, appraisal methods, and timing of evaluations for both didactic and clinical competencies. Counselor educators provide students with ongoing performance appraisal and evaluation feedback throughout the training program.

F.9.b. Limitations

Counselor educators, throughout ongoing evaluation and appraisal, are aware of and address the inability of some students to achieve counseling competencies that might impede performance. Counselor educators

1. assist students in securing remedial assistance when needed;
2. seek professional consultation and document their decision to dismiss or refer students for assistance, and
3. ensure that students have recourse in a timely manner to address decisions to require them to seek assistance or to dismiss them and provide students with due process according to institutional policies and procedures. (*See C.2.g.*)

F.9.c. Counseling for Students

If students request counseling or if counseling services are required as part of a remediation process, counselor educators provide acceptable referrals.

F.10. Roles and Relationships Between Counselor Educators and Students

F.10.a. Sexual or Romantic Relationships

Sexual or romantic interactions or relationships with current students are prohibited.

F.10.b. Sexual Harassment

Counselor educators do not condone or subject students to sexual harassment. (*See C.6.a.*)

F.10.c. Relationships With Former Students

Counselor educators are aware of the power differential in the relationship between faculty and students. Faculty members foster open discussions with former students when considering engaging in a social, sexual, or other intimate relationship. Faculty members discuss with the former student how their former relationship may affect the change in relationship.

F.10.d. Nonprofessional Relationships

Counselor educators avoid nonprofessional or ongoing professional relationships with students in which there is a risk of potential harm to the student or that may compromise the training experience or grades assigned. In addition, counselor educators do not accept any form of professional services, fees, commissions, reimbursement, or remuneration from a site for student or supervisee placement.

F.10.e. Counseling Services

Counselor educators do not serve as counselors to current students unless this is a brief role associated with a training experience.

F.10.f. Potentially Beneficial Relationships

Counselor educators are aware of the power differential in the relationship between faculty and students. If they believe a nonprofessional relationship with a student may be potentially beneficial to the student, they take precautions similar to those taken by counselors when working with clients. Examples of potentially beneficial interactions or relationships include, but are not limited to, attending a formal ceremony; hospital visits; providing support during a stressful event; or mutual membership in a professional association, organization, or community. Counselor educators engage in open discussions with students when they consider entering into relationships with students outside of their roles as teachers and supervisors. They discuss with students the rationale for such interactions, the potential benefits and drawbacks, and the anticipated consequences for the student. Educators clarify the specific nature and limitations of the additional role(s) they will have with the student prior to engaging in a nonprofessional relationship. Nonprofessional relationships with students should be time-limited and initiated with student consent.

F.11. Multicultural/Diversity Competence in Counselor Education and Training Programs

F.11.a. Faculty Diversity

Counselor educators are committed to recruiting and retaining a diverse faculty.

F.11.b. Student Diversity

Counselor educators actively attempt to recruit and retain a diverse student body. Counselor educators demonstrate commitment to multicultural/diversity competence by recognizing and valuing diverse cultures and types of abilities students bring to the training experience. Counselor educators provide appropriate accommodations that enhance and support diverse student well-being and academic performance.

F.11.c. Multicultural/Diversity Competence

Counselor educators actively infuse multicultural/diversity competency in their training and supervision practices. They actively train students to gain awareness, knowledge, and skills in the competencies of multicultural practice. Counselor educators include case examples, role-plays, discussion questions, and other classroom activities that promote and represent various cultural perspectives.

SECTION G   RESEARCH AND PUBLICATION

Introduction

Counselors who conduct research are encouraged to contribute to the knowledge base of the profession and promote a clearer understanding of the conditions that lead to a healthy and more just society. Counselors support efforts of researchers by participating fully and willingly whenever possible. Counselors minimize bias and respect diversity in designing and implementing research programs.

G.1. Research Responsibilities

G.1.a. Use of Human Research Participants

Counselors plan, design, conduct, and report research in a manner that is consistent with pertinent ethical principles, federal and state laws, host institutional regulations, and scientific standards governing research with human research participants.

G.1.b. Deviation From Standard Practice

Counselors seek consultation and observe stringent safeguards to protect the rights of research participants when a research problem suggests a deviation from standard or acceptable practices.

G.1.c. Independent Researchers

When independent researchers do not have access to an Institutional Review Board (IRB), they should consult with researchers who are familiar with IRB procedures to provide appropriate safeguards.

G.1.d. Precautions to Avoid Injury

Counselors who conduct research with human participants are responsible for the welfare of participants throughout the research process and should take reasonable precautions to avoid causing injurious psychological, emotional, physical, or social effects to participants.

G.1.e. Principal Researcher Responsibility

The ultimate responsibility for ethical research practice lies with the principal researcher. All others involved in the research activities share ethical obligations and responsibility for their own actions.

G.1.f. Minimal Interference

Counselors take reasonable precautions to avoid causing disruptions in the lives of research participants that could be caused by their involvement in research.

G.1.g. Multicultural/Diversity Considerations in Research

When appropriate to research goals, counselors are sensitive to incorporating research procedures that take into account cultural considerations. They seek consultation when appropriate.

G.2. Rights of Research Participants
(*See A.2, A.7.*)

G.2.a. Informed Consent in Research

Individuals have the right to consent to become research participants. In seeking consent, counselors use language that

1. accurately explains the purpose and procedures to be followed,
2. identifies any procedures that are experimental or relatively untried,
3. describes any attendant discomforts and risks,
4. describes any benefits or changes in individuals or organizations that might be reasonably expected,
5. discloses appropriate alternative procedures that would be advantageous for participants,
6. offers to answer any inquiries concerning the procedures,
7. describes any limitations on confidentiality,
8. describes the format and potential target audiences for the dissemination of research findings, and
9. instructs participants that they are free to withdraw their consent and to discontinue participation in the project at any time without penalty.

G.2.b. Deception

Counselors do not conduct research involving deception unless alternative procedures are not feasible and the prospective value of the research justifies the deception. If such deception has the potential to cause physical or emotional harm to research participants, the research is not conducted, regardless of prospective value. When the methodological requirements of a study necessitate concealment or deception, the investigator explains the reasons for this action as soon as possible during the debriefing.

G.2.c. Student/Supervisee Participation

Researchers who involve students or supervisees in research make clear to them that the decision regarding whether or not to participate in research activities does not affect one's academic standing or supervisory relationship. Students or supervisees who choose not to participate in educational research are provided with an appropriate alternative to fulfill their academic or clinical requirements.

G.2.d. Client Participation

Counselors conducting research involving clients make clear in the informed consent process that clients are free to choose whether or not to participate in research activities. Counselors take necessary precautions to protect clients from adverse consequences of declining or withdrawing from participation.

G.2.e. Confidentiality of Information

Information obtained about research participants during the course of an investigation is confidential. When the possibility exists that others may obtain access to such information, ethical research practice requires that the possibility, together with the plans for protecting confidentiality, be explained to participants as a part of the procedure for obtaining informed consent.

G.2.f. Persons Not Capable of Giving Informed Consent

When a person is not capable of giving informed consent, counselors provide an appropriate explanation to, obtain agreement for participation from, and obtain the appropriate consent of a legally authorized person.

G.2.g. Commitments to Participants

Counselors take reasonable measures to honor all commitments to research participants. (*See A.2.c.*)

G.2.b. Explanations After Data Collection

After data are collected, counselors provide participants with full clarification of the nature of the study to remove any misconceptions participants might have regarding the research. Where scientific or human values justify delaying or withholding information, counselors take reasonable measures to avoid causing harm.

G.2.i. Informing Sponsors

Counselors inform sponsors, institutions, and publication channels regarding research procedures and outcomes. Counselors ensure that appropriate bodies and authorities are given pertinent information and acknowledgment.

G.2.j. Disposal of Research Documents and Records

Within a reasonable period of time following the completion of a research project or study, counselors take steps to destroy records or documents (audio, video, digital, and written) containing confidential data or information that identifies research participants. When records are of an artistic nature, researchers obtain participant consent with regard to handling of such records or documents. (See B.4.a, B.4.g.)

G.3. Relationships With Research Participants (When Research Involves Intensive or Extended Interactions)

G.3.a. Nonprofessional Relationships

Nonprofessional relationships with research participants should be avoided.

G.3.b. Relationships With Research Participants

Sexual or romantic counselor-research participant interactions or relationships with current research participants are prohibited.

G.3.c. Sexual Harassment and Research Participants

Researchers do not condone or subject research participants to sexual harassment.

G.3.d. Potentially Beneficial Interactions

When a nonprofessional interaction between the researcher and the research participant may be potentially beneficial, the researcher must document, prior to the interaction (when feasible), the rationale for such an interaction, the potential benefit, and anticipated consequences for the research participant. Such interactions should be initiated with appropriate consent of the research participant. Where unintentional harm occurs to the research participant due to the nonprofessional interaction, the researcher must show evidence of an attempt to remedy such harm.

G.4. Reporting Results

G.4.a. Accurate Results

Counselors plan, conduct, and report research accurately. They provide thorough discussions of the limitations of their data and alternative hypotheses. Counselors do not engage in misleading or fraudulent research, distort data, misrepresent data, or deliberately bias their results. They explicitly mention all variables and conditions known to the investigator that may have affected the outcome of a study or the interpretation of data. They describe the extent to which results are applicable for diverse populations.

G.4.b. Obligation to Report Unfavorable Results

Counselors report the results of any research of professional value. Results that reflect unfavorably on institutions, programs, services, prevailing opinions, or vested interests are not withheld.

G.4.c. Reporting Errors

If counselors discover significant errors in their published research, they take reasonable steps to correct such errors in a correction erratum, or through other appropriate publication means.

G.4.d. Identity of Participants

Counselors who supply data, aid in the research of another person, report research results, or make original data available take due care to disguise the identity of respective participants in the absence of specific authorization from the participants to do otherwise. In situations where participants self-identify their involvement in research studies, researchers take active steps to ensure that data is adapted/changed to protect the identity and welfare of all parties and that discussion of results does not cause harm to participants.

G.4.e. Replication Studies

Counselors are obligated to make available sufficient original research data to qualified professionals who may wish to replicate the study.

G.5. Publication

G.5.a. Recognizing Contributions

When conducting and reporting research, counselors are familiar with and give recognition to previous work on the topic, observe copyright laws, and give full credit to those to whom credit is due.

G.5.b. Plagiarism

Counselors do not plagiarize, that is, they do not present another person's work as their own work.

G.5.c. Review/Republication of Data or Ideas

Counselors fully acknowledge and make editorial reviewers aware of prior publication of ideas or data where such ideas or data are submitted for review or publication.

G.5.d. Contributors

Counselors give credit through joint authorship, acknowledgment, footnote statements, or other appropriate means to those who have contributed significantly to research or concept development in accordance with such contributions. The principal contributor is listed first and minor technical or professional contributions are acknowledged in notes or introductory statements.

G.5.e. Agreement of Contributors

Counselors who conduct joint research with colleagues or students/supervisees establish

agreements in advance regarding allocation of tasks, publication credit, and types of acknowledgment that will be received.

G.5.f. Student Research

For articles that are substantially based on students course papers, projects, dissertations or theses, and on which students have been the primary contributors, they are listed as principal authors.

G.5.g. Duplicate Submission

Counselors submit manuscripts for consideration to only one journal at a time. Manuscripts that are published in whole or in substantial part in another journal or published work are not submitted for publication without acknowledgment and permission from the previous publication.

G.5.h. Professional Review

Counselors who review material submitted for publication, research, or other scholarly purposes respect the confidentiality and proprietary rights of those who submitted it. Counselors use care to make publication decisions based on valid and defensible standards. Counselors review article submissions in a timely manner and based on their scope and competency in research methodologies. Counselors who serve as reviewers at the request of editors or publishers make every effort to only review materials that are within their scope of competency and use care to avoid personal biases.

SECTION H   RESOLVING ETHICAL ISSUES

Introduction

Counselors behave in a legal, ethical, and moral manner in the conduct of their professional work. They are aware that client protection and trust in the profession depend on a high level of professional conduct. They hold other counselors to the same standards and are willing to take appropriate action to ensure that these standards are upheld.

Counselors strive to resolve ethical dilemmas with direct and open communication among all parties involved and seek consultation with colleagues and supervisors when necessary. Counselors incorporate ethical practice into their daily professional work. They engage in ongoing professional development regarding current topics in ethical and legal issues in counseling.

H.1. Standards and the Law
(*See F.9.a.*)

H.1.a. Knowledge

Counselors understand the *ACA Code of Ethics* and other applicable ethics codes from other professional organizations or from certification and licensure bodies of which they are members. Lack of knowledge or misunderstanding of an ethical responsibility is not a defense against a charge of unethical conduct.

H.1.b. Conflicts Between Ethics and Laws

If ethical responsibilities conflict with law, regulations, or other governing legal authority, counselors make known their commitment to the *ACA Code of Ethics* and take steps to resolve the conflict. If the conflict cannot be resolved by such means, counselors may adhere to the requirements of law, regulations, or other governing legal authority.

H.2. Suspected Violations

H.2.a. Ethical Behavior Expected

Counselors expect colleagues to adhere to the *ACA Code of Ethics*. When counselors possess knowledge that raises doubts as to whether another counselor is acting in an ethical manner, they take appropriate action. (*See H.2.b., H.2.c.*)

H.2.b. Informal Resolution

When counselors have reason to believe that another counselor is violating or has violated an ethical standard, they attempt first to resolve the issue informally with the other counselor if feasible, provided such action does not violate confidentiality rights that may be involved.

H.2.c. Reporting Ethical Violations

If an apparent violation has substantially harmed, or is likely to substantially harm a person or organization and is not appropriate for informal resolution or is not resolved properly, counselors take further action appropriate to the situation. Such action might include referral to state or national committees on professional ethics, voluntary national certification bodies, state licensing boards, or to the appropriate institutional authorities. This standard does not apply when an intervention would violate confidentiality rights or when counselors have been retained to review the work of another counselor whose professional conduct is in question.

H.2.d. Consultation

When uncertain as to whether a particular situation or course of action may be in violation of the *ACA Code of Ethics,* counselors consult with other counselors who are knowledgeable about ethics and the *ACA Code of Ethics,* with colleagues, or with appropriate authorities.

H.2.e. Organizational Conflicts

If the demands of an organization with which counselors are affiliated pose a conflict with the *ACA Code of Ethics,* counselors specify the nature of such conflicts and express to their supervisors or other responsible officials their commitment to the *ACA Code of Ethics*. When possible, counselors work toward change within the organization to allow full adherence to the *ACA Code of Ethics*. In doing so, they address any confidentiality issues.

H.2.f. Unwarranted Complaints

Counselors do not initiate, participate in, or encourage the filing of ethics complaints that are made with reckless disregard or willful ignorance of facts that would disprove the allegation.

H.2.g. Unfair Discrimination Against Complainants and Respondents

Counselors do not deny persons employment, advancement, admission to academic or other programs, tenure, or promotion based solely upon their having made or their being the subject of an ethics complaint. This does not preclude taking action based upon the outcome of such proceedings or considering other appropriate information.

H.3. Cooperation With Ethics Committees

Counselors assist in the process of enforcing the *ACA Code of Ethics*. Counselors cooperate with investigations, proceedings, and requirements of the ACA Ethics Committee or ethics committees of other duly constituted associations or boards having jurisdiction over those charged with a violation. Counselors are familiar with the *ACA Policy and Procedures for Processing Complaints of Ethical Violations* and use it as a reference for assisting in the enforcement of the *ACA Code of Ethics*.

GLOSSARY OF TERMS

Advocacy   promotion of the well-being of individuals and groups, and the counseling profession within systems and organizations. Advocacy seeks to remove barriers and obstacles that inhibit access, growth, and development.

Assent   to demonstrate agreement, when a person is otherwise not capable or competent to give formal consent (e.g., informed consent) to a counseling service or plan.

Client   an individual seeking or referred to the professional services of a counselor for help with problem resolution or decision making.

Counselor   a professional (or a student who is a counselor-in-training) engaged in a counseling practice or other counseling-related services. Counselors fulfill many roles and responsibilities such as counselor educators, researchers, supervisors, practitioners, and consultants.

Counselor Educator   a professional counselor engaged primarily in developing, implementing, and supervising the educational preparation of counselors-in-training.

Counselor Supervisor   a professional counselor who engages in a formal relationship with a practicing counselor or counselor-in-training for the purpose of overseeing that individual's counseling work or clinical skill development.

Culture   membership in a socially constructed way of living, which incorporates collective values, beliefs, norms, boundaries, and lifestyles that are cocreated with others who share similar worldviews comprising biological, psychosocial, historical, psychological, and other factors.

Diversity   the similarities and differences that occur within and across cultures, and the intersection of cultural and social identities.

Documents   any written, digital, audio, visual, or artistic recording of the work within the counseling relationship between counselor and client.

Examinee   a recipient of any professional counseling service that includes educational, psychological, and career appraisal utilizing qualitative or quantitative techniques.

Forensic Evaluation   any formal assessment conducted for court or other legal proceedings.

Multicultural/Diversity Competence   a capacity whereby counselors possess cultural and diversity awareness and knowledge about self and others, and how this awareness and knowledge is applied effectively in practice with clients and client groups.

Multicultural/Diversity Counseling   counseling that recognizes diversity and embraces approaches that support the worth, dignity, potential, and uniqueness of individuals within their historical, cultural, economic, political, and psychosocial contexts.

Student   an individual engaged in formal educational preparation as a counselor-in-training.

Supervisee   a professional counselor or counselor-in-training whose counseling work or clinical skill development is being overseen in a formal supervisory relationship by a qualified trained professional.

Supervisor   counselors who are trained to oversee the professional clinical work of counselors and counselors-in-training.

Teaching   all activities engaged in as part of a formal educational program designed to lead to a graduate degree in counseling.

Training   the instruction and practice of skills related to the counseling profession. Training contributes to the ongoing proficiency of students and professional counselors.

ASCA CODE OF ETHICS

Ethical Standards for School Counselors

ASCA's Ethical Standards for School Counselors were adopted by the ASCA Delegate Assembly, March 19, 1984, revised March 27, 1992, June 25, 1998 and June 26, 2004.

PREAMBLE

The American School Counselor Association (ASCA) is a professional organization whose members are certified/licensed in school counseling with unique qualifications and skills to address the academic, personal/social and career development needs of all students. Professional school counselors are advocates, leaders, collaborators and consultants who create opportunities for equity in access and success in educational opportunities by connecting their programs to the mission of schools and subscribing to the following tenets of professional responsibility:

- Each person has the right to be respected, be treated with dignity and have access to a comprehensive school counseling program that advocates for and affirms all students from diverse populations regardless of ethnic/racial status, age, economic status, special needs, English as a second language or other language group, immigration status, sexual orientation, gender, gender identity/expression, family type, religious/spiritual identity and appearance.

- Each person has the right to receive the information and support needed to move toward self-direction and self-development and affirmation within one's group identities, with special care being given to students who have historically not received adequate educational services: students of color, low socio-economic students, students with disabilities and students with nondominant language backgrounds.

- Each person has the right to understand the full magnitude and meaning of his/her educational choices and how those choices will affect future opportunities.

- Each person has the right to privacy and thereby the right to expect the counselor-student relationship to comply with all laws, policies and ethical standards pertaining to confidentiality in the school setting.

In this document, ASCA specifies the principles of ethical behavior necessary to maintain the high standards of integrity, leadership and professionalism among its members. The Ethical Standards for School Counselors were developed to clarify the nature of ethical responsibilities

---

held in common by school counseling professionals. The purposes of this document are to:

- Serve as a guide for the ethical practices of all professional school counselors regardless of level, area, population served or membership in this professional association;
- Provide self-appraisal and peer evaluations regarding counselor responsibilities to students, parents/guardians, colleagues and professional associates, schools, communities and the counseling profession; and
- Inform those served by the school counselor of acceptable counselor practices and expected professional behavior.

A.1. Responsibilities to Students

The professional school counselor:

a. Has a primary obligation to the student, who is to be treated with respect as a unique individual.
b. Is concerned with the educational, academic, career, personal and social needs and encourages the maximum development of every student.
c. Respects the student's values and beliefs and does not impose the counselor's personal values.
d. Is knowledgeable of laws, regulations and policies relating to students and strives to protect and inform students regarding their rights.

A.2. Confidentiality

The professional school counselor:

a. Informs students of the purposes, goals, techniques and rules of procedure under which they may receive counseling at or before the time when the counseling relationship is entered. Disclosure notice includes the limits of confidentiality such as the possible necessity for consulting with other professionals, privileged communication, and legal or authoritative restraints. The meaning and limits of confidentiality are defined in developmentally appropriate terms to students.

b. Keeps information confidential unless disclosure is required to prevent clear and imminent danger to the student or others or when legal requirements demand that confidential information be revealed. Counselors will consult with appropriate professionals when in doubt as to the validity of an exception.
c. In absence of state legislation expressly forbidding disclosure, considers the ethical responsibility to provide information to an identified third party who, by his/her relationship with the student, is at a high risk of contracting a disease that is commonly known to be communicable and fatal. Disclosure requires satisfaction of all of the following conditions:
  - Student identifies partner or the partner is highly identifiable
  - Counselor recommends the student notify partner and refrain from further high-risk behavior
  - Student refuses
  - Counselor informs the student of the intent to notify the partner
  - Counselor seeks legal consultation as to the legalities of informing the partner
d. Requests of the court that disclosure not be required when the release of confidential information may potentially harm a student or the counseling relationship.
e. Protects the confidentiality of students' records and releases personal data in accordance with prescribed laws and school policies. Student information stored and transmitted electronically is treated with the same care as traditional student records.
f. Protects the confidentiality of information received in the counseling relationship as specified by federal and state laws, written policies and applicable ethical standards. Such information is only to be revealed to others with the informed consent of the student, consistent with the counselor's ethical obligation.
g. Recognizes his/her primary obligation for confidentiality is to the student but balances that obligation with an understanding of the legal and inherent rights of parents/guardians to be the guiding voice in their children's lives.

A.3. Counseling Plans

The professional school counselor:

a. Provides students with a comprehensive school counseling program that includes a strong emphasis on working jointly with all students to develop academic and career goals.

b. Advocates for counseling plans supporting students right to choose from the wide array of options when they leave secondary education. Such plans will be regularly reviewed to update students regarding critical information they need to make informed decisions.

A.4. Dual Relationships

The professional school counselor:

a. Avoids dual relationships that might impair his/her objectivity and increase the risk of harm to the student (e.g., counseling one's family members, close friends or associates). If a dual relationship is unavoidable, the counselor is responsible for taking action to eliminate or reduce the potential for harm. Such safeguards might include informed consent, consultation, supervision and documentation.

b. Avoids dual relationships with school personnel that might infringe on the integrity of the counselor/student relationship.

A.5. Appropriate Referrals

The professional school counselor:

a. Makes referrals when necessary or appropriate to outside resources. Appropriate referrals may necessitate informing both parents/guardians and students of applicable resources and making proper plans for transitions with minimal interruption of services. Students retain the right to discontinue the counseling relationship at any time.

A.6. Group Work

The professional school counselor:

a. Screens prospective group members and maintains an awareness of participants' needs and goals in relation to the goals of the group. The counselor takes reasonable precautions to protect members from physical and psychological harm resulting from interaction within the group.

b. Notifies parents/guardians and staff of group participation if the counselor deems it appropriate and if consistent with school board policy or practice.

c. Establishes clear expectations in the group setting and clearly states that confidentiality in group counseling cannot be guaranteed. Given the developmental and chronological ages of minors in schools, the counselor recognizes the tenuous nature of confidentiality for minors renders some topics inappropriate for group work in a school setting.

d. Follows up with group members and documents proceedings as appropriate.

A.7. Danger to Self or Others

The professional school counselor:

a. Informs parents/guardians or appropriate authorities when the student's condition indicates a clear and imminent danger to the student or others. This is to be done after careful deliberation and, where possible, after consultation with other counseling professionals.

b. Will attempt to minimize threat to a student and may choose to 1) inform the student of actions to be taken, 2) involve the student in a three-way communication with parents/guardians when breaching confidentiality or 3) allow the student to have input as to how and to whom the breach will be made.

A.8. Student Records

The professional school counselor:

a. Maintains and secures records necessary for rendering professional services to the student as required by laws, regulations, institutional procedures and confidentiality guidelines.

b. Keeps sole-possession records separate from students' educational records in keeping with state laws.

c. Recognizes the limits of sole-possession records and understands these records are a memory aid for the creator and in absence of privilege communication may be subpoenaed and may become educational records when they (1) are shared with others in verbal or written form, (2) include information other than professional opinion or personal observations and/or (3) are made accessible to others.

d. Establishes a reasonable timeline for purging sole-possession records or case notes. Suggested guidelines include shredding sole-possession records when the student transitions to the next level, transfers to another school or graduates. Careful discretion and deliberation should be applied before destroying sole-possession records that may be needed by a court of law such as notes on child abuse, suicide, sexual harassment or violence.

A.9. Evaluation, Assessment and Interpretation

The professional school counselor:

a. Adheres to all professional standards regarding selecting, administering and interpreting assessment measures and only utilizes assessment measures that are within the scope of practice for school counselors.

b. Seeks specialized training regarding the use of electronically based testing programs in administering, scoring and interpreting that may differ from that required in more traditional assessments.

c. Considers confidentiality issues when utilizing evaluative or assessment instruments and electronically based programs.

d. Provides interpretation of the nature, purposes, results and potential impact of assessment/evaluation measures in language the student(s) can understand.

e. Monitors the use of assessment results and interpretations, and takes reasonable steps to prevent others from misusing the information.

f. Uses caution when utilizing assessment techniques, making evaluations and interpreting

the performance of populations not represented in the norm group on which an instrument is standardized.

g. Assesses the effectiveness of his/her program in having an impact on students' academic, career and personal/social development through accountability measures especially examining efforts to close achievement, opportunity and attainment gaps.

A.10. Technology

The professional school counselor:

a. Promotes the benefits of and clarifies the limitations of various appropriate technological applications. The counselor promotes technological applications (1) that are appropriate for the student's individual needs, (2) that the student understands how to use and (3) for which follow-up counseling assistance is provided.

b. Advocates for equal access to technology for all students, especially those historically underserved.

c. Takes appropriate and reasonable measures for maintaining confidentiality of student information and educational records stored or transmitted over electronic media including although not limited to fax, electronic mail and instant messaging.

d. While working with students on a computer or similar technology, takes reasonable and appropriate measures to protect students from objectionable and/or harmful online material.

e. Who is engaged in the delivery of services involving technologies such as the telephone, videoconferencing and the Internet takes responsible steps to protect students and others from harm.

A.11. Student Peer Support Program

The professional school counselor:

Has unique responsibilities when working with student-assistance programs. The school counselor is responsible for the welfare of students participating in peer-to-peer programs under his/her direction.

keep both parents informed with regard to critical information with the exception of a court order.

B. RESPONSIBILITIES TO PARENTS/GUARDIANS

B.1. Parent Rights and Responsibilities

The professional school counselor:

a. Respects the rights and responsibilities of parents/guardians for their children and endeavors to establish, as appropriate, a collaborative relationship with parents/guardians to facilitate the student's maximum development.
b. Adheres to laws, local guidelines and ethical standards of practice when assisting parents/guardians experiencing family difficulties that interfere with the student's effectiveness and welfare.
c. Respects the confidentiality of parents/guardians.
d. Is sensitive to diversity among families and recognizes that all parents/guardians, custodial and noncustodial, are vested with certain rights and responsibilities for the welfare of their children by virtue of their role and according to law.

B.2. Parents/Guardians and Confidentiality

The professional school counselor:

a. Informs parents/guardians of the counselor's role with emphasis on the confidential nature of the counseling relationship between the counselor and student.
b. Recognizes that working with minors in a school setting may require counselors to collaborate with students' parents/guardians.
c. Provides parents/guardians with accurate, comprehensive and relevant information in an objective and caring manner, as is appropriate and consistent with ethical responsibilities to the student.
d. Makes reasonable efforts to honor the wishes of parents/guardians concerning information regarding the student, and in cases of divorce or separation exercises a good-faith effort to

C. RESPONSIBILITIES TO COLLEAGUES AND PROFESSIONAL ASSOCIATES

C.1. Professional Relationships

The professional school counselor:

a. Establishes and maintains professional relationships with faculty, staff and administration to facilitate an optimum counseling program.
b. Treats colleagues with professional respect, courtesy and fairness. The qualifications, views and findings of colleagues are represented to accurately reflect the image of competent professionals.
c. Is aware of and utilizes related professionals, organizations and other resources to whom the student may be referred.

C.2. Sharing Information with Other Professionals

The professional school counselor:

a. Promotes awareness and adherence to appropriate guidelines regarding confidentiality, the distinction between public and private information and staff consultation.
b. Provides professional personnel with accurate, objective, concise and meaningful data necessary to adequately evaluate, counsel and assist the student.
c. If a student is receiving services from another counselor or other mental health professional, the counselor, with student and/or parent/guardian consent, will inform the other professional and develop clear agreements to avoid confusion and conflict for the student.
d. Is knowledgeable about release of information and parental rights in sharing information.

D. RESPONSIBILITIES TO THE SCHOOL AND COMMUNITY

D.1. Responsibilities to the School

The professional school counselor:

a. Supports and protects the educational program against any infringement not in students' best interest.

b. Informs appropriate officials in accordance with school policy of conditions that may be potentially disruptive or damaging to the school's mission, personnel and property while honoring the confidentiality between the student and counselor.

c. Is knowledgeable and supportive of the school's mission and connects his/her program to the school's mission.

d. Delineates and promotes the counselor's role and function in meeting the needs of those served. Counselors will notify appropriate officials of conditions that may limit or curtail their effectiveness in providing programs and services.

e. Accepts employment only for positions for which he/she is qualified by education, training, supervised experience, state and national professional credentials and appropriate professional experience.

f. Advocates that administrators hire only qualified and competent individuals for professional counseling positions.

g. Assists in developing: (1) curricular and environmental conditions appropriate for the school and community, (2) educational procedures and programs to meet students' developmental needs and (3) a systematic evaluation process for comprehensive, developmental, standards-based school counseling programs, services and personnel. The counselor is guided by the findings of the evaluation data in planning programs and services.

D.2. Responsibility to the Community

The professional school counselor:

a. Collaborates with agencies, organizations and individuals in the community in the best interest of students and without regard to personal reward or remuneration.

b. Extends his/her influence and opportunity to deliver a comprehensive school counseling program to all students by collaborating with community resources for student success.

E. RESPONSIBILITIES TO SELF

E.1. Professional Competence

The professional school counselor:

a. Functions within the boundaries of individual professional competence and accepts responsibility for the consequences of his/her actions.

b. Monitors personal well-being and effectiveness and does not participate in any activity that may lead to inadequate professional services or harm to a student.

c. Strives through personal initiative to maintain professional competence including technological literacy and to keep abreast of professional information. Professional and personal growth are ongoing throughout the counselor's career.

E.2. Diversity

The professional school counselor:

a. Affirms the diversity of students, staff and families.

b. Expands and develops awareness of his/her own attitudes and beliefs affecting cultural values and biases and strives to attain cultural competence.

c. Possesses knowledge and understanding about how oppression, racism, discrimination and stereotyping affects her/him personally and professionally.

d. Acquires educational, consultation and training experiences to improve awareness, knowledge, skills and effectiveness in working with diverse populations: ethnic/racial status, age, economic status, special needs, ESL or ELL, immigration status, sexual orientation, gender, gender identity/expression, family type, religious/spiritual identity and appearance.

F. RESPONSIBILITIES TO THE PROFESSION

F.1. Professionalism

The professional school counselor:

a. Accepts the policies and procedures for handling ethical violations as a result of maintaining membership in the American School Counselor Association.

b. Conducts herself/himself in such a manner as to advance individual ethical practice and the profession.

c. Conducts appropriate research and report findings in a manner consistent with acceptable educational and psychological research practices. The counselor advocates for the protection of the individual student's identity when using data for research or program planning.

d. Adheres to ethical standards of the profession, other official policy statements, such as ASCA's position statements, role statement and the ASCA National Model, and relevant statutes established by federal, state and local governments, and when these are in conflict works responsibly for change.

e. Clearly distinguishes between statements and actions made as a private individual and those made as a representative of the school counseling profession.

f. Does not use his/her professional position to recruit or gain clients, consultees for his/her private practice or to seek and receive unjustified personal gains, unfair advantage, inappropriate relationships or unearned goods or services.

F.2. Contribution to the Profession

The professional school counselor:

a. Actively participates in local, state and national associations fostering the development and improvement of school counseling.

b. Contributes to the development of the profession through the sharing of skills, ideas and expertise with colleagues.

c. Provides support and mentoring to novice professionals.

G. MAINTENANCE OF STANDARDS

Ethical behavior among professional school counselors, association members and nonmembers, is expected at all times. When there exists serious doubt as to the ethical behavior of colleagues or if counselors are forced to work in situations or abide by policies that do not reflect the standards as outlined in these Ethical Standards for School Counselors, the counselor is obligated to take appropriate action to rectify the condition. The following procedure may serve as a guide:

1. The counselor should consult confidentially with a professional colleague to discuss the nature of a complaint to see if the professional colleague views the situation as an ethical violation.

2. When feasible, the counselor should directly approach the colleague whose behavior is in question to discuss the complaint and seek resolution.

3. If resolution is not forthcoming at the personal level, the counselor shall utilize the channels established within the school, school district, the state school counseling association and ASCA's Ethics Committee.

4. If the matter still remains unresolved, referral for review and appropriate action should be made to the Ethics Committees in the following sequence:
   • state school counselor association
   • American School Counselor Association

5. The ASCA Ethics Committee is responsible for:
   • educating and consulting with the membership regarding ethical standards
   • periodically reviewing and recommending changes in code
   • receiving and processing questions to clarify the application of such standards; Questions must be submitted in writing to the ASCA Ethics chair.
   • handling complaints of alleged violations of the ethical standards. At the national level, complaints should be submitted in writing to the ASCA Ethics Committee, c/o the Executive Director, American School Counselor Association, 1101 King St., Suite 625, Alexandria, VA 22314.

APPENDIX C

NATIONAL STANDARDS FOR SCHOOL COUNSELING PROGRAMS

OVERVIEW

The purpose of a counseling program in a school setting is to promote and enhance the learning process. To that end, the School Counseling Program facilitates Student Development in three broad areas: Academic Development, Career Development, and Personal/Social Development. The following chart describes the standards for each area.

I. Academic Development

Standard A: Students will acquire the attitudes, knowledge, and skills that contribute to effective learning in school and across the life span.

Standard B: Students will complete school with the academic preparation essential to choose from a wide range of substantial post-secondary options, including college.

Standard C: Students will understand the relationship of academics to the world of work, and to life at home and in the community.

II. Career Development

Standard A: Students will acquire the skills to investigate the world of work in relation to knowledge of self and to make informed career decisions.

Standard B: Students will employ strategies to achieve future career success and satisfaction.

Standard C: Students will understand the relationship between personal qualities, education and training, and the world of work.

III. Personal/Social Development

Standard A: Students will acquire the attitudes, knowledge, and interpersonal skills to help them understand and respect self and others.

Standard B: Students will make decisions, set goals, and take necessary action to achieve goals.

Standard C: Students will understand safety and survival skills.

The standards for each content area are intended to provide guidance and direction for states, school systems, and individual schools to develop quality and effective school counseling programs. The emphasis is on success for *all students,* not only those students who are motivated, supported, and ready to learn. The school counseling program based upon national standards enables *all students* to achieve success in school and to develop into contributing members of our society.

Source: Standards from the National Standards for School Counseling Programs by the American School Counselor Association, 1997, Alexandria, VA: American School Counselor Association. © 1998 American School Counselor Association.

420

School success requires that students make successful transitions from elementary school to middle/junior high school to high school. Graduates from high school have acquired the attitudes, skills, and knowledge that are essential to the competitive workplace of the 21st century.

A school counseling program based upon national standards provides the elements for all students to achieve success in school. School counselors continuously assess their students' needs to identify barriers and obstacles that may be hindering success and also advocate for programmatic efforts to eliminate these barriers.

Each standard is followed by a list of student competencies which articulate desired student learning outcomes. Student competencies define the specific knowledge, attitudes, and skills that students should obtain or demonstrate as a result of participating in a school counseling program. These listings are not meant to be all inclusive, nor is any individual program expected to include all of the competencies in the school counseling program. The competencies offer a foundation for what a standards-based program should address and deliver. These can be used as a basis to develop measurable indicators of student performance.

The program standards for academic development guide the school counseling program to implement strategies and activities to support and maximize each student's ability to learn. Academic development includes acquiring skills, attitudes, and knowledge which contribute to effective learning in school and across the life span; employing strategies to achieve success in school; and understanding the relationship of academics to the world of work, and to life at home and in the community. Academic development standards and competencies support the premise that all students meet or exceed the local, state, and national academic standards.

The purpose of a counseling program in a school setting is to promote and enhance the learning process.

The program standards for career development guide the school counseling

program to provide the foundation for the acquisition of skills, attitudes, and knowledge that enable students to make a successful transition from school to the world of work, and from job to job across the life span. Career development includes the employment of strategies to achieve future career success and job satisfaction as well as fostering understanding of the relationship between personal qualities, education and training, and the world of work. Career development standards and competencies ensure that students develop career goals as a result of participation in a comprehensive plan of career awareness, exploration, and preparation activities.

The program standards for personal/social development guide the school counseling program to provide the foundation for personal and social growth as students progress through school and into adulthood. Personal/social development contributes to academic and career success. Personal/social development includes the acquisition of skills, attitudes, and knowledge which help students understand and respect self and others, acquire effective interpersonal skills, understand safety and survival skills, and develop into contributing members of our society. Personal/social development standards and competencies ensure that students have learned to successfully and safely negotiate their way in the increasingly complex and diverse world of the 21st century.

NATIONAL STANDARDS FOR SCHOOL COUNSELING PROGRAMS

I. Academic Development

Standards in this area guide the school counseling program to implement strategies and activities to support and enable the student to experience academic success, maximize learning through commitment, produce high-quality work, and be prepared for a full range of options and opportunities after high school.

The academic development area includes the acquisition of skills in decision making, problem solving and goal setting, critical thinking, logical reasoning, and interpersonal communication and the application of these skills to academic achievement.

The school counseling program enables all students to achieve success in school and to develop into contributing members of our society.

Standard A: Students will acquire the attitudes, knowledge, and skills that contribute to effective learning in school and across the life span.

Standard B: Students will complete school with the academic preparation essential to choose from a wide range of substantial post-secondary options, including college.

Standard C: Students will understand the relationship of academics to the world of work, and to life at home and in the community.

Academic Development: Standard A

Students will acquire the attitudes, knowledge, and skills that contribute to effective learning in school and across the life span.

Student Competencies

Improve Academic Self-Concept
Students will:
- articulate feelings of competence and confidence as a learner
- display a positive interest in learning
- take pride in work and in achievement
- accept mistakes as essential to the learning process
- identify attitudes and behaviors which lead to successful learning

Acquire Skills for Improving Learning
Students will:
- apply time management and task management skills
- demonstrate how effort and persistence positively affect learning

- use communication skills to know when and how to ask for help when needed
- apply knowledge of learning styles to positively influence school performance

Achieve School Success
Students will:
- take responsibility for their actions
- demonstrate the ability to work independently, as well as the ability to work cooperatively with other students
- develop a broad range of interests and abilities
- demonstrate dependability, productivity, and initiative
- share knowledge

Academic Development: Standard B

Students will complete school with the academic preparation essential to choose from a wide range of substantial post-secondary options, including college.

Student Competencies

Improve Learning
Students will:
- demonstrate the motivation to achieve individual potential
- learn and apply critical thinking skills
- apply the study skills necessary for academic success at each level
- seek information and support from faculty, staff, family, and peers
- organize and apply academic information from a variety of sources
- use knowledge of learning styles to positively influence school performance
- become self-directed and independent learners

Plan to Achieve Goals
Students will:
- establish challenging academic goals in elementary, middle/junior high, and high school
- use assessment results in educational planning
- develop and implement an annual plan of study to maximize academic ability and achievement
- apply knowledge of aptitudes and interests to goal setting

- use problem-solving and decision-making skills to assess progress toward educational goals
- understand the relationship between classroom performance and success in school
- identify post-secondary options consistent with interests, achievement, aptitude, and abilities

---

Academic Development: Standard C

Students will understand the relationship of academics to the world of work, and to life at home and in the community.

Student Competencies

Relate School to Life Experiences
Students will:

- demonstrate the ability to balance school, studies, extracurricular activities, leisure time, and family life
- seek co-curricular and community experiences to enhance the school experience
- understand the relationship between learning and work
- demonstrate an understanding of the value of lifelong learning as essential to seeking, obtaining, and maintaining life goals
- understand that school success is the preparation to make the transition from student to community member
- understand how school success and academic achievement enhance future career and avocational opportunities

II. Career Development

Standards in this area guide the school counseling program to implement strategies and activities to support and enable the student to develop a positive attitude toward work, and to develop the necessary skills to make a successful transition from school to the world of work, and from job to job across the life career span. Also, standards in this area help students to understand the relationship between success in school and future success in the world of work. The career development standards reflect the recommendations of the Secretary's Commission on Achieving Necessary Skills (SCANS, 1991) and the content of the *National Career Development Guidelines* (*NOICC*, 1989).

The school counseling program enables all students to achieve success in school and to develop into contributing members of our society.

Standard A: Students will acquire the skills to investigate the world of work in relation to knowledge of self and to make informed career decisions.
Standard B: Students will employ strategies to achieve future career goals with success and satisfaction.
Standard C: Students will understand the relationship between personal qualities, education, training, and the world of work.

Career Development: Standard A

Students will acquire the skills to investigate the world of work in relation to knowledge of self and to make informed career decisions.

Student Competencies

Develop Career Awareness
Students will:

- develop skills to locate, evaluate, and interpret career information
- learn about the variety of traditional and non-traditional occupations
- develop an awareness of personal abilities, skills, interests, and motivations
- learn how to interact and work cooperatively in teams
- learn to make decisions
- learn how to set goals
- understand the importance of planning
- pursue and develop competency in areas of interest
- develop hobbies and avocational interests balance between work and leisure time

Develop Employment Readiness
Students will:
- acquire employability skills such as working on a team, problem-solving, and organizational skills
- apply job readiness skills to seek employment opportunities
- demonstrate knowledge about the changing workplace
- learn about the rights and responsibilities of employers and employees
- learn to respect individual uniqueness in the workplace
- learn how to write a resume
- develop a positive attitude toward work and learning
- understand the importance of responsibility, dependability, punctuality, integrity, and effort in the workplace
- utilize time- and task-management skills

Career Development: Standard B

Students will employ strategies to achieve future career goals with success and satisfaction.

Student Competencies

Acquire Career Information
Students will:
- apply decision-making skills to career planning, course selection, and career transitions
- identify personal skills, interests, and abilities and relate them to current career choices
- demonstrate knowledge of the career planning process
- know the various ways which occupations can be classified
- use research and information resources to obtain career information
- learn to use the Internet to access career planning information
- describe traditional and non-traditional occupations and how these relate to career choice
- understand how changing economic and societal needs influence employment trends and future training

Identify Career Goals
Students will:
- demonstrate awareness of the education and training needed to achieve career goals
- assess and modify their educational plan to support career goals
- use employability and job readiness skills in internship, mentoring, shadowing, and/or other world of work experiences
- select course work that is related to career interests
- maintain a career planning portfolio

Career Development: Standard C

Students will understand the relationship between personal qualities, education, training, and the world of work.

Student Competencies

Acquire Knowledge to Achieve Career Goals
Students will:
- understand the relationship between educational achievement and career success
- explain how work can help to achieve personal success and satisfaction
- identify personal preferences and interests which influence career choices and success
- understand that the changing workplace requires lifelong learning and acquiring new skills
- describe the effect of work on lifestyles
- understand the importance of equity and access in career choice
- understand that work is an important and satisfying means of personal expression

Apply Skills to Achieve Career Goals
Students will:
- demonstrate how interests, abilities, and achievement relate to achieving personal, social, educational, and career goals
- learn how to use conflict management skills with peers and adults
- learn to work cooperatively with others as a team member

- apply academic and employment readiness skills in work-based learning situations such as internships, shadowing, and/or mentoring experiences

III. Personal/Social Development

Standards in the personal/social area guide the school counseling program to implement strategies and activities to support and maximize each student's personal growth and enhance the educational and career development of the student.

The school counseling program enables all students to achieve success in school and develop into contributing members of our society.

Standard A: Students will acquire the knowledge, attitudes, and interpersonal skills to help them understand and respect self and others.

Standard B: Students will make decisions, set goals, and take necessary action to achieve goals.

Standard C: Students will understand safety and survival skills.

Personal/Social Development: Standard A

Students will acquire the knowledge, attitudes, and interpersonal skills to help them understand and respect self and others.

Student Competencies

Acquire Self-Knowledge
Students will:

- develop a positive attitude toward self as a unique and worthy person
- identify values, attitudes, and beliefs
- learn the goal-setting process
- understand change as a part of growth
- identify and express feelings
- distinguish between appropriate and inappropriate behaviors
- recognize personal boundaries, rights, and privacy needs
- understand the need for self-control and how to practice it

- demonstrate cooperative behavior in groups
- identify personal strengths and assets
- identify and discuss changing personal and social roles
- identify and recognize changing family roles

Acquire Interpersonal Skills
Students will:

- recognize that everyone has rights and responsibilities
- respect alternative points of view
- recognize, accept, respect, and appreciate individual differences
- recognize, accept, and appreciate ethnic and cultural diversity
- recognize and respect differences in various family configurations
- use effective communication skills
- know that communication involves speaking, listening, and nonverbal behavior
- learn how to make and keep friends

Personal/Social Development: Standard B

Students will make decisions, set goals, and take necessary action to achieve goals.

Students Competencies

Self-Knowledge Applications
Students will:

- use a decision-making and problem-solving model
- understand consequences of decisions and choices
- identify alternative solutions to a problem
- develop effective coping skills for dealing with problems
- demonstrate when, where, and how to seek help for solving problems and making decisions
- know how to apply conflict resolution skills
- demonstrate a respect and appreciation for individual and cultural differences
- know when peer pressure is influencing a decision
- identify long- and short-term goals
- identify alternative ways of achieving goals

- use persistence and perseverance in acquiring knowledge and skills
- develop an action plan to set and achieve realistic goals

Personal/Social Development: Standard C

Students will understand safety and survival skills.

Student Competencies

Acquire Personal Safety Skills
Students will:
- demonstrate knowledge of personal information (i.e., telephone number, home address, emergency contact)
- learn about the relationship between rules, laws, safety, and the protection of an individual's rights
- learn the difference between appropriate and inappropriate physical contact
- demonstrate the ability to assert boundaries, rights, and personal privacy
- differentiate between situations requiring peer support and situations requiring adult professional help
- identify resource people in the school and community, and know how to seek their help
- apply effective problem-solving and decision-making skills to make safe and healthy choices
- learn about the emotional and physical dangers of substance use and abuse
- learn how to cope with peer pressure
- learn techniques for managing stress and conflict
- learn coping skills for managing life events

ASCA/AACE COMPETENCIES IN ASSESSMENT AND EVALUATION FOR SCHOOL COUNSELORS

Approved by the American School Counselor Association on September 21, 1998, and by the Association for Assessment in Counseling on September 10, 1998.*

The purpose of these competencies is to provide a description of the knowledge and skills that school counselors need in the areas of assessment and evaluation. Because effectiveness in assessment and evaluation is critical to effective counseling, these competencies are important for school counselor education and practice. Although consistent with existing Council for Accreditation of Counseling and Related Educational Programs (CACREP) and National Association of State Directors of Teacher Education and Certification (NAS-DTEC) standards for preparing counselors, they focus on competencies of individual counselors rather than content of counselor education programs.

The competencies can be used by counselor and assessment educators as a guide in the development and evaluation of school counselor preparation programs, workshops, inservice, and other continuing education opportunities. They may also be used by school counselors to evaluate their own professional development and continuing education needs.

School counselors should meet each of the nine numbered competencies and have the specific skills listed under each competency.

COMPETENCY 1. SCHOOL COUNSELORS ARE SKILLED IN CHOOSING ASSESSMENT STRATEGIES

a. They can describe the nature and use of different types of formal and informal assessments, including questionnaires, checklists, interviews, inventories, tests, observations, surveys, and performance assessments, and work with individuals skilled in clinical assessment.

b. They can specify the types of information most readily obtained from different assessment approaches.

---

*A joint committee of the American School Counselor Association (ASCA) and the Association for Assessment in Counseling (AAC) was appointed by the respective presidents in 1993 with the charge to draft a statement about school counselor preparation in assessment and evaluation. Committee members were Ruth Ekstrom (AAC), Patricia Elmore (AAC, Chair, 1997–1999), Daren Hutchinson (ASCA), Marjorie Mastie (AAC), Kathy O'Rourke (ASCA), William Schafer (AAC, Chair, 1993–1997), Thomas Trotter (ASCA), and Barbara Webster (ASCA).

c. They are familiar with resources for critically evaluating each type of assessment and can use them in choosing appropriate assessment strategies.

d. They are able to advise and assist others (e.g., a school district) in choosing appropriate assessment strategies.

COMPETENCY 2. SCHOOL COUNSELORS CAN IDENTIFY, ACCESS, AND EVALUATE THE MOST COMMONLY USED ASSESSMENT INSTRUMENTS

a. They know which assessment instruments are most commonly used in school settings to assess intelligence, aptitude, achievement, personality, work values, and interests, including computer-assisted versions and other alternate formats.

b. They know the dimensions along which assessment instruments should be evaluated, including purpose, validity, utility, norms, reliability and measurement error, score reporting method, and consequences of use.

c. They can obtain and evaluate information about the quality of those assessment instruments.

COMPETENCY 3. SCHOOL COUNSELORS ARE SKILLED IN THE TECHNIQUES OF ADMINISTRATION AND METHODS OF SCORING ASSESSMENT INSTRUMENTS

a. They can implement appropriate administration procedures, including administration using computers.

b. They can standardize administration of assessments when interpretation is in relation to external norms.

c. They can modify administration of assessments to accommodate individual differences consistent with publisher recommendations and current statements of professional practice.

d. They can provide consultation, information, and training to others who assist with administration and scoring.

e. They know when it is necessary to obtain informed consent from parents or guardians before administering an assessment.

COMPETENCY 4. SCHOOL COUNSELORS ARE SKILLED IN INTERPRETING AND REPORTING ASSESSMENT RESULTS

a. They can explain scores that are commonly reported, such as percentile ranks, standard scores, and grade equivalents. They can interpret a confidence interval for an individual score based on a standard error of measurement.

b. They can evaluate the appropriateness of a norm group when interpreting the scores of an individual or a group.

c. They are skilled in communicating assessment information to others, including teachers, administrators, students, parents, and the community. They are aware of the rights students and parents have to know assessment results and decisions made as a consequence of any assessment.

d. They can evaluate their own strengths and limitations in the use of assessment instruments and in assessing students with disabilities or linguistic or cultural differences. They know how to identify professionals with appropriate training and experience for consultation.

e. They know the legal and ethical principles about confidentiality and disclosure of assessment information and recognize the need to abide by district policy on retention and use of assessment information.

COMPETENCY 5. SCHOOL COUNSELORS ARE SKILLED IN USING ASSESSMENT RESULTS IN DECISION-MAKING

a. They recognize the limitations of using a single score in making an educational decision and know how to obtain multiple sources of information to improve such decisions.

b. They can evaluate their own expertise for making decisions based on assessment results. They also can evaluate the limitations of conclusions provided by others, including the reliability and validity of computer-assisted assessment interpretations.

c. They can evaluate whether the available evidence is adequate to support the intended use of an assessment result for decision-making, particularly when that use has not been recommended by the developer of the assessment instrument.

d. They can evaluate the rationale underlying the use of qualifying scores for placement in educational programs or courses of study.

e. They can evaluate the consequences of assessment-related decisions and avoid actions that would have unintended negative consequences.

COMPETENCY 6. SCHOOL COUNSELORS ARE SKILLED IN PRODUCING, INTERPRETING, AND PRESENTING STATISTICAL INFORMATION ABOUT ASSESSMENT RESULTS

a. They can describe data (e.g., test scores, grades, demographic information) by forming frequency distributions, preparing tables, drawing graphs, and calculating descriptive indices of central tendency, variability, and relationship.

b. They can compare a score from an assessment instrument with an existing distribution, describe the placement of a score within a normal distribution, and draw appropriate inferences.

c. They can interpret statistics used to describe characteristics of assessment instruments, including difficulty and discrimination indices, reliability and validity coefficients, and standard errors of measurement.

d. They can identify and interpret inferential statistics when comparing groups, making predictions, and drawing conclusions needed for educational planning and decisions.

e. They can use computers for data management, statistical analysis, and production of tables and graphs for reporting and interpreting results.

COMPETENCY 7. SCHOOL COUNSELORS ARE SKILLED IN CONDUCTING AND INTERPRETING EVALUATIONS OF SCHOOL COUNSELING PROGRAMS AND COUNSELING-RELATED INTERVENTIONS

a. They understand and appreciate the role that evaluation plays in the program development process throughout the life of a program.

b. They can describe the purposes of an evaluation and the types of decisions to be based on evaluation information.

c. They can evaluate the degree to which information can justify conclusions and decisions about a program.

d. They can evaluate the extent to which student outcome measures match program goals.

e. They can identify and evaluate possibilities for unintended outcomes and possible impacts of one program on other programs.

f. They can recognize potential conflicts of interest and other factors that may bias the results of evaluations.

COMPETENCY 8. SCHOOL COUNSELORS ARE SKILLED IN ADAPTING AND USING QUESTIONNAIRES, SURVEYS, AND OTHER ASSESSMENTS TO MEET LOCAL NEEDS

a. They can write specifications and questions for local assessments.

b. They can assemble an assessment into a usable format and provide directions for its use.

c. They can design and implement scoring processes and procedures for information feedback.

COMPETENCY 9. SCHOOL COUNSELORS KNOW HOW TO ENGAGE IN PROFESSIONALLY RESPONSIBLE ASSESSMENT AND EVALUATION PRACTICES

a. They understand how to act in accordance with ACA's *Code of Ethics and Standards of Practice* and ASCA's *Ethical Standards for School Counselors.*

b. They can use professional codes and standards, including the *Code of Fair Testing Practices in Education, Code of Professional Responsibilities in Educational Measurement, Responsibilities of Users of Standardized Tests,* and *Standards for Educational and Psychological Testing,* to evaluate counseling practices using assessments.

c. They understand test fairness and can avoid the selection of biased assessment instruments and biased uses of assessment instruments. They can evaluate the potential for unfairness when tests are used incorrectly and for possible bias in the interpretation of assessment results.

d. They understand the legal and ethical principles and practices regarding test security, copying copyrighted materials, and unsupervised use of assessment instruments that are not intended for self-administration.

e. They can obtain and maintain available credentialing that demonstrates their skills in assessment and evaluation.

f. They know how to identify and participate in educational and training opportunities to maintain competence and acquire new skills in assessment and evaluation.

DEFINITIONS OF TERMS

Competencies describe skills or understandings that a school counselor should possess to perform assessment and evaluation activities effectively.

Assessment is the gathering of information for decision making about individuals, groups, programs, or processes. Assessment targets include abilities, achievements, personality variables, aptitudes, attitudes, preferences, interests, values, demographics, and other characteristics. Assessment procedures include but are not limited to standardized and unstandardized tests, questionnaires, inventories, checklists, observations, portfolios, performance assessments, rating scales, surveys, interviews, and other clinical measures.

Evaluation is the collection and interpretation of information to make judgments about individuals, programs, or processes that lead to decisions and future actions.

REFERENCES

Abrams, K., Theberge, S. K., & Karan, O. C. (2005). Children and adolescents who are depressed: An ecological approach. *Professional School Counseling, 8,* 284–292.

Achenbach, T. M., & Rescorla, L. A. (2001). *Manual for the Achenbach System of Empirically Based Assessment (ASEBA)*. Burlington: University of Vermont, Research Center for Children, Youth, and Families.

Ad Council. (2000). *The real deal*. New York: Author.

Adams, M., Bell, L. A., & Griffin, P. (Eds.) (1997). *Teaching for diversity and social justice: A sourcebook*. New York: Routledge.

Agnew, C. M., Nystul, M., & Conner, M. C. (1998). Seizure disorders: An alternative explanation for students' inattention. *Professional School Counseling, 2,* 54–59.

Agras, W. S. (1987). *Eating disorders*. New York: Pergamon.

Akos, P., Goodnough, G. E., & Milsom, A. S. (2004). Preparing school counselors for group work. *Journal for Specialists in Group Work, 29,* 127–136.

Akos, P., & Martin, M. (2003). Transition groups for preparing students for middle school. *Journal for Specialists in Group Work, 28,* 139–154.

Albert, L. (1996). *Cooperative discipline*. Circle Pines, MN: American Guidance Service.

Allen, J. M. (1994). *School counselors collaborating for student success* (Report No. EDO-CG-94-27). Greensboro, NC: ERIC Clearinghouse on Counseling and Student Services. (ERIC Document Reproduction Service No. ED377414)

Allen, M., Burt, K., Bryan, E., Carter, D., Orsi, R., & Durkan, L. (2002). School counselors' preparation for and participation in crisis intervention. *Professional School Counseling, 6,* 96–101.

Amatea, E. S., Daniel, H., Bringman, N., & Vandiver, F. M. (2004). Strengthening counselor-teacher-family connections: The family-school collaborative consultation project. *Professional School Counseling, 8,* 47–55.

Amato, P. R. (1993). Children's adjustment of divorce: Theories, hypotheses, and empirical support. *Journal of Marriage and Family, 55,* 23–38.

Amato, P. R. (1994). Life-span adjustment of children to their parents' divorce. *Future of Children: Children and Divorce, 4,* 143–164.

Amato, P. R. (2000). The consequences of divorce for adults and children. *Journal of Marriage and the Family, 62,* 1269–1287.

Amato, P. R., & Gilbreth, J. G. (1999). Non-resident fathers and children's well-being: A meta-analysis. *Journal of Marriage and the Family, 61,* 557–573.

American Counseling Association. (1995). *Code of ethics and standards of practice*. Alexandria, VA: Author.

American Counseling Association. (1997, May 31). *Know your rights: Mental health, private practice and the law*. ACA national videoconference. Alexandria, VA: Author.

American Counseling Association. (2000a, January). $20 million set aside for school counseling. *Counseling Today, 42*(7), 1, 19.

American Counseling Association. (2000b). *Public awareness ideas and strategies for professional counselors*. Alexandria, VA: Author.

American Counseling Association. (2005a). *Code of ethics*. Alexandria, VA: Author.

American Counseling Association (2005b). *Position statement on high stakes testing*. Alexandria, VA: Author.

American Psychiatric Association. (2000). *Diagnostic and statistical manual of mental disorders* (Text rev.). Washington, DC: Author.

American Psychological Association. (2004). *Report on the Task Force on Psychology's Agenda for Child and Adolescent Mental Health,* 1–15. Washington, DC: Author.

American School Counselor Association. (1993). *The American School Counselor Association position statements*. Alexandria, VA: Author.

American School Counselor Association. (1999a). *Role statement*. Retrieved July 1, 2002, from www.schoolcounselor.org/role.htm

American School Counselor Association. (1999b). *Position statements*. Retrieved July 1, 2002, from www.schoolcounselor.org/pubs/position.htm

American School Counselor Association. (1999c). *The professional school counselor and comprehensive school counseling programs*. Retrieved July 1, 2002, from www.schoolcounselor.org/pubs/position.htm

American School Counselor Association. (2000). *Position statement: Critical incident response in schools*. Retrieved May 18, 2005, from www.schoolcounselor.org

American School Counselor Association. (2003a). *The ASCA national model: A framework for school counseling programs*. Alexandria, VA: Author.

American School Counselor Association. (2003b). The ASCA national model: A framework for school counseling programs. *Professional School Counseling, 6,* 165–168.

American School Counselor Association (2004a). *Ethical standards for school counselors*. Alexandria, VA: Author.

American School Counselor Association. (2004b). *Position statement: The professional school counselor and students with special needs*. Retrieved August 20, 2005, from www.schoolcounselor.org/ content.asp?contentid=218

American School Counselor Association. (2005a). *ASCA mission*. Retrieved August 10, 2005, from www.schoolcounselor.org

American School Counselor Association. (2005b). *State certification requirements*. Retrieved May 24, 2005, from www.schoolcounselor.org/ content.asp?contentid=242

Anastopoulos, A. D., Shelton, T., DuPaul, G. J., & Guevremont, D. C. (1993). Parent training for attention-deficit hyperactivity disorder: Its impact on parent functioning. *Journal of Abnormal Child Psychology, 21,* 581–596.

Anderson, B. (1988). Cognitive styles and multicultural populations. *Journal of Teacher Education, 39,* 2–9.

Anderson, B. S. (1996). *The counselor and the law* (4th ed.). Alexandria, VA: American Counseling Association.

Angaran, S., & Beckwith, K. (1999). Elementary school peer mediation. *The Education Digest, 65*(1), 23–25.

Aponte, J. F., & Crouch, R. T. (2000). The changing ethnic profile of the United States in the twenty-first century. In J. F. Aponte & J. Wohl (Eds.),

Psychological interventions and cultural diversity (2nd ed.) (pp. 1–19). Needham Heights, MA: Allyn & Bacon.

Applequist, K. L., & Bailey, D. B. (2000). Navajo caregivers' perceptions of early intervention services. *Journal of Early Intervention Services, 23,* 47–61.

Arman, J. F. (2000). In the wake of tragedy at Columbine High School. *Professional School Counseling, 2,* 218–220.

Arman, J. F., & McNair, R. (2000). A small group model for working with elementary school children of alcoholics. *Professional School Counseling, 3,* 290–293.

Armstrong, T. (1994). *Multiple intelligences in the classroom*. Alexandria, VA: Association for Supervision and Curriculum Development.

Arnett, J., & Balle-Jansen, L. (1993). Cultural bases of risk behavior: Danish adolescents. *Child Development, 64,* 1842–1855.

Arnold, M. S., Chen–Hayes, S. F., & Lewis, J. (2002, June). *Unlearning oppression: Learning skills to challenge the barriers of racism, classism, and other "-isms."* Paper presented at the Education Trust Summer School Counseling Academy, Chicago, IL.

Aronson, J. (1996). How schools can recruit hard-to-reach parents. *Education Leadership, 53*(7), 58–61.

Arredondo, D. E., & Butler, F. S. (1994). Affective comorbidity in psychiatrically hospitalized adolescents with Conduct Disorder or Oppositional Defiant Disorder: Should Conduct Disorder be treated with mood stabilizer? *Journal of Child and Adolescent Psychopharmacology, 4,* 151–158.

Arredondo, P., & D'Andrea, M. (1995, September). AMCD approves multicultural counseling competency standards. *Counseling Today,* 28–32.

Arredondo, P., & Locke, D. C. (1999, August). *Counselors academy*. Athens: University of Georgia Press.

Arredondo, P., Toporek, R., Brown, S., Jones, J., Locke, D. C., Sanchez, J., et al. (1996). *Operationalization of the multicultural counseling competencies*. Alexandria, VA: Association for Multicultural Counseling and Development.

Asarnow, J. R., Tompson, M. C., & McGrath, E. P. (2004). Annotation: Childhood-onset schizophrenia: Clinical and treatment issues. *Journal of Child Psychology and Psychiatry, 45,* 180–194.

Association for Assessment in Counseling and Education (AACE). (2004). Responsibilities of users of standardized tests (RUST) (3rd ed.). Alexandria, VA: Author.

Association for Specialists in Group Work. (1999). ASGW principles for diversity-competent group workers. *Journal for Specialists in Group Work, 24,* 7–14.

Association for Specialists in Group Work. (2000). Association for Specialists in Group Work: Professional standards for the training of group workers. *Journal for Specialists in Group Work, 25,* 327–342.

Atkins, M. S., McKay, M., Arvanitis, P., London, L., Madison, S., Costigan, C., et al. (1998). An ecological model for school-based mental health services for urban low-income aggressive children. *Journal of Behavioral Health Services Research, 5,* 64–75.

Atkinson, D. A., & Juntunen, C. L. (1994). School counselors and school psychologists as school-home-community liaisons in ethnically diverse schools. In P. Pedersen & J. C. Carey (Eds.), *Multicultural counseling in schools: A practical handbook* (pp. 103–119). Needham Heights, MA: Allyn & Bacon.

Atkinson, D. R., Furlong, M., & Janoff, D. S. (1979). A four-component model for proactive accountability in school counseling. *The School Counselor, 26,* 222–228.

Atkinson, D. R., & Lowe, S. M. (1995). The role of ethnicity, culture, knowledge, and conventional techniques in counseling and psychotherapy. In J. C. Ponterotto, J. M. Casas, L. A. Sazuki, & C. M. Alexander (Eds.), *Handbook of multicultural counseling* (pp. 387–414). Newbury Park, CA: Sage.

Aubrey, R. F. (1977). Historical development of guidance and counseling and implications for the future. *Personnel and Guidance Journal, 55,* 288–295.

Auger, R. W., Seymour, J. W., & Roberts, W. B., Jr. (2004). Responding to terror: The impact of September 11 on K–12 schools and schools' responses. *Professional School Counseling, 7,* 222–230.

Azrin, N. H., & Peterson, A. L. (1990). Treatment of Tourette's syndrome by habit reversal: A waiting-list control group comparison. *Behavior Therapy, 21,* 305–318.

Baba, M. L., & Darga, L. L. (1981). The genetic myth of racial classification. In M. S. Collins, I. W. Wainer, & T. A. Bremmer (Eds.), *Science and the question of human equality* (pp. 1–19). Boulder, CO: Westview Press.

Bachay, J. B., & Rigby, E. (1997). Welcome to our school community: A career development intervention for the newcomer. *Professional School Counseling, 1* (2), 13–14.

Bagenholm, A., & Gillberg, C. (1991). Psychosocial effects on siblings of children with autism and mental retardation: A population-based study. *Journal of Mental Deficiency Research, 35,* 291–307.

Baggerly, J., & Borkowski, T. (2004). Applying the ASCA National Model to elementary school students who are homeless: A case study. *Professional School Counseling, 8,* 116–123.

Bailey, D. F., & Bradbury-Bailey, M. (2004). Respecting differences: Racial and ethnic groups. In R. Perusse & G. E. Goodnough (Eds.), *Leadership, advocacy, and direct service strategies for professional school counselors* (pp. 157–186). Belmont, CA: Brooks/Cole-Thomson Learning.

Baker, B. L., & Feinfield, K. A. (2003). Early intervention. *Current Opinion in Psychiatry, 16* (5), 503–509.

Baker, S. B. (1994). Mandatory teaching experience for school counselors: An impediment to uniform certification standards for school counselors. *Counselor Education and Supervision, 33,* 314–326.

Baker, S. B. (2000). *School counseling for the twenty-first century* (3rd ed.). Upper Saddle River, NJ: Prentice Hall.

Baker, S. B., Swisher, J. D., Nadenichek, P. E., & Popowicz, C. L. (1984). Measured effects of primary prevention strategies. *Personnel and Guidance Journal, 62,* 459–464.

Baker, S. B., & Taylor, J. G. (1998). Effects of career education interventions: A meta-analysis. *Career Development Quarterly, 46,* 376–385.

Bardick, A. D., Bernes, K. B., McCulloch, A.R.M., Witko, K.D., Spriddle, J. W., & Roest, A. R. (2004). Eating disorder intervention, prevention, and treatment: Recommendations for school counselors. *Professional School Counseling, 8,* 168–175.

Barker, J., & Satcher, J. (2000). School counselors' perceptions of required workplace skills and career development competencies. *Professional School Counseling, 4,* 134–139.

Barkley, R. A. (1996). Attention deficit hyperactivity disorder. In E. J. Mash & R. A. Barkley (Eds.), *Child psychopathology* (pp. 63–112). New York: Guilford Press.

Barnes, P. E., Friehe, M. J. M., & Radd, T. R. (2003). Collaboration between speech-language pathologists and school counselors. *Communication Disorders Quarterly, 24*(3), 137–142.

Barry, B., & Wright, S. (1996). *The real game series* (Vols. 1–6). New Brunswick, Canada: Real Game International.

Baruth, L. G., & Robinson, E. H. (1987). *An introduction to the counseling profession.* Englewood Cliffs, NJ: Prentice Hall.

Bauer, S. R., Sapp, M., & Johnson, D. (2000). Group counseling strategies for rural at-risk high school students. *The High School Journal, 83,* 41–50.

Baumeister, A. A., & Baumeister, A. A. (2000). Mental retardation: Causes and effects. In M. Hersen & R. T. Ammerman (Eds.), *Advanced abnormal child psychology* (2nd ed.). Mahwah, NJ: Lawrence Erlbaum Associates.

Bauserman, R. (2002). Child adjustment in joint-custody versus sole-custody arrangements: A meta-analytic review. *Journal of Family Psychology, 16,* 91–102.

Beale, A. V., & Scott, P. C. (2001). "Bullybusters": Using drama to empower students to take a stand against bullying behavior. *Professional School Counseling, 4,* 300–305.

Beck, A. T., & Steer, R. A. (1991). *Beck Scale for Suicide Ideation (BSSI) manual.* San Antonio, TX: Psychological Corporation.

Beck, A. T., & Steer, R. A. (1993). *Beck Hopelessness Scale (BHS) manual.* San Antonio, TX: Psychological Corporation.

Beck, A. T., & Weishaar, M. E. (2000). Cognitive therapy. In R. J. Corsini & D. Wedding (Eds.), *Current psychotherapies* (6th ed., pp. 241–272). Itasca, IL: F. E. Peacock.

Bellack, A., & Mueser, K. T. (1993). Psychosocial treatment for schizophrenia. *Schizophrenia Bulletin, 19,* 317–336.

Bemak, F. (1997). Keeping the faith while counseling at-risk populations. In J. Kottler (Ed.), *Finding your way as a counselor* (pp. 75–81). Alexandria, VA: American Counseling Association.

Bemak, F. (1998). Interdisciplinary collaboration for social change: Redefining the counseling profession. In C. C. Lee & G. R. Walz (Eds.), *Social action: A mandate for counselors* (pp. 279–292). Alexandria, VA: American Counseling Association & ERIC/CASS.

Bemak, F. (2000). Transforming the role of the counselor to provide leadership in educational reform through collaboration. *Professional School Counseling, 3,* 323–331.

Bemak, F., & Chung, R. C. (2002). Multicultural counseling with immigrant students in schools. In P. B. Pedersen & J. Carey (Eds.), *Multicultural counseling in schools.* Needham Heights, MA: Allyn & Bacon.

Bemak, F., & Chung, R. C. (2004). Teaching multicultural group counseling: Perspectives for a new era. *Journal for Specialists in Group Work, 29,* 31–42.

Bemak, F., & Keys, S. (2000). *Violent and aggressive youth: Intervention and prevention strategies for changing times.* Thousand Oaks, CA: Corwin Press.

Bemak, F., Murphy, S., & Kaffenberger, C. (2005). Community-focused consultation: New directions and practice. In C. Sink (Ed.), *Contemporary school counseling: Theory, research and practice* (pp. 206–228). Boston: Houghton Mifflin.

Bennett, K. J., Brown, K. S., Boyle, M., Racine, Y., & Offord, D. (2003). Does low reading achievement at school entry cause conduct problems? *Social Science & Medicine, 56,* 2443–2448.

Benson, F. (2004). *Empowering teachers with best instructional practices.* New York: New Millenium.

Berg, I. K., & Miller, S. (1992). *Working with the problem drinker.* New York: Norton.

Berg, I. K., & Steiner, T. (2003). *Children's solution work.* New York: Norton.

Bergan, J. (1977). *Behavioral consultation.* Columbus, OH: Charles E. Merrill.

Bergan, J., & Kratochwill, T. (1990). *Behavioral consultation and therapy.* New York: Plenum Press.

Berger, E. H. (2000). Parents as partners in education. Upper Saddle River, NJ: Merrill.

Bergin, J. J. (1999). Small-group counseling. In A. Vernon (Ed.), *Counseling children and adolescents* (2nd ed., pp. 299–332). Denver, CO: Love.

Bergin, J. J. (2004). Small-group counseling. In A. Vernon (Ed.), *Counseling children and adolescents* (3rd ed., pp. 355–390). Denver, CO: Love.

Berk, L. E. (2001). *Development through the lifespan* (2nd ed.). Needham Heights, MA: Allyn & Bacon.

Biederman, J., Petty, C., Faraone, S. V., & Seidman, L. (2004). Phenomenology of childhood psychosis: Findings from a large sample of psychiatrically referred youth. *Journal of Nervous and Mental Disease, 192,* 607–613.

Bierman, K. L., Coie, H. D., Dodge, K. A., Greenberg, M. T., Lochman, J. E., McMahon, R. J., et al. (2002). Evaluation of the first 3 years of the Fast Track prevention trial with children at high risk for adolescent conduct problems. *Journal of Abnormal Child Psychology, 30,* 19.

Birmaher, B., Ryan, N. D., Williamson, D. E., Brent, D. A., & Kaufman, J. (1996). Childhood and adolescent depression: A review of the past 10 years: Part II. *Journal of the American Academy of Child and Adolescent Psychiatry, 35,* 1575–1583.

Bjorklund, D. F. (2000). *Children's thinking: Developmental function and individual differences* (3rd ed.). Belmont, CA: Wadsworth.

Black, B., & Uhde, T. W. (1995). Psychiatric characteristics of children with selective mutism: A pilot study. *Journal of the American Academy of Child and Adolescent Psychiatry, 34,* 847–856.

Black, J., & Underwood, J. (1998). Young, female, and gay: Lesbian students and the school environment. *Professional School Counseling, 1*(3), 15–20.

Blackhurst, A. E., Auger, R. W., & Wahl, K. H. (2003). Children's perceptions of vocational preparation requirements. *Professional School Counseling, 7,* 58–67.

Bloom, B. (n.d.). *Bloom's taxonomy.* Retrieved February 2, 2005, from www.au.af.mil/au/awc/awcgate/edref/bloom.htm

Bloomfield, M. (1915). *Readings in vocational guidance.* Cambridge, MA: Harvard University Press.

Blue-Banning, M., Summers, J. P., Frankland, H. C., Nelson, L. L., & Beegle, G. (2004). Dimensions of family and professional partnerships: Constructive guidelines for collaboration. *Exceptional Children, 70,* 167–184.

Blustein, D. (1994). "Who am I?" The question of self and identity in career development. In M. L. Savickas & R. W. Lent (Eds.), *Convergence in career development theories* (pp. 139–154). Palo Alto, CA: Consulting Psychologists Press.

Bobo, M., Hildreth, B. L., & Durodoye, B. (1998). Changing patterns in career choices among African-American, Hispanic, and Anglo children. *Professional School Counseling, 1,* 43–47.

Bodenhorn, N. (2005). American School Counselor Association ethical code changes relevant to family work. *The Family Journal, 13,* 316–320.

Bodine, R. J. (1996). From peer mediation to peaceable schools. *Update on Law-Related Education, 20,* 7–9.

Bodine, R. J., & Crawford, D. K. (1998). *The handbook of conflict resolution education: A guide to building quality programs in schools.* San Francisco: Jossey-Bass.

Bögels, S. M., Snieder, N., & Kindt, M. (2003). Specificity of dysfunctional thinking in children with symptoms of social anxiety, separation anxiety, and generalized anxiety. *Behavior Change, 20,* 160–169.

Bolyard, K. L., & Jensen–Scott, R. L. (1996). Worldview and culturally sensitive crisis intervention. In J. L. DeLucia-Waack (Ed.), *Multicultural counseling competencies: Implications for training and practice* (pp. 217–236). Alexandria, VA: Association for Counselor Education and Supervision.

Bonnington, S. B. (1993). Solution-focused brief therapy: Helpful interventions for school counselors. *The School Counselor, 41,* 126–128.

Borders, L. D., & Drury, S. M. (1992). Comprehensive school counseling programs: A review for policy-makers and practitioners. *Journal of Counseling and Development, 70,* 487–498.

Borodovsky, L. G., & Ponterotto, J. G. (1994). A family-based approach to multicultural career development. In P. Pedersen & J. Carey (Eds.), *Multicultural counseling in schools* (pp. 195–206). Boston: Allyn & Bacon.

Borum, R. (2000). Assessing violence risk among youth. *Journal of Clinical Psychology, 56,* 1263–1288.

Bostic, J. Q., & Rauch, P. K. (1999). The 3 R's of school consultation. *American Academy of Child and Adolescent Psychiatry, 38,* 339–341.

Bowen, M. L., & Glenn, E. E. (1998). Counseling interventions for students who have mild disabilities. *Professional School Counseling, 2,* 16–25.

Boyer, E. L. (1983). *High school: A report on secondary education in America.* New York: Harper & Row.

Boykin, A. W. (1986). The triple quandary and the schooling of Afro-American children. In U. Neisser (Ed.), *The school achievement of minority children* (pp. 57–92). Hillsdale, NJ: Lawrence Erlbaum Associates.

Braback, M., Walsh, M., Kenny, M., & Comilang, K. (1997). Interprofessional collaboration for children and families: Opportunities for counseling psychology in the 21st century. *The Counseling Psychologist, 25,* 615–636.

Bradley, L. J., Gould, L. J., & Hendricks, C. B. (2004). Using innovative techniques for counseling children and adolescents. In A. Vernon (Ed.), *Counseling children and adolescents* (4th ed., pp. 75–110). Denver, CO: Love.

Brantley, L. S., Brantley, P. S., & Baer-Barkley, K. (1996). Transforming acting-out behavior: A group counseling program for inner-city elementary school pupils. *Elementary School Guidance and Counseling, 31,* 96–105.

Brennan, J. (1999). *They can and they do: Low income students and high academic achievement.* Retrieved July 1, 2005, from www.edtrust.org/Low_Income.html

Bretherton, I. (1985). Attachment theory: Retrospect and prospect. *Monographs of the Society for Research on Child Development, 50*(1, Serial No. 209).

Brewer, J. M. (1942). *History of vocational guidance.* New York: Harper & Brothers.

Brigman, G., & Campbell, C. (2003). Helping students improve academic achievement and school success behavior. *Professional School Counseling, 7,* 91–98.

Brinson, J. A., Kottler, J. A., & Fisher, T. A. (2004). Cross-cultural conflict resolution in the schools: Some practical intervention strategies for counselors. *Journal of Counseling and Development, 82,* 294–301.

Britzman, M. J. (2005). Improving our moral landscape via character education: An opportunity for school counselor leadership. *Professional School Counseling, 8,* 293–295.

Brock, S. E. (1998). Helping classrooms cope with traumatic events. *Professional School Counseling, 2,* 110–116.

Brotherton, W. D., & Clarke, K. A. (1997). Special friends: The use of community resources in comprehensive school counseling programs. *Professional School Counseling, 1*(2), 41–44.

Brott, P. E., & Myers, J. E. (1999). Development of professional school counselor identity: A grounded theory. *Professional School Counseling, 2,* 339–348.

Brown, A., & Mistry, T. (1994). Group work with mixed membership groups: Issues of race and gender. *Social Work With Groups, 17,* 5–21.

Brown, D. (1993). Training consultants: A call to action. *Journal of Counseling and Development, 72,* 139–143.

Brown, D. (1996). Brown's values-based, holistic model of career and life-role choices and satisfaction. In D. Brown & L. Brooks (Eds.), *Career choice and development* (3rd ed., pp. 337–368). San Francisco: Jossey-Bass.

Brown, D., Galassi, J. P., & Akos, P. (2004). School counselors' perception of the impact of high stakes testing. *Professional School Counseling, 8,* 31–39.

Brown, D., Pryzwansky, W. B., & Schultz, A. C. (2000). *Psychological consultation: Introduction to theory and practice* (5th ed.). Needham Heights, MA: Allyn & Bacon.

Brown, D. B., & Trusty, J. (2005). *Designing and leading comprehensive school counseling programs: Promoting student competence and meeting student needs.* Belmont, CA: Thomson Brooks/Cole.

Brown, K. S., & Parsons, R. D. (1998). Accurate identification of childhood aggression: A key to successful intervention. *Professional School Counseling, 2,* 135–140.

Brown, T. A., O'Leary, T. A., & Barlow, D. H. (1993). Generalized anxiety disorder. In D. H. Barlow (Ed.). *Clinical handbook of psychological disorders* (2nd ed., pp. 137–188). New York: Guilford Press.

Bruce, M. A. (1995). Brief counseling: An effective model for change. *The School Counselor, 42,* 353–363.

Bruce, M. A., Shade, R. A., & Cossairt, A. (1996). Classroom-tested guidance activities for promoting inclusion. *The School Counselor, 43,* 224–231.

Bruner, A. B., & Fishman, M. (1998). Adolescents and illicit drug use. *Journal of the American Medical Association, 280,* 597–598.

Bruner, C. (1991). *Thinking collaboratively: Ten questions and answers to help policy makers improve children's services.* Washington, DC: Education and Human Resources Consortium.

Bryan, J. (2005). Fostering educational resilience and academic achievement in urban schools through school-family-community partnerships. *Professional School Counseling, 8,* 219–227.

Bryan, J., & Holcomb-McCoy, C. (2004). School counselors' perceptions of their involvement in school-family-community partnerships. *Professional School Counseling, 7,* 162–171.

Bucher, K. T., & Manning, M. L. (2003, Jan./Feb.). Challenges and suggestions for safe schools. *The Clearing House, 76,* 160–164.

Buckley, M. A. (2000). Cognitive-developmental considerations in violence prevention and intervention. *Professional School Counseling, 4,* 60–70.

Budman, C. L., Bruun, R. D., Park, K. S., Lesser, M., & Olson, M. (2000). Explosive outbursts in children with Tourette's disorder. *Journal of the American Academy of Child & Adolescent Psychiatry, 39,* 1270–1276.

Burgess, G., & Burgess, H. (1996). *Constructive confrontation theoretical framework.* Retrieved March 2, 2002, from www.Colorado.EDU/conflict/peace/essay/con_conf.htm

Burstyn, J., & Stevens, R. (2001). Involving the whole school in violence prevention. In J. Burstyn, G. Bender, R. Castella, H. Gordon, D. Guerra, K. Luschen, et al. (Ed.), *Preventing violence in schools: A challenge to American democracy* (pp. 139–158). Mahwah, NJ: Lawrence Erlbaum Associates.

Bussing, R., Zima, B. T., Perwien, A. R., Belin, T. R., & Widawski, M. (1998). Children in special education: Attention deficit hyperactivity disorder, use of services, and unmet need. *American Journal of Public Health, 88,* 1–7.

Butler, R. J. (2004). Childhood nocturnal enuresis: Developing a conceptual framework. *Clinical Psychology Review, 24,* 909–931.

REFERENCES   **437**

Cali, C. C. (1997). Creatures of character: Winning with character education. *Professional School Counseling, 1*(2), 19–21.

Califano, J. A., & Booth, A. (1998). *1998 CASA national survey of teens, teachers, and principals.* New York: National Center on Addiction and Substance Abuse at Columbia University.

Campbell, C. A., & Brigman, G. (2005). Closing the achievement gap: A structured approach to group counseling. *The Journal for Specialists in Group Work, 30,* 67–82.

Campbell, C., & Dahir, C. (1997). *The national standards for school counseling programs.* Alexandria, VA: American School Counselor Association.

Campbell, D. T., & Stanley, J. C. (1963). *Experimental and quasi-experimental designs for research.* Boston: Houghton Mifflin.

Campbell, M., Cueva, J. E., & Hallin, A. (1996). Autism and pervasive developmental disorders. In J. M. Wiener (Ed.), *Diagnosis and psychopharmacology of childhood and adolescent disorders* (2nd ed., pp. 151–192). New York: John Wiley & Sons.

Campbell, M., Schopler, E., Cueva, J. E., & Hallin, A. (1996). Treatment of autistic disorder. *Journal of the American Academy of Child and Adolescent Psychiatry, 35,* 134–141.

Canfield, B. S., Ballard, M. B., Osmon, B. C., & McCune, C. (2004). School and family counselors work together to reduce fighting at school. *Professional School Counseling, 8,* 40–46.

Cantwell, P. D. (1996). Attention deficit disorder: A review of the past 10 years. *Journal of the American Academy of Child and Adolescent Psychiatry, 35,* 978–987.

Capuzzi, D. (1998). Addressing the needs of at-risk youth: Early prevention and systemic intervention. In C. C. Lee & G. R. Walz (Eds.), *Social action: A mandate for counselors* (pp. 99–116). Alexandria, VA: American Counseling Association.

Carlat, D. J., Carmago, C. A., & Herzog, D. B. (1997). Eating disorders in males: A report on 135 patients. *American Journal of Psychiatry, 154,* 1127–1132.

Carlson, L. A. (2003). Existential theory: Helping school counselors attend to youth at risk for violence. *Professional School Counseling, 6,* 310–315.

Carnegie Corporation of New York. (1984–1985). Renegotiating society's contract with the public schools. *Carnegie Quarterly, 29/30*(1), 1–4, 6–11.

Carnegie Council on Adolescent Development. (1996). *Great transitions: Preparing adolescents for a new century.* New York: Carnegie Corporation.

Carnevale, A. P., & Desrochers, D. M. (2003). Preparing students for the knowledge economy: What school counselors need to know. *Professional School Counseling, 6,* 228–237.

Carney, C. G., & Kahn, K. B. (1984). Building competencies for effective cross-cultural counseling: A developmental view. *The Counseling Psychologist, 12,* 111–119.

Carney, J. V. (2000). Bullied to death: Perceptions of peer abuse and suicidal behavior during adolescents. *School Psychology International, 21,* 213–223.

Carpenter, S. L., King-Sears, M. E., & Keys, S. G. (1998). Counselors + educators + families as a transdisciplinary team = more effective inclusion for students with disabilities. *Professional School Counseling, 2,* 1–9.

Carruthers, W. L., Sweeney, B., Kmitta, D., & Harris, G. (1996). Conflict resolution: An examination of the research literature and a model for program evaluation. *The School Counselor, 44,* 5–18.

Carter, G. R. (2004, February). *Connecting the world of education. Is it good for the kids?* (Editorial) Retrieved December 23, 2004, from www.ascd.org

Carter, R. B., & El Hindi, A. E. (1999). Counseling Muslim children in school settings. *Professional School Counseling, 2,* 183–188.

Carter, R. B., & Vuong, T. K. (1997). Unity through diversity: Fostering cultural awareness. *Professional School Counseling, 1*(1), 47–51.

Carter, R. C., & Mason, P. S. (1998). The selection and use of puppets in counseling. *Professional School Counseling, 1*(5), 50–53.

Casella, R. (2001). What is violent about "school violence"?: The nature of violence in a city high school. In J. N. Burstyn, G. Bender, R. Casella, H. W. Gordon, D. P. Guerra, K. V. Luschen, et al. (Eds.), *Preventing violence in schools: A challenge to American democracy* (pp. 15–46). Mahwah, NJ: Lawrence Erlbaum Associates.

Catalano, R. F., Loeber, R., & McKinney, K. C. (1999, October). School and community interventions to prevent serious and violent offending. *OJJDP Juvenile Justice Bulletin.*

Center for Mental Health in Schools. (1999). *School-community partnerships: A guide.* Los Angeles: Author.

Centers for Disease Control and Prevention. (1999). *Youth risk behavior survey.* Washington, DC: U.S. Department of Health and Human Services.

Centers for Disease Control and Prevention, National Center for Injury Prevention and Control. (2000). *Dating violence.* Available at www.cdc.gov/ncipc/factsheets/datviol.htm

Charkow, W. B. (1998). Inviting children to grieve. *Professional School Counseling, 2,* 117–122.

Charles, C. M., & Senter G. W. (2005). *Building classroom discipline.* New York: Longman.

Charlesworth, J. R., & Jackson, C. M. (2004). Solution-focused brief counseling: An approach for school counselors. In B. T. Erford (Ed.), *Professional school counseling: A handbook of theories, programs, and practices* (pp. 139–148). Austin, TX: PRO-ED.

Charney, R. S. (1992). *Teaching children to care.* Greenfield, MA: Northeast Foundation for Children.

Chen–Hayes, S. F. (2000). Social justice advocacy with lesbian, bisexual, gay, and transgendered persons. In J. Lewis & L. Bradley (Eds.), *Advocacy in counseling: Counselors, clients, & community* (pp. 89–98). Greensboro, NC: CAPS & ERIC/CASS.

Chen–Hayes, S. F. (2005). *Multicultural counseling class lecture.* Bronx: Lehman College of the City University of New York.

Chen-Hayes, S. F., Chen, M., & Athar, N. (2000). Challenging linguicism: Action strategies for counselors and client-colleagues. In J. Lewis & L. Bradley (Eds.), *Advocacy in counseling: Counselors, clients, & community* (pp. 25–36). Greensboro, NC: CAPS & ERIC/CASS.

Cherniss, C. (1997). Teacher empowerment, consultation, and the creation of new programs in schools. *Journal of Educational and Psychological Consultation, 8,* 135–152.

Christenson, S. L., & Sheridan, S. M. (2001). *Schools and families: Creating essential connections for learning.* New York: Guilford Press.

Christle, C. A., Jolivette, K., & Nelson, C. M. (2000). *Youth aggression and violence: Risk, resilience, and prevention* (Report No. E602). Arlington, VA: ERIC Clearinghouse on Disabilities and Gifted Education, Council for Exceptional Children. (ERIC Document Reproduction Service No. ED449632)

Chung, Y. B., & Katayama, M. (1998). Ethnic and sexual identity development of Asian-American lesbian and gay adolescents. *Professional School Counseling, 1*(3), 21–25.

Clark, D. B., Smith, M. G., Neighbors, D. B., Skerlec, L. M., & Randall, J. (1994). Anxiety disorders in adolescence: Characteristics, prevalence, and comorbidities. *Clinical Psychology Review, 14,* 113–137.

Clark, D. C., & Fawcett, J. (1992). Review of empirical risk factors for evaluation of the suicidal patient. In B. Bongar (Ed.), *Suicide: Guidelines for assessment, management, and treatment* (pp. 16–48). New York: Oxford University Press.

Clark, L. A. (1987). Mutual relevance of mainstream and cross-cultural psychology. *Journal of Consulting and Clinical Psychology, 55,* 461–470.

Clark, M., & Stone, C. (2000, May). Evolving our image: School counselors as educational leaders. *Counseling Today, 21 & 46.*

Clark, R. M. (1993). Homework-focused parenting practices that positively affect student achievement. In N. F. Chavkin (Ed.), *Families and schools in a pluralistic society* (pp. 85–105). Albany: State University of New York Press.

Close, C. L., & Lechman, K. (1997). Fostering youth leadership: Students train students and adults in conflict resolution. *Theory into Practice, 36,* 11–16.

Cobia, D. C., Carney, J. S., & Waggoner, I. M. (1998). Children and adolescents with HIV disease: Implications for school counselors. *Professional School Counseling, 1*(5), 41–45.

Cobia, D. C., & Henderson, D. A. (2003). *Handbook of school counseling.* Upper Saddle River, NJ: Merrill/Prentice Hall.

Cochran, J. L., & Cochran, N. H. (1999). Using the counseling relationship to facilitate change in students with conduct disorder. *Professional School Counseling, 2,* 395–403.

Coffey, B. J., Biederman, J., Geller, D., Frazier, J., Spencer, T., Doyle, R., et al. (2004). Reexamining tic persistence and tic-associated impairment in Tourette's disorder: Findings from a naturalistic follow-up study. *The Journal of Nervous and Mental Disease, 192,* 776–780.

Coffey B. J., Biederman, J., Geller, D. A., Spencer, T. J., Kim, G. S., Bellordre, C. A., et al. (2000). Distinguishing illness severity from tic severity in children and adolescents with Tourette's disorder. *Journal of the American Academy of Child & Adolescent Psychiatry, 39,* 556–561.

Coker, J. K. (2004). Alcohol and other substance abuse: A comprehensive approach. In R. Perusse & G. E. Goodnough, (Eds.), *Leadership, advocacy, and direct service strategies for professional school counselors* (pp. 284–327). Belmont, CA: Brooks/Cole-Thomson Learning.

Colbert, R. D. (1996). The counselor's role in advancing school and family partnerships. *The School Counselor, 44,* 100–104.

Coleman, P. K. (2003). Reactive attachment disorder in the context of the family: A review and call for future research. *Emotional and Behavioral Difficulties, 8,* 205–216.

Coleman, P. T., & Deutsch, M. (2000). Cooperation, conflict resolution, and school violence: A systems approach (Choices Briefs No. 5). New York:

Columbia University, Institute for Urban and Minority Education.

College Board. (1999a). *Reaching the top: A report of the national task force on minority high achievement.* New York: Author.

College Board. (1999b). *Priming the pump: Strategies for increasing the achievement of underrepresented minority graduates.* New York: Author.

Collins, B. G., & Collins, T. M. (1994). Child and adolescent mental health: Building a system of care. *Journal of Counseling and Development, 72,* 239–243.

Comer, J. P. (1984). Home-school relationships as they affect the academic success of children. *Education and Urban Society, 16,* 323–337.

Committee for Children. (2002a). *Second Step: A violence prevention curriculum* (3rd ed.). Seattle, WA: Author.

Committee for Children. (2002b). *Second Step: A violence prevention program.* Available at www.cfchildren.org/

Compton, R. (2000). *Infusing and integrating conflict resolution into the school curriculum and culture.* Retrieved March 2, 2002, from www.crenet.org/Research/infusing.htm

Conant, J. B. (1959). *The American high school today: A first report to interested citizens.* New York: McGraw-Hill.

Conflict Research Consortium. (2000a). *Denial of identity.* Retrieved March 2, 2002, from www.colorado.EDU/conflict/peace/problem/denyid.htm

Conflict Research Consortium. (2000b). *Domination conflicts.* Retrieved March 2, 2002, from www.colorado.EDU/conflict/peace/problem/domination.htm

Conflict Research Consortium. (2000c). *The denial of other human needs.* Retrieved March 2, 2002, from www.colorado.EDU/conflict/peace/problem/needs.htm

Conflict Research Consortium. (2000d). *Treatment list 2: Treating core conflict problems.* Retrieved March 2, 2002, from http://colorado.EDU/conflict/peace/!treating_core.htm

Connecticut State Department of Education. (2004). Retrieved March 28, 2004, from www.csde.state.ct.us/public/der/schools/nclb_reports.htm

Conners, C. K. (1997). *Manual for the Conners' Rating Scales–Revised.* North Tonawanda, NY: Mental Health Systems.

Conoley, J. C., & Conoley, C. W. (1992). *School consultation practice and training* (2nd ed.). Boston: Allyn & Bacon.

Constantine, M. G. (2001). Theoretical orientation, empathy, and multicultural counseling competence in school counselor trainees. *Professional School Counseling, 4,* 342–348.

Constantine, M. G., & Yeh, C. J. (2001). Multicultural training, self-construals, and multicultural competence of school counselors. *Professional School Counseling, 4,* 202–207.

Conyne, R. K. (1996). The Association for Specialists in Group Work training standards: Some considerations and suggestions for training. *Journal for Specialists in Group Work, 21,* 155–162.

Cook, D. W. (1989). Systematic needs assessment: A primer. *Journal of Counseling and Development, 67,* 462–464.

Cook, J. B., & Kaffenberger, C. J. (2003). Solution shop: A solution-focused counseling and study skills program for middle school. *Professional School Counseling, 7,* 116–121.

Cook-Cottone, C. (2004). Childhood posttraumatic stress disorder: Diagnosis, treatment, and school reintegration. *School Psychology Review, 33*(1), 127–139.

Cooley, J. J. (1998). Gay and lesbian adolescents: Presenting problems and the counselor's role. *Professional School Counseling, 1*(3), 30–34.

Cooley-Quille, M., Boyd, R. C., Frantz, E., & Walsh, J. (2001). Emotional and behavioral impact of exposure to community violence in inner-city adolescents. *Journal of Clinical Child Psychology, 30*(1), 199–206.

Corey, G. (2004). *Theory and practice of group counseling* (6th ed.). Belmont, CA: Brooks/Cole-Thomson Learning.

Corey, G., Corey, M. S., & Callanan, P. (1998). *Issues and ethics in the helping professions* (4th ed.). Pacific Grove, CA: Brooks/Cole.

Corey, M. S., & Corey, G. (2002). *Groups: Process and practice* (6th ed.). Pacific Grove, CA: Brooks/Cole.

Cormany, R. B., & Brantley, W. A. (1996). It's our problem: An administrator looks at school guidance. *The School Counselor, 43,* 171–173.

Cornett, C. E., & Cornett, C. F. (1980). *Bibliotherapy: The right book at the right time.* Bloomington, IN: Phi Delta Kappa Educational Foundation.

Costello, E. J., Angold, A., Burns, B. J., Stangl, D. K., Tweed, D.L., Erkanli, A., et al. (1996). The Great Smoky Mountains Study of Youth: Goals, design, methods, and the prevalence of *DSM–III–R* disorders. *Archives of General Psychiatry, 53,* 1129–1136.

Cottone, R. R., & Tarvydas, V. M. (2003). *Ethical and professional issues in counseling* (2nd ed.). Upper Saddle River, NJ: Merrill/Prentice Hall.

Coulter, W. A. (1996, April). *Alarming or disarming? The status of ethnic differences with exceptionalities.* Paper presented at the annual convention of the Council for Exceptional Children, Orlando, FL.

Council for Accreditation of Counseling and Related Educational Programs. (2001). *CACREP accreditation standards and procedures manual.* Alexandria, VA: Author.

Council on Rehabilitations Education. (2003–2004). *Accreditation manual.* Available from www.core-rehab.org

Cousins, L., & Weiss, G. (1993). Parent training and social skills training for children with attention-deficit hyperactivity disorder: How can they be combined for greater effectiveness? *Canadian Journal of Psychiatry-Revue Canadienne de Psychiatrie, 38,* 449–457.

Cowley, W. H. (1937). Preface to the principles of student counseling. *Educational Record, 18,* 218–234.

Coyle, J. T., Pine, D. S., Charney, D. S., Lewis, L, Nemeroff, C. B., Carlson, G. A., et al. (2003). Depression and Bipolar Support Alliance consensus statement on the unmet needs in diagnosis and treatment of mood disorders in children and adolescents. *Journal of the American Academy of Child and Adolescent Psychiatry, 42,* 1494–1503.

Cremin, L. A. (1964). The progressive heritage of the guidance movement. In E. Landy & L. Perry (Eds.), *Guidance in American education: Backgrounds and prospects* (pp. 11–19). Cambridge, MA: Harvard University Graduate School of Education.

CRENet. (2000). *History of conflict resolution education.* Retrieved March 2, 2002, from www.crenet.org.What_is_CR/history.htm

Crites, J. O. (1978). *Theory and research handbook for the career maturity inventory.* Monterey, CA: CTB-McGraw Hill.

Crockett, L. J., & Crouter, A. C. (1995). Pathways through adolescence: An overview. In L. J. Crockett & A. C. Crouter (Eds.), *Pathways through adolescence* (pp. 1–12). Mahway, NJ: Lawrence Erlbaum Associates.

Cronbach, L. J. (1983). Course improvement through evaluation. In C. F. Madaus, M. Scriven, & D. L. Stufflebeam (Eds.), *Evaluation models* (pp. 101–116). Boston: Kluwer-Nijhoff.

Cull, J. G., & Gill, W. S. (1992). *Suicide Probability Scale.* Los Angeles: Western Psychology Service.

Cunconan-Lahr, R., & Brotherson, M. (1996). Advocacy in disability policy: Parents and consumers. *Mental Retardation, 34,* 352–358.

Cunningham, N. J., & Singh Sandhu, D. (2000). A comprehensive approach to school-community violence prevention. *Professional School Counseling, 4,* 126–133.

Curcio, C. C., Mathai, C., & Roberts, J. (2003). Evaluation of a school district's secondary counseling program. *Professional School Counseling, 6,* 296–303.

Cuthbert, B. (2001). Involving and responding to parents: Opportunities and challenges. In P. Henderson & N. Gysbers (Eds.), *Implementing comprehensive school guidance programs: Critical leadership issues and successful responses* (pp. 79–87). Greensboro, NC: ERIC–CASS.

Cutrona, C., & Guerin, D. (1994). Confronting conflict peacefully: Peer mediation in schools. *Educational Horizons, 72,* 95–104.

Dahir, C. A. (2001). The National Standards for School Counseling Programs: Development and implementation. *Professional School Counseling, 4,* 320–327.

Dahir, C. A., Sheldon, C. B., & Valiga, M. J. (1998). *Vision into action: Implementing the National Standards for School Counseling Programs.* Alexandria, VA: American School Counselor Association.

Dahir, C. A., & Stone, C. B. (2003). Accountability: A M.E.A.S.U.R.E. of the impact school counselors have on student achievement. *Professional School Counseling, 6,* 214–221.

Dana, R. H. (2001). Clinical diagnosis of multicultural populations in the United States. In L. A. Suzuki, J. G. Ponterotto, & P. J. Meller (Eds.), *Handbook of multicultural assessment: Clinical, psychological, and educational applications* (2nd ed., pp. 101–132). San Francisco: Jossey-Bass.

D'Andrea, M., & Daniels, D. (1995). Helping students to learn to get along: Assessing the effectiveness of a multicultural developmental guidance project. *Elementary School Guidance and Counseling, 30,* 143–154.

Darling, S., & Westberg, L. (2004). Parent involvement in children's acquisition of reading. *The Reading Teacher, 57,* 774–776.

Davis, L. E., Galinsky, M. J., & Schopler, J. H. (1995). RAP: A framework for leadership of multiracial groups. *Social work, 40* (20), 155–165.

Day-Vines, N. L., Day-Hairston, B. O., Carruthers, W. L., Wall, J. A., & Lupton-Smith, H. A. (1996). Conflict resolution: The value of diversity in the recruitment, selection, and training of peer mediators. *The School Counselor, 43,* 392–410.

Day-Vines, N. L., Patton, J. M., & Baytops, J. L. (2003). Counseling African American adolescents: The impact of race, culture, and middle class status. *Professional School Counseling, 7,* 40–51.

Deblinger, E., McLeer, S. V., Atkins, M. S., Ralphe, D., & Foa, E. B. (1989). Posttraumatic stress in sexually abused, physically abused and nonabused children. *Child Abuse and Neglect, 13,* 403–408.

Delpit, L. (1995). *Other people's children: Cultural conflict in the classroom.* New York: New Press.

Del Prete, T. (2000). Unsafe schools: Perception or reality. *Professional School Counseling, 3,* 375–377.

DeLucia–Waack, J. L. (1999). What makes an effective group leader? *Journal for Specialists in Group Work, 24,* 131–132.

DeLucia–Waack, J. L., DiCarlo, N. J., Parker-Sloat, E. L., & Rice, K. G. (1996). Multiculturalism: Understanding at the beginning of the process, rather than the ending. In J. DeLucia-Waack (Ed.), *Multicultural counseling competencies: Implications for training and practice* (pp. 237–243). Alexandria, VA: Association for Counselor Education and Supervision.

Demo, D. H., & Acock, A. C. (1996). Family structure, family process, and adolescent well-being. *Journal of Research on Adolescence, 6,* 457–488.

De Shazer, S. (1985). *Keys to solution in brief therapy.* New York: Norton.

DeVoe, J. F., Peter, K., Kaufman, P., Miller, A., Noonan, M., Snyder, T. D., et al. (2004). *Indicators of school crime and safety: 2004* (NCES 2005-002/NCJ 205290). U.S. Departments of Education and Justice. Washington, DC: U.S. Government Printing Office.

Dewey, J. (1910). *How we think.* Retrieved July 6, 2005, from http://spartan.ac.brocku.ca/~lward/ Dewey/Dewey_1910a/Dewey_1910_toc.html

DeWit, D. J., Offord, D. R., Sanford, M., Rye, B. J., Shain, M., & Wright, R. (2000). The effect of school culture on adolescent behavior problems: Self-esteem, attachment to learning, and peer approval of deviance as mediating mechanisms. *Canadian Journal of School Psychology, 16,* 15–38.

Diamond, G. S., Serrano, A. C., Dickey, M., & Sonis, W. (1996). Current status of family-based outcome and process research. *Journal of the American Academy of Child and Adolescent Psychiatry, 35,* 6–17.

Dimmitt, C. (2003). Transforming school counseling practice through collaboration and the use of data: A study of academic failure in high school. *Professional School Counseling, 6,* 340–349.

Dinkmeyer, D. (1975). *Systematic training for effective parenting.* Circle Pines, MN: American Guidance Service.

Dinkmeyer, D., & Carlson, J. (2001). *Consultation: Creating school-based interventions* (2nd ed.). Philadelphia: Brunner-Routledge.

Doll, B. (1996). Prevalence of psychiatric disorders in children and youth: An agenda for advocacy by school psychology. *School Psychology Quarterly, 11,* 20–46.

Dougherty, A. M. (1999). *Psychological consultation and collaboration in school and community settings* (3rd ed.). Pacific Grove, CA: Brooks/Cole.

Douglas, L. S. (1997). *The new IDEA and opportunities for school mental health.* Baltimore: Center for School Mental Health Assistance.

Dow, M. J., & Mehring, T. A. (2001). Inservice training for educators of individuals with autism. *Autistic Spectrum Disorders: Educational and Clinical Interventions, 14,* 89–107.

Driekurs, R., & Cassell, P. (1974). *Discipline without tears.* New York: Hawthorne Books.

Druliner, J. K., & Prichard, H. E. (2003). "We can handle this ourselves": Learning to negotiate conflicts. In T. S. Jones & R. Compton (Eds.), *Kids working it out: Strategies and stories for making peace in our schools* (pp. 89–108). San Francisco: Jossey-Bass.

Dryfoos, J. G. (1990). *Adolescents at risk.* New York: Oxford University Press.

Dryfoos, J. G. (1994). *Full-service schools: A revolution in health and social services for children, youth and families.* San Francisco: Jossey-Bass.

Dryfoos, J. G. (1996). Adolescents at-risk: Shaping programs to fit the need. *Journal of Negro Education, 65,* 5–17.

Dryfoos, J. G. (1998). *Safe passage: Making it through adolescence in a risky society.* New York: Oxford University Press.

Dudley, G., & Ruff, E. (1970). School counselor certification: A study of current requirements. *The School Counselor, 17,* 304–311.

Dulmus, C. N., & Wodaraski, J. S. (1996). Assessment and effective treatments of childhood psychopathology: Responsibilities and implications for practice. *Journal of Child and Adolescent Group Therapy, 6,* 75–99.

Dumont, F., & Carson, A. (1995). Precursors of vocational psychology in ancient civilizations. *Journal of Counseling and Development, 73,* 371–378.

Duncan, C. F. (1995). Cross-cultural school consultation. In C. Lee (Ed.), *Counseling for diversity* (pp. 129–139). Boston: Allyn & Bacon.

Dunn, N. A., & Baker, S. B. (2002). Readiness to serve students with disabilities: A survey of elementary school counselors. *Professional School Counseling, 5,* 277–284.

DuPaul, G. J., Guevremont, D. C., & Barkley, R. A. (1992). Behavioral treatment of attention-deficit hyperactivity disorder in the classroom: The use of the attention training system. *Behavior Modification, 16,* 204–225.

Durdoyle, B. (1998). Fostering multicultural awareness among teachers: A tripartite model. *Professional School Counseling, 1* (5), 9–13.

Durodoye, B. A., Combes, B. H., & Bryant, R. M. (2004). Counselor intervention in the post-secondary planning of African American students with learning disabilities. *Professional School Counseling, 7,* 133–140.

Dworkin, E. P., & Dworkin, A. L. (1971). The activist as counselor. *Personnel and Guidance Journal, 49,* 748–754.

Dwyer, K., Osher, D., & Wargar, C. (1998). *Early warning signs, timely response: A grid to safe schools.* Washington, DC: U.S. Department of Education.

Dykeman, C. (1995). The privatization of school counseling. *The School Counselor, 43,* 29–34.

Dykeman, C., Wood, C., Ingram, M. A., Pehrsson, D., Mandsager, N., & Herr, E. L. (2003). The structure of school career development interventions: Implications for school counselors. *Professional School Counseling, 6,* 272–279.

Eaves, L., Rutter, M., Silberg, J. L., Shillady, L., Maes, H., & Pickles, A. (2000). Genetic and environmental cause of covariation in interview assessments of disruptive behavior in child and adolescent twins. *Behavior Genetics, 30,* 321–334.

Eccles, J. S., & Harold, R. D. (1996). Family involvement in children's and adolescents' schooling. In A. Booth & J. F. Dunn (Eds.), *Family-school links: How do they affect educational outcomes?* (pp. 3–34). Mahwah, NJ: Lawrence Erlbaum Associates.

Edens, J. H. (1997). Home visitation programs with ethnic minority families. Cultural issues in parent consultation. *Journal of Educational and Psychological Consultation, 8,* 373–383.

Edmondson, J. H., & White, J. (1998). A tutorial and counseling program: Helping students at risk of dropping out of school. *Professional School Counseling, 1,* 43–47.

Education Trust. (1996a). *Education watch: The 1996 Education Trust state and national databook.* Washington, DC: Author.

Education Trust. (1996b). *National institute for transforming school counseling.* Retrieved March 21, 2004, from www.edtrust.org/

Education Trust. (1997). *The national guidance and counseling reform program.* Washington, DC: Author.

Education Trust. (2000). *National initiative for transforming school counseling summer academy for counselor educators proceedings.* Washington, DC: Author.

Education Trust (2004). *Edwatch online 2004 state summary reports.* Retrieved August 15, 2005, from www2.edtrust.org/edtrust/summaries2004/USA.pdf

Education Trust. (2005a). *Achievement in America: 2005* [Computer diskette]. Washington, DC: Author.

Education Trust. (2005b). The Education Trust's National Center for Transforming School Counseling Initiative Web site. Retrieved April 14, 2005, from www2.edtrust.org/EdTrust/Transforming+School+Counseling

Education Trust. (2005c). *Mission statement.* Retrieved August 19, 2005, from www2.edtrust.org/EdTrust/Transforming+School+Counseling/main

Education Watch. (1998). *The Education Trust state and national data book* (Vol. II). Washington, DC: Education Trust.

Edwards, D., & Mullis, F. (2003). Classroom meetings: Encouraging a climate of cooperation. *Professional School Counseling, 7,* 20–28.

Eisel v. Board of Education, 597 A.2d 447 (Md. Ct. App. 1991).

Ekstrom, R. B., Elmore, P. B., Schafer, W. D., Trotter, T. V., & Webster, B. (2004). A survey of assessment and evaluation activities of school counselors. *Professional School Counseling, 8,* 24–30.

Elam, S. (Ed.). (1993). *The state of the nation's public schools.* Bloomington, IN: Phi Delta Kappa.

Elias, M. J., Blum, L., Gager, P. T., Hunter, L., & Kress, J. S. (1998). Group interventions for students with mild disorders: Classroom inclusion approaches. In K. C. Stoiber & T. R. Kratochwill (Eds.), *Handbook of group intervention for children and families.* Boston: Allyn & Bacon.

Elkind, D. (1984). *All grown up and no place to go: Teenagers in crisis.* Reading, MA: Addison-Wesley.

Emery, R. E., Kitzman, K. M., & Waldron, M. (1999). Psychological interventions for separated and divorced families. In E. M. Hetherington (Ed.), *Coping with divorce, single parenting, and remarriage.* Mahwah, NJ: Lawrence Erlbaum Associates.

Emslie, G. J., & Mayes, T. L. (2001). Mood disorders in children and adolescents: Psychopharmacological treatment. *Biological Psychology, 49,* 1082–1090.

Epstein, J. L. (1986). Parents' reactions to teacher practices of parent involvement. *Elementary School Journal, 86,* 3.

Erdman, P., & Lampe, R. (1996). Adapting basic skills to counsel children. *Journal of Counseling and Development, 74,* 374–377.

Erford, B. T. (1995). Reliability and validity of the Conners' Teacher Rating Scale–28 (CTRS–28). *Diagnostique, 21*(1), 19–28.

Erford, B. T. (1996a). Reliability and validity of mother responses to the Disruptive Behavior Rating Scale–Parent Version (DBRS–P). *Diagnostique, 21*(2), 17–33.

Erford, B. T. (1996b). Analysis of the Conners' Teacher Rating Scale–28 (CTRS–28). *Assessment, 3*(1), 27–36.

Erford, B. T. (1997). Reliability and validity of scores on the Disruptive Behavior Rating Scale–Teacher Version (DBRS–T). *Educational and Psychological Measurement, 57,* 329–339.

Erford, B. T. (1998). Technical analysis of father responses to the Disruptive Behavior Rating Scale–Parent Version (DBRS–P). *Measurement and Evaluation in Counseling and Development, 30,* 199–210.

Erford, B. T. (1999). A modified time-out procedure for children with noncompliant or defiant behaviors. *Professional School Counseling, 2,* 205–210.

Erford, B. T. (Ed.). (In press). *Research and evaluation in counseling.* Boston: Houghton Mifflin.

Erford, B. T., & McKechnie, J. A. (2004). How to write learning objectives. In B. T. Erford (Ed.), *Professional school counseling: A handbook of theories, programs and practices* (pp. 279–286). Austin, TX: PRO-ED.

Erford, B. T., Peyrot, M., & Siska, L. (1998). Analysis of teacher responses to the Conners' Abbreviated Symptoms Questionnaire (ASQ). *Measurement and Evaluation in Counseling and Development, 31,* 2–14.

Erikson, E. H. (1963). *Childhood and society.* New York: Norton.

Erikson, E. H. (1968). *Identity: Youth and crisis.* New York: Norton.

Erk, R. R. (1999). Attention deficit hyperactivity disorders: Counselors, laws, and implications for practice. *Professional School Counseling, 2,* 318–326.

Eschenauer, R., & Chen–Hayes, S. F. (2005). The transformative individual school counseling model: An accountability model for urban school counselors. *Professional School Counseling, 8,* 244–248.

Esters, I., & Ledoux, C. (2001). At-risk high school students' preferences for counselor characteristics. *Professional School Counseling, 4,* 165–170.

Esters, I. G., & Ittenbach, R. F. (1999). Contemporary theories and assessments of intelligence: A primer. *Professional School Counseling, 2,* 373–377.

Evans, J. E., & Hines, P. L. (1997). Lunch with school counselors: Reaching parents through their workplace. *Professional School Counseling, 1*(2), 45–47.

Evans, J. R., Van Velsor, P., & Schumacher, J. E. (2002). Addressing adolescent depression: A role for school counselors. *Professional School Counseling, 5,* 211–219.

Ezell, M. (2001). *Advocacy in the human services.* Belmont, CA: Wadsworth.

Fairchild, T. N. (1986). Time analysis: Accountability tool for school counselors. *The School Counselor, 34,* 36–43.

Fallon, M. V. (1997). The school counselor's role in first generation students' college plans. *The School Counselor, 44,* 385–393.

Family Educational Rights and Privacy Act. (FERPA). (1974). 20 U.S.C. § 1232g.

Fantuzzo, J. W., Davis, G. Y., & Ginsberg, M. O. (1995). Effects of parent involvement in isolation or in combination with peer tutoring on student self-concept and mathematics achievement. *Journal of Educational Psychology, 87,* 272–281.

Federal Bureau of Investigation. (2005). *The School shooter: A threat assessment perspective.* Retrieved on September 2, 2005, from www.fbi.gov/publications/school/school2.pdf

Feller, R. W. (2003). Aligning school counseling, the changing workplace, and career development assumptions. *Professional School Counseling, 6,* 262–271.

Field, J. E., & Baker, S. (2004). Defining and examining school counselor advocacy. *Professional School Counseling, 8,* 56–63.

Field, S., Martin, J., Miller, R., Ward, M., & Wehmeyer, M. (n.d.). *Self-determination for persons with disabilities: A position statement of the Division on Career Development and Transition.* Council for Exceptional Children. Available from http://dcdt.org/pdf/self_deter.pdf

Fields, L. (2004, Jan./Feb.). Handling student fights: Advice for teachers and administrators. *The Clearing House, 77*(3), 108–110.

Figueroa, R. A. (1990). Best practices in the assessment of bilingual children. In A. Thomas & J. Grimes (Eds.), *Best practices in school psychology* (pp. 93–106). Washington, DC: National Association of School Psychologists.

Fischer, L., Schimmel, D., & Kelly, C. (1999). *Teachers and the law* (5th ed.). White Plains, NY: Longman.

Fischer, L., & Sorenson, G. P. (1997). *School law for counselors, psychologists, and social workers* (3rd ed.). White Plains, NY: Longman.

Fitch, T. J., & Marshall, J. L. (2004). What counselors do in high-achieving schools: A study on the role of the school counselor. *Professional School Counseling, 7,* 172–177.

Flaherty, L. T. (2001). School violence and the school environment. In M. Shafii & S. L. Shafii, (Eds.), *School violence: Assessment, management, prevention* (pp. 25–51). Washington, DC: American Psychiatric Publishing.

Flaherty, L. T., Garrison, E. G., Waxman, R., Uris, P. F., Keys, S. G., Glass-Siegel, M., & Weist, M. D. (1998). Optimizing the roles of school mental health professionals. *Journal of School Health, 68,* 420–424.

Flavell, J. H. (1985). *Cognitive development* (2nd ed.). Englewood Cliffs, NJ: Prentice Hall.

Fleming, V. M. (1999). Group counseling in the schools: A case for basic training. *Professional School Counseling, 2,* 409–413.

Flynn, J. P. (1995). Social justice in social agencies. In R. C. Edwards (Ed.), *Encyclopedia of social work.* Washington, DC: NASW.

Fontaine, J. H. (1998). Evidencing a need: School counselors' experiences with gay and lesbian students. *Professional School Counseling, 1* (3), 8–14.

Ford, D. Y. (1996). *Reversing underachievement among gifted black students: Promising practices and programs.* New York: Teachers College Press.

Forester-Miller, H., & Davis, T. (1996). *A practioners guide to ethical decision making.* Retrieved August 4, 2005, from www.counseling.org/Content/NavigationMenu/RESOURCES/ETHICS/APRACTIONERSGUIDETOETHICALDECISIONMAKING/Practioner_s_Guide.htm

Forte, J. A., Franks, D. D., Forte, J. A., & Rigsby, D. (1996). Asymmetrical role-taking: Comparing battered and non-battered women. *Social Work, 41,* 59–73.

Frances, R. J., & Allen, M. J. (1986). The interaction of substance-use disorders with nonpsychotic psychiatric disorders. In A. M. Cooper, A. J. Cooper, A. J. Frances, & M. H. Sacks (Eds.), *The personality disorders and neuroses* (pp. 425–437). Philadelphia: Lippincott.

Freeman, S. J. (2000). *Ethics: An introduction to philosophy and practice.* Belmont, CA: Wadsworth.

Friend, M., & Cook, L. (1996). *Interactions: Collaboration skills for school professionals* (2nd ed.). White Plains, NY: Longman.

Friesen, B., & Huff, B. (1990). Parents and professional school counselors as advocacy partners. *Preventing School Failure, 34,* 31–35.

Froeschle, J., & Moyer, M. (2004). Just cut it out: Legal and ethical challenges in counseling students who self-multilate. *Professional School Counseling, 7,* 231–235.

Fryxell, D., & Smit, D. C. (2000). Personal, social, and family characteristics of angry students. *Professional School Counseling, 4,* 86–94.

Furr, S. R. (2000). Structuring the group experience: A format for designing psychoeducational groups. *Journal for Specialists in Group Work, 25,* 29–49.

Fusick, L., & Bordeau, W. C. (2004). Counseling at-risk Afro-American youth: An examination of contemporary issues and effective school-based strategies. *Professional School Counseling, 8,* 102–115.

Gabel, K. A., & Kearney, K. (1998). Promoting reasonable perspectives of body weight: Issues for school counselors. *Professional School Counseling, 1*(5), 32–35.

Gadow, K. D., Nolan, E. E., Sprafkin, J., & Schwartz, J. (2002). Tics and psychiatric comorbidity in children and adolescents. *Developmental Medicine & Child Neurology, 44,* 330–338.

Gandara, P. (1995). *Over the ivy walls: The educational mobility of low-income Chicanos.* Albany: State University of New York Press.

Garcia, J. G., Krankowski, T., & Jones, L. L. (1998). Collaborative interventions for assisting students with acquired brain injuries in school. *Professional School Counseling, 2,* 33–38.

Gardner, H. (1999). *The disciplined mind.* New York: Simon & Schuster.

Gardner, R., & Miranda, A. H. (2001). Improving outcomes for urban African American students. *The Journal of Negro Education, 70* (4), 255–263.

Gates, B. (2005, March 3). Fixing obsolete high schools. *The Washington Post,* 3B.

Gatta, L., McCabe, N., & Edgar, S. (1997). A student advocacy program: A means of expanding the role and effectiveness of teachers. *The High School Journal, 80,* 273–278.

Gazda, G. M., Ginter, E. J., & Horne, A. M. (2001). *Group counseling and group psychotherapy: Theory and application.* Boston: Allyn & Bacon.

George, Y., Dagnese, D., Halpin, G., Halpin, G., & Keiter, R. (1996, October). *Peer mediation training: A solution to violence in schools.* Paper presented at the annual meeting of the Mid-South Educational Research Association, Tuscaloosa, AL.

Gerber, S., & Terry-Day, B. (1999). Does peer mediation really work? *Professional School Counseling, 2,* 169–171.

Gerler, E. R. (1985). Elementary school counseling research and the classroom learning environment. *Elementary School Guidance and Counseling, 20,* 39–40.

Gerler, E. R., Jr. (1992). Consultation and school counseling. *Elementary School Guidance and Counseling, 26,* 162.

Geroski, A. M., Rodgers, K. A., & Breen, D. T. (1997). Using the *DSM–IV* to enhance collaboration among school counselors, clinical counselors, and primary care physicians. *Journal of Counseling and Development, 75,* 231–239.

Gershon, J. (2002). A meta-analytic review of gender differences in ADHD. *Journal of Attention Disorders, 5* (3), 143–154.

Getch, Y. Q. (1996). *An evaluation of the self-advocacy strategy for students who are deaf.* Unpublished dissertation, University of Arkansas.

Gibelman, M. (1993). School social workers, counselors, and psychologists in collaboration: A shared agenda. *Social Work in Education, 15,* 45–53.

Gibson, R. L., & Mitchell, M. H. (1999). *Introduction to counseling and guidance* (5th ed.). Upper Saddle River, NJ: Merrill.

Gilbert, A. (2003). Group counseling in an elementary school. In K. R. Greenberg (Ed.), *Group counseling in K–12 schools: A handbook for school counselors* (pp. 56–80). Boston: Allyn & Bacon.

Giles, H. C. (2005). Three narratives of parent-educator relationships: Toward counselor repertoires for bridging the urban parent-school divide. *Professional School Counseling, 8,* 228–235.

Gillberg, C. (1991). Outcome in autism and autistic-like conditions. Special section: Longitudinal research. *Journal of the American Academy of Child and Adolescent Psychiatry, 30,* 375–382.

Gilliland, B. E., & James, R. K. (2004). *Theories and strategies in counseling and psychotherapy* (5th ed.). Needham Heights, MA: Allyn & Bacon.

Gladding, S. T. (1997). The creative arts in groups. In H. Forester-Miller & J. A. Kottler (Eds.), *Issues and challenges for group practitioners* (pp. 214–239). Denver, CO: Love.

Gladding, S. T. (2003). *Group work: A counseling specialty* (4th ed.). Upper Saddle River, NJ: Merrill/Prentice Hall.

Gladding, S. T. (2004). *Counseling: A comprehensive profession* (5th ed.). Upper Saddle River, NJ: Merrill/Prentice Hall.

Gladding, S. T. (2005). *Counseling as an art: The creative arts in counseling* (3rd ed.). Alexandria, VA: American Counseling Association.

Gladding, S. T., & Newsome, D. W. (2004). *Community and agency counseling* (2nd ed.). Upper Saddle River, NJ: Merrill/Prentice Hall.

Glasser, W. (1984). *Control theory: A new explanation of how we control our lives.* New York: Harper & Row.

Glasser, W. (2000a). School violence from the perspective of William Glasser. *Professional School Counseling, 4,* 77–80.

Glasser, W. (2000b). *Reality therapy in action.* New York: Harper Collins.

Glen, E. E., & Smith, T. T. (1998). Building self-esteem of children and adolescents with communication disorders. *Professional School Counseling, 2,* 39–46.

Glickman, C. D., Gordon, S. P., & Ross-Gordon, J. M. (1995). *Supervision of instruction: A developmental approach* (3rd ed.). Boston: Allyn & Bacon.

Glosoff, H. L., Herlihy, B., & Spence, E. B. (2000). Privileged communication in the counselor-client relationship. *Journal of Counseling and Development, 78,* 454–462.

Goldman, L. (1990). Qualitative assessment. *The Counseling Psychologist, 18,* 205–213.

Goldstein, A. P., & McGinnis, E. (1997). *Skillstreaming the adolescent.* Champaign, IL: Research Press.

Goldstein, B. S. C., & Harris, K. C. (2000). Consultant practices in two heterogeneous Latino schools. *School Psychology Review, 29,* 368–377.

Good, B. J. (1996). Culture and *DSM–IV:* Diagnosis, knowledge and power. *Culture, Medicine and Psychiatry, 20,* 127–132.

Goodenough, W. H. (1981). *Culture, language, and society.* Menlo Park, CA: Benjamin/Cummings.

Goodnough, G. E., & Dick, J. R. (1998). What a school administrator needs to know about the school counselor's curriculum at the secondary school level. In C. Dykeman (Ed.), *Maximizing school guidance program effectiveness* (pp. 15–20). Greensboro, NC: ERIC-CASS.

Goodnough, G. E., & Lee, V. V. (2004). Group counseling in schools. In B. T. Erford (Ed.), *Professional school counseling: A handbook of theories, programs, and practices* (pp. 173–182). Austin, TX: PRO-ED.

Goodwin, R., Lipsitz, J. D., Chapman, T. F., Mannuzza, S., & Fyer, A. J. (2001). Obssessive-compulsive disorder, separation anxiety co-morbidity in early onset panic disorder. *Psychological Medicine, 31,* 1307–1310.

Gothelf, D., Aharonovsky, O., Horesh, N., Carty, T., & Apter, A. (2004). Life events and personality factors in children and adolescents with obsessive-compulsive disorder and other anxiety disorders. *Comprehensive Psychiatry, 45,* 192–198.

Gottfredson, L. S. (1996). Gottfredson's theory of circumscription and compromise. In D. Brown & L. Brooks (Eds.), *Career choice and development: Applying contemporary theories to practice* (3rd ed., pp. 179–232). San Francisco: Jossey-Bass.

Graham, B. C., & Pulvino, C. (2000). Multicultural conflict resolution: Development, implementation, and assessment of a program for third graders. *Professional School Counseling, 3,* 172–181.

Granello, D. H., & Sears, S. J. (1999). The school to work opportunities act and the role of the school counselor. *Professional School Counseling, 3,* 108–115.

Green, A., & Keys, S. (2001). Expanding the school counseling paradigm: Meeting the needs of the 21st century student. *Professional School Counseling, 5,* 84–95.

Green, B. L., Grace, M. C., Vary, M. G., Kramer, T. L., Gleser, G. C., & Leonard, A. C. (1994). Children of disaster in the second decade: A 17-year follow-up of Buffalo Creek survivors. *Journal of the American Academy of Child and Adolescent Psychiatry, 33,* 71–79.

Greenberg, K. R. (2003). *Group counseling in K–12 schools: A handbook for school counselors.* Boston: Allyn & Bacon.

Greer, B. B., Greer, J. G., & Woody, D. E. (1995). The inclusion movement and its impact on counselors. *The School Counselor, 43,* 124–132.

Gresham, F. M., & Kendell, G. K. (1987). School consultation research: Methodological critique and future research direction. *School Psychology Review, 16,* 306–316.

Gribbons, M. M., & Shoffner, M. F. (2004). Prospective first-generation college students: Meeting their needs through social cognitive career theory. *Professional School Counseling, 8,* 91–97.

Griffith, J. (1998). The relation of school structure and social environment to parent involvement in elementary schools. *Elementary School Journal, 99,* 53–80.

Grolnick, W. S., Benjet, C., Kurinski, C. O., & Apostoleris, N. H. (1997). Predictors of parent involvement in children's schooling. *Journal of Educational Psychology, 89,* 538–548.

Grych, J. H., & Fincham, F. O. (2001). *Interparental conflict and child development: Theory, research*

and applications. Cambridge, England: Cambridge University Press.

Guillot-Miller, L., & Partin, P. W. (2003). Web-based resources for legal and ethical issues in school counseling. *Professional School Counseling, 7,* 52–60.

Gutierrez, L. (1995). Understanding the empowerment process: Does consciousness make a difference? *Social Work Research, 19,* 229–237.

Gutierrez, L., & Ortega, R. (1991). Developing methods to empower Latinos: The importance of groups. *Social Work with Groups, 14,* 23–43.

Guttmacher Institute. (2005a). *State policies in brief: Minors' access to contraceptive services.* Washington, DC: Author.

Guttmacher Institute. (2005b). *State policies in brief: Sex and STD/HIV education.* Washington, DC: Author.

The Guttmacher Report on Public Policy. (2000, August). *Minors and the right to consent to health care.* The Alan Guttmacher Institute (Vol. 34). Retrieved April 25, 2005, from www. agi-usa.org/pubs/journals/gr030303.html

Gysbers, N. C. (2004). Comprehensive guidance and counseling programs: The evolution of accountability. *Professional School Counseling, 7,* 1–14.

Gysbers, N., & Henderson, P. (1994). *Developing and managing your school guidance program* (2nd ed.). Alexandria, VA: American Association for Counseling and Development.

Gysbers, N. C., & Henderson, P. (2000). *Developing and managing your school counseling program* (3rd ed.). Alexandria, VA: American Counseling Association.

Gysbers, N. C., & Henderson, P. (2001). Comprehensive guidance and counseling programs: A rich history and a bright future. *Professional School Counseling, 4,* 246–256.

Gysbers, N. C., Lapan, R. T., & Blair, M. (1999). Closing in on the statewide implementation of a comprehensive guidance program model. *Professional School Counseling, 2,* 357–366.

Gysbers, N. C., Lapan, R. T., & Jones, B. A. (2000). School board policies for guidance and counseling: A call to action. *Professional School Counseling, 3,* 349–355.

Hadley, H. R. (1988). Improving reading scores through a self-esteem intervention program. *Elementary School Guidance and Counseling, 22,* 248–252.

Hagborg, W. J. (1993). Middle-school student satisfaction with group counseling: An initial study. *Journal for Specialists in Group Work, 18,* 80–85.

Hale-Benson, J. E. (1986). *Black children: Their roots, culture, and learning styles* (2nd ed.). Baltimore: Johns Hopkins University Press.

Halverson, S. (1999). "And now I'm addicted!": A counselor's plan to teach kids about addiction. *Professional School Counseling, 3,* 147–149.

Hanish, L. D., & Guerra, N. G. (2000). Children who get victimized at school: What is known? What can be done? *Professional School Counseling, 4,* 113–119.

Hansen, L. S. (1999). Beyond school-to-work: Continuing contributions of theory and practice to career development of youth. *Career Development Quarterly, 47,* 353–358.

Hanson, R. F., & Spratt, E. G. (2000). Reactive Attachment Disorder: What we know about the disorder and implications for treatment. *Child Maltreatment, 5,* 137–145.

Hardesty, P., & Dillard, J. (1994). The role of elementary school counselors compared with their middle and secondary school counterparts. *The School Counselor, 29,* 83–90.

Hardiman, R., & Jackson, B. W. (1997). Conceptual foundations for social justice courses. In M. Adams, L. A. Bell, & P. Griffin (Eds.), *Teaching for diversity and social justice: A sourcebook* (pp. 16–29). New York: Routledge.

Hardman, M. L., Drew, C. J., & Egan, M. W. (1996). *Human exceptionality: Society, school, and family* (5th ed.). Needham Heights, MA: Allyn & Bacon.

Harris, J. C. (1995). Psychiatric disorders in mentally retarded persons. In G. O. Gabbard (Ed.), *Treatments of psychiatric disorders* (pp. 95–122). Washington, DC: American Psychiatric Press.

Harris, S. L. (2000). Pervasive developmental disorders: The spectrum of autism. In M. Hersen & R. T. Ammerman (Eds.), *Advanced abnormal child psychology* (2nd ed. pp. 315–333). Mahwah, NJ: Lawrence Erlbaum Associates.

Hart, P. J., & Jacobi, M. (1992). *From gatekeeper to advocate: Transforming the role of the school counselor.* New York: College Entrance Examination Board.

Haugaard, J. J., & Hazan, C. (2004). Recognizing and treating uncommon behavioral and emotional disorders in children and adolescents who have been severely maltreated: Reactive attachment disorder. *Child Maltreatment, 9,* 154–160.

Havighurst, R. J. (1972). *Developmental tasks and education* (3rd ed.). New York: David McKay.

Hawes, D. J. (2000). Resource: The PASSPORT program: A journey through emotional, social, cognitive, and self-development. *Professional School Counseling, 3,* 229–230.

Hayes, R. L., Dagley, J. C., & Horne, A. M. (1996). Restructuring school counselor education: Work in progress. *Journal of Counseling and Development, 74,* 378–384.

Hayes, R. L., Nelson, J. L., Tabin, M., Pearson, G., & Worthy, C. (2002). Using school-wide data to advocate for student success. *Professional School Counseling, 62,* 86–95.

Hayes, R. L., Paisley, P. O., Phelps, R. E., Pearson, G., & Salter, R. (1997). Integrating theory and practice: Counselor educator-school counselor collaborative. *Professional School Counseling, 1*(1), 9–12.

Hayward, C., Wilson, K. A., Lagle, K., Killen, J. D., & Taylor, C. B. (2004). Parent-reported predictors of adolescent panic attacks. *Journal of the American Academy of Child and Adolescent Psychiatry, 4,* 613–620.

Hazler, R. J. (1998). Promoting personal investment in systematic approaches to school violence. *Education, 119,* 222–231.

Hazler, R. J., & Carney, J. V. (2000). When victims turn aggressors: Factors in the development of deadly school violence. *Professional School Counseling, 4,* 105–112.

Hazler, R. J., & Denham, S. A. (2002). Social isolation of youth at risk: Conceptualization and practical solutions. *Journal of Counseling and Development, 80,* 403–409.

Hazler, R. J., Miller, D., Carney, J. V., & Green, S. (2001). Adult recognition of school bullying situations. *Educational Research, 43,* 133–146.

Heatherington, E. M. (1989). Coping with family transitions: Winners, losers and survivors. *Child Development, 60,* 1–14.

Heatherington, E. M. (1993). An overview of the Virginia longitudinal study of divorce and remarriage with a focus on early adolescence. *Journal of Family Psychology, 7,* 39–56.

Heatherington, E. M. (1999). Social capital and the development of youth from divorced, nondivorced, and remarried families. In W. A. Collins & B. Laursen (Eds.), *Relationships as developmental contexts: The Minnesota symposium on child psychology* (Vol. 30, pp. 177–210). Mahwah, NJ: Lawrence Erlbaum Associates.

Hedges, L. V., & Olkin, I. (1985). *Statistical methods for meta-analysis.* Orlando, FL: Academic Press.

Heide, K. M. (1999). *Young killers: The challenge of juvenile homicide.* Thousand Oaks, CA: Sage.

Helms, J. E. (1994). The conceptualization of racial identity and other racial constructs. In E. J. Trickett, R. J. Watts, & D. Birman (Eds.), *Human diversity:*

Perspectives on people in context (pp. 185–311). San Francisco: Jossey-Bass.

Henderson, P. A. (1987). Terminating the counseling relationship with children. *Elementary School Guidance and Counseling, 22,* 143–148.

Henderson, P., & Gysbers, N. C. (1998). *Leading and managing your school guidance staff: A manual for school administrators and directors of guidance.* Alexandria, VA: American Counseling Association.

Henggeler, S. W. (1994). A consensus: Conclusions of the APA Task Force Report on innovative models of mental health services for children, adolescents and their families. *Journal of Clinical Child Psychology, 23* (Suppl.), 3–6.

Henning-Stout, M. (1994). Thoughts on being a white consultant. *Journal of Educational and Psychological Consultation, 5,* 269–273.

Henry, M. (1996). *Parent-school collaboration.* Albany: State University of New York Press.

Heppner, P. P., Kivlighan, D. M., Jr., & Wampold, B. E. (1992). *Research design in counseling.* Pacific Grove, CA: Brooks/Cole.

Herlihy, B., & Corey, G. (1996). *ACA ethical standards casebook* (5th ed.). Alexandria, VA: American Counseling Association.

Hernandez, T. J., & Seem, S. R. (2004). A safe school climate: A systematic approach and the school counselor. *Professional School Counseling, 7,* 256–262.

Herr, E. L. (1979). *Guidance and counseling in the schools. Perspectives on the past, present, and future.* Falls Church, VA: American Personnel and Guidance Association.

Herr, E. L. (1989). *Counseling in a dynamic society: Opportunities and challenges.* Alexandria, VA: American Counseling Association.

Herr, E. L. (1998). *Counseling in a dynamic society: Contexts and practices in the 21st century* (2nd ed.). Alexandria, VA: American Counseling Association.

Herr, E. L. (1999). *Counseling in a dynamic society. Contexts and practices for the 21st century.* Alexandria, VA: American Counseling Association.

Herr, E. L. (2001). The impact of national policies, economics, and school reform on comprehensive guidance programs. *Professional School Counseling, 2,* 236–245.

Herr, E. L. (2002). School reform and perspectives on the role of school counselors: A century of proposals for change. *Professional School Counseling, 5,* 220–234.

Herr, E. L., & Cramer, S. H. (1996). *Career guidance and counseling through the lifespan* (5th ed.). New York: Harper Collins.

Herr, E. L., Cramer, S. H., & Niles, S. G. (2004). *Career guidance and counseling through the lifespan* (6th ed.). Boston: Allyn & Bacon.

Herring, R. D. (1997a). *Multicultural counseling in schools.* Alexandria, VA: American Counseling Association.

Herring, R. (1997b). *Counseling diverse ethnic youth: Synergetic strategies and interventions for school counselors.* Fort Worth, TX: Harcourt Brace.

Hijazi, Y., Tatar, M., & Gati, I. (2004). Career decision-making difficulties among Israeli and Palestinian Arab high-school seniors. *Professional School Counseling, 8,* 64–72.

Hines, P. L., & Fields, T. H. (2002). Pregroup screening issues for school counselors. *Journal for Specialists in Group Work, 27,* 358–376.

Hixson, J., & Tinzmann, M. B. (1990). *Essay: Who are the "at-risk" students of the 1990s?* Retrieved January 5, 2002, from www.ncrel.org/sdrs/areas/rpl_esys/equity.htm

Hoagwood, K. (1999). *Summary sheet: Major research findings on child and adolescent mental health.* Washington, DC: National Institute of Mental Health.

Hoagwood, K., & Erwin, H. D. (1997). Effectiveness of school-based mental health services for children: A 10-year research review. *Journal of Child and Family Studies, 6,* 425–451.

Hoagwood, K., Kelleher, K. J., Feil, M., & Comer, D. M. (2000). Treatment services for children with AD/HD: A national perspective. *American Academy of Child and Adolescent Psychiatry, 39,* 198–206.

Hobbs, B. B., & Collison, B. B. (1995). School-community collaboration: Implications for the school counselor. *The School Counselor, 43,* 58–65.

Hoberman, H. M. (1992). Ethnic minority status and adolescent mental health services utilization. *Journal of Mental Health Administration, 19,* 246–267.

Hobson, S. M., & Phillips, G. A. (2004). Educational planning: Helping students build lives by choice, not chance. In B. T Erford (Ed.), *Professional school counseling: A handbook of theories, programs, & practices* (pp. 325–340). Austin, TX: PRO-ED.

Hodgkinson, H. L. (1985). *All one system. Demographics of education, kindergarten through graduate school.* Washington, DC: The Institute for Educational Leadership.

Hodgkinson, H. L. (1995). The changing face of tomorrow's student. *Change, 17,* 38–39.

Holcomb–McCoy, C. (2001). Exploring the self-perceived multicultural counseling competence of elementary school counselors. *Professional School Counseling, 4,* 195–201.

Holcomb–McCoy, C. (2004). Assessing the multicultural competence of school counselors: A checklist. *Professional School Counseling, 7,* 178–186.

Holcomb–McCoy, C., & Myers, J. E. (1999). Multicultural competence and counselor training: A national survey. *Journal of Counseling and Development, 77,* 294–302.

Holland, J. L. (1992). *Making vocational choices* (2nd ed.). Odessa, FL: Psychological Assessment Resources.

Hopkins, B. R., & Anderson, B. S. (1990). *The counselor and the law* (3rd ed.). Alexandria, VA: American Counseling Association.

House, A. E. (1999). DSM–IV *diagnosis in the schools.* New York: Guilford Press.

House, R. M., & Hayes, R. L. (2002). School counselors: Becoming key players in school reform. *Professional School Counseling, 5,* 249–256.

House, R. M., & Martin, P. J. (1998). Advocating for better futures for all students: A new vision for school counselors. *Education, 119,* 284–291.

Howard, D. E., & Wang, M. Q. (2003). Risk profiles of adolescent girls who were victims of dating violence. *Adolescence, 38*(149), 1–14.

Howell, K. W., & Rueda, R. (1996). Achievement testing with culturally and linguistically diverse students. In L. A. Suzuki, P. J. Meller, & J. G. Ponterotto (Eds.), *Handbook of multicultural assessment* (pp. 253–290). San Francisco: Jossey-Bass.

Hughes, C., Kim, H., Hwang, B., Killian, D. J., Fischer, G. M., Brock, M. L., et al. (1997). Practitioner-validated secondary transition support strategies. *Education and Training in Mental Retardation and Developmental Disabilities, 32,* 201–212.

Hughes, D. K., & James, S. H. (2001). Using account-ability data to protect a school counseling program: One counselor's experience. *Professional School Counseling, 4,* 306–310.

Hughey, K. F., Lapan, R. T., & Gysbers, N. C. (1993). Evaluating a high school guidance–language arts career unit: A qualitative approach. *The School Counselor, 41,* 96–101.

Hulnick, H. R. (1977). Counselor: Know thyself. *Counselor Education and Supervision, 17,* 69–72.

Humphries, T. L. (1999). Improving peer mediation programs: Student experiences and suggestions. *Professional School Counseling, 3,* 13–20.

Hussey, D. L., & Guo, S. (2003). Measuring behavior change in young children receiving intensive school-based mental health services. *Journal of Community Psychology, 31,* 629–639.

Hutchinson, R., & Reagan, C. (1989). Problems for which seniors would seek help from school counselors. *The School Counselor, 36,* 271–280.

Hutson, P. W. (1958). *The guidance function in education* (2nd ed.). New York: Appleton-Century-Crofts.

Idol, L., Nevin, A., & Paolucci-Whitcomb, P. (1994). *Collaborative consultation.* Austin, TX: PRO-ED.

Individuals With Disabilities Education Improvement Act. (2004). *IDEA 2004 resources.* Retrieved August 28, 2005, from www.ed.gov/policy/speced/guid/idea/idea2004.html

Ingraham, C. L. (2000). Consultation through a multicultural lens: Multicultural and cross-cultural consultation in schools. *School Psychology Review, 29,* 320–343.

Institute of Medicine. (1997). *Schools and health.* Washington, DC: National Academy Press.

Irvine, J. J. (1991). *Black students and school failure: Policies, practices, and prescriptions.* New York: Praeger.

Isaacs, M. L. (2003). Data-driven decision making: The engine of accountability. *Professional School Counseling, 6,* 288–295.

Isaacs, M. L., Greene, M., & Valesky, T. (1998). Elementary counselors and inclusion: A statewide attitudinal survey. *Professional School Counseling, 2,* 68–76.

Isaacs, M. L., & Stone, C. (1999). School counselors and confidentiality: Factors affecting professional choices. *Professional School Counseling, 2,* 258–266.

Isely, P. J., Busse, W., & Isely, P. (1998). Sexual assault of males in late adolescence: A hidden phenomenon. *Professional School Counseling, 2,* 153–160.

Izzo, C. V., Weissberg, R. P., Kasprow, N. J., & Fendrich, M. (1999). A longitudinal assessment of teacher perception of parent involvement in children's education and school performance. *American Journal of Community Psychology, 27,* 817–839.

Jackson, A. P. (1990). *Multicultural counseling class lecture notes.* Kent, OH: Kent State University.

Jackson, M., & Grant, D. (2004). Equity, access, and career development: Contextual conflicts. In R. Perusse & G. E. Goodnough (Eds.), *Leadership, advocacy, and direct service strategies for profes-sional school counselors* (pp. 125–153). Belmont, CA: Brooks/Cole-Thomson Learning.

Jacobi, C., Hayward, C., de Zwaan, M., Kraemer, H., & Agras, W. S. (2004). Coming to terms with risk factors for Eating Disorders: Application of risk terminology and suggestions for a general taxonomy. *Psychological Bulletin, 130,* 19–65.

Jacobs, E. E., Masson, R. L., & Harvill, R. L. (2006). *Group counseling: Strategies and skills* (5th ed.). Belmont, CA: Thompson Brooks/Cole.

Jacobs, E., & Schimmel, C. (2005). Small group counseling. In C. Sink (Ed.), *Contemporary school counseling: Theory, research, and practice* (pp. 82–115). Boston: Houghton Mifflin/Lahaska.

James, R. K., & Gilliland, B. E. (2001). *Crisis intervention strategies* (4th ed.). Pacific Grove, CA: Brooks/Cole.

Janson, G. (2000). *Exposure to repetitive abuse: Psychological distress and physiological reactivity in bystanders as compared to victims.* Unpublished doctoral dissertation, Ohio University, Athens.

Jarvis, P. S., & Keeley, E. S. (2003). From vocational decision making to career building: Blueprint, real games, and school counseling. *Professional School Counseling, 6,* 244–251.

Jensen, P. S., Kettle, L., Roper, M. T., Sloan, M. T., Dulcan, M. K., Hoven, C., et al. (1999). Are stimulants overprescribed? Treatment of AD/HD in four U.S. communities. *American Academy of Child and Adolescent Psychiatry, 38,* 797–804.

Jimerson, S., Engeland, B., & Teo, A. (1999). A longitudinal study of achievement trajectories. Factors associated with change. *Journal of Educational Psychology, 9,* 116–126.

Johnson, C. D., & Johnson, S. (2003). Results based guidance: A systems approach to student support. *Professional School Counseling, 6,* 180–185.

Johnson, C. R., & Slomka, G. (2000). Learning, motor, and communication disorders. In M. Hersen & R. T. Ammerman (Eds.), *Advanced abnormal child psychology* (2nd ed., pp. 371–385). Mahwah, NJ: Lawrence Erlbaum Associates.

Johnson, D. (1995). Specific developmental disorders. In M. Hersen & R. T. Ammerman (Eds.), *Advanced abnormal child psychology* (pp. 95–122). Washington, DC: American Psychiatric Press.

Johnson, D. W., & Johnson, R. T. (1995a). *Reducing school violence through conflict resolution.* Alexandria, VA: Association for Supervision and Curriculum Development.

Johnson, D. W., & Johnson, R. T. (1995b). Teaching students to be peacemakers: Results of five years of research. *Peace and Conflict: Journal of Peace Psychology, 1,* 417–438.

Johnson, D. W., & Johnson, R. T. (1996). Teaching all students how to manage conflicts constructively: The peacemakers program. *Journal of Negro Education, 65,* 322–335.

Johnson, D. W., & Johnson, R. T. (2002, February). Teaching students to resolve their own and their schoolmates' conflicts. *Counseling and Human Development, 34* (6), 1–12.

Johnson, D. W., Johnson, R. T., & Dudley, B. (1992). Effects of peer mediation training on elementary school students. *Mediation Quarterly, 10,* 89–99.

Johnson, D. W., Johnson, R., Dudley, B., Ward, M., & Magnuson, D. (1995). The impact of peer mediation training on the management of school and home conflicts. *American Educational Research Journal, 32,* 829–844.

Johnson, L. S. (2000). Promoting professional identity in an era of educational reform. *Professional School Counseling, 4,* 31–40.

Johnson, R. (1996). *Setting our sights: Measuring equity in school change.* Los Angeles: The Achievement Council.

Johnson, R. S. (2002). *Using data to close the achievement gap: How to measure equity in schools* (2nd ed.). Thousand Oaks, CA: Corwin Press.

Johnson, S. D. (1990). Toward clarifying culture, race, and ethnicity in the context of multicultural counseling. *Journal of Multicultural Counseling and Development, 18,* 41–50.

Johnson, S., & Johnson, C. D. (2003). Results-based guidance: A systems approach to student support programs. *Professional School Counseling, 6,* 180–185.

Johnson, V. A. (1996). Factors impacting the job retention and advancement of workers who are deaf. *Volta Review, 9,* 341–356.

Joint Committee on Testing Practices. (2004). *Code of fair testing practices* (2nd ed.). Washington, DC: Author.

Jones, A. J. (1930). *Principles of guidance.* New York: McGraw-Hill.

Jones, A. J. (1934). *Principles of guidance* (2nd ed.). New York: McGraw-Hill.

Jones, L. K. (2004). *The Career Key.* Retrieved on May 1, 2005, from www.careerkey.org

Jones, L. K., Sheffield, D., & Joyner, B. (2000). Comparing the effects of the Career Key with Self-Directed Search and Job-OE among eighth-grade students. *Professional School Counseling, 3,* 238–247.

Jones, T. S., & Compton, R. (2003). *Kids working it out: Stories and strategies for making peace in our schools.* San Francisco: Jossey-Bass.

Jordan, G. E., Snow, C. E., & Porche, M. V. (2000). Project EASE: The effect of a family literacy project on kindergarten students' early literacy skills. *Reading Research Quarterly, 35,* 524–546.

Juvenile Offenders & Victims National Report. (1999). *Juvenile offenders and victims: 1999 national report* (NCJ 178257). Washington, DC: U.S. Department of Justice.

Juvonen, J. (2001). *School violence: Prevalence, fears, and prevention* (RAND IP-219-EDU). Retrieved May 31, 2005, from www.rand.org.

Kadesjo, B., & Gillberg, C. (2000). Tourette's disorder: Epidemiology and comorbidity in primary school children. *Journal of the American Academy of Child and Adolescent Psychiatry, 39,* 548–555.

Kagan, J., & Gall, S. B. (Eds.). (1998). *The Gale encyclopedia of childhood and adolescence.* Detroit, MI: Gale Research.

Kahn, B. B. (1999). Art therapy with adolescents: Making it work for school counselors. *Professional School Counseling, 2,* 291–298.

Kahn, B. B. (2000). A model of solution-focused consultation for school counselors. *Professional School Counseling, 3,* 248–254.

Kampwirth, T. J. (2002). *Collaborative consultation in the schools. Effective practices for students with learning and behavior problems* (2nd ed.). Upper Saddle River, NJ: Prentice Hall.

Kann, L., Kinchen, S. A., Williams, B., Ross, J. G., Lowry, R., & Grunbaum, J. A. (2000). Youth risk behavior surveillance: United States, 1999. *Journal of School Health, 70,* 271–285.

Kaplan, H., Sadock, B., & Grebb, J. (1994). *Synopsis of psychiatry* (7th ed.). Baltimore: Williams & Wilkins.

Kaplan, L. S. (1996). Outrageous or legitimate concerns: What some parents are saying about school counseling. *The School Counselor, 43,* 165–170.

Kareck, T. J. (1998). Making the time to counsel students. *Professional School Counseling, 1*(5), 56–57.

Kataoka, S. H., Zhang, L., & Wells, K. B. (2002). Unmet need for mental health care among U.S. children: Variation by ethnicity and insurance status. *American Journal of Psychiatry, 159,* 1548–1555.

Katzman, M. A., & Lee, S. (1997). Beyond body image: The integration of feminist and transcultural theories in the understanding of self starvation. *International Journal of Eating Disorders, 22,* 385–394.

Kazdin, A. E. (1994). Methodology, design, and evaluation in psychotherapy research. In A. E. Bergin & S. L. Garfield (Eds.), *Handbook of psychotherapy and behavior change* (pp. 19–71). New York: John Wiley & Sons.

Kazdin, A. E. (1997). Psychosocial treatments for conduct disorder in children. *Journal of Child Psychology and Psychiatry and Allied Professions, 38,* 161–178.

Kearney, C. A., Sims, K. E., Pursell, C. R., & Tillotson, C. A. (2003). Separation anxiety disorder in young children: A longitudinal and family analysis. *Journal of Clinical Child and Adolescent Psychology, 32,* 593–598.

Keel, P. K., & Klump, K. L. (2003). Are eating disorders culture-bound syndromes? Implications for conceptualizing their etiology. *Psychological Bulletin, 129,* 747–769.

Kehle, T. J., Madaus, M. R., Baratta, V. S., & Bray, M. A. (1998). Augmented self-modeling as a treatment for children with selective mutism. *Journal of School Psychology, 36,* 247–260.

Keith, T. Z., Keith, P. B., Quirk, K. J., Speeduto, J., Santillo, S., & Killings, S. (1998). Longitudinal effects of parent involvement on high school grades: Similarities and differences across gender and ethnic groups. *Journal of School Psychology, 36,* 335–363.

Kellough, R. D., & Roberts, P. L. (2002). *A resource guide for elementary school teaching* (5th ed.). Upper Saddle River, NJ: Merrill.

Kelly, J. A. (1982). *Social-skills training: A practical guide for interventions.* New York: Springer.

Kelly, J. B., & Emery, R. E. (2003). Children's adjustment following divorce: Risk and resilience perspectives. *Family Relations, 52,* 352–362.

Kendall, P. (1993). Cognitive-behavioral therapies with youth: Guiding theory, current status, and emerging developments. *Journal of Consulting and Clinical Psychology, 61,* 235–247.

Kendall, P. C., Chu, B. C., Pimentel, S. S., & Choudhury, M. (2000). Treating anxiety disorders in youth. In P. C. Kendall (Ed.), *Child and adolescent therapy: Cognitive behavioral procedures* (pp. 235–287). New York: Guilford Press.

Kendall, P. C., Safford, S., Flannery-Schroeder, E., & Webb, A. (2004). Child anxiety treatment: Outcomes and impact on substance use and depression at 7.4-year follow-up. *Journal of Consulting and Clinical Psychology, 72,* 276–287.

Kessler, R. C., & Walters, E. E. (1998). Epidemiology of *DSM–III–R* major depression and minor depression among adolescents and young adults in the National Comorbidity Survey. *Depression & Anxiety, 7,* 3–14.

Keys, S. G. (2000). Foreword: Special edition: Collaborating for safe schools and safe communities. *Professional School Counseling, 3,* iv–v.

Keys, S. G., & Bemak, F. (1997). School-family-community linked services: A school counseling role for the changing times. *The School Counselor, 44,* 255–263.

Keys, S. G., Bemak, F., Carpenter, S. L., & King–Sears, M. F. (1998). Collaborative consultants: A new role for counselors serving at-risk youth. *Journal of Counseling and Development, 76,* 123–133.

Keys, S. G., Bemak, F., & Lockhart, E. J. (1998). Transforming school counseling to serve the mental health needs of at-risk youth. *Journal of Counseling and Development, 76,* 381–388.

Keys, S. G., & Lockhart, E. J. (1999). The school counselor's role in facilitating multi-systemic change. *Professional School Counseling, 3,* 101–107.

King, K. A., Price, J. H., Telljohann, S. K., & Wahl, J. (2000). Preventing adolescent suicide: Do high school counselors know the risk factors? *Professional School Counseling, 3,* 255–263.

King, K. A., Tribble, J. L., & Price, J. H. (1999). School counselors' perceptions of nonconsensual sexual activity among high school students. *Professional School Counseling, 2,* 286–290.

King, K. A., Wagner, D. I., & Hedrick, B. (2001). Safe and Drug-Free School coordinators' perceived needs to improve violence and drug prevention programs. *Journal of School Health, 71,* 236–241.

King, R. A., & Noshpitz, J. D. (1991). *Pathways of growth: Essentials of child psychiatry.* New York: John Wiley & Sons.

Kirst, M. (1991). Improving children's services: Overcoming barriers, creating new opportunities. *Phi Delta Kappan, 72,* 615–618.

Kiselica, M. S., Baker, S. B., Thomas, R. N., & Reddy, S. (1994). Effects of stress inoculation training on anxiety, stress, and academic performance among adolescents. *Journal of Counseling Psychology, 41,* 335–342.

Kitchener, K. S. (1984). Intuition, critical evaluation and ethical principles: The foundation for ethical decisions in counseling psychology. *The Counseling Psychologist, 12* (3), 43–55.

Kizner, L. R., & Kizner, S. R. (1999). Small group counseling with adopted children. *Professional School Counseling, 2,* 226–229.

Klein, R. G. (1993). Clinical efficacy of methylphenidate in children and adolescents. *Encephale, 19,* 89–93.

Klein, R. G. (1994). Anxiety disorders. In M. Rutter, E. Taylor, & L. Hersov (Eds.), *Child and adolescent psychiatry: Modern approaches* (pp. 351–374). Cambridge, MA: Blackwell.

Klein, T., Thornburg, K. R., & Kilmer, D. (1993). *Step by step: Toward Missouri's future.* Columbia: Missouri Youth Initiative.

Kluckhohn, C. (1985). *Mirror for man: The relation of anthropology to modern life.* Tucson: University of Arizona Press.

Kochman, T. (1981). *Black and white styles in conflict.* Chicago: University of Chicago Press.

Kovacs, M., Akiskal, S., Gatsonis, C., & Parrone, P. (1994). Childhood-onset dysthymic disorder. *Archives of General Psychiatry, 51,* 365–374.

Kraus, L. J., & Hughey, K. F. (1999). The impact of intervention on career decision-making self-efficacy and career indecision. *Professional School Counseling, 2,* 384–390.

Krentz, A., & Arthur, N. (2001). Counseling culturally diverse students with eating disorders. *Journal of College Student Psychotherapy, 15,* 7–21.

Kress, V. E., Erikson, K. P., Rayle, A. D., & Ford, S. J. W. (2005). The *DSM–IV–TR* and culture: Consideration for counselors. *Journal of Counseling and Development, 83,* 97–104.

Kress, V. E., Gibson, D. M., & Reynolds, C. A. (2004). Adolescents who self-injure: Implications and strategies for school counselors. *Professional School Counseling, 7,* 195–201.

Krishnakumer, A., & Buehler, C. (2000). Interparental conflict and parenting behaviors: A meta-analytic review. *Family Relations, 49,* 25–44.

Kronenberger, W. G., & Meyer, R. G. (1996). *The child clinician's handbook.* Needham Heights, MA: Allyn & Bacon.

Krumboltz, J. D. (1974). An accountability model for counselors. *Personnel and Guidance Journal, 52,* 639–646.

Krumboltz, J. D., & Worthington R. (1999). The school-to-work transition from a learning theory perspective. *Career Development Quarterly, 47,* 312–325.

Krysanski, V. L. (2003). A brief review of selective mutism literature. *The Journal of Psychology, 137,* 29–40.

Kulic, K. R., Dagley, J. C., & Horne, A. M. (2001). Prevention groups with children and adolescents. *Journal for Specialists in Group Work, 26,* 211–218.

Kumra, S., Sporn, A., Hommer, D. W., Nicolson, R., Thaker, G., Israel, E., et al. (2001). Smooth pursuit eye-tracking impairment in childhood-onset psychotic disorders. *The American Journal of Psychiatry, 158,* 1291–1298.

Kupper, L. (1999). *Questions often asked by parents about special education services* (4th ed. briefing paper). Washington, DC: National Information Center for Children and Youth with Disabilities.

Kurlan, R., Como, P. G., Miller, B., Palumbo, D., Deeley, C., Andersen, E. M., et al. (2002). The behavioral spectrum of tic disorders: A community-based study. *Neurology, 59,* 414–420.

Kurpius, D. J. (1985). Consultation interventions: Successes, failures and proposals. *The Counseling Psychologist, 13,* 368–389.

Kurpius, D. J., & Fuqua, D. R. (1993). Consultation I: Conceptual, structural, and operational dimensions. *Journal of Counseling and Development, 71,* 596–708.

Kurpius, D. J., & Rozecki, T. (1992). Outreach, advocacy, and consultation: A framework for prevention and intervention. *Elementary School Guidance and Counseling, 26,* 176–189.

Kush, K., & Cochran, L. (1993). Enhancing a sense of agency through career planning. *Journal of Counseling Psychology, 40,* 434–451.

Lachat, M. A. (2002). *Data-driven high school reform: The breaking ranks model.* Hampton, NH: Center for Resource Management.

LaFountain, R. M., & Garner, N. E. (1998). *A school with solutions: Implementing a solution-focused/Adlerian-based comprehensive school counseling program.* Alexandria, VA: ASCA.

Lambert, M. J. (1991). Introduction to psychotherapy research. In L. E. Beutler & M. Crago (Eds.), *Psychotherapy research: An international review of programmatic studies* (pp. 1–23). Washington, DC: American Psychological Association.

Lambie, G. W. (2004). Motivational Enhancement Therapy: A tool for professional school counselors working with adolescents. *Professional School Counseling, 7,* 268–276.

Lambie, G. W. (2005). Child abuse and neglect: A practical guide for professional school counselors. *Professional School Counseling, 8,* 249–259.

Lambie, G. W., & Rokutani, L. J. (2002). A systems approach to substance abuse identification and intervention for school counselors. *Professional School Counseling, 5,* 353–359.

Lambie, G. W., & Sias, S. M. (2005). Children of alcoholics: Implications for school counseling. *Professional School Counseling, 8,* 266–273.

Landreth, G. (1993). Child-centered play therapy. *Elementary School Guidance and Counseling, 28,* 17–29.

Landreth, G. (2002). *Play therapy: The art of the relationship* (2nd ed.). New York: Brunner-Routledge.

Lane, P. S., & McWhirter, J. J. (1992). A peer mediation model: Conflict resolution for elementary and middle school children. *Elementary School Guidance and Counseling, 27,* 15–23.

Lapan, R. T. (2001). Results-based comprehensive guidance and counseling programs: A framework for planning and evaluation. *Professional School Counseling, 4,* 289–299.

Lapan, R. (2004). *Career development across the K–16 years: Bridging the present to satisfying and successful futures.* Alexandria, VA: American Counseling Association.

Lapan, R. T., Gysbers, N., Hughey, K., & Arni, T. J. (1993). Evaluating a guidance and language arts unit for high school juniors. *Journal of Counseling and Development, 71,* 444–451.

Lapan, R. T., Gysbers, N. C., & Petroski, G. F. (2003). Helping seventh graders be safe and successful: A statewide study of the impact of comprehensive guidance and counseling programs. *Professional School Counseling, 6,* 186–197.

Lapan, R. T., Gysbers, N. C., & Sun, Y. (1997). The impact of more fully implemented guidance programs on the school experiences of high school students: A statewide evaluation study. *Journal of Counseling and Development, 75,* 292–302.

Larmann-Billings, L., & Emery, R. E. (2000). Distress among young adults in divorced families. *Journal of Family Psychology, 14,* 671–687.

Last, C. G., Perrin, S., Hersen, M., & Kazdin, A. E. (1992). DSM–III–R anxiety disorders in children: Sociodemographic and clinical characteristics. *Journal of the American Academy of Child and Adolescent Psychiatry, 31,* 1070–1076.

Last, C. G., Strauss, C., & Francis, G. (1987). Comorbidity among childhood anxiety disorders. *Journal of Nervous and Mental Disease, 175,* 726–730.

Lavin, M., & Rifkin, A. (1993). Diagnosis and pharmacotherapy of conduct disorder. *Progress in Neuro-psychopharmacology and Biological Psychiatry, 17,* 875–885.

Lavoritano, J. E., & Segal, P. B. (1992). Evaluating the efficacy of short-term counseling on adolescents in a school setting. *Adolescence, 27*(107), 535–543.

Leckman, J. F., & Cohen, D. J. (1994). Tic disorders. In M. Rutter, E. Taylor, & L. Hersov (Eds.), *Child and adolescent psychiatry: Modern approaches* (pp. 455–466). Cambridge, MA: Blackwell.

Lee, C. C. (Ed.). (1985). *Counseling for diversity: A guide for school counselors and related professionals.* Needham Heights, MA: Allyn & Bacon.

Lee, C. C. (1991). New approaches to diversity: Implications for multicultural counselor training and research. In C. C. Lee & B. L. Richardson (Eds.), *Multicultural issues in counseling: New approaches to diversity* (pp. 209–213). Alexandria, VA: American Association for Counseling and Development.

Lee, C. C. (1997, January). Empowerment through social action. *Counseling Today,* pp. 5, 26.

Lee, C. C. (1998). Counselors as agents of social change. In C. C. Lee & G. R. Walz (Eds.), *Social action: A mandate for counselors* (pp. 3–14). Alexandria, VA: American Counseling Association & ERIC/CASS.

Lee, C. C. (2001a). Culturally responsive school counselors and programs: Addressing the needs of all students. *Professional School Counseling, 4,* 257–261.

Lee, C. C. (2001b). Defining and responding to racial and ethnic diversity. In D. C. Locke, J. E. Myers, & E. L. Herr (Eds.), *The handbook of counseling* (pp. 581–599). Thousand Oaks, CA: Sage.

Lee, C. C. (2005). Urban school counseling: Context, characteristics, and competencies. *Professional School Counseling, 8,* 184–188.

Lee, C., & Walz, G. (1998). *Social action: A mandate for school counselors.* Alexandria, VA: American School Counselor Association.

Lee, J., & Cramond, B. (1999). The positive effects of mentoring economically disadvantaged students. *Professional School Counseling, 2,* 172–178.

Lee, R. S. (1993). Effects of classroom guidance on student achievement. *Elementary School Guidance and Counseling, 27,* 163–171.

Leff, S. S., Power, T. J., Manz, P. H., Costigan, T. E., & Nabors, L. A. (2001). School-based aggression prevention programs for young children: Current status and implications for violence prevention. *School Psychology Review, 30,* 344–362.

Lehr, C. A., Hansen, A., Sinclair, M. F., & Christenson, S. L. (2003). Moving beyond dropout prevention to school completion: An integrative review of data-based interventions. *School Psychology Review, 32,* 342–364.

Lehr, C. A., Johnson, D. R., Bremer, C. D., Cosio, A., & Thomson, M. (2004). *Essential tools — Increasing rates of school completion. Moving from policy and research to practice. A manual for policymakers, administrators, and educators.* National Center on Secondary Education and Transition (NCSET). Retrieved August 28, 2005, from www.ncset.org/publications/essentialtools/dropout/default.asp

Lenhardt, M. C., & Young, P. A. (2001). Proactive strategies for advancing elementary school counseling programs: A blueprint for the new millennium. *Professional School Counseling, 4,* 187–194.

Leon, G. R., Fulkerson, J. A., Perry, C.L., Keel, P.K., & Klump, K. L. (1999). Three to four year prospective evaluation of personality and behavioral risk factors for later disordered eating in adolescent girls and boys. *Journal of Youth and Adolescence, 28,* 181–197.

Lerner, R. M. (1995). *America's youth in crisis: Challenges and opportunities for programs and policies.* Thousand Oaks, CA: Sage.

Leviton, S. C., & Greenstone, J. L. (1997). *Elements of mediation.* Pacific Grove, CA: Brooks/Cole.

Lewinsohn, P. M., Clarke, G. N., Hops, H., & Andrews, J. (1990). Cognitive behavioral group treatment of depression in adolescents. *Behavior Therapy, 21,* 385–401.

Lewinsohn, P. M., Rohde, P., Seeley, J. R., Klein, D. N., & Gotlib, I. H. (2000). Natural course of adolescent major depressive disorder in a community sample: Predictors of recurrence in young adults. *American Journal of Psychiatry, 157,* 1584–1591.

Lewis, J. A., & Arnold, M. S. (1998). From multiculturalism to social action. In C. C. Lee & G. R. Walz (Eds.), *Social action: A mandate for counselors* (pp. 51–65). Alexandria, VA: American Counseling Association.

Lewis, J. A., & Bradley, L. (Eds.). (2000). *Advocacy in counseling: Counselors, clients, and community.* Greensboro, NC: CAPS & ERIC/CASS.

Lewis, M. W., & Lewis, A. C. (1996). Peer helping programs: Helper role, supervisor training, and suicidal behavior. *Journal of Counseling and Development, 74,* 307–313.

Libsch, M., & Freedman-Doan, P. (1995). Perceptions of high school counseling activities: Response differences according to college plans. *NASSP Bulletin, 79,* 53–55.

Lin, M., Kelly, K. R., & Nelson, R. C. (1996). A comparative analysis of the interpersonal process in school-based counseling and consultation. *Journal of Counseling Psychology, 43,* 389–393.

Linde, L. E. (2003). Ethical, legal, and professional issues in school counseling. In B. T. Erford (Ed.), *Transforming the school counseling profession* (pp. 39–62). Upper Saddle River, NJ: Merrill/Prentice Hall.

Littrell, J. M., Malia, J. A., & Vanderwood, M. (1995). Single session brief counseling in a high school. *Journal of Counseling and Development, 73,* 451–458.

Locke, D. C. (1990). A not so provincial view of multicultural counseling. *Counselor Education and Supervision, 30,* 18–25.

Lockhart, E. J., & Keys, S. G. (1998). The mental health counseling role of school counselors. *Professional School Counseling, 1,* 3–6.

Loeber, R., & Stouthamer-Loeber, M. (1998). Development of juvenile aggression and violence: Some common misconceptions and controversies. *American Psychologist, 53,* 242–259.

Loesch, L. C., & Ritchie, M. H. (2004). *The accountable school counselor.* Austin, TX: PRO-ED.

Lofaro, G. A. (1982). Disability and counselor education. *Counselor Education and Supervision, 21,* 200–207.

Lombana, J. H. (1985). Guidance accountability: A new look at an old problem. *The School Counselor, 32,* 340–346.

Long, J. J., Fabricus, W. V., Musheno, M., & Palumbo, D. (1998). Exploring the cognitive and affective capacities of child mediators in a "successful" inner-city peer mediation program. *Mediation Quarterly, 15,* 289–302.

Lopez, E. C. (2000). Conducting instructional consultation through interpreters. *School Psychology Review, 29,* 378–388.

Lord, C., & Rutter, M. (1994). Autism and pervasive developmental disorders. In M. Rutter, E. Taylor, & L. Hersov (Eds.), *Child and adolescent psychiatry: Modern approaches* (pp. 596–593). Cambridge, MA: Blackwell.

Löwe, B., Zipfel, S., Buchholz, C., Dupont, Y., Reas, D. L., & Herzog, W. (2001). Long-term outcomes of anorexia nervosa in a prospective 21-year follow-up study. *Psychological Medicine, 31,* 881–890.

Luongo, P. F. (2000). Partnering child welfare, juvenile justice, and behavioral health with schools. *Professional School Counseling, 3,* 308–314.

Ly, T. M., & Hodapp, R. M. (2002). Maternal attribution of child noncompliance in children with mental retardation: Down syndrome versus other causes. *Journal of Developmental and Behavioral Pediatrics, 23,* 322–329.

Lyons-Ruth, K., Zeanah, C. H., & Benoit, D. (1996). Disorder and risk for disorder during infancy and todlerhood. In E. J. Mash & R. A. Barkley (Eds.), *Child psychopathology* (pp. 457–491). New York: Guilford Press.

Maag, J. W., & Katsiyannis, A. (1996). Counseling as a related service for students with emotional and behavioral disorders: Issues and recommendations. *Behavioral Disorders, 21,* 293–305.

Macmillan, D. L., Gresham, F. M., Spierstein, G. N., & Bocian, K. M. (1996). The labyrinth of IDEA: School decisions on referred students with sub-average general intelligence. *American Journal of Mental Retardation, 101,* 161–174.

Mahoney, J. S., & Merritt, S. R. (1993). Educational hopes of black and white high school seniors in Virginia. *Journal of Educational Research, 87,* 31–38.

Maital, S. L. (2000). Reciprocal distancing: A systems model of interpersonal processes in cross-cultural consultation. *School Psychology Review, 29,* 389–400.

Manning, M. L. (2000). Benchmarks of student-friendly middle schools. *Education Digest, 66*(2), 21–26.

March, J. S., & Leonard, H. L. (1996). Obsessive-compulsive disorder in children and adolescents: A review of the past 10 years. *Journal of the American Academy of Child and Adolescent Psychiatry, 34,* 1265–1273.

Marcia, J. E. (1989). Identity and intervention. *Journal of Adolescence, 12,* 401–410.

Marinoble, R. M. (1998). Homosexuality: A blind spot in the school mirror. *Professional School Counseling, 1*(3), 4–7.

Marshall, P. L. (2002). *Cultural diversity in our schools.* Belmont, CA: Wadsworth/Thomson Learning.

Maryland State Department of Education. (1998). *Skills for success: Core learning goals.* Retrieved March 28, 2005, from http://mdk12.org/mspp/high_ school/what_will/skillsforsuccess/skills_goals99.pdf

Masi, G., Mucci, M., & Millepiedi, S. (2001). Separation anxiety disorder in children and adolescents: Epidemiology, diagnosis and management. *CNS Drugs, 15,* 94–104.

Masi, G., Perugi, G., Toni, C., Millepiedi, S., Mucci, M., Bertini, N., et al. (2004). Obsessive-compulsive bipolar co-morbidity: Focus on children and adolescents. *Journal of Affective Disorders, 78,* 175–183.

Maslow, A. (1968). *Toward a psychology of being* (2nd ed.). New York: Van Nostrand Reinhold.

Maslow, A. (1987) *Motivation and personality* (3rd ed.). New York: Harper & Row.

Masten, A., Best, K. M., & Garmezy, N. (1991). Resiliency and development: Contributions from the study of children to overcome adversity. *Development and Psychopathology, 2,* 425–444.

Masten, A., & Coatworth, J. D. (1998). The development of competence in favorable and unfavorable environments: Lessons from research on successful children. *American Psychologist, 53,* 205–220.

Mattingley, D. J., Prislin, R., McKenzie, T. L., Rodriquez, J. L., & Kayzar, R. (2002). Evaluating evaluations: The case of parental involvement programs. *Review of Educational Research, 72,* 549–576.

Mau, W., Hitchcock, R., & Calvert, C. (1998). High school students' career plans: The influence of others' expectations. *Professional School Counseling, 2,* 161–166.

Maxman, J. S., & Ward, N. G. (1995). *Essential psychopathology and its treatment* (2nd ed.). New York: Norton.

Mayfield, D., McLeod, G., & Hall, P. (1974). The CAGE questionnaire: Validation of a new alcoholism screening instrument. *American Journal of Psychiatry, 131* (10), 1121–1123.

McAdams, C. R., III, & Lambie, G. W. (2003). A changing profile of aggression in schools: Its impact and implications for school personnel. *Preventing School Failure, 47* (3), 122–130.

McCabe, P., Sheard, C., & Code, C. (2002). Acquired communication impairment in people with HIV. *Journal of Medical Speech-Language Pathology, 10,* 183–199.

McCall-Perez, Z. (2000). The counselor as advocate for English language learners: An action research approach. *Professional School Counseling, 4,* 13–22.

McCauley, J., Kern, D. E., Kolodner, K., Dill, L., Schroeder, A. F., DeChant, H. K., et al. (1997). Clinical characteristics of women with a history of childhood abuse: Unhealed wounds. *Journal of the American Medical Association, 277,* 1362–1368.

McClellan, J., McCurry, C., Speltz, M. L., & Jones, K. (2002). Symptom factors in early-onset psychotic disorders. *Journal of the American Academy of Child and Adolescent Psychiatry, 41,* 791–798.

McClelland, G. M., Elkington, K. S., Teplin, L. A., & Abram, K. M. (2004). Multiple substance use disorders in juvenile detainees. *Journal of the American Academy of Child and Adolescent Psychiatry, 43,* 1215–1224.

McClure, F. H., & Teyber, E. (2003). *Casebook in child and adolescent treatment: Cultural and familial contexts.* Pacific Grove, CA: Brooks/Cole.

McEachern, A. G. (2003). School counselor preparation to meet the guidance needs of exceptional students: A national study. *Counselor Education and Supervision, 42,* 314–325.

McFarland, W. P. (1998). Gay, lesbian and bisexual student suicide. *Professional School Counseling, 1* (3), 26–29.

McFarland, W. P., & Dupuis, M. (2001). The legal duty to protect gay and lesbian students from violence in school. *Professional School Counseling, 4,* 171–179.

McFarland, W. P., & Oliver, J. (1999). Empowering professional school counselors in the war against AIDS. *Professional School Counseling, 2,* 267–274.

McGinnis, E., & Goldstein, A. P. (1997). *Skillstreaming the elementary school child.* Champaign, IL: Research Press.

McGlauflin, H. (1998). Helping children grieve at school. *Professional School Counseling, 1* (5), 46–49.

McGoldrick, M., & Giordano, J. (1996). Overview: Ethnicity and family therapy. In M. McGoldrick, J. Giordano, & J. K. Pierce (Eds.), *Ethnicity and family therapy* (2nd ed., pp. 1–27). New York: Guilford Press.

McLanahan, S. S. (1999). Father absence and children's welfare. In E. M. Heatherington (Ed.), *Coping with divorce, single parenting and remarriage: A risk and resiliency perspective* (pp. 117–146). Mahwah, NJ: Erlbaum.

McWhirter, J. J., McWhirter, B. T., McWhirter, A. M., & McWhirter, E. H. (1998). *At-risk youth: A comprehensive response for counselors, teachers, psychologists, and human service professionals* (2nd ed.). Pacific Grove, CA: Brooks/Cole.

Melaville, A., & Blank, M. J. (1998). *Learning together: The developing field of school-community initiatives.* Flint, MI: Mott Foundation.

Merriam-Webster's Collegiate Dictionary (10th ed.). (1993). Springfield, MA: Merriam-Webster.

Metcalf, L. (1995). *Counseling toward solutions: A practical solution-focused program for working with students, teachers, and parents.* West Nyack, NY: The Center for Applied Research.

Mezirow, J. (1994). Understanding transformation theory. *Adult Education Quarterly, 44,* 222–244.

Mezzich, J. E., Kirmayer, L. J., Kleinman, A, Fabrega, H., Parron, D. L., Good, B. J., et al. (1999). The place of culture in *DSM–IV. The Journal of Nervous and Mental Disease, 187,* 457–464.

Miano, G., Forrest, A., & Gumaer, J. (1997). A collaborative program to assist at-risk youth. *Professional School Counseling, 1* (1), 16–20.

Michlowski, A. (1999). From conflict to congruence. *Kappa Delta Pi Record, 35* (3), 108–111.

Midgette, T. E., & Meggert, S. S. (1991). Multicultural counseling instruction: A challenge for faculties in the 21st century. *Journal of Counseling and Development, 70,* 136–141.

Mikkelsen, E. J. (2001). Enuresis and encopresis: Ten years of progress. *Journal of the American Academy of Child and Adolescent Psychiatry, 40,* 1146–1158.

Miller, C. H. (1961). *Foundations of guidance.* New York: Harper & Brothers.

Miller, F. G. (2001). *The SASSI-A2 manual.* Springfield, IN: SASSI Institute.

Miller, J. (1992). *Coping with chronic illness.* Philadelphia: Davis.

Miller, K. E. (2003, January 1). Effectiveness of school-based violence prevention programs. *American Family Physician, 67*(1), 161.

Milsom, A. S. (2002). Students with disabilities: School counselor involvement and preparation. *Professional School Counseling, 5,* 331–339.

Minden, J., Henry, D. B., Tolan, P. H., & Gorman-Smith, D. (2000). Urban boys' social networks and school violence. *Professional School Counseling, 4,* 95–104.

Mitchell, C. W., & Rogers, R. E. (2003). Rape, statutory rape, and child abuse: Legal distinctions and counselor duties. *Professional School Counseling, 6,* 332–339.

Mohrman, S. A., & Lawler, E. E. (1996). Motivation for school reform. In S. H. Fuhrman & J. A. O'Day (Eds.), *Rewards and reform: Creating educational incentives that work* (pp. 115–143). San Francisco: Jossey-Bass.

Morley, E., & Rossman, S. B. (1998). *Helping at-risk youth: Lessons from community-based initiatives.* Washington, DC: Urban Institute Press.

Morrison, J. (1995). DSM–IV *made easy.* New York: Guilford Press.

Morse, P. S., & Andrea, R. (1994). Peer mediation in the schools: Teaching conflict resolution techniques to students. *NASSP Bulletin, 78* (560), 75–82.

Mosconi, J., & Emmett, J. (2003). Effects of a values clarification curriculum on high school students' definition of success. *Professional School Counseling, 7,* 68–78.

Mostert, D. L., Johnson, E., & Mostert, M. P. (1997). The utility of solution-focused, brief counseling in schools: Potential from an initial study. *Professional School Counseling, 1*(1), 21–24.

Motta, R. W., & Basile, D. M. (1998). Pica. In L. Phelps (Ed.), *Health-related disorders in children and adolescents: A compilation of 96 rare and common disorders* (pp. 524–527). Washington, DC: American Psychological Association.

Mulick, J. A., & Butter, E. M. (2002). Educational advocacy for children with autism. *Behavioral Interventions, 17,* 57–74.

Mullis, F., & Otwell, P. (1998). Who gets the kids? Consulting with parents about child custody decisions. *Professional School Counseling, 2,* 103–108.

Muro, J. J., & Kottman, T. (1995). *Guidance and counseling in the elementary and middle schools.* Madison, WI: Brown & Benchmark.

Murphy, G. (1955). The cultural concept of guidance. *Personnel and Guidance Journal, 34,* 4–9.

Murphy, J. J. (1997). *Solution-focused counseling in middle and high schools.* Alexandria, VA: American Counseling Association.

Murphy, J. J. (1999). Common factors of school-based change. In M. A. Hubble & B. L. Duncan (Eds.), *The heart and soul of change: What works in therapy* (pp. 361–386). Washington, DC: American Psychological Association.

Murphy, J. P., DeEsch, J. B., & Strein, W. O. (1998). School counselors and school psychologists: Partners in student services. *Professional School Counseling, 2,* 85–87.

Murphy, S., & Carney, T. (2004). The classification of soiling and encopresis and a possible treatment protocol. *Child and Adolescent Mental Health, 9,* 125–129.

Murrow-Taylor, C. (1999). A multicultural career fair for elementary school students. *Professional School Counseling, 2,* 241–243.

Muuss, R. E. (1998). Marcia's expansion of Erickson's theory of identity formation. In R. Muuss & H. Porton (Eds.), *Adolescent behavior and society: A book of readings* (5th ed., pp. 260–270). New York: McGraw-Hill.

Myrick, R. D. (1993). *Developmental guidance and counseling: A practical approach.* Minneapolis: Educational Media Corporation.

Myrick, R. D. (1997). *Developmental guidance and counseling: A practical approach* (3rd ed.). Minneapolis: Educational Media Corporation.

Myrick, R. D. (2002). *Developmental guidance and counseling: A practical approach* (4th ed.). Minneapolis: Educational Media.

Myrick, R. D. (2003). Accountability: Counselors count. *Professional School Counseling, 6,* 174–179.

Nader, K. O., Pynoos, R. S., Fairbanks, L. A., al-Ajeel, M., & al-Asfour, A. (1993). A preliminary study of PTSD and grief among the children of Kuwait following the Gulf Crisis. *British Journal of Clinical Psychology, 32,* 407–416.

National Career Development Association. (1997). *Career counseling competencies.* Retrieved August 20, 2005, from www.ncda.org/about/polccc.html

The National Center for Chronic Disease Prevention and Health Promotion, Division of Adolescent and School Health's Information Service. (2000). *Fact sheets: Youth risk behavior trends 1991–1999.* Retrieved April 25, 2002, from www.cdc.gov/nccdphp/dash/yrbs/trend.htm

National Center for Education Statistics. (2001, May). *Statistics in brief.* Washington, DC: U.S. Department of Education, Office of Educational Research and Improvement.

The National Center for Public Policy and Higher Education. (2000). *Measuring up 2000*. Washington, DC: Author.

National Council on Disability. (2004). *Improving educational outcomes for students with disabilities*. Retrieved August 28, 2005, from www.ncd.gov/newsroom/publications/2004educationoutcomes.htm

National Dissemination Center for Children with Disabilities. (2001). *Related services news digest 16* (2nd ed.) Retrieved August 20, 2005, from www.nichcy.org/pubs/newsdig/nd16txt.htm

National Dissemination Center for Children with Disabilities (NICHCY). (2002). *Disability information*. Retrieved July 1, 2002, from www.nichcy.org/pubs/factshe/

National Education Association. (2002). *Crisis communications guide and toolkit*. Washington, DC: Author.

National Institute of Mental Health. (1999). *Teens—The company they keep: Preventing destructive behavior by harnessing the power of peers* (NIH Publication No. 99–4588). Washington, DC: Author.

National Institute of Mental Health. (2000). *Depression research at the National Institute of Mental Health*. Bethesda, MD: Author.

National Institute of Mental Health. (2005). *America's children: Parents report estimated 2.7 million children with emotional and behavioral problems*. Retrieved on September 2, 2005, from www.nimh.nih.gov/healthinformation/childhood_indicators.cfm

National Institutes of Health. (1998). *NIH consensus statement: Diagnosis and treatment of attention deficit hyperactivity disorder* (Vol. 16, no. 2). Bethesda, MD: Author.

National Institutes of Health. (2005). *The national children's study*. Retrieved on September 2, 2005, from www.national childrensstudy.gov

National Occupational Information Coordinating Committee, U.S. Department of Labor. (1992). *The national career development guidelines project*. Washington, DC: U.S. Department of Labor.

Nearpass, E. L. (1990). Counseling and guidance effectiveness in North American high schools: A meta-analysis of the research findings (Doctoral dissertation, University of Colorado at Boulder, 1989). *Dissertation Abstracts International, 50,* 1984A.

Nelson, C. M. (1988). Social skills training for handicapped students. *Teaching Exceptional Children, 20* (4), 19–23.

Nelson, D. E., Gardner, J. L., & Fox, D. G. (1998). *Contrast between students in high implementation and low implementation high schools in the Utah Comprehensive Guidance Program*. Salt Lake City, UT: The Institute for Behavioral Research in Creativity.

Nelson, J. R., Dykeman, C., Powell, S., & Petty, D. (1996). The effects of a group counseling intervention on students with behavioral adjustment problems. *Elementary School Guidance and Counseling, 31,* 21–33.

Newcomb, M. D., & Richardson, M. A. (2000). Substance-use disorders. In M. Hersen & R. T. Ammerman (Eds.), *Advanced abnormal child psychology* (2nd ed., pp. 467–492). Mahwah, NJ: Lawrence Erlbaum Associates.

Newport News Public Schools. (2002). *Secondary counselor handbook*. Retrieved March 28, 2005, from http://sbo.nn.k12.va.us/guidance/handbooks/counshandbook.pdf

Nicholson, J. I., & Pearson, Q. M. (2003). Helping children cope with fears: Using children's literature in classroom guidance. *Professional School Counseling, 7,* 15–19.

Nicoll, W. G. (1994). Developing effective classroom guidance programs: An integrative framework. *The School Counselor, 41,* 360–364.

Niedringhaus, J. J. (2000). *Counseling children: Some practical suggestions*. Unpublished manuscript.

Nieto, S. (1996). *Affirming diversity: The sociopolitical context of multicultural education* (2nd ed.). White Plains, NY: Longman.

Nieto, S. (1999). *The light in their eyes: Creating multicultural learning communities*. New York: Teachers College, Columbia University.

Nieto, S. (2004). *Affirming diversity: The sociopolitical context of multicultural education* (4th ed.). Boston: Pearson/Allyn & Bacon.

Niles, S. G. (1998). Developing life-role readiness in a multicultural society: Topics to consider. *International Journal for the Advancement of Counseling, 20,* 71–77.

Niles, S. G., Erford, B. T., Hunt, B., & Watts, R. (1997). Decision-making styles and career development in college students. *Journal of College Student Development, 38,* 479–488.

Niles, S. G., & Goodnough, G. E. (1996). Life-role salience and values: A review of recent research. *The Career Development Quarterly, 45,* 65–86.

Nims, D., James, S., & Hughey, A. (1998). The challenge of accountability: A survey of Kentucky school counselors. *Kentucky Counseling Association Journal, 17,* 31–37.

Nystul, M. S. (1999). *Introduction to counseling: An art and science perspective.* Needham Heights, MA: Allyn & Bacon.

O'Connor, K. P. (2001). Clinical and psychological features distinguishing obsessive-compulsive and chronic tic disorders. *Clinical Psychology Review, 21,* 631–660.

Oetting, E. R., & Beavais, F. (1990). Adolescent drug use: Findings of national and local surveys. *Journal of Consulting and Clinical Psychology, 58,* 385–394.

Office of Juvenile Justice and Delinquency Prevention. (1999). *OJJDP annual report 1999.* Washington, DC: U. S. Department of Justice.

Office of Juvenile Justice and Delinquency Prevention. (2000). *The effectiveness of family counseling.* Washington, DC: Author.

Office of Special Education Programs. (2005). *IDEA 2004 resources.* Available at www.ed.gov/policy/speced/guid/idea/idea2004.html

Offord, D. R., & Bennett, K. J. (1994). Conduct disorders: Long-term outcomes and intervention effectiveness. *Journal of the American Academy of Child and Adolescent Psychiatry, 33,* 1069–1079.

O'Hanlon, W. H., & Weiner–Davis, M. (1989). *In search of solutions: A new direction in psychotherapy.* New York: Guilford Press.

Oliver, L. W., & Spokane, A. R. (1988). Career-intervention outcome: What contributes to client gain? *Journal of Counseling Psychology, 35,* 447–462.

Ollendick, T. H., & King, N. J. (1998). Empirically supported treatments for children with phobic and anxiety disorders: Current status. *Journal of Clinical Child Psychology, 27,* 156–167.

Olson, M. J., & Allen, D. A. (1993). Principals' perceptions of the effectiveness of school counselors with and without teaching experience. *Counselor Education and Supervision, 33,* 10–21.

Omizo, M. M., & Omizo, S. A. (1988). The effects of participation in group counseling on self-esteem and locus of control among adolescents from divorced families. *The School Counselor, 16,* 54–60.

Omizo, M. M., Omizo, S. A., & D'Andrea, M. J. (1992). Promoting wellness among elementary school children. *Journal of Counseling and Development, 71,* 194–198.

Omizo, M. M., Omizo, S. A., & Okamoto, C. M. (1998). Gay and lesbian adolescents: A phenomenological study. *Professional School Counseling, 1*(3), 35–37.

Opffer, E. (1997). Toward cultural transformation: Comprehensive approaches to conflict resolution. *Theory Into Practice, 36,* 46–52.

Orton, G. L. (1997). *Strategies for counseling with children and their parents.* Pacific Grove, CA: Brooks/Cole.

Osborne, J. L., & Collison, B. B. (1998). School counselors and external providers: Conflict or complement. *Professional School Counseling, 1,* 7–11.

Osborne, J. L., Collison, B. B., House, R. M., Gray, L. A., Firthe, J., & Lou, M. (1998). Developing a social advocacy model for counselor education. *Counselor Education and Supervision, 37,* 190–202.

O'Shea, A. J., & Harrington, T. F. (2003). Using the Career Decision-Making System–Revised to enhance students' career development. *Professional School Counseling, 6,* 280–287.

Osher, D., Dwyer, K., & Jackson, S. (2004). *Safe, supportive and successful schools: Step by step.* Longmont, CO: Sopris West Educational Services.

Otwell, P. S., & Mullis, F. (1997). Counselor-led staff development: An efficient approach to teacher consultation. *Professional School Counseling, 1,* 25–30.

Ozer, E. J., & Weinstein, R. S. (2004). Urban adolescents' exposure to community violence: The role of support, school safety, and social constraints in a school-based sample of boys and girls. *Journal of Clinical Child and Adolescent Psychology, 33,* 463–476.

Paisley, P. O. (2001). Maintaining and enhancing the developmental focus in school counseling programs. *Professional School Counseling, 4,* 271–277.

Paisley, P. O., & Borders, L. D. (1995). School counseling: An evolving specialty. *Journal of Counseling and Development, 74,* 150–152.

Palmer, S., & Cochran, L. (1988). Parents as agents of career development. *Journal of Counseling Psychology, 35,* 71–76.

Parsons, F. (1909). *Choosing a vocation.* Boston: Houghton Mifflin.

Parsons, R. (1991). Empowerment: Purpose and practice in principle in social work. *Social Work in Groups, 14,* 7–21.

Parsons, R. (1996). *The skilled consultant: A systematic approach to the theory and practice of consultation.* Boston: Allyn & Bacon.

Pasteur, A. B., & Toldson, I. L. (1982). *The roots of soul: The psychology of Black expressiveness.* New York: Anchor Press.

Payzant, T. W. (1992). New beginnings in San Diego: Developing a strategy for interagency collaboration. *Phi Delta Kappan, 74,* 139–146.

Pederson, P. B. (1988). *A handbook for developing multicultural awareness.* Alexandria, VA: American Association for Counseling and Development.

Pederson, P. B., & Leafley, H. P. (1986). Introduction to cross-cultural training. In H. P. Leafley & P. B. Pederson (Eds.), *Cross-cultural training for mental health professionals* (pp. 5–10). Springfield, IL: Charles C. Thomas.

Pedro-Carroll, J. L., & Alpert-Gillis, L. J. (1997). Preventive interventions for children of divorce: A developmental model for 5 and 6 year old children. *Journal of Primary Prevention, 18,* 5–23.

Pedro-Carroll, J. L., Sutton, S. E., & Wyman, P. A. (1999). A two-year follow-up of a preventive intervention for young children of divorce. *School Psychology Review, 28,* 467–476.

Pelcovitz, D., Kaplan, S. J., DeRosa, R. R., Mandel, F. S., & Salziner, S. (2000). Psychiatric disorders in adolescents exposed to domestic violence and physical abuse. *American Journal of Orthopsychiatry, 70,* 360–369.

Pelham, W. E., Carlson, C. L., Sams, S. E., Vallano, G., Dixon, M. J., & Hoza, B. (1993). Separate and combined effects of methylphenidate and behavior modification on boys with attention-deficit hyperactivity disorder in the classroom. *Journal of Consulting and Clinical Psychology, 61,* 506–515.

Perlstein, R., & Thrall, G. (1996). *Ready to use conflict resolution activities for secondary school students.* West Nyack, NY: The Center for Applied Research in Education.

Perusse, R., & Goodnough, G. E. (Eds.). (2004). *Leadership, advocacy, and direct service strategies for professional school counselors.* Belmont, CA: Brooks/Cole-Thomson Learning.

Peterson, A. A., Campise, R. L., & Azrin, N. H. (1994). Behavioral and pharmacological treatments for tic and habit disorders: A review. *Journal of Developmental and Behavioral Pediatrics, 15,* 430–441.

Peterson, G. W., Long, K. L., & Billups, A. (1999). The effect of three career interventions on educational choices of eighth grade students. *Professional School Counseling, 3,* 34–42.

Peterson, J. (2004). The individual counseling process. In A. Vernon (Ed.), *Counseling children and adolescents* (3rd ed., pp. 35–74). Denver, CO: Love.

Peterson, R. L., & Skiba, R. (2001, July/Aug.). Creating school climates that prevent school violence. *The Social Studies, 92,* 167–175.

Pietrzak, D., Peterson, G. J., & Speaker, K. M. (1998). Perceptions of school violence by elementary and middle school personnel. *Professional School Counseling, 1,* 23–29.

Piran, N. (2004). Teachers: On "being" (rather than "doing") prevention. *Eating Disorders, 12,* 1–9.

Polivy, J., & Herman, C. P. (2002). Causes of eating disorders. *Annual Review of Psychology, 27,* 187.

Ponec, D. L., Poggi, J. A., & Dickel, T. A. (1998). Unity: Developing relationships between school and community counselors. *Professional School Counseling, 2,* 95–102.

Ponterotto, J. G., & Casas, J. M. (1987). In search of multicultural competence within counselor education programs. *Journal of Counseling and Development, 65,* 430–434.

Ponterotto, J. G., Casas, J. M., Suzuki, L. A., & Alexander, C. M. (1995). *Handbook of multicultural counseling.* Thousand Oaks, CA: Sage.

Ponterotto, J. G., & Pederson, P. B. (1993). *Preventing prejudice: A guide for counselors and educators.* Newbury Park, CA: Sage.

Pope–Davis, D. B., Reynolds, A. L., Dings, J. G., & Ottavi, T. M. (1994). Multicultural competencies of doctoral interns at university counseling centers: An exploratory investigation. *Professional Psychology: Research and Practice, 25,* 466–470.

Popenhagen, M. P., & Qualley, R. M. (1998). Adolescent suicide: Detection, intervention, and prevention. *Professional School Counseling, 1,* 30–36.

Popper, C. W., & Gherardi, P. C. (1996). Anxiety disorders. In J. M. Wiener (Ed.), *Diagnosis and psychopharmacology of children and adolescent disorders* (2nd ed., pp. 294–348). New York: John Wiley & Sons.

Porter, G., Epp, L., & Bryant, S. (2000). Collaboration among school mental health professionals: A necessity, not a luxury. *Professional School Counseling, 3,* 315–322.

Post, P., & Robinson, B. E. (1998). School-age children of alcoholics and non-alcoholics: Their anxiety, self-esteem, and locus of control. *Professional School Counseling, 1*(5), 36–40.

Power, T. J., DuPaul, G. J., Shapiro, E. S., & Parrish, J. M. (1998). Role of the school-based professional in health-related services. In L. Phelps (Ed.), *Health-related disorders in children and adolescents* (pp. 15–26). Washington, DC: American Psychological Association.

Poynton, T., & Dimmitt, C. (2004). *An evidence-based violence prevention curriculum for elementary school children.* Retrieved on May 25, 2005, from www.umass.edu/schoolcounseling/briefs.htm

Price, J. H., Telljohann, S. K., Dake, J. A., Marsico, L., & Zyla, C. (2002). Urban elementary school students' perceptions of fighting behavior and concerns for personal safety. *Journal of School Health, 72,* 184–191.

Prout, H. T., & DeMartino, R. A. (1986). A meta-analysis of school-based studies of psychotherapy. *Journal of School Psychology, 24,* 285–292.

Prout, S. M., & Prout, H. T. (1998). A meta-analysis of school-based studies of counseling and psychotherapy: An update. *Journal of School Psychology, 36,* 121–136.

Quarto, C. J. (1999). Teachers' perceptions of school counselors with and without teaching experience. *Professional School Counseling, 2,* 378–383.

Quigney, T. A., & Studer, J. R. (1998). Touching strands of the educational web: The professional school counselor's role in inclusion. *Professional School Counseling, 2,* 77–82.

Quinn, M. M., Gable, R. A., Rutherford, R. B., Nelson, C. M., & Howell, K. W. (1998). *Addressing student problem behavior: An IEP team's introduction to functional behavioral assessment and behavioral intervention plans* (2nd ed.). Washington, DC: Center for Effective Collaboration and Practice, American Institutes for Research.

Rainey, L. M., Hensley, F. A., & Crutchfield, L. B. (1997). Implementation of support groups in elementary and middle school student assistance programs. *Professional School Counseling, 1*(2), 36–40.

Randall, P. R. (1997). *Adult bullying: Perpetrators and victims.* London: Routledge.

Randolph, D. L., & Masker, T. (1997). Teacher certification and the counselor: A follow-up survey of school counselor certification requirements. *ACES Spectrum, 57*(4), 6–8.

The Random House dictionary of the English language (2nd ed., unabridged). (1987). New York: Random House.

Rapin, I. (1999). Autism in search of a home in the brain. *Neurology, 52,* 902–904.

Rapoport, J. L., & Ismond, D. R. (1996). DSM–IV *training guide for diagnosis of childhood disorders.* Levittown, PA: Brunner/Mazel.

Rapoport, J. L., Leonard, H., Swedo, S. E., & Lenane, M. C. (1993). Obsessive compulsive disorder in children and adolescents: Issues in management. *Journal of Clinical Psychiatry, 54,* 27–29.

Rappaport, J. (1987). Terms of empowerment/examples of prevention: Toward a theory for community psychology. *American Journal of Community Psychology, 15,* 121–144.

Rapport, M. D. (1995). Attention-deficit hyperactivity disorder. In M. Hersen & R. T. Ammerman (Eds.), *Advanced abnormal child psychology* (pp. 353–375). Hillsdale, NJ: Laurence Erlbaum Associates.

Ray, S. L. (2004). Eating disorders in adolescent males. *Professional School Counseling, 8,* 98–101.

Rayle, A. D., & Myers, J. E. (2004). Counseling adolescents toward wellness: The roles of ethnic identity, acculturation, and mattering. *Professional School Counseling, 8,* 81–90.

Reeder, J., Douzenis, C., & Bergin, J. J. (1997). The effects of small group counseling on the racial attitudes of second grade students. *Professional School Counseling, 1*(2), 15–18.

Reis, S. M., & Colbert, R. (2004). Counseling needs of academically talented students with learning disabilities. *Professional School Counseling, 8,* 156–167.

Remley, T., & Herlihy, B. (2001). *Ethical, legal, and professional issues in counseling.* Upper Saddle River, NJ: Merrill/Prentice Hall.

Remley, T., & Huey, W. C. (2002). An ethics quiz for school counselors. *Professional School Counseling, 6,* 3–11.

Rey, J. M. (1993). Oppositional defiant disorder. *American Journal of Psychiatry, 150,* 1769–1778.

Reynolds, W. M. (1988). *Suicide Ideation Questionnaire.* Lutz, FL: Psychological Assessment Resources.

Ribak-Rosenthal, N. (1994). Reasons individuals become school administrators, school counselors, and teachers. *The School Counselor, 41,* 158–164.

Richmond Public Schools. (n.d.). *Guidance and school counseling services making a difference.* Retrieved July 6, 2005, from www.richmond.k12.va.us/guidance/mission.cfm

Ridley, C. R., Mendoza, D. W., Kanitz, B. E., Angermeier, L., & Zenk, R. (1994). Cultural sensitivity in multicultural counseling: A perceptual schema model. *Journal of Counseling Psychology, 41,* 125–136.

Rigby, K. & Slee, P. (1999). Suicidal ideation among adolescent school children, involvement in bully-victim problems, and perceived social support. *Suicide and Life Threatening Behavior, 29,* 119–130.

Riley, P. L., & McDaniel, J. (2000). School violence prevention, intervention, and crisis response. *Professional School Counseling, 4,* 120–125.

Ringel, J. S., & Sturm, R. (2001). National estimates of mental health utilization and expenditures for children in 1998. *Journal of Behavioral Health Services and Research, 28,* 319–333.

Ripley, V. V., & Goodnough, G. E. (2001). Planning and implementing group counseling in a high school. *Professional School Counseling, 5,* 62–65.

Ritchie, M. H., & Huss, S. N. (2000). Recruitment and screening of minors for group counseling. *Journal for Specialists in Group Work, 25,* 146–156.

Roache, M., Shore, J., Gouleta, E., & de Obaldia Butkevich, E. (2003). An investigation of collaboration among school professionals in serving culturally and linguistically diverse students with exceptionalities. *Bilingual Research Journal, 27,* 117–136.

Roberts, M. L., Marshall, J., Nelson, J. R., & Albers, C. A. (2001). Curriculum-based assessment procedures embedded within functional behavioral assessments: Identifying escape-motivated behaviors in a general education classroom. *School Psychology Review, 30,* 264–278.

Rockney, R. M., McQuade, W. H., Days, A. L., Linn, H. E., & Alario, A. J. (1996). Encopresis treatment outcome: Long-term follow-up of 45 cases. *Journal of Developmental and Behavioral Pediatrics, 17,* 380–385.

Rogers, C. R. (1942). *Counseling and psychotherapy: Newer concepts in practice.* New York: Houghton Mifflin.

Rogers, M. R. (2000). Examining the cultural context of consultation. *School Psychology Review, 29,* 414–418.

Rogers, M. R., Ingraham, C. L., Bursztyr, A., Cajigas-Segredo, N., Esquival, G., Hess, R., et al. (1999). Providing psychological services to racially, ethnically, culturally, and linguistically diverse individuals in the schools: Recommendations for practice. *School Psychology International, 20,* 243–264.

Roid, G. H. (2003). *The Stanford–Binet Intelligence Scale–5th Edition (SBIS).* Itasca, IL: Riverside.

Rollin, S. A., Kaiser-Ulrey, C., Potts, I., & Creason, A. H. (2003). A school-based violence prevention model for at-risk eighth grade youth. *Psychology in the Schools, 40,* 403–416.

Rosenbaum, J. E., & Person, A. E. (2003). Beyond college for all: Policies and practices to improve transitions into college and jobs. *Professional School Counseling, 6,* 252–261.

Rosenberg, M. S., & Jackman, L. A. (2003). Development, implementation, and sustainability of comprehensive school-wide behavior management systems. *Intervention in School and Clinic, 39,* 10–21.

Roth, A., & Fonagy, P. (1996). *What works for whom?* New York: Guilford Press.

Rowley, W. J., Sink, C. A., & MacDonald, G. (2002). An experiential and systemic approach to encourage collaboration and community building. *Professional School Counseling, 5,* 360–365.

Rowley, W. J., Stroh, H. R., & Sink, C. A. (2005). Comprehensive guidance and counseling programs' use of guidance curricula materials: A survey of national trends. *Professional School Counseling, 8,* 296–304.

Sabella, R. A. (1998). World Wide Web resources for counseling children and adolescents with disabilities. *Professional School Counseling, 2,* 47–53.

Salend, S. J. (1994). Strategies for assessing attitudes toward individuals with disabilities. *The School Counselor, 41,* 338–342.

Salo, M. M., & Shumate, S. G. (1993). *The ACA legal series: Vol. 4: Counseling minor clients.* Alexandria, VA: ACA.

Sanchez, A. (2001). *Rainbow boys.* New York: Simon & Schuster.

Sandhu, D. S. (2000). Alienated students: Counseling strategies to curb school violence. *Professional School Counseling, 4,* 81–85.

Saphier, J., & Gower, R. (1997). *The skillful teacher.* Carlisle, MA: Research for Better Teaching.

Savickas, M. L. (1999). The transition from school to work: A developmental perspective. *Career Development Quarterly, 47,* 326–336.

Savickas, M. (2004). Toward a taxonomy of human strengths: Career counseling's contribution to positive psychology. In W. Walsh (Ed.), *Counseling psychology and optimal human functioning* (pp. 229–249). Mahwah, NJ: Lawrence Erlbaum Associates.

Scarborough, J. L. (1997). The SOS club: A practical peer helper program. *Professional School Counseling, 1*(2), 25–28.

Scarborough, J. L., & Deck, M. D. (1998). The challenges of working for students with disabilities: A view from the front lines. *Professional School Counseling, 2,* 10–15.

Schaefer, R. T. (1990). *Racial and ethnic groups* (4th ed.). Glenview, IL: Scott, Foresman/Little.

Schaefer-Schiumo, K., & Ginsberg, A. P. (2003). The effectiveness of the warning signs program in educating youth about violence prevention: A study with urban high school students. *Professional School Counseling, 7,* 1–8.

Schave, D., & Schave, B. F. (1989). *Early adolescence and the search for self: A developmental perspective.* New York: Praeger.

Schein, E. (1969). *Process consultation: Its role in organizational development.* Reading, MA: Addison-Wesley.

Schlossberg, S. M., Morris, J. D., & Lieberman, M. G. (2001). The effects of a counselor-led guidance intervention on students' behaviors and attitudes. *Professional School Counseling, 4,* 156–174.

Schmidt, J. J. (1995). Assessing school counseling programs through external reviews. *The School Counselor, 43,* 114–115.

Schmidt, J. J. (2003). *Counseling in schools: Essential services and comprehensive programs* (4th ed.). Boston: Allyn & Bacon.

Schwallie-Giddis, P., Anstrom, K., Sanchez, P., Sardi, V. A., & Granato, L. (2004). Counseling the linguistically and culturally diverse student: Meeting school counselors' professional development needs. *Professional School Counseling, 8,* 15–23.

Schweibert, V. L., Sealander, K. A., & Bradshaw, M. (1998). Preparing students with attention deficit disorders for entry into the workplace and postsecondary education. *Professional School Counseling, 2,* 26–32.

Scruggs, M. Y., Wasielewski, R. A., & Ash, M. J. (1999). Comprehensive evaluation of a K–12 counseling program. *Professional School Counseling, 2,* 244–247.

Sealander, K. A., Schwiebert, V. L., Oren, T. A., & Weeley, J. L. (1999). Confidentiality and the law. *Professional School Counseling, 3,* 122–127.

Selekman, M. D. (1997). *Pathways to change: Brief therapy solutions with difficult adolescents.* New York: Guilford Press.

Seligman, L. (1998). *Selecting effective treatments: A comprehensive, systematic guide to treating mental disorders* (Rev. ed.). San Francisco: Jossey-Bass.

Seligman, L. (2004). *Diagnosis and treatment planning in counseling* (3rd ed.). New York: Kluwer.

Seligman, M., & Darling, R. (1989). *Ordinary families, special children: A systems approach to childhood disability.* New York: Guilford Press.

Sellers, N., Satcher, J., & Comas, R. (1999). Children's occupational aspirations: Comparisons by gender, gender role identity, and socioeconomic status. *Professional School Counseling, 2,* 314–317.

Sexton, T. L. (1996). The relevance of counseling outcome research: Current trends and practical implications. *Journal of Counseling and Development, 74,* 590–600.

Sexton, T. L., & Alexander, J. (2002). Family-based interventions: Empirically supported treatments and applications. *The Counseling Psychologist, 30,* 238–261.

Sexton, T. L., Whiston, S. C., Bleuer, J. C., & Walz, G. R. (1997). *Integrating outcome research into counseling practice and training.* Alexandria, VA: American Counseling Association.

Shade, B. J. (1982). Afro-American cognitive style: A variable in school success? *Review of Educational Research, 52,* 219–244.

Shaffer, D., & Pfeffer, C. R. (2001). Practice parameter for the assessment and treatment of children with suicidal behavior. *Journal of the American Academy of Child and Adolescent Psychiatry, 40* (Suppl. 7), 24S–51S.

Shaffer, D., & Waslick, B. (1995). Elimination disorders. In G. O. Gabbard (Ed.), *Treatments of psychiatric disorders* (pp. 219–228). Washington, DC: American Psychiatric Press.

Shaver, A. V., & Walls, R. T. (1998). Effect of Title I parent involvement on student reading and mathematics achievement. *Journal of Research and Development in Education, 31,* 90–97.

Shechtman, Z. (2002). Child group psychotherapy in the school at the threshold of a new millennium. *Journal of Counseling and Development, 80,* 293–299.

Sheperis, C. J., Renfro-Michel, E. L., & Doggett, R. A. (2003). In-home treatment of reactive attachment disorder in a therapeutic foster care system: A case example. *Journal of Mental Health Counseling, 25,* 76–88.

Shepherd, K. K. (1994). Stemming conflict through peer mediation. *School Administrator, 51,* 14–17.

Shepherd-Tew, D., & Creamer, D. A. (1998). Elementary school integrated services teams: Applying case-management techniques. *Professional School Counseling, 2,* 141–144.

Sheridan, S. M. (2000). Considerations of multiculturalism and diversity in behavioral consultation with parents and teachers. *School Psychology Review, 29,* 389–400.

Sheridan, S. M., Welch, M., & Orme, S. F. (1996). Is consultation effective? A review of outcome research. *Remedial and Special Education, 17,* 341–354.

Sigman, M., & Capps, L. (1997). *Children with autism: A developmental perspective.* Cambridge, MA: Harvard University Press.

Silver, L. B. (1989). Elective mutism. In H. Kaplan & B. Sadock (Eds.), *Comprehensive textbook of psychiatry* (5th ed., pp. 1887–1889). Baltimore: Williams & Wilkins.

Silver, L. B. (1991). Developmental learning disorders. In M. Lewis (Ed.), *Comprehensive textbook of psychiatry* (5th ed., pp. 1887–1889). Baltimore: Williams & Wilkins.

Silver, L. B. (1992). *The misunderstood child: A guide for parents of children with learning disabilities* (2nd ed.). Blue Ridge Summit, PA: TAB Books.

Silver, L. B. (1995). Learning disorders. In G. O. Gabbard (Ed.), *Treatments of psychiatric disorders* (pp. 123–140). Washington, DC: American Psychiatric Press.

Silverman, J. G., Raj, A., Mucci, L. A., & Hathaway, J. E. (2001). Dating violence against adolescent girls and associated substance abuse, unhealthy weight control, sexual risk behavior, pregnancy, and suicidality. *Journal of the American Medical Association, 286,* 1263–1288.

Silverstein, D. M. (2004). Enuresis in children: Diagnosis and management. *Clinical Pediatrics, 43,* 217–221.

Sink, C. (Ed.). (2005). *Contemporary school counseling: Theory, research, and practice.* Boston: Houghton Mifflin/Lahaska.

Sink, C. A., & MacDonald, G. (1998). The status of comprehensive guidance and counseling in the United States. *Professional School Counseling, 2,* 88–94.

Sink, C. A., & Stroh, H. R. (2003). Raising achievement test scores of early elementary school students through comprehensive school counseling programs. *Professional School Counseling, 6,* 350–364.

Sink, C. A., & Yillik-Downer, A. (2001). School counselors' perceptions of comprehensive guidance and counseling programs: A national survey. *Professional School Counseling, 4,* 278–288.

Sitlington, P. L., Clark, G. M., & Kolstoe, O. P. (2000). *Transition education and services for adolescents with disabilities* (3rd ed.). Boston: Allyn & Bacon.

Skinner, M. E., & Lindstrom, B. D. (2003). Bridging the gap between high school and college: Strategies for the successful transition of students with learning disabilities. *Preventing School Failure, 47,* 132–137.

Sklare, G. B. (1997). *Brief counseling that works: A solution-focused approach for school counselors and administrators.* Thousand Oaks, CA: Corwin Press.

Sklare, G. B. (2005). *Brief counseling that works: A solution-focused approach for school counselors and administrators* (2nd ed.). Thousand Oaks, CA: Corwin Press.

Skovholt, T., Cognetta, P., Ye, G., & King, L. (1997). Violence prevention strategies of inner-city student experts. *Professional School Counseling, 1*(1), 35–38.

Slowinksi, J. (2002). *Data-driven equity: Eliminating the achievement gap and improving learning for all students.* Unpublished manuscript, Vinalhaven Schools, Vinalhaven, ME.

Smith, C. (2001). Using social stories to enhance behavior in children with autistic spectrum difficulties. *Educational Psychology in Practice, 17,* 337–345.

Smith, P. K., Morita, Y., Junger-Tas, J., Olwers, D., Catalano, R., & Slee, P. (Eds.). (1999). *The nature of school bullying: A cross-cultural perspective.* New York: Routledge.

Smith, S. D., & Chen-Hayes, S. F. (2004). Leadership and advocacy for lesbian, bisexual, gay, transgendered,

and questioning (LBGTQ) students: Academic, career, and interpersonal success strategies. In R. Perusse & G. E. Goodnough (Eds.), *Leadership, advocacy, and direct service strategies for professional school counselors* (pp. 187–221). Belmont, CA: Brooks/Cole-Thomson Learning.

Smith, S. L., Crutchfield, L. B., & Culbreth, J. R. (2001). Teaching experience for school counselors: Counselor educators' perceptions. *Professional School Counseling, 4,* 216–224.

Smith, S. R., Reddy, L. A., & Wingenfeld, S. A. (2002). Assessment of psychotic disorders in inpatient children and adolescents: Use of the Devereux Scales of Mental Disorders. *Journal of Psychopathology and Behavioral Assessment, 24,* 269–273.

Smith, S. W., Daunic, A. P., Miller, M. D., & Robinson, T. R. (2002). Conflict resolution and peer mediation in middle schools: Extending the process and outcome knowledge base. *The Journal of Social Psychology, 142,* 567–586.

Snowling, M. J. (2002). Reading and other learning difficulties. In M. Rutter, E. Taylor, & L. Hersov (Eds.), *Child and adolescent psychiatry: Modern approaches* (4th ed., pp. 682–696). Cambridge, MA: Blackwell.

Snyder, H. (2001). Child delinquents. In R. Loeber & D. P. Farrington (Eds.), *Risk factors and successful interventions* (pp. 173–195). Thousand Oaks, CA: Sage.

Sommers-Flanagan, J., & Sommers-Flanagan, R. (1997). *Tough kids, cool counseling.* Alexandria, VA: American Counseling Association.

Spaulding, F. E. (1915). Problems of vocational guidance. In M. Bloomfield (Ed.), *Readings in vocational guidance.* Cambridge, MA: Harvard University Press.

Speight, S. L., Myers, L. J., Cox, C. E., & Highlen, P. S. (1991). A redefinition of multicultural counseling. *Journal of Counseling and Development, 70,* 29–36.

Speltz, M. (1990). The treatment of preschool conduct problems: An integration of behavioral and attachment concepts. In M. Greenburg, D. Cicchetti, & E. M. Cummings (Eds.), *Attachment in the preschool years* (pp. 399–426). Chicago: University of Chicago Press.

Sprague, J. R., & Golly, A. (2004). *Best behavior: Building positive behavior supports in schools.* Longmont, CO: Sopris West Educational Services.

Sprague, J. R., & Walker, H. M. (2004). *Safe and healthy schools: Practical prevention strategies.* New York: Guilford Press.

Sprinthall, N. A. (1981). A new model for research in the science of guidance and counseling. *Personnel and Guidance Journal, 59,* 487–493.

St. Claire, K. L. (1989). Middle school counseling research: A resource for school counselors. *Elementary School Guidance and Counseling, 23,* 219–226.

State, M. W., King, B. H., & Dykens, E. (1997). Mental retardation: A review of the past 10 years. Part II. *Journal of the American Academy of Child and Adolescent Psychiatry, 36,* 1664–1671.

Steigerwald, F. (2004a). Crisis intervention with individuals in the schools. In B. T. Erford (Ed.), *Professional school counseling: A handbook of theories, programs, and practices* (pp. 829–841). Austin, TX: PRO-ED.

Steigerwald, F. (2004b). Systemic crisis intervention in the schools. In B. T. Erford (Ed.), *Professional school counseling: A handbook of theories, programs, and practices* (pp. 843–849). Austin, TX: PRO-ED.

Stelmacher, Z. T. (1995). Assessing suicidal clients. In J. N. Butcher (Ed.), *Clinical personality assessment: Practical approaches* (pp. 366–379). New York: Oxford University Press.

Stephens, W. R. (1970). *Social reform and the origins of vocational guidance.* Washington, DC: National Career Development Association.

Sterling–Turner, H. E., Watson, T. S., & Moore, J. W. (2002). The effects of direct training and treatment integrity on treatment outcomes in school consultation. *School Psychology Quarterly, 17,* 47–77.

Sterling–Turner, H. E., Watson, T. S., Wildmon, M., Watkins, C., & Little, E. (2001). Investigating the relationship between training type and treatment integrity. *School Psychology Quarterly, 16,* 56–67.

Stevahn, L., Johnson, D. W., Johnson, R. T., Laginski, A., & O'Coin, I. (1996). Effects on high school students of integrating conflict resolution and peer mediation training into an academic unit. *Mediation Quarterly, 14,* 21–36.

Stevenson, D. L., & Baker, D. P. (1987). The family-school relations and the child's school performances. *Child Development, 58,* 1348–1357.

Stewart, A., Copeland, A., Chester, N., Malley, J., & Barenbaum, N. (1997). *Separating together: How divorce transforms families.* New York: Guilford Press.

Stomfay-Stitz, A. M. (1994). Conflict resolution and peer mediation: Pathways to safer schools. *Childhood Education, 70,* 279–282.

Stone, C. B. (2000). Advocacy for sexual harassment victims: Legal support and ethical aspects. *Professional School Counseling, 4,* 23–30.

Stone, C. B. (2004). School counselors as leaders and advocates in addressing sexual harassment. In R. Perusse & G. E. Goodnough (Eds.),

Leadership, advocacy, and direct service strategies for professional school counselors (pp. 353–380). Belmont, CA: Brooks/Cole-Thomson Learning.

Stone, C. B. (2005). *School counseling and principles: Ethics and law.* Alexandria, VA: American School Counselor Association.

Stone, C. B., & Clark, M. (2001). School counselors and principals: Partners in support of academic achievement. *National Association of Secondary School Principals Bulletin, 85* (24), 46–53.

Stone, L. A. (1996, March). Violence and children: What we can do. *Psychiatric Times, 13* (3), 1–5.

Stone, L. A., & Bradley, F. O. (1994). *Foundations of elementary and middle school counseling.* White Plains, NY: Longman.

Stout, E. J., & Frame, M. W. (2004). Body image disorder in adolescent males: Strategies for school counselors. *Professional School Counseling, 8,* 176–181.

Strauss, S. (1994). Sexual harassment at an early age. *Principal, 74* (1), 26–29.

Stroh, H. R., & Sink, C. A. (2002). Applying APA's learner-centered principles to school-based group counseling. *Professional School Counseling, 6,* 71–78.

Stroul, B. A., & Friedman, R. M. (1996). *A system of care for children and youth with severe emotional disturbances.* Washington, DC: Center for Mental Health Services.

Substance Abuse and Mental Health Services Administration. (1995). *Cost of addictive and mental disorders and effectiveness of treatment.* Washington, DC: SAMHSA, Department of Health and Human Services.

Substance Abuse and Mental Health Services Administration. (1998). *National expenditures for mental health, alcohol, and other drug abuse treatment.* Washington, DC: SAMHSA, Department of Health and Human Services.

Substance Abuse and Mental Health Services Administration. (2002). *Substance use and the risk of suicide among youths.* Washington, DC: U.S. Department of Health and Human Services Office of Applied Studies. Retrieved February 16, 2005, from http://oas.samhsa.gov/2k2/suicide/suicide.html

Sue, D. W. (1991). A conceptual model for cultural diversity training. *Journal of Counseling and Development, 70,* 99–105.

Sue, D. W., Arredondo, P., & McDavis, R. J. (1992). Multicultural competencies/standards: A pressing need. *Journal of Counseling and Development, 70,* 477–486.

Sue, D. W., Bernier, J. E., Durran, A., Feinberg, L., Pederson, P., Smith, E. J., et al. (1982). Position paper: Cross-cultural counseling competencies. *The Counseling Psychologist, 10,* 45–52.

Sue, D. W., & Sue, D. (1990). *Counseling the culturally different: Theory and practice.* New York: John Wiley & Sons.

Sue, S. (1998). In search of cultural competence in psychotherapy and counseling. *American Psychologist, 53,* 440–448.

Sugai, G., Horner, R. H., Dunlap, G., Hieneman, M., Lewis, T. J., Nelson, C. M., et al. (2000). Applying positive behavior support and functional behavioral assessment in schools. *Journal of Positive Behavior Interventions, 2,* 131–143.

Sugai, G., Horner, R. H., & Gresham, F. M. (2002). Behaviorally effective school environments. In M. R. Shinn, H. M. Walker, & G. Stoner (Eds.), *Interventions for academic and behavior problems 11: Preventive and remedial approaches* (pp. 315–341). Bethesda, MD: National Association of School Psychologists.

Super, D. E. (1957). *A psychology of careers.* New York: Harper & Row.

Super, D. E. (1977). Vocational maturity in midcareer. *Vocational Guidance Quarterly, 25,* 294–302.

Super, D. E. (1980). A life span, life space approach to career development. *Journal of Vocational Behavior, 16,* 282–298.

Super, D. E. (1990). Career and life development. In D. Brown & L. Brooks (Eds.), *Career choice and development: Applying contemporary theories to practice* (2nd ed., pp. 197–261). San Francisco: Jossey-Bass.

Super, D. E., Savickas, M. L., & Super, C. M. (1996). The life span, life-space approach to careers. In D. Brown & L. Brooks (Eds.), *Career choice and development: Applying contemporary theories to practice* (3rd ed., pp. 121–178). San Francisco: Jossey-Bass.

Super, D. E., Thompson, A. S., & Lindeman, R. H. (1988). *Adult Career Concerns Inventory: Manual for research and exploratory use in counseling.* Palo Alto, CA: Consulting Psychologists Press.

Sutton, J. M., Jr., & Pearson, R. (2002). The practice of school counseling in rural and small town schools. *Professional School Counseling, 5,* 266–276.

Swadener, B. B., & Lubeck, S. (Eds.). (1995). *Children and families "at promise": Deconstructing the discourse of risk.* Albany: State University of New York Press.

Swanson, J. L. (1995). The process and outcome of career counseling. In W. B. Walsh & S. H. Osipow (Eds.), *The handbook of vocational psychology* (pp. 217–259). Mahwah, NJ: Lawrence Erlbaum Associates.

Sweeney, B., & Carruthers, W. L. (1996). Conflict resolution: History, philosophy, theory, and educational applications. *The School Counselor, 43,* 326–344.

Sweeney, T. J. (2001). Counseling: Historical origins and philosophical roots. In D. C. Locke, J. Myers, & E. L. Herr (Eds.), *The handbook of counseling* (pp. 1–13). Thousand Oaks, CA: Sage Publications.

Tarver-Behring, S., & Gelinas R. T. (1996). School consultation with Asian American children and families. *The California School Psychologist, 1,* 13–20.

Tarver-Behring, S., & Ingraham, C. L. (1998). Culture as a central component to consultation: A call to the field. *Journal of Educational and Psychological Consultation, 9,* 57–72.

Tarver-Behring, S., Spagna, M. E., & Sullivan, J. (1998). School counselors and full inclusion for children with special needs. *Professional School Counseling, 1*(3), 51–55.

Taylor, L., & Adelman, H. (2000). Connecting schools, families, and communities. *Professional School Counseling, 3,* 298–307.

Taylor, M. C., & Foster, G. A. (1986). Bad boys and school suspension: Public policy implications for Black males. *Sociological Inquiry, 56,* 498–506.

Teele, S. (2000). *Rainbow of intelligence: Exploring how students learn.* Thousand Oaks, CA: Corwin Press.

Terry, J. (1999). A community/school mentoring program for elementary students. *Professional School Counseling, 2,* 237–240.

Thabet, A. A. M., Abed, Y., & Vostanis, P. (2004). Comorbidity of PTSD and depression among refugee children during war conflict. *Journal of Child Psychology and Psychiatry, 45,* 533–542.

Theberge, S. K., & Karan, O. (2004). Six factors inhibiting the use of peer mediation in a junior high school. *Professional School Counseling, 7,* 283–290.

Thomas, R. M. (2000). *Comparing theories of child development* (5th ed.). Belmont, CA: Wadsworth.

Thompson, C. L., Rudolph, L. B., & Henderson, D. A. (2004). *Counseling children* (6th ed.). Belmont, CA: Wadsworth.

Thompson, R., & Littrell, J. M. (1998). Brief counseling for students with learning disabilities. *Professional School Counseling, 2,* 60–67.

Tobias, A. K., & Myrick, R. D. (1999). A peer facilitator-led intervention with middle school problem-behavior students. *Professional School Counseling, 3,* 27–33.

Toporek, R. L. (1999, June). Advocacy: A voice for our clients and communities. Developing a framework for understanding advocacy in counseling. *Counseling Today,* pp. 34–35, 39.

Towbin, K. E., & Cohen, D. J. (1996). Tic disorders. In J. M. Wiener (Ed.), *Diagnosis and psychopharmacology of childhood and adolescent disorders* (2nd ed., pp. 349–369). New York: John Wiley & Sons.

Towbin, K. E., Cohen, D. J., & Lechman, J. F. (1995). Tic disorders. In G. O. Gabbard (Ed.), *Treatments of psychiatric disorders* (pp. 201–218). Washington, DC: American Psychiatric Press.

Traxler, A. E., & North, R. D. (1996). *Techniques of guidance*. New York: Harper & Row.

Trevisan, M. S., & Hubert, M. (2001). Implementing comprehensive guidance program evaluation support. Lessons learned. *Professional School Counseling, 2,* 225–228.

Trusty, J. (1999). Effects of eighth-grade parental involvement on late adolescents' educational experiences. *Journal of Research and Development in Education, 32,* 224–233.

Trusty, J., & Brown, D. (2005). Advocacy competencies for professional school counselors. *Professional School Counseling, 8,* 259–265.

Trusty, J., & Niles, S. G. (2004). High-school math courses and completion of the bachelor's degree. *Professional School Counseling, 7,* 108–115.

Tyrrell, F., Scully, T., & Halligan, J. (1998). Building peaceful schools. *Thrust for Educational Leadership, 28,* 30–33.

U.S. Bureau of Census. (1992). *Statistical abstract of the United States. The national data book* (112th ed.). Washington, DC: Author.

U.S. Bureau of Census. (1999). *The official statistics.* Washington, DC: Author.

U.S. Department of Education. (1998). *Digest of educational statistics.* Washington, DC: Author.

U.S. Department of Education. (2001). Congress of the United States of America. *PL 107–110, The No Child Left Behind Act of 2001.* Retrieved January 3, 2005, at www.ed.gov/policy/elsec/leg/esea02/index.html

U.S. Department of Education. (2002). *No Child Left Behind.* Retrieved August 20, 2005, from www.ed.gov/nclb/landing.jhtml?src=pb

U.S. Department of Education. (2003a). Twenty-fifth annual report to Congress on the implementation of the Individuals with Disabilities Education Act. Retrieved August 20, 2005, from www.ed.gov/about/reports/annual/osep/2003

U.S. Department of Education (2003b). *National Assessment of Educational Progress (NAEP).* Washington, DC: Author.

U.S. Department of Education. (2005). *Digest of educational statistics.* Washington, DC: Author.

U.S. Department of Education, National Center for Education Statistics. (2005). *The condition of education 2005.* Washington, DC: U.S. Government Printing Office.

U.S. Department of Education, Office of Civil Rights. (2005). *Regulations enforced by the Office of Civil Rights (Section 504).* Retrieved August 20, 2005, from www.ed.gov/policy/rights/reg/ocr/index.html

U.S. Department of Education, Office of Educational Research and Improvement. (1996). *Reaching all families: Creating family friendly schools.* Washington, DC: Author.

U.S. Department of Education, Office of Special Education and Rehabilitative Services. (1999). *IDEA '97 amendments, final regulations.* Retrieved April 1, 2005, at www.ed.gov/policy/speced/reg/regulations.html

U.S. Department of Health and Human Services. (2000). *Report of the Surgeon General's Conference on Children's Mental Health: A national action agenda.* Rockville, MD: Author.

U.S. Department of Health and Human Services. (2001). Youth violence: A report of the surgeon general. Rockville, MD: U.S. Department of Health and Human Services, Centers for Disease Control and Prevention, National Center for Injury Prevention and Control, National Institutes of Health, National Institute of Mental Health, Substance Abuse and Mental Health Services Administration, Center for Mental Health Services. Retrieved December 23, 2004, from www.surgeongeneral.gov/library/youthviolence/toc.htm

U.S. Department of Health and Human Services. (2004). *Your rights under Section 504 of the Rehabilitation Act.* Washington, DC: Author. Retrieved July 9, 2005, at www.hhs.gov/ocr/504.html

U.S. Department of Labor, Bureau of Labor Statistics. (1949). *Occupational outlook handbook.* Washington, DC: Author.

U.S. Department of Labor, Manpower Administration, Bureau of Employment Security. (1939). *Dictionary of occupational titles.* Washington, DC: Author.

U.S. House of Representatives, 103rd Congress. (1994). *H. R. 6, Improving America's Schools Act of 1994* (Version: 7; Version Date: 10/16/94). Text from: Full Text of Bills. Available from Congressional Universe, at www.ed.gov/legislation/ESEA/toc.html

U.S. Public Health Service Office of Surgeon General. (2001). *Youth violence: A report of the surgeon general.* Washington, DC: Department of Health and Human Services.

Utah State Office of Education. (2000). *1989–1999: A decade of progress and change in the delivery of comprehensive guidance programs grades 7–12.* Salt Lake City, UT: Author.

Utah State Office of Education. (2004). Retrieved March 28, 2004, from http://beeaserv.usoe.k12.ut.:8080/U-PassWeb/SelectDistrictSchool.jsp

Vacc, N. A., Rhyne-Winkler, M. C., & Poidevant, J. M. (1993). Evaluation and accountability of counseling services: Possible implications for a mid-size district. *The School Counselor, 40,* 260–266.

Vail, K. (1998). Give peace a chance. *American School Board Journal, 185* (8), 22–24.

Van Reusen, A. K., Bos, C., Schumaker, J. B., & Deshler, D. D. (1994). *The self-advocacy strategy for education and transition planning.* Lawrence, KS: Edge Enterprises.

Vatalaro, M. (1999). Enhancing learning and interpersonal relationships. *Kappa Delta Pi Record, 35* (3), 115–117.

Vera, E. M., Shin, R. Q., Montgomery, G. P., Mildner, C., & Speight, S. L. (2004). Conflict resolution styles, self-efficacy, self-control, and future orientation of urban adolescents. *Professional School Counseling, 8,* 73–80.

Vernon, A. (1993). *Developmental assessment and intervention with children and adolescents.* Alexandria, VA: American Counseling Association.

Vernon, A. (1998). *The PASSPORT program: A journey through emotional, social, cognitive, and self-development.* Champaign, IL: Research Press.

Vernon, A. (2004). Working with children, adolescents, and their parents: Practical application of developmental theory. In A. Vernon (Ed.), *Counseling children and adolescents* (4th ed., pp. 1–34). Denver, CO: Love.

Villalba, J. A. (2003). A psychoeducational group for limited-English proficient Latino/Latina children. *Journal for Specialists in Group Work, 38,* 261–276.

Virginia Department of Education. (2004). Retrieved March 28, 2004, from www.pen.k12.va.us/Div/index.html1#Schl

Volkmar, F. R. (1996). Childhood and adolescent psychosis: A review of the past 10 years. *Journal of the American Academy of Child and Adolescent Psychiatry, 35,* 843–851.

Vontress, C. C. (1970). Counseling blacks. *Personnel and Guidance Journal, 48,* 713–719.

Vontress, C. E. (1988). An existential approach to cross-cultural counseling. *Journal of Multicultural Counseling and Development, 16,* 73–83.

Voydanoff, P., & Donnelly, B. W. (1998). Parents' risk and protective factors as predictors of parental well-being and behavior. *Journal of Marriage and Family, 60,* 344–355.

Vygotsky, L. S. (1978). *Mind in society: The development of higher psychological processes.* Cambridge, MA: Harvard University Press.

Wagner, M., Blackorby, J., Cameto, R., & Newman, L. (1993). *What makes a difference? Influences on postschool outcomes of youth with disabilities.* Menlo Park, CA: SRI International.

Wagner, M., Newman, L., & Cameto, R. (2004). *Changes over time in the secondary school experiences of students with disabilities.* A Special Topic Report of Findings from the National Longitudinal Transition Study-2 (NLTS2). Menlo Park, CA: SRI International. Available at www.nits2.org/pdfs/changestime_compreport.pdf

Wahl, K. H., & Blackhurst, A. (2000). Factors affecting the occupational and educational aspirations of children and adolescents. *Professional School Counseling, 3,* 367–374.

Wakeling, A. (1996). Epidemiology of anorexia nervosa. *Psychiatry Research, 62,* 3–9.

Walker, J. L., Lahey, B. B., Russo, M. F., Christ, M. A. G., McBurnett, K., Loeber, R., et al. (1991). Anxiety, inhibition and conduct disorder in children. I: Relation to social impairment. *Journal of American Academy of Child and Adolescent Psychiatry, 30,* 187–191.

Walsh, M. E., Howard, K. A., & Buckley, M. A. (1999). School counselors in school-community partnerships: Opportunities and challenges. *Professional School Counseling, 2,* 349–356.

Walter, J. L., & Peller, J. E. (1992). *Becoming solution-focused in brief therapy.* New York: Brunner/Mazel.

Waterman, A. S. (1985). Identity in the context of adolescent psychology. In A. S. Waterman (Ed.), *Identity in adolescence: Processes and contents* (pp. 5–24). San Francisco, CA: Jossey-Bass.

Watson, T. S., Butler, T. S., Weaver, A. D., & Foster, N. (2004). Direct behavioral consultation: An effective method for promoting school collaboration. In B. T. Erford (Ed.), *Professional school counseling: A handbook of theories, programs, and practices* (pp. 341–347). Austin, TX: PRO-ED.

Weaver, E. W. (1918). *Choosing a career.* Brooklyn, NY: Brooklyn Vocational Guidance Association.

Webb, L. D., & Myrick, R. D. (2003). A group counseling intervention for children with attention deficit hyperactivity disorder. *Professional School Counseling, 7,* 108–115.

Webster-Stratton, C., & Dahl, R. W. (1995). Conduct disorders. In M. Hersen & R. T. Ammerman (Eds.), *Advanced abnormal child psychology* (pp. 333–352). Hillsdale, NJ: Laurence Erlbaum Associates.

Webster-Stratton, C., & Taylor, T. (2001). Nipping early risk factors in the bud: Preventing substance abuse, delinquency, and violence in adolescence through interventions targeted at young children (0–8 years). *Prevention Science, 2* (3), 165–192.

Wechsler, D. (2001). *Wechsler Intelligence Scale for Children–4th edition*. San Antonio, TX: Psychological Corporation.

Weems, C. F., & Carrion, V. G. (2003). The treatment of separation anxiety disorder employing attachment theory and cognitive behavior therapy techniques. *Clinical Case Studies, 2*, 188–198.

Wehrly, B. (1995). *Pathways to multicultural counseling competence: A developmental journey*. Pacific Grove, CA: Brooks/Cole.

Weiss, C. (1998). *Evaluation* (2nd ed.). Upper Saddle River, NJ: Prentice Hall.

Weissburg, R. P., Caplan, M., & Harwood, R. L. (1991). Promoting competent young people in competence-enhancing environments: A systems-based perspective on primary prevention. *Journal of Consulting and Clinical Psychology, 59*, 830–841.

Weissman, M. M., Wolk, S., Goldstein, R. B., Moreau, D., Adams, P., Greenwald, S., et al. (1999). Depressed adolescents grown up. *Journal of the American Medical Association, 282*, 1701–1713.

Weist, M. (1997). Expanded school mental health services: A national movement in progress. In T. Ollendick & R. Prinz (Eds.), *Advances in clinical child psychology* (Vol. 19, pp. 319–352). New York: Plenum Press.

Weisz, J. R., Weiss, B., Han, S. S., Grander, D. A., & Morton, T. (1995). Effects of psychotherapy with children and adolescents revisited: A meta-analysis of treatment outcome studies. *Psychological Bulletin, 117*, 450–468.

Weitzman, S. (1998). *Upscale violence: The lived experience of domestic abuse among upper socioeconomic status*. Unpublished doctoral dissertation, Loyola University, Chicago.

Wells, R., & Giannetti, V. (1990). *Handbook of the brief psychotherapies*. New York: Plenum Press.

Werner, E. E. (1992). The children of Kauai: Resiliency and recovery in adolescence and adulthood. *Journal of Adolescent Health, 13*, 262–268.

Wessler, S. L., & Preble, W. (2003). *The respectful school: How educators and students can conquer hate and harassment*. Alexandria, VA: Association for Supervision and Curriculum Development.

Westat, P., & Policy Studies Associates. (2001). *The longitudinal evaluation of school change and performance in Title I schools*. Washington, DC: U.S. Department of Education.

Whalen, C. K., & Henker, B. (1991). Therapies for hyperactive children: Comparisons, combinations, and compromises. *Journal of Consulting and Clinical Psychology, 59*, 126–137.

Whiston, S. C. (2002). Response to the past, present, and future of school counseling: Raising some issues. *Professional School Counseling, 5*, 148–155.

Whiston, S. C., Brecheisen, B. K., & Stephens, J. (2003). Does treatment modality affect career counseling effectiveness? *Journal of Vocational Behavior, 62*, 390–410.

Whiston, S. C., Eder, K., Rahardja, D., & Tai, W. L. (2005, June). *Research supporting school counseling: Comprehensive findings*. Paper presented at the annual meeting of the American School Counselor Association, Orlando, FL.

Whiston, S. C., & Oliver, L. (2005). Career counseling process and outcome. In W. B. Walsh & M. Savickas (Eds.), *Handbook of vocational psychology* (3rd ed., pp. 155–194). Hillsdale, NJ: Lawrence Erlbaum Associates.

Whiston, S. C., & Sexton, T. L. (1998). A review of school counseling outcome research: Implications for practice. *Journal of Counseling and Development, 76*, 412–426.

Whiston, S. C., Sexton, T. L., & Lasoff, D. L. (1998). Career intervention outcome: A replication and extension. *Journal of Counseling Psychology, 45*, 150–165.

White, K. R., Taylor, M. J., & Moss, V. T. (1992). Does research support claims about the benefits of involving parents in early intervention programs? *Review of Educational Research, 62*, 91–125.

Whiteside, M. F., & Becker, B. J. (2000). Parent factors and the young child's post divorce adjustment: A meta-analysis with implications for parenting arrangements. *Journal of Family Psychology, 14*, 5–26.

Wicks-Nelson, R., & Israel, A. C. (2003). *Behavior disorders of childhood*. Upper Saddle River, NJ: Prentice Hall.

Wiggins, J. D., & Moody, A. H. (1987). Student evaluations of counseling programs: An added dimension. *The School Counselor, 34*, 353–361.

Wiggins, J. D., & Wiggins, A. H. (1992). Elementary students' self-esteem and behavioral ratings related to counselor time-task emphases. *The School Counselor, 39*, 377–381.

Wilburn, K. O., & Bates, M. L. (1997). Conflict resolution in America's schools: Defusing an approaching crisis. *Dispute Resolution Journal, 52*, 67–71.

Wiles, J., & Bondi, J. C. (1984). *Curriculum development: A guide to practice* (2nd ed.). Columbus, OH: Merrill.

Wilkinson, J., & Canter, S. (1982). *Social skills training manual: Assessment, program design, and management of training*. New York: John Wiley & Sons.

Williams, F. C., & Butler, S. K. (2003). Concerns of newly arrived immigrant students: Implications for school counselors. *Professional School Counseling, 7,* 9–14.

Williams, K. M. (2001). "Frontin' It": School violence, and relationships in the hood. In J. N. Burstyn, G. Bender, R. Casella, H. W. Gordon, D. P. Guerra, K. V. Luschen, et al. (Eds.), *Preventing violence in schools: A challenge to American democracy* (pp. 95–108). Mahwah, NJ: Lawrence Erlbaum Associates.

Williamson, E. G. (1965). *Vocational counseling. Some historical, philosophical, and theoretical perspectives.* New York: McGraw-Hill.

Wilson, F. R. (2004, September). *Assessing violence risk: An ecological analysis.* Paper presented at the Association for Assessment in Counseling (AACE) 2004 National Assessment Conference, Charleston, SC.

Wilson, N. S. (1986). Counselor interventions with low-achieving and underachieving elementary, middle, and high school students: A review of literature. *Journal of Counseling and Development, 64,* 628–634.

Wilson, S. J., Lipsey, M. W., Derzon, J. H. (2003). The effects of school-based intervention programs on aggressive behavior: A meta-analysis. *Journal of Consulting and Clinical Psychology, 71,* 136–149.

Wolfe, D. A., Sas, L., & Wekerle, C. (1994). Factors associated with the development of posttraumatic stress disorder among child victims of sexual abuse. *Child Abuse and Neglect, 18,* 37–50.

Wolraich, M. L., Hannah, J. N., Pinnock, T. Y., Baumgaertel, A., & Brown, J. (1996). Comparison of diagnostic criteria for attention deficit hyperactivity disorder in a county-wide sample. *Journal of the American Academy of Child and Adolescent Psychiatry, 35,* 319–324.

Wood Dunn, N. A., & Baker, S. B. (2002). Readiness to serve students with disabilities: A survey of elementary school counselors. *Professional School Counseling, 5,* 277–284.

Worden, W. (1991). *Grief counseling and grief therapy: A handbook for the mental health professional.* London: Routledge.

Worthen, B. B., Sanders, J. R., & Fitzpatrick, J. L. (1997). *Program evaluation: Alternative approaches and practical guidelines* (2nd ed.). New York: Longman.

Wrenn, C. G. (1962). *The counselor in a changing world.* Washington, DC: American Personnel and Guidance Association.

Wright, J. C., Zakriski, A. L., & Fisher, P. (1996). Age differences in the correlates of perceived dominance. *Social Development, 5,* 24–40.

Wright, K., & Stegelin, D. A. (2003). *Building school and community partnerships through parent involvement* (2nd ed.). Upper Saddle River, NJ: Merrill/Prentice Hall.

Wu, P., Hoven, C. W., Liu, X., Cohen, P., Fuller, C. J., & Shaffer, D. (2004). Substance use, suicidal ideation and attempts in children and adolescents. *Suicide and Life-Threatening Behavior, 34,* 408–420.

Yalom, I. D. (1995). *The theory and practice of group psychotherapy* (4th ed.). New York: Basic Books.

Yeh, C. J. (2001). An exploratory study of school counselors' experiences with and perceptions of Asian-American students. *Professional School Counseling, 4,* 349–356.

Young, A. R., & Beitchman, J. H. (2002). Reading and other specific learning difficulties. In P. Howlin & O. Udwin (Eds.), *Outcomes in neurodevelopmental and genetic disorders* (pp. 405–438). New York: Cambridge University Press.

Young, D. S. (2005). Today's lesson by . . . Roosevelt? The use of character portrayal in classroom guidance. *The Professional School Counselor, 8,* 366–371.

Young, I. M. (1990). *Justice and the politics of difference.* Princeton, NJ: Princeton University Press.

Young, T. L., & Zimmerman, R. (1998). Clueless: Parental knowledge of risk behaviors of middle school students. *Archives of Pediatrics and Adolescent Medicine, 152,* 1138–1139.

Zeanah, C. H., & Emde, R. N. (1994). Attachment disorders in infancy and childhood. In M. Rutter, E. Taylor, & L. Hersov (Eds.), *Child and adolescent psychiatry: Modern approaches* (pp. 490–504). Cambridge, MA: Blackwell.

Zimmerman, M. A. (2000). Empowerment theory: Psychological, organizational and community levels of analysis. In J. Rappaport & E. Seidman (Eds.), *Handbook of community psychology* (pp. 43–64). New York: Plenum.

Zinck, K., & Littrell, J. M. (2000). Action research shows group counseling effective with at-risk adolescent girls. *Professional School Counseling, 4,* 50–59.

Zinn, H. (2003). *A people's history of the United States 1492–present* (Rev. ed.). New York: Perennial Classics.

Zins, J. E. (1993). Enhancing consultee problem-solving skills in consultative interactions. *Journal of Counseling and Development, 72,* 185–190.

Name Index

SUBJECT INDEX

Systemic accountability, 128
Systemic advocacy, 7, 108, 111, 116–117
Systemic assessment, 124–125, 126
Systemic intolerance of students, 128
Systemic oppression, 78
Systemic/systematic, compared, 122–123
Systems-level intervention, 137

Tarasoff case, 65, 71. *See also* Duty-to-warn
    standard
Target behaviors, discipline for, 336
Task groups, 183
Teachers. *See* Educators
Teaching Students to Be Peacemakers program, 312
Teaming, 65, 392. *See also* Collaboration
Technology
    career counseling and, 45, 198–199
    confidentiality and, 65, 70, 392
    educational development and, 198–199
    ethical considerations, 389–391, 417
    history of use in counseling, 26
    learning disorders and, 361
    testing and, 257, 276, 399, 400
    violence and, 294, 295
Technology-assisted distance counseling
    services, 390
Teenager's Guide to the Real World Careers, 345
Telephone calls, positive, 234
Terminally ill clients, 388
Termination of client relationship, 181, 226,
    389, 393
Termination of practice, 395
Test Critiques, 276
Testimonials, client, 395
Testing programs, schoolwide, 260, 275–276
Tests. *See also* Assessment; NCLB
    automated interpretation of, 401
    content validity, 249
    counselor knowledge of, 36
    culture and, 81, 84–85
    curriculum-based, 260
    educator-made, 257
    English-language learners and, 85
    ethics and, 275, 276
    ethnicity/gender and, 240–241
    high-stakes, 237, 275
    history of, 19, 20
    intelligence, 358
    performance, 240–241
    reviews of, 276
    score interpretation, 239
    selecting, 276, 332
    standardized, 81, 84–86, 237, 257, 275

    standards-based, 260
    teaching skills needed for, 109
    technology and, 257, 276
Tests in Print, 276
Thinking Collaboratively (Bruner), 229
Third-parties, confidentiality and, 65, 392, 397
Thought disorders, 293
Threat assessment, 291, 292–295
Three "Cs," 4, 6
Tic disorders, 369–371, 379
Ticket to Work Program, 346
Time logs, 249
Time series design outcome studies, 255
Title I (amendment to ESEA), 237, 286, 321
Title IV (amendment to ESEA), 286
Title V-A (amendment to ESEA), 22
Title V-B (amendment to ESEA), 22, 23
Title IX (amendment to ESEA), 130
Title X (amendment to ESEA), 286
Tobacco use, 283
Token economies, 365
"Tossed salad," view of America as, 102
Tourette's disorder, 369, 370
Tracking, academic, 106, 313
Tractable conflict, 307
Training, counselor
    antioppression, 81
    changes needed in, 4, 6, 142–143
    crisis-management, 288
    diversity in, 404, 407
    ethical guidelines, 402, 404–407
    history of, 22–23
    subjects included in, 382
Training, educator, 113, 143
Training, parent, 46–47
Training, staff, 113
Training, student
    cognitive coping skills, 44
    communication skills, 44
    interpersonal skills, 43, 344
    peer mediation, 315
    self-determination, 331, 346–347
    social skills, 43, 46
    vocational skills, 286, 344, 346
Transforming School Counseling Initiative (TSCI),
    6, 81, 144
Transgenderism, 79, 99
Transient tic disorder, 369, 370
Transition enhancement assistance, 203
Transitions, 137, 203–204, 329, 331, 339, 342–347
Transportation resources, connecting families
    with, 109
Traumatic brain injury, 324